CORPORATE FINANCE: THE CORE

JONATHAN BERK
UNIVERSITY OF CALIFORNIA, BERKELEY

PETER DEMARZO
STANFORD UNIVERSITY

PEARSON

Prentice
Hall

Boston San Francisco New York
London Toronto Sydney Tokyo Singapore Madrid
Mexico City Munich Paris Cape Town Hong Kong Montreal

Editor in Chief: Denise Clinton
Executive Editor: Donna Battista
Development Editor: Rebecca Ferris-Caruso
Market Development Manager: Dona Kenly
Assistant Editor: Kerri McQueen
Managing Editor: Nancy Fenton
Senior Production Supervisor: Meredith Gertz
Cover Designers: Charles Spaulding and Christina Gleason
Supplements Coordinator: Heather McNally
Director of Media: Michelle Neil
Software Project Manager: Susan Schoenberg
Content Lead, MyFinanceLab: Michael Griffin
Senior Marketing Manager: Jodi Basset
Marketing Assistant: Ian Gold
Senior Prepress Supervisor: Caroline Fell
Senior Author Support/Technology Specialist: Joe Vetere
Rights and Permissions Advisors: Dana Weightman, Shannon Barbe
Senior Manufacturing Buyer: Carol Melville
Production Coordination, Composition, Illustrations, and Text Design: Thompson Steele Inc.
Cover Image: © Getty Images, David McNew

Credits

Back cover and p. xxii: Photo of authors overlooking the Financial District, San Francisco, CA: ©2006 Nancy Warner; **p. 395:** Nobel Prize: William Sharpe on the CAPM, excerpts from "Revisiting the Capital Asset Pricing Model," Jonathan Burton, *Dow Jones Asset Manager*, May/June 1998, pp. 20–28; **p. 403:** Figure 13.1, "Excess Return of Size Portfolios (1926–2005)," Historical return data from Kenneth French's Web site; **p. 404:** Figure 13.2, "Excess Return of Book-to-Market Portfolios (1926–2005)," Historical return data from Kenneth French's Web site; **p. 414:** Table 13.1: "FFC Portfolio Average Monthly Returns (1926–2005), Historical return data from Kenneth French's Web site; **p. 420:** Figure 13.5, "How Firms Calculate the Cost of Capital," reprinted from "The Theory and Practice of Corporate Finance: Evidence from the Field," J. R. Graham and C. R. Harvey, *Journal of Financial Economics* 60 (©2001), pp. 187–243, with permission from Elsevier; **p. 479:** Figure 15.7, "Debt-to-Value Ratio [$D/(E + D)$] for Select Industries," data from Reuters, 2005; **p. 564:** Figure 17.8, "Distribution of Stock Prices for NYSE Firms (April 2005)," data from Reuters, April 2005.

Library of Congress Cataloguing-in-Publication Data

CIP data on file at Library of Congress

ISBN-13: 978-0-321-54009-6
ISBN-10: 0-321-54009-3

2 3 4 5 6 7 8 9 10—QWT—11 10 09 08

To Rebecca, Natasha, and Hannah

for the love and for being there

—J. B.

To Kaui, Pono, Koa, and Kai

for all the love and laughter

—P. D.

Brief Contents

Contents

xiv   **Contents**

About the Authors

Jonathan Berk is the Sylvan Coleman Professor of Finance in the Haas School of Business at the University of California, Berkeley, and is a Research Associate at the National Bureau of Economic Research. He currently teaches the introductory Corporate Finance course for first-year MBA students at Berkeley. Before getting his Ph.D., he worked as an Associate at Goldman Sachs, where his education in finance really began.

Professor Berk is an Associate Editor of the *Journal of Finance*. His research interests in finance include corporate valuation, capital structure, mutual funds, asset pricing, experimental economics, and labor economics. His work has won a number of research awards including the TIAA-CREF Paul A. Samuelson Award, the Smith Breeden Prize, Best Paper of the Year in *The Review of Financial Studies*, and the FAME Research Prize. His paper, "A Critique of Size Related Anomalies," was recently selected as one of the two best papers ever published in *The Review of Financial Studies*. In recognition of his influence on the practice of finance he has received the Bernstein-Fabozzi/Jacobs Levy Award, the Graham and Dodd Award of Excellence, and the Roger F. Murray Prize.

Born in Johannesburg, South Africa, Professor Berk is married, with two daughters aged 10 and 14, and is an avid skier and biker.

Peter DeMarzo and Jonathan Berk

Peter DeMarzo is the Mizuho Financial Group Professor of Finance at the Stanford Graduate School of Business and is a Research Associate at the National Bureau of Economic Research. He currently teaches the "turbo" core finance course for Stanford's first-year MBA students. In addition to his experience at the Stanford Graduate School of Business, Professor DeMarzo has taught at the Haas School of Business and the Kellogg Graduate School of Management, and he was a National Fellow at the Hoover Institution.

Professor DeMarzo received the Sloan Teaching Excellence Award at Stanford in 2004 and 2006, and the Earl F. Cheit Outstanding Teaching Award at U.C. Berkeley in 1998. Professor DeMarzo has served as an Associate Editor for *The Review of Financial Studies*, *Financial Management*, and the *B.E. Journals in Economic Analysis and Policy*, as well as a Director of the Western Finance Association. Professor DeMarzo's research is in the area of corporate finance, asset securitization, and contracting, as well as market structure and regulation. His recent work has examined issues of the optimal design of securities, the regulation of insider trading and broker-dealers, and the influence of information asymmetries on corporate investment. He has received numerous awards including the Western Finance Association Corporate Finance Award and the Barclays Global Investors/Michael Brennan best-paper award from *The Review of Financial Studies*.

Professor DeMarzo was born in Whitestone, New York, and is married with three boys. He and his family enjoy hiking, biking, and skiing.

Preface

When we told our friends and colleagues that we had decided to write a corporate finance textbook, most of them had the same response: *Why now?* There are three main reasons.

Pedagogy

As any student of the subject will attest to, corporate finance is challenging. Consequently, as the popularity of corporate finance has grown, textbook authors have attempted to make the subject more accessible by de-emphasizing the core theoretical ideas and instead concentrating on the results. In our over 30 years of combined teaching experience, we have found that leaving out core material deemed "too hard" actually makes the subject matter less accessible. The core concepts in finance are simple and intuitive. What makes the subject challenging is that it is often difficult for a novice to distinguish between these core ideas and other intuitively appealing approaches that, if used in financial decision making, will lead to incorrect decisions. De-emphasizing the core concepts that underlie finance strips students of the essential intellectual tools they need to differentiate between good and bad decision making. Therefore, our primary motivation for writing this book was to equip students with a solid grounding in the core financial concepts and tools needed to make good decisions.

In our experience, students learn best when the material in a course is presented as one unified whole rather than a series of separate ideas. As such, this book presents corporate finance as an application of a subset of simple, powerful ideas. At the heart of this core is the principle of the absence of arbitrage opportunities, or Law of One Price. We use the Law of One Price as a compass; it keeps financial decision makers on the right track.

Perspective

The past 30 years have witnessed an evolution in both the sophistication of the students taking the course and the field itself. Today's students arrive with first-hand knowledge of financial markets, either through their participation in stock markets or in their interaction with widely available financial products. Many students encounter financial concepts in their entry-level jobs out of college; they often have experience implementing financial decisions for the firms they work for, some receive stock and options as part of their compensation, and almost all have the option to make retirement plan contributions. We capitalize on the background that students bring to the classroom in our choice of terminology and examples, our use of real data, and by relating methodology to practice.

Much of the empirical evidence in financial economics amassed in the last 30 years supports the existing theory and strengthens the importance of understanding and applying corporate finance principles. However, in a number of applications, the evidence has not supported the theory. Although puzzles have emerged, none of them has invalidated the core principles of corporate finance that this book is built on. So rather than state theory as fact, we carefully evaluate the evidence and build on the sophistication students bring with them on the first day of class. By clearly communicating these subtleties to the student, we expose them to the dynamism of the field and avoid giving them false impressions that contradict their own experience.

Technology

Even though the Internet is now commonplace, we do not feel that it has been properly exploited in the field of education. The technology breakthrough in this book has the potential to fundamentally change the way students learn. MyFinanceLab is as much a part of the learning experience as classroom lectures and the textbook itself.

This product fundamentally changes how students learn finance. In the traditional approach, students learn by working end-of-chapter problems, yet the time lag between when the problem is worked and when feedback is received marginalizes the benefit of the feedback. MyFinanceLab completely removes this inefficiency by providing students with immediate feedback at the very point that they are most receptive to the knowledge.

These reasons motivated us to write a textbook that we hope will shape the way students learn corporate finance for years to come.

Corporate Finance: The Core

You may be familiar with our 31-chapter textbook, *Corporate Finance*. We geared that text to the many schools and programs that choose one textbook for use throughout the corporate finance curriculum; that is, in the core, intermediate, and advanced classes. Many instructors have favorite topics, perhaps tied to research interests that they want to cover in the first course. *Corporate Finance* therefore provides the flexibility of topic choice and the depth and breadth of coverage they look for. However, other programs and individual professors desire a streamlined book that is specifically tailored to the topics covered in the first one-semester course. For those programs, we are pleased to offer *Corporate Finance: The Core*.

Corporate Finance: The Core's Innovative Approach

Corporate Finance: The Core carefully balances the latest advancements in research and practice with thorough coverage of core finance topics. Several key themes and innovations distinguish this textbook.

1. Using the Law of One Price as the Unifying Principle of Valuation

This book presents corporate finance as an application of a small set of simple core ideas. Modern finance theory and practice is grounded in the idea of the absence of arbitrage (or the Law of One Price) as the unifying concept in valuation. Chapter 3, "Arbitrage and Financial Decision Making," explicitly introduces the Law of One Price concept as the basis for NPV, the time value of money, and the evaluation of risk. The rest of the book relates major concepts to the Law of One Price, creating a framework to ground the student reader. Each part of the textbook begins by highlighting the Law of One Price connection. This methodology directly connects theory to practice and presents a unified approach to what might appear to students as disparate ideas.

2. Improving on the Basics: Timelines and Interest Rates

We introduce timelines in Chapter 4, "The Time Value of Money," and stress the importance of creating timelines for every problem that involves cash flows. Each subsequent example involving cash flows includes a timeline as the critical first step.

In Chapter 5, "Interest Rates," we explicitly walk students through the mechanics of adjusting discount rates for different time periods and explain how to interpret interest rate quotes. Separating the mechanics of how to compute the discount rate from the time value of money concept allows us to more effectively communicate these basic tools.

3. Emphasizing Capital Budgeting and Valuation

The capital budgeting decision is one of the most important decisions in finance and as such is the focus of many instructors' courses. We present capital budgeting and valuation in two stages.

The first stage comes early and focuses on identifying cash flows. Chapter 7, "Fundamentals of Capital Budgeting," examines the valuation of projects within a firm and provides a clear and systematic presentation of the difference between earnings and free cash flow. These concepts are then applied to stocks in Chapter 9, providing a unifying treatment of projects within the firm and the valuation of the firm as a whole. This early introduction into capital budgeting allows us to conceptually present the idea of the cost of capital, which we then use to motivate the risk and return coverage. In this way, we relate the cost of capital to risk and return, an otherwise challenging connection for new students of finance.

The second stage follows the discussion of the pricing of risk and capital structure. Chapter 18, "Capital Budgeting and Valuation with Leverage," presents the three main methods for capital budgeting with leverage and market imperfections: the weighted average cost of capital (WACC) method, the adjusted present value (APV) method, and the flow-to-equity (FTE) method. We communicate these traditionally difficult but important ideas by emphasizing the underlying assumptions and core principles behind them. This approach allows us to present these concepts in the context of progressively more complex financing policies for the firm, which allows students and professors to delve as deeply into these techniques as is appropriate for their needs. Next, Chapter 19, "Valuation and Financial Modeling: A Case Study" serves as a capstone chapter for the first six parts of the book and applies the financial tools developed thus far to build a valuation model for a case study, Ideko Corp. This chapter walks future financial managers through the process of building a financial valuation model using Excel.

4. Rethinking the Teaching of Risk and Return

Chapter 3 briefly introduces the concept of risk and return. Using the no-arbitrage concept alone, we explain conceptually one of the core principles of finance: that risk must be evaluated relative to a benchmark. Later, the flexible structure of Part IV allows professors to tailor coverage of risk and return to fit their course.

For those looking for a brief introduction to risk and return before moving directly to corporate finance topics, Chapter 10, "Capital Markets and the Pricing of Risk," provides the key intuition and motivation for the relation between risk and return. The chapter also explains the distinction between diversifiable and systematic risk, and introduces the CAPM in the way it is used in practice, as a means of identifying systematic risk and determining risk premia. This comprehensive yet succinct treatment allows instructors to skip subsequent risk and return chapters without sacrificing continuity.

Those opting for in-depth coverage of risk and return can include the following chapters:

- Chapter 11, "Optimal Portfolio Choice," develops the details of mean-variance portfolio optimization separately from the CAPM as they are of independent usefulness.

- Chapter 12, "The Capital Asset Pricing Model," presents the equilibrium argument for the CAPM, emphasizing that the CAPM is simply a means of identifying the market portfolio as an efficient portfolio, and discusses a number of practical issues that arise when implementing the CAPM.

- Chapter 13, "Alternative Models of Systematic Risk," moves beyond the CAPM, examining the relative strengths and weaknesses of other models, including multi-factor models and characteristic variable models. Because we have separated the discussion of mean-variance optimization from the CAPM in Chapters 11 and 12, this chapter is able to clearly differentiate the core concept that remains valid from the applications called into question by the empirical evidence. That is, the expected return of a stock is still given by its beta with an efficient portfolio but that portfolio might not be the standard proxies used for the market portfolio.

5. Stressing the Capital Structure Decision

We place heavy emphasis on the firm's capital structure in Chapters 14–17, but also allow instructors to tailor the coverage as suits them by presenting Modigliani and Miller in a perfect world at the outset and then layering on frictions in subsequent chapters. We tie the classic Modigliani and Miller results to the Law of One Price and maintain that central theme throughout our discussion of capital structure. Our full-chapter treatment of this foundational material highlights its importance to students and sets the stage for the remainder of this part of the text. Our in-depth look at the role of taxation, financial distress, and agency costs fully prepares the financial manager to account for real-world market imperfections in the capital budgeting process.

Organization

Corporate Finance: The Core offers coverage of the major topical areas for introductory-level MBA students as well as the depth required in a reference textbook for upper-division courses. Our focus is on financial decision making related to the corporation's choice of which investments to make or how to raise the capital required to fund an investment.

Part-by-Part Overview

Parts I and II lay the foundation for our study of corporate finance. In Chapter 1, we introduce the corporation and other business forms. We examine how stock markets facilitate trading among investors, the role of the financial manager, and conflicts surrounding ownership and control of corporations. Chapter 2 reviews basic corporate accounting principles and the financial statements on which the financial manager relies. Chapter 3, "Arbitrage and Financial Decision Making," introduces the core ideas on which finance is built—the Law of One Price, net present value, and risk—that are the basis of the unifying framework that will guide the student throughout the course. This brief introduction to risk is an important innovation that allows us to discuss risk in the early chapters, in particular in the context of the early introduction to capital budgeting.

Part II presents the basic tools that are the cornerstones of corporate finance. Chapter 4 introduces the time value of money and describes methods for estimating the timing of cash flows and computing the net present value of various types of cash flow patterns. Chapter 5, "Interest Rates," provides an extensive overview of issues that arise in estimating the appropriate discount rate. In Chapter 6, "Investment Decision Rules," we present and critique alternatives to net present value for evaluating projects.

Part III applies these newly learned valuation principles for discounting cash flows developed from Part II to both real and financial assets. We explain the basics of valuation for capital projects (Chapter 7), bonds (Chapter 8), and stocks (Chapter 9). In Chapter 9 we also discuss the issue of market efficiency and implications for financial managers.

In Part IV, we look at the critical concept of risk and return. Chapter 10, "Capital Markets and the Pricing of Risk," introduces the relation between risk and return. Some professors may choose to cover only this one-chapter treatment of risk and return before proceeding directly to the capital structure unit. In Chapter 11, "Optimal Portfolio Choice," we introduce mean-variance optimization. In Chapter 12, we derive the Capital Asset Pricing Model. Chapter 13 examines the strengths and weaknesses of alternative models of risk and return.

Part V addresses how a firm should raise the funds it needs to undertake its investments and the firm's resulting capital structure. We focus on examining how the choice of capital structure affects the value of the firm in the perfect world in Chapter 14 and with frictions such as taxes and agency issues in Chapters 15 and 16. Payout policy is the focus of Chapter 17.

In Part VI, we return to the capital budgeting decision with the complexities of the real world. Chapter 18, "Capital Budgeting and Valuation with Leverage," introduces the three main methods for capital budgeting with leverage and market imperfections: the weighted average cost of capital (WACC) method, the adjusted present value (APV) method, and the flow-to-equity (FTE) method. Chapter 19, "Valuation and Financial Modeling: A Case Study," presents a capstone case that applies the techniques developed up to this point to build a valuation model for a firm.

Customize Your Approach

Although *Corporate Finance: The Core* provides the central topics for the first course, we realize many professors will still cover chapters selectively. In reviewing hundreds of syllabi in planning for this textbook, we came to appreciate that few professors work through a textbook linearly from start to finish. The vast majority of professors customize their classes by selecting a subset of chapters reflecting the subject matter they consider most important. We therefore designed the book from the outset with this need for flexibility in mind. Instructors are free to emphasize the topics they find most interesting.

We consider Parts II through VI as the core chapters in the book. We envision that most MBA programs will cover this material in the courses they teach. However, even within these core chapters instructors can pick and choose. Universities that teach corporate finance in a single quarter will likely cover Chapters 3–15. If time allows, or if students enter the course already familiar with the time value of money concepts, Chapters 16–19 can be added. Finally, the book allows for a stripped-down treatment of finance essentials for programs that only have a single mini-semester core finance course. In this case, we suggest covering Chapters 3–10, 14, and perhaps 15 if time allows. For professors interested in coverage of advanced topics such as options, risk management, and international finance, and other topics such as working capital, we invite you to consult our 31-chapter textbook, *Corporate Finance*.

A Complete Instructor and Student Support Package

MyFinanceLab

MyFinanceLab is a critical component of the text. This resource, a premium product that is available for packaging, will give all students the practice and tutorial help they need to learn finance efficiently. For more details, see pages xxxiv–xxxv.

Solutions Manual

This essential companion to the text provides detailed, accuracy-verified solutions to every chapter problem. All the solutions, like the problems themselves, were written by the textbook authors, class tested by 10 MBA finance classes over the course of a semester, and scrutinized by Mark Simonson, Arizona State University, to guarantee unparalleled quality.

Study Guide

Written by Mark Simonson, Arizona State University, the Study Guide provides the learning tools students need to cement their understanding of the central concepts. Corresponding to each chapter, students will find a chapter synopsis that overviews the contents and a review of selected concepts and key terms to focus study time on the most critical topics. A handful of worked examples in each chapter with step-by-step solutions walk students through the thought process for arriving at each solution, instilling in them the intuition they need to tackle problems successfully on their own. A section of 5–10 questions and problems per chapter tests students' grasp of the main concepts and ability to apply them to solve problems.

Instructor's Manual

The Instructor's Manual was written by Janet Payne and William Chittenden of Texas State University. Corresponding to each chapter, these authors provide: chapter overview and outline correlated to the PowerPoint Lecture Notes; learning objectives; guide to fresh worked examples in the PowerPoint Lecture Notes; and listing of end-of-chapter problems with an Excel icon (EXCEL) for which Spreadsheets are available via the online Instructor Resource Center and Instructor's Resource CD-ROM.

Test Bank

Prepared by James Nelson, East Carolina University, the Test Bank provides a wealth of accuracy-verified testing material. Each chapter offers a wide selection of multiple-choice, short-answer, and essay questions. Questions are qualified by difficulty level and skill type and correlated to the chapter topics. Numerical-based problems include step-by-step solutions.

Instructor's Resource Disk with PowerPoint Lecture Presentations

Compatible with Windows and Macintosh computers, this CD-ROM provides numerous resources for students and professors alike.

We offer PowerPoint Lecture Presentations, authored by Janet Payne and William Chittenden of Texas State University, tailored to both instructors and students. The instructor version offers outlines of each chapter with graphs, tables, key terms, and concepts from each chapter. To enliven classroom presentations, selected figures, tables, and timelines are incorporated. Fresh worked examples provide detailed, step-by-step solutions for students in the same format as the boxed examples from the text. New examples are correlated to the parallel examples from the textbook and include calculator keystrokes and Spreadsheet Solutions as appropriate. The student version of the presentation contains selected deletions and fill-in-the blanks to encourage active student listening and participation in the lectures.

For added convenience, the CD-ROM also includes Microsoft Word files for the entire contents of the Instructor's Manual and computerized Test Bank files. The easy-to-use testing software (TestGen with QuizMaster for Windows and Macintosh) is a valuable text preparation tool that allows professors to view, edit, and add questions.

Resources Available for Packaging with This Text

The following supplementary materials are available to aid and enhance students' mastery of concepts:

Wall Street Journal Edition

When packaged with this text, Addison-Wesley offers students a reduced-cost, 10- or 15-week subscription to the *Wall Street Journal* print edition and the *Wall Street Journal* Interactive Edition.

The Financial Times Edition

Featuring international news and analysis from journalists in more than 50 countries, *The Financial Times* will provide your students with insights and perspectives on economic developments around the world. For a small charge, a 15-week subscription to *The Financial Times* can be included with each new textbook.

Acknowledgments

Now that we have explained why we chose to write the text and how to use it, we can turn to thanking the people that made it happen. As any textbook writer will tell you, you cannot write a textbook of this scope without a substantial amount of help. First and foremost we thank Donna Battista, whose leadership, talent, and market savvy are imprinted on all aspects of the project and central to its success; Denise Clinton, a friend and a leader in fact not just in name, whose experience and knowledge are indispensable; Rebecca Ferris-Caruso, for her unparalleled expertise in managing the complex writing, reviewing, and editing processes and patience in keeping us on track; Dona Kenly, for spearheading the market development work; Michelle Neil, for embracing our vision for MyFinanceLab; and Kay Ueno, for her tireless efforts during the last leg of the textbook marathon. We were blessed to be approached by the best publisher in the business and we are both truly thankful for the indispensable help provided by these and other professionals, including Nancy Fenton, Nancy Freihofer, Meredith Gertz, Marianne Groth, Roxanne Hoch, Christine Lyons, Heather McNally, Jason Miranda, Bridget Page, Margaret Monahan-Pashall, Susan Schoenberg, Charles Spaulding, Allison Stendardi, and Sally Steele.

Without Jennifer Koski's help, we would have been unable to realize our vision for this textbook. Like us, she took on much more than she bargained for, but we will be forever grateful for her willingness to stick with us and provide her critical insights and knowledge that ultimately moved the book through the second and third drafts. Her belief in this project, tireless effort, and commitment ensured that it met her very high standards. Without her, there would not have been a book.

Many of the later, non-core chapters required specific detailed knowledge. Nigel Barradale, Reid Click, Jarrad Harford, and Marianne Plunkert ensured that this knowledge was effectively communicated. Joseph Vu and Vance P. Lesseig contributed their talents to the Concept Check questions and Data Cases, respectively.

Thomas Gilbert and Miguel Palacios worked every example and end-of-chapter problem in this book. In addition, they provided numerous insights that have greatly improved the exposition. They were both indispensable, and we are very grateful for their help. Creating a truly error-free text is a challenge we could not have lived up to without our team of expert error checkers. Anand Goel and Mark Simonson each subjected the text to their exacting standards throughout the manuscript and production processes. Ting-Heng Chu, Robert James, Siddarth Tenneti, and Joseph Vu also contributed their sharp eyes.

The development of MyFinanceLab was an enormous undertaking, sometimes rivaling the book itself. Mike Griffin managed the whole process; without his financial experience and his attention to detail, MyFinanceLab would still be simply a nice idea. In addition, Shannon Donovan, Arline Savage, Patricia Bancroft, Hilary Bancroft, and Carlos Bazan provided invaluable support and we are very grateful to both of them.

A corporate finance textbook is the product of the talents and hard work of many talented colleagues. We are especially gratified with the work of those who developed an impressive array of print supplements to accompany the book: Mark Simonson, for the Solutions Manual and Study Guide; Janet Payne and William Chittenden, for the Instructor's Manual and PowerPoint; and James Nelson, for the Test Bank.

We're also appreciative Marlene Bellamy's work conducting the lively interviews that provide a critically important perspective, and to the interviewees who graciously provided their time and insights, including Andrew Balson, Lisa Black, John Bogle, Jonathan Clements, John Connors, Marilyn G. Fedak, Sue Frieden, Richard Grannis, Lawrence E. Harris, Randall P. Lert, Scott Mathews, Joseph L. Rice III, Joel Stern, Rex Sinquefield, and David Viniar.

As a colleague of both of us, Mark Rubinstein inspired us with his passion to get the history of finance right by correctly attributing the important ideas to the people who first enunciated them. Inspiration is one thing; actually undertaking the task is another. His book, *A History of the Theory of Investments: My Annotated Bibliography*, was indispensable—it provided the only available reference of the history of finance. As will be obvious to any reader, we have used it extensively in this text and we, as well as the profession as a whole, owe him a debt of gratitude for taking the time to write it all down.

We could not have written this text if we were not once ourselves students of finance. As any student knows, the key to success is having a great teacher. In our case we are lucky to have been taught and advised by the people who helped create modern finance: Ken Arrow, Darrell Duffie, Mordecai Kurz, Stephen Ross, and Richard Roll. It was from them that we learned the importance of the core principles of finance, including the Law of One Price, on which this book is based. The learning process does not end at graduation and like most people we have had especially influential colleagues and mentors from which we learned a great deal during our careers and we would like to recognize them explicitly here: Mike Fishman, Richard Green, Vasant Naik, Art Raviv, Mark Rubinstein, Joe Williams, and Jeff Zwiebel. We continue to learn from all of our colleagues and we are grateful to all of them. Finally, we would like to thank those with whom we have taught finance classes over the years: Anat Admati, Ming Huang, Robert Korajczyk, Paul Pfleiderer, Sergio Rebelo, Richard Stanton, and Raman Uppal. Their ideas and teaching strategies have without a doubt influenced our own sense of pedagogy and found their way into this text.

Finally, and most importantly, we owe our biggest debt of gratitude to our spouses, Rebecca Schwartz and Kaui Chun DeMarzo. Little did we (or they) know how much this project would impact our lives, and without their continued love and support—and especially their patience and understanding—this text could not have been completed. We owe a special thanks to Kaui DeMarzo, for her inspiration and support at the start of this project, and for her willingness to be our in-house editor, contributor, advisor, and overall sounding-board throughout each stage of its development.

Jonathan Berk
Peter DeMarzo

Contributors

We are truly thankful to have had so many manuscript reviewers, class testers, and focus group participants. We list all of these contributors below, but Gordon Bodnar, James Conover, Anand Goel, James Linck, Evgeny Lyandres, Marianne Plunkert, Mark Simonson, and Andy Terry went so far beyond the call of duty that we would like to single them out. We strived to incorporate every contributor's input and are truly grateful for the time each individual took to provide comments and suggestions. The book has benefited enormously from this input.

Reviewers

Ashok B. Abbott, *West Virginia University*
Michael Adams, *Jacksonville University*
Ibrahim Affaneh, *Indiana University of Pennsylvania*
Kevin Ahlgrim, *Illinois State University*
Confidence Amadi, *Florida A&M University*
Christopher Anderson, *University of Kansas*
Tom Arnold, *University of Richmond*
Nigel Barradale, *University of California, Berkeley*
Peter Basciano, *Augusta State University*
Thomas Bates, *University of Arizona*
Paul Bayes, *East Tennessee State University*
Gordon Bodnar, *Johns Hopkins University*

Waldo Born, *Eastern Illinois University*
Alex Boulatov, *Bauer College of Business, University of Houston*
George Chang, *Bradley University*
Ting-Heng Chu, *East Tennessee State University*
John H. Cochrane, *University of Chicago*
James Conover, *University of North Texas*
Henrik Cronqvist, *Ohio State University*
Maddur Daggar, *Citigroup*
Hazem Daouk, *Cornell University*
Daniel Deli, *Arizona State University*
Andrea DeMaskey, *Villanova University*
B. Espen Eckbo, *Dartmouth College*
Larry Eisenberg, *University of Southern Mississippi*

T. Hanan Eytan, *Baruch College*
Michael Fishman, *Northwestern University*
Michael Gallmeyer, *Texas A&M University*
Diego Garcia, *University of North Carolina*
Tom Geurts, *Marist College*
Frank Ghannadian, *Mercer University*
Thomas Gilbert, *University of California, Berkeley*
Marc Goergen, *University of Sheffield*
David Goldenberg, *Rensselaer Polytechnic Institute*
Milton Harris, *University of Chicago*
Christopher Hennessy, *University of California, Los Angeles*
Vanessa Holmes, *Xavier University*
Wenli Huang, *Boston University School of Management*
Mark Hutchinson, *University College Cork*
Stuart Hyde, *University of Manchester*
Robert James, *Babson College*
Keith Johnson, *University of Kentucky*
Ayla Kayhan, *Louisiana State University*
Doseong Kim, *University of Akron*
Kenneth Kim, *State University of New York–Buffalo*
Halil Kiymaz, *Rollins College*
Brian Kluger, *University of Cincinnati*
John Knopf, *Seton Hall University*
George Kutner, *Marquette University*
Vance P. Lesseig, *Texas State University*
Martin Lettau, *New York University*
James Linck, *University of Georgia*
David Lins, *University of Illinois at Urbana–Champaign*
Michelle Lowry, *Pennsylvania State University*
Deborah Lucas, *Northwestern University*
Peng Lui, *University of California, Berkeley*
Evgeny Lyandres, *Rice University*
Balasundram Maniam, *Sam Houston State University*
Suren Mansinghka, *University of California, Irvine*
Daniel McConaughy, *California State University, Northridge*
Robert McDonald, *Northwestern University*
Mark McNabb, *University of Cincinnati*
Ilhan Meric, *Rider University*
Timothy Michael, *James Madison University*
Dag Michalsen, *Norwegian School of Management*
James Miles, *Penn State University*
Arjen Mulder, *RSM Erasmus University*
Michael Muoghalu, *Pittsburg State University*
Jeryl Nelson, *Wayne State College*
Tom Nelson, *University of Colorado*
Chee Ng, *Fairleigh Dickinson University*
Ben Nunnally, *University of North Carolina, Charlotte*
Frank O'Hara, *University of San Francisco*
Henry Oppenheimer, *University of Rhode Island*
Miguel Palacios, *University of California, Berkeley*
Mitchell Petersen, *Northwestern University*

Marianne Plunkert, *University of Colorado at Denver*
Paul Povel, *University of Minnesota*
Michael Provitera, *Barry University*
Brian Prucyk, *Marquette University*
P. Raghavendra Rau, *Purdue University*
Charu Raheja, *Vanderbilt University*
Latha Ramchand, *University of Houston*
William A. Reese, Jr., *Tulane University*
Ali Reza, *San Jose State University*
Steven P. Rich, *Baylor University*
Antonio Rodriguez, *Texas A&M International University*
Bruce Rubin, *Old Dominion University*
Mark Rubinstein, *University of California, Berkeley*
Harley E. Ryan, Jr., *Georgia State University*
Jacob A. Sagi, *University of California, Berkeley*
Harikumar Sankaran, *New Mexico State University*
Frederik Schlingemann, *University of Pittsburgh*
Mark Seasholes, *University of California, Berkeley*
Eduardo Schwartz, *University of California, Los Angeles*
Mark Shackleton, *Lancaster University*
Jay Shanken, *Emory University*
Dennis Sheehan, *Penn State University*
Anand Shetty, *Iona College*
Mark Simonson, *Arizona State University*
Rajeev Singhal, *Oakland University*
Erik Stafford, *Harvard Business School*
David Stangeland, *University of Manitoba*
Richard H. Stanton, *University of California, Berkeley*
Mark Hoven Stohs, *California State University, Fullerton*
Ilya A. Strebulaev, *Stanford University*
Ryan Stever, *Bank for International Settlements*
John Strong, *College of William and Mary*
Diane Suhler, *Columbia College*
Lawrence Tai, *Loyola Marymount University*
Mark Taranto, *University of Pennsylvania*
Amir Tavakkol, *Kansas State University*
Andy Terry, *University of Arkansas at Little Rock*
John Thornton, *Kent State University*
Alex Triantis, *University of Maryland*
Sorin Tuluca, *Fairleigh Dickinson University*
Joe Walker, *University of Alabama at Birmingham*
Edward Waller, *University of Houston, Clear Lake*
Peihwang Wei, *University of New Orleans*
Peter Went, *Bucknell University*
John White, *Georgia Southern University*
Michael Williams, *University of Denver*
Annie Wong, *Western Connecticut State University*
K. Matthew Wong, *St. John's University*
Bob Wood, Jr., *Tennessee Tech University*
Lifan Wu, *California State University, Los Angeles*
Tzyy-Jeng Wu, *Pace University*
Jaime Zender, *University of Colorado*
Jeffrey H. Zwiebel, *Stanford University*

Chapter Class Testers

Jack Aber, *Boston University*
John Adams, *University of South Florida*
James Conover, *University of North Texas*
Lou Gingerella, *Rensselaer Polytechnic Institute*
Tom Geurts, *Marist College*
Keith Johnson, *University of Kentucky*
Gautum Kaul, *University of Michigan*
Doseong Kim, *University of Akron*
Jennifer Koski, *University of Washington*
George Kutner, *Marquette University*
Larry Lynch, *Roanoke College*
Vasil Mihov, *Texas Christina University*
Jeryl Nelson, *Wayne State College*
Chee Ng, *Fairleigh Dickinson University*
Ben Nunnally, *University of North Carolina, Charlotte*
Michael Proviteria, *Barry University*
Charu G. Raheja, *Vanderbilt University*
Bruce Rubin, *Old Dominion University*
Mark Seasholes, *University of California, Berkeley*
Dennis Sheehan, *Pennsylvania State University*
Ravi Shukla, *Syracuse University*
Mark Hoven Stohs, *California State University, Fullerton*
Andy Terry, *University of Arkansas*
Sorin Tuluca, *Fairleigh Dickinson University*
Joe Ueng, *University of Saint Thomas*
Bob Wood, *Tennessee Technological University*

End-of-Chapter Problems Class Testers

James Angel, *Georgetown University*
Ting-Heng Chu, *East Tennessee State University*
Robert Kravchuk, *Indiana University*
George Kutner, *Marquette University*
James Nelson, *East Carolina University*
Don Panton, *University of Texas at Arlington*
P. Raghavendra Rau, *Purdue University*
Carolyn Reichert, *University of Texas at Dallas*
Mark Simonson, *Arizona State University*
Diane Suhler, *Columbia College*

Focus Group Participants

Christopher Anderson, *University of Kansas*
Chenchu Bathala, *Cleveland State University*
Matthew T. Billett, *University of Iowa*
Andrea DeMaskey, *Villanova University*
Anand Desai, *Kansas State University*
Ako Doffou, *Sacred Heart University*
Shannon Donovan, *Bridgewater State University*
Ibrahim Elsaify, *Goldey-Beacom College*
Mark Holder, *Kent State University*
Steve Isberg, *University of Baltimore*

Arun Khanna, *Butler University*
Brian Kluger, *University of Cincinnati*
Greg LaBlanc, *University of California, Berkeley*
Dima Leshchinskii, *Rensselaer Polytechnic University*
James S. Linck, *University of Georgia*
Larry Lynch, *Roanoke College*
David C. Mauer, *Southern Methodist University*
Alfred Mettler, *Georgia State University*
Stuart Michelson, *Stetson University*
Vassil Mihov, *Texas Christian University*
Jeryl Nelson, *Wayne State College*
Chee Ng, *Fairleigh Dickinson University*
Ben Nunnally, *University of North Carolina at Charlotte*
Sunny Onyiri, *Campbellsville University*
Janet Payne, *Texas State University*
Michael Provitera, *Barry University*
Avri Ravid, *Rutgers University*
William A. Reese, Jr., *Tulane University*
Mario Reyes, *University of Idaho*
Hong Rim, *Shippensburg University*
Robert Ritchey, *Texas Tech University*
Antonio Rodriquez, *Texas A&M International University*
Dan Rogers, *Portland State University*
Harley E. Ryan, Jr., *Georgia State University*
Harikumar Sankaran, *New Mexico State University*
Sorin Sorescu, *Texas A&M University*
David Stangeland, *University of Manitoba*
Jonathan Stewart, *Abilene Christian University*
Mark Hoven Stohs, *California State University, Fullerton*
Tim Sullivan, *Bentley College*
Olie Thorp, *Babson College*
Harry Turtle, *Washington State University*
Joseph Vu, *DePaul University*
Joe Walker, *University of Alabama at Birmingham*
Jill Wetmore, *Saginaw Valley State University*
Jack Wolf, *Clemson University*
Bob Wood, Jr., *Tennessee Tech University*
Donald H. Wort, *California State University, East Bay*
Scott Wright, *Ohio University*
Tong Yao, *University of Arizona*

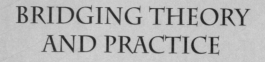

BRIDGING THEORY AND PRACTICE

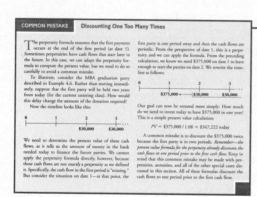

The Law of One Price as the Unifying Valuation Framework

The Law of One Price framework reflects the modern idea that the absence of arbitrage is the unifying concept of valuation. This critical insight is introduced in Chapter 3, revisited in each Part Opener, and integrated throughout the text—motivating all major concepts and connecting theory to practice.

Study Aids with a Practical Focus

To be successful, students need to master the core concepts and learn to identify and solve problems that today's practitioners face.

- **Common Mistake** boxes alert students to frequently made mistakes stemming from misunderstanding core concepts and calculations, as well as mistakes made in practice.

- **Worked Examples** accompany every important concept using a step-by-step procedure that illustrates both Problem and Solution. Clear labels make them easy to find for help with homework or studying. Many include an Excel spreadsheet calculator.

Computing a Loan Payment

Problem

Your firm plans to buy a warehouse for $100,000. The bank offers you a 30-year loan with equal annual payments and an interest rate of 8% per year. The bank requires that your firm pay 20% of the purchase price as a down payment, so you can borrow only $80,000. What is the annual loan payment?

Solution

We start with the timeline (from the bank's perspective):

Using Eq. 4.12, we can solve for the loan payment, C, as follows:

$$C = \frac{P}{\frac{1}{r}\left(1 - \frac{1}{(1+r)^N}\right)} = \frac{80,000}{\frac{1}{0.08}\left(1 - \frac{1}{(1.08)^{30}}\right)}$$

$$= \$7106.19$$

Using the annuity spreadsheet:

	NPER	RATE	PV	PMT	FV	Excel Formula
Given	30	8.00%	−80,000		0	
Solve for PMT				7106		=PMT(0.08,30,−80000,0)

Your firm will need to pay $7106.19 each year to repay the loan.

Applications That Reflect Real Practice

Corporate Finance: The Core features actual companies and leaders in the field.

- Real-company examples open each chapter.

- Interviews with notable practitioners are featured in many chapters.

- General Interest boxes highlight timely material from financial publications that shed light on business problems and real-company practices.

TEACHING STUDENTS TO THINK FINANCE

With a consistency in presentation and an innovative set of learning aids, *Corporate Finance: The Core* simultaneously meets the needs of both future financial managers and non-financial managers. This textbook truly shows every student how to "think finance."

Simplified Presentation of Mathematics

One of the hardest parts of learning finance is mastering the jargon, math, and non-standardized notation. *Corporate Finance: The Core* systematically uses:

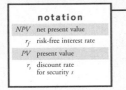

- **Notation Boxes:** Each chapter begins with a Notation box that defines the variables and the acronyms used in the chapter and serves as "legend" for students' reference.

- **Numbered and Labeled Equations:** The first time a full equation is given in notation form it is numbered. Key equations are titled and revisited in the summary and in end papers.

Future Value of an Annuity

$$FV(\text{annuity}) = PV \times (1 + r)^N$$

$$= \frac{C}{r}\left(1 - \frac{1}{(1 + r)^N}\right) \times (1 + r)^N$$

$$= C \times \frac{1}{r}\left((1 + r)^N - 1\right) \tag{4.8}$$

- **Spreadsheet Tables:** Select tables are available on the textbook Web site as Excel files, enabling students to change inputs and manipulate the underlying calculations.

Practice Finance to Learn Finance

Working problems is the proven way to cement and demonstrate an understanding of finance.

- **Concept Check questions** at the end of each section enable students to test their understanding and target areas in which they need further review.

- **End-of-chapter problems written personally by Jonathan Berk and Peter DeMarzo** offer instructors the opportunity to assign first-rate materials to students for homework and practice with the confidence that the problems are consistent with the chapter content. Both the problems and solutions, which were also written by the authors, have been class-tested and accuracy checked to ensure quality.

End-of-Chapter Materials Reinforce Learning

Testing understanding of central concepts is crucial to learning finance.
- **Chapter Summaries and Key Terms lists** are vital aids for studying and review.
- **Data Cases** present in-depth scenarios in a business setting with questions designed to guide students' analysis. Many questions involve the use of Internet resources.
- **Further Readings** direct the student reader to seminal studies and late-breaking research to encourage independent study.

Data Case

Assume today is August 1, 2006. Natasha Kingery is 30 years old and has a Bachelor of Science degree in computer science. She is currently employed as a Tier 2 field service representative for a telephony corporation located in Seattle, Washington, and earns $38,000 a year that she anticipates will grow at 3% per year. Natasha hopes to retire at age 65 and has just begun to think about the future.

Natasha has $75,000 that she recently inherited from her aunt. She invested this money in 10-year Treasury Bonds. She is considering whether she should further her education and would use her inheritance to pay for it.

She has investigated a couple of options and is asking for your help as a financial planning intern to determine the financial consequences associated with each option. Natasha has already been accepted to both of these programs, and could start either one soon.

One alternative that Natasha is considering is attaining a certification in network design. This certification would automatically promote her to a Tier 3 field service representative in her company. The base salary for a Tier 3 representative is $10,000 more than what she currently earns and she anticipates that this salary differential will grow at a rate of 3% a year as long as she keeps working. The certification program requires the completion of 20 Web-based courses and a score of 80% or better on an exam at the end of the course work. She has learned that the average amount of time necessary to finish the program is one year. The total cost of the program is $5,000, due when she enrolls in the program. Because she will do all the work for the certification on her own time, Natasha does not expect to lose any income during the certification.

Another option is going back to school for an MBA degree. With an MBA degree, Natasha expects to be promoted to a managerial position in her current firm. The managerial position

Because practice with homework problems is crucial to learning finance, each copy of *Corporate Finance: The Core* is available with MyFinanceLab, a fully integrated homework and tutorial system.

MyFinanceLab revolutionizes homework and practice with a unique hint and partial credit system written and developed by Jonathan Berk and Peter DeMarzo.

Online Assessment Using End-of-Chapter Problems

The seamless integration among the textbook, assessment materials, and online resources sets a new standard in corporate finance education.

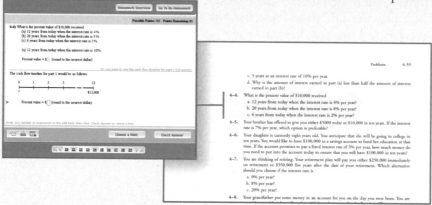

- **End-of-chapter problems** appear online. The values in the problems are algorithmically generated, giving students many opportunities for practice and mastery. Problems can be assigned by professors and completed online by students.

- **Helpful tutorial tools**, along with the same pedagogical aids from the text, support students as they study. Links to the eText direct students right to the material they most need to review.

Revolutionary Hint and Partial Credit System

MyFinanceLab provides "hints" that coach students through difficult problems. Rather than scoring an entire problem right or wrong, the partial credit system rewards students for their efforts.

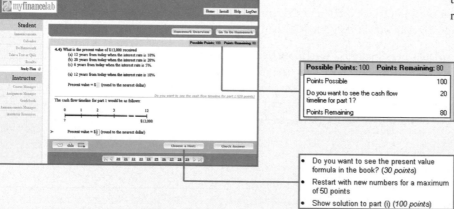

To learn more about MyFinanceLab, contact your local Pearson representative or go online to www.myfinancelab.com

HANDS-ON PRACTICE, HANDS-OFF GRADING

Hands-on, Targeted Practice

Students can take pre-loaded Practice Tests for each chapter, and their test results will generate an individualized Study Plan. With the Study Plan, students learn to focus their energies on the topics they need to be successful in class, on exams, and, ultimately, in their future careers.

Powerful Instructor Tools

MyFinanceLab provides flexible tools that enable instructors to easily customize the online course materials to suit their needs.

- **Easy-to-Use Homework Manager.** Instructors can easily create and assign tests, quizzes, or graded homework assignments. In addition to pre-loaded MyFinanceLab questions, the Test Bank is also available so that instructors have ample material with which to create assignments.

- **Flexible Gradebook.** MyFinanceLab saves time by automatically grading students' work and tracking results in an online Gradebook.

- **Downloadable Classroom Resources.** Instructors also have access to online versions of each instructor supplement, including the Instructor's Manual, PowerPoint Lecture Notes, and Test Bank.

CORPORATE FINANCE: THE CORE

PART

I

Introduction

The Law of One Price Connection. Why study Corporate Finance? No matter what your role in a corporation, an understanding of why and how financial decisions are made is essential. The focus of this book is how to make optimal corporate financial decisions. In this part of the book we lay the foundation for our study of corporate finance. We begin, in Chapter 1, by introducing the corporation and related business forms. We then examine the role of financial managers and outside investors in decision making for the firm. To make optimal decisions, a decision maker needs information. As a result, in Chapter 2 we review an important source of information for corporate decision making—the firm's accounting statements. Then, in Chapter 3 we introduce the most important idea in this book, the concept of *the absence of arbitrage* or *Law of One Price.* The Law of One Price states that we can use market prices to determine the value of an investment opportunity to the firm.

We will demonstrate that the Law of One Price is the one unifying principle that underlies all of financial economics and links all of the ideas throughout this book. We will return to this theme throughout our study of Corporate Finance.

The Corporation

The modern U.S. corporation was born in a courtroom in Washington, D.C., on February 2, 1819. On that day the U.S. Supreme Court established the legal precedent that the property of a corporation, like that of a person, is private and entitled to protection under the U.S. Constitution. Today, it is hard to entertain the possibility that a corporation's private property would not be protected by the Constitution. However, before the 1819 Supreme Court ruling, the owners of a corporation were exposed to the possibility that the state could take their business. This concern was real enough to stop most businesses from incorporating and, indeed, in 1816 that concern was realized: The state seized Dartmouth College.

Dartmouth College was incorporated in 1769 as a private educational institution governed by a self-perpetuating board of trustees. By 1816, this board of trustees was largely made up of Federalists (the political party most closely associated with George Washington), but the state government of New Hampshire was dominated by Republicans (the political party of Thomas Jefferson, later to become the modern Democratic Party). Unhappy with the political leanings of the college, the state legislature effectively took control of Dartmouth by passing legislation that established a governor-appointed board of overseers to run the school. The legislation had the effect of turning a private university under private control into a state university under state control. If such an act were constitutional, it implied that any state (or the federal government) could, at will, nationalize any corporation.

Dartmouth sued for its independence and the case made it to the Supreme Court in 1818. The chief justice at the time, John Marshall, delayed rendering a decision until 1819 to allow time to garner a nearly unanimous 5–1 ruling. He realized the importance of this decision and wanted the court to speak with a single voice. The court first ruled that a corporation was a "contract." Then, under Article 1 of the Constitution, the court noted that, "the state legislatures were forbidden to pass any law impairing the obligation of contracts" and struck down the New Hampshire law.[1] The precedent was clear: An owner of businesses could incorporate and thereby enjoy the protection of private property, as well as protection from seizure, both guaranteed by the U.S. Constitution. The modern business corporation was born.

The effect of this decision was dramatic. In 1800, the number of corporations that produced goods in the whole of the United States stood at eight. By 1830, more than 1400 corporations were involved in commerce and production in New England alone. In 1890, the number of U.S. chartered business corporations had risen to 50,000. Today the corporate structure is ubiquitous, not only in the United States (where they are responsible for 85% of business revenue), but all over the world.

This book is about how corporations make financial decisions. The purpose of this chapter is to introduce the corporation, as well as explain alternative business organizational forms. A key factor in the success of corporations is the ability to easily trade ownership shares, and so we will also explain the role of stock markets in facilitating trading among investors in a corporation and the implications that has for the ownership and control of corporations.

1.1   The Four Types of Firms

We begin by introducing the four major types of firms: sole proprietorships, partnerships, limited liability companies, and corporations. We explain each organizational form in turn, but our primary focus is on the most important form—the corporation. In addition to describing what a corporation is, we also provide an overview of why corporations are so successful.

Sole Proprietorships

A **sole proprietorship** is a business owned and run by one person. Sole proprietorships are usually very small with few, if any, employees. Although they do not account for much sales revenue in the economy, they are the most common type of firm in the world, as shown in Figure 1.1. Statistics indicate that 72% of businesses in the United States are sole proprietorships, although they generate only 5% of the revenue.[2] Contrast this with corporations which make up only 20% of firms but are responsible for 85% of U.S. revenue. Other organizational forms such as partnerships and limited liability companies make up the remaining 8% of firms and are responsible for 10% of U.S. revenue.

The advantage of a sole proprietorship is that it is straightforward to set up. Consequently, many new businesses use this organizational form. The principal limitation of a sole proprietorship is that there is no separation between the firm and the owner—the

---

1. The full text of John Marshall's decision can be found at http://www.constitution.org/dwebster/dartmouth_decision.htm.

2. This information, as well as other small business statistics, can be found at www.bizstats.com/businesses.htm. See their on-site disclosures page for a description of their methodology.

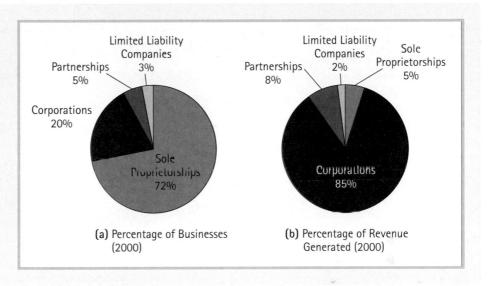

FIGURE 1.1

Types of U.S. Firms
There are four different types of firms in the United States. As (a) and (b) show, although the majority of U.S. firms are sole proprietorships, they generate only a small fraction of total revenue, in contrast to corporations.
Source: www.bizstats.com

firm can have only one owner. If there are other investors, they cannot hold an ownership stake in the firm. The owner has unlimited personal liability for any of the firm's debts. That is, if the firm defaults on any debt payment, the lender can (and will) require the owner to repay the loan from personal assets. If the owner cannot afford to repay the loan, he or she must declare personal bankruptcy. In addition, the life of a sole proprietorship is limited to the life of the owner. It is also difficult to transfer ownership of a sole proprietorship.

For most businesses, the disadvantages of a sole proprietorship outweigh the advantages. As soon as the firm reaches the point at which it can borrow without the owner agreeing to be personally liable, the owners typically convert the business into a form that limits the owner's liability.

Partnerships

A **partnership** is like a sole proprietorship but with more than one owner. In a partnership, *all* partners are liable for the firm's debt. That is, a lender can require *any* partner to repay all the firm's outstanding debts. The partnership ends on the death or withdrawal of any single partner. However, partners can avoid liquidation if the partnership agreement provides for alternatives such as a buyout of a deceased or withdrawn partner.

Some old and established businesses remain partnerships or sole proprietorships. Often these firms are the types of businesses in which the owners' personal reputations are the basis for the businesses. For example, law firms, groups of doctors, and accounting firms are often organized as partnerships. For such enterprises, the partners' personal liability increases the confidence of the firm's clients that the partners will continue to work to maintain their reputation.

A **limited partnership** is a partnership with two kinds of owners, general partners and limited partners. General partners have the same rights and privileges as partners in a (general) partnership—they are personally liable for the firm's debt obligations. Limited partners, however, have **limited liability**—that is, their liability is limited to their investment. Their private property cannot be seized to pay off the firm's outstanding debts. Furthermore, the death or withdrawal of a limited partner does not dissolve the

INTERVIEW WITH
David Viniar

D avid Viniar is Chief Financial Officer and head of the Operations, Technology and Finance Division at Goldman Sachs—the last major investment bank to convert from a partnership to a corporation. He joined the firm in 1980 and worked in Investment Banking, Treasury, and Controllers. In his role as the firm's CFO he played a leading role in the firm's conversion to a corporation in 1999.

QUESTION: *What are the advantages of partnerships and corporations?*

ANSWER: We debated this question at length when we were deciding whether to go public or stay a private partnership in the mid-1990s. There were good arguments on both sides, and smart people were taking strong positions for and against.

Those in favor of going public argued we needed greater financial and strategic flexibility to achieve our aggressive growth and market leadership goals. As a public corporation, we would have a more stable equity base to support growth and disperse risk; increased access to large public debt markets; publicly traded securities with which to undertake acquisitions and reward and motivate our employees; and a simpler and more transparent structure with which to increase scale and global reach.

Those against going public argued our private partnership structure worked well and would enable us to achieve our financial and strategic goals. As a private partnership, we could generate enough capital internally and in the private placement markets to fund growth; take a longer-term view of returns on our investments with less focus on earnings volatility, which is not valued in public companies; and retain voting control and alignment of the partners and the firm.

A big perceived advantage of our private partnership was its sense of distinctiveness and mystique, which reinforced our culture of teamwork and excellence and helped differentiate us from our competitors. Many questioned whether the special qualities of our culture would survive if the firm went public.

QUESTION: *What was the driving force behind the conversion?*

ANSWER: We ultimately decided to go public for three main reasons: to secure permanent capital to grow; to be able to use publicly traded securities to finance strategic acquisitions; and to enhance the culture of ownership and gain compensation flexibility.

QUESTION: *Did the conversion achieve its goals?*

ANSWER: Yes. As a public company, we have a simpler, bigger and more permanent capital base, including enhanced long-term borrowing capacity in the public debt markets. We have drawn on substantial capital resources to serve clients, take advantage of new business opportunities, and better control our own destiny though changing economic and business conditions. We have been able to use stock to finance key acquisitions and support large strategic and financial investments. Given how the stakes in our industry changed, how the capital demands grew, going public when we did fortunately positioned us to compete effectively through the cycle.

Our distinctive culture of teamwork and excellence has thrived in public form, and our equity compensation programs turned out better than we could have hoped. Making everyone at Goldman Sachs an owner, rather than just 221 partners, energized all our employees. The growing size and scope of our business—not the change to public form—has presented the greatest challenges to the positive aspects of our culture.

QUESTION: *Goldman Sachs was the last of the major banks to convert. Why was that and in retrospect, should it have converted sooner?*

ANSWER: We were very successful as a private partnership, and it took time to reach a consensus among the partners that an IPO would permit us to achieve even greater success. We looked at going public many times in the years leading up to our conversion—and believe we chose the right moment for the IPO in view of our business, financial and strategic needs.

partnership, and a limited partner's interest is transferable. However, a limited partner has no management authority and cannot legally be involved in the managerial decision making for the business.

Limited Liability Companies

A **limited liability company** (LLC) is a limited partnership without a general partner. That is, all the owners have limited liability, but unlike limited partners, they can also run the business.

The LLC is a relatively new phenomenon in the United States. The first state to pass a statute allowing the creation of an LLC was Wyoming in 1977; the last was Hawaii in 1997. Internationally, companies with limited liability are much older and established. LLCs rose to prominence first in Germany over 100 years ago as a *Gesellschaft mit beschränkter Haftung* (GmbH) and then in other European and Latin American countries. An LLC is known in France as a *Société à responsabilité limitée* (SAR), and by similar names in Italy (SRL) and Spain (SL).

Corporations

The distinguishing feature of a **corporation** is that it is a legally defined, artificial being (a judicial person or legal entity), separate from its owners. As such, it has many of the legal powers that people have. It can enter into contracts, acquire assets, incur obligations, and, as we have already established, it enjoys protection under the U.S. Constitution against the seizure of its property. Because a corporation is a legal entity separate and distinct from its owners, it is solely responsible for its own obligations. Consequently, the owners of a corporation (or its employees, customers, etc.) are not liable for any obligations the corporation enters into. Similarly, the corporation is not liable for any personal obligations of its owners.

Formation of a Corporation. Corporations must be legally formed, which means that the state in which it is incorporated must formally give its consent to the incorporation by chartering it. Setting up a corporation is therefore considerably more costly than setting up a sole proprietorship. The state of Delaware has a particularly attractive legal environment for corporations, so many corporations choose to incorporate there. For jurisdictional purposes, a corporation is a citizen of the state in which it is incorporated. Most firms hire lawyers to create a corporate charter that includes formal articles of incorporation and a set of bylaws. The corporate charter specifies the initial rules that govern how the corporation is run.

Ownership of a Corporation. There is no limit on the number of owners a corporation can have. Because most corporations have many owners, each owner owns only a fraction of the corporation. The entire ownership stake of a corporation is divided into shares known as **stock**. The collection of all the outstanding shares of a corporation is known as the **equity** of the corporation. An owner of a share of stock in the corporation is known as a **shareholder**, **stockholder**, or **equity holder** and is entitled to **dividend payments**, that is, payments made at the discretion of the corporation to its equity holders. Shareholders usually receive a share of the dividend payments that is proportional to the amount of stock they own. For example, a shareholder who owns 25% of the firm's shares will be entitled to 25% of the total dividend payment.

A unique feature of a corporation is that there is no limitation on who can own its stock. That is, an owner of a corporation need not have any special expertise or qualification. This feature allows free trade in the shares of the corporation and provides one of the most important advantages of organizing a firm as a corporation rather than as sole proprietorship, partnership, or LLC. Corporations can raise substantial amounts of capital because they can sell ownership shares to anonymous outside investors.

The availability of outside funding has enabled corporations to dominate the economy (see Figure 1.1b). Let's take one of the world's largest firms, Microsoft Corporation, as an example. Microsoft reported annual revenue of $39.8 billion over the 12 months from July 2004 through June 2005. The total value of the company (the wealth in the company the owners collectively owned) as of September 2005 was $284.7 billion. It employed 61,000 people. Let's put these numbers into perspective. The $39.8 billion in gross domestic product (GDP) in 2004 would rank Microsoft (with Kazakhstan) as the 59th richest *country* (out of more than 200).[3] Kazakhstan has almost 15 million people, about 250 times as many people as employees at Microsoft. Indeed, if the number of employees were used as the "population" of Microsoft, Microsoft would rank with the Marshall Islands as the tenth least populous country on earth!

Tax Implications for Corporate Entities

An important difference between the types of organizational forms is the way they are taxed. Because a corporation is a separate legal entity, a corporation's profits are subject to taxation separate from its owners' tax obligations. In effect, shareholders of a corporation pay taxes twice. First, the corporation pays tax on its profits, and then when the remaining profits are distributed to the shareholders, the shareholders pay their own personal income tax on this income. This system is sometimes referred to as double taxation.

EXAMPLE 1.1

Taxation of Corporate Earnings

Problem

You are a shareholder in a corporation. The corporation earns $5 per share before taxes. After it has paid taxes, it will distribute the rest of its earnings to you as a dividend. The dividend is income to you, so you will then pay taxes on these earnings. The corporate tax rate is 40% and your tax rate on dividend income is 15%. How much of the earnings remains after all taxes are paid?

Solution

First, the corporation pays taxes. It earned $5 per share, but must pay $0.40 \times \$5 = \$2$ to the government in corporate taxes. That leaves $3 to distribute. However, you must pay $0.15 \times \$3 = 45$ cents in income taxes on this amount, leaving $\$3 - \$0.45 = \$2.55$ per share after all taxes are paid. As a shareholder you only end up with $2.55 of the original $5 in earnings; the remaining $\$2 + \$0.45 = \$2.45$ is paid as taxes. Thus, your total effective tax rate is $2.45 / 5 = 49\%$.

---

3. World Development Indicators database, July 15, 2005. For quick reference tables on GDP, go to http://www.worldbank.org/data/quickreference.html.

In most countries, there is some relief from double taxation. Thirty countries make up the Organization for Economic Co-operation and Development (OECD), and of these countries, only Ireland and Switzerland offer no relief from double taxation. The United States offers some relief by having a lower tax rate on dividend income than on other sources of income. As of 2005, dividend income is taxed at 15%, which, for most investors, is significantly below their personal income tax rate. A few countries, including Australia, Finland, Mexico, New Zealand, and Norway, offer complete relief by effectively not taxing dividend income.

The corporate organizational structure is the only organizational structure subject to double taxation. In addition, the U.S. Internal Revenue Code allows an exemption from double taxation for certain corporations. These corporations are called **"S" corporations** because they elect subchapter S tax treatment. Under these tax regulations, the firm's profits (and losses) are not subject to corporate taxes, but instead are allocated directly to shareholders based on their ownership share. The shareholders must include these profits as income on their individual tax returns (even if no money is distributed to them). However, after the shareholders have paid income taxes on these profits, no further tax is due.

EXAMPLE 1.2

Taxation of S Corporation Earnings

Problem
Rework Example 1.1 assuming the corporation in that example has elected subchapter S treatment and your tax rate on non-dividend income is 30%.

Solution
In this case, the corporation pays no taxes. It earned $5 per share. Whether or not the corporation chooses to distribute or retain this cash, you must pay $0.30 \times \$5 = \$1.50$ in income taxes, which is substantially lower than the $2.45 you paid in Example 1.1.

The government places strict limitations on the qualifications for subchapter S tax treatment. In particular, the shareholders of such corporations must be individuals who are U.S. citizens or residents, and there can be no more than 100 of them. Because most corporations have no restrictions on who owns their shares or the number of shareholders, they cannot qualify for subchapter S treatment. Thus most corporations are **"C" corporations**, which are corporations subject to corporate taxes.

CONCEPT CHECK

1. What are the advantages and disadvantages of organizing a business as a corporation?

2. What is a limited liability company (LLC)? How does it differ from a limited partnership?

1.2 Ownership Versus Control of Corporations

Unlike the owner of a sole proprietorship, which has direct control of the firm, it is often not feasible for the owners of a corporation to have direct control of the firm because there are many owners of a corporation, each of whom can freely trade their stock. That is, in a corporation, direct control and ownership are often separate. Rather than the owners the *board of directors* and *chief executive officer* possess direct control of the corporation. In this section, we explain how the responsibilities for the corporation are divided between these two entities.

The Corporate Management Team

The shareholders of a corporation exercise their control by electing a **board of directors**, a group of people who have the ultimate decision-making authority in the corporation. In most corporations, each share of stock gives a shareholder one vote in the election of the board of directors, so investors with more shares have more influence. When one or two shareholders own a very large proportion of the outstanding stock, these shareholders might either themselves be on the board of directors, or they may have the right to appoint a number of directors.

The board of directors makes rules on how the corporation should be run (including how the top managers in the corporation are compensated), sets policy, and monitors the performance of the company. The board of directors delegates most decisions that involve day-to-day running of the corporation to its management, which is headed by the **chief executive officer (or CEO)**. This person is charged with running the corporation by instituting the rules and policies set by the board of directors. The size of the rest of the management team varies from corporation to corporation. The separation of powers within corporations is not always distinct. In fact, it is not uncommon for the CEO also to be the chairman of the board of directors.

Ownership and Control of Corporations

In theory, the goal of a firm should be determined by the firm's owners. A sole proprietorship has a single owner who runs the firm, so the goals of a sole proprietorship are the same as the owner's goals. But in organizational forms with multiple owners, the goal of the firm is not as clear.

Many corporations have thousands of owners (shareholders). Each owner is likely to have different interests and priorities. Whose interests and priorities determine the goals of the firm? Later in the book, we examine this question in more detail. However, you might be surprised to learn that the interests of shareholders are aligned for many, if not most, important decisions. For example, if the decision is whether to develop a new product that will be a profitable investment for the corporation, all shareholders will very likely agree that developing this product is a good idea.

Even when all the owners of a corporation agree on the goals of the corporation, these goals must be implemented. In a simple organizational form like a sole proprietorship, the owner, who runs the firm, can ensure that the firm's goals match his own. But a corporation is run by a management team, separate from its owners. How can the owners of a corporation ensure that the management team will implement their goals?

Principal-Agent Problem.   Many people claim that because of the separation of ownership and control in a corporation, managers have little incentive to work in the interests of the shareholders when this means working against their own self-interest. Economists call this a **principal-agent problem**. The most common way the principal-agent problem is addressed in practice is by minimizing the number of decisions managers make that require putting their self-interest against the interests of the shareholders. For example, managers' compensation contracts are designed to ensure that most decisions in the shareholders' interest are also in the managers' interests; shareholders often tie the compensation of top managers to the corporation's profits or perhaps to its stock price. There is, however, a limitation to this strategy. By tying compensation too closely to performance, the shareholders might be asking managers to take on more risk than they are comfortable taking and so the managers may not make decisions that the shareholders want them to, or it might be hard to find talented managers willing to accept the job.

The CEO's Performance.   Another way shareholders can encourage managers to work in the interests of shareholders is to discipline them if they don't. If shareholders are unhappy with a CEO's performance, they could, in principle, pressure the board to oust the CEO. However, directors and top executives are very rarely replaced through a grass-roots shareholder uprising. Instead, dissatisfied investors often choose to sell their shares. Of course, somebody must be willing to buy the shares from the dissatisfied shareholders. If enough shareholders are dissatisfied, the only way to entice investors to buy (or hold) the shares is to offer them a low price. Similarly, investors who see a well-managed corporation will want to purchase shares, which drives the stock price up. Thus, the stock price of the corporation is a barometer for corporate leaders that continuously gives them feedback on their shareholders' opinion of their performance.

When the stock performs poorly, the board of directors might react by replacing the CEO. In some corporations, however, the senior executives are entrenched because boards of directors do not have the will to replace them. Often the reluctance to fire results because the board is comprised of people who are close friends of the CEO and lack objectivity. In corporations in which the CEO is entrenched and doing a poor job, the expectation of continued poor performance will cause the stock price to be low. Low stock prices create a profit opportunity. In a **hostile takeover**, an individual or organization—sometimes known as a corporate raider—can purchase a large fraction of the stock and in doing so get enough votes to replace the board of directors and the CEO. With a new superior management team, the stock is a much more attractive investment, which would likely result in a price rise and a profit for the corporate raider and the other shareholders. Although the words "hostile" and "raider" have negative connotations, corporate raiders themselves provide an important service to shareholders. The mere threat of being removed as a result of a hostile takeover is often enough to discipline bad managers and motivate boards of directors to make difficult decisions. Consequently, the fact that a corporation's shares can be publicly traded creates a "market for corporate control" that encourages managers and boards of directors to act in the interests of their shareholders.

Corporate Bankruptcy.   Because a corporation is a separate legal entity, when it fails to repay its debts, the people who lent to the firm, the debt holders, are entitled to seize the assets of the corporation in compensation for the default. To prevent such a seizure, the firm may attempt to renegotiate with the debt holders, or file for bankruptcy protection in a federal court. We describe the details of the bankruptcy process and its implications for corporate decisions in much more detail in Part V of the text, but because of its importance in corporate decision making, it is useful to understand some of the main aspects of default and corporate bankruptcy even at this early stage.

In bankruptcy, management is given the opportunity to reorganize the firm and renegotiate with debt holders. If this process fails, control of the corporation generally passes to the debt holders. In most cases, the original equity holders are left with little or no stake in the firm. Thus, when a firm fails to repay its debts, the end result is often a change in ownership of the firm, with control passing from equity holders to debt holders. Importantly, bankruptcy need not result in a **liquidation** of the firm, which involves shutting down the business and selling off its assets. Even if control of the firm passes to the debt holders, it is in the debt holders' interest to run the firm in the most profitable way

Shareholder Activism and Voting Rights

In reaction to poor stock market performance and several accounting scandals, the number of *shareholder initiatives* (when shareholders request that a specific firm policy or decision be put to a direct vote of all shareholders) has increased dramatically in recent years. According to the Investor Responsibility Research Center, the number of shareholder proposals increased from about 800 during 2002 to over 1100 during 2004. Shareholder initiatives have covered a range of topics, including shareholder voting rights, takeovers and anti-takeover provisions, election of members of the board of directors, and changes in the time or location of shareholder meetings.

One of the recent trends in shareholder activism is to withhold voting support for nominees to the board of directors. In March 2004, shareholders withheld support for Michael Eisner (the Disney CEO) as chairman of the board. As a result, he lost the Disney chairmanship but retained his position as CEO. The California Public Employees' Retirement System (Calpers), the world's largest pension fund, has withheld votes for at least one of the directors in 90% of the 2700 companies in which it invests.

Source: Adapted from John Goff, "Who's the Boss?" *CFO Magazine,* September 1, 2004, pp. 56–66.

possible. Doing so often means keeping the business operating. For example, in 1990, Federated Department Stores declared bankruptcy. One of its best known assets at the time was Bloomingdale's, a nationally known department store. Because Bloomingdale's was a profitable business, neither equity holders nor debt holders had any desire to shut it down, and it continued to operate in bankruptcy. In 1992, when Federated Department Stores was reorganized and emerged from bankruptcy, Federated's original equity holders had lost their stake in Bloomingdale's, but this flagship chain continued to perform well for its new owners, and its value as a business was not adversely affected by the bankruptcy.

Thus, a useful way to understand corporations is to think of there being two sets of investors with claims to its cash flows—debt holders and equity holders. As long as the corporation can satisfy the claims of the debt holders, ownership remains in the hands of the equity holders. If the corporation fails to satisfy debt holders' claims, debt holders may take control of the firm. Thus a corporate bankruptcy is best thought of as a *change in ownership* of the corporation, and not necessarily as a failure of the underlying business.

CONCEPT CHECK
1. What is a principal-agent problem that may exist in a corporation?
2. How does the board of directors control a corporation?
3. How may a corporate bankruptcy filing affect the ownership of a corporation?

1.3 The Stock Market

From an outside investors' point of view, an important feature of an investment in the equity of a corporation is its *liquidity*. An investment is said to be **liquid** if it is possible to easily sell it for close to the price you can contemporaneously buy it for. The shares of many corporations are liquid because they trade on organized markets, called **stock markets (or stock exchanges)**. These kinds of corporations are known as **public companies**.

An investor in a public company can easily and quickly turn his investment into cash by simply selling his shares on one of these markets. However, not all corporations are public companies. Some corporations known as **private companies** do not allow trading or limit trading to privately brokered transactions among investors.

The Largest Stock Markets

The best known U.S. stock market and the largest stock market in the world is the New York Stock Exchange (NYSE). Billions of dollars of stock are exchanged every day on the NYSE. Other U.S. stock markets include the American Stock Exchange (AMEX), Nasdaq (which stands for the National Association of Security Dealers Automated Quotation), and regional exchanges such as the Midwest Stock Exchange. Most other countries have at least one stock market. Outside the United States, the biggest stock markets are the London Stock Exchange (LSE) and the Tokyo Stock Exchange (TSE).

Figure 1.2 ranks the world's largest stock markets by two of the most common measures: the total value of all domestic corporations listed on the exchange and the total annual volume of shares traded on the exchange.

NYSE

The NYSE is a physical place. On the floor of the NYSE, **market makers** (known on the NYSE as **specialists**) match buyers and sellers. They post two prices for every stock they make a market in: the price they stand willing to buy the stock at (the **bid price**) and a price they stand willing to sell the stock for (the **ask price**). If a customer comes to them wanting to make a trade at these prices, they will honor the price (up to a limited number of shares) and make the trade even if they do not have another customer willing to take the other side of the trade. In this way, they ensure that the market is liquid because customers can always be assured they can trade at the posted prices. The exchange has rules that attempt to ensure that bid and ask prices do not get too far apart and that large price changes take place through a series of small changes, rather than one big jump.

Ask prices exceed bid prices. This difference is called the **bid-ask spread**. Because customers always buy at the ask (the higher price) and sell at the bid (the lower price), the bid-ask spread is a **transaction cost** investors have to pay in order to trade. Because specialists in a physical market like the NYSE take the other side of the trade from their customers, this cost accrues to them as a profit. It is the compensation they demand for providing a liquid market by standing ready to honor any quoted price. Investors also pay other forms of transactions costs like commissions.

Nasdaq

In today's economy, a stock market does not need to have a physical location. Stock transactions can be made (perhaps more efficiently) over the phone or by computer network. Consequently, some stock markets are a collection of dealers or market makers connected by computer network and telephone. The most famous example of such a market is Nasdaq. An important difference between the NYSE and Nasdaq is that on the NYSE, each stock has only one market maker. On Nasdaq, stocks can and do have multiple market makers who compete with each other. Each market maker must post bid and ask prices in the Nasdaq network where they can be viewed by all participants. The Nasdaq system posts the best prices first and fills orders accordingly. This process guarantees investors the best possible price at the moment, whether they are buying or selling.

FIGURE 1.2

Worldwide Stock Markets Ranked by Two Common Measures

The 10 biggest stock markets in the world ranked (a) by total value of all domestic corporations listed on the exchange at year-end 2004 and (b) by total volume of shares traded on exchange in 2004.

Source: www.world-exchanges.org

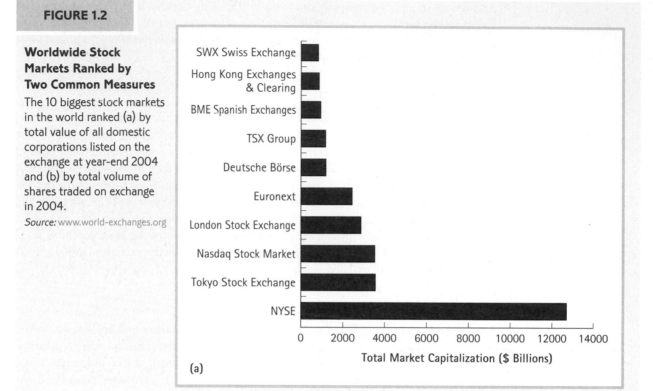

(a)

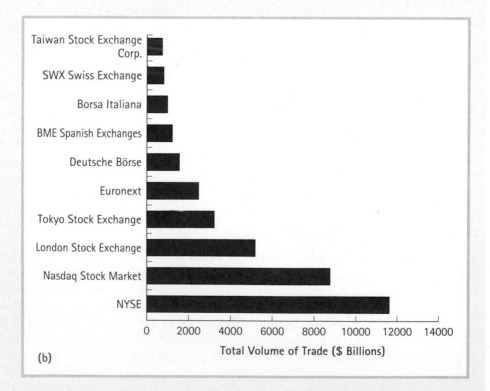

(b)

CONCEPT CHECK   1. What is the New York Stock Exchange (NYSE)?

2. What advantage does a stock market provide to corporate investors?

Summary

1. There are four types of firms in the United States: sole proprietorships, partnerships, limited liability companies, and corporations.

2. Firms with unlimited personal liability include sole proprietorships and partnerships.

3. Firms with limited liability include limited partnerships, limited liability companies, and corporations.

4. A corporation is a legally defined artificial being (a judicial person or legal entity) that has many of the legal powers people have. It can enter into contracts, acquire assets, incur obligations, and, as we have already established, it enjoys the protection under the U.S. Constitution against the seizure of its property.

5. The shareholders in a C corporation effectively must pay tax twice. The corporation pays tax once and then investors must pay personal tax on any funds that are distributed.

6. S corporations are exempt from the corporate income tax.

7. The ownership of a corporation is divided into shares of stock collectively known as equity. Investors in these shares are called shareholders, stockholders, or equity holders.

8. The ownership and control of a corporation are separated. Shareholders exercise their control indirectly through the board of directors.

9. Corporate bankruptcy can be thought of as a change in ownership and control of the corporation. The equity holders give up their ownership and control to the debt holders.

10. The shares of public corporations are traded on stock markets. The shares of private corporations do not trade on a stock market.

Key Terms

ask price *p. 13*
bid price *p. 13*
bid-ask spread *p. 13*
board of directors *p. 10*
"C" corporations *p. 9*
chief executive officer (or CEO) *p. 10*
corporation *p. 7*
dividend payments *p. 7*
equity *p. 7*
equity holder *p. 7*
hostile takeover *p. 11*
limited liability *p. 5*
limited liability company *p. 7*
limited partnership *p. 5*
liquid *p. 12*

liquidation *p. 11*
market makers *p. 13*
partnership *p. 5*
principal-agent problem *p. 10*
private companies *p. 13*
public companies *p. 12*
"S" corporations *p. 9*
shareholder *p. 7*
sole proprietorship *p. 4*
specialists *p. 13*
stock *p. 7*
stockholder *p. 7*
stock markets (or stock exchanges) *p. 12*
transaction cost *p. 13*

Further Reading

Readers interested in John Marshall's decision in the Dartmouth College case can find a more detailed description of the decision in J. E. Smith, *John Marshall: Definer of a Nation* (New York: Henry Holt, 1996), pp. 433–38.

An informative discussion that describes the objective of a corporation can be found in M. Jensen, "Value Maximization, Stakeholder Theory, and the Corporate Objective Function," *Journal of Applied Corporate Finance* (Fall 2001): 8–21.

Readers interested in what determines the goals of corporate managers and how they differ from shareholder's goals can either wait until we discuss these issues in more detail or can read M. C. Jensen and W. Meckling, "Theory of the Firm: Managerial Behavior, Agency Costs and Ownership Structure," *Journal of Financial Economics* 3(4), (1976): 305–60; J. E. Core, W. R. Guay, and D. F. Larker, "Executive Equity Compensation and Incentives: A Survey," *Federal Reserve Bank of New York Economic Policy Review* 9 (April 2003): 27–50.

The following papers explain corporate governance and ownership around the world: F. Barca and M. Becht, *The Control of Corporate Europe* (Oxford University Press, 2001); D. K. Denis and J. S. McConnell, "International Corporate Governance," *Journal of Financial Quantitative Analysis* 38 (March 2003); R. La Porta, F. Lopez-De-Silanes, and A. Shleifer, "Corporate Ownership Around the World," *Journal of Finance* 54(2) (1999): 471–517. Readers interested in a more detailed discussion of how taxes affect incorporation can consult J. K. Mackie-Mason and R. H. Gordon, "How Much Do Taxes Discourage Incorporation?" *Journal of Finance* 52(2) (1997): 477–505.

Problems

A blue box (■) indicates problems available in MyFinanceLab.

The Four Types of Firms

1. What is the most important difference between a corporation and *all* other organization forms?

2. What does the phrase *limited liability* mean in a corporate context?

3. Which organizational forms give their owners limited liability?

4. What are the main advantages and disadvantages of organizing a firm as a corporation?

5. Explain the difference between an S and a C corporation.

6. You are a shareholder in a C corporation. The corporation earns $2 per share before taxes. Once it has paid taxes it will distribute the rest of its earnings to you as a dividend. The corporate tax rate is 40% and the personal tax rate on (both dividend and non-dividend) income is 30%. How much is left for you after all taxes are paid?

7. Repeat Problem 6 assuming the corporation is an S corporation.

Ownership Versus Control of Corporations

8. Corporate managers work for the owners of the corporation. Consequently, they should make decisions that are in the interests of the owners, rather than their own. What strategies are available to shareholders to help ensure that managers are motivated to act this way?

9. What is the difference between a public and private corporation?

10. Explain why the bid-ask spread is a transaction cost.

11. The following quote on Yahoo! stock appeared on August 30, 2004, on Yahoo! Finance:

YAHOO! INC (NasdaqNM: YHOO) Quote data by Reuters				Edit
Last Trade:	**28.69**	Day's Range:	28.35 — 29.07	YHOO 30–Aug @ 11:45am (C)Yahoo!
Trade Time:	11:42AM ET	52wk Range:	16.56 — 36.51	
Change:	↓ 0.61 (2.08%)	Volume:	7,374,448	
Prev Close:	29.30	Avg Vol (3m)	20,232,318	
Open:	29.04	Market Cap:	39.03B	
Bid:	28.69 × 1000	P/E (ttm):	112.51	1d 5d 3m 6m 1y 2y 5y max
Ask:	28.70 × 5800	EPS (ttm):	0.255	Annual Report for YHOO
1y Target Est:	36.53	Div & Yield:	N/A (N/A)	

If you wanted to buy Yahoo!, what price would you pay? How much would you receive if you wanted to sell Yahoo!?

Introduction to Financial Statement Analysis

As we discussed in Chapter 1, one of the great advantages of the corporate organizational form is that it places no restriction on who can own shares in the corporation. Anyone with money to invest is a potential investor. As a result, corporations are often widely held, with investors ranging from individuals who hold 100 shares to mutual funds and institutional investors who own millions of shares. For example, in 2004, International Business Machines Corporation (IBM) had over 1.6 billion shares outstanding held by over 670,000 stockholders. Although the corporate organizational structure greatly facilitates the firm's access to investment capital, it also means that stock ownership is most investors' sole tie to the company. How, then, do investors learn enough about a company to know whether or not they should invest in it? How can financial managers assess the success of their own firm and compare it to competitors? One way firms evaluate their performance and communicate this information to investors is through their *financial statements.*

Firms issue financial statements regularly to communicate financial information to the investment community. A detailed description of the preparation and analysis of these statements is sufficiently complicated that to do it justice would require an entire book. Here we briefly review the subject, emphasizing only the material that investors and corporate financial managers need in order to make the corporate-finance decisions we discuss in the text.

We review the four main types of financial statements, present examples of these statements for a firm, and discuss where an investor or manager might find various types of information about the company. We also discuss some of the financial ratios that investors and analysts use to assess a firm's performance and value. We close the chapter with a look at highly publicized financial reporting abuses at Enron and WorldCom.

2.1 The Disclosure of Financial Information

Financial statements are firm-issued accounting reports with past performance information that a firm issues periodically (usually quarterly and annually). U.S. public companies are required to file their financial statements with the U.S. Securities and Exchange Commission (SEC) on a quarterly basis on form **10-Q** and annually on form **10-K**. They must also send an **annual report** with their financial statements to their shareholders each year. Private companies often also prepare financial statements, but they usually do not have to disclose these reports to the public. Financial statements are important tools through which investors, financial analysts, and other interested outside parties (such as creditors) obtain information about a corporation. They are also useful for managers within the firm as a source of information for corporate financial decisions. In this section, we examine the guidelines for preparing financial statements and the types of financial statements.

Preparation of Financial Statements

Reports about a company's performance must be understandable and accurate. **Generally Accepted Accounting Principles (GAAP)** provide a common set of rules and a standard format for public companies to use when they prepare their reports. This standardization also makes it easier to compare the financial results of different firms.

International Financial Reporting Standards

Because Generally Accepted Accounting Principles (GAAP) differ among countries, companies face tremendous accounting complexities when they operate internationally. Investors also face difficulty interpreting financial statements of foreign companies, which is often considered a major barrier to international capital mobility. As companies and capital markets become more global, however, interest in harmonization of accounting standards across countries has increased.

The most important harmonization project began in 1973 when representatives of ten countries (including the United States) established the International Accounting Standards Committee. This effort led to the creation of the International Accounting Standards Board (IASB) in 2001, with headquarters in London. Now the IASB has issued a set of International Financial Reporting Standards (IFRS).

The IFRS are taking root throughout the world. The European Union (EU) approved an accounting regulation in 2002 requiring all publicly traded EU companies to follow IFRS in their consolidated financial statements starting in 2005. Many other countries have adopted IFRS for all listed companies, including Australia and several countries in Latin America and Africa. Indeed all major stock exchanges around the world accept IFRS except the United States and Japan, which maintain their local GAAP.

The main conceptual difference between U.S. GAAP and IFRS is that U.S. GAAP are based primarily on accounting rules with specific guidance in applying them, whereas IFRS are based more on principles requiring professional judgment by accountants, and specific guidance in application is limited. In implementation, the main difference is how assets and liabilities are valued. Whereas U.S. GAAP is based primarily on historical cost accounting, IFRS places more emphasis on "fair value" of assets and liabilities, or estimates of market values.

Effort to achieve convergence between U.S. GAAP and IFRS was spurred by the Sarbanes-Oxley Act of 2002 in the United States. It included a provision that U.S. accounting standards move toward international convergence on high-quality accounting standards. Currently SEC regulations require companies using IFRS to reconcile to U.S. GAAP in order to list in U.S. financial markets, but in 2005, the U.S. SEC and the EU reached an agreement to eliminate this requirement, possibly by 2007, but no later than 2009.

Investors also need some assurance that the financial statements are prepared accurately. Corporations are required to hire a neutral third party, known as an **auditor**, to check the annual financial statements, ensure they are prepared according to GAAP, and verify that the information is reliable.

Types of Financial Statements

Every public company is required to produce four financial statements: the *balance sheet,* the *income statement,* the *statement of cash flows,* and the *statement of stockholders' equity.* These financial statements provide investors and creditors with an overview of the firm's financial performance. In the sections that follow, we take close look at the content of these financial statements.

CONCEPT CHECK

1. What are the four financial statements that all public companies must produce?
2. What is the role of an auditor?

2.2 The Balance Sheet

The **balance sheet** lists the firm's *assets* and *liabilities*, providing a snapshot of the firm's financial position at a given point in time. Table 2.1 shows the balance sheet for a fictitious company, Global Conglomerate Corporation. Notice that the balance sheet is divided into two parts ("sides"): the assets on the left side and the liabilities on the right. The **assets** list the cash, inventory, property, plant and equipment, and other investments the company has made; the **liabilities** show the firm's obligations to creditors. Also shown with liabilities on the right side of the balance sheet is the *stockholders' equity*. **Stockholders' equity**, the difference between the firm's assets and liabilities, is an accounting measure of the firm's net worth.

The assets on the left side show how the firm uses its capital (its investments), and the right side summarizes the sources of capital, or how a firm raises the money it needs. Because of the way stockholders' equity is calculated, the left and right sides must balance:

The Balance Sheet Identity

$$\text{Assets} = \text{Liabilities} + \text{Stockholders' Equity} \tag{2.1}$$

In Table 2.1, total assets for 2005 ($177.7 million) are equal to total liabilities ($155.5 million) plus stockholders' equity ($22.2 million).

We now examine the assets, liabilities, and stockholders' equity in more detail. Finally, we evaluate the firm's financial standing by analyzing the information contained in the balance sheet.

Assets

In Table 2.1, Global's assets are divided into current and long-term assets. We discuss each in turn.

Current Assets.   **Current assets** are either cash or assets that could be converted into cash within one year. This category includes:

1. Cash and other **marketable securities**, which are short-term, low-risk investments that can be easily sold and converted to cash (such as money market investments like government debt that matures within a year);

TABLE 2.1	Global Conglomerate Corporation Balance Sheet for 2005 and 2004

GLOBAL CONGLOMERATE CORPORATION
Consolidated Balance Sheet
Year ended December 31 (in $ millions)

Assets	2005	2004	Liabilities and Stockholders' Equity	2005	2004
Current Assets			Current Liabilities		
Cash	21.2	19.5	Accounts payable	29.2	24.5
Accounts receivable	18.5	13.2	Notes payable / short-term debt	3.5	3.2
Inventories	15.3	14.3	Current maturities of long-term debt	13.3	12.3
Other current assets	2.0	1.0	Other current liabilities	2.0	4.0
Total current assets	57.0	48.0	Total current liabilities	48.0	44.0
Long-Term Assets			Long-Term Liabilities		
Land	22.2	20.7	Long-term debt	99.9	56.3
Buildings	36.5	30.5	Capital lease obligations	—	—
Equipment	39.7	33.2	Total debt	99.9	56.3
Less accumulated depreciation	(18.7)	(17.5)	Deferred taxes	7.6	7.4
Net property, plant, and equipment	79.7	66.9	Other long-term liabilities	—	—
Goodwill	20.0	—	Total long-term liabilities	107.5	63.7
Other long-term assets	21.0	14.0	**Total Liabilities**	155.5	107.7
Total long-term assets	120.7	80.9	**Stockholders' Equity**	22.2	21.2
Total Assets	177.7	128.9	**Total Liabilities and Stockholders' Equity**	177.7	128.9

2. **Accounts receivable**, which are amounts owed to the firm by customers who have purchased goods or services on credit;

3. **Inventories**, which are composed of raw materials as well as work-in-progress and finished goods;

4. Other current assets, which is a catch-all category that includes items such as prepaid expenses (expenses, such as rent or insurance, that have been paid in advance).

Long-Term Assets. The first category of long-term assets is net property, plant, and equipment. These include assets such as real estate or machinery that produce tangible benefits for more than one year. If Global spends $2 million on new equipment, this $2 million will be included with property, plant, and equipment on the balance sheet. Because equipment tends to wear out or become obsolete over time, Global will reduce the value recorded for this equipment each year by deducting an amount called **depreciation**. The firm reduces the value of fixed assets (other than land) over time according to a depreciation schedule that depends on the asset's life span. Depreciation is not an actual cash expense that the firm pays; it is a way of recognizing that buildings and equipment wear out and thus become less valuable the older they get. The **book value** of an asset is equal to its acquisition cost less accumulated depreciation. Net property, plant, and equipment shows the total book value of these assets.

When a firm acquires another company, it will acquire a set of assets that will then be listed on its balance sheet. In many cases, however, the firm may pay more for the company than the total book value of the assets it acquires. In this case, the difference between the price paid for the company and the book value assigned to its assets is recorded as **goodwill**. For example, Global paid $25 million in 2005 for a firm whose assets had a book value of $5 million. Thus, $20 million is recorded as goodwill in Table 2.1. Goodwill captures the value of other "intangibles" that the firm acquired through the acquisition. If the value of these intangible assets declines over time, the amount of goodwill listed on the balance sheet will be reduced by an **amortization** charge that captures the change in value of the acquired assets. Like depreciation, amortization is not an actual cash expense.

Other long-term assets can include such items as property not used in business operations, start-up costs in connection with a new business, trademarks and patents, and property held for sale. The sum of all the firms' assets is the total assets at the bottom of the left side of the balance sheet in Table 2.1.

Liabilities

We now examine the liabilities shown on the right side of the balance sheet, which are divided into *current* and *long-term liabilities*.

Current Liabilities.   Liabilities that will be satisfied within one year are known as **current liabilities**. They include:

1. **Accounts payable**, the amounts owed to suppliers for products or services purchased with credit;
2. Notes payable, short-term debt, and current maturities of long-term debt, which are all repayments of debt that will occur within the next year;
3. Items such as salary or taxes that are owed but have not yet been paid, and deferred or unearned revenue, which is revenue that has been received for products that have not yet been delivered.

The difference between current assets and current liabilities is the firm's **net working capital**, the capital available in the short term to run the business. For example, in 2005, Global's net working capital totaled $9.0 million ($57.0 million in current assets − $48.0 million in current liabilities). Firms with low (or negative) net working capital may face a shortage of funds.

Long-term Liabilities.   Long-term liabilities are liabilities that extend beyond one year. We describe the main types below.

1. **Long-term debt** is any loan or debt obligation with a maturity of more than a year. When a firm needs to raise funds to purchase an asset or make an investment, it may borrow those funds through a long-term loan.
2. **Capital leases** are long-term lease contracts that obligate the firm to make regular lease payments in exchange for use of an asset.[1] They allow a firm to gain use of an asset by leasing it from the asset's owner. For example, a firm may lease a building to serve as its corporate headquarters.

---

1. See Chapter 25 for a precise definition of a capital lease.

3. **Deferred taxes** are taxes that are owed but have not yet been paid. Firms generally keep two sets of financial statements: one for financial reporting and one for tax purposes. Occasionally, the rules for the two types of statements differ. Deferred tax liabilities generally arise when the firm's financial income exceeds its income for tax purposes. Because deferred taxes will eventually be paid, they appear as a liability on the balance sheet.[2]

Stockholders' Equity

The sum of the current liabilities and long-term liabilities is total liabilities. The difference between the firm's assets and liabilities is the stockholders' equity; it is also called the **book value of equity**. As we stated earlier, it represents the net worth of the firm from an accounting perspective.

Ideally, the balance sheet would provide us with an accurate assessment of the true value of the firm's equity. Unfortunately, this is unlikely to be the case. First, many of the assets listed on the balance sheet are valued based on their historical cost rather than their true value today. For example, an office building is listed on the balance sheet according to its historical cost net of depreciation. But the actual value of the office building today may be very different than this amount, and it may be much *more* than the amount the firm paid for it years ago. The same is true for other property, plant, and equipment, as well as goodwill: The true value today of an asset may be very different from, and even exceed, its book value. A second, and probably more important, problem is that *many of the firm's valuable assets are not captured on the balance sheet.* For example, the expertise of the firm's employees, the firm's reputation in the marketplace, the relationships with customers and suppliers, and the quality of the management team are all assets that add to the value of the firm that do not appear on the balance sheet.

For these reasons, the book value of equity is an inaccurate assessment of the actual value of the firm's equity. Thus, it is not surprising that it will often differ substantially from the amount investors are willing to pay for the equity. The total market value of a firm's equity equals the market price per share times the number of shares, referred to as the company's **market capitalization**. The market value of a stock does not depend on the historical cost of the firm's assets; instead, it depends on what investors expect those assets to produce in the future.

EXAMPLE 2.1

Market Versus Book Value

Problem

If Global has 3.6 million shares outstanding, and these shares are trading for a price of $14 per share, what is Global's market capitalization? How does the market capitalization compare to Global's book value of equity?

Solution

Global's market capitalization is (3.6 million shares) $\times$ ($14 / share) = $50.4 million. This market capitalization is significantly higher than Global's book value of equity of $22.2 million. In fact, the ratio of its market value to its book value is 50.4 / 22.2 = 2.27, meaning that investors are willing to pay more than twice the amount Global's shares are "worth" according to their book value.

---

2. A firm may also have deferred tax assets related to tax credits it has earned that it will receive in the future.

Finally, we note that the book value of equity can be negative (liabilities exceed assets), and that a negative book value of equity is not necessarily an indication of poor performance. Successful firms are often able to borrow in excess of the book value of their assets because creditors recognize that the market value of the assets is far higher. For example, in June 2005, Amazon.com had total liabilities of $2.6 billion and a book value of equity of −$64 million. At the same time, the market value of its equity was over $15 billion. Clearly, investors recognized that Amazon's assets were worth far more than their book value.

Balance Sheet Analysis

What can we learn from analyzing a firm's balance sheet? Although the book value of a firm's equity is not a good estimate of its true value as an ongoing firm, it is sometimes used as an estimate of the **liquidation value** of the firm, the value that would be left if its assets were sold and liabilities paid. We can also learn a great deal of useful information from a firm's balance sheet that goes beyond the book value of the firm's equity. We now discuss analyzing the balance sheet to assess the firm's value, its leverage, and its short-term cash needs.

Market-to-Book Ratio. In Example 2.1, we computed the **market-to-book ratio** (also called the **price-to-book [P/B] ratio**) for Global, which is the ratio of its market capitalization to the book value of stockholders' equity.

$$\text{Market-to-Book Ratio} = \frac{\text{Market Value of Equity}}{\text{Book Value of Equity}} \qquad (2.2)$$

It is one of many financial ratios used by analysts to evaluate a firm. The market-to-book ratio for most successful firms substantially exceeds 1, indicating that the value of the firm's assets when put to use exceeds their historical cost (or liquidation value). Variations in this ratio reflect differences in fundamental firm characteristics as well as the value added by management.

In early 2006, General Motors Corporation (GM) had a market-to-book ratio of 0.5, a reflection of investors' assessment that many of GM's plants and other assets were unlikely to be profitable and were worth less than their book value. At the same time, the average market-to-book ratio for the auto industry was about 1.5, and for large U.S. firms it was close to 4.0. In contrast, consider that Google (GOOG) had a market-to-book ratio of over 15, and the average for technology firms was about 6.0. Analysts often classify firms with low market-to-book ratios as **value stocks**, and those with high market-to-book ratios as **growth stocks**.

Debt-Equity Ratio. Another important piece of information that we can learn from a firm's balance sheet is the firm's **leverage**, or the extent to which it relies on debt as a source of financing. The **debt-equity ratio** is a common ratio used to assess a firm's leverage. We calculate this ratio by dividing the total amount of short- and long-term debt (including current maturities) by the total stockholders' equity:

$$\text{Debt-Equity Ratio} = \frac{\text{Total Debt}}{\text{Total Equity}} \qquad (2.3)$$

We can calculate this ratio using either book or market values for equity and debt. From Table 2.1, note Global's debt in 2005 includes notes payable ($3.5 million), current maturities of long-term debt ($13.3 million), and long-term debt ($99.9 million), for a total of $116.7 million. Therefore, its *book* debt-equity ratio is 116.7 / 22.2 = 5.3, using the book value of equity. Note the large increase from 2004, when the book debt-equity ratio was only (3.2 + 12.3 + 56.3) / 21.2 = 3.4.

Because of the difficulty interpreting the book value of equity, the book debt-equity ratio is not especially useful. It is more informative to compare the firm's debt to the market value of its equity. Global's debt-equity ratio in 2005 using the market value of equity (from Example 2.1) is 116.7 / 50.4 = 2.3, which means Global's debt is a bit more than double the market value of its equity.[3] As we see later in the text, a firm's *market* debt-equity ratio has important consequences for the risk and return of its stock.

Enterprise Value.   A firm's market capitalization measures the market value of the firm's equity, or the value that remains after the firm has paid its debts. But what is the value of the business itself? The **enterprise value** of a firm assesses the value of the underlying business assets, unencumbered by debt and separate from any cash and marketable securities. We compute it as follows:

$$\text{Enterprise Value} = \text{Market Value of Equity} + \text{Debt} - \text{Cash} \qquad (2.4)$$

For example, given its market capitalization from Example 2.1, Global's enterprise value in 2005 is 50.4 + 116.7 − 21.2 = $145.9 million. The enterprise value can be interpreted as the cost to take over the business. That is, it would cost 50.4 + 116.7 = $167.1 million to buy all of Global's equity and pay off its debts, but because we would acquire Global's $21.2 million in cash, the net cost is only 167.1 − 21.2 = $145.9 million.

EXAMPLE
2.2

Computing Enterprise Value

Problem

In April 2005, H.J. Heinz Co. (HNZ) had a share price of $36.87, 347.6 million shares outstanding, a market-to-book ratio of 4.93, a book debt-equity ratio of 1.80, and cash of $1.08 billion. What was Heinz's market capitalization? What was its enterprise value?

Solution

Heinz had a market capitalization of $36.87 × 347.6 million shares = $12.82 billion. We divide the market value of equity by Heinz's market-to-book ratio to calculate Heinz's book value of equity as 12.82 / 4.93 = $2.60 billion. Given a book debt-equity ratio of 1.80, Heinz had total debt of 1.80 × 2.60 = $4.68 billion. Thus, Heinz's enterprise value was 12.82 + 4.68 − 1.08 = $16.42 billion.

Other Balance Sheet Information.   Creditors often compare a firm's current assets and current liabilities to assess whether the firm has sufficient working capital to meet its short-term needs. This comparison is sometimes summarized in the firm's **current ratio**, the ratio of current assets to current liabilities, or its **quick ratio**, the ratio of current assets other than inventory to current liabilities. A higher current or quick ratio implies less risk of the firm experiencing a cash shortfall in the near future.

---

3. In this calculation, we have compared the market value of equity to the book value of debt. Strictly speaking, it would be best to use the market value of debt. But because the market value of debt is generally not very different from its book value, this distinction is often ignored in practice.

Analysts also use the information on the balance sheet to watch for trends that could provide information regarding the firm's future performance. For example, an unusual increase in inventory could be an indicator that the firm is having difficulty selling its products.

1. The book value of a company's assets usually does not equal the market value of those assets. What are some reasons for this difference?

2. What is a firm's enterprise value?

2.3 The Income Statement

When you want somebody to get to the point, you might ask them for the "bottom line." This expression comes from the *income statement*. The **income statement** lists the firm's revenues and expenses over a period of time. The last or "bottom" line of the income statement shows the firm's **net income**, which is a measure of its profitability during the period. The income statement is sometimes called a profit and loss, or "P&L," statement, and the net income is also referred to as the firm's **earnings**. In this section, we examine the components of the income statement in detail and introduce ratios we can use to analyze this data.

Earnings Calculations

Whereas the balance sheet shows the firm's assets and liabilities at a given point in time, the income statement shows the flow of revenues and expenses generated by those assets and liabilities between two dates. Table 2.2 shows Global's income statement for 2005. We examine each category on the statement.

Gross Profit.   The first two lines of the income statement list the revenues from sales of products and the costs incurred to make and sell the products. The third line is **gross profit**, the difference between sales revenues and the costs.

Operating Expenses.   The next group of items is operating expenses. These are expenses from the ordinary course of running the business that are not directly related to producing the goods or services being sold. They include administrative expenses and overhead, salaries, marketing costs, and research and development expenses. The third type of operating expense, depreciation and amortization, is not an actual cash expense but represents an estimate of the costs that arise from wear and tear or obsolescence of the firm's assets.[4] The firm's gross profit net of operating expenses is called **operating income**.

Earnings Before Interest and Taxes.   We next include other sources of income or expenses that arise from activities that are not the central part of a company's business. Cash flows from the firm's financial investments are one example of other income that would be listed here. After we have adjusted for other sources of income or expenses, we have the firm's earnings before interest and taxes, or **EBIT**.

---

4. Only certain types of amortization are deductible as a pretax expense (e.g., amortization of the cost of an acquired patent). Amortization of goodwill is not a pretax expense and is generally included as an extraordinary item after taxes are deducted.

TABLE 2.2	Global Conglomerate Corporation Income Statement Sheet for 2005 and 2004

GLOBAL CONGLOMERATE CORPORATION
Income Statement
Year ended December 31 (in $ millions)

	2005	2004
Total sales	186.7	176.1
Cost of sales	(153.4)	(147.3)
Gross Profit	33.3	28.8
Selling, general, and administrative expenses	(13.5)	(13.0)
Research and development	(8.2)	(7.6)
Depreciation and amortization	(1.2)	(1.1)
Operating Income	10.4	7.1
Other income	—	—
Earnings before interest and taxes (EBIT)	10.4	7.1
Interest income (expense)	(7.7)	(4.6)
Pretax income	2.7	2.5
Taxes	(0.7)	(0.6)
Net Income	2.0	1.9
Earnings per share:	$0.556	$0.528
Diluted earnings per share:	$0.526	$0.500

Pretax and Net Income.   From EBIT, we deduct the interest paid on outstanding debt to compute Global's pretax income, and then we deduct corporate taxes to determine the firm's net income.

Net income represents the total earnings of the firm's equity holders. It is often reported on a per-share basis as the firm's **earnings per share (EPS)**. We compute EPS by dividing net income by the total number of shares outstanding:

$$\text{EPS} = \frac{\text{Net Income}}{\text{Shares Outstanding}} = \frac{\$2.0\,\text{million}}{3.6\,\text{million shares}} = \$0.556 \text{ per share} \qquad (2.5)$$

Although Global has only 3.6 million shares outstanding as of the end of 2005, the number of shares outstanding may grow if Global compensates its employees or executives with **stock options** that give the holder the right to buy a certain number of shares by a specific date at a specific price. If the options are "exercised," the company issues new stock and the number of shares outstanding will grow. The number of shares may also grow if the firm issues **convertible bonds**, a form of debt that can be converted to shares. Because there will be more total shares to divide the same earnings, this growth in the number of shares is referred to as **dilution**. Firms disclose the potential for dilution from options they have awarded by reporting **diluted EPS**, which shows the earnings per share the company would have if the stock options were exercised. For example, if Global has awarded 200,000 stock options to its key executives, its diluted EPS is $2.0 million / 3.8 million shares = $0.526.

Income Statement Analysis

The income statement provides very useful information regarding the profitability of a firm's business and how it relates to the value of the firm's shares. We now discuss several ratios that are often used to evaluate a firm's performance and value.

Profitability Ratios. The **operating margin** of a firm is the ratio of operating income to revenues:

$$\text{Operating Margin} = \frac{\text{Operating Income}}{\text{Total Sales}} \tag{2.6}$$

The operating margin reveals how much a company earns before interest and taxes from each dollar of sales. Global's operating margin in 2005 was $10.4 / 186.7 = 5.57\%$, an increase from its 2004 operating margin of $7.1 / 176.1 = 4.03\%$. By comparing operating margins across firms within an industry, we can assess the relative efficiency of firms' operations. For example, in 2004, American Airlines (AMR) had an operating margin of -0.77% (i.e., they lost 0.77 cents for each dollar in revenues). However, competitor Southwest Airlines (LUV) had an operating margin of 8.48%.

Differences in operating margins can also result from differences in strategy. For example, in 2004, high-end retailer Neiman Marcus had an operating margin of 9.8%; Wal-Mart Stores had an operating margin of only 5.9%. In this case, Wal-Mart's lower operating margin is not a result of its inefficiency but is part of its strategy of offering lower prices to sell common products in high volume. Indeed, Wal-Mart's sales were more than 80 times higher than those of Neiman Marcus.

A firm's **net profit margin** is the ratio of net income to revenues:

$$\text{Net Profit Margin} = \frac{\text{Net Income}}{\text{Total Sales}} \tag{2.7}$$

The net profit margin shows the fraction of each dollar in revenues that is available to equity holders after the firm pays interest and taxes. Global's net profit margin in 2005 was $2.0 / 186.7 = 1.07\%$. Differences in net profit margins can be due to differences in efficiency, but they can also result from differences in leverage, which determines the amount of interest payments.

Working Capital Days. We can use the combined information in the firm's income statement and balance sheet to gauge how efficiently the firm is utilizing its net working capital. For example, we can express the firm's accounts receivable in terms of the number of days' worth of sales that it represents, called the **accounts receivable days**:[5]

$$\text{Accounts Receivable Days} = \frac{\text{Accounts Receivable}}{\text{Average Daily Sales}} \tag{2.8}$$

Given average daily sales of $\$186.7$ million $/ 365 = \$0.51$ million in 2005, Global's receivables of $\$18.5$ million represent $18.5 / 0.51 = 36$ days' worth of sales. In other words, Global takes a little over one month to collect payment from its customers, on average. In 2004, Global's accounts receivable represented only 27 days worth of sales. Although the number of receivable days can fluctuate seasonally, a significant unexplained

---

5. Accounts Receivable Days can also be calculated based on the average accounts receivable at the end of current and prior year.

increase could be a cause for concern (perhaps indicating the firm is doing a poor job collecting from its customers or is trying to boost sales by offering generous credit terms). Accounts payable can also be expressed in terms of the number of days' worth of cost of goods sold, as can inventory.

EBITDA. Financial analysts often compute a firm's earnings before interest, taxes, depreciation, and amortization, or **EBITDA**. Because depreciation and amortization are not cash expenses for the firm, EBITDA reflects the cash a firm has earned from its operations. Global's EBITDA in 2005 was $10.4 + 1.2 = \$11.6$ million.

Leverage Ratios. Lenders often assess a firm's leverage by computing an **interest coverage ratio**. Common ratios consider operating income, EBIT, or EBITDA as a multiple of the firm's interest expenses. When this ratio is high, it indicates that the firm is earning much more than is necessary to meet its required interest payments.

Investment Returns. Analysts often evaluate the firm's return on investment by comparing its income to its investment using ratios such as the firm's **return on equity (ROE)**:[6]

$$\text{Return on Equity} = \frac{\text{Net Income}}{\text{Book Value of Equity}} \qquad (2.9)$$

Global's ROE in 2005 was $2.0 / 22.2 = 9.0\%$. The ROE provides a measure of the return that firm has earned on its past investments. A high ROE may indicate the firm is able to find investment opportunities that are very profitable. Of course, one weakness of this measure is the difficulty in interpreting the book value of equity. Another common measure is the **return on assets (ROA)**, which is net income divided by the total assets.

Valuation Ratios. Analysts use a number of ratios to gauge the market value of the firm. The most important is the firm's **price-earnings ratio (P/E)**:

$$\text{P / E Ratio} = \frac{\text{Market Capitalization}}{\text{Net Income}} = \frac{\text{Share Price}}{\text{Earnings per Share}} \qquad (2.10)$$

COMMON MISTAKE   **Mismatched Ratios**

When considering valuation (and other) ratios, be sure that the items you are comparing both represent amounts related to the entire firm or that both represent amounts related solely to equity holders. For example, a firm's share price and market capitalization are values associated with the firm's equity. Thus, it makes sense to compare them to the firm's earnings per share or net income, which are amounts to equity holders after interest has been paid to debt holders. We must be careful, however, if we compare a firm's market capitalization to its revenues, operating income, or EBITDA because these amounts are related to the whole firm, and both debt and equity holders have a claim to them. Thus, it is better to compare revenues, operating income, or EBITDA to the enterprise value of the firm, which includes both debt and equity.

---

6. Because net income is measured over the year, the ROE can also be calculated based on the average book value of equity at the end of the current and prior year.

That is, the P/E ratio is the ratio of the value of equity to the firm's earnings, either on a total basis or on a per-share basis. For example, Global's P/E ratio in 2005 was 50.4 / 2.0 = 14 / 0.56 = 25.2. The P/E ratio is a simple measure that is used to assess whether a stock is over- or under-valued based on the idea that the value of a stock should be proportional to the level of earnings it can generate for its shareholders. P/E ratios can vary widely across industries and tend to be higher for industries with high growth rates. For example, in 2005, the average large U.S. firm had a P/E ratio of about 21. But biotechnology firms, which have low current earnings but the promise of high future earnings if they develop successful drugs, had an average P/E ratio of 48.

The P/E ratio considers the value of the firm's equity and so depends on its leverage. To assess the market value of the underlying business, it is common to consider valuation ratios based on the firm's enterprise value. Common ratios include the ratio of enterprise value to revenue, or enterprise value to operating income or EBITDA. These ratios compare the value of the business to its sales, operating profits, or cash flow. Like the P/E ratio, these ratios are used to make intra-industry comparisons of how firms are priced in the market.

The P/E ratio is not useful when the firm's earnings are negative. In this case, it is common to look at the firm's enterprise value relative to sales. The risk in doing so, however, is that earnings might be negative because the firm's underlying business model is fundamentally flawed, as was the case for many Internet firms in the late 1990s.

**EXAMPLE
2.3**

Computing Profitability and Valuation Ratios

Problem

Consider the following data from 2004 for Wal-Mart Stores and Target Corporation ($ billions):

	Wal-Mart Stores (WMT)	Target Corporation (TGT)
Sales	288	47
Operating Income	17	3.6
Net Income	10	1.9
Market Capitalization	228	45
Cash	5	1
Debt	32	9

Compare Wal-Mart and Target's operating margin, net profit margin, P/E ratio, and the ratio of enterprise value to operating income and sales.

Solution

Wal-Mart had an operating margin of 17 / 288 = 5.9%, a net profit margin of 10 / 288 = 3.5%, and a P/E ratio of 228 / 10 = 22.8. Its enterprise value was 228 + 32 − 5 = $255 billion, which has a ratio of 255 / 17 = 15.0 to operating income and 255 / 288 = 0.89 to sales.

Target had an operating margin of 3.6 / 47 = 7.7%, a net profit margin of 1.9 / 47 = 4.0%, and a P/E ratio of 45 / 1.9 = 23.7. Its enterprise value was 45 + 9 − 1 = $53 billion, which has a ratio of 53 / 3.6 = 14.7 to operating income and 53 / 47 = 1.13 to sales.

Note that despite their large difference in size, Target and Wal-Mart's P/E and enterprise value to operating income ratios were very similar. Target's profitability was somewhat higher than Wal-Mart's, however, explaining the difference in the ratio of enterprise value to sales.

1. What is the diluted earnings per share?

2. How do you use the price-earnings (P/E) ratio to gauge the market value of a firm?

2.4 The Statement of Cash Flows

The income statement provides a measure of the firm's profit over a given time period. However, it does not indicate the amount of *cash* the firm has earned. There are two reasons that net income does not correspond to cash earned. First, there are non-cash entries on the income statement, such as depreciation and amortization. Second, certain uses of cash, such as the purchase of a building or expenditures on inventory, are not reported on the income statement. The firm's **statement of cash flows** utilizes the information from the income statement and balance sheet to determine how much cash the firm has generated, and how that cash has been allocated, during a set period. As we will see, from the perspective of an investor attempting to value the firm, the statement of cash flows provides what may be the most important information of the four financial statements.

The statement of cash flows is divided into three sections: operating activities, investment activities, and financing activities. The first section, operating activity, starts with net income from the income statement. It then adjusts this number by adding back all non-cash entries related to the firm's operating activities. The next section, investment activity, lists the cash used for investment. The third section, financing activity, shows the flow of cash between the firm and its investors. Global Conglomerate's statement of cash flows is shown in Table 2.3. In this section, we take a close look at each component of the statement of cash flows.

Operating Activity

The first section of Global's statement of cash flows adjusts net income by all non-cash items related to operating activity. For instance, depreciation is deducted when computing net income, but it is not an actual cash expense. Thus, we add it back to net income when determining the amount of cash the firm has generated. Similarly, we add back any other non-cash expenses (for example, deferred taxes).

Next, we adjust for changes to net working capital that arise from changes to accounts receivable, accounts payable, or inventory. When a firm sells a product, it records the revenue as income even though it may not receive the cash from that sale immediately. Instead, it may grant the customer credit and let the customer pay in the future. The customer's obligation adds to the firm's accounts receivable. Because this sale was recorded as part of net income, but the cash has not yet been received from the customer, we must adjust the cash flows by *deducting* the increases in accounts receivable. This increase represents additional lending by the firm to its customers, and it reduces the cash available to the firm. Similarly, we *add* increases in accounts payable. Accounts payable represents borrowing by the firm from its suppliers. This borrowing increases the cash available to the firm. Finally, we *deduct* increases to inventory. Increases to inventory are not recorded as an expense and do not contribute to net income (the cost of the goods are only included in net income when the goods are actually sold). However, the cost of increasing inventory is a cash expense for the firm and must be deducted.

The changes in these working capital items can be found from the balance sheet. For example, from Table 2.1, Global's accounts receivable increased from $13.2 million in 2004 to $18.5 million in 2005. We deduct the increase of $18.5 - 13.2 = \$5.3$ million on the statement of cash flows. Note that although Global showed positive net income on

TABLE 2.3	Global Conglomerate Corporation Statement of Cash Flows for 2005 and 2004

GLOBAL CONGLOMERATE CORPORATION
Statement of Cash Flows
Year ended December 31 (in $ millions)

	2005	2004
Operating activities		
Net Income	2.0	1.9
Depreciation and amortization	1.2	1.1
Other non-cash items	(2.8)	(1.0)
Cash effect of changes in		
Accounts receivable	(5.3)	(0.3)
Accounts payable	4.7	(0.5)
Inventory	(1.0)	(1.0)
Cash from operating activities	(1.2)	0.2
Investment activities		
Capital expenditures	(14.0)	(4.0)
Acquisitions and other investing activity	(27.0)	(2.0)
Cash from investing activities	(41.0)	(6.0)
Financing activities		
Dividends paid	(1.0)	(1.0)
Sale or purchase of stock	—	—
Increase in short-term borrowing	1.3	3.0
Increase in long-term borrowing	43.6	2.5
Cash from financing activities	43.9	4.5
Change in Cash and Cash Equivalents	1.7	(1.3)

the income statement, it actually had a negative $1.2 million cash flow from operating activity, in large part because of the increase in accounts receivable.

Investment Activity

The next section of the statement of cash flows shows the cash required for investment activities. Purchases of new property, plant, and equipment are referred to as **capital expenditures**. Recall that capital expenditures do not appear immediately as expenses on the income statement. Instead, the firm depreciates these assets and deducts depreciation expenses over time. To determine the firm's cash flow, we already added back depreciation because it is not an actual cash expense. Now, we subtract the actual capital expenditure that the firm made. Similarly, we also deduct other assets purchased or investments made by the firm, such as acquisitions. In Table 2.3, we see that in 2005, Global spent $41 million in cash on investing activities.

Financing Activity

The last section of the statement of cash flows shows the cash flows from financing activities. Dividends paid to shareholders are a cash outflow. Global paid $1 million to its shareholders as dividends in 2005. The difference between a firm's net income and the amount it spends on dividends is referred to as the firm's **retained earnings** for that year:

$$\text{Retained Earnings} = \text{Net Income} - \text{Dividends} \qquad (2.11)$$

Global retained $2 million − $1 million = $1 million, or 50% of its earnings in 2005.

Also listed under financing activity is any cash the company received from the sale of its own stock, or cash spent buying (repurchasing) its own stock. Global did not issue or repurchase stock during this period.

The last items to include in this section result from changes to Global's short-term and long-term borrowing. Global raised money by issuing debt, so the increases in short-term and long-term borrowing represent cash inflows. The last line of the statement of cash flows combines the cash flows from these three activities to calculate the overall change in the firm's cash balance over the period of the statement. In this case, Global had cash inflows of $1.7 million. By looking at the statement in Table 2.3 as a whole, we can determine that Global chose to borrow (mainly in the form of long-term debt) to cover the cost of its investment and operating activities. Although the firm's cash balance has increased, Global's negative operating cash flows and relatively high expenditures on investment activities might give investors some reasons for concern. If that pattern continues, Global will need to continue to borrow to remain in business.

EXAMPLE 2.4	**The Impact of Depreciation on Cash Flow**

Problem

Suppose Global had an additional $1 million depreciation expense in 2005. If Global's tax rate on pretax income is 26%, what would be the impact of this expense on Global's earnings? How would it impact Global's cash at the end of the year?

Solution

Depreciation is an operating expense, so Global's operating income, EBIT, and pretax income would fall by $1 million. This decrease in pretax income would reduce Global's tax bill by 26% × $1 million = $0.26 million. Therefore, net income would fall by 1 − 0.26 = $0.74 million.

On the statement of cash flows, net income would fall by $0.74 million, but we would add back the additional depreciation of $1 million because it is not a cash expense. Thus, cash from operating activities would rise by −0.74 + 1 = $0.26 million. Thus, Global's cash balance at the end of the year would increase by $0.26 million, the amount of the tax savings that resulted from the additional depreciation deduction.

CONCEPT CHECK

1. Why does a firm's net income not correspond to cash earned?

2. What are the components of the statement of cash flows?

2.5 Other Financial Statement Information

The most important elements of a firm's financial statements are the balance sheet, income statement, and the statement of cash flows, which we have already discussed. Several other pieces of information contained in the financial statements warrant brief mention: the management discussion and analysis, the statement of stockholders' equity, and notes to the financial statement.

INTERVIEW WITH
Sue Frieden

S ue Frieden is Ernst & Young's Global Managing Partner, Quality & Risk Management. A member of the Global Executive board, she is responsible for every aspect of quality and risk management—employees, services, procedures, and clients.

QUESTION: *Do today's financial statements give the investing public what they need?*

ANSWER: Globally, we are seeing an effort to provide more forward-looking information to investors. But fundamental questions remain, such as how fully do investors understand financial statements and how fully do they read them? Research shows that most individual investors don't rely on financial statements much at all. We need to determine how the financial statement and related reporting models can be improved. To do that we will need a dialogue involving investors, regulators, analysts, auditors, stock exchanges, academics and others to ensure that financial statements and other reporting models are as relevant as they can be.

QUESTION: *Ernst & Young is a global organization. How do accounting standards in the U.S. compare to those elsewhere?*

ANSWER: In January of 2005, 100 countries outside the U.S. began the process of adopting new accounting standards (International Financial Reporting Standards) that would in large measure be based on principles rather than rules. As global markets become more complex, it is clear that we all need to be playing by the same set of rules, but as a first step we need to have consistency from country to country. There are definite challenges to overcome in reconciling principle-based and rules-based systems, but we are optimistic that these challenges will inevitably get resolved. At the same time, there are efforts underway to ensure that auditing standards are globally consistent. Ultimately, financial statements prepared under global standards and audited under consistent global auditing standards will better serve investors.

QUESTION: *What role does the audit firm play in our financial markets, and how has that changed since the collapse of Arthur Anderson?*

ANSWER: All of us—the entire business community—have gone through a pivotal, historic moment. And certainly the accounting profession has seen unprecedented change in the past few years as well. The passage of Sarbanes-Oxley and other changes are helping to restore public trust. Things are certainly very different from what we've known before. We're now engaging on a regular basis with a wider range of stakeholders—companies, boards, policy-makers, opinion leaders, investors and academia. And we've had the chance to step back and ask ourselves why we do what we do as accounting professionals, and why it matters. In terms of the services we offer, much of what we do helps companies comply with regulations, guard against undue risks, and implement sound transactions. And part of the value in what we do is providing the basis to all stakeholders to understand whether companies are playing by the rules—whether it is accounting rules, financial reporting rules, or tax rules. We help create confidence in financial data. The public may not fully understand precisely what auditors do or how we do it, but they care that we exist because it provides them the confidence they so badly need and want.

QUESTION: *How does a global accounting firm such as Ernst & Young ensure that each of its partners adheres to the appropriate standards?*

ANSWER: People often tell me, as the global leader for quality and risk management, how hard my job is and how much is on my shoulders. The truth is, doing the right thing—adhering and often exceeding the standards expected of us as independent public auditors—rests on the shoulders of everyone in the organization. All of our more than 107,000 people around the world know it is their responsibility to make this happen. What's more, they know it is their responsibility to raise questions when they have concerns. Perhaps most importantly, all of our people know that no client is too big to walk away from if we sense the company's management is not committed to doing the right thing.

Management Discussion and Analysis

The **management discussion and analysis (MD&A)** is a preface to the financial statements in which the company's management discusses the recent year (or quarter), providing a background on the company and any significant events that may have occurred. Management may also discuss the coming year, and outline goals and new projects.

Management should also discuss any important risks that the firm faces or issues that may affect the firm's liquidity or resources. Management is also required to disclose any **off-balance sheet transactions**, which are transactions or arrangements that can have a material impact on the firm's future performance yet do not appear on the balance sheet. For example, if a firm has made guarantees that it will compensate a buyer for losses related to an asset purchased from the firm, these guarantees represent a potential future liability for the firm that must be disclosed as part of the MD&A.

Statement of Stockholders' Equity

The **statement of stockholders' equity** breaks down the stockholders' equity computed on the balance sheet into the amount that came from issuing new shares versus retained earnings. Because the book value of stockholders' equity is not a useful assessment of value for financial purposes, the information contained in the statement of stockholders' equity is also not particularly insightful.

Notes to the Financial Statements

In addition to the four financial statements, companies provide extensive notes with further details on the information provided in the statements. For example, the notes document important accounting assumptions that were used in preparing the statements. They often provide information specific to a firm's subsidiaries or its separate product lines. They show the details of the firm's stock-based compensation plans for employees and the different types of debt the firm has outstanding. Details of acquisitions, spin-offs, leases, taxes, and risk management activities are also given. The information provided in the notes is often very important to interpret fully the firm's financial statements.

EXAMPLE 2.5

Sales by Product Category

Problem

In the notes to its financial statements, H. J. Heinz (HNZ) reported the following sales revenues by product category ($ thousands):

	2005	2004
Ketchup, condiments, and sauces	$3,234,229	$3,047,662
Frozen foods	2,209,586	1,947,777
Convenience meals	2,005,468	1,874,272
Infant foods	855,558	908,469
Other	607,456	636,358

Which category showed the highest percentage growth? If Heinz has the same percentage growth by category from 2005 to 2006, what will its total revenues be in 2006?

Solution

The percentage growth in ketchup and condiment sales was $(3,234,229 - 3,047,662) / 3,047,662 = 6.1\%$. Similarly, growth in frozen foods was 13.4% and in convenience meals was 7.0%. However, sales of infant foods fell by 5.8% and other sales fell by 4.5%. Thus, frozen foods showed the highest growth.

If these growth rates continue for another year, ketchup and condiment sales will be $3,234,229 \times 1.061 = \$3.43$ billion, and the other categories will be \$2.51 billion, \$2.15 billion, \$0.81 billion, and \$0.58 billion, respectively, for total revenues of \$9.48 billion.

CONCEPT CHECK

1. Where do off-balance sheet transactions appear in a firm's financial statements?

2. What information do the notes to financial statements provide?

2.6 Accounting Manipulation

The various financial statements we have examined are of critical importance to investors and financial managers alike. Even with safeguards such as GAAP and auditors, though, financial reporting abuses unfortunately do take place. We now review two of the most infamous recent examples.

Enron

Enron was the most well known of the accounting scandals of the early 2000s. Enron started as an operator of natural-gas pipelines but evolved into a global trader dealing in a range of products including gas, oil, electricity, and even broadband Internet capacity. A series of events unfolded that led Enron to file the largest bankruptcy filing in U.S. history in December 2001. By the end of 2001, the market value of Enron's shares had fallen by over \$60 billion.

Interestingly, throughout the 1990s and up to late 2001, Enron was touted as one of the most successful and profitable companies in America. *Fortune* rated Enron "The Most Innovative Company in America" for six straight years, from 1995 to 2000. But while many aspects of Enron's business were successful, subsequent investigations suggest that Enron executives had been manipulating Enron's financial statements to mislead investors and artificially inflate the price of Enron's stock and maintain its credit rating. In 2000, for example, 96% of Enron's reported earnings were the result of accounting manipulation.[7]

Although the accounting manipulations that Enron used were quite sophisticated, the essence of most of the deceptive transactions was surprisingly simple. Enron sold assets at inflated prices to other firms (or, in many cases, business entities that Enron's CFO Andrew Fastow had created), together with a promise to buy back those assets at an even higher future price. Thus, Enron was effectively borrowing money, receiving cash today in exchange for a promise to pay more cash in the future. But Enron recorded the incoming cash as revenue and then hid the promises to buy them back in a variety of ways.[8] In the end, much of their revenue growth and profits in the late 1990s were the result of this type of manipulation.

---

7. John R. Kroger, "Enron, Fraud and Securities Reform: An Enron Prosecutor's Perspective," *University of Colorado Law Review* (December 2005): pp. 57–138.

8. In some cases, these promises were called "price risk management liabilities" and hidden with other trading activities; in other cases they were off-balance sheet transactions that were not fully disclosed.

WorldCom

On July 21, 2002, WorldCom entered the largest bankruptcy of all time. At its peak, WorldCom had a market capitalization of $120 billion. Again, a series of accounting manipulations beginning in 1998 hid the firm's financial problems from investors.

In WorldCom's case, the fraud was to reclassify $3.85 billion in operating expenses as long-term investment. The immediate impact of this change was to boost WorldCom's reported earnings: Operating expenses are deducted from earnings immediately, whereas long-term investments are depreciated slowly over time. Of course, this manipulation would not boost WorldCom's cash flows, because long-term investments must be deducted on the cash flow statement at the time they are made.

Some investors were concerned by WorldCom's excessive investment compared to the rest of the industry. As one investment advisor commented, "Red flags [were] things like big deviations between reported earnings and excess cash flow . . . [and] excessive capital expenditures for a long period of time. That was what got us out of WorldCom in 1999."[9]

Sarbanes-Oxley Act

Enron and WorldCom highlight the importance to investors of accurate and up-to-date financial statements for firms they choose to invest in. In 2002, Congress passed the Sarbanes-Oxley Act that requires, among other things, that CEOs and CFOs certify the accuracy and appropriateness of their firm's financial statements and increases the penalties against them if the financial statements later prove to be fraudulent.[10]

CONCEPT CHECK

1. Describe the transactions Enron used to increase its reported earnings.

2. What is the Sarbanes-Oxley Act?

Summary

1. Financial statements are accounting reports that a firm issues periodically to describe its past performance.

2. Investors, financial analysts, managers, and other interested parties such as creditors rely on financial statements to obtain reliable information about a corporation.

3. The main types of financial statements are the balance sheet, the income statement, and the statement of cash flows.

4. The balance sheet shows the current financial position (assets, liabilities, and stockholders' equity) of the firm at a single point in time.

5. The two sides of the balance sheet must balance:

$$\text{Assets} = \text{Liabilities} + \text{Stockholders' Equity} \qquad (2.1)$$

6. Stockholders' equity is the book value of the firm's equity. It differs from market value of the firm's equity, its market capitalization, because of the way assets and liabilities are recorded for accounting purposes. A successful firm's market-to-book ratio typically exceeds 1.

---

9. Robert Olstein, as reported in the *Wall Street Journal*, August 23, 2002.

10. We discuss these and other related corporate governance issues further in Chapter 29.

7. A common ratio used to assess a firm's leverage is

$$\text{Debt-Equity Ratio} = \frac{\text{Total Debt}}{\text{Total Equity}} \qquad (2.3)$$

This ratio is most informative when computed using the market value of equity. It indicates the degree of leverage of the firm.

8. The enterprise value of a firm is the total value of its underlying business operations:

$$\text{Enterprise Value} = \text{Market Capitalization} + \text{Debt} - \text{Cash} \qquad (2.4)$$

9. The income statement reports the firm's revenues and expenses, and it computes the firm's bottom line of net income, or earnings.

10. Net income is often reported on a per-share basis as the firms earnings per share:

$$\text{Earnings per share (EPS)} = \text{Net Income / Shares Outstanding} \qquad (2.5)$$

We compute diluted EPS by adding to the number of shares outstanding the possible increase in the number of shares from the exercise of stock options the firm has awarded.

11. Profitability ratios show the firm's operating or net income as a fraction of sales, and they are an indication of a firm's efficiency and its pricing strategy.

12. Working capital ratios express the firm's working capital as a number of days of sales (for receivables) or cost of sales (for inventory or payables).

13. Interest coverage ratios indicate the ratio of the firm's income or cash flows to its interest expenses, and they are a measure of financial strength.

14. Return on investment ratios such as ROE or ROA express the firm's net income as a return on the book value of its equity or total assets.

15. Valuation ratios compute market capitalization or enterprise value of the firm relative to its earnings or operating income.

16. The P/E ratio computes the value of a share of stock relative to the firm's EPS. P/E ratios tend to be high for fast-growing firms.

17. When comparing valuation ratios, it is important to be sure both numerator and denominator match in terms of whether they include debt.

18. The statement of cash flows reports the sources and uses of the firm's cash. It shows the adjustments to net income for non-cash expenses and changes to net working capital, as well as the cash used (or provided) from investing and financing activities.

19. The management discussion and analysis section of the financial statements contains management's overview of the firm's performance, as well as disclosure of risks the firm faces, including those from off-balance sheet transactions.

20. The statement of stockholders' equity breaks down the stockholders' equity computed on the balance sheet into the amount that came from issuing new shares versus retained earnings. It is not particularly useful for financial valuation purposes.

21. The notes to a firm's financial statements generally contain important details regarding the numbers used in the main statements.

22. Recent accounting scandals have drawn attention to the importance of financial statements. New legislation has increased the penalties for fraud, and tightened the procedures firms must use to assure that statements are accurate.

Key Terms

Further Reading

For a basic primer on financial statements, see T. R. Ittelson, *Financial Statements: A Step-By-Step Guide to Understanding and Creating Financial Reports*, 1st ed. (Career Press, 1998).

For additional information on financial accounting, there are many introductory, MBA-level financial accounting textbooks. Two examples are J. Pratt, *Financial Accounting in an Economic Context*, 5th ed. (John Wiley & Sons, 2003); and C. Stickney and R. Weil, *Financial Accounting*, 10th ed. (Thomson/South-Western, 2003).

For more on financial statement analysis, see K. G. Palepu, P. M. Healy, V. L. Bernard, *Business Analysis and Valuation: Using Financial Statements* (South-Western College Pub, 2003); and L. Revsine, D. W. Collins, W. B. Johnson, *Financial Reporting & Analysis* (Prentice Hall, 1999).

A great deal of public information is available regarding the alleged accounting abuses at Enron Corporation. A useful starting point is a report produced by a committee established by Enron's own board of directors: Report of the Special Investigative Committee of the Board of Directors of Enron (Powers Report), released February 2, 2002 (available online).

Problems

A blue box (■) indicates problems available in MyFinanceLab. An asterisk (*) indicates problems with a higher level of difficulty.

The Disclosure of Financial Information

 1. What four financial statements can be found in a firm's 10-K filing? What checks are there on the accuracy of these statements?

2. Who reads financial statements? List at least three different categories of people. For each category, provide an example of the type of information they might be interested in and discuss why.

3. Find the most recent financial statements for Starbuck's corporation (SBUX) using the following sources:

    a. From the company's Web page www.starbucks.com (*Hint:* Search for "investor relations.")

    b. From the SEC Web site www.sec.gov. (*Hint:* Search for company filings in the EDGAR database.)

    c. From the Yahoo finance Web site finance.yahoo.com.

    d. From at least one other source. (*Hint:* Enter "SBUX 10K" at www.google.com.)

The Balance Sheet

4. Consider the following potential events that might have occurred to Global Conglomerate on December 30, 2005. For each one, indicate which line items in Global's balance sheet would be affected and by how much. Also indicate the change to Global's book value of equity.

    a. Global used $20 million of its available cash to repay $20 million of its long-term debt.

    b. A warehouse fire destroyed $5 million worth of uninsured inventory.

    c. Global used $5 million in cash and $5 million in new long-term debt to purchase a $10 million building.

    d. A large customer owing $3 million for products it already received declared bankruptcy, leaving no possibility that Global would ever receive payment.

    e. Global's engineers discover a new manufacturing process that will cut the cost of its flagship product by over 50%.

    f. A key competitor announces a radical new pricing policy that will drastically undercut Global's prices.

5. What was the change in Global Conglomerate's book value of equity from 2004 to 2005 according to Table 2.1? Does this imply that the market price of Global's shares increased in 2005? Explain.

6. In March 2005, General Electric (GE) had a book value of equity of $113 billion, 10.6 billion shares outstanding, and a market price of $36 per share. GE also had cash of $13 billion, and total debt of $370 billion.

    a. What was GE's market capitalization? What was GE's market-to-book ratio?

    b. What was GE's book debt-equity ratio? What was GE's market debt-equity ratio?

    c. What was GE's enterprise value?

7. Find online the annual 10-K report for Peet's Coffee and Tea (PEET) filed in March 2005. Answer the following questions from their balance sheet:

    a. How much cash did Peet's have at the start of 2005?

    b. What was Peet's total assets?

    c. What was Peet's total liabilities? How much debt did Peet's have?

    d. What was the book value of Peet's equity?

The Income Statement

8. Find online the annual 10-K report for Peet's Coffee and Tea (PEET) filed in March 2005. Answer the following questions from the income statement:

   a. What were Peet's revenues for 2004? By what percentage did revenues grow from 2003?

   b. What was Peet's operating and net profit margin in 2004? How do they compare with its margins in 2003?

   c. What was Peet's diluted earnings per share in 2004? What number of shares is this EPS based on?

EXCEL **9.** Suppose that in 2006, Global launched an aggressive marketing campaign that boosts sales by 15%. However, their operating margin fell from 5.57% to 4.50%. Suppose that they have no other income, interest expenses are unchanged, and taxes are the same percentage of pretax income as in 2005.

   a. What is Global's EBIT in 2006?

   b. What is Global's income in 2006?

   c. If Global's P/E ratio and number of shares outstanding remains unchanged, what is Global's share price in 2006?

EXCEL **10.** Suppose a firm's tax rate is 35%.

   a. What effect would a $10 million operating expense have on this year's earnings? What effect would it have on next year's earnings?

   b. What effect would a $10 million capital expense have on this year's earnings, if the capital is depreciated at a rate of $2 million per year for 5 years? What effect would it have on next year's earnings?

*11. Quisco Systems has 6.5 billion shares outstanding and a share price of $18. Quisco is considering developing a new networking product in house at a cost of $500 million. Alternatively, Quisco can acquire a firm that already has the technology for $900 million worth (at the current price) of Quisco stock. Suppose that absent the expense of the new technology, Quisco will have EPS of $0.80.

   a. Suppose Quisco develops the product in house. What impact would the development cost have on Quisco's EPS? Assume all costs are incurred this year and are treated as an R&D expense, Quisco's tax rate is 35%, and the number of shares outstanding is unchanged.

   b. Suppose Quisco does not develop the product in house but instead acquires the technology. What effect would the acquisition have on Quisco's EPS this year? (Note that acquisition expenses do not appear directly on the income statement. Assume the acquired firm has no revenues or expenses of its own, so that the only effect on EPS is due to the change in the number of shares outstanding.)

   c. Which method of acquiring the technology has a smaller impact on earnings? Is this method cheaper? Explain.

12. In July 2005, American Airlines (AMR) had a market capitalization of $2.3 billion, debt of $14.3 billion, and cash of $3.1 billion. American Airlines had revenues of $18.9 billion. British Airways (BAB) had a market capitalization of $5.2 billion, debt of $8.0 billion, cash of $2.9 billion, and revenues of $13.6 billion.

   a. Compare the market capitalization-to-revenue ratio (also called the price-to-sales ratio) for American Airlines and British Airways.

   b. Compare the enterprise value-to-revenue ratio for American Airlines and British Airways.

   c. Which of these comparisons is more meaningful? Explain.

13. Find online the annual 10-K report for Peet's Coffee and Tea (PEET) filed in March 2005. Answer the following questions from their cash flow statement:

a. How much cash did Peet's generate from operating activities in 2004?

b. What was Peet's depreciation expense in 2004?

c. How much cash was invested in new property and equipment (net of any sales) in 2004?

d. How much did Peet's raise from the sale of shares of its stock (net of any purchases) in 2004?

14. Can a firm with positive net income run out of cash? Explain.

15. See the cash flow statement here for H.J. Heinz (HNZ) (in $ thousands):

Statement of Cash Flows:	27-Apr-05	26-Jan-05	27-Oct-04	28-Jul-04
Net Income	206,487	152,411	198,965	194,836
Operating Activities, Cash Flows Provided by or Used In				
Depreciation	67,752	65,388	60,229	59,083
Adjustments to net income	150,588	12,616	−43,557	62,140
Changes in accounts receivables	−84,612	55,787	−55,303	129,979
Changes in liabilities	135,732	−206,876	223,953	−202,123
Changes in inventories	140,434	51,280	−210,093	−6,936
Changes in other operating activities	38,266	−4,022	47,384	−50,799
Total Cash Flow From Operating Activities	654,647	126,584	221,578	186,180
Investing Activities, Cash Flows Provided by or Used In				
Capital expenditures	−109,647	−48,404	−44,180	−38,440
Investments	40,000	—	−19,179	19,179
Other cash flows from investing activities	−69,275	−24,197	45,296	−15,207
Total Cash Flows From Investing Activities	−138,922	−72,601	−18,063	−34,468
Financing Activities, Cash Flows Provided by or Used In				
Dividends paid	−99,617	−99,730	−99,552	−99,970
Sale purchase of stock	−102,286	20,903	−63,357	−67,225
Net borrowings	−11,409	−440,029	1,955	−4,520
Other cash flows from financing activities	2,629	—	—	11,323
Total Cash Flows from Financing Activities	−210,683	−518,856	−160,954	−160,392
Effect of exchange rate changes	−16,098	31,984	51,496	2,278
Change in Cash and Cash Equivalents	$288,944	($432,889)	$94,057	($6,402)

a. What was Heinz's cumulative earnings over these four quarters? What was its cumulative cash flows from operating activities?

b. What fraction of the cash from operating activities was used for investment over the four quarters?

c. What fraction of the cash from operating activities was used for financing activities over the four quarters?

16. Suppose your firm receives a $5 million order on the last day of the year. You fill the order with $2 million worth of inventory. The customer picks up the entire order the same day and pays $1 million upfront in cash; you also issue a bill for the customer to pay the remaining balance of $4 million within 30 days. Suppose your firm's tax rate is 0% (i.e., ignore taxes). Determine the consequences of this transaction for each of the following:

a. Revenues

b. Earnings

c. Receivables

d. Inventory

e. Cash

17. Nokela Industries purchases a $40 million cyclo-converter. The cyclo-converter will be depreciated by $10 million per year over four years, starting this year. Suppose Nokela's tax rate is 40%.

a. What impact will the cost of the purchase have on earnings for each of the next four years?

b. What impact will the cost of the purchase have on the firm's cash flow for the next four years?

Other Financial Statement Information

18. The balance sheet information for Clorox Co. (CLX) in 2004–2005 is shown here, with data in $ thousands:

Balance Sheet:	31-Mar-05	31-Dec-04	30-Sep-04	30-Jun-04
Assets				
Current Assets				
Cash and cash equivalents	293,000	300,000	255,000	232,000
Net receivables	401,000	362,000	385,000	460,000
Inventory	374,000	342,000	437,000	306,000
Other current assets	60,000	43,000	53,000	45,000
Total Current Assets	1,128,000	1,047,000	1,130,000	1,043,000
Long term investments	128,000	97,000	—	200,000
Property, plant, and equipment	979,000	991,000	995,000	1,052,000
Goodwill	744,000	748,000	736,000	742,000
Other assets	777,000	827,000	911,000	797,000
Total Assets	3,756,000	3,710,000	3,772,000	3,834,000
Liabilities				
Current Liabilities				
Accounts payable	876,000	1,467,000	922,000	980,000
Short/current long-term debt	410,000	2,000	173,000	288,000
Other current liabilities	—	—	—	—
Total Current Liabilities	1,286,000	1,469,000	1,095,000	1,268,000
Long-term debt	2,381,000	2,124,000	474,000	475,000
Other liabilities	435,000	574,000	559,000	551,000
Total Liabilities	4,102,000	4,167,000	2,128,000	2,294,000
Total Stockholder Equity	−346,000	−457,000	1,644,000	1,540,000
Total Liabilities & Stockholder Equity	$3,756,000	$3,710,000	$3,772,000	$3,834,000

    a. What change in the book value of Clorox's equity took place at the end of 2004?

    b. Is Clorox's market-to-book ratio meaningful? Is its book debt-equity ratio meaningful? Explain.

    c. Find online Clorox's other financial statements from that time. What was the cause of the change to Clorox's book value of equity at the end of 2004?

    d. Does Clorox's book value of equity in 2005 imply that the firm is unprofitable? Explain.

19. Find online the annual 10-K report for Peet's Coffee and Tea (PEET) filed in March 2005. Answer the following questions from the notes to their financial statements:

    a. Under stock-based compensation, what was Peet's net income in 2004 after deducting the fair value of options granted to employees?

    b. What was Peet's inventory of raw materials at the end of 2004?

    c. What was the fair value of Peet's holdings of marketable government securities at the end of 2004?

    d. What property does Peet's lease? What are the minimum lease payments due in 2005?

    e. How many stock options did Peet's grant in 2004?

    f. What fraction of Peet's 2004 sales came from coffee beans and tea products? What fraction came from beverages and pastries?

Accounting Manipulation

20. Find online the annual 10-K report for Peet's Coffee and Tea (PEET) filed in March 2005.

    a. Which auditing firm certified these financial statements?

    b. Which officers of Peet's certified the financial statements?

21. WorldCom reclassified $3.85 billion of operating expenses as capital expenditures. Explain the effect this reclassification would have on WorldCom's cash flows. (*Hint:* Consider taxes.) WorldCom's actions were illegal and clearly designed to deceive investors. But if a firm could legitimately choose how to classify an expense for tax purposes, which choice is truly better for the firm's investors?

Data Case

This is your second interview with a prestigious brokerage firm for a job as an equity analyst. You survived the morning interviews with the department manager and the Vice President of Equity. Everything has gone so well that they want to test your ability as an analyst. You are seated in a room with a computer and a list with the names of two companies—Ford (F) and Microsoft (MSFT). You have 90 minutes to complete the following tasks:

1. Download the annual income statements, balance sheets, and cash flow statements for the last four fiscal years from MarketWatch (www.marketwatch.com). Enter each company's stock symbol and then go to "financials." Export the statements to Excel by right-clicking while the cursor is inside each statement.

2. Find historical stock prices for each firm from Yahoo! Finance (http://finance.yahoo.com). Enter your stock symbol, click on "Historical Prices" in the left column, and enter the proper date range to cover the last day of the month corresponding to the date of each financial statement. Use the closing stock prices (not the adjusted close). To calculate the firm's market capitalization at each date, we multiply the number of shares outstanding (see "Basic Weighted Shares Outstanding" on the income statement) by the firm's historic stock price.

3. For each of the four years of statements, compute the following ratios for each firm:

Valuation Ratios

　　Price-Earnings Ratio (for EPS use Diluted EPS Total)

　　Market-to-Book Ratio

　　Enterprise Value-to-EBITDA

(For debt, include long-term and short-term debt; for cash, include marketable securities.)

Profitability Ratios

　　Operating Margin (Use Operating Income after Depreciation)

　　Net Profit Margin

　　Return on Equity

Financial Strength Ratios

　　Current Ratio

　　Book Debt–Equity Ratio

　　Market Debt–Equity Ratio

　　Interest Coverage Ratio (EBIT ÷ Interest Expense)

4. Obtain industry averages for each firm from Reuters.com (http://today.reuters.com/investing/default.aspx).[11] Enter the stock symbol on top of the homepage and then click on "Ratios" in the left column.

　　a. Compare each firm's ratios to the available industry ratios for the most recent year. (Ignore the "Company" column as your calculations will be different.)

　　b. Analyze the performance of each firm versus the industry and comment on any trends in each individual firm's performance. Identify any strengths or weaknesses you find in each firm.

5. Examine the Market-to-Book ratios you calculated for each firm. Which, if any, of the two firms can be considered "growth firms" and which, if any, can be considered "value firms"?

6. Compare the valuation ratios across the two firms. How do you interpret the difference between them?

7. Consider the enterprise value of each firm for each of the four years. How have the values of each firm changed over the time period?

---

11. Reuters requires free registration for access to the site. Professors may want to set up an account with a class e-mail and password.

Arbitrage and Financial Decision Making

In July 2005, Jeff Fettig, CEO of appliance maker Whirlpool, offered to buy rival Maytag Corporation for $1.43 billion in cash and stock. The same month, Hewlett-Packard CEO Mark Hurd announced that HP would cut 14,500 jobs, or 10% of its full-time staff, over the next 18 months in order to reduce costs. And Tom Gahan, CEO of Deutsche Bank Securities, authorized the firm's traders to buy and sell over $600 billion worth of the largest U.S. stocks in a strategy referred to as stock index arbitrage. How did these CEOs decide that these decisions were good for their firms?

Every decision has future consequences, and these consequences can be either beneficial or costly. For example, after raising its offer, Whirlpool ultimately succeeded in its attempt to acquire Maytag. In addition to the upfront cost of $1.73 billion for the acquisition, Whirlpool will also incur the ongoing costs of paying Maytag employees, developing and producing new Maytag products, and so on. The benefits of the acquisition include the future sales revenues that Maytag's products will generate and the possible increase in Whirlpool's sales as a result of reduced competition. Purchasing Maytag was a good decision if the future benefits justify the upfront and future costs. If the benefits exceed the costs, the decision will increase the value of the firm and therefore the wealth of its investors.

Comparing costs and benefits is complicated because they often occur at different points in time, may be in different currencies, or may have different risks associated with them. To make a valid comparison, we must use the tools of finance to express all costs and benefits in common terms. In particular, the tools we develop will allow us to take costs and benefits that occur at different times, in different currencies, or with different risks, and express them in terms of cash today. We will then be able to evaluate a decision by answering this question: *Does the cash value today of its benefits exceed the cash value today of its costs?* In addition, we will see that the difference between the cash value of the benefits and costs indicates the net amount by which the decision will increase wealth.

In this chapter, we introduce the concept of *net present value (NPV)* as a way to compare the costs and benefits of a project in terms of a common unit—namely, dollars today. We use these same tools to determine the prices of investment opportunities that trade in the market. More fundamentally, in deriving these tools we discuss strategies called *arbitrage* that allow us to exploit situations in which the prices of publicly available investment opportunities do not conform to the values that we will determine. Because investors trade rapidly to take advantage of arbitrage opportunities, we argue that equivalent investment opportunities trading simultaneously in competitive markets must have the same price. This *Law of One Price* is the unifying theme of valuation that we use throughout this text.

3.1   Valuing Costs and Benefits

The first step in evaluating a project is to identify its costs and benefits. Suppose your firm is an importer of frozen seafood, and you find the following opportunity: You can buy $1000 of frozen shrimp today and immediately resell it to a customer for $1500 today. If you were certain about these costs and benefits, the right decision would be obvious: You should seize this opportunity because the firm will gain $1500 − $1000 = $500. Thus taking this opportunity contributes $500 to the value of the firm, in the form of cash that can be paid out immediately to the firm's investors.

Of course, real-world opportunities are usually much more complex than in this example, and the costs and benefits are more difficult to quantify. The analysis will often involve skills from other management disciplines, as in the following examples:

Marketing: to determine the increase in revenues resulting from an advertising campaign

Economics: to determine the increase in demand from lowering the price of a product

Organizational Behavior: to determine the effect of changes in management structure on productivity

Strategy: to determine a competitor's response to a price increase

Operations: to determine production costs after the modernization of a manufacturing plant

For the remainder of this text, we assume that the analysis of these other disciplines has been completed to quantify the costs and benefits associated with a decision. Once that task is done, the financial manager must compare the costs and benefits and determine whether the opportunity is worthwhile. In this section, we focus on the use of market prices to determine the current cash value of different costs and benefits.

Using Market Prices to Determine Cash Values

For our shrimp trader, both costs and benefits were expressed in terms of cash today: $1000 invested and $1500 received today. In practice, benefits and costs are often expressed in different terms, and we must convert them to an equivalent cash value.

Suppose a jewelry manufacturer has the opportunity to trade 10 ounces of platinum and receive 20 ounces of gold today. Because an ounce of gold differs in value from an ounce of platinum, it is incorrect to compare 20 ounces to 10 ounces and conclude that the larger quantity is better. Instead, to compare the costs and benefits, we first need to convert them to a common unit.

Consider the gold. What is its cash value today? Suppose gold can be bought and sold for a current market price of $250 per ounce. Then the 20 ounces of gold we receive has a cash value of[1]

$$(20 \text{ ounces of gold today}) \times (\$250 \text{ today} / \text{ounce of gold today}) = \$5000 \text{ today}$$

Similarly, if the current market price for platinum is $550 per ounce, then the 10 ounces of platinum we give up has a cash value of

$$(10 \text{ ounces of platinum today}) \times (\$550 \text{ today} / \text{ounce of platinum today})$$
$$= \$5500 \text{ today}$$

Therefore, the jeweler's opportunity has a benefit of $5000 today and a cost of $5500 today. Because the benefits and costs are in the same units, they are comparable. In this case, the net value of the project is $5000 − $5500 = −$500 today. Because it is negative, the costs exceed the benefits and the jeweler should reject the trade. If he were to take it, it would be the same as giving up $500 today.

Note that for both gold and platinum, we used the current market price to convert from ounces of the metal to dollars. We did not concern ourselves with whether the jeweler thought that the price was fair or whether the jeweler would use the gold or platinum. Do such considerations matter? Suppose, for example, that the jeweler does not need the gold, or he thinks the current price of gold is too high. Would he value the gold at less than $5000? The answer is no—he can always sell the gold at the current market price and receive $5000 right now. Similarly, even if he really needs the gold or thinks the price of gold is too low, he can always buy 20 ounces of gold for $5000 and so should not value it at more than that amount.

Because the jeweler can both buy and sell gold at its current market price, his personal preferences or use for the gold and his opinion of the fair price are irrelevant in evaluating the value of this opportunity. In general, whenever a good trades in a **competitive market**—by which we mean a market in which it can be bought *and* sold at the same price—that price determines the cash value of the good. This extremely powerful and general idea is one of the foundations of all finance.

EXAMPLE 3.1	**Competitive Market Prices Determine Value**
	Problem Suppose the jeweler can produce $10,000 worth of jewelry from 20 ounces of gold but only $6000 worth of jewelry from 10 ounces of platinum. If the jeweler has a private opportunity to trade 10 ounces of platinum for 20 ounces of gold, should he take it?

---

1. You might worry about commissions or other transactions costs that are incurred when buying or selling gold, in addition to the market price. For now, we will ignore transactions costs, and discuss their effect in Section 3.7.

Solution

Given the value of the jewelry he can produce, the jeweler should exchange his platinum for gold. However, rather than accept the private trading opportunity, he can do better by using the market to trade. At current market prices the jeweler could exchange his platinum for $5500. He could then use this money to purchase $5500 ÷ ($250 / ounce of gold) = 22 ounces of gold. This amount is more than the 20 ounces he would receive if he engaged in the direct trade. As we emphasized earlier, whether this trade is attractive depends on its net cash value using market prices. Because this value is negative, the private trade is not appealing no matter what the jeweler can produce from the materials.

Because competitive markets exist for most commodities and financial assets, we can use them to determine cash values and evaluate decisions in most situations. Let's consider another example.

EXAMPLE 3.2

Calculating Cash Values Using Market Prices

Problem

You are offered the following investment opportunity: In exchange for $20,000 today, you will receive 200 shares of stock in the Coca-Cola Company today and 11,000 euros today. The current market price is $40 per share for Coca-Cola stock and the current exchange rate is 0.80 euro per dollar. Should you take this opportunity? How valuable is it? Would your decision change if you believed the value of the euro would plummet over the next month?

Solution

We need to convert the costs and benefits to their cash values. Assuming the market prices are competitive, we have

$$(200 \text{ shares}) \times (\$40 / \text{share today}) = \$8000 \text{ today}$$

$$(\text{€}11,000) \div (0.80\text{€} / \$ \text{ today}) = \$13,750 \text{ today}$$

The net value of the opportunity is $8000 + $13,750 − $20,000 = $1750 today. Because the net value is positive, we should take it. This value depends only on the *current* market prices for Coca-Cola stock and the euro. Even if we thought the value of the euro were about to plummet, because we can sell euros immediately at the current exchange rate of 0.80€ / $, the value of this investment is unchanged. Our own personal opinion about the future prospects of the euro and Coca-Cola Company does not alter the value of the decision today.

When Competitive Market Prices Are Not Available

Competitive market prices allow us to calculate the value of a decision without worrying about the tastes or opinions of the decision maker. When competitive prices are not available, we can no longer do this. Prices at retail stores, for example, are one sided: You can buy at the posted price, but you cannot sell the good to the store at that same price. We cannot use these one-sided prices to determine an exact cash value. They determine the maximum value of the good (since it can always be purchased at that price), but an individual may value it for much less depending on his or her preferences for the good.

EXAMPLE 3.3	**When Value Depends on Preferences**

Problem

The local Lexus dealer hires you as an extra in a commercial. As part of your compensation, the dealer offers to sell you today a new Lexus for $33,000. The best available retail price for the Lexus is $40,000, and the price you could sell it for in the used car market is $35,000. How would you value this compensation?

Solution

If you plan to buy a Lexus anyway, then the value to you of the Lexus is $40,000, the price you would otherwise pay for it. In this case, the value of the dealer's offer is $40,000 − $33,000 = $7000. But suppose you do not want or need a Lexus. If you were to buy it from the dealer and then sell it, the value of taking the deal would be $35,000 − $33,000 = $2000. Thus, depending on your desire to own a new Lexus, the dealer's offer is worth somewhere between $2000 (you don't want a Lexus) and $7000 (you definitely want one). Because the price of the Lexus is not competitive (you cannot buy and sell at the same price), the value of the offer is ambiguous and depends on your preferences.

CONCEPT CHECK

1. If crude oil trades in a competitive market, would an oil refiner that has a use for the oil value it differently than another investor?

3.2 Interest Rates and the Time Value of Money

For most financial decisions, unlike in the examples presented so far, costs and benefits occur at different points in time. For example, typical investment projects incur costs upfront and provide benefits in the future. In this section, we show how to account for this time difference when evaluating a project.

The Time Value of Money

Consider an investment opportunity with the following certain cash flows:

Cost: $100,000 today

Benefit: $105,000 in one year

Because both are expressed in dollar terms, it might appear that the cost and benefit are directly comparable so that the project's net value is $105,000 − $100,000 = $5000. But this calculation ignores the timing of the costs and benefits, and it treats money today as equivalent to money in one year.

In general, a dollar today is worth more than a dollar in one year. If you have $1 today, you can invest it. For example, if you deposit it in a bank account paying 7% interest, you will have $1.07 at the end of one year. We call the difference in value between money today and money in the future the **time value of money**.

The Interest Rate: An Exchange Rate Across Time

By depositing money into a savings account, we can convert money today into money in the future with no risk. Similarly, by borrowing money from the bank, we can exchange money in the future for money today. The rate at which we can exchange money today for money in the future is determined by the current interest rate. In the same way that an exchange rate allows us to convert money from one currency to another, the interest rate allows us to convert money from one point in time to another. In essence, an interest rate is like an exchange rate across time. It tells us the market price today of money in the future.

Suppose the current annual interest rate is 7%. By investing or borrowing at this rate, we can exchange $1.07 in one year for each $1 today. More generally, we define the **risk-free interest rate**, r_f, for a given period as the interest rate at which money can be borrowed or lent without risk over that period. We can exchange $(1 + r_f)$ dollars in the future per dollar today, and vice versa, without risk. We refer to $(1 + r_f)$ as the **interest rate factor** for risk-free cash flows; it defines the exchange rate across time, and has units of "$ in one year / $ today."

As with other market prices, the risk-free interest rate depends on supply and demand. In particular, at the risk-free interest rate the supply of savings equals the demand for borrowing. After we know the risk-free interest rate, we can use it to evaluate other decisions in which costs and benefits are separated in time without knowing the investor's preferences.

Let's reevaluate the investment we considered earlier, this time taking into account the time value of money. If the interest rate is 7%, then we can express our costs as

$$\text{Cost} = (\$100{,}000 \text{ today}) \times (1.07 \text{ } \$ \text{ in one year / } \$ \text{ today})$$
$$= \$107{,}000 \text{ in one year}$$

Think of this amount as the opportunity cost of spending $100,000 today: We give up the $107,000 we would have had in one year if we had left the money in the bank. Alternatively, if we were to borrow the $100,000, we would owe $107,000 in one year.

Both costs and benefits are now in terms of "dollars in one year," so we can compare them and compute the investment's net value:

$$\$105{,}000 - \$107{,}000 = -\$2000 \text{ in one year}$$

In other words, we could earn $2000 more in one year by putting our $100,000 in the bank rather than making this investment. We should reject the investment: If we took it, we would be $2000 poorer in one year than if we didn't.

The previous calculation expressed the value of the costs and benefits in terms of dollars in one year. Alternatively, we can use the interest rate factor to convert to dollars today. Consider the benefit of $105,000 in one year. What is the equivalent amount in terms of dollars today? That is, how much would we need to have in the bank today so that we would end up with $105,000 in the bank in one year? We find this amount by dividing by the interest rate factor:

$$\text{Benefit} = (\$105{,}000 \text{ in one year}) \div (1.07 \text{ } \$ \text{ in one year / } \$ \text{ today})$$
$$= \$98{,}130.84 \text{ today}$$

This is also the amount the bank would lend to us today if we promised to repay $105,000 in one year.[2] Thus, it is the competitive market price at which we can "buy" or "sell" $105,000 in one year.

Now we are ready to compute the net value of the investment:

$$\$98{,}130.84 - \$100{,}000 = -\$1869.16 \text{ today}$$

---

2. We are assuming the bank will both borrow and lend at the risk-free interest rate. We discuss the case when these rates differ in Section 3.7.

Once again, the negative result indicates that we should reject the investment. Taking the investment would make us $1869.16 poorer today because we have given up $100,000 for something worth only $98,130.84.

Thus, our decision is the same whether we express the value of the investment in terms of dollars in one year or dollars today: We should reject the investment. Indeed, if we convert from dollars today to dollars in one year,

$$(-\$1869.16 \text{ today}) \times (1.07 \ \$ \text{ in one year} / \$ \text{ today}) = -\$2000 \text{ in one year}$$

we see that the two results are equivalent, but expressed as values at different points in time. In the preceding calculation, we can interpret

$$\frac{1}{1 + r} = \frac{1}{1.07} = 0.93458$$

as the *price* today of $1 in one year. Note that the value is less than $1—money in the future is worth less today, and so its price reflects a discount. Because it provides the discount at which we can purchase money in the future, the amount $\frac{1}{1+r}$ is called the one-year **discount factor**. The risk-free interest rate is also referred to as the **discount rate** for a risk-free investment.

EXAMPLE 3.4

Comparing Costs at Different Points in Time

Problem

The cost of rebuilding the San Francisco Bay Bridge to make it earthquake-safe was approximately $3 billion in 2004. At the time, engineers estimated that if the project were delayed to 2005, the cost would rise by 10%. If the interest rate was 2%, what was the cost of a delay in terms of dollars in 2004?

Solution

If the project were delayed, it would cost $3 billion × (1.10) = $3.3 billion in 2005. To compare this amount to the cost of $3 billion in 2004, we must convert it using the interest rate of 2%:

$$\$3.3 \text{ billion in 2005} \div (\$1.02 \text{ in 2005} / \$ \text{ in 2004}) = \$3.235 \text{ billion in 2004}$$

Therefore, the cost of a delay of one year was

$$\$3.235 \text{ billion} - \$3 \text{ billion} = \$235 \text{ million in 2004}$$

That is, delaying the project for one year was equivalent to giving up $235 million in cash.

We can use the risk-free interest rate to determine values in the same way we used competitive market prices. Figure 3.1 illustrates how we use competitive market prices, exchange rates, and interest rates to convert between dollars today and other goods, currencies, or dollars in the future.

CONCEPT CHECK

1. Is the value today of money to be received in one year higher or lower when interest rates are high than when interest rates are low?

2. How do you compare costs at different points in time?

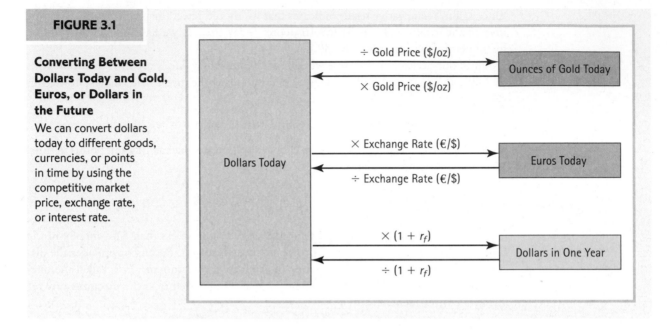

FIGURE 3.1

Converting Between Dollars Today and Gold, Euros, or Dollars in the Future

We can convert dollars today to different goods, currencies, or points in time by using the competitive market price, exchange rate, or interest rate.

3.3 Present Value and the NPV Decision Rule

In Section 3.2, we converted between cash today and cash in the future using the risk-free interest rate. As long as we convert costs and benefits to the same point in time, we can compare them to make a decision. As a matter of practice, however, most corporations prefer to measure values in terms of cash today using *net present value*, the focus of this section.

Net Present Value

When the value of a cost or benefit is computed in terms of cash today, we refer to it as the **present value (PV)**. Similarly, we define the **net present value (NPV)** of a project or investment as the difference between the present value of its benefits and the present value of its costs:

Net Present Value

$$NPV = PV(\text{Benefits}) - PV(\text{Costs}) \tag{3.1}$$

If we use positive cash flows to represent benefits and negative cash flows to represent costs, and calculate the present value of multiple cash flows as the sum of present values for individual cash flows, we can write this definition as

$$NPV = PV(\text{All project cash flows}) \tag{3.2}$$

That is, the NPV is the total of the present values of all project cash flows.

Let's consider a simple example. Suppose you are offered the following investment opportunity: In exchange for $500 today, you will receive $550 in one year with certainty. If the risk-free interest rate is 8% per year then

$$PV(\text{Benefit}) = (\$550 \text{ in one year}) \div (1.08 \, \$ \text{ in one year} / \$ \text{ today})$$

$$= \$509.26 \text{ today}$$

This PV is the amount we would need to put in the bank today to generate $550 in one year ($509.26 × 1.08 = $550). In other words, *the present value is the cash cost today of "doing it yourself"—it is the amount you need to invest at the current interest rate to recreate the cash flow.*

Once the costs and benefits are in present value terms, we can compute the investment's NPV:

$$NPV = \$509.26 - \$500 = \$9.26 \text{ today}$$

But what if you don't have the $500 needed to cover the initial cost of the project? Does the project still have the same value? Because we computed the value using competitive market prices, it should not depend on your tastes or the amount of cash you have in the bank. If you don't have the $500, suppose you borrow $509.26 from the bank at the 8% interest rate and then take the project. What are your cash flows in this case?

Today: $509.26 (loan) − $500 (invested in the project) = $9.26

In one year: $550 (from project) − $509.26 × 1.08 (loan balance) = $0

This transaction leaves you with exactly $9.26 extra cash in your pocket today and no future net obligations. So taking the project is like having an extra $9.26 in cash up front. Thus, the NPV expresses the value of an investment decision as an amount of cash received today.

The NPV Decision Rule

The NPV represents the value of the project in terms of cash today. Therefore, good projects are those with a positive NPV—they make the investor wealthier. Projects with negative NPVs have costs that exceed their benefits, and accepting them is equivalent to losing money today.

Because NPV is expressed in terms of cash today, it simplifies decision making. Decisions that increase wealth are superior to those that decrease wealth. Note that we don't need to know anything about the investor's preferences to reach this conclusion: As long as we have correctly captured all of the cash flows of a project, being wealthier increases our options[3] and makes us better off whatever our preferences are. We capture this logic in the **NPV Decision Rule**:

When making an investment decision, take the alternative with the highest NPV. Choosing this alternative is equivalent to receiving its NPV in cash today.

Accepting or Rejecting a Project. A common financial decision is whether to accept or reject a project. Because rejecting the project generally has $NPV = 0$ (there are no new costs or benefits from not doing the project), the NPV decision rule implies that we should

- Accept those projects with positive NPV because accepting them is equivalent to receiving their NPV in cash today, and

- Reject those projects with negative NPV; accepting them would reduce the wealth of investors, whereas not doing them has no cost (NPV = 0).

---

3. Including giving the extra wealth away, if one should so desire.

The NPV Is Equivalent to Cash Today

Problem

You are offered an investment opportunity in which you will receive $9500 today in exchange for paying $10,000 in one year. Suppose the risk-free interest rate is 7% per year. Is this investment a good deal? Show that its NPV represents cash in your pocket.

Solution

The benefit of $9500 today is already in PV terms. The cost, however, is in terms of dollars in one year. We therefore convert it at the risk-free interest rate:

$$PV(\text{Cost}) = (\$10{,}000 \text{ in one year}) \div (1.07 \ \$ \text{ in one year} / \$ \text{ today}) = \$9345.79 \text{ today}$$

The NPV is the difference between the benefits and the costs:

$$NPV = \$9500 - \$9345.79 = \$154.21 \text{ today}$$

The NPV is positive, so the investment is a good deal. In fact, undertaking this investment is like having an extra $154.21 in your pocket today. Suppose you undertake the investment and save $9345.79 of it in a bank paying 7% interest. Then your net cash flows are as follows:

	Date 0	Date 1
Investment	+$ 9500.00	−$ 10,000
Savings	−$ 9345.79	+$ 10,000
Net Cash Flow	$ 154.21	$ 0

Therefore, this investment is equivalent to receiving $154.21 today, without any future net obligations.

Choosing Among Projects.   We can also use the NPV decision rule to choose among projects. Suppose we must choose only one of three projects that have the risk-free cash flows depicted in Table 3.1. If the risk-free interest rate is 20%, which project is the best choice?

TABLE 3.1	Cash Flows of Three Possible Projects	
Project	**Cash Flow Today ($)**	**Cash Flow in One Year ($)**
A	42	42
B	−20	144
C	−100	225

We can find the best project by comparing the NPV of each. See the calculations in Table 3.2. All three projects have positive NPV, and we would accept all three if possible. But if we must choose only one project, Project B has the highest NPV of $100 and therefore is the best choice. It is equivalent to receiving $100 in cash today.

| | | PV of | |
Project	Cash Flow Today ($)	Cash Flow in One Year ($)	NPV ($ Today)
A	42	42 ÷ 1.20 = 35	42 + 35 = 77
B	−20	144 ÷ 1.20 = 120	−20 + 120 = 100
C	−100	225 ÷ 1.20 = 187.5	−100 + 187.5 = 87.5

TABLE 3.2 Computing the NPV of Each Project

NPV and Individual Preferences

When we compare projects with different patterns of present and future cash flows, we may have preferences regarding when to receive the cash. Some may need cash today; others may prefer to save for the future. Although Project B has the highest NPV in the last example, it does require a $20 cash outlay. Suppose we would prefer to avoid the negative cash flow today. Would Project A be a better choice in that case? Alternatively, if we would prefer to save for the future, would Project C be a better choice? In other words, should our individual preferences about present versus future cash flows affect our choice of projects?

As was true for the jeweler considering trading platinum for gold in Section 3.1, the answer is again no. As long as we are able to borrow and lend at the risk-free interest rate, Project B is superior whatever our preferences regarding the timing of the cash flows. To see why, suppose we invest in Project B and borrow $62 at the risk-free rate of 20%. Our total cash flows are shown in Table 3.3. Compare these cash flows to those for Project A. This combination generates the same initial cash flow as Project A, but with a higher final cash flow ($69.60 versus $42). Thus we are better off by investing in Project B and borrowing $62 today than we would be by accepting Project A.

TABLE 3.3 Cash Flows from Combining Project B with Borrowing

	Cash Flow Today ($)	Cash Flow in One Year ($)
Project B	−20	144
Borrow	62	−62 × (1.20) = −74.4
Total	42	69.6

Similarly, we can combine Project B with saving $80 at the risk-free rate of 20% (see Table 3.4). This combination has the same initial cash flow as Project C (see Table 3.2), but again has a higher final cash flow.

TABLE 3.4	Cash Flows from Combining Project B with Saving	
	Cash Flow Today ($)	**Cash Flow in One Year ($)**
Project B	−20	144
Save	−80	$80 \times (1.20) = 96$
Total	−100	240

Thus, no matter what pattern of cash flows we prefer, Project B is the superior choice. This example illustrates the following general principle:

Regardless of our preferences for cash today versus cash in the future, we should always maximize NPV first. We can then borrow or lend to shift cash flows through time and find our most preferred pattern of cash flows.

We illustrate this result in Figure 3.2. In the figure, the three projects are plotted such that the horizontal axis represents cash today and the vertical axis represents cash in one

FIGURE 3.2

Comparing Projects A, B, and C

The line through each project represents the combination of cash flows today and in one year that can be achieved by combining the project with borrowing or saving. By saving, we decrease today's cash flows and increase our cash flows in one year. By borrowing, we increase today's cash flows and decrease our cash flows in one year. The NPV of the project is the value of the project expressed solely in terms of cash today. The combinations attainable with the highest NPV project exceed all others.

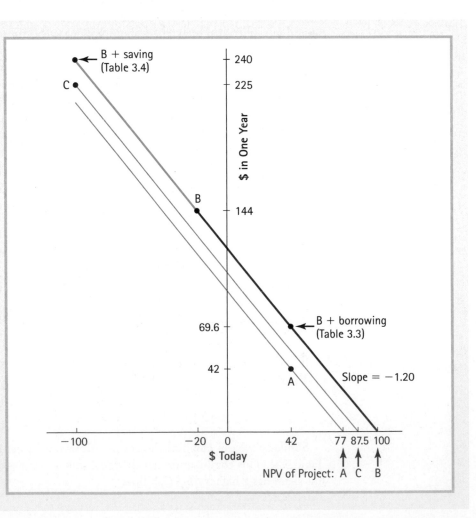

year. We determine the NPV of each project by converting the cash flows in one year to cash flows today at the risk-free rate of 20%, represented in Figure 3.2 by a line with slope −1.20, which corresponds to the conversion rate of ($1.20 in one year / $1 today). Project B has cash flows of −$20 today and +$144 in one year. If we follow the line with slope −1.20 from Project B down to the horizontal axis, we see the value of Project B expressed in today's dollars, an NPV of $100.

Notice that all points on this line are achievable by combining Project B with an appropriate amount of borrowing or lending. Similarly, all points on the line through Project A are achievable by combining Project A with either borrowing or lending, and all points on the line through Project C represent combinations of Project C with either borrowing or lending at the 20% interest rate. The project with the highest NPV, Project B, is on the highest line in Figure 3.2 and so provides the best alternatives whatever pattern of cash flows we prefer.

CONCEPT CHECK
1. What is the NPV decision rule?
2. Why doesn't the NPV decision rule depend on the investor's preferences?

3.4 Arbitrage and the Law of One Price

So far, we have emphasized the importance of using competitive market prices to compute the NPV. But is there always only one such price? What if the same good trades for different prices in different markets? Consider gold. Gold trades in many different markets, with the largest markets in New York and London. To value an ounce of gold we could look up the competitive price in either of these markets. But suppose gold is trading for $250 per ounce in New York and $300 per ounce in London. Which price should we use?

Fortunately, such situations do not arise, and it is easy to see why. Recall that these are competitive market prices, at which you can both buy *and* sell. Thus, you can make money in this situation simply by buying gold for $250 per ounce in New York and then immediately selling it for $300 per ounce in London.[4] You will make $300 − $250 = $50 per ounce for each ounce you buy and sell. Trading 1 million ounces at these prices, you would make $50 million with no risk or investment! This is a case where that old adage, "Buy low, sell high," can be followed perfectly.

Of course, you will not be the only one making these trades. Everyone who sees these prices will want to trade as many ounces as possible. Within seconds, the market in New York would be flooded with buy orders, and the market in London would be flooded with sell orders. Although a few ounces (traded by the lucky individuals who spotted this opportunity first) might be exchanged at these prices, the price of gold in New York would quickly rise in response to all the orders, and the price in London would rapidly fall.[5] Prices would continue to change until they were equalized somewhere in the middle, such as $275 per ounce. This example illustrates an *arbitrage opportunity*, the focus of this section.

---

4. There is no need to transport the gold from New York to London because investors in these markets trade ownership rights to gold that is stored securely elsewhere.

5. As economists would say, supply would not equal demand in these markets. In New York, demand would be infinite because everyone would want to buy. For equilibrium to be restored so that supply equals demand, the price in New York would have to rise. Similarly, in London there would be infinite supply until the price there fell.

An Old Joke

There is an old joke that many finance professors enjoy telling their students. It goes like this:

A finance professor and a student are walking down a street. The student notices a $100 bill lying on the pavement and leans down to pick it up. The finance professor immediately intervenes and says, "Don't bother; there is no free lunch. If that were a real $100 bill lying there, somebody would already have picked it up!"

This joke invariably generates much laughter because it makes fun of the principle of no arbitrage in competitive markets. But once the laughter dies down, the pro-fessor then asks whether anyone has ever *actually* found a real $100 bill lying on the pavement. The ensuing silence is the real lesson behind the joke.

This joke sums up the point of focusing on markets in which no arbitrage opportunities exist. Free $100 bills lying on the pavement, like arbitrage opportunities, are extremely rare for two reasons: (1) Because $100 is a large amount of money, people are especially careful not to lose it, and (2) in the rare event when someone does inadver-tently drop $100, the likelihood of your finding it before someone else does is extremely small.

Arbitrage

The practice of buying and selling equivalent goods in different markets to take advantage of a price difference is known as **arbitrage**. More generally, we refer to any situation in which it is possible to make a profit without taking any risk or making any investment as an **arbitrage opportunity**. Because an arbitrage opportunity has positive NPV, whenever an arbitrage opportunity appears in financial markets, investors will race to take advantage of it. Those investors who spot the opportunity first and who can trade quickly will have the ability to exploit it. Once they place their trades, prices will respond, causing the arbitrage opportunity to evaporate.

Arbitrage opportunities are like money lying in the street; once spotted, they will quickly disappear. Thus the normal state of affairs in markets should be that no arbitrage opportunities exist. We call a competitive market in which there are no arbitrage opportunities a **normal market**.[6]

Law of One Price

In a normal market, the price of gold at any point in time will be the same in London and New York. The same logic applies more generally whenever equivalent investment opportunities trade in two different competitive markets. If the prices in the two markets differ, investors will profit immediately by buying in the market where it is cheap and selling in the market where it is expensive. In doing so, they will equalize the prices. As a result, prices will not differ (at least not for long). This important property is the **Law of One Price**:

If equivalent investment opportunities trade simultaneously in different competitive markets, then they must trade for the same price in both markets.

---

6. The term *efficient market* is also sometimes used to describe a market that, along with other proper-ties, is without arbitrage opportunities. We avoid the term because it is often vaguely (and inconsistently) defined.

One useful consequence of the Law of One Price is that when evaluating costs and benefits to compute a net present value, we can use any competitive price to determine a cash value, without checking the price in all possible markets.

CONCEPT CHECK   **1.** If the Law of One Price were violated, how could investors profit?

   2. When investors exploit an arbitrage opportunity, how do their actions affect prices?

3.5 No-Arbitrage and Security Prices

An investment opportunity that trades in a financial market is known as a **financial security** (or, more simply, a **security**). The notions of arbitrage and the Law of One Price have important implications for security prices.

Valuing a Security

Consider a simple security that promises a one-time payment to its owner of $1000 in one year's time. Suppose there is no risk that the payment will not be made. One example of this type of security is a **bond**, a security sold by governments and corporations to raise money from investors today in exchange for the promised future payment. If the risk-free interest rate is 5%, what can we conclude about the price of this bond in a normal market?

To answer this question, consider an alternative investment that would generate the same cash flow as this bond. Suppose we invest money at the bank at the risk-free interest rate. How much do we need to invest today to receive $1000 in one year? As we saw in Section 3.3, the cost today of recreating a future cash flow on our own is its present value:

$$PV(\$1000 \text{ in one year}) = (\$1000 \text{ in one year}) \div (1.05 \text{ \$ in one year / \$ today})$$

$$= \$952.38 \text{ today}$$

If we invest $952.38 today at the 5% risk-free interest rate, we will have $1000 in one year's time with no risk.

We now have two ways to receive the same cash flow: (1) buy the bond or (2) invest $952.38 at the 5% risk-free interest rate. Because these transactions produce equivalent cash flows, the Law of One Price implies that in a normal market, they must have the same price (or cost). Therefore,

$$\text{Price(Bond)} = \$952.38$$

Recall that the Law of One Price is based on the possibility of arbitrage: If the bond had a different price, there would be an arbitrage opportunity. For example, suppose the bond traded for a price of $940. How could we profit in this situation?

In this case, we can buy the bond for $940 and at the same time borrow $952.38 from the bank. Given the 5% interest rate, we will owe the bank $952.38 × 1.05 = $1000 in one year. Our overall cash flows from this pair of transactions are as shown in Table 3.5. Using this strategy we can earn $12.38 in cash today for each bond that we buy, without taking any risk or paying any of our own money in the future. Of course, as we—and others who see the opportunity—start buying the bond, its price will quickly rise until it reaches $952.38 and the arbitrage opportunity disappears.

TABLE 3.5	Net Cash Flows from Buying the Bond and Borrowing	
	Today ($)	In One Year ($)
Buy the bond	−940.00	+1000.00
Borrow from the bank	+952.38	−1000.00
Net cash flow	+12.38	0.00

A similar arbitrage opportunity arises if the bond price is higher than $952.38. For example, suppose the bond is trading for $960. In that case, we should sell the bond and invest $952.38 at the bank. As shown in Table 3.6, we then earn $7.62 in cash today, yet keep our future cash flows unchanged by replacing the $1000 we would have received from the bond with the $1000 we will receive from the bank. Once again, as people begin selling the bond to exploit this opportunity, the price will fall until it reaches $952.38 and the arbitrage opportunity disappears.

TABLE 3.6	Net Cash Flows from Selling the Bond and Investing	
	Today ($)	In One Year ($)
Sell the bond	+960.00	−1000.00
Invest at the bank	−952.38	+1000.00
Net cash flow	+7.62	0.00

When the bond is overpriced, the arbitrage strategy involves selling the bond and investing some of the proceeds. But if the strategy involves selling the bond, does this mean that only the current owners of the bond can exploit it? The answer is no; in financial markets it is possible to sell a security you do not own by doing a *short sale*. In a **short sale**, the person who intends to sell the security first borrows it from someone who already owns it. Later, that person must either return the security by buying it back or pay the owner the cash flows he or she would have received. For example, we could short sell the bond in the example by promising to repay the current owner $1000 in one year. By executing a short sale, it is possible to exploit the arbitrage opportunity when the bond is overpriced even if you do not own it.

Determining the No-Arbitrage Price

We have shown that at any price other than $952.38, an arbitrage opportunity exists for our bond. Thus, in a normal market, the price of this bond must be $952.38. We call this price the **no-arbitrage price** for the bond.

We can apply the argument we used for the simple bond described earlier to price other securities. First, we identify the cash flows that will be paid by the security. Then, we determine the cost of replicating those cash flows on our own. This "do-it-yourself"

Nasdaq SOES Bandits

The Nasdaq stock market differs from other markets such as the NYSE in that it includes multiple dealers who all trade the same stock. For example, on a given day, as many as ten or more dealers may post prices at which they are willing to trade Apple Computer stock (AAPL). The Nasdaq also has a Small Order Execution System (SOES) that allows individual investors to execute trades of up to 1000 shares instantly through an electronic system.

A type of trader sometimes referred to as a "SOES bandit" exploits the ability to execute trades instantly. These traders watch the quotes of different dealers, waiting for arbitrage opportunities to arise. If one dealer is offering to sell AAPL at $20.25 and another is willing to buy at $20.30, the SOES bandit can profit by instantly buying 1000 shares at $20.25 from the first dealer and selling 1000 shares at $20.30 to the second dealer. Such a trade yields an arbitrage profit of $1000 \times \$0.05 = \$50$.

In the past, by making trades like this one many times per day, these traders could make a reasonable amount of money. Before long, the activity of these traders forced dealers to monitor their own quotes much more actively so as to avoid being "picked off" by these bandits. Today, this sort of arbitrage opportunity rarely appears.*

*SOES bandits can still profit by trading on information before dealers have updated their quotes. See J. Harris and P. Schultz, "The Trading Profits of SOES Bandits," *Journal of Financial Economics* 50 (2) (October 1998): 39–62.

cost is the present value of the security's cash flows. Unless the price of the security equals this present value, an arbitrage opportunity will appear. Thus, the general formula is

No Arbitrage Price of a Security

$$\text{Price(Security)} = PV(\text{All cash flows paid by the security}) \tag{3.3}$$

EXAMPLE 3.6

Computing the No-Arbitrage Price

Problem

Consider a security that pays its owner $100 today and $100 in one year, without any risk. Suppose the risk-free interest rate is 10%. What is the no-arbitrage price of the security today (before the first $100 is paid)? If the security is trading for $195, what arbitrage opportunity is available?

Solution

We need to compute the present value of the security's cash flows. In this case there are two cash flows: $100 today, which is already in present value terms, and $100 in one year. The present value of the second cash flow is

$$\$100 \text{ in one year} \div (1.10 \$ \text{ in one year} / \$ \text{ today}) = \$90.91 \text{ today}$$

Therefore, the total present value of the cash flows is $100 + $90.91 = $190.91 today, which is the no-arbitrage price of the security.

If the security is trading for $195, we can exploit its overpricing by selling it for $195. We can then use $100 of the sale proceeds to replace the $100 we would have received from the security today and invest $90.91 of the sale proceeds at 10% to replace the $100 we would have received in one year. The remaining $195 − $100 − $90.91 = $4.09 is an arbitrage profit.

Determining the Interest Rate from Bond Prices

Given the risk-free interest rate, the no-arbitrage price of a risk-free bond is determined by Eq. 3.3. The reverse is also true: If we know the price of a risk-free bond, we can use Eq. 3.3 to determine what the risk-free interest rate must be if there are no arbitrage opportunities.

For example, suppose a risk-free bond that pays $1000 in one year is currently trading with a competitive market price of $929.80 today. From Eq. 3.3, we know that the bond's price equals the present value of the $1000 cash flow it will pay:

$$\$929.80 \text{ today} = (\$1000 \text{ in one year}) \div (1 + r_f \ \$ \text{ in one year} / \$ \text{ today})$$

We can rearrange this equation to determine the risk-free interest rate:

$$1 + r_f = \frac{\$1000 \text{ in one year}}{\$929.80 \text{ today}} = 1.0755 \ \$ \text{ in one year} / \$ \text{ today}$$

That is, if there are no arbitrage opportunities, the risk-free interest rate must be 7.55%.

In practice, this method is the way interest rates are actually calculated. When financial news services report current interest rates, they have derived these rates based on the current prices of risk-free government bonds trading in the market.

Note that the risk-free interest rate equals the percentage gain that you earn from investing in the bond, which is called the bond's **return**:

$$\text{Return} = \frac{\text{Gain at end of year}}{\text{Initial Cost}}$$

$$= \frac{1000 - 929.80}{929.80} = \frac{1000}{929.80} - 1 = 7.55\% \tag{3.4}$$

Thus, if there is no arbitrage, the risk-free interest rate is equal to the return from investing in a risk-free bond. If the bond offered a higher return, then investors would earn a profit by borrowing at the risk-free interest rate and investing in the bond. If the bond had a lower return, investors would sell the bond and invest the proceeds at risk-free interest rate. No arbitrage is therefore equivalent to the idea that *all risk-free investments should offer investors the same return.*

The NPV of Trading Securities

When securities trade at no-arbitrage prices, what can we conclude about the value of trading them? We can think of buying a security as an investment decision. The cost of the decision is the price we pay for the security, and the benefit is the cash flows that we will receive from owning the security. From Eq. 3.3, these two are equal in a normal market and so the NPV of buying a security is zero:

$$NPV(\text{Buy security}) = PV(\text{All cash flows paid by the security}) - \text{Price}(\text{Security})$$
$$= 0$$

Similarly, if we sell a security, the price we receive is the benefit and the cost is the cash flows we give up. Again the NPV is zero:

$$NPV(\text{Sell security}) = \text{Price}(\text{Security}) - PV(\text{All cash flows paid by the security})$$
$$= 0$$

Thus, the NPV of trading a security in a normal market is zero. This result is not surprising. If the NPV of buying a security were positive, then buying the security would be equivalent to receiving cash today—that is, it would present an arbitrage opportunity. Because arbitrage opportunities do not exist in normal markets, the NPV of all security trades must be zero.

Another way to understand this result is to remember that every trade has both a buyer and a seller. If the trade offered a positive NPV to one, it must give a negative NPV to the other. But then one of the two parties would not agree to the trade. Because all trades are voluntary, they must occur at prices at which neither party is losing value, and therefore for which the trade is zero NPV.

In normal markets trading securities neither creates nor destroys value. Value is created by the real investment projects in which the firm engages, such as developing new products, opening new stores, or creating more efficient production methods. Financial transactions are not sources of value but merely serve to adjust the timing and risk of the cash flows to best suit the needs of the firm or its investors.

An important consequence of this result is the idea that we can evaluate a decision by focusing on its real components, rather than its financial ones. That is, we can separate the firm's investment decision from its financing choice. We refer to this concept as the **Separation Principle**:

Security transactions in a normal market neither create nor destroy value on their own. Therefore, we can evaluate the NPV of an investment decision separately from the decision the firm makes regarding how to finance the investment or any other security transactions the firm is considering.

EXAMPLE 3.7

Separating Investment and Financing

Problem

Your firm is considering a project that will require an upfront investment of $10 million today and will produce $12 million in cash flow for the firm in one year without risk. Rather than pay for the $10 million investment entirely using its own cash, the firm is considering raising additional funds by issuing a security that will pay investors $5.5 million in one year. Suppose the risk-free interest rate is 10%. Is pursuing this project a good decision without issuing the new security? Is it a good decision with the new security?

Solution

Without the new security, the cost of the project is $10 million today and the benefit is $12 million in one year. Converting the benefit to a present value

$12 million in one year ÷ (1.10 $ in one year / $ today) = $10.91 million today

we see that the project has $NPV =$ $10.91 million $-$ $10 million $=$ $0.91 million today.

Now suppose the firm issues the new security. In a normal market, the price of this security will be the present value of its future cash flow:

Price(Security) = $5.5 million ÷ 1.10 = $5 million today

Thus, after it raises $5 million by issuing the new security, the firm will only need to invest an additional $5 million to take the project.

To compute the project's NPV in this case, note that in one year the firm will receive the $12 million payout of the project, but owe $5.5 million to the investors in the new security, leaving $6.5 million for the firm. This amount has a present value of

$6.5 million in one year ÷ (1.10 $ in one year / $ today) = $5.91 million today

Thus, the project has NPV = $5.91 million − $5 million = $0.91 million today, as before.

In either case, we get the same result for the NPV. The separation principle indicates that we will get the same result for any choice of financing for the firm that occurs in a normal market. We can therefore evaluate the project without explicitly considering the different financing possibilities the firm might choose.

Valuing a Portfolio

So far, we have discussed the no-arbitrage price for individual securities. The Law of One Price also has implications for packages of securities. Consider two securities, A and B. Suppose a third security, C, has the same cash flows as A and B combined. In this case, security C is equivalent to a **portfolio** or combination, of the securities A and B. What can we conclude about the price of security C as compared to the prices of A and B?

Because security C is equivalent to the portfolio of A and B, by the Law of One Price, they must have the same price. This idea leads to the relationship known as **value additivity**; that is, the price of C must equal the price of the portfolio, which is the combined price of A and B:

Value Additivity

$$\text{Price(C)} = \text{Price(A + B)} = \text{Price(A)} + \text{Price(B)} \tag{3.5}$$

Because security C has cash flows equal to the sum of A and B, its value or price must be the sum of the values of A and B. Otherwise, an obvious arbitrage opportunity would exist. For example, if the total price of A and B were lower than the price of C, then we could make a profit buying A and B and selling C. This arbitrage activity would quickly push prices until the price of security C equals the total price of A and B.

Stock Index Arbitrage

Value additivity is the principle behind a type of trading activity known as stock index arbitrage. Common stock indices (such as the Dow Jones Industrial Average and the Standard and Poor's 500) represent portfolios of individual stocks. It is possible to trade the individual stocks in an index on the New York Stock Exchange and NASDAQ. It is also possible to trade the entire index (as a single security) on the futures exchanges in Chicago. When the price of the index in Chicago is below the total price of the individual stocks, traders buy the index and sell the stocks to capture the price difference. Similarly, when the price of the index in Chicago is above the total price of the individual stocks, traders sell the index and buy the individual stocks. The investment banks that engage in stock index arbitrage automate the process by tracking the prices and submitting the orders via computer; as a result, this activity is also referred as "program trading." It is not uncommon for 5% to 10% of the daily volume of trade on the NYSE to be due to index arbitrage activity. The actions of these arbitrageurs ensure that the index prices in Chicago and the individual stock prices track each other very closely.

More generally, value additivity implies that the value of a portfolio is equal to the sum of the values of its parts. That is, the "à la carte" price and the package price must coincide. This feature of financial markets does not hold in many other, noncompetitive markets.[7]

EXAMPLE 3.8

Valuing an Asset in a Portfolio

Problem

Holbrook Holdings is a publicly traded company with only two assets: It owns 60% of Harry's Hotcakes restaurant chain and an ice hockey team. Suppose the market value of Holbrook Holdings is $160 million, and the market value of the entire Harry's Hotcakes chain (which is also publicly traded) is $120 million. What is the market value of the hockey team?

Solution

We can think of Holbrook as a portfolio consisting of a 60% stake in Harry's Hotcakes and the hockey team. By value additivity, the sum of the value of the stake in Harry's Hotcakes and the hockey team must equal the $160 million market value of Holbrook. Because the 60% stake in Harry's Hotcakes is worth 60% × $120 million = $72 million, the hockey team has a value of $160 million − $72 million = $88 million.

Value additivity has an important consequence for the value of an entire firm. The cash flows of the firm are equal to the total cash flows of all projects and investments within the firm. Therefore, by value additivity, the price or value of the entire firm is equal to the sum of the values of all projects and investments within it. In other words, our NPV decision rule coincides with maximizing the value of the entire firm:

To maximize the value of the entire firm, managers should make decisions that maximize NPV. The NPV of the decision represents its contribution to the overall value of the firm.

CONCEPT CHECK

1. If a firm makes an investment that has a positive NPV, how does the value of the firm change?

2. What is the separation principle?

3.6 The Price of Risk

Thus far we have considered only cash flows that have no risk. But in many settings, cash flows are risky. In this section, we examine how to determine the present value of a risky cash flow.

---

7. For example, a round-trip airline ticket often costs much less than two separate one-way tickets. Of course, airline tickets are not sold in a competitive market—you cannot buy *and* sell the tickets at the listed prices. Only airlines can sell tickets, and they have strict rules against reselling tickets. Otherwise, you could make money buying round-trip tickets and selling them to people who need one-way tickets.

Risky Versus Risk-free Cash Flows

Suppose the risk-free interest rate is 4% and that over the next year the economy is equally likely to strengthen or weaken. Consider an investment in a risk-free bond, and one in the stock market index (a portfolio of all stocks in the market). The risk-free bond has no risk and will pay $1100 whatever the state of the economy. The cash flow from an investment in the market index, however, depends on the strength of the economy. Let's assume that the market index will be worth $1400 if the economy is strong but only $800 if the economy is weak. Table 3.7 summarizes these payoffs.

TABLE 3.7	Cash Flows and Market Prices (in $) of a Risk-Free Bond and an Investment in the Market Portfolio		
		Cash Flow in One Year	
Security	**Market Price Today**	**Weak Economy**	**Strong Economy**
Risk-free bond	1058	1100	1100
Market index	1000	800	1400

In Section 3.5 we saw that the no-arbitrage price of a security is equal to the present value of its cash flows. For example, the price of the risk-free bond corresponds to the 4% risk-free interest rate:

$$\text{Price(Risk-free Bond)} = \text{PV(Cash Flows)}$$
$$= (\$1100 \text{ in one year}) \div (1.04 \text{ } \$ \text{ in one year} / \$ \text{ today})$$
$$= \$1058 \text{ today}$$

Now consider the market index. An investor who buys it today can sell it in one year for a cash flow of either $800 or $1400, with an average payoff of $\frac{1}{2}$ ($800) + $\frac{1}{2}$ ($1400) = $1100. Although this average payoff is the same as the risk-free bond, the market index has a lower price today. It pays $1100 *on average*, but its actual cash flow is risky, so investors are only willing to pay $1000 for it today rather than $1058. What accounts for this lower price?

Risk Aversion and the Risk Premium

Intuitively, investors pay less to receive $1100 on average than to receive $1100 with certainty because they don't like risk. That is, *the personal cost of losing a dollar in bad times is greater than the benefit of an extra dollar in good times.* Thus, the benefit from receiving an extra $300 ($1400 versus $1100) when the economy is strong is less important than the loss of $300 ($800 versus $1100) when the economy is weak. As a result, investors prefer to receive $1100 with certainty.

The notion that investors prefer to have a safe income rather than a risky one of the same average amount is called **risk aversion**. It is an aspect of an investor's preferences, and different investors may have different degrees of risk aversion. The more risk averse investors are, the lower the current price of the market index will be compared to a risk-free bond with the same average payoff.

Because investors care about risk, we cannot use the risk-free interest rate to compute the present value of a risky future cash flow. When investing in a risky project, investors will expect a return that appropriately compensates them for the risk. For example, investors who buy the market index for its current price of $1000 receive $1100 on average at the end of the year, which is an average gain of $100, or a 10% return on their initial investment. When we compute the return of a security based on the payoff we expect to receive on average, we call it the **expected return**:

$$\text{Expected return of a risky investment} = \frac{\text{Expected Gain at end of year}}{\text{Initial Cost}} \quad (3.6)$$

Of course, although the expected return of the market index is 10%, its *actual* return will be higher or lower. If the economy is strong, the market index will rise to 1400, which represents a return of

Market return if economy is strong = (1400 − 1000) / 1000 = 40%

If the economy is weak, the index will drop to 800, for a return of

Market return if economy is weak = (800 − 1000) / 1000 = −20%

We can also calculate the 10% expected return by computing the average of these actual returns: $\frac{1}{2}(40\%) + \frac{1}{2}(-20\%) = 10\%$.

Thus, investors in the market index earn an expected return of 10% rather than the risk-free interest rate of 4% on their investment. The difference of 6% between these returns is called the market index's **risk premium**. The risk premium of a security represents the additional return that investors expect to earn to compensate them for the security's risk. Because investors are risk averse, the price of a risky security cannot be calculated by simply discounting its expected cash flow at the risk-free interest rate. Rather,

When a cash flow is risky, to compute its present value we must discount the cash flow we expect on average at a rate that equals the risk-free interest rate plus an appropriate risk premium.

The No-Arbitrage Price of a Risky Security

Just as the risk-free interest rate is determined by investors' preferences to save versus consume, the risk premium of the market index is determined by investors' preferences toward risk. The risk premium is just large enough so that the demand to invest in the market index equals the supply that is available.

In the same way we used the risk-free interest rate to determine the no-arbitrage price of other risk-free securities, we can use the risk premium of the market index to value other risky securities. For example, suppose security A will pay investors $600 if the economy is strong and nothing if it is weak. Let's see how we can determine the market price of security A using the Law of One Price.

As shown in Table 3.8, if we combine security A with a risk-free bond that pays $800 in one year, the cash flows of the portfolio in one year are identical to the cash flows of the market index. By the Law of One Price, the total market value of the bond and security A must equal $1000, the value of the market index. Given a risk-free interest rate of 4%, the market price of the bond is

($800 in one year) ÷ (1.04 $ in one year / $ today) = $769 today

Therefore, the initial market price of security A is $1000 − 769 = $231. If the price of security were higher or lower than $231, then the value of the portfolio of the bond and

TABLE 3.8	Determining the Market Price of Security A (cash flows in $)		
		Cash Flow in One Year	
Security	Market Price Today	Weak Economy	Strong Economy
Risk-free bond	769	800	800
Security A	?	0	600
Market index	1000	800	1400

security A would differ from the value of the market index, violating the Law of One Price and creating an arbitrage opportunity.

Risk Premiums Depend on Risk

Given an initial price of $231 and an expected payoff of $\frac{1}{2}(0) + \frac{1}{2}(600) = 300$, security A has an expected return of

$$\text{Expected return of security A} = \frac{300 - 231}{231} = 30\%$$

Note that this expected return exceeds the 10% expected return of the market portfolio. Investors in security A earn a risk premium of $30\% - 4\% = 26\%$ over the risk-free interest rate, compared to a 6% risk premium for the market portfolio. Why are the risk premiums so different?

The reason for the difference becomes clear if we compare the actual returns for the two securities. When the economy is weak, investors in security A lose everything, for a return of -100%, and when the economy is strong, they earn a return of $(600 - 231) / 231 = 160\%$. In contrast, the market index loses 20% in a weak economy and gains 40% in a strong economy. Given its much more variable returns, it is not surprising that security A must pay investors a higher risk premium.

Risk Is Relative to the Overall Market

The example of security A suggests that the risk premium of a security will depend on how variable its returns are. But before drawing any conclusions, it is worth considering one further example.

EXAMPLE 3.9

A Negative Risk Premium

Problem

Suppose security B pays $600 if the economy is weak and $0 if the economy is strong. What is its no-arbitrage price, expected return, and risk premium?

Solution

If we combine the market index and security B together in a portfolio, we earn the same payoff as a risk-free bond that pays $1400, as shown here (cash flows in $):

Security	Market Price Today	Cash Flow in One Year	
		Weak Economy	Strong Economy
Market index	1000	800	1400
Security B	?	600	0
Risk-free bond	1346	1400	1400

Because the market price of the risk-free bond is $1400 \div 1.04 = \$1346$ today, we can conclude from the Law of One Price that security B must have a market price of $\$1346 - 1000 = \$346$ today.

If the economy is weak, security B pays a return of $(600 - 346) / 346 = 73.4\%$. If the economy is strong, security B pays nothing, for a return of -100%. The expected return of security B is therefore $\frac{1}{2}(73.4\%) + \frac{1}{2}(-100\%) = -13.3\%$. Its risk premium is $-13.3\% - 4\% = -17.3\%$; that is, security B pays investors 17.3% *less* on average than the risk-free interest rate.

The results for security B are quite striking. Looking at securities A and B in isolation, they seem very similar—both are equally likely to pay $600 or $0. Yet security A has a much lower market price than security B ($231 vs. $346). In terms of returns, security A pays investors an expected return of 30%; security B pays −13.3%. Why are their prices and expected returns so different? And why would risk-averse investors be willing to buy a risky security with an expected return below the risk-free interest rate?

To understand this result, note that security A pays $600 when the economy is strong, and B pays $600 when the economy is weak. Recall that our definition of risk aversion is that investors value an extra dollar of income more in bad times than in good times. Thus, because security B pays $600 when the economy is weak and the market index performs poorly, it pays off when investors' wealth is low and they value money the most. In fact, security B is not really "risky" from an investor's point of view; rather, security B is an insurance policy against an economic decline. By holding security B together with the market index, we can eliminate our risk from market fluctuations. Risk-averse investors are willing to pay for this insurance by accepting a return below the risk-free interest rate.

This result illustrates an extremely important principle. The risk of a security cannot be evaluated in isolation. Even when a security's returns are quite variable, if the returns vary in a way that offsets other risks investors are holding, the security will reduce rather than increase investors' risk. As a result, risk can only be assessed relative to the other risks that investors face; that is,

The risk of a security must be evaluated in relation to the fluctuations of other investments in the economy. A security's risk premium will be higher the more its returns tend to vary with the overall economy and the market index. If the security's returns vary in the opposite direction of the market index, it offers insurance and will have a negative risk premium.

Table 3.9 compares the risk and risk premiums for the different securities we have considered thus far. For each security we compute the difference in its return when the economy is strong versus weak. Note that the risk premium for each security is proportional to this difference, and the risk premium is negative when the returns vary in the opposite direction of the market.

TABLE 3.9	**Risk and Risk Premiums for Different Securities**			
	Returns		Difference in Returns	Risk Premium
Security	**Weak Economy**	**Strong Economy**		
Risk-free bond	4%	4%	0%	0%
Market index	−20%	40%	60%	6%
Security A	−100%	160%	260%	26%
Security B	73%	−100%	−173%	−17.3%

Risk, Return, and Market Prices

We have shown that when cash flows are risky, we can use the Law of One Price to compute present values by constructing a portfolio that produces cash flows with identical risk. As shown in Figure 3.3, computing prices in this way is equivalent to converting between cash flows today and the *expected* cash flows received in the future using a discount rate r_s that includes a risk premium appropriate for the investment's risk:

$$r_s = r_f + \text{(risk premium for investment } s\text{)} \tag{3.7}$$

For the simple setting considered here with only a single source of risk (the strength of the economy), we have seen that the risk premium of an investment depends on how its returns vary with the overall economy. In Part IV of the text we show that this result holds for more general settings with many sources of risk and more than two possible states of the economy.

EXAMPLE 3.10

Using the Risk Premium to Compute a Price

Problem

Consider a risky bond with a cash flow of $1100 when the economy is strong and $1000 when the economy is weak. Suppose a 1% risk premium is appropriate for this bond. If the risk-free interest rate is 4%, what is the price of the bond today?

Solution

From Eq. 3.7, the appropriate discount rate for the bond is

$$r_b = r_f + \text{(Risk Premium for the Bond)} = 4\% + 1\% = 5\%$$

The expected cash flow of the bond is $\frac{1}{2}(\$1100) + \frac{1}{2}(\$1000) = \$1050$ in one year. Thus, the price of the bond today is

$$\text{Bond Price} = \text{(Average cash flow in one year)} \div (1 + r_b \ \$ \text{ in one year } / \$ \text{ today})$$

$$= (\$1050 \text{ in one year}) \div (1.05 \ \$ \text{ in one year } / \$ \text{ today})$$

$$= \$1000 \text{ today}$$

Given this price, the bond's return is 10% when the economy is strong, and 0% when the economy is weak. (Note that the difference in the returns is 10%, which is 1/6 as variable as the market index; see Table 3.9. Correspondingly, the risk premium of the bond is 1/6 that of the market index as well.)

FIGURE 3.3

Converting Between Dollars Today and Dollars in One Year with Risk

When cash flows are risky, Eq. (3.7) determines the expected return, r_s, that we can use to convert between prices or present values today and the expected cash flow in the future.

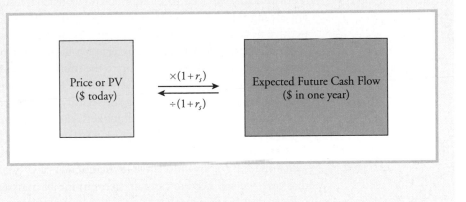

1. Why does the expected return of a risky security generally differ from the risk-free interest rate? What determines the size of its risk premium?

2. Explain why the risk of a security should not be evaluated in isolation.

3.7 Arbitrage with Transactions Costs

In our examples up to this point, we have ignored the costs of buying and selling goods or securities. In most markets, you must pay **transactions costs** to trade securities. As discussed in Chapter 1, when you trade securities in markets such as the NYSE and Nasdaq, you must pay two types of transactions costs. First, you must pay your broker a commission on the trade. Second, because you will generally pay a slightly higher price when you buy a security (the ask price) than you receive when you sell (the bid price), you will also pay the bid-ask spread. For example, a share of Dell Inc. stock (ticker symbol DELL) might be quoted as follows:

Bid: $40.50   Ask: $40.70

We can interpret these quotes as if the competitive price for DELL is $40.60, but there is a transaction cost of $0.10 per share when buying or selling.[8]

What consequence do these transaction costs have for no-arbitrage prices and the Law of One Price? Earlier we stated that the price of gold in New York and London must be identical in competitive markets. Suppose, however, that total transactions costs of $5 per ounce are associated with buying gold in one market and selling it in the other. Then if the price of gold is $250 per ounce in New York and $252 per ounce in London, the "Buy low, sell high" strategy no longer works:

Cost: $250 per ounce (buy gold in New York) + $5(transactions costs)

Benefit: $252 per ounce (sell gold in London)

NPV: $252 − $250 − $5 = −$3 per ounce

Indeed, there is no arbitrage opportunity in this case until the prices diverge by more than $5, the amount of the transactions costs.

---

8. Any price in between the bid price and the ask price could be the competitive price, with differing transaction costs for buying and selling.

In general, we need to modify our previous conclusions about no arbitrage prices by appending the phrase "up to transactions costs." In this example, there is only one competitive price for gold—up to a discrepancy of the $5 transactions cost.

The other conclusions of this chapter have the same qualifier. The package price should equal the à la carte price, up to the transaction costs associated with packaging and unpackaging. The price of a security should equal the present value of its cash flows, up to the transaction costs of trading the security and the cash flows.

Fortunately, for most financial markets, these costs are small. For example, in January 2005, typical bid-ask spreads for large NYSE stocks were between 2 and 5 cents per share. As a first approximation we can ignore these spreads in our analysis. Only in situations in which the NPV is small (relative to the transactions costs) will any discrepancy matter. In that case, we will need to carefully account for all transaction costs to decide whether the NPV is positive or negative.

EXAMPLE 3.11

The No-Arbitrage Price Range

Problem
Consider a bond that pays $1000 at the end of the year. Suppose the market interest rate for deposits is 6%, but the market interest rate for borrowing is 6.5%. What is the no-arbitrage price *range* for the bond? That is, what is the highest and lowest price the bond could trade for without creating an arbitrage opportunity?

Solution
The no-arbitrage price for the bond equals the present value of the cash flows. In this case, we can use either of two interest rates to compute the present value, depending on whether we are borrowing or lending. For example, the amount we would need to put in the bank today to receive $1000 in one year is

$$(\$1000 \text{ in one year}) \div (1.06 \text{ \$ in one year} / \text{\$ today}) = \$943.40 \text{ today}$$

where we have used the 6% interest rate that we will earn on our deposit. The amount that we can borrow today if we plan to repay $1000 in one year is

$$(\$1000 \text{ in one year}) \div (1.065 \text{ \$ in one year} / \text{\$ today}) = \$938.97 \text{ today}$$

where we have used the higher 6.5% rate that we will have to pay if we borrow.

Suppose the bond price P exceeded $943.40. Then you could profit by selling the bond at its current price and investing $943.40 of the proceeds at the 6% interest rate. You would still receive $1000 at the end of the year, but you would get to keep the difference $(P - 943.40)$ today. This arbitrage opportunity will keep the price of the bond from going higher than $943.40.

Alternatively, suppose the bond price P were less than $938.97. Then you could borrow $938.97 at 6.5% and use P of it to buy the bond. This would leave you with $(938.97 - P)$ today, and no obligation in the future because you can use the $1000 bond payoff to repay the loan. This arbitrage opportunity will keep the price of the bond from falling below $938.97.

If the bond price P is between $938.97 and $943.40, then both of the preceding strategies will lose money, and there is no arbitrage opportunity. Thus no arbitrage implies a narrow range of possible prices for the bond ($938.97 to $943.40), rather than an exact price.

To summarize, when there are transactions costs, arbitrage keeps prices of equivalent goods and securities close to each other. Prices can deviate, but not by more than the transactions cost of the arbitrage.

CONCEPT CHECK
1. In the presence of transactions costs, why might different investors disagree about the value of an investment opportunity?
2. By how much could this value differ?

Summary

1. To evaluate a decision, we must value the incremental costs and benefits associated with that decision. A good decision is one for which the value of the benefits exceeds the value of the costs.

2. To compare costs and benefits that occur at different points in time, in different currencies, or with different risks, we must put all costs and benefits in common terms. Typically, we convert costs and benefits into cash today.

3. A competitive market is one in which a good can be bought and sold at the same price. We use prices from competitive markets to determine the cash value of a good.

4. The time value of money is the difference in value between money today and money in the future. The rate at which we can exchange money today for money in the future by borrowing or investing is the current market interest rate. The risk-free interest rate, r_f, is the rate at which money can be borrowed or lent without risk.

5. The present value (PV) of a cash flow is its value in terms of cash today.

6. The net present value (NPV) of a project is

$$PV(\text{Benefits}) - PV(\text{Costs}) \tag{3.1}$$

7. A good project is one with a positive net present value. The NPV Decision Rule states that when choosing from among a set of alternatives, choose the one with the highest NPV. The NPV of a project is equivalent to the cash value today of the project.

8. Regardless of our preferences for cash today versus cash in the future, we should always first maximize NPV. We can then borrow or lend to shift cash flows through time and find our most preferred pattern of cash flows.

9. Arbitrage is the process of trading to take advantage of equivalent goods that have different prices in different competitive markets.

10. A normal market is a competitive market with no arbitrage opportunities.

11. The Law of One Price states that if equivalent goods or securities trade simultaneously in different competitive markets, they will trade for the same price in each market. This law is equivalent to saying that no arbitrage opportunities should exist.

12. The No-Arbitrage Price of a Security is

$$PV(\text{All cash flows paid by security}) \tag{3.3}$$

13. Value additivity implies that the value of a portfolio is equal to the sum of the values of its parts.

14. To maximize the value of the entire firm, managers should make decisions that maximize the NPV. The NPV of the decision represents its contribution to the overall value of the firm.

15. The Separation Principle states that security transactions in a normal market neither create nor destroy value on their own. As a consequence, we can evaluate the NPV of an investment decision separately from the security transactions the firm is considering.

16. When cash flows are risky, we cannot use the risk-free interest rate to compute present values. Instead, we can determine the present value by constructing a portfolio that produces cash flows with identical risk, and then applying the Law of One Price.

17. The risk of a security must be evaluated in relation to the fluctuations of other investments in the economy. A security's risk premium will be higher the more its returns tend to vary with the overall economy and the market index. If the security's returns vary in the opposite direction of the market index, it offers insurance and will have a negative risk premium.

18. When there are transactions costs, the prices of equivalent securities can deviate from each other, but not by more than the transactions costs of the arbitrage.

Key Terms

arbitrage *p. 60*
arbitrage opportunity *p. 60*
bond *p. 61*
competitive market *p. 49*
discount factor *p. 53*
discount rate *p. 53*
expected return *p. 69*
financial security *p. 61*
interest rate factor *p. 52*
Law of One Price *p. 60*
net present value (NPV) *p. 54*
no-arbitrage price *p. 62*
normal market *p. 60*

NPV Decision Rule *p. 55*
portfolio *p. 66*
present value (PV) *p. 54*
return *p. 64*
risk aversion *p. 68*
risk-free interest rate *p. 52*
risk premium *p. 69*
Separation Principle *p. 65*
short sale *p. 62*
time value of money *p. 51*
transactions costs *p. 73*
value additivity *p. 66*

Further Reading

Many of the fundamental principles of this chapter were developed in the classic text by I. Fisher, *The Theory of Interest: As Determined by Impatience to Spend Income and Opportunity to Invest It* (New York: Macmillan, 1930); reprinted (New York: Augustus M. Kelley, 1955).

To learn more about the principle of no arbitrage and its importance as the foundation for modern finance theory, see S. A. Ross, *Neoclassical Finance* (Princeton, NJ: Princeton University Press, 2004).

For a discussion of arbitrage and rational trading and their role in determining market prices, see M. Rubinstein, "Rational Markets: Yes or No? The Affirmative Case," *Financial Analysts Journal* (May/June 2001): 15–29.

For a discussion of some of the limitations to arbitrage that may arise in practice, see Shleifer and Vishny, "Limits of Arbitrage," *Journal of Finance*, 52 (1997): 35–55.

Problems

All problems in this chapter are available in MyFinanceLab. An asterisk (*) indicates problems with a higher level of difficulty.

Valuing Costs and Benefits

1. Honda Motor Company is considering offering a $2000 rebate on its minivan, lowering the vehicle's price from $30,000 to $28,000. The marketing group estimates that this rebate will increase sales over the next year from 40,000 to 55,000 vehicles. Suppose Honda's profit margin with the rebate is $6000 per vehicle. If the change in sales is the only consequence of this decision, what are its costs and benefits? Is it a good idea?

2. You are an international shrimp trader. A food producer in the Czech Republic offers to pay you 2 million Czech koruna today in exchange for a year's supply of frozen shrimp. Your Thai supplier will provide you with the same supply for 3 million Thai baht today. If the current competitive market exchange rates are 25.50 koruna per dollar and 41.25 baht per dollar, what is the value of this deal?

3. Suppose your employer offers you a choice between a $5000 bonus and 100 shares of the company stock. Whichever one you choose will be awarded today. The stock is currently trading for $63 per share.

   a. Suppose that if you receive the stock bonus, you are free to trade it. Which form of the bonus should you choose? What is its value?

   b. Suppose that if you receive the stock bonus, you are required to hold it for at least one year. What can you say about the value of the stock bonus now? What will your decision depend on?

Interest Rates and the Time Value of Money

 4. Suppose the risk-free interest rate is 4%.

   a. Having $200 today is equivalent to having what amount in one year?

   b. Having $200 in one year is equivalent to having what amount today?

   c. Which would you prefer, $200 today or $200 in one year? Does your answer depend on when you need the money? Why or why not?

5. You have an investment opportunity in Japan. It requires an investment of $1 million today and will produce a cash flow of ¥114 million in one year with no risk. Suppose the risk-free interest rate in the United States is 4%, the risk-free interest rate in Japan is 2%, and the current competitive exchange rate is ¥110 per $1. What is the NPV of this investment? Is it a good opportunity?

Present Value and the NPV Decision Rule

EXCEL 6. You run a construction firm. You have just won a contract to build a government office building. Building it will require an investment of $10 million today and $5 million in one year. The government will pay you $20 million in one year upon the building's completion. Suppose the cash flows and their times of payment are certain, and the risk-free interest rate is 10%.

   a. What is the NPV of this opportunity?

   b. How can your firm turn this NPV into cash today?

7. Your firm has identified three potential investment projects. The projects and their cash flows are shown here:

Project	Cash Flow Today ($)	Cash Flow in One Year ($)
A	−10	20
B	5	5
C	20	−10

Suppose all cash flows are certain and the risk-free interest rate is 10%.

   a. What is the NPV of each project?

   b. If the firm can choose only one of these projects, which should it choose?

   c. If the firm can choose any two of these projects, which should it choose?

8. Your computer manufacturing firm must purchase 10,000 keyboards from a supplier. One supplier demands a payment of $100,000 today plus $10 per keyboard payable in one year. Another supplier will charge $21 per keyboard, also payable in one year. The risk-free interest rate is 6%.

   a. What is the difference in their offers in terms of dollars today? Which offer should your firm take?

   b. Suppose your firm does not want to spend cash today. How can it take the first offer and not spend $100,000 of its own cash today?

Arbitrage and the Law of One Price

9. Suppose Bank One offers a risk-free interest rate of 5.5% on both savings and loans, and Bank Enn offers a risk-free interest rate of 6% on both savings and loans.

   a. What arbitrage opportunity is available?

   b. Which bank would experience a surge in the demand for loans? Which bank would receive a surge in deposits?

   c. What would you expect to happen to the interest rates the two banks are offering?

10. Throughout the 1990s, interest rates in Japan were lower than interest rates in the United States. As a result, many Japanese investors were tempted to borrow in Japan and invest the proceeds in the United States. Explain why this strategy does not represent an arbitrage opportunity.

11. An American Depositary Receipt (**ADR**) is security issued by a U.S. bank and traded on a U.S. stock exchange that represents a specific number of shares of a foreign stock. For example, Nokia Corporation trades as an ADR with symbol NOK on the NYSE. Each ADR represents one share of Nokia Corporation stock, which trades with symbol NOK1V on the Helsinki stock exchange. If the U.S. ADR for Nokia is trading for $17.96 per share, and Nokia stock is trading on the Helsinki exchange for 14.78 € per share, use the Law of One Price to determine the current $/€ exchange rate.

No-Arbitrage and Security Prices

EXCEL 12. The promised cash flows of three securities are listed here. If the cash flows are risk-free, and the risk-free interest rate is 5%, determine the no-arbitrage price of each security before the first cash flow is paid.

Security	Cash Flow Today ($)	Cash Flow in One Year ($)
A	500	500
B	0	1000
C	1000	0

13. An Exchange-Traded Fund (ETF) is a security that represents a portfolio of individual stocks. Consider an ETF for which each share represents a portfolio of two shares of Hewlett-Packard (HP), one share of Sears, Roebuck (S), and three shares of Ford Motor (F). Suppose the current stock prices of each individual stock are as shown here:

Stock	Current Market Price
HP	$28
S	$40
F	$14

a. What is the price per share of the ETF in a normal market?

b. If the ETF currently trades for $120, what arbitrage opportunity is available? What trades would you make?

c. If the ETF currently trades for $150, what arbitrage opportunity is available? What trades would you make?

EXCEL   14.   Consider two securities that pay risk-free cash flows over the next two years and that have the current market prices shown here:

Security	Price Today ($)	Cash Flow in One Year ($)	Cash Flow in Two Years ($)
B1	94	100	0
B2	85	0	100

a. What is the no-arbitrage price of a security that pays cash flows of $100 in one year and $100 in two years?

b. What is the no-arbitrage price of a security that pays cash flows of $100 in one year and $500 in two years?

c. Suppose a security with cash flows of $50 in one year and $100 in two years is trading for a price of $130. What arbitrage opportunity is available?

15.   Suppose a security with a risk-free cash flow of $150 in one year trades for $140 today. If there are no arbitrage opportunities, what is the current risk-free interest rate?

EXCEL   16.   Xia Corporation is a company whose sole assets are $100,000 in cash and three projects that it will undertake. The projects are risk-free and have the following cash flows:

Project	Cash Flow Today ($)	Cash Flow in One Year ($)
A	−20,000	30,000
B	−10,000	25,000
C	−60,000	80,000

Xia plans to invest any unused cash today at the risk-free interest rate of 10%. In one year, all cash will be paid to investors and the company will be shut down.

a. What is the NPV of each project? Which projects should Xia undertake and how much cash should it retain?

b. What is the total value of Xia's assets (projects and cash) today?

c. What cash flows will the investors in Xia receive? Based on these cash flows, what is the value of Xia today?

d. Suppose Xia pays any unused cash to investors today, rather than investing it. What are the cash flows to the investors in this case? What is the value of Xia now?

e. Explain the relationship in your answers to parts (b), (c), and (d).

The Price of Risk

17.   The table here shows the no-arbitrage prices of securities A and B that we calculated in Section 3.6.

Security	Market Price Today	Cash Flow in One Year	
		Weak Economy	Strong Economy
Security A	231	0	600
Security B	346	600	0

a. What are the payoffs of a portfolio of one share of security A and one share of security B?

b. What is the market price of this portfolio? What expected return will you earn from holding this portfolio?

18.   Suppose security C has a payoff of $600 when the economy is weak and $1800 when the economy is strong. The risk-free interest rate is 4%.

a. Security C has the same payoffs as what portfolio of the securities A and B in problem 17?

b. What is the no-arbitrage price of security C?

c. What is the expected return of security C if both states are equally likely? What is its risk premium?

d. What is the difference between the return of security C when the economy is strong and when it is weak?

e. If security C had a risk premium of 10%, what arbitrage opportunity would be available?

*19.   Suppose a risky security pays an expected cash flow of $80 in one year. The risk-free rate is 4%, and the expected return on the market index is 10%.

a. If the returns of this security are high when the economy is strong and low when the economy is weak, but the returns vary by only half as much as the market index, what risk premium is appropriate for this security?

b. What is the security's market price?

Arbitrage with Transactions Costs

20.   Suppose Hewlett-Packard (HP) stock is currently trading on the NYSE with a bid price of $28.00 and an ask price of $28.10. At the same time, a NASDAQ dealer posts a bid price for HP of $27.85 and an ask price of $27.95.

a. Is there an arbitrage opportunity in this case? If so, how would you exploit it?

b. Suppose the NASDAQ dealer revises his quotes to a bid price of $27.95 and an ask price of $28.05. Is there an arbitrage opportunity now? If so, how would you exploit it?

c. What must be true of the highest bid price and the lowest ask price for no arbitrage opportunity to exist?

*21.   Consider a portfolio of two securities: one share of Citigroup stock and a bond that pays $100 in one year. Suppose this portfolio is currently trading with a bid price of $131.65 and an ask price of $132.25, and the bond is trading with a bid price of $91.75 and an ask price of $91.95. In this case, what is the no-arbitrage price range for Citigroup stock?

Tools

The Law of One Price Connection. In this part of the text, we introduce the basic tools for making financial decisions. For a financial manager, evaluating financial decisions involves computing the net present value of a project's future cash flows. In Chapter 4 we use the Law of One Price to derive a central concept in financial economics—the *time value of money*. We explain how to value a stream of future cash flows and derive a few useful shortcuts for computing the net present value of various types of cash flow patterns. Chapter 5 considers how to use market interest rates to determine the appropriate discount rate for a set of cash flows. We apply the Law of One Price to demonstrate that the discount rate will depend on the rate of return of investments with maturity and risk similar to the cash flows being valued. This observation leads to the Important concept of the *cost of capital* of an investment decision. In Chapter 6, we compare the net present value rule to other investment rules firms sometimes use and explain why the net present value rule is superior.

The Time Value of Money

As discussed in Chapter 3, to evaluate a project a financial manager must compare its costs and benefits. In most cases, the cash flows in financial investments involve more than one future period. For example, early in 2003, the Boeing Company announced that it was developing the 7E7, a highly efficient, long-range airplane able to seat 200 to 250 passengers. Boeing's project involves revenues and expenses that will occur many years or even decades into the future. How can financial managers evaluate a project such as the 7E7 airplane?

As we learned in Chapter 3, Boeing should make the investment in the 7E7 if the NPV is positive. Calculating the NPV requires tools to evaluate cash flows lasting several periods. We develop these tools in this chapter. The first tool is a visual method for representing a stream of cash flows: the *timeline*. After constructing a timeline, we establish three important rules for moving cash flows to different points in time. Using these rules, we show how to compute the present and future values of the costs and benefits of a general stream of cash flows, and how to compute the NPV. Although these techniques can be used to value any type of asset, certain types of assets have cash flows that follow a regular pattern. We develop shortcuts for *annuities*, *perpetuities*, and other special cases of assets with cash flows that follow regular patterns.

notation

r	interest rate
C	cash flow
FV_n	future value on date n
PV	present value; annuity spreadsheet notation for the initial amount
C_n	cash flow at date n
N	date of the last cash flow in a stream of cash flows
NPV	net present value
P	initial principal or deposit, or equivalent present value
FV	future value; annuity spreadsheet notation for the extra final payment
g	growth rate
$NPER$	annuity spreadsheet notation for the number of periods or dates of the last cash flow
$RATE$	annuity spreadsheet notation for interest rate
PMT	annuity spreadsheet notation for cash flow
IRR	internal rate of return
PV_n	present value on date n

4.1 The Timeline

We begin our look at valuing cash flows lasting several periods with some basic vocabulary and tools. We refer to a series of cash flows lasting several periods as a **stream of cash flows**. We can represent a stream of cash flows on a **timeline**, a linear representation of the timing of the expected cash flows. Timelines are an important first step in organizing and then solving a financial problem. We use them throughout this text.

To illustrate how to construct a timeline, assume that a friend owes you money. He has agreed to repay the loan by making two payments of $10,000 at the end of each of the next two years. We represent this information on a timeline as follows:

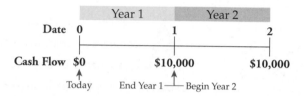

Date 0 represents the present. Date 1 is one year later and represents the end of the first year. The $10,000 cash flow below date 1 is the payment you will receive at the end of the first year. Date 2 is two years from now; it represents the end of the second year. The $10,000 cash flow below date 2 is the payment you will receive at the end of the second year.

You will find the timeline most useful in tracking cash flows if you interpret each point on the timeline as a specific date. The space between date 0 and date 1 then represents the time period between these dates—in this case, the first year of the loan. Date 0 is the beginning of the first year, and date 1 is the end of the first year. Similarly, date 1 is the beginning of the second year, and date 2 is the end of the second year. By denoting time in this way, date 1 signifies *both* the end of year 1 and the beginning of year 2, which makes sense since those dates are effectively the same point in time.[1]

In this example, both cash flows are inflows. In many cases, however, a financial decision will involve both inflows and outflows. To differentiate between the two types of cash flows, we assign a different sign to each: Inflows are positive cash flows, whereas outflows are negative cash flows.

To illustrate, suppose you're still feeling generous and have agreed to lend your brother $10,000 today. Your brother has agreed to repay this loan in two installments of $6000 at the end of each of the next two years. The timeline is:

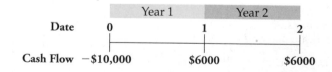

Notice that the first cash flow at date 0 (today) is represented as −$10,000 because it is an outflow. The subsequent cash flows of $6000 are positive because they are inflows.

So far, we have used timelines to show the cash flows that occur at the end of each year. Actually, timelines can represent cash flows that take place at the end of any time period.

---

1. That is, there is no real time difference between a cash flow paid at 11:59 P.M. on December 31 and one paid at 12:01 A.M. on January 1, although there may be some other differences such as taxation that we overlook for now.

For example, if you pay rent each month, you could use a timeline like the one in our first example to represent two rental payments, but you would replace the "year" label with "month."

Many of the timelines included in this chapter are very simple. Consequently, you may feel that it is not worth the time or trouble to construct them. As you progress to more difficult problems, however, you will find that timelines identify events in a transaction or investment that are easy to overlook. If you fail to recognize these cash flows, you will make flawed financial decisions. Therefore, we recommend that you approach *every* problem by drawing the timeline as we do in this chapter.

EXAMPLE 4.1

Constructing a Timeline

Problem

Suppose you must pay tuition of $10,000 per year for the next two years. Your tuition payments must be made in equal installments at the start of each semester. What is the timeline of your tuition payments?

Solution

Assuming today is the start of the first semester, your first payment occurs at date 0 (today). The remaining payments occur at semester intervals. Using one semester as the period length, we can construct a timeline as follows:

CONCEPT CHECK

1. What are the key elements of a timeline?

2. How can you distinguish cash inflows from outflows on a timeline?

4.2 The Three Rules of Time Travel

Financial decisions often require comparing or combining cash flows that occur at different points in time. In this section, we introduce three important rules central to financial decision making that allow us to compare or combine values.

Comparing and Combining Values

Our first rule is that it is only possible to compare or combine values at the same point in time. This rule restates a conclusion introduced in Chapter 3: Only cash flows in the same units can be compared or combined. *A dollar today* and *a dollar in one year* are not equivalent. Having money now is more valuable than having money in the future; if you have the money today you can earn interest on it.

To compare or combine cash flows that occur at different points in time, you first need to convert the cash flows into the same units or *move* them to the same point in time. The next two rules show how to move the cash flows on the timeline.

Moving Cash Flows Forward in Time

Suppose we have $1000 today, and we wish to determine the equivalent amount in one year's time. If the current market interest rate is 10%, we can use that rate as an exchange rate to move the cash flow forward in time. That is,

($1000 today) × (1.10 $ in one year / $ today) = $1100 in one year

In general, if the market interest rate for the year is r, then we multiply by the interest rate factor, $(1 + r)$, to move the cash flow from the beginning to the end of the year. This process of moving a value or cash flow forward in time is known as **compounding**. *Our second rule stipulates that to move a cash flow forward in time, you must compound it.*

We can apply this rule repeatedly. Suppose we want to know how much the $1000 is worth in two years' time. If the interest rate for year 2 is also 10%, then we convert as we just did:

($1100 in one year) × (1.10 $ in two years / $ in one year) = $1210 in two years

Let's represent this calculation on a timeline:

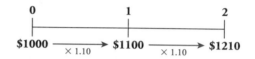

Given a 10% interest rate, all of the cash flows—$1000 at date 0, $1100 at date 1, and $1210 at date 2—are equivalent. They have the same value but are expressed in different units (different points in time). An arrow that points to the right indicates that the value is being moved forward in time—that is, compounded.

The value of a cash flow that is moved forward in time is known as its **future value**. In the preceding example, $1210 is the future value of $1000 two years from today. Note that the value grows as we move the cash flow further in the future. The equivalent value of two cash flows at two different points in time is sometimes referred to as the **time value of money**. By having money sooner, you can invest it and end up with more money later. Note also that the equivalent value grows by $100 the first year, but by $110 the second year. In the second year we earn interest on our original $1000, plus we earn interest on the $100 interest we received in the first year. This effect of earning "interest on interest" is known as **compound interest**.

How does the future value change if we move the cash flow three years? Continuing to use the same approach, we compound the cash flow a third time. Assuming the competitive market interest rate is fixed at 10%, we get

$1000 × (1.10) × (1.10) × (1.10) = $1000 × (1.10)^3 = $1331

In general, to take a cash flow C forward n periods into the future, we must compound it by the n intervening interest rate factors. If the interest rate r is constant, this calculation yields

Future Value of a Cash Flow

$$FV_n = C \times \underbrace{(1 + r) \times (1 + r) \times \cdots \times (1 + r)}_{n \text{ times}} = C \times (1 + r)^n \quad (4.1)$$

Moving Cash Flows Back in Time

The third rule describes how to move cash flows backward in time. Suppose you would like to compute the value today of $1000 you anticipate receiving in one year. If the current market interest rate is 10%, you can compute this value by converting units as we did in Chapter 3:

($1000 in one year) ÷ (1.10 $ in one year / $ today) = $909.09 today

That is, to move the cash flow backward in time, we divide it by the interest rate factor, $(1 + r)$, where r is the interest rate. This process of moving a value or cash flow backward in time—finding the equivalent value today of a future cash flow—is known as **discounting**. *Our third rule stipulates that to move a cash flow back in time, we must discount it.*

To illustrate, suppose that you anticipate receiving the $1000 two years from today rather than in one year. If the interest rate for both years is 10%, we can prepare the following timeline:

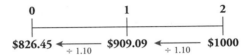

When the interest rate is 10%, all of the cash flows—$826.45 at date 0, $909.09 at date 1, and $1000 at date 2—are equivalent. They represent the same value in different units (different points in time). The arrow points to the left to indicate that the value is being moved backward in time or discounted. Note that the value decreases as we move the cash flow further back.

The value of a future cash flow at an earlier point on the timeline is its present value at the earlier point in time. That is, $826.45 is the present value at date 0 of $1000 in two years. Recall from Chapter 3 that the present value is the "do-it-yourself" price to produce a future cash flow. Thus, if we invested $826.45 today for two years at 10% interest, we would have a future value of $1000, using the second rule of time travel:

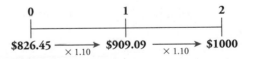

Suppose the $1000 were three years away and you wanted to compute the present value. Again, if the interest rate is 10%, we have

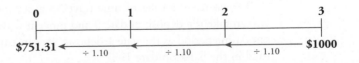

That is, the present value today of a cash flow of $1000 in three years is given by

$$\$1000 \div (1.10) \div (1.10) \div (1.10) = \$1000 \div (1.10)^3 = \$751.31$$

In general, to move a cash flow C backward n periods, we must discount it by the n intervening interest rate factors. If the interest rate r is constant, this yields

Present Value of a Cash Flow

$$PV = C \div (1 + r)^n = \frac{C}{(1 + r)^n} \qquad (4.2)$$

EXAMPLE 4.2

Present Value of a Single Future Cash Flow

Problem

You are considering investing in a savings bond that will pay $15,000 in ten years. If the competitive market interest rate is fixed at 6% per year, what is the bond worth today?

Solution

The cash flows for this bond are represented by the following timeline:

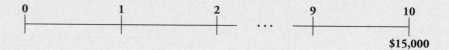

Thus, the bond is worth $15,000 in ten years. To determine the value today, we compute the present value:

$$PV = \frac{15,000}{1.06^{10}} = \$8375.92 \text{ today}$$

The bond is worth much less today than its final payoff because of the time value of money.

Applying the Rules of Time Travel

The rules of time travel allow us to compare and combine cash flows that occur at different points in time. Suppose we plan to save $1000 today, and $1000 at the end of each of the next two years. If we earn a fixed 10% interest rate on our savings, how much will we have three years from today?

Again, we start with a timeline:

The timeline shows the three deposits we plan to make. We need to compute their value at the end of three years.

We can use the rules of time travel in a number of ways to solve this problem. First, we can take the deposit at date 0 and move it forward to date 1. Because it is then in the same time period as the date 1 deposit, we can combine the two amounts to find out the total in the bank on date 1:

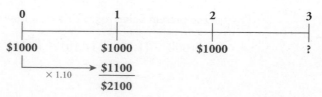

Using the first two rules of time travel, we find that our total savings on date 1 will be $2100. Continuing in this fashion, we can solve the problem as follows:

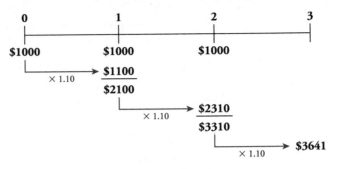

The total amount we will have in the bank at the end of three years is $3641. This amount is the future value of our $1000 savings deposits.

Another approach to the problem is to compute the future value in year 3 of each cash flow separately. Once all three amounts are in year 3 dollars, we can then combine them.

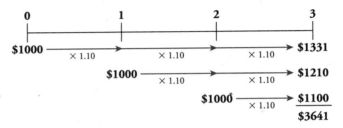

Both calculations give the same future value. As long as we follow the rules, we get the same result. The order in which we apply the rules does not matter. The calculation we choose depends on which is more convenient for the problem at hand. Table 4.1 summarizes the three rules of time travel and their associated formulas.

TABLE 4.1	The Three Rules of Time Travel	
Rule 1	Only values at the same point in time can be compared or combined.	
Rule 2	To move a cash flow forward in time, you must compound it.	Future Value of a Cash Flow $FV_n = C \times (1 + r)^n$
Rule 3	To move a cash flow backward in time, you must discount it.	Present Value of a Cash Flow $PV = C \div (1 + r)^n = \dfrac{C}{(1 + r)^n}$

EXAMPLE 4.3

Computing the Future Value

Problem

Let's revisit the savings plan we considered earlier: We plan to save $1000 today and at the end of each of the next two years. At a fixed 10% interest rate, how much will we have in the bank three years from today?

Solution

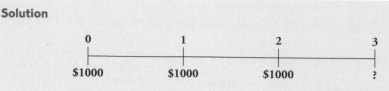

Let's solve this problem in a different way than we did in the text. First compute the present value of the cash flows. There are several ways to perform this calculation. Here we treat each cash flow separately and then combine the present values.

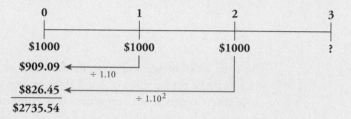

Saving $2735.54 today is equivalent to saving $1000 per year for three years. Now let's compute its future value in year 3:

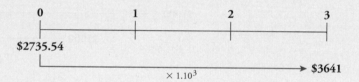

This answer of $3641 is precisely the same result we found earlier. As long as we apply the three rules of time travel, we will always get the correct answer.

CONCEPT CHECK   1. Can you compare or combine cash flows at different times?

2. How do you move a cash flow backward and forward in time?

4.3 The Power of Compounding: An Application

When you put money into a savings account and choose to leave the earned interest in the account, you will earn interest on the past interest payments. Although initially this "interest on interest" is small, it can eventually become very large. Consider putting $1000 into a bank account that earns a fixed 10% per year. At the end of the first year, you will receive $100 in interest, so your balance will grow to $1100. In the second year, the interest paid is $110, so the "interest on interest" amounts to an extra $10. What about in the twentieth year?

Using the formula for the future value, we see that after 20 years the money will have grown to

$$\$1000 \times 1.10^{20} = \$6727.50$$

The interest paid in the twenty-first year will be 10% of $6727.50, or $672.75. Of that amount, $100 corresponds to interest on the initial $1000 principal, and $572.75 is

FIGURE 4.1

The Power of Compounding

The graph illustrates the future value of $1000 invested at a 10% interest rate. Because interest is paid on past interest, the future value grows exponentially—after 50 years the money grows 117-fold and in 75 years (only 25 years later), it is 1272 times larger than the value today.

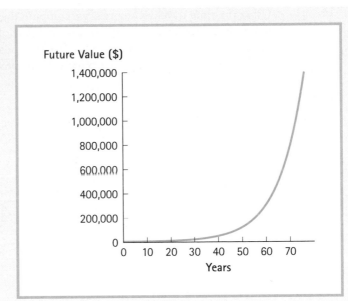

interest on accumulated interest. Note also that in 20 years the money has grown more than sixfold. What will happen over the next 20 years? You may be tempted to guess a 12-fold increase. In fact, in 40 years the amount will have grown to

$$\$1000 \times 1.10^{40} = \$1000 \times 1.10^{20} \times 1.10^{20} = \$45,259.26$$

Rather than doubling, the value of each dollar invested for 40 years is the square of the value after 20 years ($6.7^2 \approx 45$). This kind of growth is called geometric growth. Figure 4.1 shows how impressive this growth can be. After 75 years, $1000 would have grown to more than $1 million. Imagine if one of your grandparents had bequeathed $1000 to you 75 years ago, and it had grown in this way!

CONCEPT CHECK   **1.** What is compound interest?

2. Why does the future value of an investment grow faster in later years as shown in Figure 4.1?

4.4 Valuing a Stream of Cash Flows

Most investment opportunities have multiple cash flows that occur at different points in time. In Section 4.2, we applied the rules of time travel to value such cash flows. Now we formalize this approach by deriving a general formula for valuing a stream of cash flows.

Consider a stream of cash flows: C_0 at date 0, C_1 at date 1, and so on, up to C_N at date N. We represent this cash flow stream on a timeline as follows:

Using the time travel techniques, we compute the present value of this cash flow stream in two steps. First, we compute the present value of each individual cash flow. Then, once the cash flows are in common units of dollars today, we can combine them.

For a given interest rate r, we represent this process on the timeline as follows:

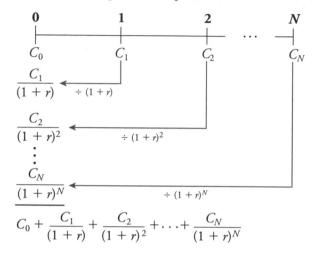

This timeline provides the general formula for the present value of a cash flow stream:

$$PV = C_0 + \frac{C_1}{(1 + r)} + \frac{C_2}{(1 + r)^2} + \cdots + \frac{C_N}{(1 + r)^N}$$

We can also write this formula as a summation:

Present Value of a Cash Flow Stream

$$PV = \sum_{n=0}^{N} PV(C_n) = \sum_{n=0}^{N} \frac{C_n}{(1 + r)^n} \tag{4.3}$$

The summation sign, $\sum$, means "sum the individual elements for each date n from 0 to N." Note that $(1 + r)^0 = 1$, so this shorthand matches precisely the previous equation. That is, the present value of the cash flow stream is the sum of the present values of each cash flow. Recall from Chapter 3 how we defined the present value as the dollar amount you would need to invest today to produce the single cash flow in the future. The same idea holds in this context. The present value is the amount you need to invest today to generate the cash flows stream $C_0, C_1, \ldots, C_N$. That is, receiving those cash flows is equivalent to having their present value in the bank today.

EXAMPLE 4.4

Present Value of a Stream of Cash Flows

Problem

You have just graduated and need money to buy a new car. Your rich Uncle Henry will lend you the money so long as you agree to pay him back within four years, and you offer to pay him the rate of interest that he would otherwise get by putting his money in a savings account. Based on your earnings and living expenses, you think you will be able to pay him $5000 in one year, and then $8000 each year for the next three years. If Uncle Henry would otherwise earn 6% per year on his savings, how much can you borrow from him?

Solution

The cash flows you can promise Uncle Henry are as follows:

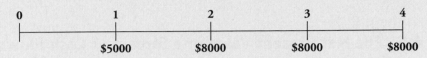

How much money should Uncle Henry be willing to give you today in return for your promise of these payments? He should be willing to give you an amount that is equivalent to these payments in present value terms. This is the amount of money that it would take him to produce these same cash flows, which we calculate as follows:

$$PV = \frac{5000}{1.06} + \frac{8000}{1.06^2} + \frac{8000}{1.06^3} + \frac{8000}{1.06^4}$$

$$= 4716.98 + 7119.97 + 6716.95 + 6336.75$$

$$= 24{,}890.65$$

Thus, Uncle Henry should be willing to lend you $24,890.65 in exchange for your promised payments. This amount is less than the total you will pay him ($5000 + $8000 + $8000 + $8000 = $29,000) due to the time value of money.

Let's verify our answer. If your uncle kept his $24,890.65 in the bank today earning 6% interest, in four years he would have

$$FV = \$24{,}890.65 \times (1.06)^4 = \$31{,}423.87 \text{ in 4 years}$$

Now suppose that Uncle Henry gives you the money, and then deposits your payments to him in the bank each year. How much will he have four years from now?

We need to compute the future value of the annual deposits. One way to do so is to compute the bank balance each year:

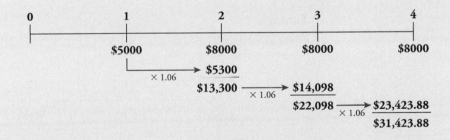

We get the same answer both ways (within a penny, which is because of rounding).

The last section of Example 4.4 illustrates a general point. If you want to compute the future value of a stream of cash flows, you can do it directly (the second approach used in Example 4.4), or you can first compute the present value and then move it to the future (the first approach). Because we obey the laws of time travel in both cases, we get the same result. This principle can be applied more generally to write the following formula for the future value in year n in terms of the present value of a set of cash flows:

Future Value of a Cash Flow Stream with a Present Value of PV

$$FV_n = PV \times (1 + r)^n \tag{4.4}$$

1. How do you calculate the present value of a cash flow stream?

2. How do you calculate the future value of a cash flow stream?

4.5 The Net Present Value of a Stream of Cash Flows

Now that we have established the rules of time travel, and determined how to compute present and future values, we are ready to address our central goal: calculating the NPV of future cash flows to evaluate an investment decision. Recall from Chapter 3 that we defined the net present value (NPV) of an investment decision as follows:

$$NPV = PV(\text{benefits}) - PV(\text{costs})$$

In this context, the benefits are the cash inflows and the costs are the cash outflows. We can represent any investment decision on a timeline as a cash flow stream where the cash outflows (investments) are negative cash flows and the inflows are positive cash flows. Thus, the NPV of an investment opportunity is also the *present value* of the stream of cash flows of the opportunity:

$$NPV = PV(\text{benefits}) - PV(\text{costs}) = PV(\text{benefits} - \text{costs})$$

EXAMPLE
4.5

Net Present Value of an Investment Opportunity

Problem

You have been offered the following investment opportunity: If you invest $1000 today, you will receive $500 at the end of each of the next three years. If you could otherwise earn 10% per year on your money, should you undertake the investment opportunity?

Solution

As always, start with a timeline. We denote the upfront investment as a negative cash flow (because it is money we need to spend) and the money we receive as a positive cash flow.

To decide whether we should accept this opportunity, we compute the NPV by computing the present value of the stream:

$$NPV = -1000 + \frac{500}{1.10} + \frac{500}{1.10^2} + \frac{500}{1.10^3} = \$243.43$$

Because the NPV is positive, the benefits exceed the costs and we should make the investment. Indeed, the NPV tells us that taking this opportunity is like getting an extra $243.43 that you can spend today. To illustrate, suppose you borrow $1000 to invest in the opportunity and an extra $243.43 to spend today. How much would you owe on the $1243.43 loan in three years? At 10% interest, the amount you would owe would be

$$FV = (\$1000 + \$243.43) \times (1.10)^3 = \$1655 \text{ in 3 years}$$

At the same time, the investment opportunity generates cash flows. If you put these cash flows into a bank account, how much will you have saved three years from now? The future value of the savings is

$$FV = (\$500 \times 1.10^2) + (\$500 \times 1.10) + \$500 = \$1655 \text{ in 3 years}$$

As you see, you can use your bank savings to repay the loan. Taking the opportunity therefore allows you to spend $243.43 today at no extra cost.

In principle, we have explained how to answer the question we posed at the beginning of the chapter: How should financial managers evaluate a project such as undertaking the development of the 7E7 airplane? We have shown how to compute the NPV of an investment opportunity such as the 7E7 airplane that lasts more than one period. In practice, when the number of cash flows exceeds four or five (as it most likely will), the calculations can become tedious. Fortunately, a number of special cases do not require us to treat each cash flow separately. We derive these shortcuts in the next section.

CONCEPT CHECK

1. How do you calculate the net present value of a cash flow stream?

2. What benefit does a firm receive when it accepts a project with a positive *NPV*?

4.6 Perpetuities, Annuities, and Other Special Cases

The formulas we have developed so far allow us to compute the present or future value of any cash flow stream. In this section we consider two types of assets, *perpetuities* and *annuities*, and learn shortcuts for valuing them. These shortcuts are possible because the cash flows follow a regular pattern.

Perpetuities

A **perpetuity** is a stream of equal cash flows that occur at regular intervals and last forever. One example is the British government bond called a **consol** (or perpetual bond). Consol bonds promise the owner a fixed cash flow every year, forever.

Here is the timeline for a perpetuity:

Note from the timeline that the first cash flow does not occur immediately; *it arrives at the end of the first period.* This timing is sometimes referred to as payment *in arrears* and is a standard convention that we adopt throughout this text.

Using the formula for the present value, the present value of a perpetuity with payment *C* and interest rate *r* is given by

$$PV = \frac{C}{(1 + r)} + \frac{C}{(1 + r)^2} + \frac{C}{(1 + r)^3} + \cdots = \sum_{n=1}^{\infty} \frac{C}{(1 + r)^n}$$

Notice that $C_n = C$ in the present value formula because the cash flow for a perpetuity is constant. Also, because the first cash flow is in one period, $C_0 = 0$.

To find the value of a perpetuity one cash flow at a time would take forever—literally! You might wonder how, even with a shortcut, the sum of an infinite number of positive terms could be finite. The answer is that the cash flows in the future are discounted for an ever increasing number of periods, so their contribution to the sum eventually becomes negligible.[2]

To derive the shortcut, we calculate the value of a perpetuity by creating our own perpetuity. We can then calculate the present value of the perpetuity because, by the Law of One Price, the value of the perpetuity must be the same as the cost we incurred to create our own perpetuity. To illustrate, suppose you could invest $100 in a bank account paying 5% interest per year forever. At the end of one year, you will have $105 in the bank—your original $100 plus $5 in interest. Suppose you withdraw the $5 interest and reinvest the $100 for a second year. Again you will have $105 after one year, and you can withdraw $5 and reinvest $100 for another year. By doing this year after year, you can withdraw $5 every year in perpetuity:

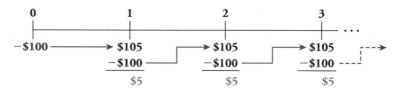

By investing $100 in the bank today, you can, in effect, create a perpetuity paying $5 per year. Recall from Chapter 3 that the Law of One Price tells us that the same good must have the same price in every market. Because the bank will "sell" us (allow us to create) the perpetuity for $100, the present value of the $5 per year in perpetuity is this "do-it-yourself" cost of $100.

Now let's generalize this argument. Suppose we invest an amount P in the bank. Every year we can withdraw the interest we have earned, $C = r \times P$, leaving the principal, P, in the bank. The present value of receiving C in perpetuity is therefore the upfront cost $P = C / r$. Therefore,

Present Value of a Perpetuity

$$PV(C \text{ in perpetuity}) = \frac{C}{r} \tag{4.5}$$

By depositing the amount $\frac{C}{r}$ today, we can withdraw interest of $\frac{C}{r} \times r = C$ each period in perpetuity.

Note the logic of our argument. To determine the present value of a cash flow stream, we computed the "do-it-yourself" cost of creating those same cash flows at the bank. This is an extremely useful and powerful approach—and is much simpler and faster than summing those infinite terms![3]

---

2. In mathematical terms, this is a geometric series, so it converges if $r > 0$.

3. Another mathematical derivation of this result exists (see the online appendix), but it is less intuitive. This case is a good example of how the Law of One Price can be used to derive useful results.

Historical Examples of Perpetuities

Companies sometimes issue bonds that they call perpetuities, but in fact are not really perpetuities. For example, according to *Dow Jones International News* (February 26, 2004), in 2004 Korea First Bank sold $300 million of debt in "the form of a so-called 'perpetual bond' that has no fixed maturity date." Although the bond has no fixed maturity date, Korea First Bank has the right to pay it back after 10 years, in 2014. Korea First Bank also has the right to extend the maturity of the bond for another 30 years after 2014. Thus, although the bond does not have a fixed maturity date, it will eventually mature—in either 10 or 40 years. The bond is not really a perpetuity because it does not pay interest forever.

Perpetual bonds were some of the first bonds ever issued. The oldest perpetuities that are still making interest payments were issued by the *Hoogheemraadschap Lekdijk Bovendams*, a seventeenth-century Dutch water board responsible for upkeep of the local dikes. The oldest bond dates from 1624. Two finance professors at Yale University, William Goetzmann and Geert Rouwenhorst, personally verified that these bonds continue to pay interest. On behalf of Yale, they purchased one of these bonds on July 1, 2003, and collected 26 years of back interest. On its issue date in 1648, this bond originally paid interest in Carolus guilders. Over the next 355 years, the currency of payment changed to Flemish pounds, Dutch guilders, and most recently euros. Currently, the bond pays interest of €11.34 annually.

Although the Dutch bonds are the oldest perpetuities still in existence, the first perpetuities date from much earlier times. For example, *cencus agreements* and *rentes*, which were forms of perpetuities and annuities, were issued in the twelfth century in Italy, France, and Spain. They were initially designed to circumvent the usury laws of the Catholic Church: Because they did not require the repayment of principal, in the eyes of the church they were not considered loans.

EXAMPLE 4.6

Endowing a Perpetuity

Problem

You want to endow an annual MBA graduation party at your alma mater. You want the event to be a memorable one, so you budget $30,000 per year forever for the party. If the university earns 8% per year on its investments, and if the first party is in one year's time, how much will you need to donate to endow the party?

Solution

The timeline of the cash flows you want to provide is

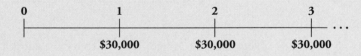

This is a standard perpetuity of $30,000 per year. The funding you would need to give the university in perpetuity is the present value of this cash flow stream. From the formula,

$$PV = C/r = \$30{,}000 / 0.08 = \$375{,}000 \text{ today}$$

If you donate $375,000 today, and if the university invests it at 8% per year forever, then the MBAs will have $30,000 every year for their graduation party.

COMMON MISTAKE   ***Discounting One Too Many Times***

The perpetuity formula assumes that the first payment occurs at the end of the first period (at date 1). Sometimes perpetuities have cash flows that start later in the future. In this case, we can adapt the perpetuity formula to compute the present value, but we need to do so carefully to avoid a common mistake.

To illustrate, consider the MBA graduation party described in Example 4.6. Rather than starting immediately, suppose that the first party will be held two years from today (for the current entering class). How would this delay change the amount of the donation required?

Now the timeline looks like this:

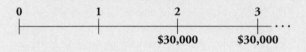

We need to determine the present value of these cash flows, as it tells us the amount of money in the bank needed today to finance the future parties. We cannot apply the perpetuity formula directly, however, because these cash flows are not *exactly* a perpetuity as we defined it. Specifically, the cash flow in the first period is "missing." But consider the situation on date 1—at that point, the

first party is one period away and then the cash flows are periodic. From the perspective of date 1, this *is* a perpetuity, and we can apply the formula. From the preceding calculation, we know we need $375,000 on date 1 to have enough to start the parties on date 2. We rewrite the timeline as follows:

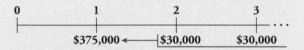

Our goal can now be restated more simply: How much do we need to invest today to have $375,000 in one year? This is a simple present value calculation:

$$PV = \$375,000 \,/\, 1.08 = \$347,222 \text{ today}$$

A common mistake is to discount the $375,000 twice because the first party is in two periods. *Remember—the present value formula for the perpetuity already discounts the cash flows to one period prior to the first cash flow.* Keep in mind that this common mistake may be made with perpetuities, annuities, and all of the other special cases discussed in this section. All of these formulas discount the cash flows to one period prior to the first cash flow.

Annuities

An **annuity** is a stream of N equal cash flows paid at regular intervals. The difference between an annuity and a perpetuity is that an annuity ends after some fixed number of payments. Most car loans, mortgages, and some bonds are annuities. We represent the cash flows of an annuity on a timeline as follows.

Note that just as with the perpetuity, we adopt the convention that the first payment takes place at date 1, one period from today. The present value of an N-period annuity with payment C and interest rate r is

$$PV = \frac{C}{(1+r)} + \frac{C}{(1+r)^2} + \frac{C}{(1+r)^3} + \cdots + \frac{C}{(1+r)^N} = \sum_{n=1}^{N} \frac{C}{(1+r)^n}$$

To find a simpler formula, we use the same approach we followed with the perpetuity: find a way to create an annuity. To illustrate, suppose you invest $100 in a bank account paying 5% interest. At the end of one year, you will have $105 in the bank—your original $100 plus $5 in interest. Using the same strategy as for a perpetuity, suppose you withdraw the $5 interest and reinvest the $100 for a second year. Once again you will have $105 after one year, and you can repeat the process, withdrawing $5 and reinvesting $100, every year. For a perpetuity, you left the principal in forever. Alternatively, you might decide after 20 years to close the account and withdraw the principal. In that case, your cash flows will look like this:

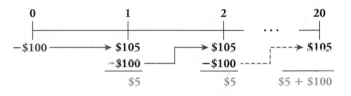

With your initial $100 investment, you have created a 20-year annuity of $5 per year, plus you will receive an extra $100 at the end of 20 years. By the Law of One Price, because it took an initial investment of $100 to create the cash flows on the timeline, the present value of these cash flows is $100, or

$$\$100 = PV(\text{20-year annuity of \$5 per year}) + PV(\$100 \text{ in 20 years})$$

Rearranging terms gives

$$PV(\text{20-year annuity of \$5 per year}) = \$100 - PV(\$100 \text{ in 20 years})$$

$$= 100 - \frac{100}{(1.05)^{20}} = \$62.31$$

So the present value of $5 for 20 years is $62.31. Intuitively, the value of the annuity is the initial investment in the bank account minus the present value of the principal that will be left in the account after 20 years.

We can use the same idea to derive the general formula. First, we invest P in the bank, and withdraw only the interest $C = r \times P$ each period. After N periods, we close the account. Thus, for an initial investment of P, we will receive an N-period annuity of C per period, *plus* we will get back our original P at the end. P is the total present value of the two sets of cash flows,[4] or

$$P = PV(\text{annuity of } C \text{ for } N \text{ periods}) + PV(P \text{ in period } N)$$

By rearranging terms, we compute the present value of the annuity:

$$PV(\text{annuity of } C \text{ for } N \text{ periods}) = P - PV(P \text{ in period } N)$$

$$= P - \frac{P}{(1+r)^N} = P\left(1 - \frac{1}{(1+r)^N}\right) \qquad (4.6)$$

Recall that the periodic payment C is the interest earned every period; that is, $C = r \times P$ or, equivalently, solving for P provides the upfront cost in terms of C,

$$P = C / r$$

Making this substitution for P, in Eq. 4.6, provides the formula for the present value of an annuity of C for N periods.

---

4. Here we are using value additivity (see Chapter 3) to separate the present value of the cash flows into separate pieces.

Present Value of an Annuity[5]

$$PV(\text{annuity of } C \text{ for } N \text{ periods with interest rate } r) = C \times \frac{1}{r}\left(1 - \frac{1}{(1+r)^N}\right) \quad (4.7)$$

EXAMPLE 4.7

Present Value of a Lottery Prize Annuity

Problem

You are the lucky winner of the $30 million state lottery. You can take your prize money either as (a) 30 payments of $1 million per year (starting today), or (b) $15 million paid today. If the interest rate is 8%, which option should you take?

Solution

Option (a) provides $30 million in prize money but paid over time. To evaluate it correctly, we must convert it to a present value. Here is the timeline:

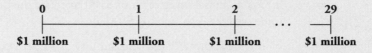

Because the first payment starts today, the last payment will occur in 29 years (for a total of 30 payments).[6] The $1 million at date 0 is already stated in present value terms, but we need to compute the present value of the remaining payments. Fortunately, this case looks like a 29-year annuity of $1 million per year, so we can use the annuity formula:

$$PV(\text{29-year annuity of \$1 million}) = \$1 \text{ million} \times \frac{1}{0.08}\left(1 - \frac{1}{1.08^{29}}\right)$$

$$= \$1 \text{ million} \times 11.16$$

$$= \$11.16 \text{ million today}$$

Thus, the total present value of the cash flows is $1 million + $11.16 million = $12.16 million. In timeline form:

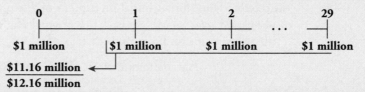

Option (b), $15 million upfront, is more valuable—even though the total amount of money paid is half that of option (a). The reason for the difference is the time value of money. If you have the $15 million today, you can use $1 million immediately and invest the remaining $14 million at an 8% interest rate. This strategy will give you $14 million × 8% = $1.12 million per year in perpetuity! Alternatively, you can spend $15 million − $11.16 million = $3.84 million today, and invest the remaining $11.16 million, which will still allow you to withdraw $1 million each year for the next 29 years before your account is depleted.

---

5. An early derivation of this formula is attributed to the astonomer Edmond Halley ("Of Compound Interest," published after Halley's death by Henry Sherwin, Sherwin's Mathematical Tables, London: W. and J. Mount, T. Page and Son, 1761).

6. An annuity in which the first payment occurs immediately is sometimes called an *annuity due*. Throughout this text, we always use the term "annuity" to mean one that is paid in arrears.

Now that we have derived a simple formula for the present value of an annuity, it is easy to find a simple formula for the future value. If we want to know the value N years in the future, we move the present value N periods forward on the timeline; that is, we compound the present value for N periods at interest rate r:

Future Value of an Annuity

$$FV(\text{annuity}) = PV \times (1 + r)^N$$

$$= \frac{C}{r}\left(1 - \frac{1}{(1 + r)^N}\right) \times (1 + r)^N$$

$$= C \times \frac{1}{r}\left((1 + r)^N - 1\right) \tag{4.8}$$

This formula is useful if we want to know how a savings account will grow over time.

EXAMPLE 4.8

Retirement Savings Plan Annuity

Problem
Ellen is 35 years old, and she has decided it is time to plan seriously for her retirement. At the end of each year until she is 65, she will save $10,000 in a retirement account. If the account earns 10% per year, how much will Ellen have saved at age 65?

Solution
As always, we begin with a timeline. In this case, it is helpful to keep track of both the dates and Ellen's age:

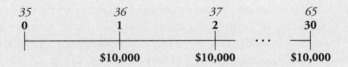

Ellen's savings plan looks like an annuity of $10,000 per year for 30 years. (*Hint:* It is easy to become confused when you just look at age, rather than at both dates and age. A common error is to think there are only $65 - 36 = 29$ payments. Writing down both dates and age avoids this problem.)

To determine the amount Ellen will have in the bank at age 65, we compute the future value of this annuity:

$$FV = \$10,000 \times \frac{1}{0.10}(1.10^{30} - 1)$$

$$= \$10,000 \times 164.49$$

$$= \$1.645 \text{ million at age 65}$$

Growing Cash Flows

So far, we have considered only cash flow streams that have the same cash flow every period. If instead the cash flows are expected to grow at a constant rate in each period, we can also derive a simple formula for the present value of the future stream.

Growing Perpetuity. A **growing perpetuity** is a stream of cash flows that occur at regular intervals and grow at a constant rate forever. For example, a growing perpetuity with a first payment of $100 that grows at a rate of 3% has the following timeline:

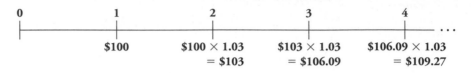

In general, a growing perpetuity with a first payment C and a growth rate g will have the following series of cash flows:

0	1	2	3	4	
	C	$C \times (1 + g)$	$C \times (1 + g)^2$	$C \times (1 + g)^3$	$\cdots$

As with perpetuities with equal cash flows, we adopt the convention that the first payment occurs at date 1. Note a second important convention: *The first payment does not grow.* That is, the first payment is C, even though it is one period away. Similarly, the cash flow in period n undergoes only $n - 1$ periods of growth. Substituting the cash flows from the preceding timeline into the general formula for the present value of a cash flow stream gives

$$PV = \frac{C}{(1 + r)} + \frac{C(1 + g)}{(1 + r)^2} + \frac{C(1 + g)^2}{(1 + r)^3} + \cdots = \sum_{n=1}^{\infty} \frac{C(1 + g)^{n-1}}{(1 + r)^n}$$

Suppose $g \geq r$. Then the cash flows grow even faster than they are discounted; each term in the sum gets larger, rather than smaller. In this case, the sum is infinite! What does an infinite present value mean? Remember that the present value is the "do-it-yourself" cost of creating the cash flows. An infinite present value means that no matter how much money you start with, it is *impossible* to reproduce those cash flows on your own. Growing perpetuities of this sort cannot exist in practice because no one would be willing to offer one at any finite price. A promise to pay an amount that forever grew faster than the interest rate is also unlikely to be kept (or believed by any savvy buyer).

The only viable growing perpetuities are those where the growth rate is less than the interest rate, so that each successive term in the sum is less than the previous term and the overall sum is finite. Consequently, we assume that $g < r$ for a growing perpetuity.

To derive the formula for the present value of a growing perpetuity, we follow the same logic used for a regular perpetuity: Compute the amount you would need to deposit today to create the perpetuity yourself. In the case of a regular perpetuity, we created a constant payment forever by withdrawing the interest earned each year and reinvesting the principal. To increase the amount we can withdraw each year, the principal that we reinvest each year must grow. We can accomplish this by withdrawing less than the full amount of interest earned each period, using the remaining interest to increase our principal.

Let's consider a specific case. Suppose you want to create a perpetuity growing at 2%, so you invest $100 in a bank account that pays 5% interest. At the end of one year, you will have $105 in the bank—your original $100 plus $5 in interest. If you withdraw only $3, you will have $102 to reinvest—2% more than the amount you had initially. This amount will then grow to $102 \times 1.05 = 107.10 in the following year, and you can withdraw $3 \times 1.02 = \$3.06$, which will leave you with principal of $\$107.10 - \$3.06 = \$104.04$. Note that $\$102 \times 1.02 = \$104.04$. That is, both the amount you withdraw and the principal you reinvest grow by 2% each year. On a timeline, these cash flows look like this:

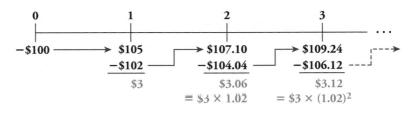

By following this strategy, you have created a growing perpetuity that starts at $3 and grows 2% per year. This growing perpetuity must have a present value equal to the cost of $100.

We can generalize this argument. In the case of an equal-payment perpetuity, we deposited an amount P in the bank and withdrew the interest each year. Because we always left the principal P in the bank, we could maintain this pattern forever. If we want to increase the amount we withdraw from the bank each year by g, then the principal in the bank will have to grow by the same factor g. That is, instead of reinvesting P in the second year, we should reinvest $P(1 + g) = P + gP$. In order to increase our principal by gP, we can only withdraw $C = rP - gP = P(r - g)$.

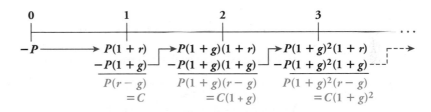

From the timeline, we see that after one period we can withdraw $C = P(r - g)$ and keep our account balance and cash flow growing at a rate of g forever. Solving this equation for P gives

$$P = \frac{C}{r - g}$$

The present value of the growing perpetuity with initial cash flow C is P, the initial amount deposited in the bank account:

Present Value of a Growing Perpetuity

$$PV(\text{growing perpetuity}) = \frac{C}{r - g} \tag{4.9}$$

To understand the formula for a growing perpetuity intuitively, start with the formula for a perpetuity. In the earlier case, you had to put enough money in the bank to ensure that the interest earned matched the cash flows of the regular perpetuity. In the case of a growing perpetuity, you need to put more than that amount in the bank because you have to finance the growth in the cash flows. How much more? If the bank pays interest at a rate of 10%, then all that is left to take out if you want to make sure the principal grows

3% per year is the difference: 10% − 3% = 7%. So instead of the present value of the perpetuity being the first cash flow divided by the interest rate, it is now the first cash flow divided by the *difference* between the interest rate and the growth rate.

Endowing a Growing Perpetuity

Problem

In Example 4.6, you planned to donate money to your alma mater to fund an annual $30,000 MBA graduation party. Given an interest rate of 8% per year, the required donation was the present value of

$$PV = \$30{,}000 / 0.08 = \$375{,}000 \text{ today}$$

Before accepting the money, however, the MBA student association has asked that you increase the donation to account for the effect of inflation on the cost of the party in future years. Although $30,000 is adequate for next year's party, the students estimate that the party's cost will rise by 4% per year thereafter. To satisfy their request, how much do you need to donate now?

Solution

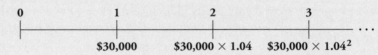

The cost of the party next year is $30,000, and the cost then increases 4% per year forever. From the timeline, we recognize the form of a growing perpetuity. To finance the growing cost, you need to provide the present value today of

$$PV = \$30{,}000 / (0.08 - 0.04) = \$750{,}000 \text{ today}$$

You need to double the size of your gift!

Growing Annuity.   A **growing annuity** is a stream of N growing cash flows, paid at regular intervals. It is a growing perpetuity that eventually comes to an end. The following timeline shows a growing annuity with initial cash flow C, growing at rate g every period until period N:

The conventions used earlier still apply: (1) The first cash flow arrives at the end of the first period, and (2) the first cash flow does not grow. The last cash flow therefore reflects only $N − 1$ periods of growth.

The present value of an N-period growing annuity with initial cash flow C, growth rate g, and interest rate r is given by

Present Value of a Growing Annuity

$$PV = C \times \frac{1}{r - g}\left(1 - \left(\frac{1 + g}{1 + r}\right)^{N}\right) \tag{4.10}$$

Because the annuity has only a finite number of terms, Eq. 4.10 also works when $g > r$.[7] The process of deriving this simple expression for the present value of a growing annuity is the same as for a regular annuity. Interested readers may consult the online appendix for details.

EXAMPLE 4.10

Retirement Savings with a Growing Annuity

Problem

In Example 4.8, Ellen considered saving $10,000 per year for her retirement. Although $10,000 is the most she can save in the first year, she expects her salary to increase each year so that she will be able to increase her savings by 5% per year. With this plan, if she earns 10% per year on her savings, how much will Ellen have saved at age 65?

Solution

Her new savings plan is represented by the following timeline:

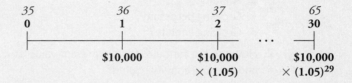

This example involves a 30-year growing annuity, with a growth rate of 5%, and an initial cash flow of $10,000. The present value of this growing annuity is given by

$$PV = \$10,000 \times \frac{1}{0.10 - 0.05} \left(1 - \left(\frac{1.05}{1.10} \right)^{30} \right)$$

$$= \$10,000 \times 15.0463$$

$$= \$150,463 \text{ today}$$

Ellen's proposed savings plan is equivalent to having $150,463 in the bank *today*. To determine the amount she will have at age 65, we need to move this amount forward 30 years:

$$FV = \$150,463 \times 1.10^{30}$$

$$= \$2.625 \text{ million in 30 years}$$

Ellen will have saved $2.625 million at age 65 using the new savings plan. This sum is almost $1 million more than she had without the additional annual increases in savings.

The formula for the growing annuity is a general solution. In fact, we can deduce all of the other formulas in this section from the expression for a growing annuity. To see how to derive the other formulas from this one, first consider a growing perpetuity. It is a growing annuity with $N = \infty$. If $g < r$, then

$$\frac{1 + g}{1 + r} < 1$$

---

7. Eq. 4.10 does not work for $g = r$. But in that case, growth and discounting cancel out, and the present value is equivalent to receiving all the cash flows at date 1: $PV = C \times N/(1 + r)$.

and so

$$\left(\frac{1+g}{1+r}\right)^N \to 0 \text{ as } N \to \infty$$

The formula for a growing annuity when $N = \infty$ therefore becomes

$$PV = \frac{C}{r-g}\left(1 - \left(\frac{1+g}{1+r}\right)^N\right) = \frac{C}{r-g}(1-0) = \frac{C}{r-g}$$

which is the formula for a growing perpetuity. The formulas for a regular annuity and perpetuity also follow from the formula if we let the growth rate $g = 0$.

CONCEPT CHECK

1. How do you calculate the present value of a
   a. Perpetuity?
   b. Annuity?
   c. Growing perpetuity?
   d. Growing annuity?

2. How are the formulas for the present value of a perpetuity, annuity, growing perpetuity, and growing annuity related?

4.7 Solving Problems with a Spreadsheet Program

In the previous section, we derived formulas that were shortcuts for computing the present values of cash flows that have special patterns. Two other kinds of shortcuts simplify the calculation of present values—the use of spreadsheets and financial calculators. In this section we focus on spreadsheets.

Spreadsheet programs such as Excel have a set of functions that perform the calculations that finance professionals do most often. In Excel, the functions are called NPER, RATE, PV, PMT, and FV. The functions are all based on the timeline of an annuity:

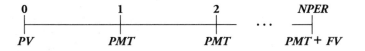

together with an interest rate, denoted by *RATE*. Thus, there are a total of five variables: *NPER, RATE, PV, PMT,* and *FV.* Each function takes four of these variables as inputs and returns the value of the fifth one that ensures that the NPV of the cash flows is zero. That is, the functions all solve the problem

$$NPV = PV + PMT \times \frac{1}{RATE}\left(1 - \frac{1}{(1+RATE)^{NPER}}\right) + \frac{FV}{(1+RATE)^{NPER}} = 0 \quad (4.11)$$

In words, the present value of the annuity payments *PMT,* plus the present value of the final payment *FV,* plus the initial amount *PV,* has a net present value of zero. Let's tackle a few examples.

EXAMPLE

4.11

Computing the Future Value In Excel

Problem

Suppose you plan to invest $20,000 in an account paying 8% interest. How much will you have in the account in 15 years?

Solution

We represent this problem with the following timeline:

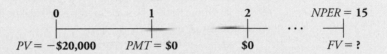

To compute the solution, we enter the four variables we know ($NPER = 15$, $RATE = 8\%$, $PV = -20,000$, $PMT = 0$) and solve for the one we want to determine (FV) using the Excel function FV (RATE, NPER, PMT, PV). The spreadsheet here calculates a future value of $63,443.

	NPER	RATE	PV	PMT	FV	Excel Formula
Given	15	8.00%	−20,000	0		
Solve for FV					63,443	=FV(0.08,15,0,−20000)

Note that we entered PV as a negative number (the amount we are putting *into* the bank), and FV is shown as a positive number (the amount we can take *out* of the bank). It is important to use signs correctly to indicate the direction in which the money is flowing when using the spreadsheet functions.

To check the result, we can solve this problem directly:

$$FV = \$20,000 \times 1.08^{15} = \$63,443$$

This Excel spreadsheet in Example 4.11 is available at the text Web site and is set up to allow you to compute any one of the five variables. We refer to this spreadsheet as the **annuity spreadsheet**. You simply enter the four input variables on the top line and leave the variable you want to compute blank. The spreadsheet computes the fifth variable and displays the answer on the bottom line. The spreadsheet also displays the Excel function that is used to get the answers. Let's work through a more complicated example that illustrates the convenience of the annuity spreadsheet.

EXAMPLE

4.12

Using the Annuity Spreadsheet

Problem

Suppose that you invest $20,000 in an account paying 8% interest. You plan to withdraw $2000 at the end of each year for 15 years. How much money will be left in the account after 15 years?

Solution

Again, we start with the timeline:

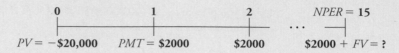

The timeline indicates that the withdrawals are an annuity payment that we receive from the bank account. Note that PV is negative (money *into* the bank), while PMT is positive (money *out* of the bank). We solve for the final balance in the account, FV, using the annuity spreadsheet:

	NPER	RATE	PV	PMT	FV	Excel Formula
Given	15	8.00%	−20,000	2000		
Solve for FV					9139	=FV(0.08,15,2000,−20000)

We will have $9139 left in the bank after 15 years.

We can also compute this solution directly. One approach is to think of the deposit and the withdrawals as being separate accounts. In the account with the $20,000 deposit, our savings will grow to $63,443 in 15 years, as we computed in Example 4.11. Using the formula for the future value of an annuity, if we borrow $2000 per year for 15 years at 8%, at the end our debt will have grown to

$$\$2000 \times \frac{1}{0.08}(1.08^{15} - 1) = \$54,304$$

After paying off our debt, we will have $63,443 − $54,304 = $9139 remaining after 15 years.

You can also use a handheld financial calculator to do the same calculations. The calculators work in much the same way as the annuity spreadsheet. You enter any four of the five variables, and the calculator calculates the fifth variable.

CONCEPT CHECK   1. What are the two shortcuts that you can use to simplify the calculation of present values?

2. How do you use a spreadsheet to simplify financial calculations?

4.8 Solving for Variables Other Than Present Value or Future Value

So far, we have calculated the present value or future value of a stream of cash flows. Sometimes, however, we know the present value or future value but do not know one of the variables we have previously been given as an input. For example, when you take out a loan, you may know the amount you would like to borrow, but may not know the loan payments that will be required to repay it. Or, if you make a deposit into a bank account, you may want to calculate how long it will take before your balance reaches a certain level. In such situations, we use the present and/or future values as inputs, and solve for the variable we are interested in. We examine several special cases in this section.

Solving for the Cash Flows

Let's consider an example where we know the present value of an investment, but do not know the cash flows. The best example is a loan—you know how much you want to borrow (the present value) and you know the interest rate, but you do not know how much you need to repay each year. Suppose you are opening a business that requires an initial investment of $100,000. Your bank manager has agreed to lend you this money. The terms of the loan state that you will make equal annual payments for the next ten years and will pay an interest rate of 8% with the first payment due one year from today. What is your annual payment?

From the bank's perspective, the timeline looks like this:

The bank will give you $100,000 today in exchange for ten equal payments over the next decade. You need to determine the size of the payment C that the bank will require. For the bank to be willing to lend you $100,000, the loan cash flows must have a present value of $100,000 when evaluated at the bank's interest rate of 8%. That is,

$$100,000 = PV(\text{10-year annuity of } C \text{ per year, evaluated at the loan rate})$$

Using the formula for the present value of an annuity,

$$100,000 = C \times \frac{1}{0.08}\left(1 - \frac{1}{1.08^{10}}\right) = C \times 6.71$$

Solving this equation for C gives

$$C = \frac{100,000}{6.71} = \$14,903$$

You will be required to make ten annual payments of $14,903 in exchange for $100,000 today.

We can also solve this problem with the annuity spreadsheet:

	NPER	RATE	PV	PMT	FV	Excel Formula
Given	10	8.00%	100,000		0	
Solve for PMT				−14,903		=PMT(0.08,10,100000,0)

In general, when solving for a loan payment, think of the amount borrowed (the loan principal) as the present value of the payments. If the payments of the loan are an annuity, we can solve for the payment of the loan by inverting the annuity formula. Writing this procedure formally, we begin with the timeline (from the bank's perspective) for a loan with principal P, requiring N periodic payments of C and interest rate r:

Setting the present value of the payments equal to the principal,

$$P = PV(\text{annuity of } C \text{ for } N \text{ periods}) = C \times \frac{1}{r}\left(1 - \frac{1}{(1 + r)^N}\right)$$

Solving this equation for C gives the general formula for the loan payment in terms of the outstanding principal (amount borrowed), P; interest rate, r; and number of payments, N:

Loan Payment

$$C = \frac{P}{\frac{1}{r}\left(1 - \frac{1}{(1 + r)^N}\right)}$$ (4.12)

EXAMPLE 4.13

Computing a Loan Payment

Problem
Your firm plans to buy a warehouse for $100,000. The bank offers you a 30-year loan with equal annual payments and an interest rate of 8% per year. The bank requires that your firm pay 20% of the purchase price as a down payment, so you can borrow only $80,000. What is the annual loan payment?

Solution
We start with the timeline (from the bank's perspective):

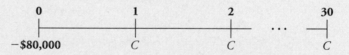

Using Eq. 4.12, we can solve for the loan payment, C, as follows:

$$C = \frac{P}{\frac{1}{r}\left(1 - \frac{1}{(1 + r)^N}\right)} = \frac{80,000}{\frac{1}{0.08}\left(1 - \frac{1}{(1.08)^{30}}\right)}$$

$$= \$7106.19$$

Using the annuity spreadsheet:

	NPER	RATE	PV	PMT	FV	Excel Formula
Given	30	8.00%	−80,000		0	
Solve for PMT				7106		=PMT(0.08,30,−80000,0)

Your firm will need to pay $7106.19 each year to repay the loan.

We can use this same idea to solve for the cash flows when we know the future value rather than the present value. As an example, suppose you have just had a child. You decide to be prudent and start saving this year for her college education. You would like to have $60,000 saved by the time your daughter is 18 years old. If you can earn 7% per year on your savings, how much do you need to save each year to meet your goal?

The timeline for this example is

That is, you plan to save some amount C per year, and then withdraw $60,000 from the bank in 18 years. Therefore, we need to find the annuity payment that has a future value of $60,000 in 18 years. Using the formula for the future value of an annuity from Eq. 4.8,

$$60,000 = FV(\text{annuity}) = C \times \frac{1}{0.07}(1.07^{18} - 1) = C \times 34$$

Therefore, $C = \frac{60,000}{34} = \$1765$. So you need to save $1765 per year. If you do, then at a 7% interest rate your savings will grow to $60,000 by the time your child is 18 years old.

Now let's solve this problem with the annuity spreadsheet:

	NPER	RATE	PV	PMT	FV	Excel Formula
Given	18	7.00%	0		60,000	
Solve for PMT				−1765		=PMT(0.07,18,0,60000)

Once again, we find that we need to save $1765 for 18 years to accumulate $60,000.

Internal Rate of Return

In some situations, you know the present value and cash flows of an investment opportunity but you do not know the interest rate that equates them. This interest rate is called the **internal rate of return (IRR)**, defined as the interest rate that sets the net present value of the cash flows equal to zero.

For example, suppose that you have an investment opportunity that requires a $1000 investment today and will have a $2000 payoff in six years. On a timeline,

One way to analyze this investment is to ask the question: What interest rate, r, would you need so that the NPV of this investment is zero?

$$NPV = -1000 + \frac{2000}{(1 + r)^6} = 0$$

Rearranging gives

$$1000 \times (1 + r)^6 = 2000$$

That is, r is the interest rate you would need to earn on your $1000 to have a future value of $2000 in six years. We can solve for r as follows:

$$1 + r = \left(\frac{2000}{1000}\right)^{1/6} = 1.1225$$

or $r = 12.25\%$. This rate is the IRR of this investment opportunity. Making this investment is like earning 12.25% per year on your money for six years.

When there are just two cash flows, as in the preceding example, it is easy to compute the IRR. Consider the general case in which you invest an amount P today, and receive FV in N years. Then

$$P \times (1 + \text{IRR})^N = FV$$
$$1 + \text{IRR} = (FV/P)^{1/N}$$

That is, we take the total return of the investment over N years, FV/P, and convert it to an equivalent one-year rate by raising it to the power $1/N$.

Now let's consider a more sophisticated example. Suppose your firm needs to purchase a new forklift. The dealer gives you two options: (1) a price for the forklift if you pay cash and (2) the annual payments if you take out a loan from the dealer. To evaluate the loan that the dealer is offering you, you will want to compare the rate on the loan with the rate that your bank is willing to offer you. Given the loan payment that the dealer quotes, how do you compute the interest rate charged by the dealer?

In this case, we need to compute the IRR of the dealer's loan. Suppose the cash price of the forklift is $40,000, and the dealer offers financing with no down payment and four annual payments of $15,000. This loan has the following timeline:

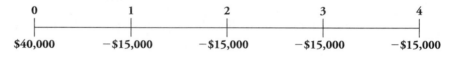

From the timeline it is clear that the loan is a four-year annuity with a payment of $15,000 per year and a present value of $40,000. Setting the NPV of the cash flows equal to zero requires that the present value of the payments equals the purchase price:

$$40,000 = 15,000 \times \frac{1}{r}\left(1 - \frac{1}{(1+r)^4}\right)$$

The value of r that solves this equation, the IRR, is the interest rate charged on the loan. Unfortunately, in this case there is no simple way to solve for the interest rate r.[8] The only way to solve this equation is to guess values of r until you find the right one.

Start by guessing $r = 10\%$. In this case, the value of the annuity is

$$15,000 \times \frac{1}{0.10}\left(1 - \frac{1}{(1.10)^4}\right) = 47,548$$

The present value of the payments is too large. To lower it, we need to use a higher interest rate. We guess 20% this time:

$$15,000 \times \frac{1}{0.20}\left(1 - \frac{1}{(1.20)^4}\right) = 38,831$$

Now the present value of the payments is too low, so we must pick a rate between 10% and 20%. We continue to guess until we find the right rate. Let us try 18.45%:

---

8. With five or more periods and general cash flows, there is *no* general formula to solve for r; trial and error (by hand or computer) is the *only* way to compute the IRR.

$$15{,}000 \times \frac{1}{0.1845}\left(1 - \frac{1}{(1.1845)^4}\right) = 40{,}000$$

The interest rate charged by the dealer is 18.45%.

An easier solution than guessing the IRR and manually calculating values is to use a spreadsheet or calculator to automate the guessing process. When the cash flows are an annuity, as in this example, we can use the annuity spreadsheet in Excel to compute the IRR. Recall that the annuity spreadsheet solves Eq. 4.11. It ensures that the NPV of investing in the annuity is zero. When the unknown variable is the interest rate, it will solve for the interest rate that sets the NPV equal to zero—that is, the IRR. For this case,

	NPER	RATE	PV	PMT	FV	Excel Formula
Given	4		40,000	−15,000	0	
Solve for Rate		18.45%				=RATE(4,−15000,40000,0)

The annuity spreadsheet correctly computes an IRR of 18.45%.

EXAMPLE 4.14

Computing the Internal Rate of Return with the Annuity Spreadsheet in Excel

Problem

Jessica has just graduated with her MBA. Rather than take the job she was offered at a prestigious investment bank—Baker, Bellingham, and Botts—she has decided to go into business for herself. However, Baker, Bellingham, and Botts was so impressed with Jessica that it has decided to fund her business. In return for an initial investment of $1 million, Jessica has agreed to pay the bank $125,000 at the end of each year for the next 30 years. What is the internal rate of return on Baker, Bellingham, and Botts's investment in Jessica's company, assuming she fulfills her commitment?

Solution

Here is the timeline (from Baker, Bellingham, and Botts's perspective):

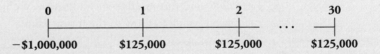

The timeline shows that the future cash flows are a 30-year annuity. Setting the NPV equal to zero requires

$$1{,}000{,}000 = \frac{125{,}000 \times 1}{r}\left(1 - \frac{1}{(1+r)^{30}}\right)$$

Using the annuity spreadsheet to solve for r,

	NPER	RATE	PV	PMT	FV	Excel Formula
Given	30		−1,000,000	125,000	0	
Solve for Rate		12.09%				=RATE(30,125000,−1000000,0)

The IRR on this investment is 12.09%.

In a few cases, it is possible to solve for the IRR directly. The next example demonstrates one such case.

EXAMPLE 4.15

Computing the Internal Rate of Return Directly

Problem
Baker, Bellingham, and Botts offers Jessica a second option for repayment of the loan. She can pay $100,000 the first year, increase the amount by 4% each year, and continue to make these payments forever, rather than for 30 years. What is the IRR in this case?

Solution
The timeline is

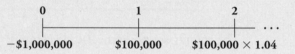

The timeline shows that the future cash flows are a growing perpetuity with a growth rate of 4%. Setting the NPV equal to zero requires

$$1,000,000 = \frac{100,000}{r - 0.04}$$

We can solve this equation for r

$$r = 0.04 + \frac{100,000}{1,000,000} = 0.14$$

The IRR on this investment is 14%.

Solving for the Number of Periods

In addition to solving for cash flows or the interest rate, we can solve for the amount of time it will take a sum of money to grow to a known value. In this case, the interest rate, present value, and future value are all known. We need to compute how long it will take for the present value to grow to the future value.

Suppose we invest $10,000 in an account paying 10% interest, and we want to know how long it will take for the amount to grow to $20,000.

We want to determine N.

In terms of our formulas, we need to find N so that the future value of our investment equals $20,000:

$$FV = \$10,000 \times 1.10^N = \$20,000 \tag{4.13}$$

One approach is to use trial and error to find N, as with the IRR. For example, with $N = 7$ years, $FV = \$19,487$, so it will take longer than 7 years. With $N = 8$ years, $FV = \$21,436$, so it will take between 7 and 8 years.

COMMON MISTAKE   Excel's NPV and IRR Functions

Although spreadsheets and financial calculators can simplify the process of solving problems, their designers have adopted specific conventions that you will need to be aware of to avoid making mistakes. In particular, before using any built-in financial function, always read the documentation for that function carefully to be aware of the correct format and any assumptions that are made by the software. Here we describe two functions in Excel, NPV and IRR, and some pitfalls to watch out for.

NPV

Excel's NPV function has the format, NPV(rate, value1, value2, . . .) where "rate" is the interest rate per period used to discount the cash flows, and "value1", "value2", etc. are the cash flows (or ranges of cash flows). The NPV function computes the present value of the cash flows *assuming the first cash flow occurs at date 1*. Therefore, if a project's first cash flow occurs at date 0, we cannot use the NPV function by itself to compute the NPV. We can use the NPV function to compute the present value of the cash flows from date 1 onwards, and then must add the date 0 cash flow to that result to calculate the NPV.

Another pitfall with the NPV function is that cash flows that are left blank are treated differently from cash flows that are equal to zero. If the cash flow is left blank, *both the cash flow and the period are ignored*. For example, the NPV function is used to evaluate the two equivalent cash flow streams shown below. In the second case, the NPV function ignores the blank cell at date 2 and assumes the cash flow is 10 at date 1 and 110 at date 2, which is clearly not what is intended and is incorrect.

NPV @ 10%	Date		
	1	2	3
$91.74	10	0	110
$100.00	10		110

Because of these idiosyncrasies, we avoid using Excel's NPV function, and find it to be more reliable to compute the present value of each cash flow separately in Excel, and then sum them to determine the NPV.

IRR

Excel's IRR function has the format, IRR(values, guess), where "values" is the range containing the cash flows, and "guess" is an optional starting guess where Excel begins its search for an IRR. There are two things to note about the IRR function. First, the values given to the IRR function should include all of the cash flows of the project, including the one at date 0. In this sense, the IRR and NPV functions in Excel are inconsistent. Second, like the NPV function, the IRR ignores the period associated with any blank cells.

Alternatively, this problem can be solved on the annuity spreadsheet. In this case, we solve for *N*:

	NPER	RATE	PV	PMT	FV	Excel Formula
Given		10.00%	−10,000	0	20,000	
Solve for NPER	7.27					=NPER(0.10,0,−10000,20000)

It will take about 7.3 years for our savings to grow to $20,000.

Finally, this problem can be solved mathematically. Dividing both sides of Eq. 4.13 by $10,000, we have

$$1.10^N = 20,000 / 10,000 = 2$$

To solve for an exponent, we take the logarithm of both sides, and use the fact that $\ln(x^y) = y \ln(x)$:

$$N \ln(1.10) = \ln(2)$$

$$N = \ln(2) / \ln(1.10) = 0.6931 / 0.0953 \approx 7.3 \text{ years}$$

**EXAMPLE
4.16**

Solving for the Number of Periods in a Savings Plan

Problem

You are saving to make a down payment on a house. You have $10,050 saved already, and you can afford to save an additional $5000 per year at the end of each year. If you earn 7.25% per year on your savings, how long will it take you to save $60,000?

Solution

The timeline for this problem is

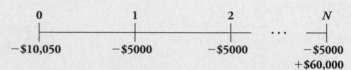

We need to find N so that the future value of our current savings plus the future value of our planned additional savings (which is an annuity) equals our desired amount:

$$10{,}050 \times 1.0725^N + 5000 \times \frac{1}{0.0725}(1.0725^N - 1) = 60{,}000$$

To solve mathematically, rearrange the equation to

$$1.0725^N = \frac{60{,}000 \times 0.0725 + 5000}{10{,}050 \times 0.0725 + 5000} = 1.632$$

We can then solve for N:

$$N = \frac{\ln(1.632)}{\ln(1.0725)} = 7 \text{ years}$$

It will take seven years to save the down payment. We can also solve this problem using the annuity spreadsheet:

	NPER	RATE	PV	PMT	FV	Excel Formula
Given		7.25%	−10,050	−5000	60,000	
Solve for N	7.00					=NPER(0.0725,−5000,−10050,60000)

Rule of 72

Another way to think about the effect of compounding and discounting is to consider how long it will take your money to double given different interest rates. Suppose we want to know how many years it will take for $1 to grow to a future value of $2. We want the number of years, N, to solve

$$FV = \$1 \times (1 + r)^N = \$2$$

If you solve this formula for different interest rates, you will find the following approximation:

Years to double $\approx 72 \div$ (interest rate in percent)

This simple "Rule of 72" is fairly accurate (i.e., within one year of the exact doubling time) for interest rates higher than 2%. For example, if the interest rate is 9%, the doubling time should be about $72 \div 9 = 8$ years. Indeed, $1.09^8 = 1.99$! So, given a 9% interest rate, your money will approximately double every 8 years.

CONCEPT CHECK   1. How do you calculate the cash flow of an annuity?

2. What is the internal rate of return, and how do you calculate it?

3. How do you solve for the number of periods to pay off an annuity?

Summary

1. Timelines are a critical first step in organizing the cash flows in a financial problem.

2. There are three rules of time travel:
   a. Only cash flows that occur at the same point in time can be compared or combined.
   b. To move a cash flow forward in time, you must compound it.
   c. To move a cash flow backward in time, you must discount it.

3. The future value in n years of a cash flow C today is

$$C \times (1 + r)^n \tag{4.1}$$

4. The present value today of a cash flow C received in n years is

$$C \div (1 + r)^n \tag{4.2}$$

5. The present value of a cash flow stream is

$$PV = \sum_{n=0}^{N} \frac{C_n}{(1 + r)^n} \tag{4.3}$$

6. The future value on date n of a cash flow stream with a present value of PV is

$$FV_n = PV \times (1 + r)^n \tag{4.4}$$

7. The NPV of an investment opportunity is $PV(\text{benefits} - \text{costs})$.

8. A perpetuity is a constant cash flow C paid every period, forever. The present value of a perpetuity is

$$\frac{C}{r} \tag{4.5}$$

9. An annuity is a constant cash flow C paid every period for N periods. The present value of an annuity is

$$C \times \frac{1}{r} \left(1 - \frac{1}{(1 + r)^N} \right) \tag{4.7}$$

   The future value of an annuity at the end of the annuity is

$$C \times \frac{1}{r} \left((1 + r)^N - 1 \right) \tag{4.8}$$

10. In a growing perpetuity or annuity, the cash flows grow at a constant rate g each period. The present value of a growing perpetuity is

$$\frac{C}{r - g} \tag{4.9}$$

The present value of a growing annuity is

$$C \times \frac{1}{r-g}\left(1 - \left(\frac{1+g}{1+r}\right)^N\right) \qquad (4.10)$$

11. The annuity and perpetuity formulas can be used to solve for the annuity payments when either the present value or the future value is known. The periodic payment on an N-period loan with principal P and interest rate r is

$$C = \frac{P}{\dfrac{1}{r}\left(1 - \dfrac{1}{(1+r)^N}\right)} \qquad (4.12)$$

12. The internal rate of return (IRR) of an investment opportunity is the interest rate that sets the NPV of the investment opportunity equal to zero.

13. The annuity formulas can be used to solve for the number of periods it takes to save a fixed amount of money.

Key Terms

annuity *p. 98*
annuity spreadsheet *p. 107*
compounding *p. 86*
compound interest *p. 86*
consol *p. 95*
discounting *p. 87*
future value *p. 86*

growing annuity *p. 104*
growing perpetuity *p. 102*
internal rate of return (IRR) *p. 111*
perpetuity *p. 95*
stream of cash flows *p. 84*
timeline *p. 84*
time value of money *p. 86*

Further Reading

The earliest known published work that introduces the ideas in this chapter was in 1202 by the famous Italian mathematician Fibonacci (or Leonardo of Pisa) in Liber Abaci (recently translated into English by Laurence Sigler, *Fibonacci's Liber Abaci, A Translation into Modern English of Leonardo Pisano's Book of Calculation*, New York: Springer-Verlag, 2002). In this book, Fibonacci provides examples demonstrating the rules of time travel for cash flows.

Students who are interested in the early origins of finance and the historical development of the annuity formula will be interested in reading (1) M. Rubinstein, *A History of the Theory of Investments: My Annotated Bibliography* (Hoboken: John Wiley and Sons, 2006) and (2) W. N. Goetzmann and K. G. Rouwenhorst, eds., *Origins of Value: Innovations in the History of Finance* (New York: Oxford University Press, 2005).

The material in this chapter should provide the foundation you need to understand the time value of money. For assistance using Excel, other spreadsheet programs, or financial calculators to compute present values, consult available help files and user manuals for additional information and examples.

Students in the lucky position of having to decide how to receive lottery winnings may consult A. B. Atkins and E. A. Dyl, "The Lotto Jackpot: The Lump Sum versus the Annuity," *Financial Practice and Education* (Fall/Winter 1995): 107–11.

Problems

All problems in this chapter are available in MyFinanceLab. An asterisk (*) indicates problems with a higher level of difficulty.

The Timeline

1. You have just taken out a five-year loan from a bank to buy an engagement ring. The ring costs $5000. You plan to put down $1000 and borrow $4000. You will need to make annual payments of $1000 at the end of each year. Show the timeline of the loan from your perspective. How would the timeline differ if you created it from the bank's perspective?

2. You currently have a four-year-old mortgage outstanding on your house. You make monthly payments of $1500. You have just made a payment. The mortgage has 26 years to go (i.e., it had an original term of 30 years). Show the timeline from your perspective. How would the timeline differ if you created it from the bank's perspective?

The Three Rules of Time Travel

3. Calculate the future value of $2000 in
   a. 5 years at an interest rate of 5% per year.
   b. 10 years at an interest rate of 5% per year.
   c. 5 years at an interest rate of 10% per year.
   d. Why is the amount of interest earned in part (a) less than half the amount of interest earned in part (b)?

4. What is the present value of $10,000 received
   a. 12 years from today when the interest rate is 4% per year?
   b. 20 years from today when the interest rate is 8% per year?
   c. 6 years from today when the interest rate is 2% per year?

5. Your brother has offered to give you either $5000 today or $10,000 in ten years. If the interest rate is 7% per year, which option is preferable?

The Power of Compounding: An Application

6. Your daughter is currently 8 years old. You anticipate that she will be going to college in ten years. You would like to have $100,000 in a savings account to fund her education at that time. If the account promises to pay a fixed interest rate of 3% per year, how much money do you need to put into the account today to ensure that you will have $100,000 in ten years?

7. You are thinking of retiring. Your retirement plan will pay you either $250,000 immediately on retirement or $350,000 five years after the date of your retirement. Which alternative should you choose if the interest rate is
   a. 0% per year?
   b. 8% per year?
   c. 20% per year?

8. Your grandfather put some money in an account for you on the day you were born. You are now 18 years old and are allowed to withdraw the money for the first time. The account currently has $3996 in it and pays an 8% interest rate.
   a. How much money would be in the account if you left the money there until your 25th birthday?
   b. What if you left the money until your 65th birthday?
   c. How much money did your grandfather originally put in the account?

Valuing a Stream
of Cash Flows

EXCEL **9.** You have just received a windfall from an investment you made in a friend's business. He will be paying you $10,000 at the end of this year, $20,000 at the end of the following year, and $30,000 at the end of the year after that (three years from today). The interest rate is 3.5% per year.

    a. What is the present value of your windfall?

    b. What is the future value of your windfall in three years (on the date of the last payment)?

EXCEL **10.** You have a loan outstanding. It requires making three annual payments at the end of the next three years of $1000 each. Your bank has offered to allow you to skip making the next two payments in lieu of making one large payment at the end of the loan's term in three years. If the interest rate on the loan is 5%, what final payment will the bank require you to make so that it is indifferent between the two forms of payment?

The Net Present Value of a
Stream of Cash Flows

EXCEL **11.** You have been offered a unique investment opportunity. If you invest $10,000 today, you will receive $500 one year from now, $1500 two years from now, and $10,000 ten years from now.

    a. What is the NPV of the opportunity if the interest rate is 6% per year? Should you take the opportunity?

    b. What is the NPV of the opportunity if the interest rate is 2% per year? Should you take it now?

EXCEL **12.** Marian Plunket owns her own business and is considering an investment. If she undertakes the investment, it will pay $4000 at the end of each of the next three years. The opportunity requires an initial investment of $1000 plus an additional investment at the end of the second year of $5000. What is the NPV of this opportunity if the interest rate is 2% per year? Should Marian take it?

Perpetuities, Annuities,
and Other Special Cases

13. Your buddy in mechanical engineering has invented a money machine. The main drawback of the machine is that it is slow. It takes one year to manufacture $100. However, once built, the machine will last forever and will require no maintenance. The machine can be built immediately, but it will cost $1000 to build. Your buddy wants to know if he should invest the money to construct it. If the interest rate is 9.5% per year, what should your buddy do?

14. How would your answer to Problem 4.13 change if the machine takes one year to build?

15. The British government has a consol bond outstanding paying £100 per year forever. Assume the current interest rate is 4% per year.

    a. What is the value of the bond immediately after a payment is made?

    b. What is the value of the bond immediately before a payment is made?

16. What is the present value of $1000 paid at the end of each of the next 100 years if the interest rate is 7% per year?

*17. You are head of the Schwartz Family Endowment for the Arts. You have decided to fund an arts school in the San Francisco Bay area in perpetuity. Every five years, you will give the school $1 million. The first payment will occur five years from today. If the interest rate is 8% per year, what is the present value of your gift?

*18. When you purchased your house, you took out a 30-year annual-payment mortgage with an interest rate of 6% per year. The annual payment on the mortgage is $1200. You have just made a payment and have now decided to pay the mortgage off by repaying the outstanding balance. What is the payoff amount if

a. You have lived in the house for 12 years (so there are 18 years left on the mortgage)?

b. You have lived in the house for 20 years (so there are 10 years left on the mortgage)?

c. You have lived in the house for 12 years (so there are 18 years left on the mortgage) and you decide to pay off the mortgage immediately *before* the twelfth payment is due?

EXCEL **19.** Your grandmother has been putting $1000 into a savings account on every birthday since your first (that is, when you turned 1). The account pays an interest rate of 3%. How much money will be in the account on your 18th birthday immediately after your grandmother makes the deposit on that birthday?

EXCEL **20.** A rich relative has bequeathed you a growing perpetuity. The first payment will occur in a year and will be $1000. Each year after that, you will receive a payment on the anniversary of the last payment that is 8% larger than the last payment. This pattern of payments will go on forever. If the interest rate is 12% per year,

a. What is today's value of the bequest?

b. What is the value of the bequest immediately after the first payment is made?

*21. You are thinking of building a new machine that will save you $1000 in the first year. The machine will then begin to wear out so that the savings *decline* at a rate of 2% per year forever. What is the present value of the savings if the interest rate is 5% per year?

22. You work for a pharmaceutical company that has developed a new drug. The patent on the drug will last 17 years. You expect that the drug's profits will be $2 million in its first year and that this amount will grow at a rate of 5% per year for the next 17 years. Once the patent expires, other pharmaceutical companies will be able to produce the same drug and competition will likely drive profits to zero. What is the present value of the new drug if the interest rate is 10% per year?

EXCEL **23.** Your oldest daughter is about to start kindergarten at a private school. Tuition is $10,000 per year, payable at the *beginning* of the school year. You expect to keep your daughter in private school through high school. You expect tuition to increase at a rate of 5% per year over the 13 years of her schooling. What is the present value of the tuition payments if the interest rate is 5% per year?

EXCEL **24.** A rich aunt has promised you $5000 one year from today. In addition, each year after that, she has promised you a payment (on the anniversary of the last payment) that is 5% larger than the last payment. She will continue to show this generosity for 20 years, giving a total of 20 payments. If the interest rate is 5%, what is her promise worth today?

EXCEL ***25.** You are running a hot Internet company. Analysts predict that its earnings will grow at 30% per year for the next five years. After that, as competition increases, earnings growth is expected to slow to 2% per year and continue at that level forever. Your company has just announced earnings of $1,000,000. What is the present value of all future earnings if the interest rate is 8%? (Assume all cash flows occur at the end of the year.)

Solving for Variables
Other Than Present Value
or Future Value

26. You have decided to buy a perpetuity. The bond makes one payment at the end of every year forever and has an interest rate of 5%. If you initially put $1000 into the bond, what is the payment every year?

EXCEL **27.** You are thinking of purchasing a house. The house costs $350,000. You have $50,000 in cash that you can use as a down payment on the house, but you need to borrow the rest of the purchase price. The bank is offering a 30-year mortgage that requires annual payments and has an interest rate of 7% per year. What will your annual payment be if you sign up for this mortgage?

*28. You are thinking about buying a piece of art that costs $50,000. The art dealer is proposing the following deal: He will lend you the money, and you will repay the loan by making the same payment every two years for the next 20 years (i.e., a total of 10 payments). If the interest rate is 4%, how much will you have to pay every two years?

EXCEL ***29.** You would like to buy the house and take the mortgage described in Problem 4.27. You can afford to pay only $23,500 per year. The bank agrees to allow you to pay this amount each year, yet still borrow $300,000. At the end of the mortgage (in 30 years), you must make a *balloon* payment; that is, you must repay the remaining balance on the mortgage. How much will this balloon payment be?

EXCEL **30.** You are saving for retirement. To live comfortably, you decide you will need to save $2 million by the time you are 65. Today is your 30th birthday, and you decide, starting today and continuing on every birthday up to and including your 65th birthday, that you will put the same amount into a savings account. If the interest rate is 5%, how much must you set aside each year to make sure that you will have $2 million in the account on your 65th birthday?

EXCEL ***31.** You realize that the plan in Problem 4.30 has a flaw. Because your income will increase over your lifetime, it would be more realistic to save less now and more later. Instead of putting the same amount aside each year, you decide to let the amount that you set aside grow by 7% per year. Under this plan, how much will you put into the account today? (Recall that you are planning to make the first contribution to the account today.)

32. You have an investment opportunity that requires an initial investment of $5000 today and will pay $6000 in one year. What is the IRR of this opportunity?

33. You are shopping for a car and read the following advertisement in the newspaper: "Own a new Spitfire! No money down. Four annual payments of just $10,000." You have shopped around and know that you can buy a Spitfire for cash for $32,500. What is the interest rate the dealer is advertising (what is the IRR of the loan in the advertisement)? Assume that you must make the annual payments at the end of each year.

34. A local bank is running the following advertisement in the newspaper: "For just $1000 we will pay you $100 forever!" The fine print in the ad says that for a $1000 deposit, the bank will pay $100 every year in perpetuity, starting one year after the deposit is made. What interest rate is the bank advertising (what is the IRR of this investment)?

*35. The Tillamook County Creamery Association manufactures Tillamook Cheddar Cheese. It markets this cheese in four varieties: aged 2 months, 9 months, 15 months, and 2 years. At the shop in the dairy, it sells 2 pounds of each variety for the following prices: $7.95, $9.49, $10.95, and $11.95, respectively. Consider the cheese maker's decision whether to continue to age a particular 2-pound block of cheese. At 2 months, he can either sell the cheese immediately or let it age further. If he sells it now, he will receive $7.95 immediately. If he ages the cheese, he must give up the $7.95 today to receive a higher amount in the future. What is the IRR (expressed in percent per month) of the investment of giving up $79.50 today by choosing to store 20 pounds of cheese that is currently 2 months old and instead selling 10 pounds of this cheese when it has aged 9 months, 6 pounds when it has aged 15 months, and the remaining 4 pounds when it has aged 2 years?

*36. Your grandmother bought an annuity from Rock Solid Life Insurance Company for $200,000 when she retired. In exchange for the $200,000, Rock Solid will pay her $25,000 per year until she dies. The interest rate is 5%. How long must she live after the day she retired to come out ahead (that is, to get more in *value* than what she paid in)?

EXCEL ***37.** You are thinking of making an investment in a new plant. The plant will generate revenues of $1 million per year for as long as you maintain it. You expect that the maintenance cost will start at $50,000 per year and will increase 5% per year thereafter. Assume that all revenue and maintenance costs occur at the end of the year. You intend to run the plant as long as it continues to make a positive cash flow (as long as the cash generated by the plant exceeds the maintenance costs). The plant can be built and become operational immediately. If the plant costs $10 million to build, and the interest rate is 6% per year, should you invest in the plant?

EXCEL *38. You have just turned 30 years old, have just received your MBA, and have accepted your first job. Now you must decide how much money to put into your retirement plan. The plan works as follows: Every dollar in the plan earns 7% per year. You cannot make withdrawals until you retire on your sixty-fifth birthday. After that point, you can make withdrawals as you see fit. You decide that you will plan to live to 100 and work until you turn 65. You estimate that to live comfortably in retirement, you will need $100,000 per year starting at the end of the first year of retirement and ending on your one hundredth birthday. You will contribute the same amount to the plan at the end of every year that you work. How much do you need to contribute each year to fund your retirement?

EXCEL *39. Problem 4.38 is not very realistic because most retirement plans do not allow you to specify a fixed amount to contribute every year. Instead, you are required to specify a fixed percentage of your salary that you want to contribute. Assume that your starting salary is $75,000 per year and it will grow 2% per year until you retire. Assuming everything else stays the same as in Problem 4.38, what percentage of your income do you need to contribute to the plan every year to fund the same retirement income?

Data Case

Assume today is August 1, 2006. Natasha Kingery is 30 years old and has a Bachelor of Science degree in computer science. She is currently employed as a Tier 2 field service representative for a telephony corporation located in Seattle, Washington, and earns $38,000 a year that she anticipates will grow at 3% per year. Natasha hopes to retire at age 65 and has just begun to think about the future.

Natasha has $75,000 that she recently inherited from her aunt. She invested this money in 10-year Treasury Bonds. She is considering whether she should further her education and would use her inheritance to pay for it.[9]

She has investigated a couple of options and is asking for your help as a financial planning intern to determine the financial consequences associated with each option. Natasha has already been accepted to both of these programs, and could start either one soon.

One alternative that Natasha is considering is attaining a certification in network design. This certification would automatically promote her to a Tier 3 field service representative in her company. The base salary for a Tier 3 representative is $10,000 more than what she currently earns and she anticipates that this salary differential will grow at a rate of 3% a year as long as she keeps working. The certification program requires the completion of 20 Web-based courses and a score of 80% or better on an exam at the end of the course work. She has learned that the average amount of time necessary to finish the program is one year. The total cost of the program is $5,000, due when she enrolls in the program. Because she will do all the work for the certification on her own time, Natasha does not expect to lose any income during the certification.

Another option is going back to school for an MBA degree. With an MBA degree, Natasha expects to be promoted to a managerial position in her current firm. The managerial position

---

9. If Natasha lacked the cash to pay for her tuition up front, she could borrow the money. More intriguingly, she could sell a fraction of her future earnings, an idea that has received attention from researchers and entrepreneurs; see Miguel Palacios, *Investing in Human Capital: A Capital Markets Approach to Student Funding*, Cambridge University Press, 2004.

pays $20,000 a year more than her current position. She expects that this salary differential will also grow at a rate of 3% per year for as long as she keeps working. The evening program, which will take three years to complete, costs $25,000 per year, due at the beginning of each of her three years in school. Because she will attend classes in the evening, Natasha doesn't expect to lose any income while she is earning her MBA if she chooses to undertake the MBA.

1. Determine the interest rate she is currently earning on her inheritance by going to Yahoo! Finance (http://finance.yahoo.com) and clicking on the 10-year bond link in the market summary. Then go to "Historical Prices" and enter the appropriate date, August 1, 2006, to obtain the closing yield or interest rate that she is earning. Use this interest rate as the discount rate for the remainder of this problem.

2. Create a timeline in Excel for her current situation, as well as the certification program and MBA degree options, using the following assumptions:
   - Salaries for the year are paid only once, at the end of the year.
   - The salary increase becomes effective immediately upon graduating from the MBA program or being certified. That is, because the increases become effective immediately but salaries are paid at the end of the year, the first salary increase will be paid exactly one year after graduation or certification.

3. Calculate the present value of the salary differential for completing the certification program. Subtract the cost of the program to get the NPV of undertaking the certification program.

4. Calculate the present value of the salary differential for completing the MBA degree. Calculate the present value of the cost of the MBA program. Based on your calculations, determine the NPV of undertaking the MBA.

5. Based on your answers to Questions 3 and 4, what advice would you give to Natasha? What if the two programs are mutually exclusive?—if Natasha undetakes one of the programs there is no further benefit to undertaking the other program. Would your advice change?

Interest Rates

In Chapter 4, we explored the mechanics of computing present values and future values given a market interest rate. But how do we determine that interest rate? In practice, interest is paid and interest rates are quoted in different ways. For example, in mid-2006, ING Direct offered savings accounts with an interest rate of 5.25% paid at the end of one year, while New Century Bank offered an interest rate of 5.12%, but with the interest paid on a daily basis. Interest rates can also differ depending on the investment horizon. In January 2004, investors earned only about 1% on one-year risk-free investments, but could earn more than 5% on fifteen-year risk-free investments. Interest rates can also vary due to risk or tax consequences. For example, the U.S. government is able to borrow at a much lower interest rate than General Motors Corporation.

In this chapter, we consider the factors that affect interest rates and discuss how to determine the appropriate discount rate for a set of cash flows. We begin by looking at the way interest is paid and interest rates are quoted, and we show how to calculate the effective interest paid in one year given different quoting conventions. We then consider some of the main determinants of interest rates—namely, inflation and government policy. Because interest rates tend to change over time, investors will demand different interest rates for different investment horizons based on their expectations. Finally, we examine the role of risk in determining interest rates and show how to adjust interest rates to determine the effective amount received (or paid) after accounting for taxes.

5.1 Interest Rate Quotes and Adjustments

To determine the appropriate discount rate from an interest rate, we need to understand the ways that interest rates are quoted. Also, because interest rates may be quoted for different time intervals, such as monthly, semiannual, or annual, it is often necessary to adjust the interest rate to a time period that matches that of our cash flows. We explore these mechanics of interest rates in this section.

The Effective Annual Rate

Interest rates are often stated as an **effective annual rate (EAR)**, which indicates the total amount of interest that will be earned at the end of one year.[1] This method of quoting the interest rate is the one we have used thus far in this textbook, and in Chapter 4 we used the EAR as the discount rate r in our time value of money calculations. For example, with an EAR of 5%, a $100,000 investment grows to

$$\$100,000 \times (1 + r) = \$100,000 \times (1.05) = \$105,000$$

in one year. After two years it will grow to

$$\$100,000 \times (1 + r)^2 = \$100,000 \times (1.05)^2 = \$110,250$$

Adjusting the Discount Rate to Different Time Periods

The preceding example shows that earning an effective annual rate of 5% for two years is equivalent to earning 10.25% in total interest over the entire period:

$$\$100,000 \times (1.05)^2 = \$100,000 \times 1.1025 = \$110,250$$

In general, by raising the interest rate factor $(1 + r)$ to the appropriate power, we can compute an equivalent interest rate for a longer time period.

We can use the same method to find the equivalent interest rate for periods shorter than one year. In this case, we raise the interest rate factor $(1 + r)$ to the appropriate fractional power. For example, earning 5% interest in one year is equivalent to receiving

$$(1 + r)^{0.5} = (1.05)^{0.5} = \$1.0247$$

for each $1 invested every six months. That is, a 5% effective annual rate is equivalent to an interest rate of approximately 2.47% earned every six months. We can verify this result by computing the interest we would earn in one year by investing for two six-month periods at this rate:

$$(1 + r)^2 = (1.0247)^2 = \$1.05$$

In general, we can convert a discount rate of r for one period to an equivalent discount rate for n periods using the following formula:

$$\text{Equivalent } n\text{-Period Discount Rate} = (1 + r)^n - 1 \qquad (5.1)$$

In this formula, n can be larger than 1 (to compute a rate over more than one period) or smaller than 1 (to compute a rate over a fraction of a period). When computing present

---

1. The effective annual rate is often referred to as the *effective annual yield* (EAY) or the *annual percentage yield* (APY).

or future values, it is convenient to adjust the discount rate to match the time period of the cash flows. This adjustment is *necessary* to apply the perpetuity or annuity formulas, as in the following example.

EXAMPLE 5.1

Valuing Monthly Cash Flows

Problem

Suppose your bank account pays interest monthly with an effective annual rate of 6%. What amount of interest will you earn each month? If you have no money in the bank today, how much will you need to save at the end of each month to accumulate $100,000 in 10 years?

Solution

From Eq. 5.1, a 6% EAR is equivalent to earning $(1.06)^{1/12} - 1 = 0.4868\%$ per month. To determine the amount to save each month to reach the goal of $100,000 in 10 years, we must determine the amount C of the monthly payment that will have a future value of $100,000 in 10 years, given an interest rate of 0.4868% per month. We can use the annuity formula from Chapter 4 to solve this problem if we write the timeline for our savings plan using *monthly* periods:

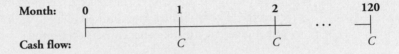

That is, we can view the savings plan as a monthly annuity with $10 \times 12 = 120$ monthly payments. From the future value of an annuity formula, Eq. 4.8:

$$FV(\text{annuity}) = C \times \frac{1}{r}[(1 + r)^n - 1]$$

We can solve for the payment C using the equivalent monthly interest rate $r = 0.4868\%$, and $n = 120$ months:

$$C = \frac{FV(\text{annuity})}{\frac{1}{r}[(1 + r)^n - 1]} = \frac{\$100,000}{\frac{1}{0.004868}[(1.004868)^{120} - 1]} = \$615.47 \text{ per month}$$

We can also compute this result using the annuity spreadsheet:

	NPER	RATE	PV	PMT	FV	Excel Formula
Given	120	0.4868%	0		100,000	
Solve for PMT				−615.47		=PMT(0.004868,120,0,100000)

Thus, if we save $615.47 per month and we earn interest monthly at an effective annual rate of 6%, we will have $100,000 in 10 years.

Annual Percentage Rates

Banks also quote interest rates in terms of an **annual percentage rate (APR)**, which indicates the amount of **simple interest** earned in one year, that is, the amount of interest earned *without* the effect of compounding. Because it does not include the effect of compounding, the APR quote is typically less than the actual amount of interest that you will earn. To compute the actual amount that you will earn in one year, the APR must first be converted to an effective annual rate.

For example, suppose Granite Bank advertises savings accounts with an interest rate of "6% APR with monthly compounding." In this case, you will earn 6% / 12 = 0.5% every month. So an APR with monthly compounding is actually a way of quoting a *monthly* interest rate, rather than an annual interest rate. Because the interest compounds each month, you will earn

$$\$1 \times (1.005)^{12} = \$1.061678$$

at the end of one year, for an effective annual rate of 6.1678%. The 6.1678% that you earn on your deposit is higher than the quoted 6% APR due to compounding: In later months, you earn interest on the interest paid in earlier months.

It is important to remember that because the APR does not reflect the true amount you will earn over one year, *the APR itself cannot be used as a discount rate.* Instead, the APR with k compounding periods is a way of quoting the actual interest earned each compounding period:

$$\text{Interest Rate per Compounding Period} = \frac{\text{APR}}{k \, \text{periods / year}} \tag{5.2}$$

Once we have computed the interest earned per compounding period from Eq. 5.2, we can compute the equivalent interest rate for any other time interval using Eq. 5.1. Thus the effective annual rate corresponding to an APR with k compounding periods per year is given by the following conversion formula:

Converting an APR to an EAR

$$1 + EAR = \left(1 + \frac{APR}{k}\right)^k \tag{5.3}$$

Table 5.1 shows the effective annual rates that correspond to an APR of 6% with different compounding intervals. The EAR increases with the frequency of compounding because of the ability to earn interest on interest sooner. Investments can compound even more frequently than daily. In principle, the compounding interval could be hourly or every second. In the limit we approach the idea of **continuous compounding**, in which we compound the interest every instant.[2] As a practical matter, compounding more frequently than daily has a negligible impact on the effective annual rate and is rarely observed.

TABLE 5.1	Effective Annual Rates for a 6% APR with Different Compounding Periods
Compounding Interval	**Effective Annual Rate**
Annual	$(1 + 0.06 / 1)^1 - 1 = 6\%$
Semiannual	$(1 + 0.06 / 2)^2 - 1 = 6.09\%$
Monthly	$(1 + 0.06 / 12)^{12} - 1 = 6.1678\%$
Daily	$(1 + 0.06 / 365)^{365} - 1 = 6.1831\%$

---

2. A 6% APR with continuous compounding results in an EAR of approximately 6.1837%, which is almost the same as daily compounding. See the appendix for further discussion of continuous compounding.

When working with APRs, we must first convert the APR to a discount rate per compounding interval using Eq. 5.2, or to an EAR using Eq. 5.3, before evaluating the present or future value of a set of cash flows.

EXAMPLE 5.2

Converting the APR to a Discount Rate

Problem

Your firm is purchasing a new telephone system, which will last for four years. You can purchase the system for an upfront cost of $150,000, or you can lease the system from the manufacturer for $4000 paid at the end of each month.[3] Your firm can borrow at an interest rate of 5% APR with semiannual compounding. Should you purchase the system outright or pay $4000 per month?

Solution

The cost of leasing the system is a 48-month annuity of $4000 per month:

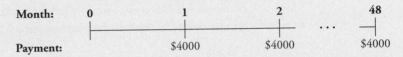

Month:	0	1	2		48
Payment:		$4000	$4000	...	$4000

We can compute the present value of the lease cash flows using the annuity formula, but first we need to compute the discount rate that corresponds to a period length of one month. To do so, we convert the borrowing cost of 5% APR with semiannual compounding to a monthly discount rate. Using Eq. 5.2, the APR corresponds to a six-month discount rate of 5% / 2 = 2.5%. To convert a six-month discount rate into a one-month discount rate, we compound the six-month rate by 1/6 using Eq. 5.1:

$$(1.025)^{1/6} - 1 = 0.4124\% \text{ per month}$$

(Alternatively, we could first use Eq. 5.3 to convert the APR to an EAR: $1 + EAR = (1 + 0.05 / 2)^2 = 1.050625$. Then we can convert the EAR to a monthly rate using Eq. 5.1: $(1.050625)^{1/12} - 1 = 0.4124\%$ per month.)

Given this discount rate, we can use the annuity formula (Eq. 4.7) to compute the present value of the monthly payments:

$$PV = 4000 \times \frac{1}{0.004124} \left(1 - \frac{1}{1.004124^{48}} \right) = \$173,867$$

We can also use the annuity spreadsheet:

	NPER	RATE	PV	PMT	FV	Excel Formula
Given	48	0.4124%		−4,000	0	
Solve for PV			173,867			=PV(0.004124,48,−4000,0)

Thus paying $4000 per month for 48 months is equivalent to paying a present value of $173,867 today. This cost is $173,867 − $150,000 = $23,867 higher than the cost of purchasing the system, so it is better to pay $150,000 for the system rather than lease it. One way to interpret this result is as follows: At a 5% APR with semiannual compounding, by promising to repay $4000 per month your firm can borrow $173,867 today. With this loan it could purchase the phone system and have an additional $23,867 to use for other purposes.

---

3. In addition to these cash flows, there may be tax and accounting considerations when comparing a purchase with a lease. We ignore these complications in this example, and consider leases in detail in Chapter 25.

Application: Discount Rates and Loans

Now that we have explained how to compute the discount rate from an interest rate quote, let's apply the concept to solve two common financial problems: calculating a loan payment and calculating the remaining balance on a loan.

Computing Loan Payments.   To calculate a loan payment, we first compute the discount rate from the quoted interest rate of the loan, and then equate the outstanding loan balance with the present value of the loan payments and solve for the loan payment.

Many loans, such as mortgages and car loans, have monthly payments and are quoted in terms of an APR with monthly compounding. These types of loans are **amortizing loans**, which means that each month you pay interest on the loan plus some part of the loan balance. Each monthly payment is the same, and the loan is fully repaid with the final payment. Typical terms for a new car loan might be "6.75% APR for 60 months." When the compounding interval for the APR is not stated explicitly, it is equal to the interval between the payments, or one month in this case. Thus this quote means that the loan will be repaid with 60 equal monthly payments, computed using a 6.75% APR with monthly compounding. Consider the timeline for a $30,000 car loan with these terms:

Month:	0	1	2		60
Cash flow:	$30,000	$-C$	$-C$	$\cdots$	$-C$

The payment, C, is set so that the present value of the cash flows, evaluated using the loan interest rate, equals the original principal amount of $30,000. In this case, the 6.75% APR with monthly compounding corresponds to a one-month discount rate of 6.75% / 12 = 0.5625%. Because the loan payments are an annuity, we can use Eq. 4.12 to find C:

$$C = \frac{P}{\frac{1}{r}\left(1 - \frac{1}{(1 + r)^{N}}\right)} = \frac{30,000}{\frac{1}{0.005625}\left(1 - \frac{1}{(1 + 0.005625)^{60}}\right)} = \$590.50$$

Alternatively, we can solve for the payment C using the annuity spreadsheet:

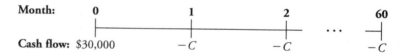

	NPER	RATE	PV	PMT	FV	Excel Formula
Given	60	0.5625%	30,000		0	
Solve for PMT				−590.50		=PMT(0.005625,60,30000,0)

Computing the Outstanding Loan Balance.   The outstanding balance on a loan, also called the outstanding principal, is equal to the present value of the remaining future loan payments, again evaluated using the loan interest rate. We calculate the outstanding loan balance by determining the present value of the remaining loan payments using the loan rate as the discount rate.

EXAMPLE 5.3

Computing the Outstanding Loan Balance

Problem

Ten years ago your firm borrowed $3 million to purchase an office building using a loan with a 7.80% APR and monthly payments for 30 years. How much do you owe on the loan today? How much interest was paid on the loan in the past year?

Solution

The first step is to solve for the monthly loan payment. Here is the timeline (in months):

An APR of 7.80% with monthly compounding is equivalent to 7.80% / 12 = 0.65% per month. The monthly payment is then

$$C = \frac{P}{\frac{1}{r}\left(1 - \frac{1}{(1 + r)^n}\right)} = \frac{3,000,000}{\frac{1}{0.0065}\left(1 - \frac{1}{(1.0065)^{360}}\right)} - \$21,596$$

The remaining balance on the loan is the present value of the remaining 20 years, or 240 months, of payments:

$$\text{Balance after 10 years} = \$21,596 \times \frac{1}{0.0065}\left(1 - \frac{1}{1.0065^{240}}\right) = \$2,620,759$$

Thus, after 10 years, you owe $2,620,759 on the loan.

During the past year, your firm made total payments of $21,596 × 12 = $259,152 on the loan. To determine how much of that amount was interest, it is easiest to first determine the amount that was used to repay the principal. Your loan balance one year ago, with 21 years (252 months) remaining, was

$$\text{Balance after 9 years} = \$21,596 \times \frac{1}{0.0065}\left(1 - \frac{1}{1.0065^{252}}\right) = \$2,673,248$$

Therefore, the balance declined by $2,673,248 − $2,620,759 = $52,489 in the past year. Of the total payments made, $52,489 was used to repay the principal and the remaining $259,152 − $52,489 = $206,663 was used to pay interest.

CONCEPT CHECK   1. What is the difference between an EAR and an APR quote?

2. Why can't the APR be used as a discount rate?

5.2 The Determinants of Interest Rates

How are interest rates determined? Fundamentally, interest rates are determined in the market based on individuals' willingness to borrow and lend. In this section, we look at some of the factors that may influence interest rates, such as inflation, government policy, and expectations of future growth.

Inflation and Real Versus Nominal Rates

The interest rates that are quoted by banks and other financial institutions, and that we have used for discounting cash flows, are **nominal interest rates**, which indicate the rate at which your money will grow if invested for a certain period. Of course, if prices in the economy are also growing due to inflation, the nominal interest rate does not represent the increase in purchasing power that will result from investing. The rate of growth of your purchasing power, after adjusting for inflation, is determined by the **real interest rate**, which we denote by r_r. If r is the nominal interest rate and i is the rate of inflation, we can calculate the rate of growth of purchasing power as follows:

$$\text{Growth in Purchasing Power} = 1 + r_r = \frac{1 + r}{1 + i} = \frac{\text{Growth of Money}}{\text{Growth of Prices}} \quad (5.4)$$

We can rearrange Eq. 5.4 to find the following formula for the real interest rate, together with a convenient approximation for the real interest rate when inflation rates are low:

The Real Interest Rate

$$r_r = \frac{r - i}{1 + i} \approx r - i \quad (5.5)$$

That is, the real interest rate is approximately equal to the nominal interest rate less the rate of inflation.[4]

EXAMPLE 5.4

Calculating the Real Interest Rate

Problem

In the year 2000, short-term U.S. government bond rates were about 5.8% and the rate of inflation was about 3.4%. In 2003, interest rates were about 1% and inflation was about 1.9%. What was the real interest rate in 2000 and 2003?

Solution

Using Eq. 5.5, the real interest rate in 2000 was $(5.8\% - 3.4\%) / (1.034) = 2.32\%$ (which is approximately equal to the difference between the nominal rate and inflation: $5.8\% - 3.4\% = 2.4\%$). In 2003, the real interest rate was $(1\% - 1.9\%) / (1.019) = -0.88\%$. Note that the real interest rate was negative in 2003, indicating that interest rates were insufficient to keep up with inflation: Investors in U.S. government bonds were able to buy less at the end of the year than they could have purchased at the start of the year.

Figure 5.1 shows the history of nominal interest rates and inflation rates in the United States since 1955. Note that the nominal interest rate tends to move with inflation. Intuitively, individuals' willingness to save will depend on the growth in purchasing power they can expect (given by the real interest rate). Thus, when the inflation rate is high, a higher nominal interest rate is needed to induce individuals to save.

Investment and Interest Rate Policy

Interest rates affect not only individuals' propensity to save, but also firms' incentive to raise capital and invest. Consider a risk-free investment opportunity that requires an upfront investment of $10 million and generates a cash flow of $3 million per year for four years. If the risk-free interest rate is 5%, this investment has an NPV of

$$NPV = -10 + \frac{3}{1.05} + \frac{3}{1.05^2} + \frac{3}{1.05^3} + \frac{3}{1.05^4} = \$0.638 \text{ million}$$

---

4. The real interest rate should not be used as a discount rate for future cash flows. It can be used as a discount rate only if the cash flows are not the expected cash flows that will be paid, but are the equivalent cash flows before adjusting them for growth due to inflation (in that case, we say the cash flows are in *real terms*). This approach is error prone, however, so throughout this book we will always forecast cash flows including any growth due to inflation, and discount using nominal interest rates.

U.S. Interest Rates and Inflation Rates, 1955–2005

Interest rates are average three-month Treasury bill rates and inflation rates are based on annual increases in the U.S. Bureau of Labor Statistics' consumer price index. Note that interest rates tend to be high when inflation is high.

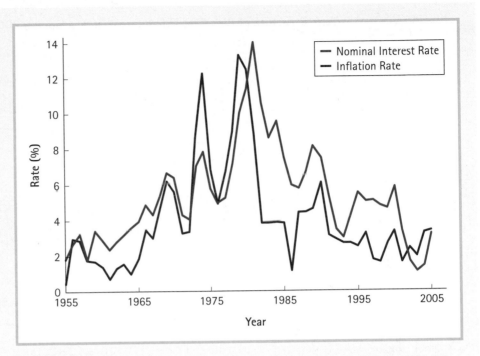

If the interest rate is 9%, the NPV falls to

$$NPV = -10 + \frac{3}{1.09} + \frac{3}{1.09^2} + \frac{3}{1.09^3} + \frac{3}{1.09^4} = -\$0.281 \text{ million}$$

and the investment is no longer profitable. The reason, of course, is that we are discounting the positive cash flows at a higher rate, which reduces their present value. The cost of $10 million occurs today, however, so its present value is independent of the discount rate.

More generally, when the costs of an investment precede the benefits, an increase in the interest rate will decrease the investment's NPV. All else equal, higher interest rates will therefore tend to shrink the set of positive-NPV investments available to firms. The Federal Reserve in the United States and central banks in other countries use this relationship between interest rates and investment incentives when trying to guide the economy. They can lower interest rates to stimulate investment if the economy is slowing, and they can raise interest rates to reduce investment if the economy is "overheating" and inflation is on the rise.

The Yield Curve and Discount Rates

You may have noticed that the interest rates that banks offer on investments or charge on loans depend on the horizon, or *term*, of the investment or loan. The relationship between the investment term and the interest rate is called the **term structure** of interest rates. We can plot this relationship on a graph called the **yield curve**. Figure 5.2 shows the term structure and corresponding yield curve of risk-free U.S. interest rates that was available to investors in January of 2004, 2005, and 2006. In each case, note that the interest rate depends on the horizon, and that the difference between short-term and long-term interest rates was especially pronounced in 2004.

FIGURE 5.2   **Term Structure of Risk-Free U.S. Interest Rates, January 2004, 2005, and 2006**

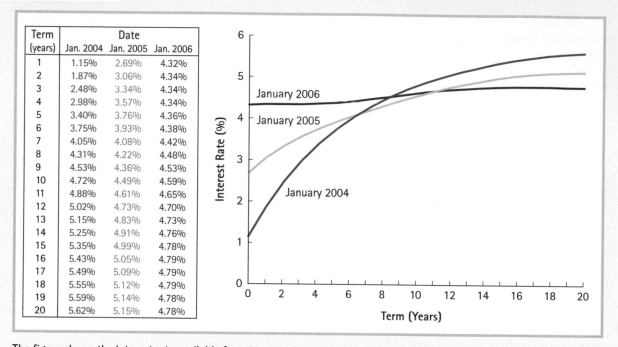

Term (years)	Date		
	Jan. 2004	Jan. 2005	Jan. 2006
1	1.15%	2.69%	4.32%
2	1.87%	3.06%	4.34%
3	2.48%	3.34%	4.34%
4	2.98%	3.57%	4.34%
5	3.40%	3.76%	4.36%
6	3.75%	3.93%	4.38%
7	4.05%	4.08%	4.42%
8	4.31%	4.22%	4.48%
9	4.53%	4.36%	4.53%
10	4.72%	4.49%	4.59%
11	4.88%	4.61%	4.65%
12	5.02%	4.73%	4.70%
13	5.15%	4.83%	4.73%
14	5.25%	4.91%	4.76%
15	5.35%	4.99%	4.78%
16	5.43%	5.05%	4.79%
17	5.49%	5.09%	4.79%
18	5.55%	5.12%	4.79%
19	5.59%	5.14%	4.78%
20	5.62%	5.15%	4.78%

The figure shows the interest rate available from investing in risk-free U.S. Treasury securities with different investment terms. In each case, the interest rates differ depending on the horizon. (Data from U.S. Treasury STRIPS.)

We can use the term structure to compute the present and future values of a risk-free cash flow over different investment horizons. For example, $100 invested for one year at the one-year interest rate in January 2004 would grow to a future value of

$$\$100 \times 1.0115 = \$101.15$$

at the end of one year, and $100 invested for ten years at the ten-year interest rate in January 2004 would grow to[5]

$$\$100 \times (1.0472)^{10} = \$158.60$$

The same logic can be applied when computing the present value of cash flows with different maturities. A risk-free cash flow received in two years should be discounted at the two-year interest rate, and a cash flow received in ten years should be discounted at the ten-year interest rate. In general, a risk-free cash flow of C_n received in n years has present value

$$PV = \frac{C_n}{(1 + r_n)^n} \tag{5.6}$$

where r_n is the risk-free interest rate for an n-year term. In other words, when computing a present value we must match the term of the cash flow and term of the discount rate.

---

5. We could also invest for ten years by investing at the one-year interest rate for ten years in a row. However, because we do not know what future interest rates will be, our ultimate payoff would not be risk free.

Combining Eq. 5.6 for cash flows in different years leads to the general formula for the present value of a cash flow stream:

Present Value of a Cash Flow Stream Using a Term Structure of Discount Rates

$$PV = \frac{C_1}{1 + r_1} + \frac{C_2}{(1 + r_2)^2} + \cdots + \frac{C_N}{(1 + r_N)^N} = \sum_{n=1}^{N} \frac{C_n}{(1 + r_n)^n} \quad (5.7)$$

Note the difference between Eq. 5.7 and Eq. 4.3. Here, we use a different discount rate for each cash flow, based on the rate from the yield curve with the same term. When the yield curve is relatively flat, as it was in January 2006, this distinction is relatively minor and is often ignored by discounting using a single "average" interest rate r. But when short-term and long-term interest rates vary widely, as they did in January 2004, Eq. 5.7 should be used.

Warning: All of our shortcuts for computing present values (annuity and perpetuity formulas, the annuity spreadsheet) are based on discounting all of the cash flows *at the same rate*. They *cannot* be used in situations in which cash flows need to be discounted at different rates.

| EXAMPLE 5.5 | **Using the Term Structure to Compute Present Values** |

Problem

Compute the present value of a risk-free five-year annuity of $1000 per year, given the yield curve for January 2005 in Figure 5.2.

Solution

To compute the present value, we discount each cash flow by the corresponding interest rate:

$$PV = \frac{1000}{1.0269} + \frac{1000}{1.0306^2} + \frac{1000}{1.0334^3} + \frac{1000}{1.0357^4} + \frac{1000}{1.0376^5} = \$4522$$

Note that we cannot use the annuity formula here because the discount rates differ for each cash flow.

COMMON MISTAKE   **Using the Annuity Formula When Discount Rates Vary**

When computing the present value of an annuity, a common mistake is to use the annuity formula with a single interest rate even though interest rates vary with the investment horizon. For example, we *cannot* compute the present value of the five-year annuity in Example 5.5 using the five-year interest rate from January 2005:

$$PV \neq \$1000 \times \frac{1}{0.0376} \left(1 - \frac{1}{1.0376^5}\right) = \$4482$$

If we want to find the single interest rate that we could use to value the annuity, we must first compute the present value of the annuity using Eq. 5.7 and then solve for its IRR. For the annuity in Example 5.5, we use the annuity spreadsheet below to find its IRR of 3.45%. The IRR of the annuity is always between the highest and lowest discount rates used to calculate its present value, as is the case in this example.

	NPER	RATE	PV	PMT	FV	Excel Formula
Given	5		−4,522	1,000	0	
Solve for Rate		3.45%				=RATE(5,1000,−4522,0)

The Yield Curve and the Economy

As Figure 5.3 illustrates, the yield curve changes over time. Sometimes, short-term rates are close to long-term rates, and at other times they may be very different. What accounts for the changing shape of the yield curve?

The Federal Reserve determines very short-term interest rates through its influence on the **federal funds rate**, which is the rate at which banks can borrow cash reserves on an overnight basis. All other interest rates on the yield curve are set in the market and are adjusted until the supply of lending matches the demand for borrowing at each loan term. As we shall see in a moment, expectations of future interest rate changes have a major effect on investors' willingness to lend or borrow for longer terms and, therefore, on the shape of the yield curve.

Suppose short-term interest rates are equal to long-term interest rates. If interest rates are expected to rise in the future, investors would not want to make long-term investments. Instead, they could do better by investing on a short-term basis and then reinvesting after interest rates rose. Thus, if interest rates are expected to rise, long-term interest rates will tend to be higher than short-term rates to attract investors.

Similarly, if interest rates are expected to fall in the future, then borrowers would not wish to borrow at long-term rates that are equal to short-term rates. They would do better

FIGURE 5.3	Short-Term Versus Long-Term U.S. Interest Rates and Recessions

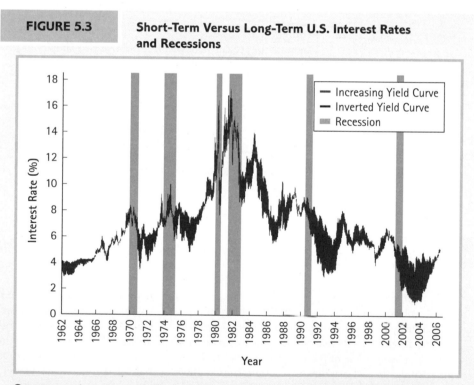

One-year and ten-year U.S. Treasury rates are plotted, with the spread between them shaded in blue if the shape of the yield curve is increasing (the one-year rate is below the ten-year rate) and in red if the yield curve is inverted (the one-year rate exceeds the ten-year rate). Gray bars show the dates of U.S. recessions as determined by the National Bureau of Economic Research. Note that inverted yield curves tend to precede recessions . In recessions, interest rates tend to fall, with short-term rates dropping further. As a result, the yield curve tends to be steep coming out of a recession.

by borrowing on a short-term basis, and then taking out a new loan after rates fall. So, if interest rates are expected to fall, long-term rates will tend to be lower than short-term rates to attract borrowers.

These arguments imply that the shape of the yield curve will be strongly influenced by interest rate expectations. A sharply increasing (*steep*) yield curve, with long-term rates much higher than short-term rates, generally indicates that interest rates are expected to rise in the future. A decreasing (*inverted*) yield curve, with long-term rates lower than short-term rates, generally signals an expected decline in future interest rates. Because interest rates tend to drop in response to a slowdown in the economy, an inverted yield curve is often interpreted as a negative forecast for economic growth. Indeed, as Figure 5.3 illustrates, each of the last six recessions in the United States was preceded by a period in which the yield curve was inverted. Conversely, the yield curve tends to be steep as the economy comes out of a recession and interest rates are expected to rise.[6]

Clearly, the yield curve provides extremely important information for a business manager. In addition to specifying the discount rates for risk-free cash flows that occur at different horizons, it is also a potential leading indicator of future economic growth.

EXAMPLE 5.6

Comparing Short- and Long-Term Interest Rates

Problem

Suppose the current one-year interest rate is 1%. If it is known with certainty that the one-year interest rate will be 2% next year and 4% the following year, what will the interest rates r_1, r_2, and r_3 of the yield curve be today? Is the yield curve flat, increasing, or inverted?

Solution

We are told already that the one-year rate $r_1 = 1\%$. To find the two-year rate, note that if we invest $1 for one year at the current one-year rate and then reinvest next year at the new one-year rate, after two years we will earn

$$\$1 \times (1.01) \times (1.02) = \$1.0302$$

We should earn the same payoff if we invest for two years at the current two-year rate r_2:

$$\$1 \times (1 + r_2)^2 = \$1.0302$$

Otherwise, there would be an arbitrage opportunity: If investing at the two-year rate led to a higher payoff, investors could invest for two years and borrow at the one-year rate. If investing at the two-year rate led to a lower payoff, investors could invest at the one-year rate and borrow at the two-year rate.

Solving for r_2, we find that

$$r_2 = (1.0302)^{1/2} - 1 = 1.499\%$$

Similarly, investing for three years at the one-year rates should have the same payoff as investing at the current three-year rate:

$$(1.01) \times (1.02) \times (1.04) = 1.0714 = (1 + r_3)^3$$

We can solve for $r_3 = (1.0714)^{1/3} - 1 = 2.326\%$. Therefore, the current yield curve has $r_1 = 1\%$, $r_2 = 1.499\%$, and $r_3 = 2.326\%$. The yield curve is increasing as a result of the anticipated higher interest rates in the future.

---

6. Other factors besides interest rate expectations—most notably risk—can have an impact on the shape of the yield curve. See Chapter 8, pages 231–233, for further discussion.

1. What is the difference between a nominal and real interest rate?

2. How are interest rates and the level of investment made by businesses related?

5.3 Risk and Taxes

In this section, we discuss two other factors that are important when evaluating interest rates: risk and taxes.

Risk and Interest Rates

We have already seen that interest rates vary with the investment horizon. Interest rates also vary based on the identity of the borrower. For example, Table 5.2 lists the interest rates paid by a number of different borrowers in mid-2006 for a five-year loan.

Why do these interest rates vary so widely? The lowest interest rate is the rate paid on U.S. Treasury notes. U.S. Treasury securities are widely regarded to be risk-free because there is virtually no chance the government will fail to pay the interest and default on these bonds. Thus, when we refer to the "risk-free interest rate," we mean the rate on U.S. Treasuries.

All other borrowers have some risk of default. For these loans, the stated interest rate is the *maximum* amount that investors will receive. Investors may receive less if the company has financial difficulties and is unable to fully repay the loan. To compensate for the risk that they will receive less if the firm defaults, investors demand a higher interest rate than the rate on U.S. Treasuries. The difference between the interest rate of the loan and the Treasury rate will depend on investors' assessment of the likelihood that the firm will default.

Later in the textbook we will develop tools to evaluate the risk of different investments and determine the interest rate or discount rate that appropriately compensates investors for the level of risk they are taking. For now, we should remember that when discounting future cash flows, it is important to use a discount rate that matches both the horizon and the risk of the cash flows. Specifically, *the right discount rate for a cash flow is the rate of return available in the market on other investments of comparable risk and term.*

TABLE 5.2	Interest Rates on Five-Year Loans for Various Borrowers, June 2006

Borrower	Interest Rate
U.S. government (Treasury Notes)	4.94%
J. P. Morgan Chase & Co.	5.44%
Abbott Laboratories	5.45%
Time Warner	5.86%
RadioShack Corp.	6.60%
General Motors Acceptance Corp.	8.22%
Goodyear Tire and Rubber Co.	8.50%

EXAMPLE 5.7	**Discounting Risky Cash Flows**

Problem

Suppose the U.S. government owes your firm $1000, to be paid in five years. Based on the interest rates in Table 5.2, what is the present value of this cash flow? Suppose instead Goodyear Tire and Rubber Company owes your firm $1000. Estimate the present value in this case.

Solution

Assuming we can regard the government's obligation as risk free (there is no chance you won't be paid), then we discount the cash flow using the risk-free interest rate of 4.94%:

$$PV = \$1000 \div (1.0494)^5 = \$785.77$$

The obligation from Goodyear is not risk-free. There is no guarantee that Goodyear will not have financial difficulties and fail to pay the $1000. Because the risk of this obligation is likely to be comparable to the five-year loan quoted in Table 5.2, the 8.50% interest rate of the loan is a more appropriate discount rate to use to compute the present value in this case:

$$PV = \$1000 \div (1.0850)^5 = \$665.05$$

Note the substantially lower present value in this case, due to the risk of default.

After-Tax Interest Rates

If the cash flows from an investment are taxed, the actual cash flow that the investor will get to keep will be reduced by the amount of the tax payments. We will discuss the taxation of corporate investments in detail in later chapters. Here, we consider the effect of taxes on the interest earned on savings (or paid on borrowing). Taxes reduce the amount of interest the investor can keep, and we refer to this reduced amount as the **after-tax interest rate**.

Consider an investment that pays 8% interest (EAR) for one year. If you invest $100 at the start of the year, you will earn 8% × $100 = $8 in interest at year-end. This interest may be taxable as income.[7] If you are in a 40% tax bracket, you will owe

$$(40\% \text{ income tax rate}) \times (\$8 \text{ interest}) = \$3.20 \text{ tax liability}$$

Thus you will receive only $8 − $3.20 = $4.80 after paying taxes. This amount is equivalent to earning 4.80% interest and not paying any taxes, so the after-tax interest rate is 4.80%.

In general, if the interest rate is r and the tax rate is τ, then for each $1 invested you will earn interest equal to r and owe tax of $\tau \times r$ on the interest. The equivalent after-tax interest rate is therefore

After-Tax Interest Rate

$$r - (\tau \times r) = r(1 - \tau) \tag{5.8}$$

Applying this formula to our previous example of an 8% interest rate and a 40% tax rate, we find the interest rate is 8% × (1 − 0.40) = 4.80% after taxes.

---

7. In the United States, interest income for individuals is taxable as income unless the investment is held in a tax-sheltered retirement account or the investment is from tax-exempt securities (such as municipal bonds). Interest from U.S. Treasury securities is exempt from state and local taxes. Interest income earned by a corporation is also taxed at the corporate tax rate.

The same calculation can be applied to loans. In some cases, the interest on loans is tax deductible.[8] In that case, the cost of paying interest on the loan is offset by the benefit of the tax deduction. The net effect is that when interest on a loan is tax deductible, the effective after-tax interest rate is $r(1 - \tau)$. In other words, the ability to deduct the interest expense lowers the effective after-tax interest rate paid on the loan.

EXAMPLE 5.8

Comparing After-Tax Interest Rates

Problem

Suppose you have a credit card with a 14% APR with monthly compounding, a bank savings account paying 5% EAR, and a home equity loan with a 7% APR with monthly compounding. Your income tax rate is 40%. The interest on the savings account is taxable, and the interest on the home equity loan is tax deductible. What is the effective after-tax interest rate of each instrument, expressed as an EAR? Suppose you are purchasing a new car and are offered a car loan with a 4.8% APR and monthly compounding (which is not tax deductible). Should you take the car loan?

Solution

Because taxes are typically paid annually, we first convert each interest rate to an EAR to determine the actual amount of interest earned or paid during the year. The savings account has a 5% EAR. Using Eq. 5.3, the EAR of the credit card is $(1 + 0.14 / 12)^{12} - 1 = 14.93\%$, and the EAR of the home equity loan is $(1 + 0.07 / 12)^{12} - 1 = 7.23\%$.

Next, we compute the after-tax interest rate for each. Because the credit card interest is not tax deductible, its after-tax interest rate is the same as its pre-tax interest rate, 14.93%. The after-tax interest rate on the home equity loan, which is tax deductible, is 7.23% $\times$ $(1 - 0.40) = 4.34\%$. The after-tax interest rate that we will earn on the savings account is 5% $\times (1 - 0.40) = 3\%$.

Now consider the car loan. Its EAR is $(1 + 0.048 / 12)^{12} - 1 = 4.91\%$. It is not tax deductible, so this rate is also its after-tax interest rate. Therefore, the car loan is not our cheapest source of funds. It would be best to use savings, which has an opportunity cost of foregone after-tax interest of 3%. If we don't have sufficient savings, we should use the home equity loan, which has an after-tax cost of 4.34%. And we should never borrow using our credit card!

CONCEPT CHECK

1. Why do corporations pay higher interest rates on their loans than the U.S. government?

2. How do taxes affect the interest earned on an investment? What about the interest paid on a loan?

5.4 The Opportunity Cost of Capital

As we have seen in this chapter, the interest rates we observe in the market will vary based on quoting conventions, the term of the investment, and risk. The actual return kept by an investor will also depend on how the interest is taxed. In this chapter, we have devel-

---

8. In the United States, interest is tax deductible for individuals only for home mortgages or home equity loans (up to certain limits), some student loans, and loans made to purchase securities. Interest on other forms of consumer debt is not tax deductible. Interest on debt is tax deductible for corporations.

oped the tools to account for these differences and gained some insights into how interest rates are determined.

In Chapter 3, we argued that the "market interest rate" provides the exchange rate that we need to compute present values and evaluate an investment opportunity. But with so many interest rates to choose from, the term "market interest rate" is inherently ambiguous. Therefore, going forward in the textbook, we will base the discount rate that we use to evaluate cash flows on the investor's **opportunity cost of capital** (or more simply, the **cost of capital**), which is *the best available expected return offered in the market on an investment of comparable risk and term to the cash flow being discounted.*

The opportunity cost of capital is the return the investor forgoes when the investor takes on a new investment. For a risk-free project, it will typically correspond to the interest rate on U.S. Treasury securities with a similar term. But the cost of capital is a much more general concept that can be applied to risky investments as well.

CONCEPT CHECK

1. What is the opportunity cost of capital?

2. Why do different interest rates exist, even in a competitive market?

Summary

1. The effective annual rate (EAR) indicates the actual amount of interest earned in one year. The EAR can be used as a discount rate for annual cash flows.

2. Given an EAR r, the equivalent discount rate for an n-year time interval, where n may be a fraction, is

$$(1 + r)^n - 1 \qquad (5.1)$$

3. An annual percentage rate (APR) indicates the total amount of interest earned in one year without considering the effect of compounding. APRs cannot be used as discount rates.

4. We need to know the compounding interval, k, of an APR to determine the EAR:

$$1 + EAR = \left(1 + \frac{APR}{k}\right)^k \qquad (5.3)$$

5. For a given APR, the EAR increases with the compounding frequency.

6. Loan rates are typically stated as APRs. The outstanding balance of a loan is equal to the present value of the loan cash flows, when evaluated using the effective interest rate per payment interval based on the loan rate.

7. Quoted interest rates are nominal interest rates, which indicate the rate of growth of the money invested. The real interest rate indicates the rate of growth of one's purchasing power after adjusting for inflation.

8. Given a nominal interest rate r and an inflation rate i, the real interest rate is

$$r_r = \frac{r - i}{1 + i} \approx r - i \qquad (5.5)$$

9. Nominal interest rates tend to be high when inflation is high and low when inflation is low.

10. Higher interest rates tend to reduce the NPV of typical investment projects. The U.S. Federal Reserve raises interest rates to moderate investment and combat inflation and lowers interest rates to stimulate investment and economic growth.

11. Interest rates differ with the investment horizon according to the term structure of interest rates. The graph plotting interest rates as a function of the horizon is called the yield curve.

12. Cash flows should be discounted using the discount rate that is appropriate for their horizon. Thus the PV of a cash flow stream is

$$PV = \frac{C_1}{1 + r_1} + \frac{C_2}{(1 + r_2)^2} + \cdots + \frac{C_N}{(1 + r_N)^N} = \sum_{n=1}^{N} \frac{C_n}{(1 + r_n)^n} \tag{5.7}$$

13. Annuity and perpetuity formulas cannot be applied when discount rates vary with the horizon.

14. The shape of the yield curve tends to vary with investors' expectations of future economic growth and interest rates. It tends to be inverted prior to recessions and to be steep coming out of a recession.

15. U.S. government Treasury rates are regarded as risk-free interest rates. Because other borrowers may default, they will pay higher interest rates on their loans.

16. The correct discount rate for a cash flow is the expected return available in the market on other investments of comparable risk and term.

17. If the interest on an investment is taxed at rate τ, or if the interest on a loan is tax deductible, then the effective after-tax interest rate is

$$r(1 - \tau) \tag{5.8}$$

Key Terms

after-tax interest rate *p. 139*
amortizing loan *p. 130*
annual percentage rate (APR) *p. 127*
continuous compounding *p. 128*
(opportunity) cost of capital *p. 141*
effective annual rate (EAR) *p. 126*

federal funds rate *p. 136*
nominal interest rate *p. 131*
real interest rate *p. 131*
simple interest *p. 127*
term structure *p. 133*
yield curve *p. 133*

Further Reading

An interesting account of the history of interest rates over the past four millennia is provided in S. Homer and R. Sylla, *A History of Interest Rates*, 4th ed. (New Jersey: John Wiley & Sons, Inc., 2005).

For a deeper understanding of interest rates, how they behave with changing market conditions, and how risk can be managed, see J. C. Van Horne, *Financial Market Rates and Flows*, 6th ed. (Prentice Hall, 2000).

For further insights into the relationship between interest rates, inflation, and economic growth, see a macroeconomics text such as A. Abel and B. Bernanke, *Macroeconomics*, 5th ed. (Boston: Pearson Addison Wesley, 2005).

For further analysis of the yield curve, and how it is measured and modeled, see M. Choudhry, *Analyzing and Interpreting the Yield Curve* (New Jersey, John Wiley & Sons, Inc., 2004).

Problems

All problems in this chapter are available in MyFinanceLab. An asterisk (*) indicates problems with a higher level of difficulty.

Interest Rate Quotes and Adjustments

1. Your bank is offering you an account that will pay 20% interest in total for a two-year deposit. Determine the equivalent discount rate for a period length of
   a. Six months.
   b. One year.
   c. One month.

EXCEL 2. Which do you prefer: a bank account that pays 5% per year (EAR) for three years or
   a. An account that pays $2\frac{1}{2}$% every six months for three years?
   b. An account that pays $7\frac{1}{2}$% every 18 months for three years?
   c. An account that pays $\frac{1}{2}$% per month for three years?

EXCEL 3. Many academic institutions offer a sabbatical policy. Every seven years a professor is given a year free of teaching and other administrative responsibilities at full pay. For a professor earning $70,000 per year who works for a total of 42 years, what is the present value of the amount she will earn while on sabbatical if the interest rate is 6% (EAR)?

4. You have found three investment choices for a one-year deposit: 10% APR compounded monthly, 10% APR compounded annually, and 9% APR compounded daily. Compute the EAR for each investment choice. (Assume that there are 365 days in the year.)

5. Your bank account pays interest with an EAR of 5%. What is the APR quote for this account based on semiannual compounding? What is the APR with monthly compounding?

6. Suppose the interest rate is 8% APR with monthly compounding. What is the present value of an annuity that pays $100 every six months for five years?

EXCEL 7. Your son has been accepted into college. This college guarantees that your son's tuition will not increase for the four years he attends college. The first $10,000 tuition payment is due in six months. After that, the same payment is due every six months until you have made a total of eight payments. The college offers a bank account that allows you to withdraw money every six months and has a fixed APR of 4% (semiannual) guaranteed to remain the same over the next four years. How much money must you deposit today if you intend to make no further deposits and would like to make all the tuition payments from this account, leaving the account empty when the last payment is made?

8. You make monthly payments on your mortgage. It has a quoted APR of 5% (monthly compounding). What percentage of the outstanding principal do you pay in interest each month?

9. Capital One is advertising a 60-month, 5.99% APR motorcycle loan. If you need to borrow $8000 to purchase your dream Harley Davidson, what will your monthly payment be?

10. Oppenheimer Bank is offering a 30-year mortgage with an EAR of $5\frac{3}{8}$%. If you plan to borrow $150,000, what will your monthly payment be?

11. You have decided to refinance your mortgage. You plan to borrow whatever is outstanding on your current mortgage. The current monthly payment is $2356 and you have made every payment on time. The original term of the mortgage was 30 years, and the mortgage is exactly four years and eight months old. You have just made your monthly payment. The mortgage interest rate is $6\frac{3}{8}$% (APR). How much do you owe on the mortgage today?

12. You have just sold your house for $1,000,000 in cash. Your mortgage was originally a 30-year mortgage with monthly payments and an initial balance of $800,000. The mortgage is currently exactly $18\frac{1}{2}$ years old, and you have just made a payment. If the interest rate on the mortgage is 5.25% (APR), how much cash will you have from the sale once you pay off the mortgage?

13. You have just purchased a home and taken out a $500,000 mortgage. The mortgage has a 30-year term with monthly payments and an APR of 6%.

    a. How much will you pay in interest, and how much will you pay in principal, during the first year?

    b. How much will you pay in interest, and how much will you pay in principal, during the twentieth year (i.e., between 19 and 20 years from now)?

EXCEL ***14.** You have an outstanding student loan with required payments of $500 per month for the next four years. The interest rate on the loan is 9% APR (monthly). You are considering making an extra payment of $100 today (that is, you will pay an extra $100 that you are not required to pay). If you are required to continue to make payments of $500 per month until the loan is paid off, what is the amount of your final payment? What effective rate of return (expressed as an APR with monthly compounding) have you earned on the $100?

EXCEL ***15.** Consider again the setting of Problem 14. Now that you realize your best investment is to prepay your student loan, you decide to prepay as much as you can each month. Looking at your budget, you can afford to pay an extra $250 per month in addition to your required monthly payments of $500, or $750 in total each month. How long will it take you to pay off the loan?

*16. If you decide to take the mortgage in Problem 10, Oppenheimer Bank will offer you the following deal: Instead of making the monthly payment you computed in that problem every month, you can make half the payment every two weeks (so that you will make 52 / 2 = 26 payments per year). How long will it take to pay off the mortgage if the EAR remains the same at $5\frac{3}{8}$%?

EXCEL ***17.** Your friend tells you he has a very simple trick for taking one-third off the time it takes to repay your mortgage: Use your Christmas bonus to make an extra payment on January 1 of each year (that is, pay your monthly payment due on that day twice). If you take out your mortgage on July 1, so your first monthly payment is due August 1, and you make an extra payment every January 1, how long will it take to pay off the mortgage? Assume that the mortgage has an original term of 30 years and an APR of 12%.

EXCEL **18.** You need a new car and the dealer has offered you a price of $20,000, with the following payment options: (a) pay cash and receive a $2000 rebate, or (b) pay a $5000 down payment and finance the rest with a 0% APR loan over 30 months. But having just quit your job and started an MBA program, you are in debt and you expect to be in debt for at least the next $2\frac{1}{2}$ years. You plan to use credit cards to pay your expenses; luckily you have one with a low (fixed) rate of 15% APR (monthly). Which payment option is best for you?

19. The mortgage on your house is 5 years old. It required monthly payments of $1402, had an original term of 30 years, and had an interest rate of 10% (APR). In the intervening 5 years, interest rates have fallen and so you have decided to refinance—that is, you will roll over the outstanding balance into a new mortgage. The new mortgage has a 30-year term, requires monthly payments, and has an interest rate of $6\frac{5}{8}$% (APR).

    a. What monthly repayments will be required with the new loan?

    b. If you still want to pay off the mortgage in 25 years, what monthly payment should you make after you refinance?

c. Suppose you are willing to continue making monthly payments of $1402. How long will it take you to pay off the mortgage after refinancing?

d. Suppose you are willing to continue making monthly payments of $1402, and want to pay off the mortgage in 25 years. How much additional cash can you borrow today as part of the refinancing?

20. You have credit card debt of $25,000 that has an APR (monthly compounding) of 15%. Each month you pay minimum monthly payment only. You are required to pay only the outstanding interest. You have received an offer in the mail for an otherwise identical credit card with an APR of 12%. After considering all your alternatives, you decide to switch cards, roll over the outstanding balance on the old card into the new card, and borrow additional money as well. How much can you borrow today on the new card without changing the minimum monthly payment you will be required to pay?

The Determinants of Interest Rates

21. In 1975, interest rates were 7.85% and the rate of inflation was 12.3% in the United States. What was the real interest rate in 1975? How would the purchasing power of your savings have changed over the year?

22. If the rate of inflation is 5%, what nominal interest rate is necessary for you to earn a 3% real interest rate on your investment?

23. Can the nominal interest rate available to an investor be negative? (*Hint:* Consider the interest rate earned from saving cash "under the mattress.") Can the real interest rate be negative? Explain.

24. Consider a project that requires an initial investment of $100,000 and will produce a single cash flow of $150,000 in five years.

   a. What is the NPV of this project if the five-year interest rate is 5% (EAR)?

   b. What is the NPV of this project if the five-year interest rate is 10% (EAR)?

   c. What is the highest five-year interest rate such that this project is still profitable?

EXCEL 25. Suppose the term structure of risk-free interest rates is as shown below:

Term	1 year	2 years	3 years	5 years	7 years	10 years	20 years
Rate (EAR, %)	1.99	2.41	2.74	3.32	3.76	4.13	4.93

   a. Calculate the present value of an investment that pays $1000 in two years and $2000 in five years for certain.

   b. Calculate the present value of receiving $500 per year, with certainty, at the end of the next five years. To find the rates for the missing years in the table, linearly interpolate between the years for which you do know the rates. (For example, the rate in year 4 would be the average of the rate in year 3 and year 5.)

   *c. Calculate the present value of receiving $2300 per year, with certainty, for the next 20 years. Infer rates for the missing years using linear interpolation. (*Hint:* Use a spreadsheet.)

EXCEL 26. Using the term structure in Problem 25, what is the present value of an investment that pays $100 at the end of each of years 1, 2, and 3? If you wanted to value this investment correctly using the annuity formula, which discount rate should you use?

EXCEL 27. What is the shape of the yield curve given the term structure in Problem 25? What expectations are investors likely to have about future interest rates?

EXCEL 28. Suppose the current one-year interest rate is 6%. One year from now, you believe the economy will start to slow and the one-year interest rate will fall to 5%. In two years, you expect the economy to be in the midst of a recession, causing the Federal Reserve to cut interest rates drastically and the one-year interest rate to fall to 2%. The one-year interest rate will then rise to 3% the following year, and continue to rise by 1% per year until it returns to 6%, where it will remain from then on.

    a. If you were certain regarding these future interest rate changes, what two-year interest rate would be consistent with these expectations?

    b. What current term structure of interest rates, for terms of 1 to 10 years, would be consistent with these expectations?

    c. Plot the yield curve in this case. How does the one-year interest rate compare to the ten-year interest rate?

Risk and Taxes

29. Based on the data in Table 5.2, which would you prefer: $500 from General Motors Acceptance Corporation paid today or a promise that the firm will pay you $700 in five years? Which would you choose if J. P. Morgan offered you the same alternatives?

30. Your best taxable investment opportunity has an EAR of 4%. You best tax-free investment opportunity has an EAR of 3%. If your tax rate is 30%, which opportunity provides the higher after-tax interest rate?

31. Your uncle Fred just purchased a new boat. He brags to you about the low 7% interest rate (APR, monthly compounding) he obtained from the dealer. The rate is even lower than the rate he could have obtained on his home equity loan (8% APR, monthly compounding). If his tax rate is 25% and the interest on the home equity loan is tax deductible, which loan is truly cheaper?

32. You are enrolling in an MBA program. To pay your tuition, you can either take out a standard student loan (so the interest payments are not tax deductible) that has an EAR of $5\frac{1}{2}$% or you can use a tax-deductible home equity loan with an APR (monthly) of 6%. You anticipate being in a very low tax bracket, so your tax rate will be only 15%. Which loan should you use?

33. Your best friend consults you for investment advice. You learn that his tax rate is 35%, and he has the following current investments and debts:

• A car loan with an outstanding balance of $5000 and a 4.8% APR (monthly compounding)

• Credit cards with an outstanding balance of $10,000 and a 14.9% APR (monthly compounding)

• A regular savings account with a $30,000 balance, paying a 5.50% EAR

• A money market savings account with a $100,000 balance, paying a 5.25% APR (daily compounding)

• A tax-deductible home equity loan with an outstanding balance of $25,000 and a 5.0% APR (monthly compounding)

    a. Which savings account pays a higher after-tax interest rate?

    b. Should your friend use his savings to pay off any of his outstanding debts? Explain.

34. Suppose you have outstanding debt with an 8% interest rate that can be repaid anytime, and the interest rate on U.S. Treasuries is only 5%. You plan to repay your debt using any cash that you don't invest elsewhere. Until your debt is repaid, what cost of capital should you use when evaluating a new risk-free investment opportunity? Why?

notation

e	$2.71828\ldots$
ln	natural logarithm
r_{cc}	continuously compounded discount rate
g_{cc}	continuously compounded growth rate
$\overline{C}_1$	total cash flows received in first year

Continuous Rates and Cash Flows

In this appendix we consider how to discount cash flows when interest is paid, or cash flows are received, on a continuous basis.

Discount Rates for a Continuously Compounded APR

Some investments compound more frequently than daily. As we move from daily to hourly ($k = 24 \times 365$) to compounding every second ($k = 60 \times 60 \times 24 \times 365$), we approach the limit of continuous compounding, in which we compound every instant ($k = \infty$). Equation 5.3 on page 128 cannot be used to compute the discount rate from an APR quote based on continuous compounding. In this case, the discount rate for a period length of one year—that is, the EAR—is given by Eq. 5A.1:

The EAR for a Continuously Compounded APR

$$(1 + EAR) = e^{APR} \tag{5A.1}$$

where the mathematical constant[9] $e = 2.71828 \ldots$. Once you know the EAR, you can compute the discount rate for any compounding period length using Eq. 5.2.

Alternatively, if we know the EAR and want to find the corresponding continuously compounded APR, we can invert Eq. 5A.1 by taking the natural logarithm (ln) of both sides:[10]

The Continuously Compounded APR for an EAR

$$APR = \ln(1 + EAR) \tag{5A.2}$$

Continuously compounded rates are not often used in practice. Sometimes, banks offer them as a marketing gimmick, but there is little actual difference between daily and continuous compounding. For example, with a 6% APR, daily compounding provides an EAR of $(1 + 0.06/365)^{365} - 1 = 6.18313\%$, whereas with continuous compounding the EAR is $e^{0.06} - 1 = 6.18365\%$.

Continuously Arriving Cash Flows

How can we compute the present value of an investment whose cash flows arrive continuously? For example, consider the cash flows of an online book retailer. Suppose the firm forecasts cash flows of $10 million per year. The $10 million will be received throughout each year, not at year-end, that is, the $10 million is paid *continuously* throughout the year.

We can compute the present value of cash flows that arrive continuously using a version of the growing perpetuity formula. If cash flows arrive, starting immediately, at an initial rate of $\$C$ per year, and if the cash flows grow at rate g per year, then given a discount rate (expressed as an EAR) of r per year, the present value of the cash flows is

Present Value of a Continuously Growing Perpetuity[11]

$$PV = \frac{C}{r_{cc} - g_{cc}} \tag{5A.3}$$

where $r_{cc} = \ln(1 + r)$ and $g_{cc} = \ln(1 + g)$ are the discount and growth rates expressed as continuously compounded APRs, respectively.

---

9. The constant e raised to a power is also written as the function *exp*. That is, $e^{APR} = exp(APR)$. This function is built into most spreadsheets and calculators.

10. Recall that $\ln(e^x) = x$

11. Given the perpetuity formula, we can value an annuity as the difference between two perpetuities.

There is another, approximate method for dealing with continuously arriving cash flows. Let $\overline{C}_1$ be the total cash flows that arrive during the first year. Because the cash flows arrive throughout the year, we can think of them arriving "on average" in the middle of the year. In that case, we should discount the cash flows by $\frac{1}{2}$ year less:

$$\frac{C}{r_{cc} - g_{cc}} \approx \frac{\overline{C}_1}{r - g} \times (1 + r)^{1/2} \tag{5A.4}$$

In practice, the approximation in Eq. 5A.4 works quite well. More generally, it implies that when cash flows arrive continuously, we can compute present values reasonably accurately by pretending that all of the cash flows for the year arrive in the middle of the year.

EXAMPLE 5A.1

Valuing Projects with Continuous Cash Flows

Problem

Your firm is considering buying an oil rig. The rig will initially produce oil at a rate of 30 million barrels per year. You have a long-term contract that allows you to sell the oil at a profit of $1.25 per barrel. If the rate of oil production from the rig declines by 3% over the year and the discount rate is 10% per year (EAR), how much would you be willing to pay for the rig?

Solution

According to the estimates, the rig will generate profits at an initial rate of (30 million barrels per year) $\times$ ($1.25 / barrel) = $37.5 million per year. The 10% discount rate is equivalent to a continuously compounded APR of $r_{cc} = \ln(1 + 0.10) = 9.531\%$; similarly, the growth rate has an APR of $g_{cc} = \ln(1 - 0.03) = -3.046\%$. From Eq. 5A.3, the present value of the profits from the rig is

$$PV(\text{profits}) = 37.5 / (r_{cc} - g_{cc}) = 37.5 / (0.09531 + 0.03046) = \$298.16 \text{ million}$$

Alternatively, we can closely approximate the present value as follows. The initial profit rate of the rig is $37.5 million per year. By the end of the year, the profit rate will have declined by 3% to $37.5 \times (1 - 0.03) = \$36.375$ million per year. Therefore, the average profit rate during the year is approximately $(37.5 + 36.375) / 2 = \$36.938$ million. Valuing the cash flows as though they occur at the middle of each year, we have

$$PV(\text{profits}) = [36.938 / (r - g)] \times (1 + r)^{1/2}$$
$$= [36.938 / (0.10 + 0.03)] \times (1.10)^{1/2} = \$298.01 \text{ million}$$

Note that both methods produce very similar results.

Investment Decision Rules

notation

r	discount rate
NPV	net present value
IRR	internal rate of return
PV	present value
EVA_n	Economic Value Added at date n
C_n	cash flow that arrives at date n
I	initial investment or initial capital committed to the project
I_n	capital committed to the project at date n

When Cisco Systems decided whether to acquire the Linksys Group in 2003, it needed to consider both the costs and the benefits of the proposed acquisition. The costs included the initial purchase price and the ongoing costs of operating the business. Benefits would be future revenues from sales of the Linksys products. The right way for Cisco to evaluate this decision was to compare the cash value today of the costs to the cash value today of the benefits by computing the NPV of this acquisition; Cisco should have undertaken the acquisition only if it had a positive NPV.

Although the NPV investment rule maximizes the value of the firm, some firms nevertheless use other techniques to evaluate investments and decide which projects to pursue. In this chapter, we explain several commonly used techniques—namely, the *payback rule*, the *internal rate of return rule*, and the *economic profit* or *EVA® rule*. In each case, we define the decision rule and compare decisions based on this rule to decisions based on the NPV rule. We also illustrate the circumstances in which some of the alternative rules are likely to lead to bad investment decisions. After establishing these rules in the context of a single, stand-alone project, we broaden our perspective to include deciding among mutually exclusive investment opportunities. We conclude with a look at project selection when the firm faces resource constraints.

6.1   NPV and Stand-Alone Projects

We begin our discussion of investment decision rules by considering a take-it-or-leave-it decision involving a single, stand-alone project. By undertaking this project, the firm does not constrain its ability to take other projects. We initiate our analysis with the familiar NPV rule.

NPV Rule

Researchers at Fredrick Feed and Farm (FFF) have made a breakthrough. They believe that they can produce a new, environmentally friendly fertilizer at a substantial cost saving over the company's existing line of fertilizer. The fertilizer will require a new plant that can be built immediately at a cost of $250 million. Financial managers estimate that the benefits of the new fertilizer will be $35 million per year, starting at the end of the first year and lasting forever, as shown by the following timeline:

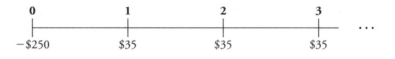

As we explained in Chapter 4, the NPV of this cash flow stream, given a discount rate *r*, is

$$NPV = -250 + \frac{35}{r}$$

Figure 6.1 plots the NPV as a function of the discount rate, *r*. Notice that the NPV is positive only for discount rates that are less than 14%, the internal rate of return (IRR). To decide whether to invest (using the NPV rule), we need to know the cost of capital. The financial managers responsible for this project estimate a cost of capital of 10% per year. Referring to Figure 6.1, we see that when the discount rate is 10%, the NPV is $100 million, which is positive. The NPV investment rule indicates that by making the investment, FFF will increase the value of the firm by $100 million, so FFF should undertake this project.

Measuring Sensitivity with IRR

If you are unsure of your cost of capital estimate, it is important to determine how sensitive your analysis is to errors in this estimate. The IRR can provide this information. For FFF, if the cost of capital estimate is more than the 14% IRR, the NPV will be negative (see Figure 6.1). In general, *the difference between the cost of capital and the IRR is the maximum amount of estimation error in the cost of capital estimate that can exist without altering the original decision.*

Alternative Rules Versus the NPV Rule

The NPV rule indicates that FFF should undertake the investment in fertilizer technology. As we evaluate alternative rules for project selection, keep in mind that sometimes other investment rules may give the same answer as the NPV rule, but at other times they may disagree. When the rules conflict, following the alternative rule means we are not taking a positive NPV project and thus we are not maximizing wealth. In these cases, the alternative rules lead to bad decisions.

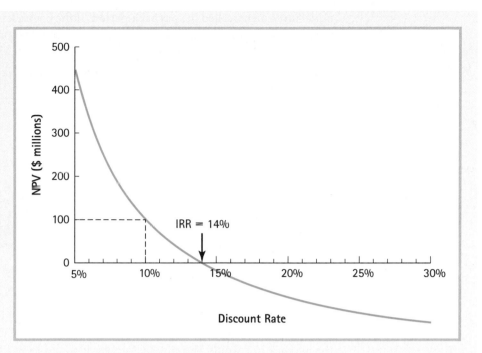

FIGURE 6.1

NPV of FFF's New Project

The graph shows the NPV as a function of the discount rate. The NPV is positive only for discount rates that are less than 14%, the internal rate of return (IRR). Given the cost of capital of 10%, the project has a positive NPV of $100 million.

CONCEPT CHECK

1. Explain the NPV rule for stand-alone projects.

2. How can you interpret the difference between the cost of capital and the IRR?

6.2 Alternative Decision Rules

In a 2001 study, John Graham and Campbell Harvey[1] found that 74.9% of the firms they surveyed used the NPV rule for making investment decisions. This result is substantially different from that found in a similar study in 1977 by L. J. Gitman and J. R. Forrester,[2] who found that only 9.8% of firms used the NPV rule. MBA students in recent years have been listening to their finance professors! Even so, Graham and Harvey's study indicates that one fourth of U.S. corporations do not use the NPV rule. Exactly why other capital budgeting techniques are used in practice is not always clear. However, because you may encounter these techniques in the business world, you should know what they are, how they are used, and how they compare to NPV. In this section, we examine alternative decision rules for single, stand-alone projects within the firm. The focus here is on the *payback rule*, *IRR rule*, and *Economic Value Added*.

The Payback Rule

The simplest investment rule is the **payback investment rule**, which is based on the notion that an opportunity that pays back its initial investment quickly is a good idea. To apply the payback rule, you first calculate the amount of time it takes to pay back the

---

1. John Graham and Campbell Harvey, "The Theory and Practice of Corporate Finance: Evidence from the Field," *Journal of Financial Economics* 60 (2001): 187–243.

2. L. J. Gitman and J. R. Forrester, Jr., "A Survey of Capital Budgeting Techniques Used by Major U.S. Firms," *Financial Management* 6 (1977): 66–71.

initial investment, called the **payback period**. If the payback period is less than a prespecified length of time—usually a few years—you accept the project. Otherwise, you turn it down. For example, a firm might adopt any project with a payback period of less than two years.

EXAMPLE 6.1

Using the Payback Rule

Problem

Assume FFF requires all projects to have a payback period of five years or less. Would the firm undertake the fertilizer project under this rule?

Solution

The sum of the cash flows from year 1 to year 5 is $35 \times 5 = \$175$ million, which will not cover the initial investment of $250 million. Because the payback period for this project exceeds 5 years, FFF will reject the project.

As a result of the payback rule analysis in Example 6.1, FFF rejected the project. However, as we saw earlier, with a cost of capital of 10%, the NPV is $100 million. Following the payback rule would be a mistake because it would leave FFF worth $100 million less.

The payback rule is not reliable because it ignores the time value of money and does not depend on the cost of capital. No rule that ignores the set of alternative investment opportunities can be optimal. Despite this failing, Graham and Harvey found that about 50% of the firms they surveyed reported using the payback rule for making decisions.

Why do some companies consider the payback rule? The answer probably relates to its simplicity. This rule is typically used for small investment decisions—for example, whether to purchase a new copy machine or to service the old one. In such cases, the cost of making an incorrect decision might not be large enough to justify the time required to calculate the NPV. The appeal of the payback rule is that it biases the decision toward short-term projects. Also, if the required payback period is short (1–2 years), then most projects that satisfy the payback rule will have a positive NPV. So firms might save effort by first applying the payback rule, and only if it fails take the time to compute NPV.

The Internal Rate of Return Rule

Like the payback rule, the **internal rate of return (IRR) investment rule** is based on an intuitive notion: If the return on the investment opportunity you are considering is greater than the return on other alternatives in the market with equivalent risk and maturity (i.e., the project's cost of capital), you should undertake the investment opportunity. We state the rule formally as follows:

IRR Investment Rule: *Take any investment opportunity where IRR exceeds the opportunity cost of capital. Turn down any opportunity whose IRR is less than the opportunity cost of capital.*

The IRR investment rule will give the correct answer (that is, the same answer as the NPV rule) in many—but not all—situations. For instance, it gives the correct answer for FFF's fertilizer opportunity. From Figure 6.1, whenever the cost of capital is below the IRR (14%), the project has a positive NPV and you should undertake the investment. In general, the IRR rule works for a stand-alone project if all of the project's negative cash flows precede its positive cash flows. But in other cases, the IRR rule may disagree with the NPV rule and thus be incorrect. Let's examine several situations in which the IRR fails.

Delayed Investments.   John Star, the founder of SuperTech, the most successful company in the last 20 years, has just retired as CEO. A major publisher has offered him a $1 million "how I did it" book deal. That is, the publisher will pay him $1 million upfront if Star agrees to write a book about his experiences. He estimates that it will take him three years to write the book. The time that he spends writing will cause him to forgo alternative sources of income amounting to $500,000 per year. Considering the risk of his alternative income sources and available investment opportunities, Star estimates his opportunity cost of capital to be 10%. The timeline of Star's investment opportunity is:

The NPV of Star's investment opportunity is

$$NPV = 1,000,000 - \frac{500,000}{1 + r} - \frac{500,000}{(1 + r)^2} - \frac{500,000}{(1 + r)^3}$$

By setting the NPV equal to zero and solving for r, we find the IRR. Using the annuity spreadsheet:

	NPER	RATE	PV	PMT	FV	Excel Formula
Given	3		1,000,000	−500,000	0	
Solve for I		23.38%				RATE(3, 500000, 1000000, 0)

The 23.38% IRR is larger than the 10% opportunity cost of capital. According to the IRR rule, Star should sign the deal. But what does the NPV rule say?

$$NPV = 1,000,000 - \frac{500,000}{1.1} - \frac{500,000}{1.1^2} - \frac{500,000}{1.1^3} = -\$243,426$$

At a 10% discount rate, the NPV is negative, so signing the deal would reduce Star's wealth. He should not sign the book deal.

Figure 6.2 plots the NPV of the investment opportunity. It shows that, no matter what the cost of capital is, the IRR rule and the NPV rule will give exactly opposite recommendations. That is, the NPV is positive only when the opportunity cost of capital is *above* 23.38% (the IRR). Star should accept the investment only when the opportunity cost of capital is greater than the IRR, the opposite of what the IRR rule recommends.

Figure 6.2 also illustrates the problem with using the IRR rule in this case. For most investment opportunities, expenses occur initially and cash is received later. In this case, Star gets cash *upfront* and incurs the costs of producing the book *later*. It is as if Star borrowed money, and when you borrow money you prefer as *low* a rate as possible. Star's optimal rule is to borrow money so long as the rate at which he borrows is *less* than the cost of capital.

Even though the IRR rule fails to give the correct answer in this case, the IRR itself still provides useful information *in conjunction* with the NPV rule. As mentioned earlier, the IRR provides information on how sensitive the investment decision is to uncertainty in the cost of capital estimate. In this case, the difference between the cost of capital and

FIGURE 6.2

NPV of Star's $1 million Book Deal

When the benefits of an investment occur before the costs, the NPV is an *increasing* function of the discount rate.

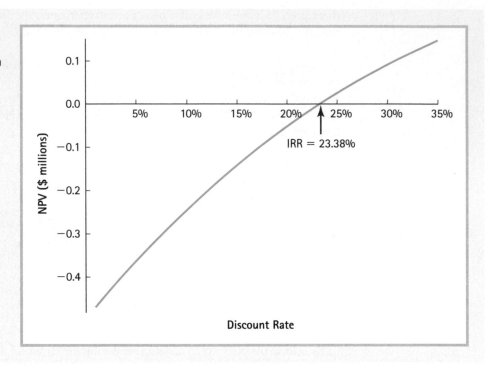

the IRR is large—13.38%. Star would have to have underestimated the cost of capital by 13.38% to make the the NPV positive.

Nonexistent IRR.   Luckily for John Star, he has other opportunities available to him. An agent has approached him and guaranteed $1 million in each of the next three years if he will agree to give four lectures per month over that period. Star estimates that preparing and delivering the lectures would take the same amount of time as writing the book—that is, the cost would be $500,000 per year. Therefore, his net cash flow will be $500,000 per year. What is the IRR of this opportunity? Here is the new timeline:

The NPV of Star's new investment opportunity is

$$NPV = \frac{500{,}000}{1 + r} + \frac{500{,}000}{(1 + r)^2} + \frac{500{,}000}{(1 + r)^3}$$

By setting the NPV equal to zero and solving for r, we find the IRR. In this case, however, there is *no* discount rate that will set the NPV equal to zero. As shown in Figure 6.3, the NPV of this opportunity is always positive, no matter what the cost of capital is. But do not be fooled into thinking that whenever the IRR does not exist the NPV will always be positive. It is quite possible for no IRR to exist when the NPV is always negative (see Problem 11).

In such situations, we cannot use the IRR rule because it provides no recommendation at all. Thus, our only choice is to rely on the NPV rule.

FIGURE 6.3

NPV of Lecture Contract

No IRR exists because the NPV is positive for all values of the discount rate. Thus the IRR rule cannot be used.

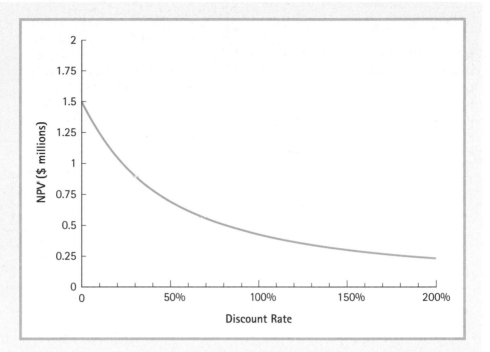

Multiple IRRs. Unfortunately, Star's lecture deal fell through. So Star has informed the publisher that it needs to sweeten the deal before he will accept it. In response, the publisher has agreed to make royalty payments. Star expects these payments to amount to $20,000 per year forever, starting once the book is published in three years. Should he accept or reject the new offer?

We begin with the new timeline:

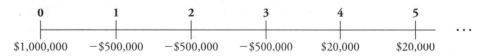

Using the annuity and perpetuity formulas, the NPV of Star's new investment opportunity is

$$NPV = 1,000,000 - \frac{500,000}{1+r} - \frac{500,000}{(1+r)^2} - \frac{500,000}{(1+r)^3} + \frac{20,000}{(1+r)^4} + \frac{20,000}{(1+r)^5} + \cdots$$

$$= 1,000,000 - \frac{500,000}{r}\left(1 - \frac{1}{(1+r)^3}\right) + \frac{1}{(1+r)^3}\left(\frac{20,000}{r}\right)$$

By setting the NPV equal to zero and solving for r, we find the IRR. In this case, there are *two* IRRs—that is, there are two values of r that set the NPV equal to zero. You can verify this fact by substituting IRRs of 4.723% and 19.619% into the equation. Because there is more than one IRR, we cannot apply the IRR rule.

For guidance, let's turn to the NPV rule. Figure 6.4 plots the NPV of the opportunity. If the cost of capital is *either* below 4.723% or above 19.619%, Star should undertake the opportunity. Otherwise, he should turn it down. Notice that even though the IRR rule

NPV of Star's Book Deal with Royalties

In this case, there is more than one IRR, invalidating the IRR rule. If the opportunity cost of capital is *either* below 4.723% or above 19.619%, Star should make the investment.

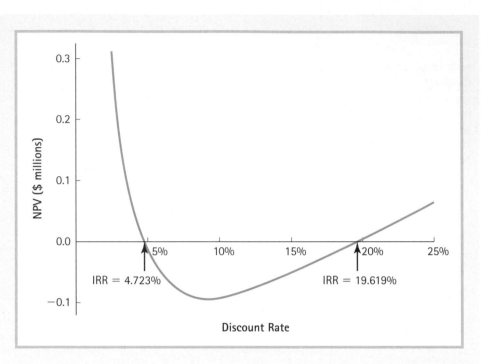

fails in this case, the two IRRs are still useful as bounds on the cost of capital. If the cost of capital estimate is wrong, and it is actually smaller than 4.723% or larger than 19.619%, the decision not to pursue the project will change. Because these bounds are far from the actual cost of capital of 10%, Star can have a high degree of confidence in his decision to reject the deal.

There is no easy fix for the IRR rule when there are multiple IRRs. Although the NPV is negative between the IRRs in this example, the reverse is also possible (see Problem 9). In this case, the project would have a positive NPV for discount rates between the IRRs rather than for discount rates lower or higher than the IRRs. Furthermore, there are situations in which more than two IRRs exist.[3] In such situations, our only choice is to rely on the NPV rule.

IRR Versus the IRR Rule.   Throughout this subsection, we have distinguished between the IRR itself and the IRR rule. While we have pointed out the shortcomings of using the IRR rule to make investment decisions, the IRR itself remains a very useful tool. Not only does the IRR measure the sensitivity of the NPV to estimation error in the cost of capital, but it also measures the average return of the investment.

Economic Profit or EVA

The concept of **economic profit** was originally suggested by Alfred Marshall more than 100 years ago. It has been popularized recently by a consulting firm, Stern Stewart, that specializes in increasing firms' efficiency. This firm renamed the concept **Economic Value Added** and even went so far as registering the acronym EVA as a trademark. EVA

---

3. In general, there can be as many IRRs as the number of times the project's cash flows change sign over time.

Joel M. Stern has been the managing partner of Stern Stewart & Company since its founding in 1982. He is a pioneer and leading advocate of the concept of managing for shareholder value and, with Bennett Stewart, developed EVA.

QUESTION: *EVA has become a popular tool among successful companies to measure performance. How does EVA work, and how does it differ from traditional performance measures?*

ANSWER: There are two popular models used for the purpose of evaluation. The first is the PV of expected future free cash flow, which is operating profit minus new investment in working capital and plant. The second model adds the PV of expected future EVA to a firm's book value, but only after adjusting the book value to include all investments in intangible assets including goodwill, acquisitions, brand value, research and development, and the training development cost in human capital. The two models provide identical answers because NPV and EVA offer identical answers. The much more interesting question, then, is, Why bother with EVA? Under NPV, there is no way to keep score year by year to see whether the project is generating positive value in that year. Because we can measure EVA year by year and quite deep into an organization, it can be used to design incentive compensation plans at almost all levels of an organization.

Virtually all methods for measuring management and determining variable compensation are tied to accounting earnings. These numbers suffer from two principal shortcomings: There is no charge for equity capital on the P&L and intangible assets are expensed. Intangible assets represent an investment that builds long-term value and should be treated as such. EVA corrects these issues by taking into account all capital costs, assessing a charge for using that capital, and capitalizing intangible assets. Managers then care about managing assets as well as income.

EVA provides a single consistent financial measure that links all decision making to improving EVA. Plus EVA cascades the incentive structure down deep into the organization. In an EVA system, people work harder and smarter. *All* employees have incentives to come up with ideas to improve the value of the firm. The first company to implement EVA throughout the organization, from the shop floor to the CEO, was Briggs and Stratton (they make lawnmower engines), and the effect was unbelievable. The U.S. Postal Service implemented EVA in 1996. After teaching more than 700,000 people to understand EVA and how the incentive program worked, the USPS eliminated more than $2.4 billion in annual losses and achieved improvements in operating efficiency.

QUESTION: *What is EVA's relevance as an investment rule* ex ante *as opposed to a performance measure* ex post?

ANSWER: NPV is a very cumbersome *measurement* process, ex post. You lay out a case today and expect cash flows in the future. How do you measure whether you've done well? You can determine this only by looking at cash outflows and inflows over the life of the project. Under NPV, there is no way to keep score year by year. EVA can be measured just as easily as NPV, but unlike NPV it allows boards of directors to design incentives that encourage wealth creation.

QUESTION: *What are the challenges to implementing EVA in a firm?*

ANSWER: To implement EVA, a firm must (1) measure EVA correctly, making adjustments to put intangibles on the balance sheet and apply a capital charge; (2) train employees about EVA and how to influence EVA and the firm's success by improving their own efficiencies; (3) set firm's priorities from greatest to least EVA opportunities, so the goal is improving EVA; (4) use EVA as the basis for incentive compensation as well as performance; and (5) communicate your EVA system and how you've designed it to the markets. All of this clearly requires a change in the management mindset and corporate culture, from "bigger is better" to "value is best."

was not originally invented as an investment rule, and even today it is not primarily used that way. Nevertheless, EVA is based on many of the same concepts underlying the NPV calculation. We will define an investment decision rule based on EVA and relate it to NPV.

EVA and Economic Profit.　　Joel Stern, of Stern Stewart, realized that some companies were rewarding managers simply because they made money for the company, without taking into account the resources the manager used while making this money. The distinction between simply making money and creating value is the essence of the NPV calculation. For example, a manager could easily make $1 million per year for a company by simply putting $20 million into a bank account paying an interest rate of 5%. He has made money, but created no value: The NPV of putting $20 million into a bank account is zero. Whereas the NPV is a measure of wealth created over the life of the project, managers are rewarded annually. As a result, Stern turned to Marshall's concept of economic profit, which rewarded managers based on the NPV they created each year. The result, EVA, measures the annual value added by the manager over and above the cost to tie up and use the capital the project requires.

EVA When Invested Capital Is Constant.　　Consider a project that requires an initial investment in capital with a cost of I dollars. Suppose that the capital lasts forever, and generates a cash flow of C_n at each future date n. The EVA in year n is the value added of the project over and above the opportunity cost of tying up the capital required to run the project. If the cost of capital is r, then the cost of tying up $\$I$ in capital in the project rather than investing it elsewhere is $r \times I$ each period (this is the expected return we could have earned). We refer to the opportunity cost associated with the project's use of capital as the **capital charge**. The EVA in period n is the difference between the project's cash flow and the capital charge:

EVA in Period n (When Capital Lasts Forever)

$$EVA_n = C_n - rI \tag{6.1}$$

The **EVA investment rule** can be stated as follows: Accept any investment opportunity in which the present value of all future EVAs is positive when we compute the present value using the project's cost of capital r.

How does the EVA investment rule compare with the NPV rule? Note that if we discount the capital charge of rI every period at rate r, the present value is simply $rI / r = I$. Thus, if we discount the project's EVA at the project's cost of capital r, then $PV(EVA_n) = PV(C_n) - PV(rI) = PV(C_n) - I = $ NPV. Thus, the EVA rule and the NPV rule will coincide.

EXAMPLE
6.2

Calculating EVA When Invested Capital Is Constant

Problem
Compute the EVA of FFF's fertilizer opportunity, which required an upfront investment of $250 million, and had a benefit of $35 million each year. Using this information, decide whether to make the investment.

Solution

The EVA in every year is

$$C_n - 250r = 35 - 250r$$

Using the perpetuity formula, the present value of these EVAs is

$$PV(EVA) = \sum_{n=1}^{\infty} \frac{35 - 250r}{(1 + r)^n} = \frac{35 - 250r}{r} = \frac{35}{r} - 250$$

This present value matches our earlier calculation of the project's NPV in Section 6.1, and so FFF should make the investment if the cost of capital is below 14%.

EVA When Invested Capital Changes. Typically, the capital invested in a project will change over time. Existing capital will tend to become less valuable over time (e.g., machines wear out with use), and new investment may need to be made. Let I_{n-1} be the amount of capital allocated to the project at date $n-1$, which is the start of period n. Then the capital charge in period n should include the opportunity cost of tying up this capital, $r I_{n-1}$. It should also take into account the cost of the wear and tear from the use of the capital, which is the amount by which the value of the capital depreciates over the period. Thus,

EVA in Period n (When Capital Depreciates)

$$EVA_n = C_n - rI_{n-1} - (\text{Depreciation in Period } n) \qquad (6.2)$$

With this definition of the EVA, the EVA and NPV rules again coincide.

EXAMPLE 6.3

Calculating EVA When Invested Capital Changes

Problem

You are considering installing new energy-efficient lighting in your firm's warehouse. The installation will cost $300,000, and you estimate total savings of $75,000 per year. The lights will depreciate evenly over the 5 years, at which point they must be replaced. The cost of capital is 7% per year. What do the NPV and EVA rules indicate about whether you should install the lights?

Solution

The timeline for the investment is (in $ thousands):

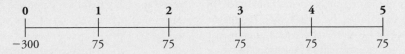

Therefore, the NPV is

$$NPV = -300 + \frac{75}{0.07}\left(1 - \frac{1}{(1.07)^5}\right) = \$7.51 \text{ thousand}$$

So, the lights should be installed. Let's see that we get the same result with EVA. If the lights depreciate by $300,000/5 = $60,000 each year, then the EVA is calculated as follows:

Year	0	1	2	3	4	5
Capital	300	240	180	120	60	0
Cash Flow		75.0	75.0	75.0	75.0	75.0
Capital Charge		(21.0)	(16.8)	(12.6)	(8.4)	(4.2)
Depreciation		(60.0)	(60.0)	(60.0)	(60.0)	(60.0)
EVA		−6.0	−1.8	2.4	6.6	10.8

For example, $EVA_1 = 75 - 7\%(300) - 60 = -6.0$, and $EVA_2 = 75 - 7\%(240) - 60 = -1.8$. The present value of the EVAs at the project's cost of capital of 7% is

$$PV(EVA) = -\frac{-6.0}{1.07} + \frac{-1.8}{1.07^2} + \frac{2.4}{1.07^3} + \frac{6.6}{1.07^4} + \frac{10.8}{1.07^5} = \$7.51 \text{ thousand}$$

Why Do Rules Other Than the NPV Rule Persist?

Professors Graham and Harvey found that a sizable minority of firms (25%) in their study do not use the NPV rule at all. In addition, about 50% of firms surveyed used the payback rule. Furthermore, it appears that most firms use *both* the NPV rule and the IRR rule. Why do firms use rules other than NPV if they can lead to erroneous decisions?

One possible explanation for this phenomenon is that Graham and Harvey's survey results might be misleading. CFOs who were using the IRR as a sensitivity measure in conjunction with the NPV rule might have checked both the IRR box and the NPV box on the survey. The question they were asked was, "How frequently does your firm use the following techniques when deciding which projects or acquisitions to pursue?" By computing the IRR and using it in conjunction with the NPV rule to estimate the sensitivity of their results, they might have felt they were using *both* techniques. Nevertheless, a significant minority of managers surveyed replied that they used only the IRR rule, so this explanation cannot be the whole story.

One common reason that managers give for using the IRR rule exclusively is that you do not need to know the opportunity cost of capital to calculate the IRR. On a superficial level, this is true: The IRR does not depend on the cost of capital. You may not need to know the cost of

capital to *calculate* the IRR, but you certainly need to know the cost of capital when you *apply* the IRR rule. Consequently, the opportunity cost is as important to the IRR rule as it is to the NPV rule.

In our opinion, some firms use the IRR rule exclusively because the IRR sums up the attractiveness of investment opportunity in a single number without requiring the person running the numbers to make an assumption about the cost of capital. However, if a CFO wants a brief summary of an investment opportunity but does not want her employee to make a cost of capital assumption, she can also request a plot of the NPV as a function of the discount rate. Neither this request nor a request for the IRR requires knowing the cost of capital, but the NPV graph has the distinct advantage of being much more informative and reliable.

If you are employed by a firm that uses the IRR rule exclusively, our advice is to always calculate the NPV. If the two rules agree, you can feel comfortable reporting the IRR rule recommendation. If they do not agree, you should investigate why the IRR rule failed by using the concepts in this section. Once you have identified the problem, you can alert your superiors to it and perhaps persuade them to adopt the NPV rule.

CONCEPT CHECK   1. When other investment rules do not give the same answer as the NPV rule, which rule should you follow? Why?

2. Explain the term *Economic Value Added* (EVA).

6.3 Mutually Exclusive Investment Opportunities

Thus far, we have considered only decisions where the choice is either to accept or to reject a single, stand-alone project. Sometimes, however, a firm must choose just one project from among several possible projects. For example, a manager may be evaluating alternative marketing campaigns for a single new product launch.

When projects, like the market campaigns, are mutually exclusive, it is not enough to determine which projects have positive NPV. With **mutually exclusive projects**, the manager's goal is to rank the projects and choose the best one. In this situation, the NPV rule provides a straightforward answer: *Pick the project with the highest NPV.*

Because the IRR is a measure of the expected return of investing in the project, you might be tempted to extend the IRR investment rule to the case of mutually exclusive projects by picking the project with the highest IRR. Unfortunately, picking one project over another simply because it has a larger IRR can lead to mistakes. Problems arise when the mutually exclusive investments have differences in scale (require different initial investments) and when they have different cash flow patterns. We discuss each of these situations in this section.

Differences in Scale

If a project has a positive NPV, then if we can double its size, its NPV will double: By the Law of One Price, doubling the cash flows of an investment opportunity must make it worth twice as much. However, the IRR rule does not have this property—it is unaffected by the scale of the investment opportunity because the IRR measures the average return of the investment. Hence the IRR rule cannot be used to compare projects of different scales. Let's illustrate this concept in the context of an example.

Identical Scale. We begin by considering two mutually exclusive projects with the same scale. Don is evaluating two investment opportunities. If he went into business with his girlfriend, he would need to invest $1000 and the business would generate incremental cash flows of $1100 per year, declining at 10%, forever. Alternatively, he could start a single-machine laundromat. The washer and dryer cost a total of $1000 and will generate $400 per year, declining, because of maintenance costs, at 20% per year, forever. The opportunity cost of capital for both opportunities is 12% and both will require all his time, so Don must choose between them. Which one should he choose?

The timeline for the investment with his girlfriend is

The future cash flows are a perpetuity with a growth rate of -10%, so the NPV of the investment opportunity when $r = 12\%$ is

$$NPV = -1000 + \frac{1100}{r + 0.1} = -1000 + \frac{1100}{0.12 + 0.1} = \$4000$$

We can determine the IRR of this investment by setting the NPV equal to zero and solving for r:

$$1000 = \frac{1100}{r + 0.1} \quad \text{implies} \quad r = 100\%$$

Thus the IRR for Don's investment in his girlfriend's business is 100%.

The timeline for his investment in the laundromat is

Once again the future cash flows are a perpetuity, this time with a negative growth rate of -20%. The NPV of the investment opportunity is

$$NPV = -1000 + \frac{400}{r + 0.2} = -1000 + \frac{400}{0.12 + 0.2} = \$250$$

The \$250 NPV of the laundromat is lower than the \$4000 NPV for his girlfriend's business, so Don should join his girlfriend in business. Luckily, it appears that Don does not need to choose between his checkbook and his relationship!

If we compare IRRs, note that for the laundromat, setting the NPV equal to zero and solving for r gives an IRR of 20%. The laundromat has a lower IRR than the investment in his girlfriend's business. As Figure 6.5 shows, in this case the project with the higher IRR has the higher NPV.

FIGURE 6.5

NPV of Don's Investment Opportunities with the Single-Machine Laundromat

The NPV of his girlfriend's business is always larger than the NPV of the single-machine laundromat. The same is true for the IRR; the IRR of his girlfriend's business is 100%, while the IRR for the laundromat is 20%.

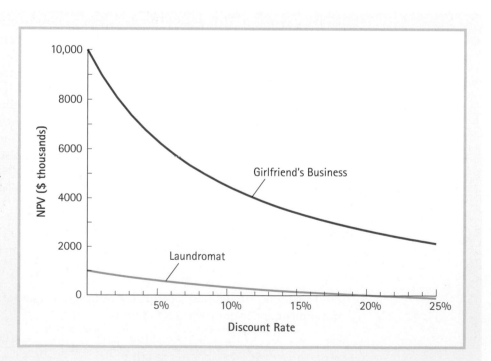

Change in Scale.   What happens if we change the scale of one of the projects? Don's finance professor points out that, given the space available in the facility, he could just as easily install 20 machines in the laundromat. What should Don do now?

Note that the IRR is unaffected by the scale. A 20-machine laundromat has exactly the same IRR as a single-machine Laundromat, so his girlfriend's business still has a higher IRR than the Laundromat. However, the NPV of the Laundromat does grow by the scale: It is 20 times larger.

$$NPV = 20\left(-1000 + \frac{400}{0.12 + 0.2}\right) = \$5000$$

Now Don should invest in the 20-machine laundromat. As Figure 6.6 shows, the NPV of the 20-machine laundromat exceeds the NPV of going into business with his girlfriend whenever the cost of capital is less than 13.9%. In this case, even though the IRR of going into business with his girlfriend exceeds the IRR of the laundromat, picking the investment opportunity with the higher IRR does not result in taking the opportunity with the higher NPV.

Percentage Return Versus Dollar Impact on Value.   This result might seem counterintuitive. Why would anyone turn down an investment opportunity with a 100% return (IRR) in favor of one with only a 20% return? The answer is that the latter opportunity makes more money. To demonstrate, consider this set of alternatives: Would you prefer a 200% return on $1 dollar or a 10% return on $1 million? The former investment certainly gives you great bragging rights, but at the end of the day you make only $2. The latter opportunity gives no bragging rights, but you make $100,000. The IRR is a measure

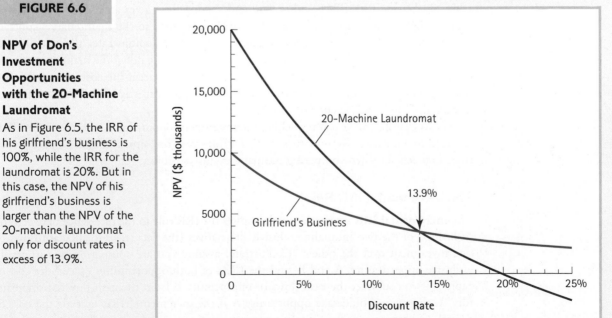

FIGURE 6.6

NPV of Don's Investment Opportunities with the 20-Machine Laundromat

As in Figure 6.5, the IRR of his girlfriend's business is 100%, while the IRR for the laundromat is 20%. But in this case, the NPV of his girlfriend's business is larger than the NPV of the 20-machine laundromat only for discount rates in excess of 13.9%.

of the average return, which can be valuable information. When you are comparing mutually exclusive projects of different scale, however, you need to know the dollar impact on value, or the NPV.

Timing of the Cash Flows

Another failing of the IRR is that it can be altered by changing the timing of the cash flows, even when that change in timing does not affect the NPV. Therefore, it is possible to alter the ranking of projects' IRRs without changing their ranking in terms of NPV. Hence you cannot use the IRR to choose between mutually exclusive investments. To see this in the context of an example, let's return to Don's laundromat.

A salesman has offered Don a maintenance contract on his machines under which Don would pay $250 per year for maintenance on each machine. With this contract, Don would not have to pay for his own maintenance and so the cash flows from the machines would not decline. The expected cash flows would then be the cash flows from the machines minus the cost of the contract: $400 − $250 = $150 per year per machine, forever.

Don must now decide between two mutually exclusive investment opportunities: the laundromat with or without the contract. We begin with the timeline:

Notice that the maintenance contract does not change the NPV:

$$NPV = 20\left(-1000 + \frac{150}{r}\right) = \$5000 \tag{6.3}$$

As a consequence, Don is indifferent between taking the maintenance contract or not taking it. Setting the NPV equal to zero and solving for r gives an IRR of 15%. Recall that the IRR without the maintenance contract was 20%, so the maintenance contract has lowered the IRR by 5 percentage points. Figure 6.7 demonstrates that picking the alternative with the higher IRR always results in Don turning down the maintenance contract. However, the correct decision is to agree to the contract if the cost of capital is less than 12% and to decline the contract if the cost of capital exceeds 12%. With a 12% cost of capital, Don is indifferent.

As this example makes clear, picking the investment opportunity with the largest IRR can lead to a mistake. We now turn our attention to a "fix" aimed at addressing the IRR rule's deficiencies when comparing mutually exclusive projects.

The Incremental IRR Rule

The **incremental IRR investment rule** applies the IRR rule to the difference between the cash flows of the two mutually exclusive alternatives (the *increment* to the cash flows of one investment over the other). To illustrate, assume you are comparing two mutually exclusive opportunities, A and B, and the IRRs of both opportunities exceed the cost of capital. If you subtract the cash flows of opportunity B from the cash flows of opportunity A, then you should take opportunity A if the incremental IRR exceeds the cost of capital. Otherwise, you should take opportunity B.

FIGURE 6.7

NPV with and Without the Maintenance Contract

The NPV without the maintenance contract exceeds the NPV with the contract for discount rates that are in excess of 12%. However, the IRR without the maintenance contract (20%) is larger than the IRR with the maintenance contract (15%).

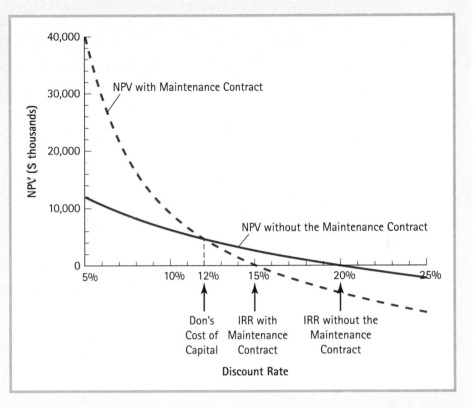

Incremental IRR Rule Application.   Let's apply the incremental IRR rule to Don's dilemma. The following timeline illustrates the incremental cash flows of the maintenance contract laundromat over the laundromat without the contract:

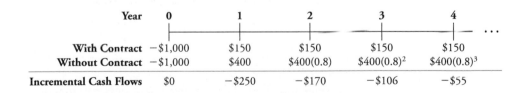

The NPV of the incremental cash flow is very difficult to calculate directly in this case, because it does not grow at a constant rate. We can compute it easily, though, as the difference of the NPV with and without the contract:

$$NPV = \frac{150}{r} - \frac{400}{r + 0.2}$$

Setting this equation equal to zero and solving for r gives an IRR of 12%. Applying the incremental IRR rule, Don should take the contract when the cost of capital is less than 12%. Because his cost of capital is 12%, he is indifferent. Recall that this finding concurs with the NPV rule, so in this case the incremental IRR rule gives the correct answer.

Shortcomings of the Incremental IRR Rule.   Although the incremental IRR rule resolves some problems with mutually exclusive investments, it still uses the IRR rule on the incremental cash flows. As a result, it shares several problems with the regular IRR rule:

- The fact that the IRR exceeds the cost of capital for both projects does not imply that both projects have positive NPV.

- The incremental IRR need not exist.

- Many incremental IRRs could exist. In fact, the likelihood of multiple IRRs is greater with the incremental IRR rule than with the regular IRR rule.

- You must keep track of which project is the incremental project and ensure that the incremental cash flows are initially negative and then become positive. Otherwise, the incremental IRR rule will have the negative initial investment problem and will give the wrong answer.

- The incremental IRR rule assumes that the riskiness of the two projects is the same. When the risks are different, the cost of capital of the incremental cash flows is not obvious, making it difficult to know whether the incremental IRR exceeds the cost of capital. In this case only the NPV rule, which allows each project to be discounted at its own cost of capital, will give a reliable answer.

In summary, although the incremental IRR rule can provide a reliable method for choosing among projects, it can be difficult to apply correctly. It is much simpler to use the NPV rule.

CONCEPT CHECK   1. What is the incremental IRR rule and what are its shortcomings?

2. For mutually exclusive projects, explain why picking one project over another because it has a larger IRR can lead to mistakes.

6.4 Project Selection with Resource Constraints

In the preceeding section, we considered the decision between two mutually exclusive investment opportunities. We implicitly assumed that both projects had *identical* resource needs—for example, that both the laundromat or his girlfriend's business demanded 100% of Don's time.

In some situations, different investment opportunities demand different amounts of a particular resource. If there is a fixed supply of the resource so that you cannot undertake all possible opportunities, simply picking the highest-NPV opportunity might not lead to the best decision.

Evaluation of Projects with Different Resource Requirements

Assume you are considering the three projects in Table 6.1, all of which require warehouse space. Table 6.1 shows the NPV of each project and the amount of available warehouse space that each project requires. Project A has the highest NPV but it uses up the entire resource (the warehouse); thus it would be a mistake to take this opportunity. Projects B and C can *both* be undertaken (together they use all the available space), and their combined NPV exceeds the NPV of project A; thus you should initiate them both. Together their NPV is $150 million, compared to just $100 million for project A alone.

TABLE 6.1		Possible Projects Requiring Warehouse Space	
Project	NPV ($ millions)	Fraction of Warehouse Required (%)	Profitability Index
A	100	100	1
B	75	60	1.25
C	75	40	1.875

Profitability Index

In this simple example, identifying the optimal combination of projects to undertake is straightforward. In actual situations replete with many projects and resources, finding the optimal combination can be difficult. Practitioners often use the **profitability index** to identify the optimal combination of projects to undertake in such situations:

Profitability Index

$$\text{Profitability Index} = \frac{\text{Value Created}}{\text{Resource Consumed}} = \frac{\text{NPV}}{\text{Resource Consumed}} \qquad (6.4)$$

The profitability index measures the "bang for your buck"—that is, the value created in terms of NPV per unit of resource consumed. After computing the profitability index, we can rank projects based on it. Starting with the project with the highest index, we move down the ranking, taking all projects until the resource is consumed. In Table 6.1, we have calculated the profitability index for each of the three projects. Note how the profitability index rule would select projects B and C.

EXAMPLE 6.4

Profitability Index with a Human Resource Constraint

Problem

Your division at NetIt, a large networking company, has put together a project proposal to develop a new home networking router. The expected NPV of the project is $17.7 million, and the project will require 50 software engineers. NetIt has a total of 190 engineers available, and the router project must compete with the following other projects for these engineers:

Project	NPV ($ millions)	Engineering Headcount
Router	17.7	50
Project A	22.7	47
Project B	8.1	44
Project C	14.0	40
Project D	11.5	61
Project E	20.6	58
Project F	12.9	32
Total	**107.5**	**332**

How should NetIt prioritize these projects?

Solution

The goal is to maximize the total NPV we can create with 190 employees (at most). We compute the profitability index for each project, using Engineering Headcount in the denominator, and then sort projects based on the index:

Project	NPV ($ millions)	Engineering Headcount (EHC)	Profitability Index (NPV per EHC)	Total EHC Required
Project A	22.7	47	0.483	47
Project F	12.9	32	0.403	79
Project E	20.6	58	0.355	137
Router	17.7	50	0.354	187
Project C	14.0	40	0.350	
Project D	11.5	61	0.189	
Project B	8.1	44	0.184	

We now assign the resource to the projects in descending order according to the profitability index. The final column shows the cumulative use of the resource as each project is taken on until the resource is used up. To maximize NPV within the constraint of 190 employees, NetIt should choose the first four projects on the list. The resource constraint forces NetIt to forgo three otherwise valuable projects.

Shortcomings of the Profitability Index

Although the profitability index is simple to compute and use, in some situations it does not give an accurate answer. For example, suppose in Example 6.4 that NetIt has an additional small project with a NPV of only $100,000 that requires 3 engineers. The profitability index in this case is $0.1/3 = 0.03$, so this project would appear at the bottom of the ranking. However, notice that 3 of the 190 employees are not being used after the first four projects are selected. As a result, it would make sense to take on this project even though it would be ranked last.

A more serious problem occurs when multiple resource constraints apply. In this case, the profitability index can break down completely. The only surefire way to find the best combination of projects is to search through all of them. Although this process may sound exceedingly time-consuming, linear and integer programming techniques have been developed specifically to tackle this kind of problem. By using these techniques on a computer, the solution can usually be obtained almost instantaneously (see Further Reading for references).

CONCEPT CHECK

1. Explain why picking the project with the highest NPV might not be optimal when you evaluate mutually exclusive projects with different resource requirements.

2. Explain why practitioners often use the profitability index to identify the optimal combinations of projects to undertake.

Summary

1. If your objective is to maximize wealth, the NPV rule always gives the correct answer.

2. The difference between the cost of capital and the IRR is the maximum amount of estimation error that can exist in the cost of capital estimate without altering the original decision.

3. Payback investment rule: Calculate the amount of time it takes to pay back the initial investment (the payback period). If the payback period is less than a prespecified length of time, accept the project. Otherwise, turn it down.

4. IRR investment rule: Take any investment opportunity whose IRR exceeds the opportunity cost of capital. Turn down any opportunity whose IRR is less than the opportunity cost of capital.

5. The IRR rule may give the wrong answer if the cash flows have an upfront payment (negative investment). When there are multiple IRRs or the IRR does not exist, the IRR rule cannot be used.

6. The EVA in year n is the cash flow in that year minus the cost of tying up and using up the capital required to run the project—it is the value added in that year over the life of the project:

$$EVA_n = C_n - rI_{n-1} - (\text{Depreciation in Period } n) \qquad (6.2)$$

7. EVA investment rule: Accept any investment opportunity in which the present value, using the project's cost of capital r, of all future EVAs is positive.

8. When choosing among mutually exclusive investment opportunities, pick the opportunity with the highest NPV. Do not use IRR to choose among mutually exclusive investment opportunities.

9. Incremental IRR rule: Assume you are comparing two mutually exclusive opportunities, A and B, and the IRRs of both opportunities exceed the cost of capital. If you subtract the cash flows of opportunity B from the cash flows of opportunity A, then you should take opportunity A if the incremental IRR exceeds the cost of capital. Otherwise, take opportunity B.

10. When choosing among projects competing for the same resource, ranking the projects by their profitability indices and picking the set of projects with the highest profitability indices that can still be undertaken given the limited resource often produces the best result.

$$\text{Profitability Index} = \frac{\text{Value Created}}{\text{Resource Consumed}} = \frac{\text{NPV}}{\text{Resource Consumed}} \qquad (6.4)$$

Key Terms

capital charge *p. 158*
economic profit *p. 156*
Economic Value Added *p. 156*
EVA investment rule *p. 158*
incremental IRR investment
    rule *p. 164*

internal rate of return (IRR) investment
    rule *p. 152*
mutually exclusive projects *p. 161*
payback investment rule *p. 151*
payback period *p. 152*
profitability index *p. 167*

Further Reading

For readers who would like to learn more about economic profit (or EVA) and how it is used, see A. Ehrbar, *EVA: The Real Key to Creating Wealth*. (New York: John Wiley and Sons, 1998).

Readers who would like to know more about what managers actually do should consult J. Graham and C. Harvey, "How CFOs Make Capital Budgeting and Capital Structure

Decisions," *Journal of Applied Corporate Finance* 15(1) (2002): 8–23; S. H. Kim, T. Crick, and S. H. Kim, "Do Executives Practice What Academics Preach?" *Management Accounting* 68 (November 1986): 49–52; and P. Ryan and G. Ryan, "Capital Budgeting Practices of the Fortune 1000: How Have Things Changed?" *Journal of Business and Management* 8(4) (2002): 355–364.

For readers interested in how to select among projects competing for the same set of resources, the following references will be helpful: M. Vanhoucke, E. Demeulemeester, and W. Herroelen, "On Maximizing the Net Present Value of a Project Under Renewable Resource Constraints," *Management Science* 47(8) (2001): 1113–1121; and H. M. Weingartner, *Mathematical Programming and the Analysis of Capital Budgeting Problems.* (Englewood Cliffs, NJ: Prentice-Hall, 1963).

Problems

All problems in this chapter are available in MyFinanceLab. An asterisk (*) indicates problems with a higher level of difficulty.

NPV and Stand-Alone Projects

1. You are considering opening a new plant. The plant will cost $100 million upfront and will take one year to build. After that, it is expected to produce profits of $30 million at the end of every year of production. The cash flows are expected to last forever. Calculate the NPV of this investment opportunity if your cost of capital is 8%. Should you make the investment? Calculate the IRR and use it to determine the maximum deviation allowable in the cost of capital estimate to leave the decision unchanged.

EXCEL 2. Bill Clinton reportedly was paid $10 million to write his book *My Way*. The book took three years to write. In the time he spent writing, Clinton could have been paid to make speeches. Given his popularity, assume that he could earn $8 million per year (paid at the end of the year) speaking instead of writing. Assume his cost of capital is 10% per year.

    a. What is the NPV of agreeing to write the book (ignoring any royalty payments)?

    b. Assume that, once the book is finished, it is expected to generate royalties of $5 million in the first year (paid at the end of the year) and these royalties are expected to decrease at a rate of 30% per year in perpetuity. What is the NPV of the book with the royalty payments?

EXCEL *3. FastTrack Bikes, Inc., is thinking of developing a new composite road bike. Development will take six years and the cost is $200,000 per year. Once in production, the bike is expected to make $300,000 per year for 10 years.

    a. Assume the cost of capital is 10%.

        i. Calculate the NPV of this investment opportunity. Should the company make the investment?

        ii. Calculate the IRR and use it to determine the maximum deviation allowable in the cost of capital estimate to leave the decision unchanged.

        iii. How long must development last to change the decision?

    b. Assume the cost of capital is 14%.

        i. Calculate the NPV of this investment opportunity. Should the company make the investment?

        ii. How much must this cost of capital estimate deviate to change the decision?

        iii. How long must development last to change the decision?

Alternative Decision Rules

4. You are a real estate agent thinking of placing a sign advertising your services at a local bus stop. The sign will cost $5000 and will be posted for one year. You expect that it will generate additional revenue of $500 per month. What is the payback period?

5. Does the IRR rule agree with the NPV rule in Problem 1?

EXCEL 6. How many IRRs are there in part (a) of Problem 2? Does the IRR rule give the right answer in this case?

EXCEL 7. How many IRRs are there in part (b) of Problem 2? Does the IRR rule work in this case?

8. Professor Wendy Smith has been offered the following deal: A law firm would like to retain her for an upfront payment of $50,000. In return, for the next year the firm would have access to 8 hours of her time every month. Smith's rate is $550 per hour and her opportunity cost of capital is 15% (EAR). What does the IRR rule advise regarding this opportunity? What about the NPV rule?

9. Innovation Company is thinking about marketing a new software product. Upfront costs to market and develop the product are $5 million. The product is expected to generate profits of $1 million per year for ten years. The company will have to provide product support expected to cost $100,000 per year in perpetuity. Assume all profits and expenses occur at the end of the year.

    a. What is the NPV of this investment if the cost of capital is 6%? Should the firm undertake the project? Repeat the analysis for discount rates of 2% and 11%.

    b. How many IRRs does this investment opportunity have?

    c. What does the IRR rule indicate about this investment?

10. You own a coal mining company and are considering opening a new mine. The mine itself will cost $120 million to open. If this money is spent immediately, the mine will generate $20 million for the next ten years. After that, the coal will run out and the site must be cleaned and maintained at environmental standards. The cleaning and maintenance are expected to cost $2 million per year in perpetuity. What does the IRR rule say about whether you should accept this opportunity? If the cost of capital is 8%, what does the NPV rule say?

EXCEL *11. You are considering investing in a new gold mine in South Africa. Gold in South Africa is buried very deep, so the mine will require an initial investment of $250 million. Once this investment is made, the mine is expected to produce revenues of $30 million per year for the next 20 years. It will cost $10 million per year to operate the mine. After 20 years, the gold will be depleted. The mine must then be stabilized on an ongoing basis, which will cost $5 million per year in perpetuity. Calculate the IRR of this investment. (*Hint:* Plot the NPV as a function of the discount rate.)

12. Calculate the present value of the EVAs in Problem 1 and determine whether the outcome with the EVA rule agrees with the outcome with the NPV rule.

EXCEL *13. You are considering constructing a new plant to manufacture a new product. You anticipate that the plant will take a year to build and cost $100 million upfront. Once built, it will generate cash flows of $15 million at the end of every year over the life of the plant. The plant will wear out 20 years after its completion. At that point you expect to get $10 million in salvage value for the plant. Using a cost of capital of 12%, calculate the present value of the EVAs and verify that they equal the NPV.

14. You are considering making a movie. The movie is expected to cost $10 million upfront and take a year to make. After that, it is expected to make $5 million in the year it is released and $2 million for the following four years. What is the payback period of this investment? If you

require a payback period of two years, will you make the movie? Does the movie have positive NPV if the cost of capital is 10%?

15. You work for a company that uses IRR exclusively. The reason is that the CEO does not like to read long memos. He is fond of saying, "I don't like two-handed economists!"[4] He likes to distill all decisions down to a single number like the IRR. Your boss has asked you to calculate the IRR of a project. He refuses to give you the cost of capital for the project, but you know that once you compute the IRR he will compare it to the cost of capital and use that information to make the investment decision. What should you do?

Mutually Exclusive Investment Opportunities

16. You are deciding between two mutually exclusive investment opportunities. Both require the same initial investment of $10 million. Investment A will generate $2 million per year (starting at the end of the first year) in perpetuity. Investment B will generate $1.5 million at the end of the first year and its revenues will grow at 2% per year for every year after that.

   a. Which investment has the higher IRR?

   b. Which investment has the higher NPV when the cost of capital is 7%?

   c. In this case, when does picking the higher IRR give the correct answer as to which investment is the best opportunity?

17. Use the incremental IRR rule to correctly choose between the investments in Problem 16 when the cost of capital is 7%.

18. You work for an outdoor play structure manufacturing company and are trying to decide between two projects:

	Year-End Cash Flows ($ thousands)			
Project	0	1	2	IRR
Playhouse	−30	15	20	10.4%
Fort	−80	39	52	8.6%

You can undertake only one project. If your cost of capital is 8%, use the incremental IRR rule to make the correct decision.

Project Selection with Resource Constraints

*19. Kartman Corporation is evaluating four real estate investments. Management plans to buy the properties today and sell them three years from today. The annual discount rate for these investments is 15%. The following table summarizes the initial cost and the sale price in three years for each property.

	Cost Today	Sale Price in Year 3
Parkside Acres	$500,000	$ 900,000
Real Property Estates	800,000	1,400,000
Lost Lake Properties	650,000	1,050,000
Overlook	150,000	350,000

Kartman has a total capital budget of $800,000 to invest in properties. Which properties should it choose?

---

4. U.S. President Harry Truman is purported to have complained that the problem with all economists is that they always have two hands. When asked to give advice, they always said, "On the one hand . . . but on the other hand . . ."

*20.   Orchid Biotech Company is evaluating several development projects for experimental drugs. Although the cash flows are difficult to forecast, the company has come up with the following estimates of the initial capital requirements and NPVs for the projects. Given a wide variety of staffing needs, the company has also estimated the number of research scientists required for each development project (all cost values are given in millions of dollars).

Project Number	Initial Capital	Number of Research Scientists	NPV
I	$10	2	$10.1
II	15	3	19.0
III	15	4	22.0
IV	20	3	25.0
V	30	10	60.2

a. Suppose that Orchid has a total capital budget of $60 million. How should it prioritize these projects?

b. Suppose that Orchid currently has 12 research scientists and does not anticipate being able to hire any more in the near future. How should Orchid prioritize these projects?

Data Case

On October 6, 2004 Sirius Satellite Radio announced that it had reached an agreement with Howard Stern to broadcast his radio show exclusively on their system. As a result of this announcement, the Sirius stock price increased dramatically. You are currently working as a stock analyst for a large investment firm and XM Radio, also a satellite radio firm, is one of the firms you track. Your boss wants to be prepared if XM follows Sirius in trying to sign a major personality. Therefore, she wants you to estimate the net cash flows the market had anticipated from the signing of Stern. She advises that you treat the value anticipated by the market as the NPV of the signing, then work backward from the NPV to determine the annual cash flows necessary to generate that value. The potential deal had been rumored for some time prior to the announcement. As a result, the stock price for Sirius increased for several days before the announcement. Thus, your boss advises that the best way to capture all of the value is to take the change in stock price from September 28, 2004 through October 7, 2004. You nod your head in agreement, trying to look like you understand how to proceed. You are relatively new to the job and the term NPV is somewhat familiar to you.

1. To determine the change in stock price over this period, go to Yahoo! Finance (http://finance.yahoo.com) and enter the stock symbol for Sirius (SIRI). Then click on "Historical Prices" and enter the appropriate dates. Use the adjusted closing prices for the two dates.

2. To determine the change in value, multiply the change in stock price by the number of shares outstanding. The number of shares outstanding around those dates can be found by going to finance.google.com and typing "SIRI" into the "Search" window. Next, select the Income Statement link on the left side of the screen, and then select "Annual Data" in the upper right-hand corner. The "Diluted Weighted Average Shares" can be found for the 12/31/2004 income statement on that page.

3. Because the change in value represents the "expected" NPV of the project, you will have to find the annual net cash flows that would provide this NPV. For this analysis, you will need to estimate the cost of capital for the project. We show how to calculate the cost of capital

in subsequent chapters; for now, use the New York University (NYU) cost of capital Web site (http://pages.stern.nyu.edu/~adamodar/New_Home_Page/datafile/wacc.htm). Locate the cost of capital in the far-right column for the "Entertainment Tech" industry.

4. Use the cost of capital from the NYU Web site and the NPV you computed to calculate the constant annual cash flow that provides this NPV. Compute cash flows for 5-, 10-, and 15-year horizons.

5. Your boss mentioned that she believes that the Howard Stern signing by Sirius was actually good for XM because it signaled that the industry has valuable growth potential. To see if she appears to be correct, find the percentage stock price reaction to XM (XMSR) over this same period.

Basic Valuation

The Law of One Price Connection.   Now that the tools for financial decision making are in place, we can begin to apply them. One of the most important decisions facing a financial manager is the choice of which investments the corporation should make. The process of allocating the firm's capital for investment is known as capital budgeting and in Chapter 7 we outline the discounted cash flow method for making such decisions. Chapter 7 provides a practical demonstration of the power of the tools that were introduced in Part II.

Firms raise the capital they need to make investments by issuing securities such as stocks and bonds. In the next two chapters, we use these same tools to explain how to value bonds and stocks. In Chapter 8, Valuing Bonds, the Law of One Price allows us to link bond prices and their yields to the term structure of market interest rates. Similarly, in Chapter 9, Valuing Stocks, we show how the Law of One Price leads to several alternative methods for valuing a firm's equity by considering its future dividends, free cash flows, or how its value compares to that of similar, publicly traded companies.

Fundamentals of Capital Budgeting

In early 2004, Kellogg Company, the world's leading producer of cereal and other convenience foods, announced the introduction of its Low-Sugar Frosted Flakes and Froot Loops cereals. As described by Jeff Montie, Morning Foods Division North America President at Kellogg, "The Frosted Flakes and Froot Loops brand extensions represent a great new option for parents and their families. Consumer research indicates that parents value the fact that Kellogg was able to maintain great taste without adding artificial sweeteners. As a result, we're confident that we have two new products that parents and kids will enthusiastically agree on." The decision by Kellogg to introduce brand extensions of two of its most popular cereals represents a classic capital budgeting decision. How did Kellogg quantify the costs and benefits of this project, and decide to introduce its new cereals? We will develop the tools to evaluate projects such as this one in this chapter.

An important responsibility of corporate financial managers is determining which projects or investments a firm should undertake. *Capital budgeting* is the process of analyzing investment opportunities and deciding which ones to accept. It requires computing the NPV and accepting projects for which the NPV is positive. The first step in this process is estimating the project's expected cash flows by forecasting the project's revenues and costs. Using these cash flows, we can then compute the project's NPV—its contribution to shareholder value. Finally, because the cash flow forecasts almost always contain uncertainty, we demonstrate how to compute the sensitivity of the NPV to the uncertainty in the forecasts.

7.1 Forecasting Earnings

A **capital budget** lists the projects and investments that a company plans to undertake during the coming year. To determine this list, firms analyze alternate projects and decide which ones to accept through a process called **capital budgeting**. This process begins with forecasts of the project's future consequences for the firm. Some of these consequences will affect the firm's revenues; others will affect its costs. Our ultimate goal is to determine the effect of the decision on the firm's cash flows.

As we emphasized in Chapter 2, *earnings are not actual cash flows.* However, as a practical matter, to derive the forecasted cash flows of a project, financial managers often begin by forecasting earnings. Thus, we *begin* by determining the **incremental earnings** of a project—that is, the amount by which the firm's earnings are expected to change as a result of the investment decision. Then, in Section 7.2, we demonstrate how to use the incremental earnings to forecast the *cash flows* of the project.

Let's consider a hypothetical capital budgeting decision faced by managers of the Linksys division of Cisco Systems, a maker of consumer networking hardware. Linksys is considering the development of a wireless home networking appliance, called HomeNet, that will provide both the hardware and the software necessary to run an entire home from any Internet connection. In addition to connecting PCs and printers, HomeNet will control new Internet-capable stereos, digital video recorders, heating and air-conditioning units, major appliances, telephone and security systems, office equipment, and so on. Linksys has already conducted an intensive, $300,000 feasibility study to assess the attractiveness of the new product.

Revenue and Cost Estimates

We begin by reviewing the revenue and cost estimates for HomeNet. HomeNet's target market is upscale residential "smart" homes and home offices. Based on extensive marketing surveys, the sales forecast for HomeNet is 100,000 units per year. Given the pace of technological change, Linksys expects the product will have a four-year life. It will be sold through high-end stereo and electronics stores for a retail price of $375, with an expected wholesale price of $260.

Developing the new hardware will be relatively inexpensive, as existing technologies can be simply repackaged in a newly designed, home-friendly box. Industrial design teams will make the box and its packaging aesthetically pleasing to the residential market. Linksys expects total engineering and design costs to amount to $5 million. Once the design is finalized, actual production will be outsourced at a cost (including packaging) of $110 per unit.

In addition to the hardware requirements, Linksys must build a new software application to allow virtual control of the home from the Web. This software development project requires coordination with each of the Web appliance manufacturers and is expected to take a dedicated team of 50 software engineers a full year to complete. The cost of a software engineer (including benefits and related costs) is $200,000 per year. To verify the compatibility of new consumer Internet-ready appliances with the HomeNet system as they become available, Linksys must also build a new lab for testing purposes. This lab will occupy existing facilities but will require $7.5 million of new equipment.

The software and hardware design will be completed, and the lab will be operational, at the end of one year. At that time, HomeNet will be ready to ship. Linksys expects to spend $2.8 million per year on marketing and support for this product.

INTERVIEW WITH
Dick Grannis

Dick Grannis is Senior Vice President and Treasurer of QUALCOMM Incorporated, a world leader in digital wireless communications technology and semiconductors, headquartered in San Diego. He joined the company in 1991 and oversees the company's $10 billion cash investment portfolio. He works primarily on investment banking, capital structure, and international finance.

QUESTION: *QUALCOMM has a wide variety of products in different business lines. How does your capital budgeting process for new products work?*

ANSWER: QUALCOMM evaluates new projects (such as new products, equipment, technologies, research and development, acquisitions, and strategic investments) by using traditional financial measurements including DCF models, IRR levels, peak funding requirements, the time needed to reach cumulative positive cash flows, and the short-term impact of the investment on our reported net earnings. For strategic investments, we consider the possible value of financial, competitive, technology and/or market value enhancements to our core businesses—even if those benefits cannot be quantified. Overall, we make capital budgeting decisions based on a combination of objective analyses and our own business judgment.

We do not engage in capital budgeting and analysis if the project represents an immediate and necessary requirement for our business operations. One example is new software or production equipment to start a project that has already received approval.

We are also mindful of the opportunity costs of allocating our internal engineering resources on one project vs. another project. We view this as a constantly challenging but worthwhile exercise, because we have many attractive opportunities but limited resources to pursue them.

QUESTION: *How often does QUALCOMM evaluate its hurdle rates and what factors does it consider in setting them? How do you allocate capital across areas and regions and assess the risk of non-U.S. investments?*

ANSWER: QUALCOMM encourages its financial planners to utilize hurdle (or discount) rates that vary according to the risk of the particular project. We expect a rate of return commensurate with the project's risk. Our finance staff considers a wide range of discount rates and chooses one that fits the project's expected risk profile and time horizon. The range can be from 6.00% to 8.00% for relatively safe investments in the domestic market to 50% or more for equity investments in foreign markets that may be illiquid and difficult to predict. We re-evaluate our hurdle rates at least every year.

We analyze key factors including: (i) market adoption risk (whether or not customers will buy the new product or service at the price and volume we expect), (ii) technology development risk (whether or not we can develop and patent the new product or service as expected), (iii) execution risk (whether we can launch the new product or service cost effectively and on time), and (iv) dedicated asset risk (the amount of resources that must be consumed to complete the work).

QUESTION: *How are projects categorized and how are the hurdle rates for new projects determined? What would happen if QUALCOMM simply evaluated all new projects against the same hurdle rate?*

ANSWER: We primarily categorize projects by risk level, but we also categorize projects by the expected time horizon. We consider short-term and long-term projects to balance our needs and achieve our objectives. For example, immediate projects and opportunities may demand a great amount of attention, but we also stay focused on long-term projects because they often create greater long-term value for stockholders.

If we were to evaluate all new projects against the same hurdle rate, then our business planners would, by default, consistently choose to invest in the highest risk projects because those projects would appear to have the greatest expected returns in DCF models or IRR analyses. That approach would probably not work well for very long.

Incremental Earnings Forecast

Given the revenue and cost estimates, we can forecast HomeNet's incremental earnings, as shown in Table 7.1 Spreadsheet. After the product is developed in year 0, it will generate sales of 100,000 units × $260 / unit = $26 million each year for the next four years. The cost of producing these units is 100,000 units × $110 / unit = $11 million per year. Thus, HomeNet will produce a gross profit of $26 million − $11 million = $15 million per year, as shown in line 3 of the spreadsheet in Table 7.1.[1]

The project's operating expenses include $2.8 million per year in marketing and support costs, which are listed as selling, general, and administrative expenses. In year 0, Linksys will spend $5 million on design and engineering, together with 50 × $200,000 = $10 million on software, for a total of $15 million in research and development expenditures.

TABLE 7.1 SPREADSHEET	HomeNet's Incremental Earnings Forecast					
Year	0	1	2	3	4	5
Incremental Earnings Forecast ($000s)						
1 Sales	—	26,000	26,000	26,000	26,000	—
2 Cost of Goods Sold	—	(11,000)	(11,000)	(11,000)	(11,000)	—
3 **Gross Profit**	—	15,000	15,000	15,000	15,000	—
4 Selling, General, and Administrative	—	(2,800)	(2,800)	(2,800)	(2,800)	—
5 Research and Development	(15,000)	—	—	—	—	—
6 Depreciation	—	(1,500)	(1,500)	(1,500)	(1,500)	(1,500)
7 **EBIT**	(15,000)	10,700	10,700	10,700	10,700	(1,500)
8 Income Tax at 40%	6,000	(4,280)	(4,280)	(4,280)	(4,280)	600
9 **Unlevered Net Income**	(9,000)	6,420	6,420	6,420	6,420	(900)

Capital Expenditures and Depreciation. HomeNet also requires $7.5 million in equipment for a new lab. Recall from Chapter 2 that while investments in plant, property, and equipment are a cash expense, they are not directly listed as expenses when calculating *earnings*. Instead, the firm deducts a fraction of the cost of these items each year as depreciation. Several different methods are used to compute depreciation. The simplest method is **straight-line depreciation**, in which the asset's cost is divided equally over its life (we discuss other methods in Section 7.2). If we assume straight-line depreciation over a five-year life for the lab equipment, HomeNet's depreciation expense is $1.5 million per year. Deducting these depreciation expenses leads to the forecast for HomeNet's earnings before interest and taxes (EBIT) shown in line 7 of Table 7.1 Spreadsheet. This treatment of capital expenditures is one of the key reasons why earnings are not an accurate representation of cash flows.

Interest Expenses. In Chapter 2, we saw that to compute a firm's net income, we must first deduct interest expenses from EBIT. When evaluating a capital budgeting decision like the HomeNet project, however, we generally *do not include interest expenses*. Any

[1]. While revenues and costs occur throughout the year, the standard convention, which we adopt here, is to list revenues and costs in the year in which they occur. Thus cash flows that occur at the end of one year will be listed in a different column than those that occur at the start of the next year, even though they may occur only weeks apart. When additional precision is required, cash flows are often estimated on a quarterly or monthly basis. (See also the Appendix to Chapter 5 for a method of converting continuously arriving cash flows to annual ones.)

incremental interest expenses will be related to the firm's decision regarding how to finance the project. Here we wish to evaluate the project on its own, separate from the financing decision.[2] Thus we evaluate the HomeNet project *as if* Cisco will not use any debt to finance it (whether or not that is actually the case), and we postpone the consideration of alternative financing choices until Part V of this book. For this reason, we refer to the net income we compute in the spreadsheet in Table 7.1 as the **unlevered net income** of the project, to indicate that it does not include any interest expenses associated with leverage.

Taxes.   The final expense we must account for is corporate taxes. The correct tax rate to use is the firm's **marginal corporate tax rate**, which is the tax rate it will pay on an *incremental* dollar of pre-tax income. In Table 7.1 Spreadsheet, we assume the marginal corporate tax rate for the HomeNet project is 40% each year. The incremental income tax expense is calculated in line 8 as

$$\text{Income Tax} = \text{EBIT} \times \tau_c \tag{7.1}$$

where τ_c is the firm's marginal corporate tax rate.

In year 1, HomeNet will contribute an additional $10.7 million to Cisco's EBIT, which will result in an additional $10.7 million $\times$ 40% = $4.28 million in corporate tax that Cisco will owe. We deduct this amount to determine HomeNet's after-tax contribution to net income.

In year 0, however, HomeNet's EBIT is negative. Are taxes relevant in this case? Yes. HomeNet will reduce Cisco's taxable income in year 0 by $15 million. As long as Cisco earns taxable income elsewhere in year 0 against which it can offset HomeNet's losses, Cisco will owe $15 million $\times$ 40% = $6 million *less* in taxes in year 0. The firm should credit this tax savings to the HomeNet project. A similar credit applies in year 5, when the firm claims its final depreciation expense for the lab equipment.

EXAMPLE 7.1

Taxing Losses for Projects in Profitable Companies

Problem
Kellogg Company plans to launch a new line of high-fiber, zero-trans-fat breakfast pastries. The heavy advertising expenses associated with the new product launch will generate operating losses of $15 million next year for the product. Kellogg expects to earn pre-tax income of $460 million from operations other than the new pastries next year. If Kellogg pays a 40% tax rate on its pre-tax income, what will it owe in taxes next year without the new pastry product? What will it owe with the new pastries?

Solution
Without the new pastries, Kellogg will owe $460 million $\times$ 40% = $184 million in corporate taxes next year. With the new pastries, Kellogg's pre-tax income next year will be only $460 million − $15 million = $445 million, and it will owe $445 million $\times$ 40% = $178 million in tax. Thus, launching the new product reduces Kellogg's taxes next year by $184 million − $178 million = $6 million.

---

2. This approach is motivated by the Separation Principle from Chapter 3: When securities are fairly priced, the net present value of a fixed set of cash flows is independent of how those cash flows are financed. Later in the text we will consider cases in which financing may influence the project's value, and we will extend our capital budgeting techniques accordingly in Chapter 18.

We can express the data in Spreadsheet 7.1 as the following shorthand formula for unlevered net income:

$$\text{Unlevered Net Income} = \text{EBIT} \times (1 - \tau_c)$$
$$= (\text{Revenues} - \text{Costs} - \text{Depreciation}) \times (1 - \tau_c) \quad (7.2)$$

That is, a project's unlevered net income is equal to its incremental revenues less costs and depreciation, evaluated on an after-tax basis.

Indirect Effects on Incremental Earnings

When computing the incremental earnings of an investment decision, we should include *all* changes between the firm's earnings with the project versus without the project. Thus far, we have analyzed only the direct effects of the HomeNet project. But HomeNet may have indirect consequences for other operations within Cisco. Because these indirect effects will also affect Cisco's earnings, we must include them in our analysis.

Opportunity Costs.   Many projects use a resource that the company already owns. Because the firm does not need to pay cash to acquire this resource for a new project, it is tempting to assume that the resource is available for free. However, in many cases the resource could provide value for the firm in another opportunity or project. The **opportunity cost** of using a resource is the value it could have provided in its best alternative use.[3] Because this value is lost when the resource is used by another project, we should include the opportunity cost as an incremental cost of the project. In the case of the HomeNet project, space will be required for the new lab. Even though the lab will be housed in an existing facility, we must include the opportunity cost of not using the space in an alternative way.

EXAMPLE 7.2

The Opportunity Cost of HomeNet's Lab Space

Problem

Suppose HomeNet's lab will be housed in warehouse space that the company would have otherwise rented out for $200,000 per year during years 1–4. How does this opportunity cost affect HomeNet's incremental earnings?

Solution

In this case, the opportunity cost of the warehouse space is the forgone rent. This cost would reduce HomeNet's incremental earnings during years 1–4 by $200,000 \times (1 - 40\%) = $120,000.

Project Externalities.   **Project externalities** are indirect effects of the project that may increase or decrease the profits of other business activities of the firm. For instance, in the Kellogg example in the chapter introduction, some purchasers of Kellogg's new Low-Sugar Frosted Flakes would otherwise have bought Kellogg's regular Frosted Flakes. When sales of a new product displace sales of an existing product, the situation is often referred to as

---

3. In Chapter 5, we defined the opportunity cost of capital as the rate you could earn on an alternative investment with equivalent risk. We similarly define the opportunity cost of using an existing asset in a project as the cash flow generated by the next-best alternative use for the asset.

A common mistake is to conclude that if an asset is currently idle, its opportunity cost is zero. For example, the firm might have a warehouse that is currently empty or a machine that is not being used. Often, the asset may have been idled in anticipation of taking on the new project, and would have otherwise been put to use by the firm. Even if the firm has no alternative use for the asset, the firm could choose to sell or rent the asset. The value obtained from the asset's alternative use, sale, or rental represents an opportunity cost that must be included as part of the incremental cash flows.

cannibalization. Suppose that approximately 25% of HomeNet's sales come from customers who would have purchased an existing Linksys wireless router if HomeNet were not available. Because this reduction in sales of the existing wireless router is a consequence of the decision to develop HomeNet, we must include it when calculating HomeNet's incremental earnings.

TABLE 7.2 SPREADSHEET — **HomeNet's Incremental Earnings Forecast Including Cannibalization and Lost Rent**

	Year	0	1	2	3	4	5
Incremental Earnings Forecast ($000s)							
1	Sales	—	23,500	23,500	23,500	23,500	—
2	Cost of Goods Sold	—	(9,500)	(9,500)	(9,500)	(9,500)	—
3	Gross Profit	—	14,000	14,000	14,000	14,000	—
4	Selling, General, and Administrative	—	(3,000)	(3,000)	(3,000)	(3,000)	—
5	Research and Development	(15,000)	—	—	—	—	—
6	Depreciation	—	(1,500)	(1,500)	(1,500)	(1,500)	(1,500)
7	EBIT	(15,000)	9,500	9,500	9,500	9,500	(1,500)
8	Income Tax at 40%	6,000	(3,800)	(3,800)	(3,800)	(3,800)	600
9	Unlevered Net Income	(9,000)	5,700	5,700	5,700	5,700	(900)

The spreadsheet in Table 7.2 recalculates HomeNet's incremental earnings forecast including the opportunity cost of the lab space and the expected cannibalization of the existing product. The opportunity cost of the lab space in Example 7.2 increases selling, general, and administrative expenses from $2.8 million to $3.0 million. For the cannibalization, suppose that the existing router wholesales for $100 so the expected loss in sales is

$$25\% \times 100{,}000 \text{ units} \times \$100/\text{unit} = \$2.5 \text{ million}$$

Compared to Table 7.1 Spreadsheet, the sales forecast falls from $26 million to $23.5 million. In addition, suppose the cost of the existing router is $60 per unit. Then the cost of goods sold is reduced by

$$25\% \times 100{,}000 \text{ units} \times (\$60 \text{ cost per unit}) = \$1.5 \text{ million}$$

Thus, because Cisco will no longer need to produce as many of its existing wireless routers, the incremental cost of goods sold of the HomeNet project drops from $11 million to $9.5 million. HomeNet's incremental gross profit therefore declines by $2.5 million − $1.5 million = $1 million once we account for this externality.

Thus, comparing the spreadsheets in Tables 7.1 and 7.2, our forecast for HomeNet's unlevered net income in years 1–4 declines from $6.42 million to $5.7 million due to the lost rent of the lab space and the lost sales of the existing router.

Sunk Costs and Incremental Earnings

A **sunk cost** is any unrecoverable cost for which the firm is already liable. Sunk costs have been or will be paid regardless of the decision whether or not to proceed with the project. Therefore, they are not incremental with respect to the current decision and should not be included in its analysis. For this reason, we did not include in our analysis the $300,000 already expended on the marketing and feasibility studies for HomeNet. Because this $300,000 has already been spent, it is a sunk cost. A good rule to remember is that *if our decision does not affect a cash flow, then the cash flow should not affect our decision.* Following are some common examples of sunk costs you may encounter.

Fixed Overhead Expenses.   **Overhead expenses** are associated with activities that are not directly attributable to a single business activity but instead affect many different areas of the corporation. These expenses are often allocated to the different business activities for accounting purposes. To the extent that these overhead costs are fixed and will be incurred in any case, they are not incremental to the project and should not be included. Only include as incremental expenses the *additional* overhead expenses that arise because of the decision to take on the project.

Past Research and Development Expenditures.   When a firm has already devoted significant resources to develop a new product, there may be a tendency to continue investing in the product even if market conditions have changed and the product is unlikely to be viable. The rationale that is sometimes given is that if the product is abandoned, the money that has already been invested will be "wasted." In other cases, a decision is made to abandon a project because it cannot possibly be successful enough to recoup the investment that has already been made. In fact, neither argument is correct: Any money that has already been spent is a sunk cost and therefore irrelevant. The decision to continue or abandon should be based only on the incremental costs and benefits of the product going forward.

Real-World Complexities

We have simplified the HomeNet example in an effort to focus on the types of effects that financial managers consider when estimating a project's incremental earnings. For a real project, however, the estimates of these revenues and costs are likely to be much more complicated. For instance, our assumption that the same number of HomeNet units will be sold each year is probably unrealistic. A new product typically has lower sales initially, as customers gradually become aware of the product. Sales will then accelerate, plateau, and ultimately decline as the product nears obsolescence or faces increased competition.

Similarly, the average selling price of a product and its cost of production will generally change over time. Prices and costs tend to rise with the general level of inflation in the economy. The prices of technology products, however, often fall over time as newer, superior technologies emerge and production costs decline. For most industries, competition tends to reduce profit margins over time. These factors should be considered when estimating a project's revenues and costs.

The Sunk Cost Fallacy

Sunk cost fallacy is a term used to describe the tendency of people to be influenced by sunk costs and to "throw good money after bad." That is, people sometimes continue to invest in a project that has a negative NPV because they have already invested a large amount in the project and feel that by not continuing it, the prior investment will be wasted. The sunk cost fallacy is also sometimes called the "Concorde effect," a term that refers to the British and French governments' decision to continue funding the joint development of the Concorde aircraft even after it was clear that sales of the plane would fall far short of what was necessary to justify its continued development. Although the project was viewed by the British government as a commercial and financial disaster, the political implications of halting the project—and thereby publicly admitting that all past expenses on the project would result in nothing—ultimately prevented either government from abandoning the project.

EXAMPLE 7.3

Product Adoption and Price Changes

Problem

Suppose sales of HomeNet were expected to be 100,000 units in year 1, 125,000 units in years 2 and 3, and 50,000 units in year 4. Suppose also that HomeNet's sale price and manufacturing cost are expected to decline by 10% per year, as with other networking products. By contrast, selling, general, and administrative expenses are expected to rise with inflation by 4% per year. Update the incremental earnings forecast in the spreadsheet in Table 7.2 to account for these effects.

Solution

HomeNet's incremental earnings with these new assumptions are shown in the spreadsheet below:

	Year	0	1	2	3	4	5
Incremental Earnings Forecast ($000s)							
1	Sales	—	23,500	26,438	23,794	8,566	—
2	Cost of Goods Sold	—	(9,500)	(10,688)	(9,619)	(3,463)	—
3	**Gross Profit**	—	14,000	15,750	14,175	5,103	—
4	Selling, General, and Administrative	—	(3,000)	(3,120)	(3,245)	(3,375)	—
5	Research and Development	(15,000)	—	—	—	—	—
6	Depreciation	—	(1,500)	(1,500)	(1,500)	(1,500)	(1,500)
7	EBIT	(15,000)	9,500	11,130	9,430	228	(1,500)
8	Income Tax at 40%	6,000	(3,800)	(4,452)	(3,772)	(91)	600
9	Unlevered Net Income	(9,000)	5,700	6,678	5,658	137	(900)

For example, sale prices in year 2 will be $260 × 0.90 = $234 per unit for HomeNet, and $100 × 0.90 = $90 per unit for the cannibalized product. Thus incremental sales in year 2 are equal to 125,000 units × ($234 per unit) − 31,250 cannibalized units × ($90 per unit) = $26.438 million.

CONCEPT CHECK

1. Should we include sunk costs in the cash flows of a project? Why or why not?

2. Explain why you must include the opportunity cost of using a resource as an incremental cost of a project.

7.2 Determining Free Cash Flow and NPV

As discussed in Chapter 2, earnings are an accounting measure of the firm's performance. They do not represent real profits: The firm cannot use its earnings to buy goods, pay employees, fund new investments, or pay dividends to shareholders. To do those things, a firm needs cash. Thus, to evaluate a capital budgeting decision, we must determine its consequences for the firm's available cash. The incremental effect of a project on the firm's available cash is the project's **free cash flow**.

In this section, we forecast the free cash flow of the HomeNet project using the earnings forecasts we developed in Section 7.1. We then use this forecast to calculate the NPV of the project.

Calculating the Free Cash Flow from Earnings

As discussed in Chapter 2, there are important differences between earnings and cash flow. Earnings include non-cash charges, such as depreciation, but do not include the cost of capital investment. To determine HomeNet's free cash flow from its incremental earnings, we must adjust for these differences.

Capital Expenditures and Depreciation.   Depreciation is not a cash expense that is paid by the firm. Rather, it is a method used for accounting and tax purposes to allocate the original purchase cost of the asset over its life. Because depreciation is not a cash flow, we do not include it in the cash flow forecast. Instead, we include the actual cash cost of the asset when it is purchased.

To compute HomeNet's free cash flow, we must add back to earnings the depreciation expense for the lab equipment (a non-cash charge) and subtract the actual capital expenditure of $7.5 million that will be paid for the equipment in year 0. We show these adjustments in lines 10 and 11 of the spreadsheet in Table 7.3 (which is based on the incremental earnings forecast of Table 7.2 Spreadsheet).

TABLE 7.3 SPREADSHEET	Calculation of HomeNet's Free Cash Flow (Including Cannibalization and Lost Rent)					

	Year	0	1	2	3	4	5
Incremental Earnings Forecast ($000s)							
1 Sales		—	23,500	23,500	23,500	23,500	—
2 Cost of Goods Sold		—	(9,500)	(9,500)	(9,500)	(9,500)	—
3 **Gross Profit**		—	14,000	14,000	14,000	14,000	—
4 Selling, General, and Administrative		—	(3,000)	(3,000)	(3,000)	(3,000)	—
5 Research and Development		(15,000)	—	—	—	—	—
6 Depreciation		—	(1,500)	(1,500)	(1,500)	(1,500)	(1,500)
7 **EBIT**		(15,000)	9,500	9,500	9,500	9,500	(1,500)
8 Income Tax at 40%		6,000	(3,800)	(3,800)	(3,800)	(3,800)	600
9 **Unlevered Net Income**		(9,000)	5,700	5,700	5,700	5,700	(900)
Free Cash Flow ($000s)							
10 Plus: Depreciation		—	1,500	1,500	1,500	1,500	1,500
11 Less: Capital Expenditures		(7,500)	—	—	—	—	—
12 Less: Increases in NWC		—	(2,100)	—	—	—	2,100
13 **Free Cash Flow**		(16,500)	5,100	7,200	7,200	7,200	2,700

Net Working Capital (NWC). We defined net working capital in Chapter 2 as the difference between current assets and current liabilities. The main components of net working capital are cash, inventory, receivables, and payables:

$$\text{Net Working Capital} = \text{Current Assets} - \text{Current Liabilities}$$
$$= \text{Cash} + \text{Inventory} + \text{Receivables} - \text{Payables} \qquad (7.3)$$

Most projects will require the firm to invest in net working capital. Firms may need to maintain a minimum cash balance[4] to meet unexpected expenditures, and inventories of raw materials and finished product to accommodate production uncertainties and demand fluctuations. Also, customers may not pay for the goods they purchase immediately. While sales are immediately counted as part of earnings, the firm does not receive any cash until the customers actually pay. In the interim, the firm includes the amount that customers owe in its receivables. Thus the firm's receivables measure the total credit that the firm has extended to its customers. In the same way, payables measure the credit the firm has received from its suppliers. The difference between receivables and payables is the net amount of the firm's capital that is consumed as a result of these credit transactions, known as **trade credit**.

Suppose that HomeNet will have no incremental cash or inventory requirements (products will be shipped directly from the contract manufacturer to customers). However, receivables related to HomeNet are expected to account for 15% of annual sales, and payables are expected to be 15% of the annual cost of goods sold (COGS).[5] HomeNet's net working capital requirements are shown in Table 7.4 Spreadsheet.

TABLE 7.4 SPREADSHEET	HomeNet's Net Working Capital Requirements					

Year	0	1	2	3	4	5
Net Working Capital Forecast ($000s)						
1 Cash Requirements	—	—	—	—	—	—
2 Inventory	—	—	—	—	—	—
3 Receivables (15% of Sales)	—	3,525	3,525	3,525	3,525	—
4 Payables (15% of COGS)	—	(1,425)	(1,425)	(1,425)	(1,425)	—
5 Net Working Capital	—	2,100	2,100	2,100	2,100	—

Table 7.4 Spreadsheet shows that the HomeNet project will require no net working capital in year 0, $2.1 million in net working capital in years 1–4, and no net working capital in year 5. How does this requirement affect the project's free cash flow? Any increases in net working capital represent an investment that reduces the cash available to

---

4. The cash included in net working capital is cash that is *not* invested to earn a market rate of return. It includes cash held in the firm's checking account, in a company safe or cash box, in cash registers (for retail stores), and other sites.

5. If customers take N days to pay on average, then accounts receivable will consist of those sales that occurred in the last N days. If sales are evenly distributed throughout the year, receivables will equal $(N/365)$ times annual sales. Thus, receivables equal to 15% of sales corresponds to an average payment period of $N = 15\% \times 365 = 55$ days. The same is true for payables. (See also Eq. 2.8 in Chapter 2.)

the firm and so reduces free cash flow. We define the increase in net working capital in year t as

$$\Delta NWC_t = NWC_t - NWC_{t-1} \qquad (7.4)$$

We can use our forecast of HomeNet's net working capital requirements to complete our estimate of HomeNet's free cash flow in Table Spreadsheet 7.3. In year 1, net working capital increases by $2.1 million. This increase represents a cost to the firm as shown in line 12 of Table Spreadsheet 7.3. This reduction of free cash flow corresponds to the fact that $3.525 million of the firm's sales in year 1, and $1.425 million of its costs, have not yet been paid.

In years 2–4, net working capital does not change, so no further contributions are needed. In year 5, when the project is shut down, net working capital falls by $2.1 million as the payments of the last customers are received and the final bills are paid. We add this $2.1 million to free cash flow in year 5, as shown in line 12 of Table 7.3 Spreadsheet

Now that we have adjusted HomeNet's unlevered net income for depreciation, capital expenditures, and increases to net working capital, we compute HomeNet's free cash flow as shown in line 13 of the spreadsheet in Table 7.3. Note that in the first two years, free cash flow is lower than unlevered net income, reflecting the upfront investment in equipment and net working capital required by the project. In later years, free cash flow exceeds unlevered net income because depreciation is not a cash expense. In the last year, the firm ultimately recovers the investment in net working capital, further boosting the free cash flow.

EXAMPLE 7.4

Net Working Capital with Changing Sales

Problem
Forecast the required investment in net working capital for HomeNet under the scenario in Example 7.3.

Solution
Required investments in net working capital are shown below:

	Year	0	1	2	3	4	5
Net Working Capital Forecast ($000s)							
1	Receivables (15% of Sales)	—	3,525	3,966	3,569	1,285	—
2	Payables (15% of COGS)	—	(1,425)	(1,603)	(1,443)	(519)	—
3	Net Working Capital	—	2,100	2,363	2,126	765	—
4	Increases in NWC	—	2,100	263	(237)	(1,361)	(765)

In this case, working capital changes each year. A large initial investment in working capital is required in year 1, followed by a small investment in year 2 as sales continue to grow. Working capital is recovered in years 3–5 as sales decline.

Calculating Free Cash Flow Directly

As we noted at the outset of this chapter, because practitioners usually begin the capital budgeting process by first forecasting earnings, we have chosen to do the same. However, we could have calculated the HomeNet's free cash flow directly by using the following shorthand formula:

Free Cash Flow

$$\overbrace{\text{Free Cash Flow} = (\text{Revenues} - \text{Costs} - \text{Depreciation}) \times (1 - \tau_c)}^{\text{Unlevered Net Income}}$$
$$+ \text{ Depreciation} - \text{CapEx} - \Delta NWC \qquad (7.5)$$

Note that we first deduct depreciation when computing the project's incremental earnings, and then add it back (because it is a non-cash expense) when computing free cash flow. Thus the only effect of depreciation is to reduce the firm's taxable income. Indeed, we can rewrite Eq. 7.5 as

$$\text{Free Cash Flow} = (\text{Revenues} - \text{Costs}) \times (1 - \tau_c) - \text{CapEx} - \Delta NWC$$
$$+ \tau_c \times \text{Depreciation} \qquad (7.6)$$

The last term in Eq. 7.6, $\tau_c \times$ Depreciation, is called the **depreciation tax shield**. It is the tax savings that results from the ability to deduct depreciation. As a consequence, depreciation expenses have a *positive* impact on free cash flow. Firms often report a different depreciation expense for accounting and for tax purposes. Because only the tax consequences of depreciation are relevant for free cash flow, we should use the depreciation expense that the firm will use for tax purposes in our forecast.

Calculating the NPV

To compute HomeNet's NPV, we must discount its free cash flow at the appropriate cost of capital.[6] As discussed in Chapter 5, the cost of capital for a project is the expected return that investors could earn on their best alternative investment with similar risk and maturity. We will develop the techniques needed to estimate the cost of capital in Part V of the text, when we discuss capital structure. For now, we assume that Cisco's managers believe that the HomeNet project will have similar risk to other projects within Cisco's Linksys division, and that the appropriate cost of capital for these projects is 12%.

Given this cost of capital, we compute the present value of each free cash flow in the future. As explained in Chapter 4, if the cost of capital $r = 12\%$, the present value of the free cash flow in year t (or FCF_t) is

$$PV(FCF_t) = \frac{FCF_t}{(1 + r)^t} = FCF_t \times \underbrace{\frac{1}{(1 + r)^t}}_{t-\text{year discount factor}} \qquad (7.7)$$

We compute the NPV of the HomeNet project in Table 7.5. Spreadsheet Line 3 calculates the discount factor, and line 4 multiplies the free cash flow by the discount factor to get the present value. The NPV of the project is the sum of the present values of each free cash flow, reported on line 5:

$$NPV = -16{,}500 + 4554 + 5740 + 5125 + 4576 + 1532$$
$$= 5027$$

We can also compute the NPV using the Excel NPV function to calculate the present value of the cash flows in year 1 through 5, and then add the cash flow in year 0 (i.e., "$= NPV(r, FCF_1:FCF_5) + FCF_0$").

---

6. Rather than draw a separate timeline for these cash flows, we can interpret the final line of Table 7.3 Spreadsheet as the timeline.

TABLE 7.5 SPREADSHEET	Computing HomeNet's NPV						
Year	0	1	2	3	4	5	
Net Present Value ($000s)							
1 Free Cash Flow	(16,500)	5,100	7,200	7,200	7,200	2,700	
2 Project Cost of Capital	12%						
3 Discount Factor		1.000	0.893	0.797	0.712	0.636	0.567
4 PV of Free Cash Flow	(16,500)	4,554	5,740	5,125	4,576	1.532	
5 NPV	5,027						

Based on our estimates, HomeNet's NPV is $5,027 million. While HomeNet's upfront cost is $16.5 million, the present value of the additional free cash flow that Cisco will receive from the project is $21.5 million. Thus, taking the HomeNet project is equivalent to Cisco having an extra $5 million in the bank today.

Choosing Among Alternatives

Thus far, we have considered the capital budgeting decision to launch the HomeNet product line. To analyze the decision, we computed the project's free cash flow and calculated the NPV. Because *not* launching HomeNet produces an additional NPV of zero for the firm, launching HomeNet is the best decision for the firm if its NPV is positive. In many situations, however, we must compare mutually exclusive alternatives, each of which has consequences for the firm's cash flows. As we explained in Chapter 6, in such cases we can make the best decision by first computing the free cash flow associated with each alternative and then choosing the alternative with the highest NPV.

Evaluating Manufacturing Alternatives.   Suppose Cisco is considering an alternative manufacturing plan for the HomeNet product. The current plan is to fully outsource production at a cost of $110 per unit. Alternatively, Cisco could assemble the product in-house at a cost of $95 per unit. However, the latter option will require $5 million in upfront operating expenses to reorganize the assembly facility, and Cisco will need to maintain inventory equal to one month's production.

To choose between these two alternatives, we compute the free cash flow associated with each choice and compare their NPVs to see which is most advantageous for the firm. When comparing alternatives, we need to compare only those cash flows that differ between them. We can ignore any cash flows that are the same under either scenario (e.g., HomeNet's revenues).

The spreadsheet in Table 7.6 compares the two assembly options, computing the NPV of the cash costs for each. The difference in EBIT results from the upfront cost of setting up the in-house facility in year 0, and the differing assembly costs: $110/unit × 100,000 units/yr = $11 million/yr outsourced, versus $95/unit × 100,000 units/yr = $9.5 million/yr in-house. Adjusting for taxes, we see the consequences for unlevered net income on lines 3 and 9.

Because the options do not differ in terms of capital expenditures (there are none associated with assembly), to compare the free cash flow for each, we only need to adjust for their different net working capital requirements. If assembly is outsourced, payables account for 15% of the cost of goods, or 15% × $11 million = $1.65 million. This amount is the credit Cisco will receive from its supplier in year 1 and will maintain until year 5. Because Cisco will borrow this amount from its supplier, net working capital *falls*

TABLE 7.6 SPREADSHEET	NPV Cost of Outsourced Versus In-House Assembly of HomeNet

Year	0	1	2	3	4	5
Outsourced Assembly ($000s)						
1 EBIT	—	(11,000)	(11,000)	(11,000)	(11,000)	—
2 Income Tax at 40%	—	4,400	4,400	4,400	4,400	—
3 Unlevered Net Income	—	(6,600)	(6,600)	(6,600)	(6,600)	—
4 Less: Increases in NWC	—	1,650	—	—	—	(1,650)
5 Free Cash Flow	—	(4,950)	(6,600)	(6,600)	(6,600)	(1,650)
6 NPV at 12%	(19,510)					

Year	0	1	2	3	4	5
In-House Assembly ($000s)						
1 EBIT	(5,000)	(9,500)	(9,500)	(9,500)	(9,500)	—
2 Income Tax at 40%	2,000	3,800	3,800	3,800	3,800	—
3 Unlevered Net Income	(3,000)	(5,700)	(5,700)	(5,700)	(5,700)	—
4 Less: Increases in NWC	—	633	—	—	—	(633)
5 Free Cash Flow	(3,000)	(5,067)	(5,700)	(5,700)	(5,700)	(633)
6 NPV at 12%	(20,107)					

by $1.65 million in year 1, adding to Cisco's free cash flow. In year 5, Cisco's net working capital will increase as Cisco pays its suppliers, and free cash flow will fall by an equal amount.

If assembly is done in-house, payables are 15% × $9.5 million = $1.425 million. However, Cisco will need to maintain inventory equal to one month's production, which has cost of $9.5 million ÷ 12 = $0.792 million. Thus Linksys's net working capital will decrease by $1.425 million − $0.792 million = $0.633 million in year 1 and will increase by the same amount in year 5.

Comparing Free Cash Flows for Cisco's Alternatives.   Adjusting for increases to net working capital, we compare the free cash flow of each alternative on lines 5 and 11 and compute their NPVs using the project's 12% cost of capital.[7] In each case, the NPV is negative, as we are evaluating only the costs of production. Outsourcing, however, is somewhat cheaper, with a present value cost of $19.5 million versus $20.1 million if the units are produced in-house.[8]

Further Adjustments to Free Cash Flow

Here we describe a number of complications that can arise when estimating a project's free cash flow.

Other Non-cash Items.   In general, other non-cash items that appear as part of incremental earnings should not be included in the project's free cash flow. The firm should

---

7. The risks of these options could potentially differ from the risk of the project overall and from the risks of each other, requiring a different cost of capital for each case. We ignore any such differences here.

8. It is also possible to compare these two cases in a single spreadsheet where we compute the difference in the free cash flows directly, rather than compute the free cash flows separately for each option. We prefer to do them separately, as it is clearer and generalizes to the case when there are more than two options.

include only actual cash revenues or expenses. For example, the firm adds back any amortization of intangible assets (such as patents) to unlevered net income when calculating free cash flow.

Timing of Cash Flows.   For simplicity, we have treated the cash flows for HomeNet as if they occur at annual intervals. In reality, cash flows will be spread throughout the year. We can forecast free cash flow on a quarterly, monthly, or even continuous basis when greater accuracy is required.

Accelerated Depreciation.   Because depreciation contributes positively to the firm's cash flow through the depreciation tax shield, it is in the firm's best interest to use the most accelerated method of depreciation that is allowable for tax purposes. By doing so, the firm will accelerate its tax savings and increase their present value. In the United States, the most accelerated depreciation method allowed by the IRS is MACRS (Modified Accelerated Cost Recovery System) depreciation. With **MACRS depreciation**, the firm first categorizes assets according to their recovery period. Based on the recovery period, MACRS depreciation tables assign a fraction of the purchase price that the firm can recover each year. We provide MACRS tables and recovery periods for common assets in the appendix.

EXAMPLE 7.5

Computing Accelerated Depreciation

Problem
What depreciation deduction would be allowed for the lab equipment using the MACRS method, assuming the lab equipment is designated to have a five-year recovery period?

Solution
Table 7A.1 in the appendix provides the percentage of the cost that can be depreciated each year. Based on the table, the allowable depreciation expense for the lab equipment is shown below (in thousands of dollars):

	Year	0	1	2	3	4	5
MACRS Depreciation							
1	Lab Equipment Cost	(7,500)					
2	MACRS Depreciation Rate	20.00%	32.00%	19.20%	11.52%	11.52%	5.76%
3	Depreciation Expense	(1,500)	(2,400)	(1,440)	(864)	(864)	(432)

Compared with straight-line depreciation, the MACRS method allows for larger depreciation deductions earlier in the asset's life, which increases the present value of the depreciation tax shield and so will raise the project's NPV. In the case of HomeNet, computing the NPV using MACRS depreciation leads to an NPV of $5.34 million.

Liquidation or Salvage Value.   Assets that are no longer needed often have a resale value, or some salvage value if the parts are sold for scrap. Some assets may have a negative liquidation value. For example, it may cost money to remove and dispose of the used equipment.

In the calculation of free cash flow, we include the liquidation value of any assets that are no longer needed and may be disposed of. When an asset is liquidated, any capital gain is taxed as income. We calculate the capital gain as the difference between the sale price and the book value of the asset:

$$\text{Capital Gain} = \text{Sale Price} - \text{Book Value} \qquad (7.8)$$

The book value is equal to the asset's original cost less the amount it has already been depreciated for tax purposes:

$$\text{Book Value} = \text{Purchase Price} - \text{Accumulated Depreciation} \qquad (7.9)$$

We must adjust the project's free cash flow to account for the after-tax cash flow that would result from an asset sale:

$$\begin{array}{c} \text{After-Tax Cash Flow from Asset Sale} = \\ \text{Sale Price} - (\tau_c \times \text{Capital Gain}) \end{array} \qquad (7.10)$$

EXAMPLE 7.6

Adding Salvage Value to Free Cash Flow

Problem

Suppose that in addition to the $7.5 million in new equipment required for HomeNet's lab, equipment will be transferred to the lab from another Linksys facility. This equipment has a resale value of $2 million and a book value of $1 million. If the equipment is kept rather than sold, its remaining book value can be depreciated next year. When the lab is shut down in year 5, the equipment will have a salvage value of $800,000. What adjustments must we make to HomeNet's free cash flow in this case?

Solution

The existing equipment could have been sold for $2 million. The after-tax proceeds from this sale are an opportunity cost of using the equipment in the HomeNet lab. Thus we must reduce HomeNet's free cash flow in year 0 by $2 million − 40% × ($2 million − $1 million) = $1.6 million.

In year 1, the remaining $1 million book value of the equipment can be depreciated, creating a depreciation tax shield of 40% × $1 million = $400,000. In year 5, the firm will sell the equipment for a salvage value of $800,000. Because the equipment will be fully depreciated at that time, the entire amount will be taxable as a capital gain, so the after-tax cash flow from the sale is $800,000 × (1 − 40%) = $480,000.

The spreadsheet below shows these adjustments to the free cash flow from Table 7.3 Spreadsheet and recalculates HomeNet's free cash flow and NPV in this case.

	Year	0	1	2	3	4	5
	Free Cash Flow and NPV ($000s)						
1	Free Cash Flow w/o equipment	(16,500)	5,100	7,200	7,200	7,200	2,700
	Adjustments for use of existing equipment						
2	After-Tax Salvage Value	(1,600)	–	–	–	–	480
3	Depreciation Tax Shield	–	400	–	–	–	–
4	Free Cash Flow with equipment	(18,100)	5,500	7,200	7,200	7,200	3,180
5	NPV at 12%	4,055					

Terminal or Continuation Value.   Sometimes the firm explicitly forecasts free cash flow over a shorter horizon than the full horizon of the project or investment. This is necessarily true for investments with an indefinite life, such as an expansion of the firm. In this case, we estimate the value of the remaining free cash flow beyond the forecast horizon by including an additional, one-time cash flow at the end of the forecast horizon called the **terminal** or **continuation value** of the project. This amount represents the market value (as of the last forecast period) of the free cash flow from the project at all future dates.

Depending on the setting, we use different methods for estimating the continuation value of an investment. For example, when analyzing investments with long lives, it is common to explicitly calculate free cash flow over a short horizon, and then assume that cash flows grow at some constant rate beyond the forecast horizon.

EXAMPLE 7.7

Continuation Value with Perpetual Growth

Problem

Base Hardware is considering opening a set of new retail stores. The free cash flow projections for the new stores are shown below (in millions of dollars):

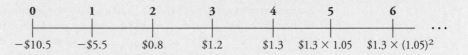

After year 4, Base Hardware expects free cash flow from the stores to increase at a rate of 5% per year. If the appropriate cost of capital for this investment is 10%, what continuation value in year 3 captures the value of future free cash flows in year 4 and beyond? What is the NPV of the new stores?

Solution

The expected free cash flow from the store in year 4 is $1.30 million, with future free cash flow beyond year 4 expected to grow at 5% per year. The continuation value in year 3 of the free cash flow in year 4 and beyond can therefore be calculated as a constant growth perpetuity:

$$\text{Continuation Value in Year 3} = \text{PV(FCF in Year 4 and Beyond)}$$

$$= \frac{FCF_4}{r - g} = \frac{\$1.30 \text{ million}}{0.10 - 0.05} = \$26 \text{ million}$$

We can restate the free cash flows of the investment as follows (in thousands of dollars):

Year	0	1	2	3
Free Cash Flow (Years 0–3)	(10,500)	(5,500)	800	1,200
Continuation Value				26,000
Free Cash Flow	(10,500)	(5,500)	800	27,200

The NPV of the investment in the new stores is

$$NPV = -10,500 - \frac{5500}{1.10} + \frac{800}{1.10^2} + \frac{27,200}{1.10^3} = \$5597$$

or $5.597 million.

Tax Carryforwards.   A firm generally identifies its marginal tax rate by determining the tax bracket that it falls into based on its overall level of pre-tax income. Two additional features of the tax code, called **tax loss carryforwards and carrybacks**, allow corporations to take losses during a current year and offset them against gains in nearby years. Since 1997, companies can "carry back" losses for two years and "carry forward" losses for 20 years. This tax rule means that the firm can offset losses during one year against income for the last two years, or save the losses to be offset against income during the next 20 years. When a firm can carry back losses, it receives a refund for back taxes in the current year. Otherwise, the firm must carry forward the loss and use it to offset future taxable income. When a firm has tax loss carryforwards well in excess of its current pre-tax income, then additional income it earns today will simply increase the taxes it owes after it exhausts its carryforwards.

EXAMPLE 7.8	**Tax Loss Carryforwards**

Problem

Verian Industries has outstanding tax loss carryforwards of $100 million from losses over the past six years. If Verian earns $30 million per year in pre-tax income from now on, when will it first pay taxes? If Verian earns an extra $5 million this coming year, in which year will its taxes increase?

Solution

With pre-tax income of $30 million per year, Verian will be able to use its tax loss carryforwards to avoid paying taxes until year 4 (in millions of dollars):

Year	1	2	3	4	5
Pre-tax Income	30	30	30	30	30
Tax Loss Carryforward	−30	−30	−30	−10	
Taxable Income	0	0	0	20	30

If Verian earns an additional $5 million the first year, it will owe taxes on an extra $5 million in year 4:

Year	1	2	3	4	5
Pre-tax Income	35	30	30	30	30
Tax Loss Carryforward	−35	−30	−30	−5	
Taxable Income	0	0	0	25	30

Thus, when a firm has tax loss carryforwards, the tax impact of current earnings will be delayed until the carryforwards are exhausted. This delay reduces the present value of the tax impact, and firms sometimes approximate the effect of tax loss carryforwards by using a lower marginal tax rate.

CONCEPT CHECK

1. Explain why it is advantageous for a firm to use the most accelerated depreciation schedule possible for tax purposes.

2. What is the continuation or terminal value of a project?

7.3 Analyzing the Project

When evaluating a capital budgeting project, financial managers should make the decision that maximizes NPV. As we have discussed, to compute the NPV for a project, you need to estimate the incremental cash flows and choose a discount rate. Given these inputs, the NPV calculation is relatively straightforward. The most difficult part of capital budgeting is deciding how to estimate the cash flows and cost of capital. These estimates are often subject to significant uncertainty. In this section, we look at methods that assess the importance of this uncertainty and identify the drivers of value in the project.

Break-Even Analysis

When we are uncertain regarding the input to a capital budgeting decision, it is often useful to determine the **break-even** level of that input, which is the level for which the investment has an NPV of zero. One example that we have already considered is the calculation of the internal rate of return (IRR). Recall from Chapter 6 that the difference between the IRR of a project and the cost of capital tells you how much error in the cost of capital it would take to change the investment decision. Using the Excel function IRR, the spreadsheet in Table 7.7 calculates an IRR of 24.1% for the free cash flow of the HomeNet project.[9] Hence, the true cost of capital can be as high as 24.1% and the project will still have positive NPV.

TABLE 7.7 SPREADSHEET	HomeNet IRR Calculation						
	Year	0	1	2	3	4	5
NPV ($000s) and IRR							
1 Free Cash Flow		(16,500)	5,100	7,200	7,200	7,200	2,700
2 NPV at 12%		5,027					
3 IRR		24.1%					

There is no reason to limit our attention to the uncertainty in the cost of capital estimate. In a **break-even analysis**, for each parameter, we calculate the value at which the NPV of the project is zero. Table 7.8 shows the break-even level for several key parameters.

TABLE 7.8	Break-Even Levels for HomeNet
Parameter	**Break-Even Level**
Units sold	79,759 units per year
Wholesale price	$232 per unit
Cost of goods	$138 per unit
Cost of capital	24.1%

---

9. The format in Excel is = IRR(FCF0:FCF5).

For example, based on the initial assumptions, the HomeNet project will break even with a sales level of just under 80,000 units per year. Alternatively, at a sales level of 100,000 units per year, the project will break even with a sales price of $232 per unit.

We have examined the break-even levels in terms of the project's NPV, which is the most useful perspective for decision making. Other accounting notions of break-even are sometimes considered, however. For example, we could compute the **EBIT break-even** for sales, which is the level of sales for which the project's EBIT is zero. While HomeNet's EBIT break-even level of sales is only about 32,000 units per year, given the large upfront investment required in HomeNet, its NPV is −$11.8 million at that sales level.

Sensitivity Analysis

Another important capital budgeting tool is sensitivity analysis. **Sensitivity analysis** breaks the NPV calculation into its component assumptions and shows how the NPV varies as the underlying assumptions change. In this way, sensitivity analysis allows us to explore the effects of errors in our NPV estimates for the project. By conducting a sensitivity analysis, we learn which assumptions are the most important; we can then invest further resources and effort to refine these assumptions. Such an analysis also reveals which aspects of the project are most critical when we are actually managing the project.

To illustrate, consider the assumptions underlying the calculation of HomeNet's NPV. There is likely to be significant uncertainty surrounding each revenue and cost assumption. Table 7.9 shows the base-case assumptions, together with the best and worst cases, for several key aspects of the project.

| TABLE 7.9 | Best- and Worst-Case Parameter Assumptions for HomeNet |

Parameter	Initial Assumption	Worst Case	Best Case
Units sold (thousands)	100	70	130
Sale price ($/unit)	260	240	280
Cost of goods ($/unit)	110	120	100
NWC ($ thousands)	2100	3000	1600
Cannibalization	25%	40%	10%
Cost of capital	12%	15%	10%

To determine the importance of this uncertainty, we recalculate the NPV of the HomeNet project under the best- and worst-case assumptions for each parameter. For example, if the number of units sold is only 70,000 per year, the NPV of the project falls to −$2.4 million. We repeat this calculation for each parameter. The result is shown in Figure 7.1, which reveals that the most important parameter assumptions are the number of units sold and the sale price per unit. These assumptions deserve the greatest scrutiny during the estimation process. In addition, as the most important drivers of the project's value, these factors deserve close attention when managing the project.

FIGURE 7.1

HomeNet's NPV Under Best- and Worst-Case Parameter Assumptions
Green bars show the change in NPV under the best-case assumption for each parameter; red bars show the change under the worst-case assumption. Also shown are the break-even levels for each parameter. Under the initial assumptions, HomeNet's NPV is $5.0 million.

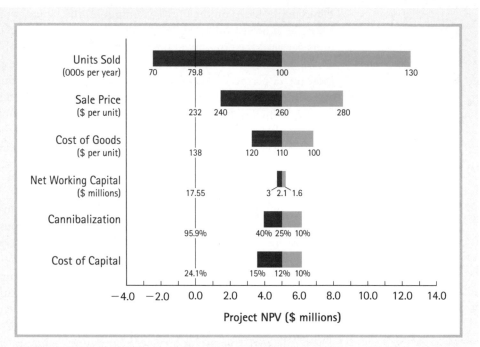

EXAMPLE 7.9

Sensitivity to Marketing and Support Costs

Problem
The current forecast for HomeNet's marketing and support costs is $3 million per year during years 1–4. Suppose the marketing and support costs may be as high as $4 million per year. What is HomeNet's NPV in this case?

Solution
We can answer this question by changing the selling, general, and administrative expense to $4 million in Table 7.3 Spreadsheet and computing the NPV of the resulting free cash flow. We can also calculate the impact of this change as follows: A $1 million increase in marketing and support costs will reduce EBIT by $1 million and will, therefore, decrease HomeNet's free cash flow by an after-tax amount of $1 million × (1 − 40%) = $0.6 million per year. The present value of this decrease is

$$PV = \frac{-0.6}{1.12} + \frac{-0.6}{1.12^2} + \frac{-0.6}{1.12^3} + \frac{-0.6}{1.12^4} = -\$1.8 \text{ million}$$

HomeNet's NPV would fall to $5.0 million − $1.8 million = $3.2 million.

Scenario Analysis

In the analysis thus far, we have considered the consequences of varying only one parameter at a time. In reality, certain factors may affect more than one parameter. **Scenario analysis** considers the effect on NPV of changing multiple project parameters. For example, lowering HomeNet's price may increase the number of units sold. We can use scenario

TABLE 7.10	Scenario Analysis of Alternative Pricing Strategies		
Strategy	**Sale Price ($ / unit)**	**Expected Units Sold (thousands)**	**NPV ($ thousands)**
Current strategy	260	100	5027
Price reduction	245	110	4582
Price increase	275	90	4937

FIGURE 7.2

Price and Volume Combinations for HomeNet with Equivalent NPV

The graph shows alternative price per unit and annual volume combinations that lead to an NPV of $5.0 million. Pricing strategies with combinations above this line will lead to a higher NPV and are superior.

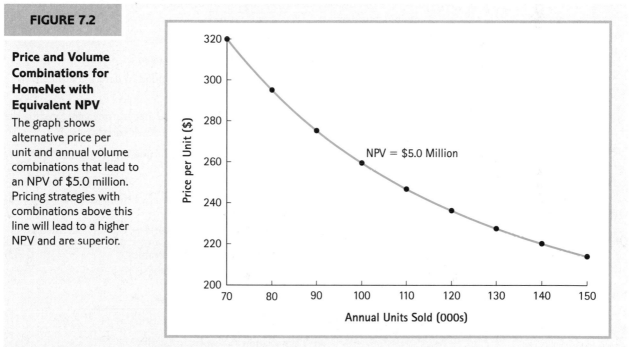

analysis to evaluate alternative pricing strategies for the HomeNet product in Table 7.10. In this case, the current strategy is optimal. Figure 7.2 shows the combinations of price and volume that lead to the same NPV of $5 million for HomeNet as the current strategy. Only strategies with price and volume combinations above the line will lead to a higher NPV.

CONCEPT CHECK

1. What is sensitivity analysis?

2. How does scenario analysis differ from sensitivity analysis?

Summary

1. Capital budgeting is the process of analyzing investment opportunities and deciding which ones to accept. A capital budget is a list of all projects that a company plans to undertake during the next period.

2. We use the NPV rule to evaluate capital budgeting decisions, making decisions that maximize NPV. When deciding to accept or reject a project, we accept projects with a positive NPV.

3. The incremental earnings of a project comprise the amount by which the project is expected to change the firm's earnings.

4. Incremental earnings should include all incremental revenues and costs associated with the project, including project externalities and opportunity costs, but excluding sunk costs and interest expenses.

   a. Project externalities are cash flows that occur when a project affects other areas of the company's business.

   b. An opportunity cost is the cost of using an existing asset.

   c. A sunk cost is an unrecoverable cost that has already been incurred.

   d. Interest and other financing-related expenses are excluded to determine the project's unlevered net income.

5. We estimate taxes using the marginal tax rate, based on the net income generated by the rest of the firm's operations, as well as any tax loss carrybacks or carryforwards.

6. We compute free cash flow from incremental earnings by eliminating all non-cash expenses and including all capital investment.

   a. Depreciation is not a cash expense, so it is added back.

   b. Actual capital expenditures are deducted.

   c. Increases in net working capital are deducted. Net working capital is defined as

$$\text{Cash} + \text{Inventory} + \text{Receivables} - \text{Payables} \qquad (7.3)$$

7. The basic calculation for free cash flow is

$$\text{Free Cash Flow} = \overbrace{(\text{Revenues} - \text{Costs} - \text{Depreciation}) \times (1 - \tau_c)}^{\text{Unlevered Net Income}}$$
$$+ \text{Depreciation} - \text{CapEx} - \Delta NWC \qquad (7.5)$$

   Free cash flow should also include the (after-tax) liquidation or salvage value of any assets that are disposed of. It may also include a terminal (continuation) value if the project continues beyond the forecast horizon.

8. Depreciation expenses affect free cash flow only through the depreciation tax shield. The firm should use the most accelerated depreciation schedule possible.

9. The discount rate for a project is its cost of capital: The expected return of securities with comparable risk and horizon.

10. Break-even analysis computes the level of a parameter that makes the project's NPV equal zero.

11. Sensitivity analysis breaks the NPV calculation down into its component assumptions, showing how the NPV varies as the values of the underlying assumptions change.

12. Scenario analysis considers the effect of changing multiple parameters simultaneously.

Key Terms

break-even *p. 196*

break-even analysis *p. 196*

cannibalization *p. 183*

capital budget *p. 178*

capital budgeting *p. 178*

depreciation tax shield *p. 189*

EBIT break-even *p. 197*

free cash flow *p. 186*

incremental earnings *p. 178*

MACRS depreciation *p. 192*

marginal corporate tax rate *p. 181*

opportunity cost *p. 182*

overhead expenses *p. 184*

project externalities *p. 182*

scenario analysis *p. 198*

sensitivity analysis *p. 197*

straight-line depreciation *p. 180*

sunk cost *p. 184*

tax loss carryforwards and carrybacks *p. 195*

terminal (continuation value) *p. 194*

trade credit *p. 187*

unlevered net income *p. 181*

Further Reading

For an excellent overview of the history of the concept of present value and its use in capital budgeting, see M. Rubinstein, "Great Moments in Financial Economics: I. Present Value," *Journal of Investment Management* (First Quarter 2003).

Irving Fisher was one of the first to apply the Law of One Price to propose that any capital project should be evaluated in terms of its present value; see I. Fisher, *The Rate of Interest: Its Nature, Determination and Relation to Economic Phenomena* (New York: Macmillan, 1907). I. Fisher, *The Theory of Interest: As Determined by Impatience to Spend Income and Opportunity to Invest It* (New York: Macmillan, 1930); reprinted (New York: Augustus M. Kelley, 1955).

The use of this approach for capital budgeting was later popularized in the following book: J. Dean, *Capital Budgeting* (New York: Columbia University Press, 1951).

We will revisit the topics of this chapter in greater depth in Part VI of this book. Additional readings for more advanced topics will be provided there.

Problems

All problems in this chapter are available in MyFinanceLab. An asterisk (*) indicates problems with a higher level of difficulty.

Forecasting Earnings

1. Pisa Pizza, a seller of frozen pizza, is considering introducing a healthier version of its pizza that will be low in cholesterol and contain no trans fats. The firm expects that sales of the new pizza will be $20 million per year. While many of these sales will be to new customers, Pisa Pizza estimates that 40% will come from customers who switch to the new, healthier pizza instead of buying the original version.

    a. Assume customers will spend the same amount on either version. What level of incremental sales is associated with introducing the new pizza?

    b. Suppose that 50% of the customers who will switch from Pisa Pizza's original pizza to its healthier pizza will switch to another brand if Pisa Pizza does not introduce a healthier pizza. What level of incremental sales is associated with introducing the new pizza in this case?

2. Kokomochi is considering the launch of an advertising campaign for its latest dessert product, the Mini Mochi Munch. Kokomochi plans to spend $5 million on TV, radio, and print advertising this year for the campaign. The ads are expected to boost sales of the Mini Mochi Munch by $9 million this year and by $7 million next year. In addition, the company expects that new consumers who try the Mini Mochi Munch will be more likely to try Kokomochi's other products. As a result, sales of other products are expected to rise by $2 million each year.

    Kokomochi's gross profit margin for the Mini Mochi Munch is 35%, and its gross profit margin averages 25% for all other products. The company's marginal corporate tax rate is 35% both this year and next year. What are the incremental earnings associated with the advertising campaign?

3. Home Builder Supply, a retailer in the home improvement industry, currently operates seven retail outlets in Georgia and South Carolina. Management is contemplating building an eighth retail store across town from its most successful retail outlet. The company already owns the land for this store, which currently has an abandoned warehouse located on it. Last month, the marketing department spent $10,000 on market research to determine the extent of customer demand for the new store. Now Home Builder Supply must decide whether to build and open the new store.

    Which of the following should be included as part of the incremental earnings for the proposed new retail store?

    a. The cost of the land where the store will be located.

    b. The cost of demolishing the abandoned warehouse and clearing the lot.

    c. The loss of sales in the existing retail outlet, if customers who previously drove across town to shop at the existing outlet become customers of the new store instead.

    d. The $10,000 in market research spent to evaluate customer demand.

    e. Construction costs for the new store.

    f. The value of the land if sold.

    g. Interest expense on the debt borrowed to pay the construction costs.

4. Hyperion, Inc., currently sells its latest high-speed color printer, the Hyper 500, for $350. It plans to lower the price to $300 next year. Its cost of goods sold for the Hyper 500 is $200 per unit, and this year's sales are expected to be 20,000 units.

    a. Suppose that if Hyperion drops the price to $300 immediately, it can increase this year's sales by 25% to 25,000 units. What would be the incremental impact on this year's EBIT of such a price drop?

    b. Suppose that for each printer sold, Hyperion expects additional sales of $75 per year on ink cartridges for the next three years, and Hyperion has a gross profit margin of 70% on ink cartridges. What is the incremental impact on EBIT for the next three years of a price drop this year?

EXCEL 5. Castle View Games would like to invest in a division to develop software for video games. To evaluate this decision, the firm first attempts to project the working capital needs for this operation. Its chief financial officer has developed the following estimates (in millions of dollars):

	Year 1	Year 2	Year 3	Year 4	Year 5
Cash	6	12	15	15	15
Accounts receivable	21	22	24	24	24
Inventory	5	7	10	12	13
Accounts payable	18	22	24	25	30

Assuming that Castle View currently does not have any working capital invested in this division, calculate the cash flows associated with changes in working capital for the first five years of this investment.

Determining Free Cash Flow and NPV

6. Elmdale Enterprises is deciding whether to expand its production facilities. Although long-term cash flows are difficult to estimate, management has projected the following cash flows for the first two years (in millions of dollars):

	Year 1	Year 2
Revenues	125	160
Cost of goods sold and operating expenses other than depreciation	40	60
Depreciation	25	36
Increase in working capital	5	8
Capital expenditures	30	40
Marginal corporate tax rate	35%	35%

a. What are the incremental earnings for this project for years 1 and 2?

b. What are the free cash flows for this project for the first two years?

EXCEL 7. You are a manager at Percolated Fiber, which is considering expanding its operations in synthetic fiber manufacturing. Your boss comes into your office, drops a consultant's report on your desk, and complains, "We owe these consultants $1 million for this report, and I am not sure their analysis makes sense. Before we spend the $25 million on new equipment needed for this project, look it over and give me your opinion." You open the report and find the following estimates (in thousands of dollars):

			Project Year		
	1	2	...	9	10
Sales revenue	30,000	30,000		30,000	30,000
− Cost of goods sold	18,000	18,000		18,000	18,000
= Gross profit	12,000	12,000		12,000	12,000
− General, sales, and administrative expenses	2,000	2,000		2,000	2,000
− Depreciation	2,500	2,500		2,500	2,500
= Net operating income	7,500	7,500		7,500	7,500
− Income tax	2,625	2,625		2,625	2,625
= Net income	4,875	4,875		4,875	4,875

All of the estimates in the report seem correct. You note that the consultants used straight-line depreciation for the new equipment that will be purchased today (year 0), which is what the accounting department recommended. The report concludes that because the project will increase earnings by $4.875 million per year for ten years, the project is worth $48.75 million. You think back to your halcyon days in finance class and realize there is more work to be done!

First, you note that the consultants have not factored in the fact that the project will require $10 million in working capital upfront (year 0), which will be fully recovered in year 10. Next, you see they have attributed $2 million of selling, general and administrative expenses to the project, but you know that $1 million of this amount is overhead that will be incurred even if the project is not accepted. Finally, you know that accounting earnings are not the right thing to focus on!

    a. Given the available information, what are the free cash flows in years 0 through 10 that should be used to evaluate the proposed project?

    b. If the cost of capital for this project is 14%, what is your estimate of the value of the new project?

8. Cellular Access, Inc., is a cellular telephone service provider that reported net income of $250 million for the most recent fiscal year. The firm had depreciation expenses of $100 million, capital expenditures of $200 million, and no interest expenses. Working capital increased by $10 million. Calculate the free cash flow for Cellular Access for the most recent fiscal year.

9. Markov Manufacturing recently spent $15 million to purchase some equipment used in the manufacture of disk drives. The firm expects that this equipment will have a useful life of five years, and its marginal corporate tax rate is 35%. The company plans to use straight-line depreciation.

    a. What is the annual depreciation expense associated with this equipment?

    b. What is the annual depreciation tax shield?

    c. Rather than straight-line depreciation, suppose Markov will use the MACRS depreciation method for five-year property. Calculate the depreciation tax shield each year for this equipment under this accelerated depreciation schedule.

    d. If Markov has a choice between straight-line and MACRS depreciation schedules, and its marginal corporate tax rate is expected to remain constant, which should it choose? Why?

    e. How might your answer to part (d) change if Markov anticipates that its marginal corporate tax rate will increase substantially over the next five years?

10. Bay Properties is considering starting a commercial real estate division. It has prepared the following four-year forecast of free cash flows for this division:

	Year 1	Year 2	Year 3	Year 4
Free cash flow	−$185,000	−$12,000	$99,000	$240,000

Assume cash flows after year 4 will grow at 3% per year, forever. If the cost of capital for this division is 14%, what is the continuation value in year 4 for cash flows after year 4? What is the value today of this division?

11. Your firm would like to evaluate a proposed new operating division. You have forecasted cash flows for this division for the next five years, and have estimated that the cost of capital is 12%. You would like to estimate a continuation value. You have made the following forecasts for the last year of your five-year forecasting horizon (in millions of dollars):

	Year 5
Revenues	1,200
Operating income	100
Net income	50
Free cash flows	110
Book value of equity	400

    a. You forecast that future free cash flows after year 5 will grow at 2% per year, forever. Estimate the continuation value in year 5, using the perpetuity with growth formula.

    b. You have identified several firms in the same industry as your operating division. The average P/E ratio for these firms is 30. Estimate the continuation value assuming the

P/E ratio for your division in year 5 will be the same as the average P/E ratio for the comparable firms today.

    c. The average market/book ratio for the comparable firms is 4.0. Estimate the continuation value using the market/book ratio.

EXCEL 12. One year ago, your company purchased a machine used in manufacturing for $110,000. You have learned that a new machine is available that offers many advantages; you can purchase it for $150,000 today. It will be depreciated on a straight-line basis over 10 years, after which it has no salvage value. You expect that the new machine will produce additional EBITDA (earnings before interest, taxes, depreciation, and amortization) of $40,000 per year for the next 10 years. The current machine is expected to produce EBITDA of $20,000 per year. The current machine is being depreciated on a straight-line basis over a useful life of 11 years, after which it will have no salvage value, so depreciation expense for the current machine is $10,000 per year. All other expenses of the two machines are identical. The market value today of the current machine is $50,000. Your company's tax rate is 45%, and the opportunity cost of capital for this type of equipment is 10%. Is it profitable to replace the year-old machine?

EXCEL 13. Beryl's Iced Tea currently rents a bottling machine for $50,000 per year, including all maintenance expenses. It is considering purchasing a machine instead, and is comparing two options:

    a. Purchase the machine it is currently renting for $150,000. This machine will require $20,000 per year in ongoing maintenance expenses.

    b. Purchase a new, more advanced machine for $250,000. This machine will require $15,000 per year in ongoing maintenance expenses and will lower bottling costs by $10,000 per year. Also, $35,000 will be spent upfront in training the new operators of the machine.

Suppose the appropriate discount rate is 8% per year and the machine is purchased today. Maintenance and bottling costs are paid at the end of each year, as is the rental of the machine. Assume also that the machines will be depreciated via the straight-line method over seven years and that they have a ten-year life with a negligible salvage value. The marginal corporate tax rate is 35%. Should Beryl's Iced Tea continue to rent, purchase its current machine, or purchase the advanced machine?

Analyzing the Project

EXCEL 14. Bauer Industries is an automobile manufacturer. Management is currently evaluating a proposal to build a plant that will manufacture lightweight trucks. Bauer plans to use a cost of capital of 12% to evaluate this project. Based on extensive research, it has prepared the following incremental free cash flow projections (in millions of dollars):

	Year 0	Years 1–9	Year 10
Revenues		100.0	100.0
− Manufacturing expenses (other than depreciation)		−35.0	−35.0
− Marketing expenses		−10.0	−10.0
− Depreciation		−15.0	−15.0
= EBIT		40.0	40.0
− Taxes (35%)		−14.0	−14.0
= Unlevered net income		26.0	26.0
+ Depreciation		+15.0	+15.0
− Increases in net working capital		−5.0	−5.0
− Capital expenditures	−150.0		
+ Continuation value			+12.0
= Free cash flow	−150.0	36.0	48.0

a. For this base-case scenario, what is the NPV of the plant to manufacture lightweight trucks?

b. Based on input from the marketing department, Bauer is uncertain about its revenue forecast. In particular, management would like to examine the sensitivity of the NPV to the revenue assumptions. What is the NPV of this project if revenues are 10% higher than forecast? What is the NPV if revenues are 10% lower than forecast?

c. Rather than assuming that cash flows for this project are constant, management would like to explore the sensitivity of its analysis to possible growth in revenues and operating expenses. Specifically, management would like to assume that revenues, manufacturing expenses, and marketing expenses are as given in the table for year 1 and grow by 2% per year every year starting in year 2. Management also plans to assume that the initial capital expenditures (and therefore depreciation), additions to working capital, and continuation value remain as initially specified in the table. What is the NPV of this project under these alternative assumptions? How does the NPV change if the revenues and operating expenses grow by 5% per year rather than by 2%?

d. To examine the sensitivity of this project to the discount rate, management would like to compute the NPV for different discount rates. Create a graph, with the discount rate on the *x*-axis and the NPV on the *y*-axis, for discount rates ranging from 5% to 30%. For what ranges of discount rates does the project have a positive NPV?

EXCEL *15. Billingham Packaging is considering expanding its production capacity by purchasing a new machine, the XC-750. The cost of the XC-750 is $2.75 million. Unfortunately, installing this machine will take several months and will partially disrupt production. The firm has just completed a $50,000 feasibility study to analyze the decision to buy the XC-750, resulting in the following estimates:

- *Marketing:* Once the XC-750 is operating next year, the extra capacity is expected to generate $10 million per year in additional sales, which will continue for the ten-year life of the machine.

- *Operations:* The disruption caused by the installation will decrease sales by $5 million this year. Once the machine is operating next year, the cost of goods for the products produced by the XC-750 is expected to be 70% of their sale price. The increased production will require additional inventory on hand of $1 million, to be added in year 0 and depleted in year 10.

- *Human Resources:* The expansion will require additional sales and administrative personnel at a cost of $2 million per year.

- *Accounting:* The XC-750 will be depreciated via the straight-line method over the ten-year life of the machine. The firm expects receivables from the new sales to be 15% of revenues and payables to be 10% of the cost of goods sold. Billingham's marginal corporate tax rate is 35%.

a. Determine the incremental earnings from the purchase of the XC-750.

b. Determine the free cash flow from the purchase of the XC-750.

c. If the appropriate cost of capital for the expansion is 10%, compute the NPV of the purchase.

d. While the expected new sales will be $10 million per year from the expansion, estimates range from $8 million to $12 million. What is the NPV in the worst case? In the best case?

e. What is the break-even level of new sales from the expansion? What is the break-even level for the cost of goods sold?

f. Billingham could instead purchase the XC-900, which offers even greater capacity. The cost of the XC-900 is $4 million. The extra capacity would not be useful in the first two years of operation, but would allow for additional sales in years 3–10. What level of additional sales (above the $10 million expected for the XC-750) per year in those years would justify purchasing the larger machine?

Data Case

You have just been hired by Dell Computers in their capital budgeting division. Your first assignment is to determine the net cash flows and NPV of a proposed new type of portable computer system similar in size to a Blackberry, a popular gadget with many MBA students, which has the operating power of a high-end desktop system.

Development of the new system will initially require an initial investment equal to 10% of net Property, Plant, and Equipment (PPE) for the fiscal year ended Feb. 3, 2006. The project will then require an additional investment equal to 10% of initial investment after the first year of the project, a 5% increase after the second year, and a 1% increase after the third, fourth, and fifth years. The product is expected to have a life of five years. First-year revenues for the new product are expected to be 3% of total revenue for Dell's fiscal year ended Feb. 3, 2006. The new product's revenues are expected to grow at 15% for the second year then 10% for the third and 5% annually for the final two years of the expected life of the project. Your job is to determine the rest of the cash flows associated with this project. Your boss has indicated that the operating costs and net working capital requirements are similar to the rest of the company and that depreciation is straight-line for capital budgeting purposes. Welcome to the "real world." Since your boss hasn't been much help, here are some tips to guide your analysis:

1. Obtain Dell's financial statements. (If you "really" worked for Dell you would already have this data, but at least you won't get fired if your analysis is off target.) Download the annual income statements, balance sheets, and cash flow statements for the last four fiscal years from MarketWatch (www.marketwatch.com). Enter Dell's ticker symbol and then go to "financials." Export the statements to Excel by right-clicking while the cursor is inside each statement.

2. You are now ready to determine the Free Cash Flow. Compute the Free Cash Flow for each year using Eq. 7.5 from this chapter:

$$\text{Free Cash Flow} = \overbrace{(\text{Revenues} - \text{Costs} - \text{Depreciation}) \times (1 - \tau_c)}^{\text{Unlevered net income}} \\ + \text{Depreciation} - \text{CapEx} - \Delta NWC$$

Set up the timeline and computation of free cash flow in separate, contiguous columns for each year of the project life. Be sure to make ouflows negative and inflows positive.

a. Assume that the project's profitbility will be similar to Dell's existing projects in 2005 and estimate (revenues − costs) each year by using the 2005 EBITDA/Sales profit margin.

b. Determine the annual depreciation by assuming Dell depreciates these assets by the straight-line method over a 10-year life.

c. Determine Dell's tax rate by using the income tax rate in 2005.

d. Calculate the net working capital required each year by assuming that the level of NWC will be a constant percentage of the project's sales. Use Dell's 2005 NWC/Sales to estimate the required percentage. (Use only accounts receivable, accounts payable, and inventory to measure working capital. Other components of current assets and liabilities are harder to interpret and not necessarily reflective of the project's required NWC—e.g., Dell's cash holdings.)

   e. To determine the free cash flow, calculate the *additional* capital investment and the *change* in net working capital each year.

3. Determine the IRR of the project and the NPV of the project at a cost of capital of 12% using the Excel functions. For the calculation of NPV, include cash flows 1 through 5 in the NPV function and then subtract the initial cost (i.e., $= NPV(\text{rate}, CF_1 : CF_5) + CF_0$). For IRR, include cash flows zero through five in the cash flow range.

MACRS Depreciation

The U.S. tax code allows for accelerated depreciation of most assets. The depreciation method that you use for any particular asset is determined by the tax rules in effect at the time you place the asset into service. (Congress has changed the depreciation rules many times over the years, so many firms that have held property for a long time may have to use several depreciation methods simultaneously.)

For most business property placed in service after 1986, the IRS allows firms to depreciate the asset using the MACRS (Modified Accelerated Cost Recovery System) method. Under this method, you categorize each business asset into a recovery class that determines the time period over which you can write off the cost of the asset. The most commonly used items are classified as shown below:

- *3-year property:* Tractor units, racehorses over 2 years old, and horses over 12 years old.

- *5-year property:* Automobiles, buses, trucks, computers and peripheral equipment, office machinery, and any property used in research and experimentation. Also includes breeding and dairy cattle.

- *7-year property:* Office furniture and fixtures, and any property that has not been designated as belonging to another class.

- *10-year property:* Water transportation equipment, single-purpose agricultural or horticultural structures, and trees or vines bearing fruit or nuts.

- *15-year property:* Depreciable improvements to land such as fences, roads, and bridges.

- *20-year property:* Farm buildings that are not agricultural or horticultural structures.

- *27.5-year property:* Residential rental property.

- *39-year property:* Nonresidential real estate, including home offices. (Note that the value of land may not be depreciated.)

Generally speaking, residential and nonresidential real estate is depreciated via the straight-line method, but other classes can be depreciated more rapidly in early years. Table 7A.1 shows the standard depreciation rates for assets in the other recovery classes; refinements of this table can be applied depending on the month that the asset was placed into service (consult IRS guidelines). The table indicates the percentage of the asset's cost that may be depreciated each year, with year 1 indicating the year the asset was first put into use.

TABLE 7A.1	MACRS Depreciation Table Showing the Percentage of the Asset's Cost That May Be Depreciated Each Year Based on Its Recovery Period

Depreciation Rate for Recovery Period

Year	3 Years	5 Years	7 Years	10 Years	15 Years	20 Years
1	33.33	20.00	14.29	10.00	5.00	3.750
2	44.45	32.00	24.49	18.00	9.50	7.219
3	14.81	19.20	17.49	14.40	8.55	6.677
4	7.41	11.52	12.49	11.52	7.70	6.177
5		11.52	8.93	9.22	6.93	5.713
6		5.76	8.92	7.37	6.23	5.285
7			8.93	6.55	5.90	4.888
8			4.46	6.55	5.90	4.522
9				6.56	5.91	4.462
10				6.55	5.90	4.461
11				3.28	5.91	4.462
12					5.90	4.461
13					5.91	4.462
14					5.90	4.461
15					5.91	4.462
16					2.95	4.461
17						4.462
18						4.461
19						4.462
20						4.461
21						2.231

Valuing Bonds

notation

CPN	coupon payment on a bond
n	number of periods
y	yield to maturity
P	initial price of a bond
FV	face value of a bond
YTM_n	yield to maturity on a zero-coupon bond with *n* periods to maturity
YTM	yield to maturity
r_n	interest rate or discount rate for a cash flow that arrives in period *n*
PV	present value

After a four-year hiatus, the U.S. government began issuing 30-year Treasury bonds again in August 2005. While the move was due in part to the government's need to borrow to fund record budget deficits, the decision to issue 30-year bonds also responded to investor requests for long-term risk-free securities backed by the U.S. government. These new 30-year Treasury bonds are part of a much larger market for publicly traded bonds. As of December 30, 2005, the value of outstanding U.S. Treasury debt was $4.17 trillion, and the value of corporate bond market debt was almost $5 trillion. If we include bonds issued by municipalities, government agencies, and other issuers, at the end of 2005, investors had almost $25 trillion invested in U.S. bond markets.[1]

In this chapter we look at the basic types of bonds and consider their valuation. Understanding bonds and their pricing is useful for several reasons. First, the prices of risk-free government bonds can be used to determine the risk-free interest rates that produce the yield curve discussed in Chapter 5. As we saw there, the yield curve provides important information for valuing risk-free cash flows and assessing expectations of inflation and economic growth. Second, firms often issue bonds to fund their own investments, and the returns investors receive on those bonds is one factor determining a firm's cost of capital. Finally, bonds provide an opportunity to begin our study of how securities are priced in a competitive market. The ideas we develop in this chapter will be helpful when we turn to the topic of valuing stocks in Chapter 9.

As we explained in Chapter 3, the Law of One Price implies that the price of a security in a competitive market should be the present value of the cash flows an investor will receive from owning it. Thus we begin the chapter by evaluating the promised cash flows for different types of bonds. If a bond is risk-free, so that the promised cash flows will be paid with certainty, we can use the Law of One Price to directly

---

1. *Source:* www.bondmarkets.com.

relate the return of a bond and its price. We also describe how bond prices change dynamically over time and examine the relationship between the prices and returns of different bonds. Finally, we consider bonds for which there is a risk of default, so that their cash flows are not known with certainty.

8.1   Bond Cash Flows, Prices, and Yields

In this section we look at how bonds are defined and then study the basic relationship between bond prices and their yield to maturity.

Bond Terminology

Recall from Chapter 3 that a bond is a security sold by governments and corporations to raise money from investors today in exchange for the promised future payment. The terms of the bond are described as part of the **bond certificate**, which indicates the amounts and dates of all payments to be made. These payments are made until a final repayment date, called the **maturity date** of the bond. The time remaining until the repayment date is known as the **term** of the bond.

Bonds typically make two types of payments to their holders. The promised interest payments of a bond are called **coupons**. The bond certificate typically specifies that the coupons will be paid periodically (for example, semiannually) until the maturity date of the bond. The principal or **face value** of a bond is the notional amount we use to compute the interest payments. Usually, the face value is repaid at maturity. It is generally denominated in standard increments such as $1000. A bond with a $1000 face value, for example, is often referred to as a "$1000 bond."

The amount of each coupon payment is determined by the **coupon rate** of the bond. This coupon rate is set by the issuer and stated on the bond certificate. By convention, the coupon rate is expressed as an APR, so the amount of each coupon payment, CPN, is

Coupon Payment

$$CPN = \frac{\text{Coupon Rate} \times \text{Face Value}}{\text{Number of Coupon Payments per Year}} \qquad (8.1)$$

For example, a "$1000 bond with a 10% coupon rate and semiannual payments" will pay coupon payments of $1000 × 10% / 2 = $50 every six months.

Zero-Coupon Bonds

The simplest type of bond is a **zero-coupon bond**, a bond that does not make coupon payments. The only cash payment the investor receives is the face value of the bond on the maturity date. **Treasury bills**, which are U.S. government bonds with a maturity of up to one year, are zero-coupon bonds. Recall from Chapter 3 that the present value of a future cash flow is less than the cash flow itself. As a result, prior to its maturity date, the price of a zero-coupon bond is always less than its face value. That is, zero-coupon bonds always trade at a **discount** (a price lower than the face value), so they are also called **pure discount bonds**.

Suppose that a one-year, risk-free, zero-coupon bond with a $100,000 face value has an initial price of $96,618.36. If you purchased this bond and held it to maturity, you would have the following cash flows:

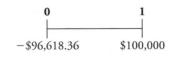

Although the bond pays no "interest" directly, as an investor you are compensated for the time value of your money by purchasing the bond at a discount to its face value.

Yield to Maturity.   Recall that the IRR of an investment opportunity is the discount rate at which the NPV of the investment opportunity is equal to zero. The IRR of an investment in zero-coupon bond is the rate of return that investors will earn on their money if they buy the bond at its current price and hold it to maturity. The IRR of an investment in a bond is given a special name, the **yield to maturity (YTM)** or just the *yield:*

The yield to maturity of a bond is the discount rate that sets the present value of the promised bond payments equal to the current market price of the bond.

Intuitively, the yield to maturity for a zero-coupon bond is the return you will earn as an investor from holding the bond to maturity and receiving the promised face value payment.

Let's determine the yield to maturity of the one-year zero-coupon bond discussed earlier. According to the definition, the yield to maturity of the one-year bond solves the following equation:

$$96,618.36 = \frac{100,000}{1 + YTM_1}$$

In this case,

$$1 + YTM_1 = \frac{100,000}{96,618.36} = 1.035$$

That is, the yield to maturity for this bond is 3.5%. Because the bond is risk free, investing in this bond and holding it to maturity is like earning 3.5% interest on your initial investment. Thus, by the Law of One Price, the competitive market risk-free interest rate is 3.5%, meaning all one-year risk-free investments must earn 3.5%.

Similarly, the yield to maturity for a zero-coupon bond with n periods to maturity, current price P, and face value FV is[2]

$$P = \frac{FV}{(1 + YTM_n)^n} \qquad (8.2)$$

---

2. In Chapter 4, we used the notation FV_n for the future value on date n of a cash flow. Conveniently, for a zero-coupon bond, the future value is also its face value, so the abbreviation FV is easy to remember.

Rearranging this expression, we get

Yield to Maturity of an *n*-Year Zero-Coupon Bond

$$YTM_n = \left(\frac{FV}{P}\right)^{1/n} - 1 \tag{8.3}$$

The yield to maturity (YTM_n) in Eq. 8.3 is the per-period rate of return for holding the bond from today until maturity on date *n*.

EXAMPLE 8.1

Yields for Different Maturities

Problem

Suppose the following zero-coupon bonds are trading at the prices shown below per $100 face value. Determine the corresponding yield to maturity for each bond.

Maturity	1 year	2 years	3 years	4 years
Price	$96.62	$92.45	$87.63	$83.06

Solution

Using Eq. 8.3, we have

$$YTM_1 = (100/96.62) - 1 \quad = 3.50\%$$
$$YTM_2 = (100/92.45)^{1/2} - 1 = 4.00\%$$
$$YTM_3 = (100/87.63)^{1/3} - 1 = 4.50\%$$
$$YTM_4 = (100/83.06)^{1/4} - 1 = 4.75\%$$

Risk-Free Interest Rates. In earlier chapters, we discussed the competitive market interest rate r_n available from today until date *n* for risk-free cash flows; we used this interest rate as the cost of capital for a risk-free cash flow that occurs on date *n*. Because a default-free zero-coupon bond that matures on date *n* provides a risk-free return over the same period, the Law of One Price guarantees that the risk-free interest rate equals the yield to maturity on such a bond.

Risk-Free Interest Rate with Maturity *n*

$$r_n = YTM_n \tag{8.4}$$

Consequently, we will often refer to the yield to maturity of the appropriate maturity, zero-coupon risk-free bond as *the* risk-free interest rate. Some financial professionals also use the term **spot interest rates** to refer to these default-free, zero-coupon yields.

In Chapter 5, we introduced the yield curve, which plots the risk-free interest rate for different maturities. These risk-free interest rates correspond to the yields of risk-free zero-coupon bonds. Thus the yield curve we introduced in Chapter 5 is also referred to as the **zero-coupon yield curve**.

Coupon Bonds

Like zero-coupon bonds, **coupon bonds** pay investors their face value at maturity. In addition, these bonds make regular coupon interest payments. Two types of U.S. Treasury coupon securities are currently traded in financial markets: **Treasury notes**, which have original maturities from one to ten years, and **Treasury bonds**, which have original maturities of more than ten years.

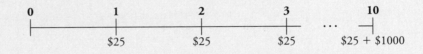

EXAMPLE 8.2

The Cash Flows of a Coupon Bond

Problem

The U.S. Treasury has just issued a five-year, $1000 bond with a 5% coupon rate and semi-annual coupons. What cash flows will you receive if you hold this bond until maturity?

Solution

The face value of this bond is $1000. Because this bond pays coupons semiannually, from Eq. 8.1 you will receive a coupon payment every six months of CPN $= \$1000 \times 5\% / 2 = \$25$. Here is the timeline, based on a six-month period:

Note that the last payment occurs five years (ten six-month periods) from now and is composed of both a coupon payment of $25 and the face value payment of $1000.

We can also compute the yield to maturity of a coupon bond. Recall that the yield to maturity for a bond is the IRR of investing in the bond and holding it to maturity; it is the *single* discount rate that equates the present value of the bond's remaining cash flows to its current price, shown in the following timeline:

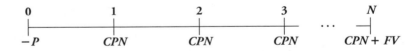

Because the coupon payments represent an annuity, the yield to maturity is the interest rate y that solves the following equation:[3]

Yield to Maturity of a Coupon Bond

$$P = CPN \times \frac{1}{y}\left(1 - \frac{1}{(1 + y)^N}\right) + \frac{FV}{(1 + y)^N} \qquad (8.5)$$

Unfortunately, unlike in the case of zero-coupon bonds, there is no simple formula to solve for the yield to maturity directly. Instead, we need to use either trial-and-error or the annuity spreadsheet we introduced in Chapter 4 (or Excel's IRR function).

---

3. In Eq. 8.5, we have assumed that the first cash coupon will be paid one period from now. If the first coupon is less than one period away, the cash price of the bond can be found by adjusting the price in Eq. 8.5 by multiplying by $(1 + y)^f$, where f is the fraction of the coupon interval that has already elapsed. (Also, bond prices are often quoted in terms of the *clean price*, which is calculated by deducting from the cash price P an amount, called *accrued interest*, equal to $f \times CPN$. See the box on page 221.)

When we calculate a bond's yield to maturity by solving Eq. 8.5, the yield we compute will be a rate *per coupon interval*. This yield is typically stated as an annual rate by multiplying it by the number of coupons per year, thereby converting it to an APR with the same compounding interval as the coupon rate.

EXAMPLE 8.3

Computing the Yield to Maturity of a Coupon Bond

Problem
Consider the five-year, $1000 bond with a 5% coupon rate and semiannual coupons described in Example 8.2. If this bond is currently trading for a price of $957.35, what is the bond's yield to maturity?

Solution
Because the bond has ten remaining coupon payments, we compute its yield y by solving:

$$957.35 = 25 \times \frac{1}{y}\left(1 - \frac{1}{(1+y)^{10}}\right) + \frac{1000}{(1+y)^{10}}$$

We can solve it by trial-and-error or by using the annuity spreadsheet:

	NPER	RATE	PV	PMT	FV	Excel Formula
Given	10		−957.35	25	1,000	
Solve for Rate		3.00%				=Rate(10,25,−957.35,1000)

Therefore, $y = 3\%$. Because the bond pays coupons semiannually, this yield is for a six-month period. We convert it to an APR by multiplying by the number of coupon payments per year. Thus the bond has a yield to maturity equal to a 6% APR with semiannual compounding.

We can also use Eq. 8.5 to compute a bond's price based on its yield to maturity. We simply discount the cash flows using the yield, as in Example 8.4.

EXAMPLE 8.4

Computing a Bond Price from Its Yield to Maturity

Problem
Consider again the five-year, $1000 bond with a 5% coupon rate and semiannual coupons in Example 8.3. Suppose you are told that its yield to maturity has increased to 6.30% (expressed as an APR with semiannual compounding). What price is the bond trading for now?

Solution
Given the yield, we can compute the price using Eq. 8.5. First, note that a 6.30% APR is equivalent to a semiannual rate of 3.15%. Therefore, the bond price is

$$P = 25 \times \frac{1}{0.0315}\left(1 - \frac{1}{1.0315^{10}}\right) + \frac{1000}{1.0315^{10}} = \$944.98$$

We can also use the annuity spreadsheet:

	NPER	RATE	PV	PMT	FV	Excel Formula
Given	10	3.15%		25	1,000	
Solve for PV			−944.98			=PV(0.0315,10,25,1000)

Because we can convert any price into a yield, and vice versa, prices and yields are often used interchangeably. For example, the bond in Example 8.4 could be quoted as having a yield of 6.30% or a price of $944.98 per $1000 face value. Indeed, bond traders generally quote bond yields rather than bond prices. One advantage of quoting the yield to maturity rather than the price is that the yield is independent of the face value of the bond. When prices are quoted in the bond market, they are conventionally quoted as a percentage of their face value. Thus the bond in Example 8.4 would be quoted as having a price of 94.498, which would imply an actual price of $944.98 given the $1000 face value of the bond.

CONCEPT CHECK

1. What is the relationship between a bond's price and its yield to maturity?

2. The risk-free interest rate for a maturity of *n*-years can be determined from the yield of what type of bond?

8.2 Dynamic Behavior of Bond Prices

As we mentioned earlier, zero-coupon bonds always trade for a discount—that is, prior to maturity, their price is less than their face value. Coupon bonds may trade at a discount, at a **premium** (a price greater than their face value), or at **par** (a price equal to their face value). In this section, we identify when a bond will trade at a discount or premium as well as how the bond's price will change due to the passage of time and fluctuations in interest rates.

Discounts and Premiums

If the bond trades at a discount, an investor who buys the bond will earn a return both from receiving the coupons *and* from receiving a face value that exceeds the price paid for the bond. As a result, if a bond trades at a discount, its yield to maturity will exceed its coupon rate. Given the relationship between bond prices and yields, the reverse is clearly also true: If a coupon bond's yield to maturity exceeds its coupon rate, the present value of its cash flows at the yield to maturity will be less than its face value, and the bond will trade at a discount.

A bond that pays a coupon can also trade at a premium to its face value. In this case, an investor's return from the coupons is diminished by receiving a face value less than the price paid for the bond. Thus, a bond trades at a premium whenever its yield to maturity is less than its coupon rate.

When a bond trades at a price equal to its face value, it is said to trade at par. A bond trades at par when its coupon rate is equal to its yield to maturity. A bond that trades at a discount is also said to trade below par, and a bond that trades at a premium is said to trade above par.

Table 8.1 summarizes these properties of coupon bond prices.

TABLE 8.1	**Bond Prices Immediately After a Coupon Payment**		
When the bond price is . . .	greater than the face value	equal to the face value	less than the face value
We say the bond trades	"above par" or "at a premium"	"at par"	"below par" or "at a discount"
This occurs when	Coupon Rate > Yield to Maturity	Coupon Rate = Yield to Maturity	Coupon Rate < Yield to Maturity

EXAMPLE 8.5

Determining the Discount or Premium of a Coupon Bond

Problem

Consider three 30-year bonds with annual coupon payments. One bond has a 10% coupon rate, one has a 5% coupon rate, and one has a 3% coupon rate. If the yield to maturity of each bond is 5%, what is the price of each bond per $100 face value? Which bond trades at a premium, which trades at a discount, and which trades at par?

Solution

We can compute the price of each bond using Eq. 8.5. Therefore, the bond prices are

$$P(10\% \text{ coupon}) = 10 \times \frac{1}{0.05}\left(1 - \frac{1}{1.05^{30}}\right) + \frac{100}{1.05^{30}} = \$176.86 \ \text{(trades at a premium)}$$

$$P(5\% \text{ coupon}) = 5 \times \frac{1}{0.05}\left(1 - \frac{1}{1.05^{30}}\right) + \frac{100}{1.05^{30}} = \$100.00 \ \text{(trades at par)}$$

$$P(3\% \text{ coupon}) = 3 \times \frac{1}{0.05}\left(1 - \frac{1}{1.05^{30}}\right) + \frac{100}{1.05^{30}} = \$69.26 \ \text{(trades at a discount)}$$

Most issuers of coupon bonds choose a coupon rate so that the bonds will *initially* trade at, or very close to, par (i.e., at face value). For example, the U.S. Treasury sets the coupon rates on its notes and bonds in this way. After the issue date, the market price of a bond generally changes over time for two reasons. First, as time passes, the bond gets closer to its maturity date. Holding fixed the bond's yield to maturity, the present value of the bond's remaining cash flows changes as the time to maturity decreases. Second, at any point in time, changes in market interest rates affect the bond's yield to maturity and its price (the present value of the remaining cash flows). We explore these two effects in the remainder of this section.

Time and Bond Prices

Let's consider the effect of time on the price of a bond. Suppose you purchase a 30-year, zero-coupon bond with a yield to maturity of 5%. For a face value of $100, the bond will initially trade for

$$P(30 \text{ years to maturity}) = \frac{100}{1.05^{30}} = \$23.14$$

Now let's consider the price of this bond five years later, when it has 25 years remaining until maturity. If the bond's yield to maturity remains at 5%, the bond price in five years will be

$$P(25 \text{ years to maturity}) = \frac{100}{1.05^{25}} = \$29.53$$

Note that the bond price is higher, and hence the discount from its face value is smaller, when there is less time to maturity. The discount shrinks because the yield has not changed, but there is less time until the face value will be received. If you purchased the bond for $23.14 and then sold it after five years for $29.53, the IRR of your investment would be

$$\left(\frac{29.53}{23.14}\right)^{1/5} - 1 = 5.0\%$$

That is, your return is the same as the yield to maturity of the bond. This example illustrates a more general property for bonds. If a bond's yield to maturity does not change, then the IRR of an investment in the bond equals its yield to maturity even if you sell the bond early.

These results also hold for coupon bonds. The pattern of price changes over time is a bit more complicated for coupon bonds, however, because as time passes most of the cash flows get closer but some of the cash flows disappear as the coupons get paid. Example 8.6 illustrates these effects.

EXAMPLE 8.6

The Effect of Time on the Price of a Coupon Bond

Problem

Consider a 30-year bond with a 10% coupon rate (annual payments) and a $100 face value. What is the initial price of this bond if it has a 5% yield to maturity? If the yield to maturity is unchanged, what will the price be immediately before and after the first coupon is paid?

Solution

We computed the price of this bond with 30 years to maturity in Example 8.5:

$$P = 10 \times \frac{1}{0.05}\left(1 - \frac{1}{1.05^{30}}\right) + \frac{100}{1.05^{30}} = \$176.86$$

Now consider the cash flows of this bond in one year, immediately before the first coupon is paid. The bond now has 29 years until it matures, and the timeline is as follows:

0	1	2		29
$10	$10	$10	...	$10 + $100

Again, we compute the price by discounting the cash flows by the yield to maturity. Note that there is a cash flow of $10 at date zero, the coupon that is about to be paid. In this case, it is easiest to treat the first coupon separately and value the remaining cash flows as in Eq. 8.5:

$$P(\text{just before first coupon}) = 10 + 10 \times \frac{1}{0.05}\left(1 - \frac{1}{1.05^{29}}\right) + \frac{100}{1.05^{29}} = \$185.71$$

Note that the bond price is higher than it was initially. It will make the same total number of coupon payments, but an investor does not need to wait as long to receive the first one. We could also compute the price by noting that because the yield to maturity remains at 5% for the bond, investors in the bond should earn a return of 5% over the year: $176.86 × 1.05 = $185.71.

What happens to the price of the bond just after the first coupon is paid? The timeline is the same as that given earlier, except the new owner of the bond will not receive the coupon at date zero. Thus, just after the coupon is paid, the price of the bond (given the same yield to maturity) will be

$$P(\text{just after first coupon}) = 10 \times \frac{1}{0.05}\left(1 - \frac{1}{1.05^{29}}\right) + \frac{100}{1.05^{29}} = \$175.71$$

The price of the bond will drop by the amount of the coupon ($10) immediately after the coupon is paid, reflecting the fact that the owner will no longer receive the coupon. In this case, the price is lower than the initial price of the bond. Because there are fewer coupon payments remaining, the premium investors will pay for the bond declines. Still, an investor who buys the bond initially, receives the first coupon, and then sells it, earns a 5% return if the bond's yield does not change: (10 + 175.71) / 176.86 = 1.05.

Figure 8.1 illustrates the effect of time on bond prices, assuming the yield to maturity remains constant. Between coupon payments, the prices of all bonds rise at a rate equal to the yield to maturity as the remaining cash flows of the bond become closer. But as

FIGURE 8.1

The Effect of Time on Bond Prices

The graph illustrates the effects of the passage of time on bond prices when the yield remains constant. The price of a zero-coupon bond rises smoothly. The price of a coupon bond also rises between coupon payments, but tumbles on the coupon date, reflecting the amount of the coupon payment. For each coupon bond, the gray line shows the trend of the bond price just after each coupon is paid.

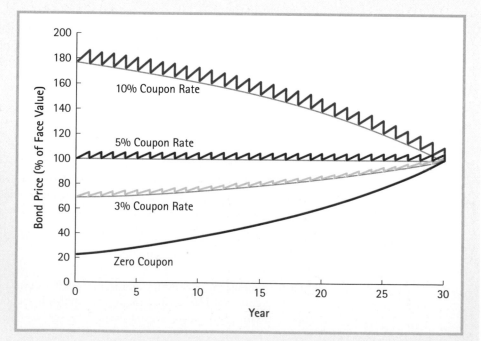

Clean and Dirty Prices for Coupon Bonds

As Figure 8.1 illustrates, coupon bond prices fluctuate around the time of each coupon payment in a sawtooth pattern: The value of the coupon bond rises as the next coupon payment gets closer and then drops after it has been paid. This fluctuation occurs even if there is no change in the bond's yield to maturity.

Because bond traders are more concerned about changes in the bond's price that arise due to changes in the bond's yield, rather than these predictable patterns around coupon payments, they often do not quote the price of a bond in terms of its actual cash price, which is also called the **dirty price** or **invoice price** of the bond. Instead, bonds are often quoted in terms of a **clean price**, which is the bond's cash price less an adjustment for accrued interest, the amount of the next coupon payment that has already accrued:

Clean price = Cash (dirty) price − Accrued interest

Accrued interest = Coupon Amount ×

$$\left(\frac{\text{days since last coupon payment}}{\text{days in current coupon period}} \right)$$

Note that immediately before a coupon payment is made, the accrued interest will equal the full amount of the coupon, whereas immediately after the coupon payment is made, the accrued interest will be zero. Thus, accrued interest will rise and fall in a saw tooth pattern as each coupon payment passes:

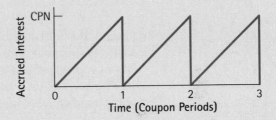

If we subtract accrued interest from the bond's cash price and compute the clean price, the sawtooth pattern is eliminated. Thus, absent changes in the bond's yield to maturity, its clean price converges smoothly over time to the bond's face value, as shown in the gray lines in Figure 8.1.

---

each coupon is paid, the price of a bond drops by the amount of the coupon. When the bond is trading at a premium, the price drop when a coupon is paid will be larger than the price increase between coupons, so the bond's premium will tend to decline as time passes. If the bond is trading at a discount, the price increase between coupons will exceed the drop when a coupon is paid, so the bond's price will rise and its discount will decline as time passes. Ultimately, the prices of all bonds approach the bonds' face value when the bonds mature and their last coupon is paid.

For each of the bonds illustrated in Figure 8.1, if the yield to maturity remains at 5%, investors will earn a 5% return on their investment. For the zero-coupon bond, this return is earned solely due to the price appreciation of the bond. For the 10% coupon bond, this return comes from the combination of coupon payments and price depreciation over time.

Interest Rate Changes and Bond Prices

As interest rates in the economy fluctuate, the yields that investors demand to invest in bonds will also change. Let's evaluate the effect of fluctuations in a bond's yield to maturity on its price.

Consider again a 30-year, zero-coupon bond with a yield to maturity of 5%. For a face value of $100, the bond will initially trade for

$$P(\text{5\% yield to maturity}) = \frac{100}{1.05^{30}} = \$23.14$$

But suppose interest rates suddenly rise so that investors now demand a 6% yield to maturity before they will invest in this bond. This change in yield implies that the bond price will fall to

$$P(\text{6\% yield to maturity}) = \frac{100}{1.06^{30}} = \$17.41$$

Relative to the initial price, the bond price changes by $(17.41 - 23.14) / 23.14 = -24.8\%$, a substantial price drop.

This example illustrates a general phenomenon. A higher yield to maturity implies a higher discount rate for a bond's remaining cash flows, reducing their present value and hence the bond's price. Therefore, *as interest rates and bond yields rise, bond prices will fall, and vice versa.*

The sensitivity of a bond's price to changes in interest rates depends on the timing of its cash flows. Because it is discounted over a shorter period, the present value of a cash flow that will be received in the near future is less dramatically affected by interest rates than a cash flow in the distant future. Thus shorter-maturity zero-coupon bonds are less sensitive to changes in interest rates than are longer-term zero-coupon bonds. Similarly, bonds with higher coupon rates—because they pay higher cash flows upfront—are less sensitive to interest rate changes than otherwise identical bonds with lower coupon rates. The sensitivity of a bond's price to changes in interest rates is measured by the bond's **duration**.[4] Bonds with high durations are highly sensitive to interest rate changes.

EXAMPLE 8.7	**The Interest Rate Sensitivity of Bonds**

Problem

Consider a 15-year zero-coupon bond and a 30-year coupon bond with 10% annual coupons. By what percentage will the price of each bond change if its yield to maturity increases from 5% to 6%?

Solution

First we compute the price of each bond for each yield to maturity:

Yield to Maturity	15-Year, Zero-Coupon Bond	30-Year, 10% Annual Coupon Bond
5%	$\dfrac{100}{1.05^{15}} = \$48.10$	$10 \times \dfrac{1}{0.05}\left(1 - \dfrac{1}{1.05^{30}}\right) + \dfrac{100}{1.05^{30}} = \$176.86$
6%	$\dfrac{100}{1.06^{15}} = \$41.73$	$10 \times \dfrac{1}{0.06}\left(1 - \dfrac{1}{1.06^{30}}\right) + \dfrac{100}{1.06^{30}} = \$155.06$

The price of the 15-year zero-coupon bond changes by $(41.73 - 48.10) / 48.10 = -13.2\%$ if its yield to maturity increases from 5% to 6%. For the 30-year bond with 10% annual

---

4. We define duration formally and discuss this concept more thoroughly in Chapter 30.

coupons, the price change is $(155.06 - 176.86) / 176.86 = -12.3\%$. Even though the 30-year bond has a longer maturity, because of its high coupon rate its sensitivity to a change in yield is actually less than that of the 15-year zero coupon bond.

In actuality, bond prices are subject to the effects of both the passage of time and changes in interest rates. Bond prices converge to the bond's face value due to the time effect, but simultaneously move up and down due to unpredictable changes in bond yields. Figure 8.2 illustrates this behavior by demonstrating how the price of the 30-year, zero-coupon bond might change over its life. Note that the bond price tends to converge to the face value as the bond approaches the maturity date, but also moves higher when its yield falls and lower when its yield rises.

FIGURE 8.2

Yield to Maturity and Bond Price Fluctuations Over Time

The graphs illustrate changes in price and yield for a 30-year zero-coupon bond over its life. The top graph illustrates the changes in the bond's yield to maturity over its life. In the bottom graph, the actual bond price is shown in blue. Because the yield to maturity does not remain constant over the bond's life, the bond's price fluctuates as it converges to the face value over time. Also shown is the price if the yield to maturity remained fixed at 4%, 5%, or 6%.

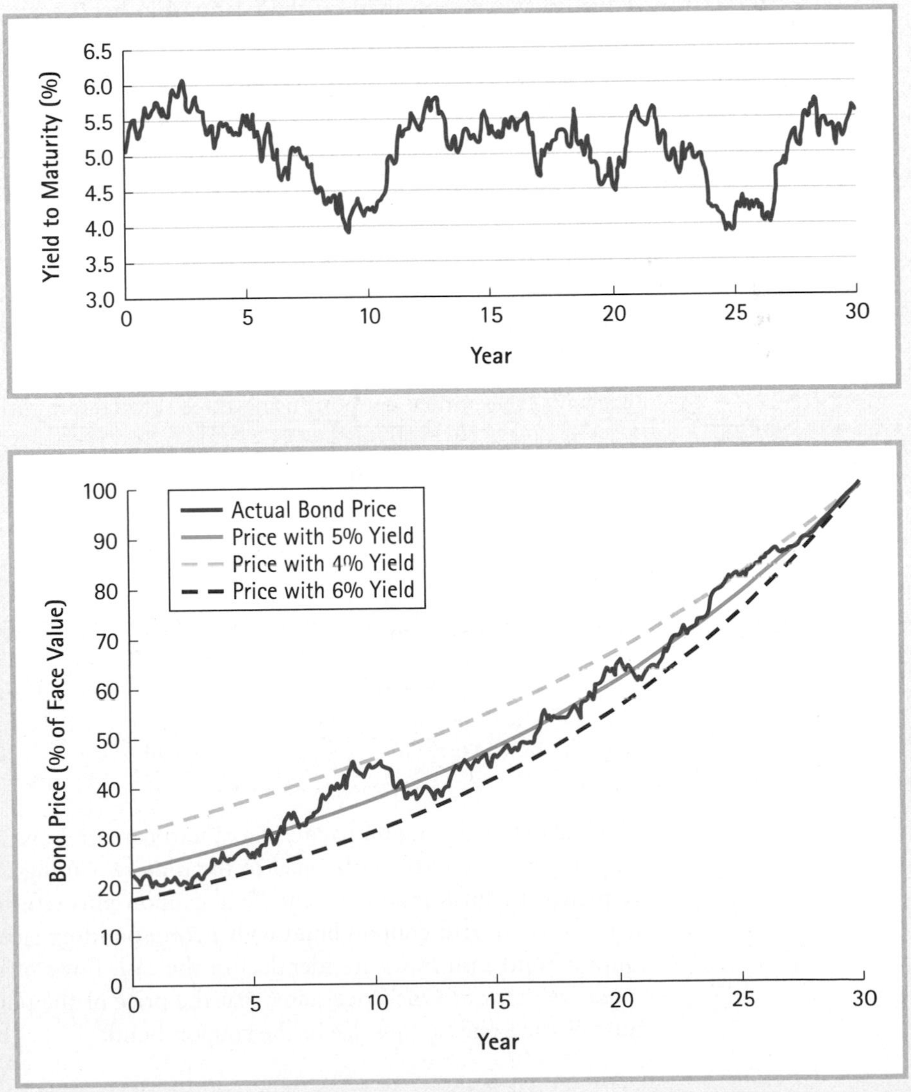

As Figure 8.2 demonstrates, prior to maturity the bond is exposed to interest rate risk. If an investor chooses to sell and the bond's yield to maturity has decreased, then the investor will receive a high price and earn a high return. If the yield to maturity has increased, the bond price is low at the time of sale and the investor will earn a low return. In the appendix to this chapter, we discuss one way corporations manage this type of risk.

CONCEPT CHECK

1. If a bond's yield to maturity does not change, how does its cash price change between coupon payments?

2. What risk does an investor in a default-free bond face if she plans to sell the bond prior to maturity?

8.3 The Yield Curve and Bond Arbitrage

Thus far, we have focused on the relationship between the price of an individual bond and its yield to maturity. In this section, we explore the relationship between the prices and yields of different bonds. Using the Law of One Price, we show that given the spot interest rates, which are the yields of default-free zero-coupon bonds, we can determine the price and yield of any other default-free bond. As a result, the yield curve provides sufficient information to evaluate all such bonds.

Replicating a Coupon Bond

Because it is possible to replicate the cash flows of a coupon bond using zero-coupon bonds, we can use the Law of One Price to compute the price of a coupon bond from the prices of zero-coupon bonds. For example, we can replicate a three-year, $1000 bond that pays 10% annual coupons using three zero-coupon bonds as follows:

	0	1	2	3
Coupon bond:		$100	$100	$1100
1-year zero:		$100		
2-year zero:			$100	
3-year zero:				$1100
Zero-coupon Bond portfolio:		$100	$100	$1100

We match each coupon payment to a zero-coupon bond with a face value equal to the coupon payment and a term equal to the time remaining to the coupon date. Similarly, we match the final bond payment (final coupon plus return of face value) in three years to a three-year, zero-coupon bond with a corresponding face value of $1100. Because the coupon bond cash flows are identical to the cash flows of the portfolio of zero-coupon bonds, the Law of One Price states that the price of the portfolio of zero-coupon bonds must be the same as the price of the coupon bond.

TABLE 8.2	Yields and Prices (per $100 Face Value) for Zero-Coupon Bonds			
Maturity	1 year	2 years	3 years	4 years
YTM	3.50%	4.00%	4.50%	4.75%
Price	$96.62	$92.45	$87.63	$83.06

To illustrate, assume that current zero-coupon bond yields and prices are as shown in Table 8.2 (they are the same as in Example 8.1). We can calculate the cost of the zero-coupon bond portfolio that replicates the three-year coupon bond as follows:

Zero-Coupon Bond	Face Value Required	Cost
1 year	100	96.62
2 years	100	92.45
3 years	1100	$11 \times 87.63 = 963.93$
	Total Cost:	$1153.00

By the Law of One Price, the three-year coupon bond must trade for a price of $1153. If the price of the coupon bond were higher, you could earn an arbitrage profit by selling the coupon bond and buying the zero-coupon bond portfolio. If the price of the coupon bond were lower, you could earn an arbitrage profit by buying the coupon bond and short selling the zero-coupon bonds.

Valuing a Coupon Bond Using Zero-Coupon Yields

To this point, we have used the zero-coupon bond *prices* to derive the price of the coupon bond. Alternatively, we can use the zero-coupon bond *yields*. Recall that the yield to maturity of a zero-coupon bond is the competitive market interest rate for a risk-free investment with a term equal to the term of the zero-coupon bond. Therefore, the price of a coupon bond must equal the present value of its coupon payments and face value discounted at the competitive market interest rates (see Eq. 5.7 in Chapter 5):

Price of a Coupon Bond

$$P = PV(\text{Bond Cash Flows})$$

$$= \frac{CPN}{1 + YTM_1} + \frac{CPN}{(1 + YTM_2)^2} + \cdots + \frac{CPN + FV}{(1 + YTM_n)^n} \tag{8.6}$$

where *CPN* is the bond coupon payment, YTM_n is the yield to maturity of a *zero-coupon* bond that matures at the same time as the *n*th coupon payment, and *FV* is the face value of the bond. For the three-year, $1000 bond with 10% annual coupons considered earlier, we can use Eq. 8.6 to calculate its price using the zero-coupon yields in Table 8.2:

$$P = \frac{100}{1.035} + \frac{100}{1.04^2} + \frac{100 + 1000}{1.045^3} = \$1153$$

This price is identical to the price we computed earlier by replicating the bond. Thus we can determine the no-arbitrage price of a coupon bond by discounting its cash flows using the zero-coupon yields. In other words, the information in the zero-coupon yield curve is sufficient to price all other risk-free bonds.

Coupon Bond Yields

Given the yields for zero-coupon bonds, we can use Eq. 8.6 to price a coupon bond. In Section 8.1, we saw how to compute the yield to maturity of a coupon bond from its price. Combining these results, we can determine the relationship between the yields of zero-coupon bonds and coupon-paying bonds.

Consider again the three-year, $1000 bond with 10% annual coupons. Given the zero-coupon yields in Table 8.2, we calculate a price for this bond of $1153. From Eq. 8.5, the yield to maturity of this bond is the rate y that satisfies

$$P = 1153 = \frac{100}{(1+y)} + \frac{100}{(1+y)^2} + \frac{100 + 1000}{(1+y)^3}$$

We can solve for the yield by using the annuity spreadsheet:

	NPER	RATE	PV	PMT	FV	Excel Formula
Given	3		−1,153	100	1,000	
Solve for Rate		4.44%				=RATE(3,100,−1153,1000)

Therefore, the yield to maturity of the bond is 4.44%. We can check this result directly as follows:

$$P = \frac{100}{1.0444} + \frac{100}{1.0444^2} + \frac{100 + 1000}{1.0444^3} = \$1153$$

Because the coupon bond provides cash flows at different points in time, the yield to maturity of a coupon bond is a weighted average of the yields of the zero-coupon bonds of equal and shorter maturities. The weights depend (in a complex way) on the magnitude of the cash flows each period. In this example, the zero-coupon bonds yields were 3.5%, 4.0%, and 4.5%. For this coupon bond, most of the value in the present value calculation comes from the present value of the third cash flow because it includes the principal, so the yield is closest to the three-year, zero-coupon yield of 4.5%.

EXAMPLE 8.8

Yields on Bonds with the Same Maturity

Problem

Given the following zero-coupon yields, compare the yield to maturity for a three-year, zero-coupon bond; a three-year, coupon bond with 4% annual coupons; and a three-year coupon bond with 10% annual coupons. All of these bonds are default free.

Maturity	1 year	2 years	3 years	4 years
Zero-coupon YTM	3.50%	4.00%	4.50%	4.75%

Solution

From the information provided, the yield to maturity of the three-year, zero-coupon bond is 4.50%. Also, because the yields match those in Table 8.2, we already calculated the yield to maturity for the 10% coupon bond as 4.44%. To compute the yield for the 4% coupon bond, we first need to calculate its price. Using Eq. 8.6, we have

$$P = \frac{40}{1.035} + \frac{40}{1.04^2} + \frac{40 + 1000}{1.045^3} = \$986.98$$

The price of the bond with a 4% coupon is $986.98. From Eq. 8.5, its yield to maturity solves the following equation:

$$\$986.98 = \frac{40}{(1 + y)} + \frac{40}{(1 + y)^2} + \frac{40 + 1000}{(1 + y)^3}$$

We can calculate the yield to maturity using the annuity spreadsheet:

	NPER	RATE	PV	PMT	FV	Excel Formula
Given	3		−986.98	40	1,000	
Solve for Rate		4.47%				=RATE(3,40,−986.98,1000)

To summarize, for the three-year bonds considered,

Coupon rate	**0%**	**4%**	**10%**
YTM	4.50%	4.47%	4.44%

Example 8.8 shows that coupon bonds with the same maturity can have different yields depending on their coupon rates. The yield to maturity of a coupon bond is a weighted average of the yields on the zero-coupon bonds. As the coupon increases, earlier cash flows become relatively more important than later cash flows in the calculation of the present value. If the yield curve is upward sloping (as it is for the yields in Example 8.8), the resulting yield to maturity decreases with the coupon rate of the bond. Alternatively, when the zero-coupon yield curve is downward sloping, the yield to maturity will increase with the coupon rate. When the yield curve is flat, all zero-coupon and coupon-paying bonds will have the same yield, independent of their maturities and coupon rates.

Treasury Yield Curves

As we have shown in this section, we can use the zero-coupon yield curve to determine the price and yield to maturity of other risk-free bonds. The plot of the yields of coupon bonds of different maturities is called the **coupon-paying yield curve**. When U.S. bond traders refer to "the yield curve," they are often referring to the coupon-paying Treasury yield curve. As we showed in Example 8.8, two coupon-paying bonds with the same maturity may have different yields. By convention, practitioners always plot the yield of the most recently issued bonds, termed the **on-the-run bonds**. Using similar methods to those employed in this section, we can apply the Law of One Price to determine the zero-coupon bond yields using the coupon-paying yield curve (see Problem 22). Thus either type of yield curve provides enough information to value all other risk-free bonds.

CONCEPT CHECK   **1.** Why does the zero-coupon yield curve for the default-free bonds provide sufficient information to value all other default-free bonds?

2. Explain why two coupon bonds with the same maturity may each have a different yield to maturity.

8.4 Corporate Bonds

So far in this chapter, we have focused on default-free bonds such as U.S. Treasury securities, for which the cash flows are known with certainty. For other bonds such as **corporate bonds** (bonds issued by corporations), the issuer may default—that is, it might not pay back the full amount promised in the bond prospectus. This risk of default, which is known as the **credit risk** of the bond, means that the bond's cash flows are not known with certainty.

Corporate Bond Yields

How does the credit risk of default affect bond prices and yields? Because the cash flows promised by the bond are the most that bondholders can hope to receive, the cash flows that a purchaser of a bond with credit risk *expects* to receive may be less than that amount. As a result, investors pay less for bonds with credit risk than they would for an otherwise identical default-free bond. Because the yield to maturity for a bond is calculated using the *promised* cash flows, the yield of bonds with credit risk will be higher than that of otherwise identical default-free bonds. Let's illustrate the effect of credit risk on bond yields and investor returns by comparing different cases.

No Default.   Suppose that the one-year, zero-coupon Treasury bill has a yield to maturity of 4%. What are the price and yield of a one-year, $1000, zero-coupon bond issued by Avant Corporation? First, suppose that all investors agree that there is *no* possibility that Avant will default within the next year. In that case, investors will receive $1000 in one year for certain, as promised by the bond. Because this bond is risk free, the Law of One Price guarantees that it must have the same yield as the one-year, zero-coupon Treasury bill. The price of the bond will therefore be

$$P = \frac{1000}{1 + YTM_1} = \frac{1000}{1.04} = \$961.54$$

Certain Default.   Now suppose that investors believe that Avant will default with certainty at the end of one year and will be able to pay only 90% of its outstanding obligations. Then, even though the bond promises $1000 at year-end, bondholders know they will receive only $900. Investors can predict this shortfall perfectly, so the $900 payment is risk free, and the bond is still a one-year risk-free investment. We therefore compute the price of the bond by discounting this cash flow using the risk-free interest rate as the cost of capital:

$$P = \frac{900}{1 + YTM_1} = \frac{900}{1.04} = \$865.38$$

The prospect of default lowers the cash flow investors expect to receive and hence the price they are willing to pay.

Given the bond's price, we can compute the bond's yield to maturity. When computing this yield, we use the *promised* rather than the *actual* cash flows. Thus

$$YTM = \frac{FV}{P} - 1 = \frac{1000}{865.38} - 1 = 15.56\%$$

The 15.56% yield to maturity of Avant's bond is much higher than the yield to maturity of the default-free Treasury bill. But this result does not mean that investors who buy the bond will earn a 15.56% return. Because Avant will default, the expected return of the bond equals its 4% cost of capital:

$$\frac{900}{865.38} = 1.04$$

Note that *the yield to maturity of a defaultable bond is not equal to the expected return of investing in the bond.* Because we calculate the yield to maturity using the promised cash flows rather than the expected cash flows, the yield will always be higher than the expected return of investing in the bond.

Risk of Default. The two Avant examples were extreme cases, of course. In the first case, we assumed the probability of default was zero; in the second case, we assumed Avant would definitely default. In reality, the chance that Avant will default lies somewhere in between these two extremes (and for most firms, is probably much closer to zero).

To illustrate, again consider the one-year, $1000, zero-coupon bond issued by Avant. This time, assume that the bond payoffs are uncertain. In particular, there is a 50% chance that the bond will repay its face value in full and a 50% chance that the bond will default and you will receive $900. Thus, on average, you will receive $950.

To determine the price of this bond, we must discount this expected cash flow using a cost of capital equal to the expected return of other securities with equivalent risk. If Avant is more likely to default if the economy is weak than if the economy is strong, the results of Chapter 3 suggest that investors will demand a risk premium to invest in this bond. Thus Avant's debt cost of capital, which is the expected return Avant's debt holders will require to compensate them for the risk of the bond's cash flows, will be higher than the 4% risk-free interest rate.

Let's suppose investors demand a risk premium of 1.1% for this bond, so that the appropriate cost of capital is 5.1%. Then the present value of the bond's cash flow is

$$P = \frac{950}{1.051} = \$903.90$$

Consequently, in this case the bond's yield to maturity is 10.63%:

$$YTM = \frac{FV}{P} - 1 = \frac{1000}{903.90} - 1 = 1.1063$$

Of course, the 10.63% promised yield is the most investors will receive. If Avant defaults, they will receive only $900, for a return of $900 / 903.90 - 1 = -0.43\%$. The average return is $0.50(10.63\%) + 0.50(-0.43\%) = 5.1\%$, the bond's cost of capital.

INTERVIEW WITH
Lisa Black

*L*isa Black is Managing Director at
Teachers Insurance and Annuity
Association, a major financial services
company. A Chartered Financial
Analyst, she oversees a variety of
fixed income funds, including money
market, intermediate bond, high-yield,
emerging market debt, and inflation-
linked bond funds.

QUESTION: *When many people
think about the financial markets,
they picture the equity markets.
How big and how active are the bond markets
compared to the equity markets?*

ANSWER: The dollar volume of bonds traded daily is
about ten times that of equity markets. For example,
a single $15 billion issue of 10 year Treasury bonds will
sell in one day. The Lehman Brothers US Universal
Index of dollar-denominated debt outstanding totals
almost $10 trillion, and its biggest component is the
$8.3 trillion US aggregate index, a broad index of invest-
ment grade debt. It includes treasuries, agencies, corporate bonds, and mortgage-backed securities. Other major
sectors include corporate high yield bonds, Eurodollar
bonds, emerging markets, and private placements.

QUESTION: *How do the bond markets operate?*

ANSWER: Firms and governments turn to bond markets
when they need to borrow money to fund new construction projects, cover budget deficits, and similar reasons.
On the other side, you have institutions like TIAA-CREF,
endowments, and foundations with funds to invest.
Wall Street investment bankers serve as intermediaries
between capital raisers and investors, matching up borrowers with creditors in terms of maturity needs and risk
appetite. Because we provide annuities for college professors, for example, we invest money for longer periods
of time than an insurance company that needs funds to
pay claims. In the institutional world, such as the bond
funds we manage, we typically trade in blocks of bonds
ranging from $5 million to $50 million at a time.

QUESTION: *What drives changes in the values of
Treasury bonds?*

ANSWER: The simple answer is that when interest rates
rise, bond prices fall. The key is to dig below that reality

to see *why* interest rates rise and fall.
A major factor is investors' expectation for inflation and economic
growth. Right now (July 2006),
the Fed Funds (overnight) rate is
5.25 percent. A 10-year Treasury
bond is yielding about 5 percent,
about 0.25 percent below the
overnight rate. This downward-
sloping yield curve is saying that
inflation is in check and won't erode
the value of that 5 percent yield.
Otherwise investors would require
a greater expected return to lend for 10 years.

Expectations of future economic growth have an
important influence on interest rates—interest rates
generally rise when the expectation is that growth will
accelerate, because inflation won't be far behind. In
2000, when the bubble burst and there was concern
that the economy would go into a recession, interest
rates fell because with the expectations of slower growth,
the inflation outlook would improve.

QUESTION: *Are there other factors that affect corporate bonds?*

ANSWER: Corporate bonds have asymmetric returns—
you expect to get principal and interest back over life
of bond, but the downside is that if the company files
for bankruptcy, you may only get 30 to 50 cents on the
dollar. Therefore, another factor that affects the values
of corporate bonds is expectations of the likelihood of
default. When the economy is very good, a company
that is strong financially will need to offer only a very
small yield spread over treasuries. For example, IBM
may need to offer just 0.35% more than 10-year treasuries to attract buyers to their bonds.

On other hand, if an issuer has credit issues, the yield
spread of its bonds over treasuries will widen. GM's
yield spreads have widened dramatically since they
announced high losses. No longer can they issue debt
at 2.5% over the 10-year treasury rate; now the yields
on GM bonds are about 5% higher than treasuries.
Investors demand higher yields to compensate them
for the higher risk that GM may default.

Table 8.3 summarizes the prices, expected return, and yield to maturity of the Avant bond under the various default assumptions. Note that the bond's price decreases, and its yield to maturity increases, with a greater likelihood of default. Conversely, *the bond's expected return, which is equal to the firm's debt cost of capital, is less than the yield to maturity if there is a risk of default. Moreover, a higher yield to maturity does not necessarily imply that a bond's expected return is higher.*

TABLE 8.3	Price, Expected Return, and Yield to Maturity of a One-Year, Zero-Coupon Avant Bond with Different Likelihoods of Default

Avant Bond (1-year, zero-coupon)	Bond Price	Yield to Maturity	Expected Return
Default Free	$961.54	4.00%	4%
50% Chance of Default	$903.90	10.63%	5.1%
Certain Default	$865.38	15.56%	4%

Bond Ratings

It would be both difficult and inefficient for every investor to privately investigate the default risk of every bond. Consequently, several companies rate the creditworthiness of bonds and make this information available to investors. By consulting these ratings, investors can assess the creditworthiness of a particular bond issue. The ratings therefore encourage widespread investor participation and relatively liquid markets. The two best-known bond-rating companies are Standard & Poor's and Moody's. Table 8.4 summarizes the rating classes each company uses. Bonds with the highest rating are judged to be least likely to default.

Bonds in the top four categories are often referred to as **investment-grade bonds** because of their low default risk. Bonds in the bottom five categories are often called **speculative bonds**, **junk bonds**, or **high-yield bonds** because their likelihood of default is high. The rating depends on the risk of bankruptcy as well as the bondholders' ability to lay claim to the firm's assets in the event of such a bankruptcy. Thus debt issues with a low-priority claim in bankruptcy will have a lower rating than issues from the same company that have a high priority in bankruptcy or that are backed by a specific asset such as a building or a plant.

Corporate Yield Curves

Just as we can construct a yield curve from risk-free Treasury securities, we can plot a similar yield curve for corporate bonds. Figure 8.3 shows the average yields of U.S. corporate coupon bonds with three different Standard & Poor's bond ratings: two curves are for investment-grade bonds (AAA and BBB) and one is for junk bonds (B). Figure 8.3 also includes the U.S. (coupon-paying) Treasury yield curve. We refer to the difference between the yields of the corporate bonds and the Treasury yields as the **default spread** or **credit spread**. Credit spreads fluctuate as perceptions regarding the probability of default change. Note that the credit spread is high for bonds with low ratings and therefore a greater likelihood of default.

TABLE 8.4		Bond Ratings
Moody's	**Standard & Poor's**	**Description (Moody's)**
Investment Grade Debt		
Aaa	AAA	Judged to be of the best quality. They carry the smallest degree of investment risk and are generally referred to as "gilt edged." Interest payments are protected by a large or an exceptionally stable margin and principal is secure. While the various protective elements are likely to change, such changes as can be visualized are most unlikely to impair the fundamentally strong position of such issues.
Aa	AA	Judged to be of high quality by all standards. Together with the Aaa group, they constitute what are generally known as high-grade bonds. They are rated lower than the best bonds because margins of protection may not be as large as in Aaa securities or fluctuation of protective elements may be of greater amplitude or there may be other elements present that make the long-term risk appear somewhat larger than the Aaa securities.
A	A	Possess many favorable investment attributes and are considered as upper-medium-grade obligations. Factors giving security to principal and interest are considered adequate, but elements may be present that suggest a susceptibility to impairment some time in the future.
Baa	BBB	Are considered as medium-grade obligations (i.e., they are neither highly protected nor poorly secured). Interest payments and principal security appear adequate for the present but certain protective elements may be lacking or may be characteristically unreliable over any great length of time. Such bonds lack outstanding investment characteristics and, in fact, have speculative characteristics as well.
Speculative Bonds		
Ba	BB	Judged to have speculative elements; their future cannot be considered as well assured. Often the protection of interest and principal payments may be very moderate, and thereby not well safeguarded during both good and bad times over the future. Uncertainty of position characterizes bonds in this class.
B	B	Generally lack characteristics of the desirable investment. Assurance of interest and principal payments of maintenance of other terms of the contract over any long period of time may be small.
Caa	CCC	Are of poor standing. Such issues may be in default or there may be present elements of danger with respect to principal or interest.
Ca	CC	Are speculative in a high degree. Such issues are often in default or have other marked shortcomings.
C	C, D	Lowest-rated class of bonds, and issues so rated can be regarded as having extremely poor prospects of ever attaining any real investment standing.

Source: www.moodys.com.

Corporate Yield Curves for Various Ratings, September 2005

This figure shows the yield curve for U.S. Treasury securities and yield curves for corporate securities with different ratings. Note how the yield to maturity is higher for lower rated bonds, which have a higher probability of default.

Source: Reuters.

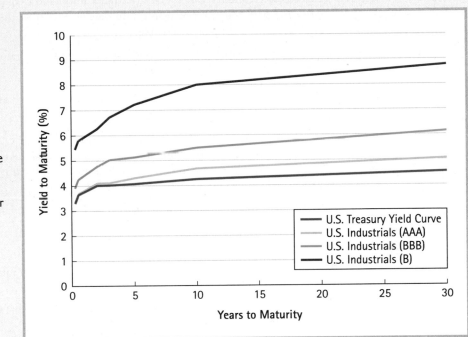

CONCEPT CHECK

1. How will the yield to maturity of a bond vary with the bond's risk of default?

2. What is a junk bond?

Summary

1. Bonds pay both coupon and principal or face value payments to investors. By convention, the coupon rate of a bond is expressed as an APR, so the amount of each coupon payment, *CPN*, is

$$CPN = \frac{\text{Coupon Rate} \times \text{Face Value}}{\text{Number of Coupon Payments per Year}} \qquad (8.1)$$

2. Zero-coupon bonds make no coupon payments, so investors receive only the bond's face value.

3. The internal rate of return of a bond is called its yield to maturity (or yield). The yield to maturity of a bond is the discount rate that sets the present value of the promised bond payments equal to the current market price of the bond.

4. The yield to maturity for a zero-coupon bond is given by

$$YTM_n = \left(\frac{FV}{P}\right)^{1/n} - 1 \qquad (8.3)$$

5. The risk-free interest rate for an investment until date n equals the yield to maturity of a risk-free zero-coupon that matures on date n. A plot of these rates against maturity is called the zero-coupon yield curve.

6. The yield to maturity for a coupon bond is the discount rate, y, that equates the present value of the bond's future cash flows with its price:

$$P = CPN \times \frac{1}{y}\left(1 - \frac{1}{(1+y)^N}\right) + \frac{FV}{(1+y)^N} \tag{8.5}$$

7. A bond will trade at a premium if its coupon rate exceeds its yield to maturity. It will trade at a discount if its coupon rate is less than its yield to maturity. If a bond's coupon rate equals its yield to maturity, it trades at par.

8. As a bond approaches maturity, the price of the bond approaches its face value.

9. If a bond's yield to maturity does not change, then the IRR of an investment in the bond equals its yield to maturity even if you sell the bond early.

10. Bond prices change as interest rates change. When interest rates rise, bond prices fall, and vice versa.

    a. Long-term zero-coupon bonds are more sensitive to changes in interest rates than are short-term zero-coupon bonds.

    b. Bonds with low coupon rates are more sensitive to changes in interest rates than similar maturity bonds with high coupon rates.

    c. The duration of a bond measures the sensitivity of its price to changes in interest rates.

11. Because we can replicate a coupon-paying bond using a portfolio of zero-coupon bonds, the price of a coupon-paying bond can be determined based on the zero-coupon yield curve using the Law of One Price:

$$P = PV(\text{Bond Cash Flows})$$

$$= \frac{CPN}{1 + YTM_1} + \frac{CPN}{(1 + YTM_2)^2} + \cdots + \frac{CPN + FV}{(1 + YTM_n)^n} \tag{8.6}$$

12. When the yield curve is not flat, bonds with the same maturity but different coupon rates will have different yields to maturity.

13. When a bond issuer does not make a bond payment in full, the issuer has defaulted.

    a. The risk that default can occur is called default or credit risk.

    b. U.S. Treasury securities are free of default risk.

14. The expected return of a corporate bond, which is the firm's debt cost of capital, equals the risk-free rate of interest plus a risk premium. The expected return is less than the bond's yield to maturity because the yield to maturity of a bond is calculated using the promised cash flows, not the expected cash flows.

15. Bond ratings summarize the creditworthiness of bonds for investors.

16. The difference between yields on Treasury securities and yields on corporate bonds is called the credit spread or default spread. The credit spread compensates investors for the difference between promised and expected cash flows and for the risk of default.

Key Terms

bond certificate *p. 212*
clean price *p. 221*
corporate bonds *p. 228*
coupon bonds *p. 214*
coupon rate *p. 212*
coupon-paying yield curve *p. 227*
coupons *p. 212*
credit risk *p. 228*
default (credit) spread *p. 231*
dirty price *p. 221*
discount *p. 212*
duration *p. 222*
face value *p. 212*
high-yield bonds *p. 231*
investment-grade bonds *p. 231*
invoice price *p. 221*

junk bonds *p. 231*
maturity date *p. 212*
on-the-run bond *p. 227*
par *p. 217*
premium *p. 217*
pure discount bond *p. 212*
speculative bonds *p. 231*
spot interest rates *p. 214*
term *p. 212*
Treasury bills *p. 212*
Treasury bonds *p. 215*
Treasury notes *p. 215*
yield to maturity (YTM) *p. 213*
zero-coupon bond *p. 212*
zero-coupon yield curve *p. 214*

Further Reading

For readers interested in more details about the bond market, the following texts will prove useful: Z. Bodie, A. Kane, and A. J. Marcus, *Investments*, 6th ed. (Boston: McGraw-Hill/Irwin, 2004); F. Fabozzi, *The Handbook of Fixed Income Securities*, 7th ed. (Boston: McGraw-Hill, 2005); W. F. Sharpe, G. J. Alexander, and J. V. Bailey, *Investments*, 6th ed. (Englewood Cliffs, NJ: Prentice-Hall, 1998); and B. Tuckman, *Fixed Income Securities: Tools for Today's Markets*, 2nd ed. (Hoboken, NJ: John Wiley & Sons, Inc., 2002).

Problems

All problems in this chapter are available in MyFinanceLab. An asterisk (*) indicates problems with a higher level of difficulty.

Bond Cash Flows, Prices, and Yields

1. A 30-year bond with a face value of $1000 has a coupon rate of 5.5%, with semiannual payments.

   a. What is the coupon payment for this bond?

   b. Draw the cash flows for the bond on a timeline.

2. Assume that a bond will make payments every six months as shown on the following timeline (using six-month periods):

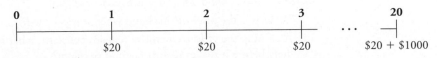

   a. What is the maturity of the bond (in years)?

   b. What is the coupon rate (in percent)?

   c. What is the face value?

EXCEL 3. The following table summarizes prices of various default-free zero-coupon bonds (expressed as a percentage of face value):

Maturity (years)	1	2	3	4	5
Price (per $100 face value)	$95.51	$91.05	$86.38	$81.65	$76.51

   a. Compute the yield to maturity for each bond.

   b. Plot the zero-coupon yield curve (for the first five years).

   c. Is the yield curve upward sloping, downward sloping, or flat?

EXCEL 4. Suppose the current zero-coupon yield curve for risk-free bonds is as follows:

Maturity (years)	1	2	3	4	5
YTM	5.00%	5.50%	5.75%	5.95%	6.05%

   a. What is the price per $100 face value of a two-year, zero-coupon, risk-free bond?

   b. What is the price per $100 face value of a four-year, zero-coupon, risk-free bond?

   c. What is the risk-free interest rate for a five-year maturity?

5. Suppose a ten-year, $1000 bond with an 8% coupon rate and semiannual coupons is trading for a price of $1034.74.

   a. What is the bond's yield to maturity (expressed as an APR with semiannual compounding)?

   b. If the bond's yield to maturity changes to 9% APR, what will the bond's price be?

6. Suppose a five-year, $1000 bond with annual coupons has a price of $900 and a yield to maturity of 6%. What is the bond's coupon rate?

Dynamic Behavior of Bond Prices

7. The prices of several bonds with face values of $1000 are summarized in the following table:

Bond	A	B	C	D
Price	$972.50	$1040.75	$1150.00	$1000.00

   For each bond, state whether it trades at a discount, at par, or at a premium.

8. Explain why the yield of a bond that trades at a discount exceeds the bond's coupon rate.

9. Suppose a seven-year, $1000 bond with an 8% coupon rate and semiannual coupons is trading with a yield to maturity of 6.75%.

   a. Is this bond currently trading at a discount, at par, or at a premium? Explain.

   b. If the yield to maturity of the bond rises to 7.00% (APR with semiannual compounding), what price will the bond trade for?

10. Suppose that General Motors Acceptance Corporation issued a bond with ten years until maturity, a face value of $1000, and a coupon rate of 7% (annual payments). The yield to maturity on this bond when it was issued was 6%.

   a. What was the price of this bond when it was issued?

   b. Assuming the yield to maturity remains constant, what is the price of the bond immediately before it makes its first coupon payment?

   c. Assuming the yield to maturity remains constant, what is the price of the bond immediately after it makes its first coupon payment?

11. Suppose you purchase a ten-year bond with 6% annual coupons. You hold the bond for four years, and sell it immediately after receiving the fourth coupon. If the bond's yield to maturity was 5% when you purchased and sold the bond,

a. What cash flows will you pay and receive from your investment in the bond per $100 face value?

b. What is the internal rate of return of your investment?

EXCEL **12.** Consider the following bonds:

Bond	Coupon Rate (annual payments)	Maturity (years)
A	0%	15
B	0%	10
C	4%	15
D	8%	10

a. What is the percentage change in the price of each bond if its yield to maturity falls from 6% to 5%?

b. Which of the bonds A–D is most sensitive to a 1% drop in interest rates from 6% to 5% and why? Which bond is least sensitive? Provide an intuitive explanation for your answer.

EXCEL **13.** Suppose you purchase a 30-year, zero-coupon bond with a yield to maturity of 6%. You hold the bond for five years before selling it.

a. If the bond's yield to maturity is 6% when you sell it, what is the internal rate of return of your investment?

b. If the bond's yield to maturity is 7% when you sell it, what is the internal rate of return of your investment?

c. If the bond's yield to maturity is 5% when you sell it, what is the internal rate of return of your investment?

d. Even if a bond has no chance of default, is your investment risk free if you plan to sell it before it matures? Explain.

The Yield Curve and Bond Arbitrage

For Problems 14–19, assume zero-coupon yields on default-free securities are as summarized in the following table:

Maturity (years)	1	2	3	4	5
Zero-coupon YTM	4.00%	4.30%	4.50%	4.70%	4.80%

14. What is the price today of a two-year, default-free security with a face value of $1000 and an annual coupon rate of 6%? Does this bond trade at a discount, at par, or at a premium?

15. What is the price of a five-year, zero-coupon, default-free security with a face value of $1000?

16. What is the price of a three-year, default-free security with a face value of $1000 and an annual coupon rate of 4%? What is the yield to maturity for this bond?

17. What is the maturity of a default-free security with annual coupon payments and a yield to maturity of 4.0%? Why?

*18. Consider a four-year, default-free security with annual coupon payments and a face value of $1000 that is issued at par. What is the coupon rate of this bond?

19. Consider a five-year, default-free bond with annual coupons of 5% and a face value of $1000.

a. Without doing any calculations, determine whether this bond is trading at a premium or at a discount. Explain.

b. What is the yield to maturity on this bond?

c. If the yield to maturity on this bond increased to 5.2%, what would the new price be?

*20. Prices of zero-coupon, default-free securities with face values of $1000 are summarized in the following table.

Maturity (years)	1	2	3
Price (per $1000 face value)	$970.87	$938.95	$904.56

Suppose you observe that a three-year, default-free security with an annual coupon rate of 10% and a face value of $1000 has a price today of $1183.50. Is there an arbitrage opportunity? If so, show specifically how you would take advantage of this opportunity. If not, why not?

*21. Assume there are four default-free bonds with the following prices and future cash flows:

Bond	Price Today	Cash Flows		
		Year 1	Year 2	Year 3
A	$ 934.58	1,000	0	0
B	881.66	0	1,000	0
C	1,118.21	100	100	1,100
D	839.62	0	0	1,000

Do these bonds present an arbitrage opportunity? If so, how would you take advantage of this opportunity? If not, why not?

EXCEL ***22.** Suppose you are given the following information about the default-free, coupon-paying yield curve:

Maturity (years)	1	2	3	4
Coupon rate (annual payments)	0.00%	10.00%	6.00%	12.00%
YTM	2.000%	3.908%	5.840%	5.783%

a. Use arbitrage to determine the yield to maturity of a two-year, zero-coupon bond.

b. What is the zero-coupon yield curve for years 1 through 4?

Corporate Bonds

23. Explain why the expected return of a corporate bond does not equal its yield to maturity.

24. The following table summarizes the yields to maturity on several one-year, zero-coupon securities:

Security	Yield (%)
Treasury	3.1
AAA corporate	3.2
BBB corporate	4.2
B corporate	4.9

a. What is the price (expressed as a percentage of the face value) of a one-year, zero-coupon corporate bond with a AAA rating?

b. What is the credit spread on AAA-rated corporate bonds?

c. What is the credit spread on B-rated corporate bonds?

d. How does the credit spread change with the bond rating? Why?

25. Andrew Industries is contemplating issuing a 30-year bond with a coupon rate of 7% (annual coupon payments) and a face value of $1000. Andrew believes it can get a rating of A from

Standard and Poor's. However, due to recent financial difficulties at the company, Standard and Poor's is warning that it may downgrade Andrew Industries bonds to BBB. Yields on A-rated, long-term bonds are currently 6.5%, and yields on BBB-rated bonds arc 6.9%.

  a. What is the price of the bond if Andrew maintains the A rating for the bond issue?

  b. What will the price of the bond be if it is downgraded?

EXCEL 26. HMK Enterprises would like to raise $10 million to invest in capital expenditures. The company plans to issue five-year bonds with a face value of $1000 and a coupon rate of 6.5% (annual payments). The following table summarizes the yield to maturity for five-year (annual-pay) coupon corporate bonds of various ratings:

Rating	AAA	AA	A	BBB	BB
YTM	6.20%	6.30%	6.50%	6.90%	7.50%

  a. Assuming the bonds will be rated AA, what will the price of the bonds be?

  b. How much total principal amount of these bonds must HMK issue to raise $10 million today, assuming the bonds are AA rated? (Because HMK cannot issue a fraction of a bond, assume that all fractions are rounded to the nearest whole number.)

  c. What must the rating of the bonds be for them to sell at par?

  d. Suppose that when the bonds are issued, the price of each bond is $959.54. What is the likely rating of the bonds? Are they junk bonds?

27. A BBB-rated corporate bond has a yield to maturity of 8.2%. A U.S. Treasury security has a yield to maturity of 6.5%. These yields are quoted as APRs with semiannual compounding. Both bonds pay semiannual coupons at a rate of 7% and have five years to maturity.

  a. What is the price (expressed as a percentage of the face value) of the Treasury bond?

  b. What is the price (expressed as a percentage of the face value) of the BBB-rated corporate bond?

  c. What is the credit spread on the BBB bonds?

Data Case

You are an intern with Sirius Satellite Radio in their corporate finance division. The firm is planning to issue $50 million of 12% annual coupon bonds with a ten-year maturity. The firm anticipates an increase in its bond rating. Your boss wants you to determine the gain in the proceeds of the new issue if the issue is rated above the firm's current bond rating. To prepare this information, you will have to determine Sirius' current debt rating and the yield curve for their particular rating. Strangely, no one at Sirius seems to have this information; apparently they are still busy trying to figure out who decided it was a good idea to hire Howard Stern.

  1. Begin by finding the current U.S. Treasury yield curve. At the Treasury Web site (www .treas.gov), search using the term "yield curve" and select "US Treasury—Daily Treasury Yield Curve." *Beware:* There will likely be two links with the same title. Look at the description below the link and select the one that does NOT say "Real Yield . . ." You want the nominal rates. The correct link is likely to be the first link on the page. Download that table into Excel by right clicking with the cursor in the table and selecting "Export to Microsoft Excel."

  2. Find the current yield spreads for the various bond ratings. Unfortunately, the current spreads are available only for a fee, so you will use old ones. Go to BondsOnline (www.bondsonline.com) and click on "Today's Market." Next click on "Corporate Bond

Spreads." Download this table to Excel and copy and paste it to the same file as the Treasury yields.

3. Find the current bond rating for Sirius. Go to Standard & Poor's Web site (www.standardandpoors.com). Select "Find a Rating" from the list at the left of the page, then select "Credit Ratings Search." At this point you will have to register (it's free) or enter the username and password provided by your instructor. Next you will be able to search by Organization Name—enter Sirius and select Sirius Satellite Radio. Use the credit rating for the organization, not the specific issue ratings.

4. Return to Excel and create a timeline with the cash flows and discount rates you will need to value the new bond issue.

   a. To create the required spot rates for Sirius' issue add the appropriate spread to the Treasury yield of the same maturity.

   b. The yield curve and spread rates you have found do not cover every year that you will need for the new bonds. Specifically, you do not have yields or spreads for four-, six-, eight-, and nine-year maturities. Fill these in by linearly interpolating the given yields and spreads. For example, the four-year spot rate and spread will be the average of the three- and five-year rates. The six-year rate and spread will be the average of the five- and seven-year rates. For years eight and nine you will have to spread the difference between years seven and ten across the two years.

   c. To compute the spot rates for Sirius' current debt rating, add the yield spread to the Treasury rate for each maturity. However, note that the spread is in basis points, which are 1/100th of a percentage point.

   d. Compute the cash flows that would be paid to bondholders each year and add them to the timeline.

5. Use the spot rates to calculate the present value of each cash flow paid to the bondholders.

6. Compute the issue price of the bond and its initial yield to maturity.

7. Repeat steps 4–6 based on the assumption that Sirius is able to raise its bond rating by one level. Compute the new yield based on the higher rating and the new bond price that would result.

8. Compute the additional cash proceeds that could be raised from the issue if the rating were improved.

**CHAPTER 8
APPENDIX**

notation

f_n one-year forward
rate for year n

Forward Interest Rates

Given the risk associated with interest rate changes, corporate managers require tools to help manage this risk. One of the most important is the interest rate forward contract. An **interest rate forward contract** (also called a **forward rate agreement**) is a contract today that fixes the interest rate for a loan or investment in the future. In this appendix, we explain how to derive forward interest rates from zero-coupon yields.

Computing Forward Rates

A **forward interest rate** (or **forward rate**) is an interest rate that we can guarantee today for a loan or investment that will occur in the future. Throughout this section, we will consider only interest rate forward contracts for investments of one year. For example, when we refer to the forward rate for year 5, we mean the rate available *today* on a one-year investment that begins four years from today and is repaid five years from today.

We can use the Law of One Price to calculate the forward rate from the zero-coupon yield curve. The forward rate for year 1 is the rate on an investment that starts today and is repaid in one year; it is equivalent to an investment in a one-year, zero-coupon bond. Therefore, by the Law of One Price, these rates must coincide:

$$f_1 = YTM_1 \qquad (8A.1)$$

Now consider the two-year forward rate. Suppose the one-year, zero-coupon yield is 5.5% and the two-year, zero-coupon yield is 7.0%. There are two ways to invest money risk free for two years. First, we can invest in the two-year, zero-coupon bond at rate of 7.0% and earn $\$(1.07)^2$ after two years per dollar invested. Second, we can invest in the one-year bond at a rate of 5.5%, which will pay \$1.055 at the end of one year, and simultaneously guarantee the interest rate we will earn by reinvesting the \$1.055 for the second year by entering into an interest rate forward contract for year 2 at rate f_2. In that case, we will earn $\$(1.055)(1 + f_2)$ at the end of two years.

Because both strategies are risk free, by the Law of One Price, they must have the same return:

$$(1.07)^2 = (1.055)(1 + f_2)$$

Rearranging, we have

$$(1 + f_2) = \frac{1.07^2}{1.055} = 1.0852$$

Therefore, in this case the forward rate for year 2 is $f_2 = 8.52\%$.

In general, we can compute the forward rate for year n by comparing an investment in an n-year, zero-coupon bond to an investment in an $(n - 1)$ year, zero-coupon bond, with the interest rate earned in the nth year being guaranteed through an interest rate forward contract. Because both strategies are risk free, they must have the same payoff or else an arbitrage opportunity would be available. Comparing the payoffs of these strategies, we have

$$(1 + YTM_n)^n = (1 + YTM_{n-1})^{n-1}(1 + f_n)$$

We can rearrange this equation to find the general formula for the forward interest rate:

$$f_n = \frac{(1 + YTM_n)^n}{(1 + YTM_{n-1})^{n-1}} - 1 \qquad (8A.2)$$

EXAMPLE

8A.1

Computing Forward Rates

Problem

Calculate the forward rates for years 1 through 5 from the following zero-coupon yields:

Maturity	1	2	3	4
YTM	5.00%	6.00%	6.00%	5.75%

Solution

Using Eqs. 8A.1 and 8A.2:

$$f_1 = YTM_1 = 5.00\%$$

$$f_2 = \frac{(1 + YTM_2)^2}{(1 + YTM_1)} - 1 = \frac{1.06^2}{1.05} - 1 = 7.01\%$$

$$f_3 = \frac{(1 + YTM_3)^3}{(1 + YTM_2)^2} - 1 = \frac{1.06^3}{1.06^2} - 1 = 6.00\%$$

$$f_4 = \frac{(1 + YTM_4)^4}{(1 + YTM_3)^3} - 1 = \frac{1.0575^4}{1.06^3} - 1 = 5.00\%$$

Note that when the yield curve is increasing in year n (that is, when $YTM_n > YTM_{n-1}$), the forward rate is higher than the zero-coupon yield, $f_n > YTM_n$. Similarly, when the yield curve is decreasing, the forward rate is less than the zero-coupon yield. When the yield curve is flat, the forward rate equals the zero-coupon yield.

Computing Bond Yields from Forward Rates

Equation 8A.2 computes the forward interest rate using the zero-coupon yields. It is also possible to compute the zero-coupon yields from the forward interest rates. To see this, note that if we use interest rate forward contracts to lock in an interest rate for an investment in year 1, year 2, and so on through year n, we can create an n-year, risk-free investment. The return from this strategy must match the return from an n-year, zero-coupon bond. Therefore:

$$(1 + f_1) \times (1 + f_2) \times \cdots \times (1 + f_n) = (1 + YTM_n)^n \qquad (8A.3)$$

For example, using the forward rates from Example 8A.1, we can compute the four-year zero-coupon yield:

$$1 + YTM_4 = [(1 + f_1)(1 + f_2)(1 + f_3)(1 + f_4)]^{1/4}$$

$$= [(1.05)(1.0701)(1.06)(1.05)]^{1/4}$$

$$= 1.0575$$

Forward Rates and Future Interest Rates

A forward rate is the rate that you contract for today for an investment in the future. How does this rate compare to the interest rate that will actually prevail in the future? It is tempting to believe that the forward interest rate should be a good predictor of future interest rates. In reality, this will generally not be the case. Instead, it is a good predictor only when investors do not care about risk.

EXAMPLE
8A.2

Forward Rates and Future Spot Rates

Problem

JoAnne Wilford is corporate treasurer for Wafer Thin Semiconductor. She must invest some of the cash on hand for two years in risk-free bonds. The current one-year, zero-coupon yield is 5%. The one-year forward rate is 6%. She is trying to decide between two possible strategies. The first strategy is risk free—she would invest the money for one year and guarantee the rate in the second year by entering into an interest rate forward contract. The second strategy is risky—she would invest in a risk-free asset for one year but would forgo the forward contract. Instead, she would take her chances and simply accept whatever one-year rate prevails in the market in one year. Under what conditions would she be better off following the risky strategy?

Solution

We first work out the future rate that would leave her indifferent. The risk-free strategy returns $(1.05)(1.06)$. The risky strategy returns $(1.05)(1 + r)$, where r is the one-year interest rate next year. If the future interest rate is 6%, then the two strategies will offer the same return. Thus Wafer Thin Semiconductor is better off with the risky strategy if the interest rate next year is greater than the forward rate—6%—and worse off if the interest rate is lower than 6%.

As Example 8A.2 makes clear, we can think of the forward rate as a break-even rate. If this rate actually prevails in the future, investors will be indifferent between investing in a two-year bond and investing in a one-year bond and rolling over the money in one year. If investors did not care about risk, then they would be indifferent between the two strategies whenever the expected one-year spot rate equals the current forward rate. However, investors *do* generally care about risk. If the expected returns of both strategies were the same, investors would prefer one strategy or the other depending on whether they want to be exposed to future interest rate risk fluctuations. In general, the expected future spot interest rate will reflect investors' preferences toward the risk of future interest rate fluctuations. Thus

Expected Future Spot Interest Rate

$$= \text{Forward Interest Rate} + \text{Risk Premium} \qquad (8A.4)$$

This risk premium can be either positive or negative depending on investors' preferences.[5] As a result, forward rates tend not be good predictors of future spot rates.

Key Terms

forward interest rate (forward rate) *p. 241*   interest rate forward contract *p. 241*
forward rate agreement *p. 241*

---

5. Empirical research suggests that the risk premium tends to be negative when the yield curve is upward sloping, and positive when it is downward sloping. See Eugene F. Fama and Robert R. Bliss, "The Information in Long-Maturity Forward Rates," *American Economic Review* 77(4) (1987): 680–692; and John Y. Campbell and Robert J. Shiller, "Yield Spreads and Interest Rate Movements: A Bird's Eye View," *Review of Economic Studies* 58(3) (1991): 495–514.

Problems

All problems in this Appendix are available in MyFinanceLab. An asterisk (*) indicates problems with a higher level of difficulty.

Problems A.1–A.4 refer to the following table:

Maturity (years)	1	2	3	4	5
Zero-coupon YTM	4.0%	5.5%	5.5%	5.0%	4.5%

A.1. What is the forward rate for year 2 (the forward rate quoted today for an investment that begins in one year and matures in two years)?

A.2. What is the forward rate for year 3 (the forward rate quoted today for an investment that begins in two years and matures in three years)? What can you conclude about forward rates when the yield curve is flat?

A.3. What is the forward rate for year 5 (the forward rate quoted today for an investment that begins in four years and matures in five years)?

*A.4. Suppose you wanted to lock in an interest rate for an investment that begins in one year and matures in five years. What rate would you obtain if there are no arbitrage opportunities?

*A.5. Suppose the yield on a one-year, zero-coupon bond is 5%. The forward rate for year 2 is 4%, and the forward rate for year 3 is 3%. What is the yield to maturity of a zero-coupon bond that matures in three years?

CHAPTER

9

Valuing Stocks

notation

P_t	stock price at the end of year t
r_E	equity cost of capital
N	terminal date or forecast horizon
g	expected dividend growth rate
Div_t	dividends paid in year t
EPS_t	earnings per share on date t
PV	present value
$EBIT$	earnings before interest and taxes
FCF_t	free cash flow on date t
V_t	enterprise value on date t
τ_c	corporate tax rate
r_{wacc}	weighted average cost of capital
g_{FCF}	expected free cash flow growth rate
$EBITDA$	earnings before interest, taxes, depreciation, and amortization

On January 16, 2006, footwear and apparel maker Kenneth Cole Productions, Inc., announced that its president, Paul Blum, had resigned to pursue "other opportunities." The price of the company's stock had already dropped more than 16% over the prior two years, and the firm was in the midst of a major undertaking to restructure its brand. News that its president, who had been with the company for more than 15 years, was now resigning was taken as a bad sign by many investors. The next day, Kenneth Cole's stock price dropped by more than 6% on the New York Stock Exchange to $26.75, with over 300,000 shares traded, more than twice its average daily volume. How might an investor decide whether to buy or sell a stock such as Kenneth Cole at this price? Why would the stock suddenly be worth 6% less on the announcement of this news? What actions can Kenneth Cole's managers take to increase the stock price?

To answer these questions, we turn to the Law of One Price. As we demonstrated in Chapter 3, the Law of One Price implies that the price of a security should equal the present value of the expected cash flows an investor will receive from owning it. In this chapter, we apply this idea to stocks. Thus, to value a stock, we need to know the expected cash flows an investor will receive and the appropriate cost of capital with which to discount those cash flows. Both of these quantities can be challenging to estimate, and many of the details needed to do so will be developed throughout the remainder of the text. In this chapter, we will begin our study of stock valuation by identifying the relevant cash flows and developing the main tools that practitioners use to evaluate them.

Our analysis begins with a consideration of the dividends and capital gains received by investors who hold the stock for different periods, from which we develop the dividend-discount model of stock valuation. Next, we apply Chapter 7's tools to value stocks based on the free cash flows generated by the firm. Having developed these stock valuation methods based on discounted cash flows, we then relate them to the practice of using valuation multiples based on comparable firms. We conclude the chapter by discussing the role of competition in the information contained in stock prices and its implications for investors and corporate managers.

9.1 Stock Prices, Returns, and the Investment Horizon

The Law of One Price implies that to value any security, we must determine the expected cash flows an investor will receive from owning it. Thus, we begin our analysis of stock valuation by considering the cash flows for an investor with a one-year investment horizon. In that case, we show how the stock's price and the investor's return from the investment are related. We then consider the perspective of investors with long investment horizons. Finally, we show that, if investors have the same beliefs, their valuation of the stock will not depend on their investment horizon.

A One-Year Investor

There are two potential sources of cash flows from owning a stock. First, the firm might pay out cash to its shareholders in the form of a dividend. Second, the investor might generate cash by choosing to sell the shares at some future date. The total amount received in dividends and from selling the stock will depend on the investor's investment horizon. Let's begin by considering the perspective of a one-year investor.

When an investor buys a stock, she will pay the current market price for a share, P_0. While she continues to hold the stock, she will be entitled to any dividends the stock pays. Let Div_1 be the total dividends paid per share of the stock during the year. At the end of the year, the investor will sell her share at the new market price, P_1. Assuming for simplicity that all dividends are paid at the end of the year, we have the following timeline for this investment:

$$
\begin{array}{ll}
0 & 1 \\
\mid\!\!\!\rule[0.5ex]{10em}{0.4pt}\!\!\!\mid & \\
-P_0 & Div_1 + P_1
\end{array}
$$

Of course, the future dividend payment and stock price in the timeline above are not known with certainty; rather, these values are based on the investor's expectations at the time the stock is purchased. Given these expectations, the investor will be willing to pay a price today up to the point that this transaction has a zero NPV—that is, up to the point at which the current price equals the present value of the expected future dividend and sale price. Because these cash flows are risky, we cannot discount them using the risk-free interest rate. Instead, we must discount them based on the **equity cost of capital**, r_E, for the stock, which is the expected return of other investments available in the market with equivalent risk to the firm's shares. Doing so leads to the following equation for the stock price:

$$
P_0 = \frac{Div_1 + P_1}{1 + r_E} \tag{9.1}
$$

If the current stock price were less than this amount, it would be a positive-NPV investment. We would therefore expect investors to rush in and buy it, driving up the stock's price. If the stock price exceeded this amount, selling it would have a positive NPV and the stock price would quickly fall.

Dividend Yields, Capital Gains, and Total Returns

We can reinterpret Eq. 9.1 if we multiply by $(1 + r_E)$, divide by P_0, and subtract 1 from both sides:

Total Return

$$r_E = \frac{Div_1 + P_1}{P_0} - 1 = \underbrace{\frac{Div_1}{P_0}}_{\text{Dividend Yield}} + \underbrace{\frac{P_1 - P_0}{P_0}}_{\text{Capital Gain Rate}} \tag{9.2}$$

The first term on the right side of Eq. 9.2 is the stock's **dividend yield**, which is the expected annual dividend of the stock divided by its current price. The dividend yield is the percentage return the investor expects to earn from the dividend paid by the stock. The second term on the right side of Eq. 9.2 reflects the **capital gain** the investor will earn on the stock, which is the difference between the expected sale price and purchase price for the stock, $P_1 - P_0$. We divide the capital gain by the current stock price to express the capital gain as a percentage return, called the **capital gain rate**.

The sum of the dividend yield and the capital gain rate is called the **total return** of the stock. The total return is the expected return that the investor will earn for a one-year investment in the stock. Thus Eq. 9.2 states that the stock's total return should equal the equity cost of capital. In other words, *the expected total return of the stock should equal the expected return of other investments available in the market with equivalent risk.*

This result is what we should expect: The firm must pay its shareholders a return commensurate with the return they can earn elsewhere while taking the same risk. If the stock offered a higher return than other securities with the same risk, investors would sell those other investments and buy the stock instead. This activity would drive up the stock's current price, lowering its dividend yield and capital gain rate until Eq. 9.2 holds true. If the stock offered a lower expected return, investors would sell the stock and drive down its price until Eq. 9.2 was again satisfied.

EXAMPLE 9.1

Stock Prices and Returns

Problem

Suppose you expect Longs Drug Stores to pay dividends of $0.56 per share in the coming year and trade for $45.50 per share at the end of the year. If investments with equivalent risk to Longs' stock have an expected return of 6.80%, what is the most you would pay today for Longs' stock? What dividend yield and capital gain rate would you expect at this price?

Solution

Using Eq. 9.1, we have

$$P_0 = \frac{Div_1 + P_1}{1 + r_E} = \frac{0.56 + 45.50}{1.0680} = \$43.13$$

At this price, Longs' dividend yield is $Div_1 / P_0 = 0.56 / 43.13 = 1.30\%$. The expected capital gain is $45.50 - \$43.13 = \$2.37$ per share, for a capital gain rate of $2.37 / 43.13 = 5.50\%$. Therefore, at this price Long's expected total return is $1.30\% + 5.50\% = 6.80\%$, which is equal to its equity cost of capital.

A Multiyear Investor

Equation 9.1 depends upon the expected stock price in one year, P_1. But suppose we planned to hold the stock for two years. Then we would receive dividends in both year 1 and year 2 before selling the stock, as shown in the following timeline:

$$
\begin{array}{ccc}
\mathbf{0} & \mathbf{1} & \mathbf{2} \\
\hline
-P_0 & Div_1 & Div_2 + P_2
\end{array}
$$

Setting the stock price equal to the present value of the future cash flows in this case implies[1]

$$P_0 = \frac{Div_1}{1 + r_E} + \frac{Div_2 + P_2}{(1 + r_E)^2} \tag{9.3}$$

Equations 9.1 and 9.3 are different: As a two-year investor we care about the dividend and stock price in year 2, but these terms do not appear in Eq. 9.1. Does this difference imply that a two-year investor will value the stock differently than a one-year investor?

The answer to this question is no. While a one-year investor does not care about the dividend and stock price in year 2 directly, she will care about them indirectly because they will affect the price for which she can sell the stock at the end of year 1. For example, suppose the investor sells the stock to another one-year investor with the same beliefs. The new investor will expect to receive the dividend and stock price at the end of year 2, so he will be willing to pay

$$P_1 = \frac{Div_2 + P_2}{1 + r_E}$$

for the stock. Substituting this expression for P_1 into Eq. 9.1, we get the same result as in Eq. 9.3:

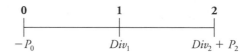

$$P_0 = \frac{Div_1 + P_1}{1 + r_E} = \frac{Div_1}{1 + r_E} + \frac{1}{1 + r_E}\overbrace{\left(\frac{Div_2 + P_2}{1 + r_E}\right)}^{P_1}$$

$$= \frac{Div_1}{1 + r_E} + \frac{Div_2 + P_2}{(1 + r_E)^2}$$

Thus the formula for the stock price for a two-year investor is the same as the one for a sequence of two one-year investors.

We can continue this process for any number of years by replacing the final stock price with the value that the next holder of the stock would be willing to pay. Doing so leads to the general **dividend-discount model** for the stock price, where the horizon N is arbitrary:

Dividend-Discount Model

$$P_0 = \frac{Div_1}{1 + r_E} + \frac{Div_2}{(1 + r_E)^2} + \cdots + \frac{Div_N}{(1 + r_E)^N} + \frac{P_N}{(1 + r_E)^N} \tag{9.4}$$

---

1. By using the same equity cost of capital for both periods, we are assuming that the equity cost of capital does not depend on the term of the cash flows. Otherwise, we would need to adjust for the term structure of the equity cost of capital (as we did with the yield curve for risk-free cash flows in Chapter 5). This step would complicate the analysis but would not change the results.

Equation 9.4 applies to a single *N*-year investor, who will collect dividends for *N* years and then sell the stock, or to a series of investors who hold the stock for shorter periods and then resell it. Note that Eq. 9.4 holds for *any* horizon *N*. Thus all investors (with the same beliefs) will attach the same value to the stock, independent of their investment horizons. How long they intend to hold the stock and whether they collect their return in the form of dividends or capital gains is irrelevant. For the special case in which the firm eventually pays dividends and is never acquired, it is possible to hold the shares forever. Consequently, we can let *N* go to infinity in Eq. 9.4 and write it as follows:

$$P_0 = \frac{Div_1}{1 + r_E} + \frac{Div_2}{(1 + r_E)^2} + \frac{Div_3}{(1 + r_E)^3} + \cdots = \sum_{n=1}^{\infty} \frac{Div_n}{(1 + r_E)^n} \qquad (9.5)$$

That is, *the price of the stock is equal to the present value of the expected future dividends it will pay.*

CONCEPT CHECK

1. How do you calculate the total return of a stock?

2. What discount rate do you use to discount the future cash flows of a stock?

9.2 The Dividend-Discount Model

Equation 9.5 expresses the value of the stock in terms of the expected future dividends the firm will pay. Of course, estimating these dividends—especially for the distant future—is difficult. A common approximation is to assume that in the long run, dividends will grow at a constant rate. In this section, we will consider the implications of this assumption for stock prices and explore the tradeoff between dividends and growth.

Constant Dividend Growth

The simplest forecast for the firm's future dividends states that they will grow at a constant rate, *g*, forever. That case yields the following timeline for the cash flows for an investor who buys the stock today and holds it:

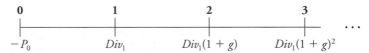

Because the expected dividends are a constant growth perpetuity, we can use Eq. 4.9 to calculate their present value. We then obtain the following simple formula for the stock price:[2]

Constant Dividend Growth Model

$$P_0 = \frac{Div_1}{r_E - g} \qquad (9.6)$$

According to the **constant dividend growth model**, the value of the firm depends on the current dividend level, divided by the equity cost of capital adjusted by the growth rate.

---

2. As we discussed in Chapter 4, this formula requires that $g < r_E$. Otherwise, the present value of the growing perpetuity is infinite. The implication here is that it is impossible for a stock's dividends to grow at a rate $g > r_E$ *forever*. If the growth rate does exceed r_E, it must be temporary, and the constant growth model cannot be applied in such a case.

EXAMPLE 9.2

Valuing a Firm with Constant Dividend Growth

Problem

Consolidated Edison, Inc. (Con Edison), is a regulated utility company servicing the New York City area. Suppose Con Edison plans to pay $2.30 per share in dividends in the coming year. If its equity cost of capital is 7% and dividends are expected to grow by 2% per year in the future, estimate the value of Con Edison's stock.

Solution

If dividends are expected to grow perpetually at a rate of 2% per year, we can use Eq. 9.6 to calculate the price of a share of Con Edison stock:

$$P_0 = \frac{Div}{r_E - g} = \frac{\$2.30}{0.07 - 0.02} = \$46.00$$

For another interpretation of Eq. 9.6, note that we can rearrange it as follows:

$$r_E = \frac{Div_1}{P_0} + g \tag{9.7}$$

Comparing Eq. 9.7 with Eq. 9.2, we see that g equals the expected capital gain rate. In other words, with constant expected dividend growth, the expected growth rate of the share price matches the growth rate of dividends.

Dividends Versus Investment and Growth

In Eq. 9.6, the firm's share price increases with the current dividend level, Div_1, and the expected growth rate, g. To maximize its share price, a firm would like to increase both these quantities. Often, however, the firm faces a tradeoff: Increasing growth may require investment, and money spent on investment cannot be used to pay dividends. We can use the constant dividend growth model to gain insight into this tradeoff.

A Simple Model of Growth.   What determines the rate of growth of a firm's dividends? If we define a firm's **dividend payout rate** as the fraction of its earnings that the firm pays as dividends each year, then we can write the firm's dividend per share at date t as follows:

$$Div_t = \underbrace{\frac{Earnings_t}{Shares\ Outstanding_t}}_{EPS_t} \times Dividend\ Payout\ Rate_t \tag{9.8}$$

That is, the dividend each year is the firm's earnings per share (EPS) multiplied by its dividend payout rate. Thus the firm can increase its dividend in three ways: (1) by increasing its earnings (net income); (2) by increasing its dividend payout rate; or (3) by decreasing its shares outstanding. Let's suppose for now that the firm does not issue new shares (or buy back its existing shares), so that the number of shares outstanding is fixed, and explore the tradeoff between options 1 and 2.

A firm can do one of two things with its earnings: It can pay them out to investors, or it can retain and reinvest them. By investing cash today, a firm can increase its future dividends. For simplicity, let's assume that if no investment is made, the firm does not grow, so the current level of earnings generated by the firm remains constant. If all increases in future earnings result exclusively from new investment made with retained earnings, then

$$\text{Change in Earnings} = \text{New Investment} \times \text{Return on New Investment} \quad (9.9)$$

New investment equals earnings multiplied by the firm's **retention rate**, the fraction of current earnings that the firm retains:

$$\text{New Investment} = \text{Earnings} \times \text{Retention Rate} \quad (9.10)$$

Substituting Eq. 9.10 into Eq. 9.9 and dividing by earnings gives an expression for the growth rate of earnings:

$$\text{Earnings Growth Rate} = \frac{\text{Change in Earnings}}{\text{Earnings}}$$

$$= \text{Retention Rate} \times \text{Return on New Investment} \quad (9.11)$$

If the firm chooses to keep its dividend payout rate constant, then the growth in dividends will equal growth of earnings:

$$g = \text{Retention Rate} \times \text{Return on New Investment} \quad (9.12)$$

Profitable Growth.   Equation 9.12 shows that a firm can increase its growth rate by retaining more of its earnings. However, if the firm retains more earnings, it will be able to pay out less of those earnings, which from Eq. 9.8 means that the firm will have to reduce its dividend. If a firm wants to increase its share price, should it cut its dividend and invest more, or should it cut investment and increase its dividend? Not surprisingly, the answer will depend on the profitability of the firm's investments. Let's consider an example.

EXAMPLE 9.3

Cutting Dividends for Profitable Growth

Problem

Crane Sporting Goods expects to have earnings per share of $6 in the coming year. Rather than reinvest these earnings and grow, the firm plans to pay out all of its earnings as a dividend. With these expectations of no growth, Crane's current share price is $60.

Suppose Crane could cut its dividend payout rate to 75% for the foreseeable future and use the retained earnings to open new stores. The return on its investment in these stores is expected to be 12%. Assuming its equity cost of capital is unchanged, what effect would this new policy have on Crane's stock price?

Solution

First, let's estimate Crane's equity cost of capital. Currently, Crane plans to pay a dividend equal to its earnings of $6 per share. Given a share price of $60, Crane's dividend yield is $6 / $60 = 10%. With no expected growth ($g = 0$), we can use Eq. 9.7 to estimate r_E:

$$r_E = \frac{Div_1}{P_0} + g = 10\% + 0\% = 10\%$$

In other words, to justify Crane's stock price under its current policy, the expected return of other stocks in the market with equivalent risk must be 10%.

Next, we consider the consequences of the new policy. If Crane reduces its dividend payout rate to 75%, then from Eq. 9.8 its dividend this coming year will fall to $Div_1 = EPS_1 \times 75\% = \$6 \times 75\% = \$4.50$. At the same time, because the firm will now retain 25% of its earnings to invest in new stores, from Eq. 9.12 its growth rate will increase to

$$g = \text{Retention Rate} \times \text{Return on New Investment} = 25\% \times 12\% = 3\%$$

Assuming Crane can continue to grow at this rate, we can compute its share price under the new policy using the constant dividend growth model of Eq. 9.6:

$$P_0 = \frac{Div_1}{r_E - g} = \frac{\$4.50}{0.10 - 0.03} = \$64.29$$

Thus Crane's share price should rise from $60 to $64.29 if it cuts its dividend to increase investment and growth, implying the investment has positive NPV.

In Example 9.3, cutting the firm's dividend in favor of growth raised the firm's stock price. But this is not always the case, as the next example demonstrates.

EXAMPLE 9.4

Unprofitable Growth

Problem

Suppose Crane Sporting Goods decides to cut its dividend payout rate to 75% to invest in new stores, as in Example 9.3. But now suppose that the return on these new investments is 8%, rather than 12%. Given its expected earnings per share this year of $6 and its equity cost of capital of 10%, what will happen to Crane's current share price in this case?

Solution

Just as in Example 9.3, Crane's dividend will fall to $6 \times 75\% = \$4.50$. Its growth rate under the new policy, given the lower return on new investment, will now be $g = 25\% \times 8\% = 2\%$. The new share price is therefore

$$P_0 = \frac{Div_1}{r_E - g} = \frac{\$4.50}{0.10 - 0.02} = \$56.25$$

Thus, even though Crane will grow under the new policy, the new investments have negative NPV and its share price will fall if it cuts its dividend to make new investments with a return of only 8%.

Comparing Example 9.3 with Example 9.4, we see that the effect of cutting the firm's dividend to grow crucially depends on the return on new investment. In Example 9.3, the return on new investment of 12% exceeds the firm's equity cost of capital of 10%, so the investment has positive NPV. In Example 9.4, the return on new investment is only 8%, so the new investment has negative NPV (even though it will lead to earnings growth). Thus *cutting the firm's dividend to increase investment will raise the stock price if, and only if, the new investments have a positive NPV.*

Changing Growth Rates

Successful young firms often have very high initial earnings growth rates. During this period of high growth, it is not unusual for these firms to retain 100% of their earnings to exploit profitable investment opportunities. As they mature, their growth slows to rates

INTERVIEW WITH
Marilyn Fedak

Marilyn G. Fedak is the Head of Global Value Equities at AllianceBernstein, a publicly-traded global asset management firm with approximately $618 billion in assets.

QUESTION: *What valuation methods do you use to identify buying opportunities?*

ANSWER: Since the early 1980s we have used the dividend discount model for U.S. large cap stocks. At its most basic level, the dividend discount model provides a way to evaluate how much we need to pay today for a company's future earnings. All things being equal, we are looking to buy as much earnings power as cheaply as we can.

It is a very reliable methodology, *if* you have the right forecasts for companies' future earnings. The key to success in using the dividend discount model is having deep fundamental research— a large team of analysts who use a consistent process for modeling earnings. We ask our analysts to provide us with 5-year forecasts for the companies they follow.

For non-U.S. stocks and for small caps, we use quantitative return models that are based upon companies' current characteristics rather than forecasts. The universes for these asset classes are too large to populate them with quality forecasts, even with our 50+ research team. The quant models encompass a variety of valuation measures, such as P/E and price-to-book ratios and selected success factors—for example, ROE and price momentum. We rank companies in their appropriate universes and focus on the stocks that rank the highest. Then the investment policy group meets with the analysts who follow these securities to determine whether the quant edge tool is correctly reflecting the likely financial future of each company.

QUESTION: *Are there drawbacks to the dividend discount model?*

ANSWER: Two things make the dividend discount model hard to use in practice. First, you need a huge research department to generate good forecasts for a large universe of stocks—in the large cap universe alone that means more than 650 companies. Since this is a relative valuation methodology, you need to have as much confidence in the forecast for the stock that ranks 450 as well as the one that ranks 15. Second, it is very hard to live by the results of the dividend discount model. At the peak of the bubble in 2000, for example, dividend discount models found tech stocks to be extremely overvalued. This was hard for most portfolio managers, because the pressure to override the model—to say it isn't working right—was enormous. That situation was extreme, but a dividend discount model almost always puts you in a contrarian position—a difficult position to constantly maintain.

QUESTION: *Why have you focused on value stocks?*

ANSWER: We don't assign labels to companies. Our valuation model is such that we will buy any company if it is selling cheaply relative to our vision of its long-term earnings. Today, for example, we own Microsoft, GE, TimeWarner—companies that were considered premier growth stocks just a few years ago. By using this consistent methodology and investing heavily in research, we have been able to produce strong investment results for our clients over long periods of time. And we believe that this process will continue to be successful in the future because it relies on enduring characteristics of human behavior (such as loss aversion) and the flows of capital in a free economic system.

more typical of established companies. At that point, their earnings exceed their investment needs and they begin to pay dividends.

We cannot use the constant dividend growth model to value the stock of such a firm, for several reasons. First, these firms often pay *no* dividends when they are young. Second, their growth rate continues to change over time until they mature. However, we can use the general form of the dividend-discount model to value such a firm by applying the constant growth model to calculate the future share price of the stock P_N once the firm matures and its expected growth rate stabilizes:

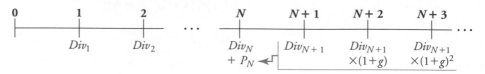

Specifically, if the firm is expected to grow at a long-term rate g after year $N + 1$, then from the constant dividend growth model:

$$P_N = \frac{Div_{N+1}}{r_E - g} \tag{9.13}$$

We can then use this estimate of P_N as a terminal (continuation) value in the dividend-discount model. Combining Eq. 9.4 with Eq. 9.13, we have

Dividend-Discount Model with Constant Long-Term Growth

$$P_0 = \frac{Div_1}{1 + r_E} + \frac{Div_2}{(1 + r_E)^2} + \cdots + \frac{Div_N}{(1 + r_E)^N} + \frac{1}{(1 + r_E)^N} \left(\frac{Div_{N+1}}{r_E - g} \right) \tag{9.14}$$

EXAMPLE 9.5

Valuing a Firm with Two Different Growth Rates

Problem

Small Fry, Inc., has just invented a potato chip that looks and tastes like a french fry. Given the phenomenal market response to this product Small Fry is reinvesting all of its earnings to expand its operations. Earnings were $2 per share this past year and are expected to grow at a rate of 20% per year until the end of year 4. At that point, other companies are likely to bring out competing products. Analysts project that at the end of year 4, Small Fry will cut investment and begin paying 60% of its earnings as dividends and its growth will slow to a long-run rate of 4%. If Small Fry's equity cost of capital is 8%, what is the value of a share today?

Solution

We can use Small Fry's projected earnings growth rate and payout rate to forecast its future earnings and dividends as shown in the following spreadsheet:

Year	0	1	2	3	4	5	6
Earnings							
1 EPS Growth Rate (versus prior year)		20%	20%	20%	20%	4%	4%
2 EPS	$2.00	$2.40	$2.88	$3.46	$4.15	$4.31	$4.49
Dividends							
3 Dividend Payout Rate		0%	0%	0%	60%	60%	60%
4 Div		$ —	$ —	$ —	$2.49	$2.59	$2.69

Starting from $2.00 in year 0, EPS grows by 20% per year until year 4, after which growth slows to 4%. Small Fry's dividend payout rate is zero until year 4, when competition reduces its investment opportunities and its payout rate rises to 60%. Multiplying EPS by the dividend payout ratio, we project Small Fry's future dividends in line 4.

From year 4 onward, Small Fry's dividends will grow at the expected long-run rate of 4% per year. Thus we can use the constant dividend growth model to project Small Fry's share price at the end of year 3. Given its equity cost of capital of 8%,

$$P_3 = \frac{Div_4}{r_E - g} = \frac{\$2.49}{0.08 - 0.04} = \$62.25$$

We then apply the dividend-discount model (Eq. 9.4) with this terminal value:

$$P_0 = \frac{Div_1}{1 + r_E} + \frac{Div_2}{(1 + r_E)^2} + \frac{Div_3}{(1 + r_E)^3} + \frac{P_3}{(1 + r_E)^3} = \frac{\$62.25}{(1.08)^3} = \$49.42$$

Limitations of the Dividend-Discount Model

The dividend-discount model values the stock based on a forecast of the future dividends paid to shareholders. But unlike a Treasury bond, whose cash flows are known with virtual certainty, a tremendous amount of uncertainty is associated with any forecast of a firm's future dividends.

Let's consider the example of Kenneth Cole Productions (KCP), mentioned in the introduction to this chapter. In early 2006, KCP paid annual dividends of $0.72. With an equity cost of capital of 11% and expected dividend growth of 8%, the constant dividend growth model implies a share price for KCP of

$$P_0 = \frac{Div_1}{r_E - g} = \frac{\$0.72}{0.11 - 0.08} = \$24$$

John Burr Williams' *Theory of Investment Value*

The first formal derivation of the dividend-discount model appeared in the *Theory of Investment Value*, written by John Burr Williams in 1938.* The book was an important landmark in the history of corporate finance, because Williams demonstrated for the first time that corporate finance relied on certain principles that could be derived using formal analytical methods. As Williams wrote in the preface:

The truth is that the mathematical method is a new tool of great power whose use promises to lead to notable advances in Investment Analysis. Always it has been the rule in the history of science that the invention of new tools is the key to new discoveries, and we may expect the same rule to hold true in this branch of Economics as well.

By the time Williams died in 1989, the importance of the mathematical method in corporate finance was indis-putable and the discoveries that resulted from this "new" tool fundamentally changed the practice of corporate finance. Academics and practitioners alike now rely on principles developed in the intervening years whose origins can be traced to Williams' book and the mathematical method he brought to bear.

What happened to Williams himself? His book comprised his Ph.D. dissertation at Harvard University, which was accepted in 1940 (legend has it that his Ph.D. committee held a lively debate as to whether the work actually met the standard at Harvard, but in the end decided it did!). After earning his degree, Williams returned to the investment industry (in his own words, he "took time off to earn a Ph.D. in economics") and died a very wealthy man, presumably applying the principles and discoveries he helped initiate.

*This book contains many other ideas that are now central to modern finance (see Chapter 14 for a further reference).

which is reasonably close to the $26.75 share price the stock had at the time. With a 10% dividend growth rate, however, this estimate would rise to $72 per share; with a 5% dividend growth rate, the estimate falls to $12 per share. As we see, even small changes in the assumed dividend growth rate can lead to large changes in the estimated stock price.

Furthermore, it is difficult to know which estimate of the dividend growth rate is more reasonable. KCP more than doubled its dividend between 2003 and 2005, but earnings have remained relatively flat over the past few years. Consequently, this rate of increase is not sustainable. From Eq. 9.8, forecasting dividends requires forecasting the firm's earnings, dividend payout rate, and future share count. But future earnings will depend on interest expenses (which in turn depend on how much the firm borrows), and its share count and dividend payout rate will depend on whether the firm uses a portion of its earnings to repurchase shares. Because borrowing and repurchase decisions are at management's discretion, they can be more difficult to forecast reliably than other, more fundamental aspects of the firm's cash flows.[3] We look at two alternative methods that avoid some of these difficulties in the next section.

CONCEPT CHECK

1. In what three ways can a firm increase its future dividend per share?

2. Under what circumstances can a firm increase its share price by cutting its dividend and investing more?

9.3 Total Payout and Free Cash Flow Valuation Models

In this section, we outline two alternative approaches to valuing the firm's shares that avoid some of the difficulties of the dividend-discount model. First, we consider the total payout model, which allows us to ignore the firm's choice between dividends and share repurchases. Then we consider the discounted free cash flow model, which focuses on the cash flows to all of the firm's investors, both debt and equity holders, and allows us to avoid estimating the impact of the firm's borrowing decisions on earnings.

Share Repurchases and the Total Payout Model

In our discussion of the dividend-discount model, we implicitly assumed that any cash paid out by the firm to shareholders takes the form of a dividend. However, in recent years, an increasing number of firms have replaced dividend payouts with share repurchases. In a **share repurchase**, the firm uses excess cash to buy back its own stock. Share repurchases have two consequences for the dividend-discount model. First, the more cash the firm uses to repurchase shares, the less it has available to pay dividends. Second, by repurchasing shares, the firm decreases its share count, which increases its earning and dividends on a per-share basis.

In the dividend-discount model, we valued a share from the perspective of a single shareholder, discounting the dividends the shareholder will receive:

$$P_0 = PV(\text{Future Dividends per Share}) \tag{9.15}$$

An alternative method that may be more reliable when a firm repurchases shares is the **total payout model**, which values *all* of the firm's equity, rather than a single share. To do so, we discount the total payouts that the firm makes to shareholders, which is the total

---

3. We discuss management's decision to borrow funs or repurchase shares in Part V of the text.

amount spent on both dividends *and* share repurchases.[4] Then we divide by the current number of shares outstanding to determine the share price.

Total Payout Model

$$P_0 = \frac{PV(\text{Future Total Dividends and Repurchases})}{\text{Shares Outstanding}_0} \tag{9.16}$$

We can apply the same simplifications that we obtained by assuming constant growth in Section 9.2 to the total payout method. The only change is that *we discount total dividends and share repurchases and use the growth rate of earnings (rather than earnings per share) when forecasting the growth of the firm's total payouts.* This method can be more reliable and easier to apply when the firm uses share repurchases.

EXAMPLE 9.6

Valuation with Share Repurchases

Problem

Titan Industries has 217 million shares outstanding and expects earnings at the end of this year of $860 million. Titan plans to pay out 50% of its earnings in total, paying 30% as a dividend and using 20% to repurchase shares. If Titan's earnings are expected to grow by 7.5% per year and these payout rates remain constant, determine Titan's share price assuming an equity cost of capital of 10%.

Solution

Titan will have total payouts this year of 50% × $860 million = $430 million. Based on the equity cost of capital of 10% and an expected earnings growth rate of 7.5%, the present value of Titan's future payouts can be computed as a constant growth perpetuity:

$$PV(\text{Future Total Dividends and Repurchases}) = \frac{\$430 \text{ million}}{0.10 - 0.075} = \$17.2 \text{ billion}$$

This present value represents the total value of Titan's equity (i.e., its market capitalization). To compute the share price, we divide by the current number of shares outstanding:

$$P_0 = \frac{\$17.2 \text{ billion}}{217 \text{ million shares}} = \$79.26 \text{ per share}$$

Using the total payout method, we did not need to know the firm's split between dividends and share repurchases. To compare this method with the dividend-discount model, note that Titan will pay a dividend of 30% × $860 million / (217 million shares) = $1.19 per share, for a dividend yield of 1.19 / 79.26 = 1.50%. From Eq. 9.7, Titan's expected EPS, dividend, and share price growth rate is $g = r_E - Div_1 / P_0 = 8.50\%$. This growth rate exceeds the 7.50% growth rate of earnings because Titan's share count will decline over time due to share repurchases.[5]

---

4. You can think of the total payouts as the amount you would receive if you owned 100% of the firm's shares: You would receive all of the dividends, plus the proceeds from selling shares back to the firm in the share repurchase.

5. We can check that an 8.5% EPS growth rate is consistent with 7.5% earnings growth and Titan's repurchase plans as follows. Given an expected share price of $79.26 × 1.085 = $86.00 next year, Titan will repurchase 20% × $860 million ÷ ($86.00 per share) = 2 million shares next year. With the decline in the number of shares from 217 million to 215 million, EPS grows by a factor of 1.075 × (217 / 215) = 1.085 or 8.5%.

The Discounted Free Cash Flow Model

In the total payout model, we first value the firm's equity, rather than just a single share. The **discounted free cash flow model** goes one step further and begins by determining the total value of the firm to all investors—both equity *and* debt holders. That is, we begin by estimating the firm's enterprise value, which we defined in Chapter 2 as[6]

$$\text{Enterprise Value} = \text{Market Value of Equity} + \text{Debt} - \text{Cash} \qquad (9.17)$$

The enterprise value is the value of the firm's underlying business, unencumbered by debt and separate from any cash or marketable securities. We can interpret the enterprise value as the net cost of acquiring the firm's equity, taking its cash, paying off all debt, and thus owning the unlevered business. The advantage of the discounted free cash flow model is that it allows us to value a firm without explicitly forecasting its dividends, share repurchases, or its use of debt.

Valuing the Enterprise.   How can we estimate a firm's enterprise value? To estimate the value of the firm's equity, we computed the present value of the firm's total payouts to equity holders. Likewise, to estimate a firm's enterprise value, we compute the present value of the *free cash flow* (FCF) that the firm has available to pay all investors, both debt and equity holders. We saw how to compute the free cash flow for a project in Chapter 7; we now perform the same calculation for the entire firm:

$$\text{Free Cash Flow} = \overbrace{EBIT \times (1 - \tau_c)}^{\text{Unlevered Net Income}} + \text{Depreciation}$$
$$- \text{Capital Expenditures} - \text{Increases in Net Working Capital} \qquad (9.18)$$

Free cash flow measures the cash generated by the firm before any payments to debt or equity holders are considered.

Thus, just as we determine the value of a project by calculating the NPV of the project's free cash flow, we estimate a firm's current enterprise value V_0 by computing the present value of the firm's free cash flow:

Discounted Free Cash Flow Model

$$V_0 = PV(\text{Future Free Cash Flow of Firm}) \qquad (9.19)$$

Given the enterprise value, we can estimate the share price by using Eq. 9.17 to solve for the value of equity and then divide by the total number of shares outstanding:

$$P_0 = \frac{V_0 + \text{Cash}_0 - \text{Debt}_0}{\text{Shares Outstanding}_0} \qquad (9.20)$$

Intuitively, the difference between the discounted free cash flow model and the dividend-discount model is that in the dividend-discount model, the firm's cash and debt are included indirectly through the effect of interest income and expenses on earnings. In the discounted free cash flow model, we ignore interest income and expenses because free cash flow is based on EBIT, but then adjust for cash and debt directly in Eq. 9.20.

Implementing the Model.   A key difference between the discounted free cash flow model and the earlier models we have considered is the discount rate. In previous calcula-

---

6. To be precise, by cash we are referring to the firm's cash in excess of its working capital needs, which is the amount of cash it has invested at a competitive market interest rate.

tions we used the firm's equity cost of capital, r_E, because we were discounting the cash flows to equity holders. Here we are discounting the free cash flow that will be paid to both debt and equity holders. Thus we should use the firm's **weighted average cost of capital (WACC)**, denoted by r_{wacc}; it is the cost of capital that reflects the risk of the overall business, which is the combined risk of the firm's equity *and* debt. For now, we interpret r_{wacc} as the expected return the firm must pay to investors to compensate them for the risk of holding the firm's debt and equity together. If the firm has no debt, then $r_{wacc} = r_E$. We will develop methods to calculate the WACC explicitly in Parts IV and V of the text.[7]

Given the firm's weighted average cost of capital, we implement the discounted free cash flow model in much the same way as we did the dividend discount model. That is, we forecast the firm's free cash flow up to some horizon, together with a terminal (continuation) value of the enterprise:

$$V_0 = \frac{FCF_1}{1 + r_{wacc}} + \frac{FCF_2}{(1 + r_{wacc})^2} + \cdots + \frac{FCF_N}{(1 + r_{wacc})^N} + \frac{V_N}{(1 + r_{wacc})^N} \quad (9.21)$$

Often, the terminal value is estimated by assuming a constant long-run growth rate g_{FCF} for free cash flows beyond year N, so that

$$V_N = \frac{FCF_{N+1}}{r_{wacc} - g_{FCF}} = \left(\frac{1 + g_{FCF}}{r_{wacc} - g_{FCF}} \right) \times FCF_N \quad (9.22)$$

The long-run growth rate g_{FCF} is typically based on the expected long-run growth rate of the firm's revenues.

| EXAMPLE 9.7 | Valuing Kenneth Cole Using Free Cash Flow |

Problem

Kenneth Cole's (KCP) had sales of $518 million in 2005. Suppose you expect its sales to grow at a 9% rate in 2006, but that this growth rate will slow by 1% per year to a long-run growth rate for the apparel industry of 4% by 2011. Based on KCP's past profitability and investment needs, you expect EBIT to be 9% of sales, increases in net working capital requirements to be 10% of any increase in sales, and capital expenditures to equal depreciation expenses. If KCP has $100 million in cash, $3 million in debt, 21 million shares outstanding, a tax rate of 37%, and a weighted average cost of capital of 11%, what is your estimate of the value of KCP's stock in early 2006?

Solution

We can estimate KCP's future free cash flow based on the estimates above as follows:

	Year	2005	2006	2007	2008	2009	2010	2011
	FCF Forecast ($ million)							
1	Sales	518.0	564.6	609.8	652.5	691.6	726.2	755.3
2	*Growth versus Prior Year*		*9.0%*	*8.0%*	*7.0%*	*6.0%*	*5.0%*	*4.0%*
3	EBIT (9% of sales)		50.8	54.9	58.7	62.2	65.4	68.0
4	Less: Income Tax (37%)		(18.8)	(20.3)	(21.7)	(23.0)	(24.2)	(25.1)
5	Plus: Depreciation		—	—	—	—	—	—
6	Less: Capital Expenditures		—	—	—	—	—	—
7	Less: Inc. in NWC (10% ΔSales)		(4.7)	(4.5)	(4.3)	(3.9)	(3.5)	(2.9)
8	**Free Cash Flow**		27.4	30.1	32.7	35.3	37.7	39.9

---

7. We can also interpret the firm's weighted average cost of capital as the average cost of capital associated with all of the firm's projects. In that sense, the WACC reflects the average risk of the firm's investments.

Note that because captial expenditures are expected to equal depreciation, lines 5 and 6 in the spreadsheet cancel out, and so we can set them both to zero rather than explicitly forecast them. Because we expect KCP's free cash flow to grow at a constant rate after 2011, we can use Eq. 9.22 to compute a terminal enterprise value:

$$V_{2011} = \left(\frac{1 + g_{FCF}}{r_{wacc} - g_{FCF}} \right) \times FCF_{2011} = \left(\frac{1.04}{0.11 - 0.04} \right) \times 39.9 = \$592.8 \text{ million}$$

From Eq. 9.21, KCP's current enterprise value is the present value of its free cash flows plus terminal value:

$$V_0 = \frac{27.4}{1.11} + \frac{30.1}{1.11^2} + \frac{32.7}{1.11^3} + \frac{35.3}{1.11^4} + \frac{37.7}{1.11^5} + \frac{39.9}{1.11^6} + \frac{592.8}{1.11^6} = \$456.9 \text{ million}$$

We can now estimate the value of a share of KCP's stock using Eq. 9.20:

$$P_0 = \frac{456.9 + 100 - 3}{21} = \$26.38$$

Connection to Capital Budgeting.   There is an important connection between the discounted free cash flow model and the NPV rule for capital budgeting that we developed in Chapter 7. Because the firm's free cash flow is equal to the sum of the free cash flows from the firm's current and future investments, we can interpret the firm's enterprise value as the total NPV that the firm will earn from continuing its existing projects and initiating new ones. Hence, the NPV of any individual project represents its contribution to the firm's enterprise value. To maximize the firm's share price, we should accept projects that have a positive NPV.

Recall also from Chapter 7 that many forecasts and estimates were necessary to estimate the free cash flows of a project. The same is true for the firm: We must forecast future sales, operating expenses, taxes, capital requirements, and other factors. On the one hand, estimating free cash flow in this way gives us flexibility to incorporate many specific details about the future prospects of the firm. On the other hand, some uncertainty inevitably surrounds each assumption. It is therefore important to conduct a sensitivity analysis, as we described in Chapter 7, to translate this uncertainty into a range of potential values for the stock.

**EXAMPLE
9.8**

Sensitivity Analysis for Stock Valuation

Problem
In Example 9.7, KCP's EBIT was assumed to be 9% of sales. If KCP can reduce its operating expenses and raise its EBIT to 10% of sales, how would your estimate of the stock's value change?

Solution
EBIT will increase by 1% of sales compared to Example 9.7. Thus, in year 1, EBIT will be 1% × $564.6 million = $5.6 million higher. After taxes, this increase will raise FCF in year 1 by (1 − 0.37) × $5.6 million = $3.5 million, to $30.9 million. Doing the same calculation for each year, we get the following revised FCF estimates:

Year	2006	2007	2008	2009	2010	2011
FCF	30.9	33.9	36.8	39.7	42.3	44.7

We can now reestimate the stock price as in the prior example. The terminal value is V_{2011} $= [1.04 / (0.11 - 0.04)] \times 44.7 = \$664.1$ million, so

$$V_0 = \frac{30.9}{1.11} + \frac{33.9}{1.11^2} + \frac{36.8}{1.11^3} + \frac{39.7}{1.11^4} + \frac{42.3}{1.11^5} + \frac{44.7}{1.11^6} + \frac{664.1}{1.11^6} = \$512.5 \text{ million}$$

The new estimate for the value of the stock is $P_0 = (512.5 + 100 - 3) / 21 = \$29.02$ per share, a difference of about 10% compared to the previous example.

Figure 9.1 summarizes the different valuation methods we have discussed thus far. The value of the stock is determined by the present value of its future dividends. We can estimate the total market capitalization of the firm's equity from the present value of the firm's total payouts, which includes dividends and share repurchases. Finally, the present value of the firm's free cash flow, which is the cash the firm has available to make payments to equity or debt holders, determines the firm's enterprise value.

FIGURE 9.1	A Comparison of Discounted Cash Flow Models of Stock Valuation

Present Value of ...	Determines the ...
Dividend Payments	Stock Price
Total Payouts (All Dividends and Repurchases)	Equity Value
Free Cash Flow (Cash available to pay all security holders)	Enterprise Value

By computing the present value of the firm's dividends, total payouts or free cash flows, we can estimate the value of the stock, the total value of the firm's equity, or the firm's enterprise value.

CONCEPT CHECK

1. How does the growth rate used in the total payout model differ from the growth rate used in the dividend-discount model?

2. Why do we ignore interest payments on the firm's debt in the discounted free cash flow model?

9.4 Valuation Based on Comparable Firms

Thus far, we have valued a firm or its stock by considering the expected future cash flows it will provide to its owner. The Law of One Price then tells us that its value is the present value of its future cash flows, because the present value is the amount we would need to invest elsewhere in the market to replicate the cash flows with the same risk.

Another application of the Law of One Price is the method of comparables. In the **method of comparables** (or "comps"), rather than value the firm's cash flows directly, we estimate the value of the firm based on the value of other, comparable firms or investments that we expect will generate very similar cash flows in the future. For example, consider the case of a new firm that is *identical* to an existing publicly traded company. If these firms will generate identical cash flows, the Law of One Price implies that we can use the value of the existing company to determine the value of the new firm.

Of course, identical companies do not exist. Even two firms in the same industry selling the same types of products, while similar in many respects, are likely to be of a different size or scale. In this section, we consider ways to adjust for scale differences to use comparables to value firms with similar business, and then discuss the strengths and weaknesses of this approach.

Valuation Multiples

We can adjust for differences in scale between firms by expressing their value in terms of a **valuation multiple**, which is a ratio of the value to some measure of the firm's scale. As an analogy, consider valuing an office building. A natural measure to consider would be the price per square foot for other buildings recently sold in the area. Multiplying the size of the office building under consideration by the average price per square foot would typically provide a reasonable estimate of the building's value. We can apply this same idea to stocks, replacing square footage with some more appropriate measure of the firm's scale.

The Price-Earnings Ratio.   The most common valuation multiple is the price-earnings (P/E) ratio, which we introduced in Chapter 2. A firm's P/E ratio is equal to the share price divided by its earnings per share. The intuition behind its use is that when you buy a stock, you are in a sense buying the rights to the firm's future earnings and differences in the scale of firms' earnings are likely to persist. Therefore, you should be willing to pay proportionally more for a stock with higher current earnings. Thus we can estimate the value of a firm's share by multiplying its current earnings per share by the average P/E ratio of comparable firms.

We can compute a firm's P/E ratio by using either **trailing earnings** (earnings over the prior 12 months) or **forward earnings** (expected earnings over the coming 12 months), with the resulting ratio called the **trailing P/E** or **forward P/E**, respectively. For valuation purposes, the forward P/E is generally preferred, as we are most concerned about future earnings.[8] We can interpret the forward P/E in terms of the dividend-discount model or total payout model that we introduced earlier. For example, in the case of constant dividend growth, dividing through Eq. 9.6 by EPS_1, we find that

$$\text{Forward P/E} = \frac{P_0}{EPS_1} = \frac{Div_1 / EPS_1}{r_E - g} = \frac{\text{Dividend Payout Rate}}{r_E - g} \tag{9.23}$$

Equation 9.23 implies that if two stocks have the same payout and EPS growth rates, as well as equivalent risk (and therefore the same equity cost of capital), then they should

---

8. Because we are interested in the persistent components of the firm's earnings, it is also common practice to exclude extraordinary items that will not be repeated when calculating a P/E ratio for valuation purposes.

have the same P/E. It also shows that firms and industries with high growth rates, and which generate cash well in excess of their investment needs so that they can maintain high payout rates, should have high P/E multiples.

EXAMPLE
9.9

Valuation Using the Price-Earnings Ratio

Problem
Suppose furniture manufacturer Herman Miller, Inc., has earnings per share of $1.38. If the average P/E of comparable furniture stocks is 21.3, estimate a value for Herman Miller using the P/E as a valuation multiple. What are the assumptions underlying this estimate?

Solution
We estimate a share price for Herman Miller by multiplying its EPS by the P/E of comparable firms. Thus $P_0 = \$1.38 \times 21.3 = \$29.39$. This estimate assumes that Herman Miller will have similar future risk, payout rates, and growth rates to comparable firms in the industry.

Enterprise Value Multiples.   It is also common practice to use valuation multiples based on the firm's enterprise value. As we discussed in Section 9.3, because it represents the total value of the firm's underlying business rather than just the value of equity, using the enterprise value is advantageous if we want to compare firms with different amounts of leverage.

Because the enterprise value represents the entire value of the firm before the firm pays its debt, to form an appropriate multiple, we divide it by a measure of earnings or cash flows before interest payments are made. Common multiples to consider are enterprise value to EBIT, EBITDA (earnings before interest, taxes, depreciation, and amortization), and free cash flow. However, because capital expenditures can vary substantially from period to period (e.g., a firm may need to add capacity and build a new plant one year, but then not need to expand further for many years), most practitioners rely on enterprise value to EBITDA multiples. From Eq. 9.22, if expected free cash flow growth is contant, then

$$\frac{V_0}{EBITDA_1} = \frac{FCF_1 \ / \ EBITDA_1}{r_{wacc} - g_{FCF}} \tag{9.24}$$

As with the P/E multiple, this valuation multiple is higher for firms with high growth rates and low capital requirements (so that free cash flow is high in proportion to EBITDA).

EXAMPLE
9.10

Valuation Using an Enterprise Value Multiple

Problem
Suppose Rocky Shoes and Boots (RCKY) has earnings per share of $2.30 and EBITDA of $30.7 million. RCKY also has 5.4 million shares outstanding and debt of $125 million (net of cash). You believe Deckers Outdoor Corporation is comparable to RCKY in terms of its underlying business, but Deckers has no debt. If Deckers has a P/E of 13.3 and an enterprise value to EBITDA multiple of 7.4, estimate the value of RCKY's shares using both multiples. Which estimate is likely to be more accurate?

> **Solution**
>
> Using Decker's P/E, we would estimate a share price for RCKY of $P_0 = \$2.30 \times 13.3 = \$30.59$. Using the enterprise value to EBITDA multiple, we would estimate RCKY's enterprise value to be $V_0 = \$30.7$ million $\times 7.4 = \$227.2$ million. We then subtract debt and divide by the number of shares to estimate RCKY's share price: $P_0 = (227.2 - 125) / 5.4 = \$18.93$. Because of the large difference in leverage between the firms, we would expect the second estimate, which is based on enterprise value, to be more reliable.

Other Multiples.   Many other valuation multiples are possible. Looking at enterprise value as a multiple of sales can be useful if it is reasonable to assume that the firms will maintain similar margins in the future. For firms with substantial tangible assets, the ratio of price to book value of equity per share is sometimes used. Some multiples are specific to an industry. In the cable TV industry, for example, it is natural to consider enterprise value per subscriber.

Limitations of Multiples

If comparables were identical, the firms' multiples would match precisely. Of course, firms are not identical. Thus the usefulness of a valuation multiple will depend on the nature of the differences between firms and the sensitivity of the multiples to these differences.

Table 9.1 lists several valuation multiples for firms in the footwear industry, as of January 2006. Also shown is the average for each multiple, together with the range around the average (in percentage terms). For all of the multiples, a fair amount of dispersion across the industry is apparent. While the enterprise value to EBITDA multiple shows the smallest variation, even with it we cannot expect to obtain a precise estimate of value.

The differences in these multiples are most likely due to differences in expected future growth rates, risk (and therefore costs of capital), and, in the case of Puma, differences in accounting conventions between the United States and Germany. Investors in the market understand that these differences exist, so the stocks are priced accordingly. But when valuing a firm using multiples, there is no clear guidance about how to adjust for these differences other than by narrowing the set of comparables used.

Another limitation of comparables is that they provide only information regarding the value of the firm *relative to* the other firms in the comparison set. Using multiples will not help us determine if an entire industry is overvalued, for example. This issue became especially important during the Internet boom of the late 1990s. Because many of these firms did not have positive cash flows or earnings, new multiples were created to value them (e.g., price to "page views"). While these multiples could justify the value of these firms in relation to one another, it was much more difficult to justify the stock prices of many of these firms using a realistic estimate of cash flows and the discounted free cash flow approach.

Comparison with Discounted Cash Flow Methods

Using a valuation multiple based on comparables is best viewed as a "shortcut" to the discounted cash flow methods of valuation. Rather than separately estimate the firm's cost of capital and future earnings or free cash flows, we rely on the market's assessment of the value of other firms with similar future prospects. In addition to its simplicity, the multiples approach has the advantage of being based on actual prices of real firms, rather than what may be unrealistic forecasts of future cash flows.

TABLE 9.1	Stock Prices and Multiples for the Footwear Industry, January 2006						
Ticker	Name	Stock Price ($)	Market Capitalization ($ million)	Enterprise Value ($ million)	P/E	Price/ Book	Enterprise Value/ Sales	Enterprise Value/ EBITDA
NKE	Nike	84.20	21,830	20,518	16.64	3.59	1.43	8.75
PMMAY	Puma AG	312.05	5,088	4,593	14.99	5.02	2.19	9.02
RBK	Reebok International	58.72	3,514	3,451	14.91	2.41	0.90	8.58
WWW	Wolverine World Wide	22.10	1,257	1,253	17.42	2.71	1.20	9.53
BWS	Brown Shoe Co.	43.36	800	1,019	22.62	1.91	0.47	9.09
SKX	Skechers U.S.A.	17.09	683	614	17.63	2.02	0.62	6.88
SRR	Stride Rite Corp.	13.70	497	524	20.72	1.87	0.89	9.28
DECK	Deckers Outdoor Corp.	30.05	373	367	13.32	2.29	1.48	7.44
WEYS	Weyco Group	19.90	230	226	11.97	1.75	1.06	6.66
RCKY	Rocky Shoes & Boots	19.96	106	232	8.66	1.12	0.92	7.55
DFZ	R.G. Barry Corp.	6.83	68	92	9.2	8.11	0.87	10.75
BOOT	LaCrosse Footwear	10.40	62	75	12.09	1.28	0.76	8.30
				Average	15.01	2.84	1.06	8.49
				Maximum	+51%	+186%	+106%	+27%
				Minimum	−42%	−61%	−56%	−22%

One shortcoming of the comparables approach is that it does not take into account the important differences among firms. The fact that a firm has an exceptional management team, has developed an efficient manufacturing process, or has just secured a patent on a new technology is ignored when we apply a valuation multiple. Discounted cash flows methods have the advantage that they allow us to incorporate specific information about the firm's cost of capital or future growth. Thus, because the true driver of value for any firm is its ability to generate cash flows for its investors, the discounted cash flow methods have the potential to be more accurate than the use of a valuation multiple.

Stock Valuation Techniques: The Final Word

In the end, no single technique provides a final answer regarding a stock's true value. All approaches require assumptions or forecasts that are too uncertain to provide a definitive assessment of the firm's value. Most real-world practitioners use a combination of these approaches and gain confidence if the results are consistent across a variety of methods.

Figure 9.2 compares the ranges of values for Kenneth Cole Productions using the different valuation methods that we have discussed in this chapter. Kenneth Cole's stock price of $26.75 in January 2006 is within the range estimated by all of these methods. Hence, based on this evidence alone we would not conclude that the stock is obviously under- or over-priced.

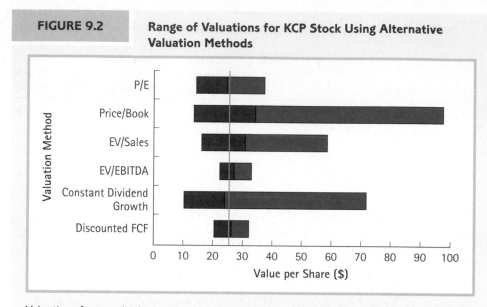

| **FIGURE 9.2** | **Range of Valuations for KCP Stock Using Alternative Valuation Methods** |

Valuations from multiples are based on the low, high, and average values of the comparable firms from Table 9.1 (see Problems 17 and 18). The constant dividend growth model is based on an 11% equity cost of capital and 5%, 8%, and 10% dividend growth rates, as discussed at the end of Section 9.2. The discounted free cash flow model is based on Example 9.7 with the range of parameters in Problem 16. (Midpoints are based on average multiples or base case assumptions. Red and blue regions show the variation between the lowest-multiple/ worst-case scenario and the highest-multiple/best-case scenario. KCP's actual share price of $26.75 is indicated by the gray line.)

CONCEPT CHECK   1. What are some common valuation multiples?

2. What implicit assumptions are made when valuing a firm using multiples based on comparable firms?

9.5 Information, Competition, and Stock Prices

As shown in Figure 9.3, the models described in this chapter link the firm's expected future cash flows, its cost of capital (determined by its risk), and the value of its shares. But what conclusions should we draw if the actual market price of a stock doesn't appear to be consistent with our estimate of its value? Is it more likely that the stock is mispriced or that we are mistaken about its risk and future cash flows? We close this chapter with a consideration of this question and the implications for corporate managers.

Information in Stock Prices

Consider the following situation. You are a new junior analyst assigned to research Kenneth Cole Productions stock and assess its value. You scrutinize the company's recent financial statements, look at the trends in the industry, and forecast the firm's future earnings, dividends, and free cash flows. You carefully run the numbers and estimate the stock's value at $30 per share. On your way to present your analysis to your boss, you run

FIGURE 9.3	The Valuation Triad

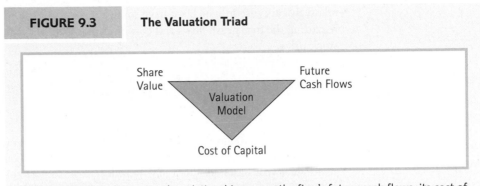

Valuation models determine the relationship among the firm's future cash flows, its cost of capital, and the value of its shares. The stock's expected cash flows and cost of capital can be used to assess its market price. Conversely, the market price can be used to assess the firm's future cash flows or cost of capital.

into a slightly more experienced colleague in the elevator. It turns out your colleague has been researching the same stock. But according to her analysis, the value of the stock is only $20 per share. What would you do?

Although you could just assume your colleague is wrong, most of us in this situation would reconsider our own analysis. The fact that someone else who has carefully studied the stock has come to a very different conclusion is powerful evidence that we might be mistaken. In the face of this information from our colleague, we would probably adjust our assessment of the stock's value downward. Of course, our colleague might also revise her opinion based on our assessment. After sharing our analyses, we would likely end up with a consensus estimate somewhere between $20 and $30 per share.

This type of encounter happens millions of times every day in the stock market. When a buyer seeks to buy a stock, the willingness of other parties to sell the same stock suggests that they value the stock differently. This information should lead buyers and sellers to revise their valuations. Ultimately, investors trade until they reach a consensus regarding the value of the stock. In this way, stock markets aggregate the information and views of many different investors.

Thus, if your valuation model suggests a stock is worth $30 per share when it is trading for $20 per share in the market, the discrepancy is equivalent to knowing that thousands of investors—many of them professionals who have access to the best information—disagree with your assessment. This knowledge should make you reconsider your original analysis. You would need a very compelling reason to trust your own estimate in the face of such contrary opinions.

What conclusion can we draw from this discussion? Recall Figure 9.3, in which a valuation model links the firm's future cash flows, its cost of capital, and its share price. In other words, given accurate information about any two of these variables, a valuation model allows us to make inferences about the third variable. Thus the way we use a valuation model will depend on the quality of our information: The model will tell us the most about the variable for which our prior information is the least reliable.

For a publicly traded firm, its market price should already provide very accurate information, aggregated from a multitude of investors, regarding the true value of its shares. Therefore, in most situations, a valuation model is best applied to tell us something about the firm's future cash flows or cost of capital, based on its current stock price. Only in the relatively rare case in which we have some superior information that other investors lack regarding the firm's cash flows and cost of capital would it make sense to second-guess the stock price.

<table><tr><td>**EXAMPLE 9.11**</td><td>**Using the Information in Market Prices**</td></tr></table>

Problem

Suppose Tecnor Industries will pay a dividend this year of $5 per share. Its equity cost of capital is 10%, and you expect its dividends to grow at a rate of about 4% per year, though you are somewhat unsure of the precise growth rate. If Tecnor's stock is currently trading for $76.92 per share, how would you update your beliefs about its dividend growth rate?

Solution

If we apply the constant dividend growth model based on a 4% growth rate, we would estimate a stock price of $P_0 = 5 / (0.10 - 0.04) = \$83.33$ per share. The market price of $76.92, however, implies that most investors expect dividends to grow at a somewhat slower rate. If we continue to assume a constant growth rate, we can solve for the growth rate consistent with the current market price using Eq. 9.7:

$$g = r_E - Div_1 / P_0 = 10\% - 5 / 76.92 = 3.5\%$$

Thus, given this market price for the stock, we should lower our expectations for the dividend growth rate unless we have very strong reasons to trust our own estimate.

Competition and Efficient Markets

The idea that markets aggregate the information of many investors, and that this information is reflected in security prices, is a natural consequence of investor competition. If information were available that indicated that buying a stock had a positive NPV, investors with that information would choose to buy the stock; their attempts to purchase it would then drive up the stock's price. By a similar logic, investors with information that selling a stock had a positive NPV would sell it and the stock's price would fall.

The idea that competition among investors works to eliminate *all* positive-NPV trading opportunities is referred to as the **efficient markets hypothesis**. It implies that securities will be fairly priced, based on their future cash flows, given all information that is available to investors.

The underlying rationale for the efficient markets hypothesis is the presence of competition. What if new information becomes available that affects the firm's value? The degree of competition, and therefore the accuracy of the efficient markets hypothesis, will depend on the number of investors who possess this information. Let's consider two important cases.

Public, Easily Interpretable Information. Information that is available to all investors includes information in news reports, financials statements, corporate press releases, or in other public data sources. If the impact of this information on the firm's future cash flows can be readily ascertained, then all investors can determine the effect of this information on the firm's value.

In this situation, we expect competition between investors to be fierce and the stock price to react nearly instantaneously to such news. A few lucky investors might be able to trade a small quantity of shares before the price fully adjusted. Most investors, however, would find that the stock price already reflected the new information before they were able to trade on it. In other words, we expect the efficient markets hypothesis to hold very well with respect to this type of information.

EXAMPLE 9.12

Stock Price Reactions to Public Information

Problem

Myox Labs announces that due to potential side effects, it is pulling one of its leading drugs from the market. As a result, its future expected free cash flow will decline by $85 million per year for the next ten years. Myox has 50 million shares outstanding, no debt, and an equity cost of capital of 8%. If this news came as a complete surprise to investors, what should happen to Myox's stock price upon the announcement?

Solution

In this case, we can use the discounted free cash flow method. With no debt, $r_{wacc} = r_E = 8\%$. Using the annuity formula, the decline in expected free cash flow will reduce Myox's enterprise value by

$$\$85 \text{ million} \times \frac{1}{0.08}\left(1 - \frac{1}{1.08^{10}}\right) = \$570 \text{ million}$$

Thus the share price should fall by $570 / 50 = $11.40 per share. Because this news is public and its effect on the firm's expected free cash flow is clear, we would expect the stock price to drop by this amount nearly instantaneously.

Private or Difficult-to-Interpret Information. Some information is not publicly available. For example, an analyst might spend time and effort gathering information from a firm's employees, competitors, suppliers, or customers that is relevant to the firm's future cash flows. This information is not available to other investors who have not devoted a similar effort to gathering it.

Even when information is publicly available, it may be difficult to interpret. Non-experts in the field may find it difficult to evaluate research reports on new technologies, for example. It may take a great deal of legal and accounting expertise and effort to understand the full consequences of a highly complicated business transaction. Certain consulting experts may have greater insight into consumer tastes and the likelihood of a product's acceptance. In these cases, while the fundamental information may be public, the interpretation of how that information will affect the firm's future cash flows is itself private information.

When private information is relegated to the hands of a relatively small number of investors, these investors may be able to profit by trading on their information.[9] In this case, the efficient markets hypothesis will not hold in the strict sense. However, as these informed traders begin to trade, they will tend to move prices, so over time prices will begin to reflect their information as well.

---

9. Even with private information, informed investors may find it difficult to profit from that information, because they must find others who are willing to trade with them; that is, the market for the stock must be sufficiently *liquid*. A liquid market requires that other investors in the market have alternative motives to trade (e.g., selling shares of a stock to purchase a house) and so be willing to trade even when facing the risk that other traders may be better informed.

If the profit opportunities from having this type of information are large, other individuals will attempt to gain the expertise and devote the resources needed to acquire it. As more individuals become better informed, competition to exploit this information will increase. Thus, in the long run, we should expect that the degree of "inefficiency" in the market will be limited by the costs of obtaining the information.

EXAMPLE 9.13

Stock Price Reactions to Private Information

Problem
Phenyx Pharmaceuticals has just announced the development of a new drug for which the company is seeking approval from the Food and Drug Administration (FDA). If approved, the future profits from the new drug will increase Phenyx's market value by $750 million, or $15 per share given its 50 million shares outstanding. If the development of this drug was a surprise to investors, and if the average likelihood of FDA approval is 10%, what do you expect will happen to Phenyx's stock price when this news is announced? What may happen to the stock price over time?

Solution
Because many investors are likely to know that the chance of FDA approval is 10%, competition should lead to an immediate jump in the stock price of 10% × $15 = $1.50 per share. Over time, however, analysts and experts in the field are likely to do their own assessments of the probable efficacy of the drug. If they conclude that the drug looks more promising than average, they will begin to trade on their private information and buy the stock, and the price will tend to drift higher over time. If the experts conclude that the drug looks less promising than average, they will tend to sell the stock, and its price will drift lower over time. Examples of possible price paths are shown in Figure 9.4.

FIGURE 9.4

Possible Stock Price Paths for Example 9.13
Phenyx's stock price jumps on the announcement based on the average likelihood of approval. The stock price then drifts up (green path) or down (gold path) as informed traders trade on their more accurate assessment of the drug's likelihood of approval.

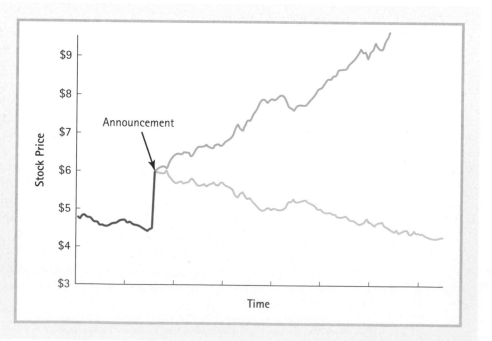

Lessons for Investors and Corporate Managers

The effect of competition based on information about stock prices has important consequences for both investors and corporate managers.

Consequences for Investors. As in other markets, investors should be able to identify positive-NPV trading opportunities in securities markets only if some barrier or restriction to free competition exists. An investor's competitive advantage may take several forms. The investor may have expertise or access to information that is known to only a few people. Alternatively, the investor may have lower trading costs than other market participants and so can exploit opportunities that others would find unprofitable. In all cases, however, the source of the positive-NPV trading opportunity must be something that is hard to replicate; otherwise, any gains would be competed away.

While the fact that positive-NPV trading opportunities are hard to come by may be disappointing, there is some good news as well. If stocks are fairly priced according to our valuation models, then investors who buy stocks can expect to receive future cash flows that fairly compensate them for the risk of their investment. Thus, in such cases the average investor can invest with confidence, even if he is not fully informed.

Implications for Corporate Managers. If stocks are fairly valued according to the models we have described, then the value of the firm is determined by the cash flows that it can pay to its investors. This result has several key implications for corporate managers:

- *Focus on NPV and free cash flow.* A manager seeking to boost the price of her firm's stock should make investments that increase the present value of the firm's free cash flow. Thus the capital budgeting methods outlined in Chapter 7 are fully consistent with the objective of maximizing the firm's share price.

- *Avoid accounting illusions.* Many managers make the mistake of focusing on accounting earnings as opposed to free cash flows. With efficient markets, the accounting consequences of a decision do not directly affect the value of the firm and should not drive decision making.

- *Use financial transactions to support investment.* With efficient markets, the firm can sell its shares at a fair price to new investors. Thus, the firm should not be constrained from raising capital to fund positive NPV investment opportunities.

The Efficient Markets Hypothesis Versus No Arbitrage

An important distinction can be drawn between the efficient markets hypothesis and the notion of a normal market that we introduced in Chapter 3, which is based on the idea of arbitrage. An arbitrage opportunity is a situation in which two securities (or portfolios) with *identical* cash flows have different prices. Because anyone can earn a sure profit in this situation by buying the low-priced security and selling the high-priced one, we expect that investors will immediately exploit and eliminate these opportunities. Thus, in a normal market, arbitrage opportunities will not be found.

The efficient markets hypothesis is best expressed in terms of returns, as in Eq. 9.2. It states that securities with *equivalent risk* should have the same *expected return*. The efficient markets hypothesis is therefore incomplete without a definition of "equivalent risk." Furthermore, different investors may perceive risks and returns differently (based on their information and preferences). There is no reason to expect the efficient markets hypothesis to hold perfectly; it is best viewed as an idealized approximation for highly competitive markets.

To test the validity of the efficient markets hypothesis and, more importantly, to implement the discounted cash flow methods of stock valuation introduced in this chapter, we need a theory of risk and return. Developing such a theory is the topic of Part IV of the text, which we turn to next.

CONCEPT CHECK
1. State the efficient market hypothesis.
2. What are the implications of the efficient market hypothesis for corporate managers?

Summary

1. The Law of One Price states that the value of a stock is equal to the present value of the dividends and future sale price the investor will receive. Because these cash flows are risky, they must be discounted at the equity cost of capital, which is the expected return of other securities available in the market with equivalent risk to the firm's equity.

2. The total return of a stock is equal to the dividend yield plus the capital gain rate. The expected total return of a stock should equal its equity cost of capital:

$$r_E = \frac{Div_1 + P_1}{P_0} - 1 = \underbrace{\frac{Div_1}{P_0}}_{\text{Dividend Yield}} + \underbrace{\frac{P_1 - P_0}{P_0}}_{\text{Capital Gain Rate}} \tag{9.2}$$

3. When investors have the same beliefs, the dividend-discount model states that, for any horizon N, the stock price satisfies the following equation:

$$P_0 = \frac{Div_1}{1 + r_E} + \frac{Div_2}{(1 + r_E)^2} + \cdots + \frac{Div_N}{(1 + r_E)^N} + \frac{P_N}{(1 + r_E)^N} \tag{9.4}$$

4. If the stock eventually pays dividends and is never acquired, the dividend-discount model implies that the stock price equals the present value of all future dividends.

5. The constant dividend growth model assumes that dividends grow at a constant expected rate g. In that case, g is also the expected capital gain rate, and

$$P_0 = \frac{Div_1}{r_E - g} \tag{9.6}$$

6. Future dividends depend on earnings, shares outstanding, and the dividend payout rate:

$$Div_t = \underbrace{\frac{\text{Earnings}_t}{\text{Shares Outstanding}_t}}_{EPS_t} \times \text{Dividend Payout Rate}_t \tag{9.8}$$

7. If the dividend payout rate and the number of shares outstanding is constant, and if earnings change only as a result of new investment from retained earnings, then the growth rate of the firm's earnings, dividends, and share price is calculated as follows:

$$g = \text{Retention Rate} \times \text{Return on New Investment} \tag{9.12}$$

8. Cutting the firm's dividend to increase investment will raise the stock price if, and only if, the new investments have a positive NPV.

9. If the firm has a long-term growth rate of g after the period $N + 1$, then we can apply the dividend-discount model and use the constant dividend growth formula to estimate the terminal stock value P_N.

10. The dividend-discount model is sensitive to the dividend growth rate, which is difficult to estimate accurately.

11. If the firm undertakes share repurchases, it is more reliable to use the total payout model to value the firm. In this model, the value of equity equals the present value of future total dividends and repurchases. To determine the stock price, we divide the equity value by the initial number of shares outstanding of the firm:

$$P_0 = \frac{PV(\text{Future Total Dividends and Repurchases})}{\text{Shares Outstanding}_0} \tag{9.16}$$

12. The growth rate of the firm's total payout is governed by the growth rate of earnings, not earnings per share.

13. When a firm has leverage, it is more reliable to use the discounted free cash flow model. In this model,

   a. The enterprise value of the firm equals the present value of the firm's future free cash flow:

$$V_0 = PV(\text{Future Free Cash Flow of Firm}) \tag{9.19}$$

   b. We discount cash flows using the weighted average cost of capital, which is the expected return the firm must pay to investors to compensate them for the risk of holding the firm's debt and equity together.

   c. We can estimate a terminal enterprise value by assuming free cash flow grows at a constant rate (typically equal to the rate of long-run revenue growth).

   d. We determine the stock price by subtracting debt and adding cash to the enterprise value, and then dividing by the initial number of shares outstanding of the firm:

$$P_0 = \frac{V_0 + \text{Cash}_0 - \text{Debt}_0}{\text{Shares Outstanding}_0} \tag{9.20}$$

14. We can also value stocks by using valuation multiples based on comparable firms. Multiples commonly used for this purpose include the P/E ratio and the ratio of enterprise value to EBITDA. Using multiples assumes that comparable firms have the same risk and future growth as the firm being valued.

15. No valuation model provides a definitive value for the stock. It is best to use several methods to identify a reasonable range for the value.

16. Stock prices aggregate the information of many investors. Therefore, if our valuation disagrees with the stock's market price, it is most likely an indication that our assumptions about the firm's cash flows are wrong.

17. Competition between investors tends to eliminate positive-NPV trading opportunities. Competition will be strongest when information is public and easy to interpret. Privately informed traders may be able to profit from their information, which is reflected in prices only gradually.

18. The efficient markets hypothesis states that competition eliminates all positive-NPV trades, which is equivalent to stating that securities with equivalent risk have the same expected returns.

19. In an efficient market, investors will not find positive-NPV trading opportunities without some source of competitive advantage. By contrast, the average investor will earn a fair return on his or her investment.

20. In an efficient market, to raise the stock price corporate managers should focus on maximizing the present value of the free cash flow from the firm's investments, rather than accounting consequences or financial policy.

Key Terms

capital gain *p. 247*
capital gain rate *p. 247*
constant dividend growth model *p. 249*
discounted free cash flow model *p. 258*
dividend-discount model *p. 248*
dividend payout rate *p. 250*
dividend yield *p. 247*
efficient markets hypothesis *p. 268*
equity cost of capital *p. 246*
forward earnings *p. 262*
forward P/E *p. 262*

method of comparables *p. 262*
retention rate *p. 251*
share repurchase *p. 256*
total payout model *p. 256*
total return *p. 247*
trailing earnings *p. 262*
trailing P/E *p. 262*
valuation multiple *p. 262*
weighted average cost of capital
  (WACC) *p. 259*

Further Reading

For a more thorough discussion of different stock valuation methods, see T. Copeland, T. Koller, and J. Murrin, *Valuation: Measuring and Managing the Value of Companies*, 3rd ed. (Hoboken: NJ: John Wiley & Sons, 2001).

For a comparison of the discounted free cash flow model and the method of comparables for a sample of 51 highly leveraged transactions, see S. N. Kaplan and R. S. Ruback "The Valuation of Cash Flow Forecasts: An Empirical Analysis," *Journal of Finance* 50 (1995): 1059–1093.

An entertaining introduction to efficient markets can be found in B. Malkiel's popular book, *A Random Walk Down Wall Street: Completely Revised and Updated Eighth Edition* (New York: W. W. Norton, 2003).

For a classic discussion of market efficiency, the arguments that support it, and important empirical tests, see E. F. Fama, "Efficient Capital Markets: A Review of Theory and Empirical Work," *Journal of Finance* 25 (1970): 383–417, and "Efficient Capital Markets: II," *The Journal of Finance* 46(5) (1991):1575–1617. Another review of the literature and apparent anomalies can be found in R. Ball, "The Development, Accomplishments and Limitations of the Theory of Stock Market Efficiency," *Managerial Finance* 20(2,3) (1994): 3–48.

For two sides of the debate of whether the price of Internet companies in the late 1990s could be justified by a valuation model, see: L. Pástor and P. Veronesi, "Was There a Nasdaq Bubble in the Late 1990s?" *Journal of Financial Economics* 2006 (in press); M. Richardson and E. Ofek, "DotCom Mania: The Rise and Fall of Internet Stock Prices," *Journal of Finance* 58 (2003): 1113–1138.

Problems

All problems in this chapter are available in MyFinanceLab. An asterisk (*) indicates problems with a higher level of difficulty.

Stock Price, Returns, and the Investment Horizon

1. Suppose Acap Corporation will pay a dividend of $2.80 per share at the end of this year and $3.00 per share next year. You expect Acap's stock price to be $52.00 in two years. If Acap's equity cost of capital is 10%:

    a. What price would you be willing to pay for a share of Acap stock today, if you planned to hold the stock for two years?

    b. Suppose instead you plan to hold the stock for one year. What price would you expect to be able to sell a share of Acap stock for in one year?

    c. Given your answer in part (b), what price would you be willing to pay for a share of Acap stock today, if you planned to hold the stock for one year? How does this compare to your answer in part (a)?

2. Krell Industries has a share price of $22.00 today. If Krell is expected to pay a dividend of $0.88 this year, and its stock price is expected to grow to $23.54 at the end of the year, what is Krell's dividend yield and equity cost of capital?

The Dividend-Discount Model

3. NoGrowth Corporation currently pays a dividend of $0.50 per quarter, and it will continue to pay this dividend forever. What is the price per share if its equity cost of capital is 15% per year?

4. Summit Systems will pay a dividend of $1.50 this year. If you expect Summit's dividend to grow by 6% per year, what is its price per share if its equity cost of capital is 11%?

5. Dorpac Corporation has a dividend yield of 1.5%. Dorpac's equity cost of capital is 8%, and its dividends are expected to grow at a constant rate.

    a. What is the expected growth rate of Dorpac's dividends?

    b. What is the expected growth rate of Dorpac's share price?

6. DFB, Inc., expects earnings this year of $5 per share, and it plans to pay a $3 dividend to shareholders. DFB will retain $2 per share of its earnings to reinvest in new projects with an expected return of 15% per year. Suppose DFB will maintain the same dividend payout rate, retention rate, and return on new investments in the future and will not change its number of outstanding shares.

    a. What growth rate of earnings would you forecast for DFB?

    b. If DFB's equity cost of capital is 12%, what price would you estimate for DFB stock?

    c. Suppose DFB instead paid a dividend of $4 per share this year and retained only $1 per share in earnings. If DFB maintains this higher payout rate in the future, what stock price would you estimate now? Should DFB raise its dividend?

7. Cooperton Mining just announced it will cut its dividend from $4 to $2.50 per share and use the extra funds to expand. Prior to the announcement, Cooperton's dividends were expected to grow at a 3% rate, and its share price was $50. With the new expansion, Cooperton's dividends are expected to grow at a 5% rate. What share price would you expect after the announcement? (Assume Cooperton's risk is unchanged by the new expansion.) Is the expansion a positive NPV investment?

8. Gillette Corporation will pay an annual dividend of $0.65 one year from now. Analysts expect this dividend to grow at 12% per year thereafter until the fifth year. After then, growth will level off at 2% per year. According to the dividend-discount model, what is the value of a share of Gillette stock if the firm's equity cost of capital is 8%?

9. Colgate-Palmolive Company has just paid an annual dividend of $0.96. Analysts are predicting an 11% per year growth rate in earnings over the next five years. After then, Colgate's earnings are expected to grow at the current industry average of 5.2% per year. If Colgate's equity cost of capital is 8.5% per year and its dividend payout ratio remains constant, what price does the dividend-discount model predict Colgate stock should sell for?

10. What is the value of a firm with initial dividend Div, growing for n years (i.e., until year $n + 1$) at rate g_1 and after that at rate g_2 forever, when the equity cost of capital is r?

11. Halliford Corporation expects to have earnings this coming year of $3 per share. Halliford plans to retain all of its earnings for the next two years. For the subsequent two years, the firm will retain 50% of its earnings. It will then retain 20% of its earnings from that point onward. Each year, retained earnings will be invested in new projects with an expected return of 25% per year. Any earnings that are not retained will be paid out as dividends. Assume Halliford's share count remains constant and all earnings growth comes from the investment of retained earnings. If Halliford's equity cost of capital is 10%, what price would you estimate for Halliford stock?

The Total Payout and Free Cash Flow Valuation Models

12. Suppose Cisco Systems pays no dividends but spent $5 billion on share repurchases last year. If Cisco's equity cost of capital is 12%, and if the amount spent on repurchases is expected to grow by 8% per year, estimate Cisco's market capitalization. If Cisco has 6 billion shares outstanding, what stock price does this correspond to?

13. Maynard Steel plans to pay a dividend of $3 this year. The company has an expected earnings growth rate of 4% per year and an equity cost of capital of 10%.

   a. Assuming Maynard's dividend payout rate and expected growth rate remains constant, and Maynard does not issue or repurchase shares, estimate Maynard's share price.

   b. Suppose Maynard decides to pay a dividend of $1 this year and use the remaining $2 per share to repurchase shares. If Maynard's total payout rate remains constant, estimate Maynard's share price.

   c. If Maynard maintains the dividend and total payout rate given in part (b), at what rate are Maynard's dividends and earnings per share expected to grow?

EXCEL 14. Heavy Metal Corporation is expected to generate the following free cash flows over the next five years:

Year	1	2	3	4	5
FCF ($ million)	53	68	78	75	82

After then, the free cash flows are expected to grow at the industry average of 4% per year. Using the discounted free cash flow model and a weighted average cost of capital of 14%:

   a. Estimate the enterprise value of Heavy Metal.

   b. If Heavy Metal has no excess cash, debt of $300 million, and 40 million shares outstanding, estimate its share price.

EXCEL **15.** Sora Industries has 60 million outstanding shares, $120 million in debt, $40 million in cash, and the following projected free cash flow for the next four years:

	Year	0	1	2	3	4
	Earnings and FCF Forecast ($ million)					
1	Sales	433.0	468.0	516.0	547.0	574.3
2	Growth versus Prior Year		8.1%	10.3%	6.0%	5.0%
3	Cost of Goods Sold		(313.6)	(345.7)	(366.5)	(384.8)
4	Gross Profit		154.4	170.3	180.5	189.5
5	Selling, General, and Administrative		(93.6)	(103.2)	(109.4)	(114.9)
6	Depreciation		(7.0)	(7.5)	(9.0)	(9.5)
7	EBIT		53.8	59.6	62.1	65.2
8	Less: Income Tax at 40%		(21.5)	(23.8)	(24.8)	(26.1)
9	Plus: Depreciation		7.0	7.5	9.0	9.5
10	Less: Capital Expenditures		(7.7)	(10.0)	(9.9)	(10.4)
11	Less: Increase in NWC		(6.3)	(8.6)	(5.6)	(4.9)
12	Free Cash Flow		25.3	24.6	30.8	33.3

a. Suppose Sora's revenue and free cash flow are expected to grow at a 5% rate beyond year 4. If Sora's weighted average cost of capital is 10%, what is the value of Sora's stock based on this information?

b. Sora's cost of goods sold was assumed to be 67% of sales. If its cost of goods sold is actually 70% of sales, how would the estimate of the stock's value change?

c. Let's return to the assumptions of part (a) and suppose Sora can maintain its cost of goods sold at 67% of sales. However, now suppose Sora reduces its selling, general, and administrative expenses from 20% of sales to 16% of sales. What stock price would you estimate now? (Assume no other expenses, except taxes, are affected.)

*d. Sora's net working capital needs were estimated to be 18% of sales (which is their current level in year 0). If Sora can reduce this requirement to 12% of sales starting in year 1, but all other assumptions remain as in part (a), what stock price do you estimate for Sora? (*Hint:* This change will have the largest impact on Sora's free cash flow in year 1.)

EXCEL **16.** Consider the valuation of Kenneth Cole Productions in Example 9.7.

a. Suppose you believe KCP's initial revenue growth rate will be between 7% and 11% (with growth slowing linearly to 4% by year 2011). What range of share prices for KCP is consistent with these forecasts?

b. Suppose you believe KCP's initial revenue EBIT margin will be between 8% and 10% of sales. What range of share prices for KCP is consistent with these forecasts?

c. Suppose you believe KCP's weighted average cost of capital is between 10.5% and 12%. What range of share prices for KCP is consistent with these forecasts?

d. What range of share prices is consistent if you vary the estimates as in parts (a), (b), and (c) simultaneously?

Valuation Based on Comparable Firms

EXCEL **17.** Suppose that in January 2006, Kenneth Cole Productions had EPS of $1.65 and a book value of equity of $12.05 per share.

a. Using the average P/E multiple in Table 9.1, estimate KCP's share price.

b. What range of share prices do you estimate based on the highest and lowest P/E multiples in Table 9.1?

c. Using the average price to book value multiple in Table 9.1, estimate KCP's share price.

d. What range of share prices do you estimate based on the highest and lowest price to book value multiples in Table 9.1?

`EXCEL` **18.** Suppose that in January 2006, Kenneth Cole Productions had sales of $518 million, EBITDA of $55.6 million, excess cash of $100 million, $3 million of debt, and 21 million shares outstanding.

    a. Using the average enterprise value to sales multiple in Table 9.1, estimate KCP's share price.

    b. What range of share prices do you estimate based on the highest and lowest enterprise value to sales multiples in Table 9.1?

    c. Using the average enterprise value to EBITDA multiple in Table 9.1, estimate KCP's share price.

    d. What range of share prices do you estimate based on the highest and lowest enterprise value to EBITDA multiples in Table 9.1?

`EXCEL` **19.** In addition to footwear, Kenneth Cole Productions designs and sells handbags, apparel, and other accessories. You decide, therefore, to consider comparables for KCP outside the footwear industry.

    a. Suppose that Fossil, Inc., has an enterprise value to EBITDA multiple of 9.73 and a P/E multiple of 18.4. What share price would you estimate for KCP using each of these multiples, based on the data for KCP in Problems 17 and 18?

    b. Suppose that Tommy Hilfiger Corporation has an enterprise value to EBITDA multiple of 7.19 and a P/E multiple of 17.2. What share price would you estimate for KCP using each of these multiples, based on the data for KCP in Problems 17 and 18?

`EXCEL` **20.** Consider the following data for the auto industry in mid-2006 (EV = enterprise value, BV = book value, NM = not meaningful because divisor is negative). Discuss the usefulness of using multiples to value an auto company.

Company Name	Market Cap	EV	EV/Sales	EV/EBITDA	EV/EBIT	P/E	P/BV
Honda Motor Co. Ltd.	55,694.1	77,212.4	0.9×	8.2×	10.8×	10.9×	1.6×
DaimlerChrysler AG	47,462.2	136,069.6	0.7×	6.6×	28.7×	13.2×	1.2×
Nissan Motor Co. Ltd.	44,463.2	93,138.3	1.2×	7.3×	11.8×	NM	NM
Volkswagen AG	25,215.6	84,922.0	0.7×	5.7×	22.3×	14.5×	1.2×
General Motors Corp.	15,077.9	274,336.9	1.4×	44.3×	NM	NM	1.1×
PSA Peugeot Citroen	13,506.7	44,015.1	0.6×	7.2×	18.6×	10.6×	1.3×
Ford Motor Co.	11,931.1	145,009.1	0.8×	11.9×	NM	490.8×	2.0×
Mitsubishi Motors Corp.	7,919.4	9,633.3	0.6×	207.2×	NM	NM	3.9×
Daihatsu Motor Co. Ltd.	3,666.3	6,913.8	0.6×	7.9×	17.7×	15.9×	1.6×

Source: Capital IQ.

Information, Competition, and Stock Prices

21. In mid-2006, Coca-Cola Company had a share price of $43. Its dividend was $1.24, and you expect Coca-Cola to raise this dividend by approximately 7% per year in perpetuity.

    a. If Coca-Cola's equity cost of capital is 8%, what share price would you expect based on your estimate of the dividend growth rate?

    b. Given Coca-Cola's share price, what would you conclude about your assessment of Coca-Cola's future dividend growth?

22. Roybus, Inc., a manufacturer of flash memory, just reported that its main production facility in Taiwan was destroyed in a fire. While the plant was fully insured, the loss of production will decrease Roybus's free cash flow by $180 million at the end of this year and by $60 million at the end of next year.

   a. If Roybus has 35 million shares outstanding and a weighted average cost of capital of 13%, what change in Roybus's stock price would you expect upon this announcement? (Assume the value of Roybus' debt is not affected by the event.)

   b. Would you expect to be able to sell Roybus's stock on hearing this announcement and make a profit? Explain.

23. Apnex, Inc., is a biotechnology firm that is about to announce the results of its clinical trials of a potential new cancer drug. If the trials were successful, Apnex stock will be worth $70 per share. If the trials were unsuccessful, Apnex stock will be worth $18 per share. Suppose that the morning before the announcement is scheduled, Apnex shares are trading for $55 per share.

   a. Based on the current share price, what sort of expectations do investors seem to have about the success of the trials?

   b. Suppose hedge fund manager Paul Kliner has hired several prominent research scientists to examine the public data on the drug and make their own assessment of the drug's promise. Would Kliner's fund be likely to profit by trading the stock in the hours prior to the announcement?

   c. What would limit the fund's ability to profit on its information?

Data Case

A new analyst for a large brokerage firm, you are anxious to demonstrate the skills you learned in your MBA program and prove that you are worth your attractive salary. Your first assignment is to analyze the stock of the General Electric Corporation. Your boss recommends determining prices based on both the dividend-discount model and discounted free cash flow valuation methods. GE uses a cost of equity of 10.5% and an after-tax weighted average cost of capital of 7.5%. The expected return on new investments is 12%. However, you are a little concerned because your finance professor has told you that these two methods can result in widely differing estimates when applied to real data. You are really hoping that the two methods will reach similar prices. Good luck with that!

1. Go to Yahoo! Finance (http://finance.yahoo.com) and enter the symbol for General Electric (GE). From the main page for GE gather the following information and enter it onto a spreadsheet:

   a. The current stock price (last trade) at the top of the page.

   b. The current dividend amount, which is in the bottom-right cell in the same box as the stock price.

2. Next click on "Key Statistics" from the left side of the page. From the Key Statistics page gather the following information and enter it on the same spreadsheet:

   a. The number of shares of stock outstanding.

   b. The Payout ratio.

3. Next click on "Analyst Estimates" from the left side of the page. From the Analyst Estimates page find the expected growth rate for the next 5 years and enter it onto your spreadsheet. It will be near the very bottom of the page.

4. Next click on "Income Statement" near the bottom of the menu on the left. Place the cursor in the middle of the income statements and right-click. Select "Export to Microsoft Excel." Copy and paste the entire three years of income statements into a new worksheet in your existing Excel file. Repeat this process for both the balance sheet and cash flow statement for General Electric. Keep all the different statements in the same Excel worksheet.

5. To determine the stock value based on the dividend-discount model:
   a. Create a timeline in Excel for five years.
   b. Use the dividend obtained from Yahoo! Finance as the current dividend to forecast the next 5 annual dividends based on the five-year growth rate.
   c. Determine the long-term growth rate based on GE's payout ratio (which is one minus the retention ratio) using Eq. 9.12.
   d. Use the long-term growth rate to determine the stock price for year five using Eq. 9.13.
   e. Determine the current stock price using Eq. 9.14.

6. To determine the stock value based on the discounted free cash flow method:
   a. Forecast the free cash flows using the historic data from the financial statements downloaded from Yahoo! to compute the three-year average of the following ratios:
      i. EBIT/Sales
      ii. Tax Rate (Income Tax Expense/Income Before Tax)
      iii. Property Plant and Equipment/Sales
      iv. Depreciation/Property Plant and Equipment
      v. Net Working Capital/Sales
   b. Create a timeline for the next seven years.
   c. Forecast future sales based on the most recent year's total revenue growing at the five-year growth rate from Yahoo! for the first five years and the long-term growth rate for years six and seven.
   d. Use the average ratios computed in part (a) to forecast EBIT, property, plant and equipment, depreciation, and net working capital for the next seven years.
   e. Forecast the free cash flow for the next seven years using Eq. 9.18.
   f. Determine the horizon enterprise value for year 5 using Eq. 9.22.
   g. Determine the enterprise value of the firm as the present value of the free cash flows.
   h. Determine the stock price using Eq. 9.20.

7. Compare the stock prices from the two methods to the actual stock price. What recommendations can you make as to whether clients should buy or sell General Electric's stock based on your price estimates?

8. Explain to your boss why the estimates from the two valuation methods differ. Specifically address the assumptions implicit in the models themselves as well as those you made in preparing your analysis. Why do these estimates differ from the actual stock price of GE?

Risk and Return

The Law of One Price Connection. To apply the Law of One Price correctly requires comparing investment opportunities of equivalent risk. The objective in this part of the book is to explain how to measure and compare risks across investment opportunities. Chapter 10 introduces the key insight that investors only demand a risk premium for risk they cannot remove themselves without cost by diversifying their portfolios. Hence, only non-diversifiable risk will matter when comparing investment opportunities. In Chapter 11, we quantify this idea and thereby derive investors' optimal investment portfolio choices. In Chapter 12 we consider the implications of assuming all investors choose their portfolio of investments optimally. This assumption leads to the Capital Asset Pricing Model (CAPM), the central model in financial economics that quantifies what an equivalent risk is and thereby provides the relation between risk and return. Chapter 13 examines the strengths and weaknesses of alternative models of risk and return.

CHAPTER 10

Capital Markets and the Pricing of Risk

notation

p_R	probability of return R
$Var(R)$	variance of return R
$SD(R)$	standard deviation of return R
$E[R]$	expectation of return R
Div_t	dividend paid on date t
P_t	price on date t
R_t	realized or total return of a security from date $t-1$ to t
$\overline{R}$	average return
β_s	beta of security s
r	Cost of capital of an investment opportunity

Over the four-year period 2001 through 2004, investors in Anheuser-Busch Companies, Inc., earned an average return of 4.4% per year. Within this period there was some variation, with the annual return ranging from almost 11% in 2003 to −2% in 2004. Over the same period, investors in Yahoo! Inc. earned an average return of 25.8%. These investors, however, lost 41% in 2001 and gained 175% in 2003. Finally, investors in three-month U.S. Treasury bills earned an average return of 1.8% during the period, with a high return of 3.3% in 2001 and a low return of 1.0% in 2003. Clearly, these three investments offered returns that were very different in terms of their average level and their variability. What accounts for these differences?

In this chapter, we will explain why these differences exist. Our goal is to develop a theory that explains the relationship between average returns and the variability of returns and thereby derive the risk premium that investors require to hold different securities and investments. We then use this theory to explain how to determine the cost of capital for an investment opportunity.

We begin our investigation of the relationship between risk and return by examining historical data for publicly traded securities. We will see, for example, that while stocks are riskier investments than bonds, they have also earned higher average returns. We can interpret the higher average return on stocks as compensation to investors for the greater risk they are taking.

But we will also find that not all risk needs to be compensated. By holding a portfolio containing many different investments, investors can eliminate risks that are specific to individual securities. It is only those risks that cannot be eliminated by holding a large portfolio that determine the risk premium required by investors. These observations will allow us to refine our definition of what risk is, how it can be measured, and how the cost of capital is determined.

10.1 A First Look at Risk and Return

Suppose your great-grandparents invested $100 on your behalf at the end of 1925. They instructed their broker to reinvest any dividends or interest earned in the account until the beginning of 2005. How would that $100 have grown if it were placed in one of the following investments?

1. Standard & Poor's 500 (S&P 500): A portfolio, constructed by Standard and Poor's, comprising 90 U.S. stocks up to 1957 and 500 U.S. stocks after that. The firms represented are leaders in their respective industries and are among the largest firms, in terms of market value, traded on U.S. markets.

2. Small Stocks: A portfolio of stocks of U.S. firms whose market values are in the bottom 10% of all stocks traded on the NYSE. (As stocks' market values change, this portfolio is updated so it always consists of the smallest 10% of stocks.)

3. World Portfolio: A portfolio of international stocks from all of the world's major stock markets in North America, Europe, and Asia.[1]

4. Corporate Bonds: A portfolio of long-term, AAA-rated U.S. corporate bonds. These bonds have a maturity of approximately 20 years.

5. Treasury Bills: An investment in three-month U.S. Treasury bills.

Figure 10.1 shows the result, through 2005, of investing $100 at the end of 1925 in each of these five investment portfolios, ignoring transactions costs. The graph is striking—had your great-grandparents invested $100 in the small stock portfolio, the investment would be worth more than $8 million in 2005! By contrast, if they had invested in Treasury bills, the investment would be worth only about $2000.

For comparison, we also show how prices changed during the same period using the consumer price index (CPI). During this period in the United States, small stocks experienced the highest long-term return, followed by the large stocks in the S&P 500, the international stocks in the world portfolio, corporate bonds, and finally Treasury bills. All of the investments grew faster than inflation (as measured by the CPI).

A second pattern is also evident in Figure 10.1. While the small stock portfolio performed the best in the long run, its value also experienced the largest fluctuations. For example, investors in small stocks had the largest loss during the Depression era of the 1930s: Had your great-grandparents put the $100 in a small stock portfolio intended for their own retirement 15 years later in 1940, they would have had only $175 to retire on, compared with $217 from the same investment in corporate bonds. Moreover, during the 15-year period, they would have seen the value of their investment drop as low as $33. On the other hand, if they had invested in Treasury bills, they would not have experienced any losses during the period, but rather would have enjoyed steady—albeit modest—gains each year. Indeed, if we were to rank the investments by the size of their increases and decreases in value, we would obtain the same ranking as before: Small stocks had the most variable returns, followed by the S&P 500, the world portfolio, corporate bonds, and finally Treasury bills.

In Chapter 3, we explained why investors are averse to fluctuations in the value of their investments and why riskier investments have higher expected returns. Investors do not

---

1. This index is based on the Morgan Stanley Capital International World Index from 1970–2005. Prior to 1970, the index is constructed by Global Financial Data, with approximate initial weights of 44% North America, 44% Europe, and 12% Asia, Africa, and Australia.

FIGURE 10.1

Value of $100 Invested at the End of 1925 in U.S. Large Stocks (S&P 500), Small Stocks, World Stocks, Corporate Bonds, and Treasury Bills

These returns assume all dividends and interest are reinvested and exclude transactions costs. Also shown is the change in the consumer price index (CPI).

Source: Chicago Center for Research in Security Prices (CRSP) for U.S. stocks and CPI, Global Finance Data for the World Index, Treasury bills and corporate bonds.

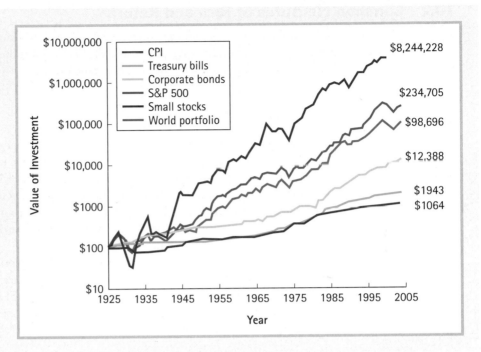

like to be hit when they are already down—when times are bad, they do not like to have their problems further compounded by experiencing losses on their investments. In fact, even if your great-grandparents had actually put the $100 into a small stock portfolio in 1925, it is unlikely you would have seen any of it. More likely, in the depths of the Great Depression your great-grandparents would have turned to their investment to get them through the bad times. Unfortunately, the small stock portfolio would not have helped much in this regard—in 1932, their original $100 investment would have been worth only $33. With the benefit of 80 years of hindsight the small stock portfolio looks like a great investment, but in 1932 it would have seemed like a huge mistake. Perhaps this is the reason your great-grandparents did not actually invest money for you in small stocks. The pleasure of knowing that your great-grandchild might one day be a millionaire may not make up for the pain of the investment going bust at precisely the time when the money is needed for other things.

Although we understand the general principle explaining why investors do not like risk and demand a risk premium to bear it, our goal in this chapter is to quantify this relationship. We would like to explain *how much* investors demand (in terms of a higher expected return) to bear a given level of risk. To quantify the relationship, we must first develop tools that will allow us to measure risk and return. That is the objective of the next section.

CONCEPT CHECK

1. From 1926 to 2005, which of the following investments had the highest return: Standard & Poor's 500, small stocks, world portfolio, corporate bonds, or Treasury bills?

2. From 1926 to 2005, which investment grew in value in every year? Which investment had the greatest variability?

10.2 Common Measures of Risk and Return

When a manager makes an investment decision or an investor purchases a security, they have some view as to the risk involved and the likely return the investment will earn. Thus we begin our discussion by reviewing the standard ways in which risks are defined and measured.

Probability Distributions

Different securities have different initial prices, pay different dividend amounts, and sell for different future amounts. To make them comparable, we express their performance in terms of their returns. The return indicates the percentage increase in the value of an investment per dollar initially invested in the security. When an investment is risky, there are different returns it may earn. Each possible return has some likelihood of occurring. We summarize this information with a **probability distribution**, which assigns a probability, P_R, that each possible return, R, will occur.

Let's consider a simple example. Suppose BFI stock currently trades for $100 per share. You believe that in one year there is a 25% chance the share price will be $140, a 50% chance it will be $110, and a 25% chance it will be $80. BFI pays no dividends, so these payoffs correspond to returns of 40%, 10%, and −20%, respectively. Table 10.1 summarizes the probability distribution for BFI's returns.

TABLE 10.1	**Probability Distribution of Returns for BFI**		
		Probability Distribution	
Current Stock Price ($)	**Stock Price in One Year ($)**	**Return, R**	**Probability, P_R**
	140	0.40	25%
100	110	0.10	50%
	80	−0.20	25%

We can also represent the probability distribution with a histogram, as shown in Figure 10.2.

Expected Return

Given the probability distribution of returns, we can compute the expected return. The **expected** (or **mean) return** is calculated as a weighted average of the possible returns, where the weights correspond to the probabilities.[2]

Expected (Mean) Return

$$\text{Expected Return} = E[R] = \sum_R p_R \times R \tag{10.1}$$

---

2. The notation $\sum_R$ means that we sum the probability that each return will occur, P_R, times the return, R, for all possible returns.

FIGURE 10.2

**Probability Distribution
of Returns for BFI**
The height of a bar in the
histogram indicates the
likelihood of the associated
outcome.

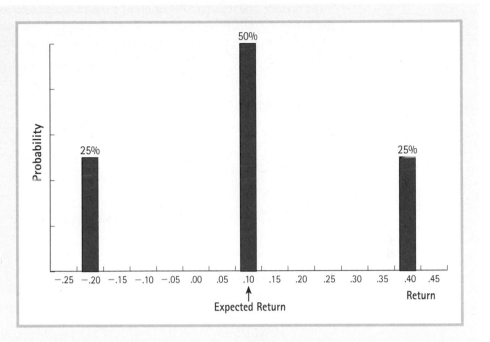

The expected return is the return we would earn on average if we could repeat the investment many times, with the return being drawn from the same distribution each time. In terms of the histogram, the expected return is the "balancing point" of the distribution, if we think of the probabilities as weights. The expected return for BFI is

$$E[R_{BFI}] = 25\%(-0.20) + 50\%(0.10) + 25\%(0.40) = 10\%$$

This expected return corresponds to the balancing point in Figure 10.2.

Variance and Standard Deviation

Two common measures of the risk of a probability distribution are its variance and standard deviation. The **variance** is the expected squared deviation from the mean, and the **standard deviation** is the square root of the variance.

Variance and Standard Deviation of the Return Distribution

$$Var(R) = E[(R - E[R])^2] = \sum_R p_R \times (R - E[R])^2$$

$$SD(R) = \sqrt{Var(R)} \tag{10.2}$$

If the return is riskless and never deviates from its mean, the variance is zero. Otherwise, the variance increases with the magnitude of the deviations from the mean. Therefore, the variance is a measure of how "spread out" the distribution of the return is. The variance of BFI's return is

$$Var(R_{BFI}) = 25\% \times (-0.20 - 0.10)^2 + 50\% \times (0.10 - 0.10)^2$$
$$+ 25\% \times (0.40 - 0.10)^2 = 0.045$$

The standard deviation of the return is the square root of the variance, so for BFI,

$$SD(R) = \sqrt{Var(R)} = \sqrt{0.045} = 21.2\% \tag{10.3}$$

In finance, the standard deviation of a return is also referred to as its **volatility**. While the variance and the standard deviation both measure the variability of the returns, the standard deviation is easier to interpret because it is in the same units as the returns themselves.[3]

EXAMPLE 10.1

Calculating the Expected Return and Volatility

Problem

Suppose AMC stock is equally likely to have a 45% return or a −25% return. What are its expected return and volatility?

Solution

First we calculate the expected return by taking the probability-weighted average of the possible returns:

$$E[R] = \sum_R p_R \times R = 50\% \times 0.45 + 50\% \times (-0.25) = 10.0\%$$

To compute the volatility, we first determine the variance:

$$Var(R) = \sum_R p_R \times (R - E[R])^2 = 50\% \times (0.45 - 0.10)^2 + 50\% \times (-0.25 - 0.10)^2$$

$$= 0.1225$$

Then the volatility or standard deviation is the square root of the variance:

$$SD(R) = \sqrt{(R)} = \sqrt{0.1225} = 35\%$$

Note that both AMC and BFI have the same expected return, 10%. However, the returns for AMC are more spread out than those for BFI—the high returns are higher and the low returns are lower, as shown by the histogram in Figure 10.3. As a result, AMC has a higher variance and volatility than BFI.

If we could observe the probability distributions that investors anticipate for different securities, we could compute their expected returns and volatilities and explore the relationship between them. Of course, in most situations we do not know the explicit probability distribution, as we did for BFI. Without that information, how can we estimate and compare risk and return? A popular approach is to extrapolate from historical data, which is a sensible strategy if we are in a stable environment and believe that future returns should mirror past returns. Let's look at the historical returns of stocks and bonds, to see what they reveal about the relationship between risk and return.

---

3. While the variance and the standard deviation are the most common measures of risk, they do not differentiate between upside and downside risk. Because investors dislike only negative resolutions of uncertainty, alternative measures that focus solely on downside risk have been developed, such as the semivariance (which measures the variance of the losses only) and the expected tail loss (the expected loss in the worst x% of outcomes). These alternative measures are more complex and cumbersome to apply, and yet in many applications produce the same ranking of risk as the standard deviation (as in Example 10.1, or if returns are normally distributed). Thus they tend to be used only in special applications in which the standard deviation alone is not a sufficient characterization of risk.

FIGURE 10.3

Probability Distribution for BFI and AMC Returns

While both stocks have the same expected return, AMC's return has a higher variance and standard deviation.

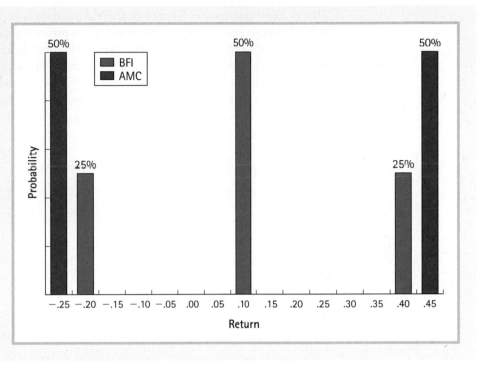

CONCEPT CHECK

1. How do we calculate the expected return of a stock?

2. What are the two most common measures of risk, and how are they related to each other?

10.3 Historical Returns of Stocks and Bonds

In this section, we explain how to compute average returns and volatilities using historical stock market data. The distribution of past returns can be helpful when we seek to estimate the distribution of returns investors may expect in the future. We begin by first explaining how to compute historical returns.

Computing Historical Returns

Of all the possible returns, the **realized return** is the return that actually occurs over a particular time period. How do we measure the realized return for a stock? Suppose you invest in a stock on date t for price P_t. If the stock pays a dividend, Div_{t+1}, on date $t + 1$, and you sell the stock at that time for price P_{t+1}, then the realized return from your investment in the stock from t to $t + 1$ is

$$R_{t+1} = \frac{Div_{t+1} + P_{t+1}}{P_t} - 1 = \frac{Div_{t+1}}{P_t} + \frac{P_{t+1} - P_t}{P_t}$$

$$= \text{Dividend Yield} + \text{Capital Gain Rate} \tag{10.4}$$

That is, as we discussed in Chapter 9, the realized return, R_{t+1}, is the total return we earn from dividends and capital gains, expressed as a percentage of the initial stock price.[4]

If you hold the stock beyond the date of the first dividend, then to compute your return you must specify how you invest any dividends you receive in the interim. To focus on the returns of a single security, let's assume that *all dividends are immediately reinvested and used to purchase additional shares of the same stock or security.* In this case, we can use Eq. 10.4 to compute the stock's return between dividend payments, and then compound the returns from each dividend interval to compute the return over a longer horizon. For example, if a stock pays dividends at the end of each quarter, with realized returns $R_{Q1}, \ldots, R_{Q4}$ each quarter, then its annual realized return, R_{annual}, is computed as

$$1 + R_{annual} = (1 + R_{Q1})(1 + R_{Q2})(1 + R_{Q3})(1 + R_{Q4}) \tag{10.5}$$

EXAMPLE 10.2

Realized Returns for GM Stock

Problem

What were the realized annual returns for GM stock in 1999 and in 2004?

Solution

First we look up GM stock price data at the start and end of the year, as well as at any dividend dates (see the book's Web site for online sources of stock price and dividend data). From these data we can construct the following table:

Date	Price ($)	Dividend ($)	Return	Date	Price ($)	Dividend ($)	Return
12/31/98	71.56			12/31/03	53.40		
2/2/99	89.44	0.50	25.68%	2/11/04	49.80	0.50	−5.81%
5/11/99	85.75	0.50	−3.57%	5/12/04	44.48	0.50	−9.68%
5/28/99[5]	69.00	13.72	−3.53%	8/11/04	41.74	0.50	−5.04%
8/10/99	60.81	0.50	−11.14%	11/4/04	39.50	0.50	−4.17%
11/8/99	69.06	0.50	14.39%	12/31/04	40.06		1.42%
12/31/99	72.69		5.26%				

We compute each period's return using Eq. 10.4. For example, the return from December 31, 1998, until February 2, 1999, is equal to

$$\frac{0.50 + 89.44}{71.56} - 1 = 25.68\%$$

---

4. We can compute the realized return for any security in the same way, by replacing the dividend payments with any cash flows paid by the security (for example, with a bond, coupon payments would replace dividends).

5. This large dividend was a special dividend related to GM's spinoff of auto parts maker Delphi Automotive Systems. For each share of GM stock owned, each GM shareholder received 0.69893 share of Delphi common stock, which had a value of $13.72 based on Delphi's closing stock price of $19.625. When we compute GM's annual return, we assume these shares of Delphi were sold and the proceeds were immediately reinvested in GM. In that way the returns reflect GM's performance exclusively.

We then determine the annual returns using Eq. 10.5:

$$R_{1999} = (1.2568)(0.9643)(0.9647)(0.8886)(1.1439)(1.0526) - 1 = 25.09\%$$

$$R_{2004} = (0.9419)(0.9032)(0.9496)(0.9583)(1.0142) - 1 = -21.48\%$$

Example 10.2 illustrates two features of the returns from holding a stock like GM. First, both dividends and capital gains contribute to the total realized return—ignoring either one would give a very misleading impression of GM's performance. Second, the returns are risky. In years like 1999 the returns are quite high, but in other years like 2004 they are negative, meaning GM's shareholders lost money over the year.

We can compute realized returns in this same way for any investment. We can also compute the realized returns for an entire portfolio, by keeping track of the interest and dividend payments paid by the portfolio during the year, as well as the change in the market value of the portfolio. For example, the realized returns for the S&P 500 index are shown in Table 10.2, which for comparison purposes also lists the returns for GM and for three-month Treasury bills.

Once we have calculated the realized annual returns, we can compare them to see which investments performed better in a given year. From Table 10.2, we can see that GM stock outperformed the S&P 500 in 1999 and 2001 through 2003. Also, in 2000 through 2002, Treasury bills performed better than both GM stock and the S&P 500. Note the overall tendency for GM's return to move in the same direction as the S&P 500.

TABLE 10.2	**Realized Return for the S&P 500, GM, and Treasury Bills, 1996–2004**				
Year End	S&P 500 Index	Dividends Paid*	S&P 500 Realized Return	GM Realized Return	3-Month T-Bill Return
1995	615.93				
1996	740.74	16.61	23.0%	8.6%	5.1%
1997	970.43	17.2	33.4%	19.6%	5.2%
1998	1229.23	18.5	28.6%	21.3%	4.9%
1999	1469.25	18.1	21.0%	25.1%	4.8%
2000	1320.28	15.7	−9.1%	−27.8%	6.0%
2001	1148.08	15.2	−11.9%	−1.0%	3.3%
2002	879.82	14.53	−22.1%	−20.8%	1.6%
2003	1111.92	20.8	28.7%	52.9%	1.0%
2004	1211.92	20.98	10.9%	−21.5%	1.4%

*Total dividends paid by the 500 stocks in the portfolio, based on the number of shares of each stock in the index, adjusted until the end of the year, assuming they were reinvested when paid.

Source: Standard & Poor's, GM, and Global Financial Data.

Over any particular period we observe only one draw from the probability distribution of returns. If the realized return in each period is drawn from the same probability distribution, however, we can observe multiple draws by observing the realized return over multiple periods. By counting the number of times the realized return falls within a particular range, we can estimate the underlying probability distribution. Let's illustrate this process with the data in Figure 10.1.

Figure 10.4 plots the annual returns for each U.S. investment in Figure 10.1 in a histogram. The height of each bar represents the number of years that the annual returns were in each range indicated on the *x*-axis. When we plot the probability distribution in this way using historical data, we refer to it as the **empirical distribution** of the returns.

Average Annual Returns

The **average annual return** of an investment during some historical period is simply the average of the realized returns for each year. That is, if R_t is the realized return of a security in year t, then the average annual return for years 1 through T is

Average Annual Return of a Security

$$\overline{R} = \frac{1}{T}(R_1 + R_2 + \cdots + R_T) = \frac{1}{T}\sum_{t=1}^{T} R_t \tag{10.6}$$

Notice that the average annual return is the balancing point of the empirical distribution—in this case, the probability of a return occurring in a particular range is measured by the number of times the realized return falls in that range. Therefore, if the probability distribution of the returns is the same over time, the average return provides an estimate of the expected return.

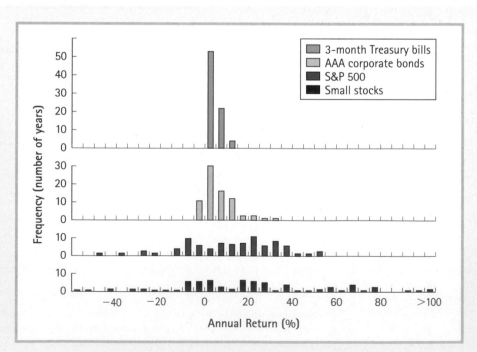

FIGURE 10.4

The Empirical Distribution of Annual Returns for U.S. Large Stocks (S&P 500), Small Stocks, Corporate Bonds, and Treasury Bills, 1926–2004.

The height of each bar represents the number of years that the annual returns were in each 5% range. Note the greater variability of stock returns (especially small stocks) compared to the returns of corporate bonds or Treasury bills.

TABLE 10.3	Average Annual Returns for U.S. Small Stocks, Large Stocks (S&P 500), Corporate Bonds, and Treasury Bills, 1926–2004

Investment	Average Annual Return
Small stocks	22.11%
S&P 500	12.32%
Corporate bonds	6.52%
Treasury bills	3.87%

For example, using the data from Table 10.2, the average return for S&P 500 for the years 1996–2004 is

$$\overline{R} = \frac{1}{9}(0.230 + 0.334 + 0.286 + 0.210 - 0.091 \\ - 0.119 - 0.221 + 0.287 + 0.109) = 11.4\%$$

The average Treasury bill return from 1996–2004 was 3.7%. Therefore, investors earned 11.4% − 3.7% = 7.7% more on average holding the S&P 500 than investing in Treasury bills during this period. Table 10.3 provides the average returns for different U.S. investments from 1926–2004.

The Variance and Volatility of Returns

Looking at Figure 10.4, we can see that the variability of the returns is very different for each investment. The distribution of small stocks' returns shows the widest spread. The large stocks of the S&P 500 have returns that vary less than those of small stocks, but much more than the returns of corporate bonds or Treasury bills.

To quantify this difference in variability, we can estimate the standard deviation of the probability distribution. As before, we will use the empirical distribution to derive this estimate. Using the same logic as we did with the mean, we estimate the variance by computing the average squared deviation from the mean. The only complication is that we do not actually know the mean, so instead we use the best estimate of the mean—the average realized return.[6]

Variance Estimate Using Realized Returns

$$Var(R) = \frac{1}{T-1} \sum_{t=1}^{T} (R_t - \overline{R})^2 \tag{10.7}$$

We estimate the standard deviation or volatility as the square root of the variance.[7]

---

6. You may wonder why we divide by $T - 1$ rather than by T here. It is because we are not computing deviations from the true expected return; instead, we are computing deviations from the estimated average return $\overline{R}$. Because the average return is derived from the same data, we lose a degree of freedom (in essence, we use up one of the data points), so that when computing the variance we really have only $T - 1$ additional data points to base it on.

7. If the returns used in Eq. 10.7 are not annual returns, the variance is typically converted to annual terms by multiplying the number of periods per year. For example, when using monthly returns, we multiply the variance by 12 and, equivalently, the standard deviation by $\sqrt{12}$.

EXAMPLE
10.3

Computing a Historical Volatility

Problem

Using the data from Table 10.2, what are the variance and volatility of the S&P 500's returns for the years 1996–2004?

Solution

Earlier we calculated the average annual return of the S&P 500 during this period to be 11.4%. Therefore,

$$Var(R) = \frac{1}{T-1}\sum_t (R_t - \bar{R})^2$$

$$= \frac{1}{9-1}[(0.230 - 0.114)^2 + (0.334 - 0.114)^2 + \cdots + (0.109 - 0.114)^2]$$

$$= 0.0424$$

The volatility or standard deviation is therefore $SD(R) = \sqrt{Var(R)} = \sqrt{0.0424} = 20.6\%$.

We can compute the standard deviation of the returns to quantify the differences in the variability of the distributions that we observed in Figure 10.4. These results are shown in Table 10.4.

TABLE 10.4   **Volatility of U.S. Small Stocks, Large Stocks (S&P 500), Corporate Bonds, and Treasury Bills, 1926–2004**

Investment	Return Volatility (Standard Deviation)
Small stocks	42.75%
S&P 500	20.36%
Corporate bonds	7.17%
Treasury bills	3.18%

Comparing the volatilities in Table 10.4 we see that, as expected, small stocks have had the most variable historical returns, followed by large stocks. The returns of corporate bonds and Treasury bills are much less variable than stocks, with Treasury bills being the least volatile investment category.

Using Past Returns to Predict the Future: Estimation Error

To estimate the cost of capital for an investment, we need to determine the expected return that investors will require to compensate them for that investment's risk. If we assume that the distribution of past returns and the distribution of future returns are the same, one approach we could take is to look at the return investors expected to earn in the past on the same or similar investments, and assume they will require the same return in the future.

Two difficulties arise with this approach. The first difficulty is that we do not know what investors expected in the past; we can only observe the actual returns that were realized. In 2002, for example, investors lost more than 22% investing in the S&P 500, which is surely not what they expected at the beginning of the year (or they would have invested in Treasury bills instead!). If we believe that investors are neither overly optimistic nor overly pessimistic on average, however, then over time the average realized return should match investors' expected return.

Armed with this assumption, we can use a security's historical average return to estimate its actual expected return. But here we encounter the second difficulty—the average return is just an estimate of the expected return. As with all statistics, an estimation error will occur. Given the volatility of stock returns, this estimation error will be large even when we have many years of data.

We measure the degree of estimation error statistically through the standard error of the estimate. The **standard error** is the standard deviation of the estimated value of the mean of the actual distribution around its true value; that is, it is the standard deviation of the average return. The standard error provides an indication of how far the sample average might deviate from the expected return. If we assume that the distribution of a stock's return is identical each year, and that each year's return is independent of prior years' returns,[8] then the standard error of the estimate of the expected return can be found from the following formula:

Standard Error of the Estimate of the Expected Return

$$SD(\text{Average of Independent, Identical Risks}) = \frac{SD(\text{Individual Risk})}{\sqrt{\text{Number of Observations}}} \quad (10.8)$$

Because the average return will be within two standard errors of the true expected return approximately 95% of the time,[9] the standard error can be used to determine a reasonable range for the true expected value. The **95% confidence interval** for the expected return is defined as

$$\text{Historical Average Return} \pm (2 \times \text{Standard Error}) \quad (10.9)$$

For example, from 1926 to 2004 the average return of the S&P 500 was 12.3% with a volatility of 20.36%. Assuming its returns are drawn from an independent and identical distribution (IID) each year, the 95% confidence interval for the expected return of the S&P 500 during this period is

$$12.3\% \pm 2\left(\frac{20.36\%}{\sqrt{79}}\right) = 12.3\% \pm 4.6\%$$

or a range from 7.7% to 16.9%. Thus, even with 79 years of data, we cannot estimate the expected return of the S&P 500 very accurately. If we believe the distribution may have changed over time and we can use only more recent data to estimate the expected return, then the estimate will be even less accurate.

---

8. The assumption that the returns of a security are independent and identically distributed (IID) means that the likelihood that this year's return has a given outcome is the same as in prior years and does not depend on past returns, in the same way that the odds of a coin coming up heads do not depend on past flips. It turns out to be a reasonable first approximation for stock returns.

9. If returns are independent and from a normal distribution, then the estimated mean will be within two standard errors of the true mean 95.44% of the time. Even if returns are not normally distributed, this formula is approximately correct with a sufficient number of independent observations.

Arithmetic Average Returns Versus Compound Annual Returns

We compute average annual returns by calculating an *arithmetic* average. An alternative is the compound annual return (also called the compound annual growth rate, or CAGR), which is computed as the *geometric* average of the annual returns $R_1, \ldots, R_T$:

Compound Annual Return =
$$[(1 + R_1) \times (1 + R_2) \times \cdots \times (1 + R_T)]^{1/T} - 1$$

In other words, we compute the return from year 1 through T by compounding the annual returns, and then convert the result to an annual yield by taking it to the power $1/T$.

For the S&P 500, the compound annual return for 1926–2004 was 10.32%. That is, $1 invested at 10.32% for the 79 years from 1926 to 2004 would grow to

$$\$100 \times (1.1032)^{79} = \$234,253$$

This is equivalent (up to rounding error) to the growth in the S&P 500 during the same period. Similarly, the compound annual return for small stocks is 15.41%, for corporate bonds is 6.29%, and for Treasury bills is 3.83%.

In each case, the compound annual return is below the average annual return shown in Table 10.3. This difference reflects the fact that returns are volatile. To see the effect of volatility, suppose an investment has annual returns of +20% one year and −20% the next year. The average annual return is $\frac{1}{2}(20\% - 20\%) = 0\%$. But the value of $1 invested after two years is

$$\$1 \times (1.20) \times (0.80) = \$0.96$$

That is, an investor would have lost money. Why? Because the 20% gain happens on a $1 investment, whereas the 20% loss happens on a larger investment of $1.20. In this case, the compound annual return is

$$(0.96)^{1/2} - 1 = -2.02\%$$

This logic implies that the compound annual return will always be below the average return, and the difference grows with the volatility of the annual returns. (Typically, the difference is about half of the variance of the returns.)

Which is a better description of an investment's return? The compound annual return is a better description of the long-run *historical* performance of an investment. It describes the equivalent risk-free return that would be required to duplicate the investment's performance over the same time period. The ranking of the long-run performance of different investments coincides with the ranking of their compound annual returns. Thus the compound annual return is the return that is most often used for comparison purposes. For example, mutual funds generally report their compound annual returns over the last five or ten years.

Conversely, we should use the arithmetic average return when we are trying to estimate an investment's *expected* return over a *future* horizon based on its past performance. If we view past returns as independent draws from the same distribution, then the arithmetic average return provides an unbiased estimate of the true expected return. However, for this result to hold we must compute the historical returns using the same time intervals as the expected return we are estimating. (E.g. we use the average of past monthly returns to estimate the future monthly return, or the average of past annual returns to estimate the future annual return.) Because of estimation error the estimate for different time intervals will generally differ from the result one would get by simply compounding the average annual return. With enough data however, the results will coincide. For example, if the investment mentioned above is equally likely to have annual returns of +20% and −20% in the future, then if we observe many 2-year periods, a $1 investment will be equally likely to grow to

$$(1.20)(1.20) = \$1.44, \ (1.20)(0.80) = \$0.96,$$
$$(0.80)(1.20) = \$0.96, \text{ or } (0.80)(0.80) = \$0.64.$$

Thus, the average 2-year return will be (1.44 + 0.96 + 0.96 + 0.64)/4 = $1, so that the average annual and 2-year returns will both be 0%.

Individual stocks tend to be even more volatile than large portfolios, and many have been in existence for only a few years, providing little data with which to estimate returns. Because of the relatively large estimation error in such cases, the average return investors earned in the past is not a reliable estimate of a security's expected return. Instead, we need to derive an alternative method to estimate the expected return—one that relies on more reliable statistical estimates. In the remainder of this chapter, the strategy we will follow is to first consider how to measure a security's risk, and then use the relationship between risk and return—which we must still determine—to estimate its expected return.

EXAMPLE
10.4

The Accuracy of Expected Return Estimates

Problem

Using the returns for the S&P 500 from 1996–2004 only (see Table 10.2), what is the 95% confidence interval for our estimate of the S&P 500's expected return?

Solution

Earlier, we calculated the average return for the S&P 500 during this period to be 11.4%, with a volatility of 20.6% (see Example 10.3). The standard error of our estimate of the expected return is $20.6\% / \sqrt{9} = 6.9\%$, and the 95% confidence interval is 11.4% ± (2 × 6.9%), or from −2.4% to 25.2%. As this example shows, with only a few years of data, we cannot reliably estimate expected returns for stocks.

CONCEPT CHECK

1. How do we estimate the average annual return of an investment?

2. We have 79 years of data on the S&P 500 returns, yet we cannot estimate the expected return of the S&P 500 very accurately. Why?

10.4 The Historical Tradeoff Between Risk and Return

In Chapter 3, we discussed the idea that investors are risk averse: The benefit they receive from an increase in income is smaller than the personal cost of an equivalent decrease in income. This idea suggests that investors would not choose to hold a portfolio that is more volatile unless they expected to earn a higher return. In this section, we quantify the historical relationship between volatility and average returns.

The Returns of Large Portfolios

In Tables 10.3 and 10.4, we computed the historical average returns and volatilities for several different types of investments. We combine those data in Table 10.5, which lists the volatility and excess return for each investment. The **excess return** is the difference between the average return for the investment and the average return for Treasury bills, a risk-free investment.

TABLE 10.5 **Volatility Versus Excess Return of U.S. Small Stocks, Large Stocks (S&P 500), Corporate Bonds, and Treasury Bills, 1926–2004**

Investment	Return Volatility (Standard Deviation)	Excess Return (Average Return in Excess of Treasury Bills)
Small stocks	42.75%	18.24%
S&P 500	20.36%	8.45%
Corporate bonds	7.17%	2.65%
Treasury bills	3.18%	0.00%

The Historical Tradeoff Between Risk and Return in Large Portfolios, 1926–2004

Also included are a mid-cap portfolio composed of the 10% of U.S. stocks whose size is just below the median of all U.S. stocks, and a world portfolio of large stocks from North America, Europe, and Asia. Note the general increasing relationship between historical volatility and average return for these large portfolios.

Source: CRSP, Morgan Stanley Capital International and Global Financial Data.

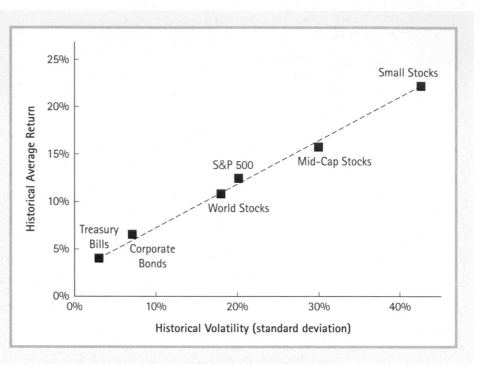

In Figure 10.5, we plot the average return versus the volatility of each type of investment given in Table 10.5. We also include data for a large portfolio of mid-cap stocks, or stocks of median size in the U.S. market, as well as a world index of the largest stocks traded in stock markets in North America, Europe, and Asia. Note the positive relationship: The investments with higher volatility have rewarded investors with higher average returns. Figure 10.5 is consistent with our view that investors are risk averse. Riskier investments must offer investors higher average returns to compensate them for the extra risk they are taking on.

The Returns of Individual Stocks

Figure 10.5 suggests the following simple model of the risk premium: Investments with higher volatility should have a higher risk premium and therefore higher returns. Indeed, looking at Figure 10.5 it is tempting to draw a line through the portfolios and conclude that all investments should lie on or near this line—that is, expected return should rise proportionately with volatility. This conclusion appears to be approximately true for the large portfolios we have looked at so far. Is it correct? Does it apply to individual stocks?

Unfortunately, the answer to both questions is no. Figure 10.6 shows that, if we look at the volatility and return of individual stocks, we do not see any clear relationship between them. Each point represents the returns from 1926 to 2004 of investing in the Nth largest stock traded in the United States (updated quarterly) for $N = 1$ to 500.

We can make several important observations from these data. First, there is a relationship between size and risk: Larger stocks have lower volatility overall. In addition, even the largest stocks are typically more volatile than a portfolio of large stocks, the S&P 500. Finally, there is no clear relationship between volatility and return. While the smallest

FIGURE 10.6

Historical Volatility and Return for 500 Individual Stocks, by Size, Updated Quarterly, 1926–2004

Unlike the case for large portfolios, there is no precise relationship between volatility and average return for individual stocks. Individual stocks have higher volatility and lower average returns than the relationship shown for large portfolios.

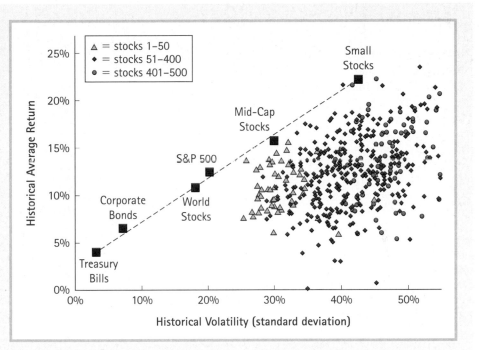

stocks have a slightly higher average return, many stocks have higher volatility and lower average returns than other stocks. And all stocks seem to have higher risk and lower returns than we would have predicted from a simple extrapolation of our data from large portfolios.

Thus, while volatility seems be a reasonable measure of risk when evaluating a large portfolio, it is not adequate to explain the returns of individual securities. What are we to make of this fact? Why wouldn't investors demand a higher return from stocks with a higher volatility? And how is it that the S&P 500—a portfolio of the 500 largest stocks—is so much less risky than all of the 500 stocks individually? To answer these questions, we need to think more carefully about how to measure risk for an investor.

CONCEPT CHECK

1. What is the excess return?

2. Is it true that expected returns for individual stocks increase proportionately with volatility?

10.5 Common Versus Independent Risk

In this section we explain why the risk of an individual security differs from the risk of a portfolio composed of similar securities. We begin with an example from the insurance industry. Consider two types of home insurance: theft insurance and earthquake insurance. Let us assume, for the purpose of illustration, that the risk of each of these two hazards is similar for a given home in the San Francisco area. Each year there is about a 1% chance that the home will be robbed and a 1% chance that the home will be damaged by an earthquake.

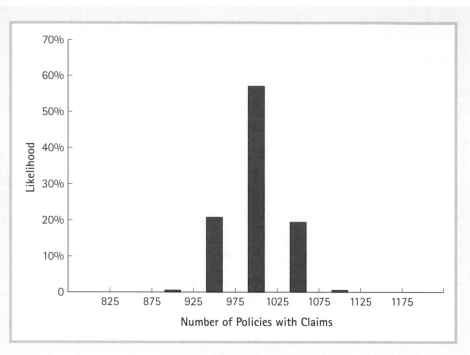

FIGURE 10.7

Likelihood of Different Numbers of Annual Claims for a Portfolio of 100,000 Theft Insurance Policies

The distribution assumes that there is a 1% chance of theft for an individual home, and that the incidence of theft is independent across homes. The number of claims is generally very close to 1000, or 1% of the policies written. The number of claims will almost always be between 875 and 1125 (0.875% and 1.125% of the number of policies written).

In this case, the chance the insurance company will pay a claim for a single home is the same for both types of insurance policies. Suppose an insurance company writes 100,000 policies of each type for homeowners in San Francisco. We know that the risks of the individual policies are similar, but are the risks of the portfolios of policies similar?

First consider theft insurance. Because the chance of a theft for any given home is 1%, we would expect about 1% of the 100,000 homes to experience a robbery. Thus the number of theft claims will be about 1000 per year. The actual number of claims may be a bit higher or lower each year, but not by much. Indeed, Figure 10.7 shows the likelihood that the insurance company will receive different numbers of claims, assuming that instances of theft are independent of one another (that is, the fact that one house is robbed does not change the odds of other houses being robbed). Figure 10.7 shows that the number of claims will almost always be between 875 and 1125 (0.875% and 1.125% of the number of policies written). In this case, if the insurance company holds reserves sufficient to cover 1200 claims, it will almost certainly have enough to meet its obligations on its theft insurance policies.

Now consider earthquake insurance. There is a 99% chance that an earthquake will not occur. All of the homes are in the same city, so if an earthquake does occur, all homes are likely to be affected and the insurance company can expect 100,000 claims. As a result, the insurance company will have to hold reserves sufficient to cover claims on all 100,000 policies it wrote to meet its obligations if an earthquake occurs.

Thus earthquake and theft insurance lead to portfolios with very different risk characteristics. For earthquake insurance, the number of claims is very risky. It will most likely be zero, but there is a 1% chance that the insurance company will have to pay claims on *all* the policies it wrote. In this case, the risk of the portfolio of insurance policies is no different from the risk of any single policy—it is still all or nothing. Conversely, for theft insurance the number of claims in a given year is quite predictable. Year in and year out, it will be very close to 1% of the total number of policies, or 1000 claims. The portfolio of theft insurance policies has almost no risk![10]

Why are the portfolios of insurance policies so different when the individual policies themselves are quite similar? Intuitively, the key difference between them is that an earthquake affects all houses simultaneously, so the risk is perfectly correlated across homes. We call risk that is perfectly correlated **common risk**. In contrast, we assume that thefts in different houses are not related to each other, so the risk of theft is uncorrelated and independent across homes. We call this type of risk **independent risk**. When risks are independent, some individual homeowners are unlucky and others are lucky, but overall the number of claims is quite predictable. The averaging out of independent risks in a large portfolio is called **diversification**.[11]

We can quantify this difference in terms of the standard deviation of the percentage of claims. First consider the standard deviation for an individual homeowner. At the beginning of the year, the homeowner expects a 1% chance of placing a claim for either type of insurance. But at the end of the year, the homeowner will have filed a claim (100%) or not (0%). Using Eq. 10.2 the standard deviation is

$$SD(\text{Claim}) = \sqrt{Var(\text{Claim})}$$
$$= \sqrt{0.99 \times (0 - 0.01)^2 + 0.01 \times (1 - 0.01)^2} = 9.95\%$$

For the homeowner, this standard deviation is the same for a loss from earthquake or theft.

Now consider the standard deviation of the percentage of claims for the insurance company. In the case of earthquake insurance, because the risk is common, the percentage of claims is either 100% or 0%, just as it was for the homeowner. Thus the percentage of claims received by the earthquake insurer is also 1% on average, with a 9.95% standard deviation.

While the theft insurer also receives 1% of claims on average, because the risk of theft is independent across households, the portfolio is much less risky. To quantify this difference, let's calculate the standard deviation of the average claim using Eq. 10.8. Recall that when risks are independent and identical, the standard deviation of the average is known as the standard error, which declines with the square root of the number of observations. Therefore,

$$SD(\text{Percentage Theft Claims}) = \frac{SD(\text{Individual Claim})}{\sqrt{\text{Number of Observations}}}$$
$$= \frac{9.95\%}{\sqrt{100,000}} = 0.03\%$$

Thus there is almost *no* risk for the theft insurer.

---

10. In the case of insurance, this difference in risk—and therefore in required reserves—can lead to a significant difference in the cost of the insurance. Indeed, earthquake insurance is generally thought to be more expensive to purchase, even though the risk to an individual household may be similar to other risks, such as theft or fire.

11. Harry Markowitz was the first to formalize the role of diversification in forming an optimal stock market portfolio. See H. M. Markowitz, "Portfolio Selection," *Journal of Finance* 7 (1952): 77–91.

The principle of diversification is used routinely in the insurance industry. In addition to theft insurance, many other forms of insurance (life, health, auto) rely on the fact that the number of claims is relatively predictable in a large portfolio. Even in the case of earthquake insurance, insurers can achieve some diversification by selling policies in different geographical regions or by combining different types of policies. Diversification is used to reduce risk in many other settings. For example, many systems are designed with redundancy to decrease the risk of a disruption: Firms often add redundancy to critical parts of the manufacturing process, NASA puts more than one antenna on its space probes, automobiles contain spare tires, and so forth.

**EXAMPLE
10.5**

Diversification and Gambling

Problem

Roulette wheels are typically marked with the numbers 1 through 36 plus 0 and 00. Each of these outcomes is equally likely every time the wheel is spun. If you place a bet on any one number and are correct, the payoff is 35 : 1; that is, if you bet $1, you will receive $36 if you win ($35 plus your original $1) and nothing if you lose. Suppose you place a $1 bet on your favorite number. What is the casino's expected profit? What is the standard deviation of this profit for a single bet? Suppose 9 million similar bets are placed throughout the casino in a typical month. What is the standard deviation of the casino's average revenues per dollar bet each month?

Solution

Because there are 38 numbers on the wheel, the odds of winning are 1 / 38. The casino loses $35 if you win, and makes $1 if you lose. Therefore, using Eq. 10.1, the casino's expected profit is

$$E[\text{Payoff}] = (1 / 38) \times (-\$35) + (37 / 38) \times (\$1) = \$0.0526$$

That is, for each dollar bet, the casino earns 5.26 cents on average. For a single bet, we calculate the standard deviation of this profit using Eq. 10.2 as

$$SD(\text{Payoff}) = \sqrt{(1 / 38) \times (-35 - 0.0526)^2 + (37 / 38) \times (1 - 0.0526)^2} = \$5.76$$

This standard deviation is quite large relative to the magnitude of the profits. But if many such bets are placed, the risk will be diversified. Using Eq. 10.8, the standard deviation of the casino's average revenues per dollar bet is only

$$SD(\text{Average Payoff}) = \frac{\$5.76}{\sqrt{9,000,000}} = \$0.0019$$

In other words, the 95% confidence interval for the casino's profits per dollar bet is $0.0526 ± (2 × 0.0019) = $0.0488 to $0.0564. Given $9 million in bets placed, the casino's monthly profits will almost always be between $439,000 and $508,000, which is very little risk. The key assumption, of course, is that the outcome of each bet is independent of each other. If the $9 million were placed in a single bet, the casino's risk would be large—losing 35 × $9 million = $315 million if the bet wins. For this reason, casinos often impose limits on the amount of any individual bet.

CONCEPT CHECK

1. What is the difference between common risk and independent risk?

2. Under what circumstances will risk be diversified in a large portfolio of insurance contracts?

10.6 Diversification in Stock Portfolios

As the insurance example indicates, the risk of a portfolio of insurance contracts depends on whether the individual risks within it are common or independent. Independent risks are diversified in a large portfolio, whereas common risks are not. Let's consider the implication of this distinction for the risk of stock portfolios.

Firm-Specific Versus Systematic Risk

Over any given time period, the risk of holding a stock is that the dividends plus the final stock price will be higher or lower than expected, which makes the realized return risky. What causes dividends or stock prices, and therefore returns, to be higher or lower than we expect? Usually, stock prices and dividends fluctuate due to two types of news:

1. *Firm-specific news* is good or bad news about the company itself. For example, a firm might announce that it has been successful in gaining market share within its industry.

2. *Market-wide news* is news about the economy as a whole and therefore affects all stocks. For instance, the Federal Reserve might announce that it will lower interest rates to boost the economy.

Fluctuations of a stock's return that are due to firm-specific news are independent risks. Like theft across homes, these risks are unrelated across stocks. This type of risk is also referred to as **firm-specific, idiosyncratic, unsystematic, unique,** or **diversifiable risk**.

Fluctuations of a stock's return that are due to market-wide news represent common risk. As with earthquakes, all stocks are affected simultaneously by the news. This type of risk is also called **systematic, undiversifiable,** or **market risk**.

When we combine many stocks in a large portfolio, the firm-specific risks for each stock will average out and be diversified. Good news will affect some stocks, and bad news will affect others, but the amount of good or bad news overall will be relatively constant. The systematic risk, however, will affect all firms—and therefore the entire portfolio—and will not be diversified.

Let's consider an example. Suppose type S firms are affected *only* by the strength of the economy, a systematic risk which has a 50–50 chance of being either strong or weak. If the economy is strong, type S stocks will earn a return of 40%; if the economy is weak, their return will be -20%. Because these firms face systematic risk (the strength of the economy), holding a large portfolio of type S firms will not diversify the risk. When the economy is strong, the portfolio will have the same return of 40% as each type S firm; when the economy is weak, the portfolio will also have a return of -20%.

Now consider type I firms, which are affected only by idiosyncratic, firm-specific risks. Their returns are equally likely to be 35% or -25%, based on factors specific to each firm's local market. Because these risks are firm specific, if we hold a portfolio of the stocks of many type I firms, the risk is diversified. About half of the firms will have returns of 35%, and half will have returns of -25%, so that the return of the portfolio will be the average return of $50\% \, (0.35) + 50\% \, (-0.25) = 5\%$.

Figure 10.8 illustrates how volatility declines with the size of the portfolio for type S and I firms. Type S firms have only systematic risk. As with earthquake insurance, the volatility of the portfolio does not change as the number of firms increases. Type I firms have only idiosyncratic risk. As with theft insurance, the risk is diversified as the number of firms increases, and volatility declines. As is evident from Figure 10.8, with a large number of firms, the risk is essentially eliminated.

Volatility of Portfolios of Type S and I Stocks

Because type S firms have only systematic risk, the volatility of the portfolio does not change. Type I firms have only idiosyncratic risk, which is diversified and eliminated as the number of firms in the portfolio increases. Typical stocks carry a mix of both types of risk, so that the risk of the portfolio declines as idiosyncratic risk is diversified away, but systematic risk still remains.

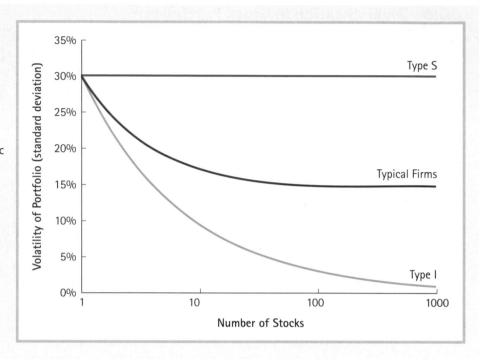

Of course, actual firms are not like type S or I firms. Firms are affected by both systematic, market-wide risks and firm-specific risks. Figure 10.8 also shows how the volatility changes with the size of a portfolio containing the stocks of typical firms. When firms carry both types of risk, only the firm-specific risk will be diversified when we combine many firm's stocks into a portfolio. The volatility will therefore decline until only the systematic risk, which affects all firms, remains.

This example explains one of the puzzles in Figure 10.6. There we saw that the S&P 500 had much lower volatility than any of the individual stocks. Now we can see why: The individual stocks each contain firm-specific risk, which is eliminated when we combine them into a large portfolio. Thus the portfolio as a whole can have lower volatility than each of the stocks within it.

EXAMPLE 10.6

Portfolio Volatility

Problem

What is the volatility of the average return of ten type S firms? What is the volatility of the average return of ten type I firms?

Solution

Type S firms have equally likely returns of 40% or -20%. Their expected return is $\frac{1}{2}(40\%) + \frac{1}{2}(-20\%) = 10\%$, so

$$SD(R_S) = \sqrt{\frac{1}{2}(0.40 - 0.10)^2 + \frac{1}{2}(-0.20 - 0.10)^2} = 30\%$$

Because all type S firms have high or low returns at the same time, the average return of ten type S firms is also 40% or -20%. Thus it has the same volatility of 30%, as shown in Figure 10.8.

Type I firms have equally likely returns of 35% or -25%. Their expected return is $\frac{1}{2}(35\%) + \frac{1}{2}(-25\%) = 5\%$, so

$$SD(R_I) = \sqrt{\frac{1}{2}(0.35 - 0.05)^2 + \frac{1}{2}(-0.25 - 0.05)^2} = 30\%$$

Because the returns of type I firms are independent, using Eq. 10.8, the average return of ten type I firms has volatility of $30\% / \sqrt{10} = 9.5\%$, as shown in Figure 10.8.

No Arbitrage and the Risk Premium

Consider again type I firms, which are affected only by firm-specific risk. Because each individual type I firm is risky, should investors expect to earn a risk premium when investing in type I firms?

In a competitive market, the answer is no. To see why, suppose the expected return of type I firms exceeds the risk-free interest rate. Then by holding a large portfolio of many type I firms, investors could diversify the firm-specific risk of these firms and earn a return above the risk-free interest rate without taking on any significant risk.

The situation just described is very close to an arbitrage opportunity, which investors would find very attractive. They would borrow money at the risk-free interest rate and invest it in a large portfolio of type I firms, which offers a higher return with only a tiny amount of risk.[12] As more investors take advantage of this situation and purchase shares of type I firms, the current share prices for type I firms would rise, lowering their expected return—recall that the current share price P_t is the denominator when computing the stock's return as in Eq. 10.4. This trading would stop only after the return of type I firms equaled the risk-free interest rate. Competition between investors drives the return of type I firms down to the risk-free return.

The preceding argument is essentially an application of the Law of One Price: Because a large portfolio of type I firms has no risk, it must earn the risk-free interest rate. This no-arbitrage argument suggests the following more general principle:

The risk premium for diversifiable risk is zero, so investors are not compensated for holding firm-specific risk.

This principle can be applied not just to type I firms, but to all stocks and securities. It implies that the risk premium of a stock is not affected by its diversifiable, firm-specific risk. If the diversifiable risk of stocks were compensated with an additional risk premium, then investors could buy the stocks, earn the additional premium, and simultaneously diversify and eliminate the risk. By doing so, investors could earn an additional premium without taking on additional risk. This opportunity to earn something for nothing would quickly be exploited and eliminated.[13]

Because investors can eliminate firm-specific risk "for free" by diversifying their portfolios, they will not require a reward or risk premium for holding it. However, diversification does not reduce systematic risk: Even holding a large portfolio, an investor will be exposed to risks that affect the entire economy and therefore affect all securities. Because investors are risk averse, they will demand a risk premium to hold systematic risk; otherwise

---

12. If investors could actually hold a large enough portfolio and completely diversify all the risk, then this would be a true arbitrage opportunity.

13. The main thrust of this argument can be found in S. Ross, "The Arbitrage Theory of Capital Asset Pricing," *Journal of Economic Theory* 13 (December 1976): 341–360.

they would be better off selling their stocks and investing in risk-free bonds. Because idiosyncratic risk can be eliminated for free by diversifying, whereas systematic risk can be eliminated only by sacrificing expected returns, it is a security's systematic risk that determines the risk premium investors require to hold it. This fact leads to a second key principle:

The risk premium of a security is determined by its systematic risk and does not depend on its diversifiable risk.

This principle implies that a stock's volatility, which is a measure of total risk (that is, systematic risk plus diversifiable risk), is not especially useful in determining the risk premium that investors will earn. For example, consider again type S and I firms. As calculated in Example 10.6, the volatility of a single type S or I firm is 30%. Although both types of firms have the same volatility, type S firms have an expected return of 10% and type I firms have an expected return of 5%. The difference in expected returns derives from the difference in the kind of risk each firm bears. Type I firms have only firm-specific risk, which does not require a risk premium, so the expected return of 5% for type I firms equals the risk-free interest rate. Type S firms have only systematic risk. Because investors will require compensation for taking on this risk, the expected return of 10% for type S firms provides investors with a 5% risk premium above the risk-free interest rate.

COMMON MISTAKE   A Fallacy of Long-Run Diversification

We have seen that investors can greatly reduce their risk by dividing their investment dollars over many different investments, eliminating the diversifiable risk in their portfolios. It is sometimes argued that the same logic applies over time: By investing for many years, we can also diversify the risk we face during any particular year. Is this correct? In the long run, does risk still matter?

Equation 10.8 tells us that if returns each year are independent, the volatility of the average annual return declines with the number of years that we invest. Of course, as long-term investors, we don't care about the volatility of our *average* return; instead, we care about the volatility of our *cumulative* return over the period. This volatility grows with the investment horizon, as illustrated in the following example.

In 1925, large U.S. stocks increased in value by about 30%. In fact, a $77 investment at the start of 1925 would have grown to $77 × 1.30 = $100 by the end of the year. We see from Figure 10.1 that if that $100 were invested in the S&P 500 from 1926 onward, it would have grown to about $234,000 by the start of 2005. But suppose that mining and transportation strikes had caused stocks to drop by 35% in 1925. Then the initial $77 invested would be worth only $77 × (1 − 35%) = $50 at the beginning of 1926. If returns from then on were unchanged, the investment would be worth half as much in 2005, or $117,000.

Thus, if future returns are not affected by today's return, then an increase or a decline in the value of our portfolio today will translate into the same percentage increase or decrease in the value of our portfolio in the future, so there is no diversification over time. The only way the length of the time horizon can reduce risk is if a below-average return this year implies that returns are more likely to be above average in the future (and vice versa), a phenomenon sometimes referred to as *mean reversion*. Mean reversion implies that past low returns can be used to predict future high returns in the stock market.

For short horizons of a few years, there is no evidence of mean reversion in the stock market. For longer horizons, there is some evidence of mean reversion historically, but it is not clear how reliable this evidence is (there are not enough decades of accurate stock market data available) or whether the pattern will continue. Even if there is long-run mean reversion in stock returns, a buy-and-hold diversification strategy is still not optimal: Because mean reversion implies that past returns can be used to predict future returns, one should invest more in stocks when returns are predicted to be high, and invest less when they are predicted to be low. This strategy is very different from the diversification we achieve by holding many stocks, where we cannot predict which stocks will have good or bad firm-specific shocks.

We now have an explanation for the second puzzle of Figure 10.6. While volatility might be a reasonable measure of risk for a large portfolio, it is not an appropriate metric for an individual security. Thus, there should be no clear relationship between volatility and average returns for individual securities. Consequently, to estimate a security's expected return, we need to find a measure of a security's systematic risk.

In Chapter 3, we used a simple example to show that an investment's risk premium depends on how its returns move in relation to the overall economy. In particular, risk-averse investors will demand a premium to invest in securities that will do poorly in bad times (recall, for example, the performance of small stocks in Figure 10.1 during the Great Depression). This idea coincides with the notion of systematic risk we have defined in this chapter. Economy-wide risk—that is, the risk of recessions and booms—is systematic risk that cannot be diversified. Therefore an asset that moves with the economy contains systematic risk and so requires a risk premium.

EXAMPLE 10.7

Diversifiable Versus Systematic Risk

Problem

Which of the following risks of a stock are likely to be firm-specific, diversifiable risks, and which are likely to be systematic risks? Which risks will affect the risk premium that investors will demand?

a. The risk that the founder and CEO retires
b. The risk that oil prices rise, increasing production costs
c. The risk that a product design is faulty and the product must be recalled
d. The risk that the economy slows, reducing demand for the firm's products

Solution

Because oil prices and the health of the economy affect all stocks, risks (b) and (d) are systematic risks. These risks are not diversified in a large portfolio, and so will affect the risk premium that investors require to invest in a stock. Risks (a) and (c) are firm-specific risks, and so are diversifiable. While these risks should be considered when estimating a firm's future cash flows, they will not affect the risk premium that investors will require and, therefore, will not affect a firm's cost of capital.

CONCEPT CHECK

1. Explain why the risk premium of diversifiable risk is zero.

2. Why is the risk premium of a security determined only by its systematic risk?

10.7 Estimating the Expected Return

When evaluating the risk of an investment, an investor will care about its systematic risk, which cannot be eliminated through diversification. In exchange for bearing systematic risk, investors want to be compensated by earning a higher return. So, to determine the expected return investors will require to undertake an investment, we must take two steps:

1. Measure the investment's systematic risk.

2. Determine the risk premium required to compensate for that amount of systematic risk.

Once we have completed steps (1) and (2), we can estimate the expected return of the investment. In this section, we outline the main method used in practice.

Measuring Systematic Risk

To measure the systematic risk of a stock, we must determine how much of the variability of its return is due to systematic, market-wide risks versus diversifiable, firm-specific risks. That is, we would like to know how sensitive the stock is to systematic shocks that affect the economy as a whole.

If we wanted to determine how sensitive a stock's return is to interest rate changes, for example, we would look at how much the return tends to change on average for each 1% change in interest rates. Similarly, if we want to determine how sensitive a stock's return is to oil prices, we would examine the average change in the return for each 1% change in oil prices. In the same way, if we wanted to determine how sensitive a stock is to systematic risk, we can look at the average change in the return for each 1% change in the return of *a portfolio that fluctuates solely due to systematic risk.*

Thus the key step to measuring systematic risk is finding a portfolio that contains *only* systematic risk. Then changes in the price of this portfolio will correspond to systematic shocks to the economy. We call such a portfolio an **efficient portfolio**. An efficient portfolio cannot be diversified further—that is, there is no way to reduce the risk of the portfolio without lowering its expected return.

As we will see over the next few chapters, the best way to identify an efficient portfolio is one of the key questions in modern finance. Because diversification improves with the number of stocks held in a portfolio, an efficient portfolio should be a large portfolio containing many different stocks. Thus it is reasonable to consider a portfolio that contains all shares of all stocks and securities in the market. We call this portfolio the **market portfolio**. Because it is difficult to find data for the returns of many bonds and small stocks, it is common in practice to use the S&P 500 portfolio as an approximation for the market portfolio, under the assumption that the S&P 500 is large enough to be essentially fully diversified.

If we assume that the market portfolio (or the S&P 500) is efficient, then changes in the value of the market portfolio represent systematic shocks to the economy. Knowing this, we can measure the systematic risk of a security's return by its beta. The **beta (β)** of a security is the sensitivity of the security's return to the return of the overall market. More precisely,

The beta is the expected percent change in the excess return of a security for a 1% change in the excess return of the market portfolio.

EXAMPLE 10.8

Estimating Beta

Problem

Suppose the market portfolio excess return tends to increase by 47% when the economy is strong and decline by 25% when the economy is weak. What is the beta of a type S firm whose excess return is 40% on average when the economy is strong and −20% when the economy is weak? What is the beta of a type I firm that bears only idiosyncratic, firm-specific risk?

Solution

The systematic risk of the strength of the economy produces a 47% − (−25%) = 72% change in the return of the market portfolio. The type S firm's return changes by 40% − (−20%) = 60% on average. Thus the firm's beta is $\beta_S = 60\% / 72\% = 0.833$. That is, each 1% change in the return of the market portfolio leads to a 0.833% change in the type S firm's return on average.

The return of a type I firm that has only firm-specific risk, however, is not affected by the strength of the economy. Its return is affected only by factors that are specific to the firm. Whether the economy is strong or weak, it will have the same expected return, and thus $\beta_I = 0\% / 72\% = 0$.

We will look at statistical techniques for estimating beta from historical data in Chapter 12. It is important to note that we can estimate beta reasonably accurately using just a few years of data (which was not the case for expected returns, as we saw in Example 10.4). Using the S&P 500 to represent the market's return, Table 10.6 shows the betas of several stocks, as well as the average betas for stocks within their industry, during 2000–2005. As shown in the table, each 1% change in the excess return of the market during this period led, on average, to a 2.17% change in the excess return for Intel, but only a 0.50% change in the excess return for Coca-Cola.

TABLE 10.6   **Betas With Respect to the S&P 500 for Individual Stocks and Average Betas for Stocks in Their Industries (based on monthly data for 2000–2005)**

Industry	Beta	Ticker	Firm	Beta
Gold and Silver	−0.04	NEM	Newmont Mining Corporation	0.02
Beverages (Alcoholic)	0.23	BUD	Anheuser-Busch Companies, Inc.	0.10
Personal and Household Prods.	0.25	PG	The Procter & Gamble Company	0.19
Food Processing	0.34	HNZ	H. J. Heinz Company	0.37
		HSY	The Hershey Company	−0.10
Beverages (Nonalcoholic)	0.43	KO	The Coca-Cola Company	0.50
Electric Utilities	0.48	EIX	Edison International	0.50
Major Drugs	0.48	PFE	Pfizer Inc.	0.54
Restaurants	0.69	SBUX	Starbucks Corporation	0.60
Retail (Grocery)	0.74	SWY	Safeway Inc.	0.67
Conglomerates	0.84	GE	General Electric Company	0.85
Forestry and Wood Products	0.95	WY	Weyerhaeuser Company	0.96
Recreational Products	1.00	HDI	Harley-Davidson, Inc.	1.14
Apparel/Accessories	1.12	LIZ	Liz Claiborne, Inc.	0.90
Retail (Home Improvement)	1.22	HD	Home Depot, Inc.	1.43
Auto and Truck Manufacturers	1.44	GM	General Motors Corporation	1.20
Computer Hardware	1.60	AAPL	Apple Computer, Inc.	1.35
Software and Programming	1.74	ADBE	Adobe Systems, Inc.	1.84
		MSFT	Microsoft Corporation	1.12
Computer Services	1.77	YHOO	Yahoo! Inc.	2.80
Communications Equipment	2.20	CSCO	Cisco Systems, Inc.	2.28
Semiconductors	2.59	AMD	Advanced Micro Devices, Inc.	3.23
		INTC	Intel Corporation	2.17

Beta measures the sensitivity of a security to market-wide risk factors. For a stock, this value is related to how sensitive its underlying revenues and cash flows are to general economic conditions. Stocks in cyclical industries, in which revenues tend to vary greatly over the business cycle, are likely to be more sensitive to systematic risk and have higher betas than stocks in less sensitive industries.

For example, notice the relatively low betas of Edison International (a utility company), Anheuser-Busch (a beer-brewing company), and H. J. Heinz (a ketchup manufacturer). Utilities tend to be stable and highly regulated, and thus are insensitive to fluctuations in the overall market. Brewing and food companies are also very insensitive—the demand for their products appears to be unrelated to the booms and busts of the economy as a whole.

At the other extreme, technology stocks tend to have the highest betas; the average for the industry is close to 2, with the betas of Internet stocks (such as Yahoo!) being even higher. Shocks in the economy have an amplified impact on these stocks: When the market as a whole is up, Intel tends to rise almost twice as much; but when the market stumbles, Intel tends to fall almost twice as far.

Recall that beta differs from volatility. Volatility measures total risk—that is, both market and firm-specific risks—so that there is no necessary relationship between volatility and beta. Consider that Pfizer (a drug company) and Intel may have similar volatilities. Pfizer, however, has a much lower beta. While drug companies face a great deal of risk related to the development and approval of new drugs, this risk is unrelated to the rest of the economy. And though health care expenditures do vary a little with the state of the economy, they vary much less than expenditures on technology.

Estimating the Risk Premium

An investment opportunity with a beta of 2 carries twice as much systematic risk as an investment in the S&P 500. That is, for each dollar we invest in the opportunity, we could invest twice that amount in the S&P 500 and be exposed to the same amount of systematic risk. In general, the beta of an investment opportunity measures its amplification of systematic risk compared to the market as a whole, and investors will require a commensurate risk premium to make such an investment.

The risk premium investors can earn by holding the market portfolio is the difference between the market portfolio's expected return and the risk-free interest rate:

$$\text{Market Risk Premium} = E[R_{Mkt}] - r_f$$

The market risk premium is the reward investors expect to earn for holding a portfolio with a beta of 1. Because the systematic risk of any traded security is proportional to its beta, its risk premium will be proportional to beta. Therefore, to compensate investors for the time value of their money as well as the systematic risk they are taking by investing in security s, the expected return of the traded security should satisfy the following formula:

Estimating a Traded Security's Expected Return from Its Beta

$$E[R] = \text{Risk-Free Interest Rate} + \text{Risk Premium}$$
$$= r_f + \beta \times (E[R_{Mkt}] - r_f) \tag{10.10}$$

As an example, suppose the market risk premium is 6% and the risk-free interest rate is 5%. According to Eq. 10.10, investors' expected return for Yahoo! and Anheuser-Busch stocks is

$$E[R_{YHOO}] = 5\% + 2.80 \times 6\% = 21.8\%$$
$$E[R_{BUD}] = 5\% + 0.10 \times 6\% = 5.6\%$$

Thus, the difference in the average returns of these two stocks reported in the introduction of this chapter is not so surprising. Investors in Yahoo! expect a much higher return on average to compensate them for Yahoo!'s much higher systematic risk.

EXAMPLE
10.9

Expected Returns and Beta

Problem

Suppose the risk-free rate is 5% and the economy is equally likely to be strong or weak. Verify that Eq. 10.10 holds for the type S firms considered in Example 10.8.

Solution

If the economy is equally likely to be strong or weak, the expected return of the market is $E[R_{Mkt}] = 50\%(0.47) + 50\%(-0.25) = 11\%$, and the market risk premium is $E[R_{Mkt}] - r_f = 11\% - 5\% = 6\%$. Given the beta of 0.833 for type S firms that we calculated in Example 10.8, the estimate of the expected return for type S firms from Eq. 10.10 is

$$E[R] = r_f + \beta \times (E[R_{Mkt}] - r_f) = 5\% + 0.833 \times (11\% - 5\%) = 10\%$$

This matches their expected return: $50\%(0.4) + 50\%(-0.2) = 10\%$.

What happens if a stock has a negative beta? According to Eq. 10.10, such a stock would have a negative risk premium—it would have an expected return below the risk-free rate. While this might seem unreasonable at first, note that stock with a negative beta will tend to do well when times are bad, so owning it will provide insurance against the systematic risk of other stocks in the portfolio. (We saw an example of such a security in Example 3.10 in Chapter 3.) Risk-averse investors are willing to pay for this insurance by accepting a return below the risk-free interest rate.

CONCEPT CHECK
1. What is the market portfolio?
2. Define the beta of a security.

10.8 Risk and the Cost of Capital

Now that we have a means to measure systematic risk and determine the expected return of a traded security, we can turn to the final goal of this chapter: explaining how to calculate the cost of capital for an investment.

Recall that a firm's cost of capital for an investment or project is the expected return that its investors could earn on other securities with the same risk and maturity. Because the risk that determines expected returns is systematic risk, which is measured by beta, the cost of capital for an investment is the expected return available on securities with the same beta. Equation 10.10 gives the expected return for investing in such a traded security, so it also is the cost of capital for investing in the project. Hence, the cost of capital, r, for investing in a project with a beta, β, is

Cost of Capital of a Project

$$r = r_f + \beta \times (E[R_{Mkt}] - r_f) \tag{10.11}$$

Thus, to determine a project's cost of capital, we need to estimate its beta. Estimating the beta of the project requires knowing the systematic risk of the project. A common assumption is to assume that the project has the same risk as the firm, or other firms whose investments are similar. If the firm has no debt, we can then use the beta of the firm's equity to estimate the beta for the project.[14] Betas for different stocks in the market can be obtained from online sources or from firms that specialize in calculating betas. In Chapter 12, we will develop statistical methods to estimate betas from historical returns.

EXAMPLE 10.10

Computing the Cost of Capital

Problem

Suppose that in the coming year, you expect Microsoft stock to have a volatility of 23% and a beta of 1.28, and McDonald's stock to have a volatility of 37% and a beta of 0.99. Which stock carries more total risk? Which has more systematic risk? If the risk-free interest rate is 4% and the market's expected return is 10%, estimate the cost of capital for a project with the same beta as McDonald's stock and a project with the same beta as Microsoft stock. Which project has a higher cost of capital?

Solution

Total risk is measured by volatility; therefore, McDonald's stock has more total risk. Systematic risk is measured by beta. Microsoft has a higher beta, so it has more systematic risk.

Given the estimated beta for Microsoft of 1.28, we expect the price for Microsoft's stock to move by 1.28% for every 1% move of the market. Therefore, Microsoft's risk premium will be 1.28 times the risk premium of the market, and the cost of capital for investing in a project with the same risk as Microsoft stock is

$$E[R_{MSFT}] = r_f + 1.28 \times 6\% = 4\% + 7.7\% = 11.7\%$$

McDonald's stock has a lower beta of 0.99. The cost of capital for investing in a project with the same risk as McDonald's stock is

$$E[R_{McD}] = r_f + 0.99 \times 6\% = 4\% + 5.9\% = 9.9\%$$

Because systematic risk cannot be diversified, it is systematic risk that determines the cost of capital; thus Microsoft has a higher cost of capital than McDonald's, even though it is less volatile.

Equations 10.10 and 10.11 for estimating the expected return and cost of capital are often referred to as the **Capital Asset Pricing Model (CAPM)**.[15] It is the most important method for estimating the cost of capital that is used in practice. We explore this model in detail in the next two chapters.

---

14. If the firm has debt, the beta of its equity will be affected by its leverage. We show how to adjust betas to correct for the firm's leverage in Chapter 14.

15. The CAPM was first developed independently by Lintner and Sharpe. See L. Lintner "The Valuation of Risk Assets and the Selection of Risky Investments in Stock Portfolios and Capital Budgets," *Review of Economics and Statistics* 47 (1965): 13–37; and W. F. Sharpe, "Capital Asset Prices: A Theory of Market Equilibrium under Conditions of Risk," *Journal of Finance* 19 (1964): 425–442.

1. What is the cost of capital of a project?

2. Is the cost of capital related to the systematic risk or unsystematic risk?

10.9 Capital Market Efficiency

In Chapter 9, we introduced the efficient markets hypothesis, which states that the expected return of any security should equal its cost of capital, and thus the NPV of trading a security is zero. Testing this hypothesis requires a method of determining the cost of capital of an investment, which we established in this chapter. With this additional background in place, we're prepared to reconsider the efficient markets hypothesis.

Notions of Efficiency

In this chapter, we have developed two important ideas regarding the cost of capital. First, the cost of capital of an investment should depend only on its systematic risk, and not its diversifiable risk. When this property holds, we refer to the market as an **efficient capital market**.

But even if the capital market is efficient, to determine a cost of capital we need a method to measure systematic risk. The Capital Asset Pricing Model provides such a method, and states that the expected return of any security, and thus the cost of capital of any investment, depends upon its beta with the market portfolio. The underlying assumption of the CAPM is that the *market portfolio is an efficient portfolio*—there is no way to reduce its risk without lowering its return. Note that the CAPM is a much stronger hypothesis than an efficient capital market. The CAPM states that the cost of capital depends only on systematic risk *and* that systematic risk can be measured precisely by an investment's beta with the market portfolio.

Empirical Evidence on Capital Market Competition

In the next three chapters, we will explore the theoretical motivations behind these notions of efficiency as well as their empirical support. But before doing so it is useful to discuss briefly here whether or not the assumption that the market portfolio is efficient is a good working approximation. That is, is it reasonable for a corporate manager to rely on the CAPM?

Intuitively, the efficiency of the market portfolio should result from competition. If the market portfolio were not efficient, investors could find strategies that would "beat the market" with higher average returns and lower risk. Investors will want to adopt these strategies. But not all investors can beat the market, because the sum of all investors' portfolios *is* the market portfolio. Hence security prices must change, and the returns from adopting these strategies must fall so that these strategies are no longer superior to the market portfolio.

The performance of active portfolio provides evidence that actual markets are very competitive. An active portfolio manager advertises his ability to pick stocks with average returns that exceed the return necessary to compensate for their systematic risk. By holding a portfolio of such stocks, a portfolio manager should be able to outperform the market portfolio. While many managers do have some ability to beat the market,[16] once we take

---

16. For recent evidence, see, for example, R. Wermers, "Mutual Fund Performance: An Empirical Decomposition into Stock-Picking Talent, Style, Transactions Costs and Expenses," *Journal of Finance* 55 (2000):1655-1695.

INTERVIEW WITH
Randall Lert

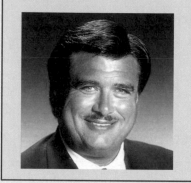

Randall P. Lert is the chief portfolio strategist for Russell Investment Group, the creators of the Russell 2000® Index. Randy is involved in the formation and implementation of investment policy for the firm, which manages more than $170 billion in assets (as of June 30, 2006) and advises clients who represent more than $2.4 trillion.

QUESTION: *How does diversification affect portfolio strategy and the risk-return tradeoff?*

ANSWER: Holding a large, strategically allocated portfolio across many asset classes maximizes your return for a given level of risk, because different markets are not perfectly correlated to each other. The *number* of stocks per se does not drive diversification; *weighting* does. A 1,000-stock portfolio with very divergent weightings from the market index will have more idiosyncratic risk than a 100-stock portfolio whose weights approximate the index. If I hold 100 stocks but underweight the 50 largest, which constitute half the market capitalization of the index, my portfolio will diverge more from the benchmark than a 100 stock portfolio holding the top 50 relatively close to market weight but scattering the other 50 stocks.

QUESTION: *In the U.S., history shows a relatively large reward for taking systematic equity risk versus holding bonds. What is your firm's view of this risk—reward tradeoff going forward?*

ANSWER: We believe that the reward for holding equity risk will be smaller in the future. The economic environment is less volatile, given the current-day regulatory climate and more stable central bank policy worldwide. For strategic asset allocation modeling purposes, we define the equity risk premium as the expected return for holding a well-diversified equity portfolio minus the risk free rate. We assume there is a premium for longer-maturity bonds and fixed income securities with credit risk—currently we, and others in the industry, believe that risk premium is about 3 percent relative to cash, and the risk premium of stocks relative to long-term bonds is another 3 percent, for about 6 percent equity risk premium.

QUESTION: *Historical evidence suggests that it is difficult for active fund managers to "beat the market." Why is this the case?*

ANSWER: Active management—trying to generate performance in excess of the market index—is a zero sum game, because "the market" is nothing more than the collection of investors participating in that asset class. Before transactions costs, the average investor's return must equal the market return. When measured against a correctly specified index, about half of all managers should outperform and half should under-perform. However, active managers have much higher transaction costs than an unmanaged index, so the number of underperforming managers is often higher. However, in a world where everybody indexed, there would be no market activity forcing securities to their current valuation levels. This process of active management, then, serves as the primary price discovery mechanism in modern capital markets.

QUESTION: *Given these challenges, how do you manage the risk of the portfolio yet still maximize performance?*

ANSWER: Active portfolio managers focus on idiosyncratic risk, which is normally measured as the standard deviation of a portfolio's return relative to the benchmark index. Most establish a *risk budget* that sets targets for this risk and then seek to generate the highest returns possible within that band of risk. Managers take that risk in two ways. They can bet on industry or economic sectors—for example, the airline industry—and overweight their portfolio to that industry. Or they can take a broader view and hold most economic sectors at roughly market weights, picking specific stocks in sectors that they think will outperform—say, Southwest Airlines. Generally, a larger number of small bets is better than a few large bets. If you bet on two sectors and they are the wrong ones, you are out of luck. Spreading the bet over many sectors gives you a greater chance of some working and balancing out the ones that don't. It diversifies your active management risk.

into account the fees that are charged by these funds, the empirical evidence indeed shows that active portfolio managers appear to have no ability to provide returns to their investors that outperform the market portfolio.[17]

The inability of portfolio managers to outperform the market is likely driven by competition. Investors flock to invest with mutual funds that have done well in the past. As a result, active portfolio managers who do well experience an inflow of new capital.[18] This inflow of capital, however, reduces the fund's returns: Now managers are forced to make larger trades (that have a greater impact on prices) or spread their trades over more (and potentially less attractive) stocks. In practice, successful funds do not continue to outperform other active funds, as competition among investors drives down their future returns.[19]

These arguments and results suggest that capital markets are competitive and so the market portfolio should be approximately efficient. As a result, for a corporate manager who is not a skilled portfolio manager, the assumption that the market portfolio is efficient is a reasonable first approximation.

CONCEPT CHECK

1. What is an efficient capital market?
2. How is the CAPM a stronger hypothesis than an efficient capital market?

Summary

1. A probability distribution summarizes information about possible different returns and their likelihood of occurring.

   a. The expected, or mean, return is the return we expect to earn on average:

   $$\text{Expected Return} = E[R] = \sum_R p_R \times R \tag{10.1}$$

   b. The variance or standard deviation measures the variability of the returns:

   $$Var(R) = E[(R - E[R])^2] = \sum_R p_R \times (R - E[R])^2$$

   $$SD(R) = \sqrt{Var(R)} \tag{10.2}$$

   c. The standard deviation of a return is also called its volatility.

---

17. This widely supported result was first documented by I Friend, F. E. Brown, E. S. Herman and D. Vickers, "A Study of Mutual Funds: Investment Policy and Investment Company Performance," Report No. 2274, 87th Congress, Second Session (August 28, 1962) and I. Horowitz, "The Varying Quality of Investment Trust Management," *Journal of the American Statistical Association* 58 (1963):1011–1032.

18. See M. J. Gruber, "Another Puzzle: The Growth in Actively Managed Mutual Funds," *Journal of Finance* 51 (1996): 783–810; E. R. Sirri and P. Tufano, "Costly Search and Mutual Fund Flows," *Journal of Finance* 53 (1998): 1589–1622; J. Chevalier and G. Ellison, "Risk Taking by Mutual Funds as a Response to Incentives," *Journal of Political Economy* 105 (1997): 1167–1200. For a theoretical model that considers the equilibrium impact of these fund flows, see J. B. Berk and R. C. Green, "Mutual Fund Flows and Performance in Rational Markets," *Journal of Political Economy* 112 (2004): 1269–1295.

19. See M. Carhart, "On Persistence in Mutual Fund Performance," *Journal of Finance* 52 (1997): 57–82.

2. The realized or total return for an investment is the total of the dividend yield and the capital gain rate.

   a. Using the empirical distribution of realized returns, we can estimate the expected return and variance of the distribution of returns by calculating the average annual return and variance of realized returns:

   $$\bar{R} = \frac{1}{T}(R_1 + R_2 + \cdots + R_T) = \frac{1}{T}\sum_{t=1}^{T} R_t \qquad (10.6)$$

   $$Var(R) = \frac{1}{T-1}\sum_{t=1}^{T}(R_t - \bar{R})^2 \qquad (10.7)$$

   b. The square root of the estimated variance is an estimate of the volatility of returns.

   c. Because a security's historical average return is only an estimate of its true expected return, we use the standard error of the estimate to gauge the amount of estimation error:

   $$SD(\text{Average of Independent, Identical Risks}) = \frac{SD(\text{Individual Risk})}{\sqrt{\text{Number of Observations}}} \qquad (10.8)$$

3. Based on historical data, small stocks have had higher volatility and higher average returns than large stocks, which have had higher volatility and higher average returns than bonds.

4. There is no clear relationship between the volatility and return of individual stocks.

   a. Larger stocks tend to have lower overall volatility, but even the largest stocks are typically more risky than a portfolio of large stocks.

   b. All stocks seem to have higher risk and lower returns than would be predicted based on extrapolation of data for large portfolios.

5. The total risk of a security represents both idiosyncratic risk and systematic risk.

   a. Variation in a stock's return due to firm-specific news is called idiosyncratic risk. This type of risk is also called firm-specific, unsystematic, unique, or diversifiable risk.

   b. Systematic risk is risk due to market-wide news that affect all stocks simultaneously. Common risk is also called market or undiversifiable risk.

6. Diversification eliminates idiosyncratic risk but does not eliminate systematic risk.

   a. Because investors can eliminate idiosyncratic risk, they do not require a risk premium for taking it on.

   b. Because investors cannot eliminate systematic risk, they must be compensated for holding it. As a consequence, the risk premium for a stock depends on the amount of its systematic risk rather than its total risk.

7. An efficient portfolio is a portfolio that contains only systematic risk and cannot be diversified further—that is, there is no way to reduce the risk of the portfolio without lowering its expected return.

8. The market portfolio is a portfolio that contains all shares of all stocks and securities in the market. The market portfolio is often assumed to be efficient.

9. If the market portfolio is efficient, we can measure the systematic risk of a security by its beta (β). The beta of a security is the sensitivity of the security's return to the return of the overall market.

10. The expected return for a risky security equals the risk-free rate plus a risk premium. The Capital Asset Pricing Model (CAPM) states that the risk premium equals the security's beta times the market risk premium:

$$E[R] = r_f + \beta \times (E[R_{Mkt}] - r_f) \tag{10.10}$$

11. The cost of capital, r, for investing in a project with a beta, β, is

$$r = r_f + \beta \times (E[R_{Mkt}] - r_f) \tag{10.11}$$

12. The efficient markets hypothesis states that the expected return of any security should equal its cost of capital. In an efficient capital market the cost of capital depends on systematic risk, and not on diversifiable risk.

13. The CAPM is a stronger hypothesis than an efficient capital market. It states that an investment's systematic risk, and therefore its cost of capital, depends only on its beta with the market portfolio.

Key Terms

average annual return *p. 292*
beta (β) *p. 308*
Capital Asset Pricing Model (CAPM) *p. 312*
common risk *p. 301*
diversification *p. 301*
efficient capital market *p. 313*
efficient portfolio *p. 308*
empirical distribution *p. 292*
excess return *p. 297*
expected (mean) return *p. 286*
firm-specific, idiosyncratic, unsystematic, unique, or diversifiable risk *p. 303*

independent risk *p. 301*
market portfolio *p. 308*
95% confidence interval *p. 295*
probability distribution *p. 286*
realized return *p. 289*
standard deviation *p. 287*
standard error *p. 295*
systematic, undiversifiable, or market risk *p. 303*
variance *p. 287*
volatility *p. 288*

Further Reading

The original work on diversification was developed in the following papers: H. M. Markowitz, "Portfolio Selection," *Journal of Finance* 7 (1952): 77–91; A. D. Roy, "Safety First and the Holding of Assets," *Econometrica* 20, No. 3 (July 1952): 431–449; and, in the context of insurance, B. deFinetti, "Il problema de pieni," *Giornale dell'Istituto Italiano degli Attuari*, 11 (1940): 1–88.

Readers who are interested in historical returns of different types of assets can find useful information in the following sources: E. Dimson, P. R. Marsh, and M. Staunton, *Triumph of the Optimist: 101 Years of Global Equity Returns* (Princeton, NJ: Princeton University Press, 2002); and Ibbotson Associates, Inc., *Stocks, Bonds, Bills, and Inflation*, 2005 Yearbook (Chicago: Ibbotson Associates, 2005).

Many books address the topics of this chapter in more depth: E. J. Elton, M. J. Gruber, S. J. Brown, and W. N. Goetzmann, *Modern Portfolio Theory and Investment Analysis*, 6th ed. (New York: John Wiley & Sons, 2002); J. C. Francis, *Investments: Analysis and Management* (New York: McGraw-Hill, 1991); R. C. Radcliffe, *Investment: Concepts, Analysis, and Strategy* (New York: Harper-Collins, 1994); and F. Reilly and K. C. Brown, *Investment Analysis and Portfolio Management* (Fort Worth, TX: Dryden Press, 1996).

Problems

All problems in this chapter are available in MyFinanceLab. An asterisk (*) indicates problems with a higher level of difficulty.

Common Measures of Risk and Return

EXCEL   **1.**   The figure below shows the one-year return distribution for RCS stock. Calculate
   a. The expected return.
   b. The standard deviation of the return.

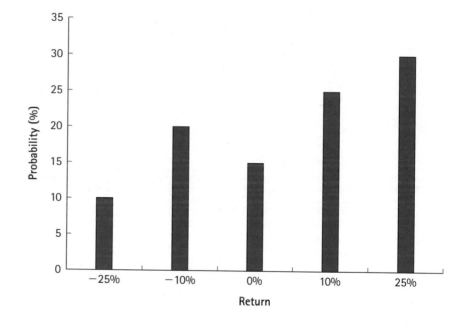

EXCEL   **2.**   The table below shows the one-year return distribution of Startup Inc. Calculate
   a. The expected return.
   b. The standard deviation of the return.

Return	Probability
−100%	40%
− 75%	20%
− 50%	20%
− 25%	10%
1000%	10%

3.   Characterize the difference between the two stocks in Problems 1 and 2. What tradeoffs would you face in choosing one to hold?

Historical Returns of Stocks and Bonds

EXCEL   **4.**   Using the data in the table below, calculate the return for investing in Boeing stock from January 2, 2003, to January 2, 2004, assuming all dividends are reinvested in the stock immediately.

Historical Stock and Dividend Data for Boeing

Date	Price	Dividend
1/2/03	33.88	
2/5/03	30.67	0.17
5/14/03	29.49	0.17
8/13/03	32.38	0.17
11/12/03	39.07	0.17
1/2/04	41.99	

EXCEL   **5.** Download the spreadsheet from www.aw-bc.com/berk_demarzo that contains historical monthly prices and dividends (paid at the end of the month) for Ford Motor Company stock (Ticker: F) from August 1994 to August 1998. Calculate the realized return over this period, expressing your answer in percent per month.

EXCEL   **6.** Using the same data as in Problem 5, compute the

   a. Average monthly return over this period.

   b. Monthly volatility (or standard deviation) over this period.

7. Explain the difference between the average return you calculated in Problem 6(a) and the realized return you calculated in Problem 5. Are both numbers useful? If so, explain why.

EXCEL   ***8.** Compute the 95% confidence interval of the estimate of the average monthly return you calculated in Problem 6(a).

The Historical Tradeoff between Risk and Return

9. How does the relationship between the average return and the historical volatility of individual stocks differ from the relationship between the average return and the historical volatility of large, well-diversified portfolios?

Common Versus Independent Risk

10. Consider two local banks. Bank A has 100 loans outstanding, each for $1 million, that it expects will be repaid today. Each loan has a 5% probability of default, in which case the bank has not repaid anything. The chance of default is independent across all the loans. Bank B has only one loan of $100 million outstanding, which it also expects will be repaid today. It also has a 5% probability of not being repaid. Explain the difference between the type of risk each bank faces. Which bank faces less risk? Why?

***11.** Using the data in Problem 10, calculate

   a. The expected overall payoff of each bank.

   b. The standard deviation of the overall payoff of each bank.

Diversification in Stock Portfolios

12. You are a risk-averse investor who is considering investing in one of two economies. The expected return and volatility of all stocks in both economies is the same. In the first economy, all stocks move together—in good times all prices rise together and in bad times they all fall together. In the second economy, stock returns are independent—one stock increasing in price has no effect on the prices of other stocks. Which economy would you choose to invest in? Explain.

13. Consider an economy with two types of firms, S and I. S firms all move together. I firms move independently. For both types of firms, there is a 60% probability that the firms will have a 15% return and a 40% probability that the firms will have a −10% return. What is the volatility (standard deviation) of a portfolio that consists of an equal investment in 20

   a. Type S firms?

   b. Type I firms?

*14. Using the data in Problem 13, plot the volatility as a function of the number of firms in the two portfolios.

15. Explain why the risk premium of a stock does not depend on its diversifiable risk.

16. Identify each of the following risks as either systematic risk or diversifiable risk:

   a. The risk that the CEO of your firm is killed in a plane accident

   b. The risk that the economy slows, decreasing demand for your firm's products

   c. The risk that your best employees will be hired away

   d. The risk that the new product you expect your R&D division to produce will not materialize.

Estimating the Cost of Capital in Practice

17. What is an efficient portfolio?

18. What does the beta of a stock measure?

19. Suppose the market portfolio is equally likely to increase by 30% or decrease by 10%.

   a. Calculate the beta of a firm that goes up on average by 43% when the market goes *up* and goes down by 17% when the market goes *down*.

   b. Calculate the beta of a firm that goes up on average by 18% when the market goes *down* and goes down by 22% when the market goes *up*.

   c. Calculate the beta of a firm that is expected to go up by 4% *independently* of the market.

20. Suppose the risk-free interest rate is 4%.

   a. i. Use the beta you calculated for the stock in Problem 19 (a) to estimate its expected return.

      ii. How does this compare with the stock's actual expected return?

   b. i. Use the beta you calculated for the stock in Problem 19 (b) to estimate its expected return.

      ii. How does this compare with the stock's actual expected return?

EXCEL 21. Suppose the market risk premium is 6% and the risk-free interest rate is 4%. Using the data in Table 10.6, calculate the expected return of investing in

   a. H. J. Heinz stock

   b. Cisco Systems stock

   c. General Electric stock

22. Suppose the market risk premium is 6.5% and the risk-free interest rate is 5%. Calculate the cost of capital of investing in a project with a beta of 1.2.

Capital Market Efficiency

23. State whether each of the following is inconsistent with an efficient capital market, the CAPM, or both:

   a. A security with only diversifiable risk has an expected return that exceeds the risk-free interest rate.

b. A security with a beta of 1 had a return last year of 15% when the market had a return of 9%.

c. Small stock with a beta of 1.5 tend to have higher returns on average than large stocks with a beta of 1.5.

Data Case

Today is May 24, 2006, and you have just started your new job with a financial planning firm. You have just started your new job with a financial planning firm. In addition to studying for all your license exams, you have been asked to review a portion of a client's stock portfolio to determine the risk/return profiles of 12 stocks in the portfolio. Unfortunately, your small firm cannot afford the expensive databases that would provide all this information with a few simple keystrokes, but that's why they have you. Specifically, you have been asked to determine the monthly average returns and standard deviations for the 12 stocks for the past five years. In the following chapters, you will be asked to do more extensive analyses on these same stocks.

The stocks (with their symbols in parentheses) are:

> Apple Computer (AAPL)
> Archer Daniels Midland (ADM)
> Boeing (BA)
> Citigroup (C)
> Caterpillar (CAT)
> Deere & Co. (DE)
> Hershey (HSY)
> Motorola (MOT)
> Proctor and Gamble (PG)
> Sirius Satellite Radio (SIRI)
> Wal-Mart (WMT)
> Yahoo! (YHOO)

1. Collect price information for each stock from Yahoo! Finance (http://finance.yahoo.com) as follows:

   a. Enter the stock symbol. On the page for that stock, click "Historical Prices" on the left side of the page.

   b. Enter the "start date" as May 24, 2001 and the "end date" as May 1, 2006 to cover the five-year period. Make sure you click "monthly" next to the date.

   c. After hitting "Get Prices," scroll to the bottom of the first page and click "Download to Spreadsheet." If you are asked if you want to open or save the file, click open.

   d. Copy the entire spreadsheet, open Excel, and paste the Web data into a spreadsheet. Delete all the columns except the date and the adjusted close (the first and last columns).

   e. Keep the Excel file open and go back to the Yahoo! Finance Web page and hit the back button. If you are asked if you want to save the data, click no.

   f. When you return to the prices page, enter the next stock symbol and hit "Get Prices" again. Do not change the dates or frequency, but make sure you have the same dates for all the stocks you will download. Again, click "Download to Spreadsheet" and then open the file. Copy the last column, "Adj. Close," paste it into the Excel file and change "Adj. Close" to the stock symbol. Make sure that the first and last prices are in the same rows as the first stock.

g. Repeat these steps for the remaining ten stocks, pasting each closing price right next to the other stocks, again making sure that the correct prices on the correct dates all appear on the same rows.

2. Convert these prices to monthly returns as the percentage change in the monthly prices. (*Hint:* Create a separate worksheet within the Excel file.) Note that to compute a return for each month, you need a beginning and ending price, so you will not be able to compute the return for the first month.

3. Compute the mean monthly returns and standard deviations for the monthly returns of each of the stocks.[20] Convert the monthly statistics to annual statistics for easier interpretation (muliply the mean monthly return by 12, and multiply the monthly standard deviation by $\sqrt{12}$).

4. Add a column in your Excel worksheet with the average return across stocks for each month. This is the monthly return to an equally weighted portfolio of these 12 stocks. Compute the mean and standard deviation of monthly returns for the equally weighted portfolio. Double check that the average return on this equally weighted portfolio is equal to the average return of all of the individual stocks. Convert these monthly statistics to annual statistics (as described in Step 3) for interpretation.

5. Using the annual statistics, create an Excel plot with standard deviation (volatility) on the *x*-axis and average return on the *y*-axis as follows:

   a. Create three columns on your spreadsheet with the statistics you created in questions 3 and 4 for each of the individual stocks and the equally weighted portfolio. The first column will have the ticker, the second will have annual standard deviation, and the third will have the annual mean return.

   b. Highlight the data in the last two columns (standard deviation and mean), choose >Insert>Chart>XY Scatter Plot. Complete the chart wizard to finish the plot.

6. What do you notice about the volatilities of the individual stocks, compared to the volatility of the equally weighted portfolio?

---

20. In Eq. 10.4, we showed how to compute returns with stock price and dividend data. The "adjusted close" series from Yahoo! Finance is already adjusted for dividends and splits, so we may compute returns based on the percentage change in monthly adjusted prices.

Optimal Portfolio Choice

notation

R_P return of portfolio P

R_i return of security i

x_i fraction invested in security i

$E[R]$ expected return

r_f risk-free interest rate

$Corr(R_i, R_j)$ correlation between returns of i and j

$Cov(R_i, R_j)$ covariance between returns of i and j

$SD(R)$ standard deviation (volatility) of return R

$Var(R)$ variance of return R

R_{xP} return of portfolio with fraction x invested in portfolio P and $(1 - x)$ invested in the risk-free security

β_i^P beta or sensitivity of the investment i to the fluctuations of the portfolio P

r_i required return or cost of capital of security i

I n this chapter, we quantify the ideas we introduced in Chapter 10, and explain how an investor can choose an efficient portfolio. In particular, we will see how to find the optimal portfolio for an investor who wants to earn the highest possible return given the level of volatility he or she is willing to accept. To do so, we will develop the statistical techniques of *mean-variance portfolio optimization.* These techniques were developed by Harry Markowitz, who was awarded the Nobel Prize in 1990 for his work, and are used routinely by professional investors, money managers, and financial institutions.

In our exploration of these concepts, we take the perspective of a stock market investor. These concepts, however, are also important for a corporate financial manager. After all, financial managers are also investors, investing money on behalf of their shareholders. When a company makes a new investment, financial managers must ensure that the investment has a positive NPV. Doing so requires knowing the cost of capital of the investment opportunity and, as we saw in Chapter 10, calculating the cost of capital requires identifying an efficient portfolio.

In Chapter 10, we explained how to calculate the expected return and volatility of a single stock. To find the efficient portfolio, we must understand how to do the same thing for a portfolio of stocks. We begin this chapter by explaining how to calculate the expected return and volatility of a portfolio. With these statistical tools in hand, we then describe how an investor can create an efficient portfolio out of individual stocks, and consider the implications for the cost of capital for an investment.

11.1   The Expected Return of a Portfolio

To find an optimal portfolio, we need a method to define a portfolio and analyze its return. We can describe a portfolio by its **portfolio weights**, the fraction of the total investment in the portfolio held in each individual investment in the portfolio:

$$x_i = \frac{\text{Value of investment } i}{\text{Total value of portfolio}} \tag{11.1}$$

These portfolio weights add up to 1 (that is, $\sum_i x_i = 1$), so that they represent the way we have divided our money between the different individual investments in the portfolio.

As an example, consider a portfolio with 200 shares of the Walt Disney Company worth $30 per share and 100 shares of Coca-Cola worth $40 per share. The total value of the portfolio is $200 \times \$30 + 100 \times \$40 = \$10,000$, and the corresponding portfolio weights x_D and x_C are

$$x_D = \frac{200 \times \$30}{10,000} = 60\%$$

$$x_C = \frac{100 \times \$40}{10,000} = 40\%$$

Given the portfolio weights, the return on the portfolio is easy to calculate. Suppose $x_1, \ldots, x_n$ are the portfolio weights of the n investments in a portfolio, and these investments have returns $R_1, \ldots, R_n$. Then the return on the portfolio, R_P, is the weighted average of the returns on the investments in the portfolio, where the weights correspond to portfolio weights:

$$R_P = x_1 R_1 + x_2 R_2 + \cdots + x_n R_n = \sum_i x_i R_i \tag{11.2}$$

The return of a portfolio is straightforward to compute if we know the returns of the individual stocks and the portfolio weights.

EXAMPLE 11.1

Calculating Portfolio Returns

Problem

Suppose you invest $10,000 by buying 200 shares of the Walt Disney Company at $30 per share and 100 shares of Coca-Cola stock at $40 per share. If Disney's share price goes up to $36 and Coca-Cola's share price falls to $38, what is the new value of the portfolio, and what return did the portfolio earn? Show that Eq. 11.2 holds. If you don't buy or sell any shares after the price change, what are the new portfolio weights?

Solution

The new value of the portfolio is $200 \times \$36 + 100 \times \$38 = \$11,000$, for a gain of $1000 or a 10% return on your initial $10,000 investment. The return on Disney stock was $36 / 30 - 1 = 20\%$, and the return on Coca-Cola stock was $38 / 40 - 1 = -5\%$. Given the initial portfolio weights of 60% Disney and 40% Coca-Cola, we can also compute the return of the portfolio from Eq. 11.2:

$$R_P = x_D R_D + x_C R_C = 60\% \times 0.2 + 40\% \times (-0.05) = 10\%$$

After the price change, the new portfolio weights are

$$x_D = \frac{200 \times \$36}{11{,}000} = 65.45\%$$

$$x_C = \frac{100 \times \$38}{11{,}000} = 34.55\%$$

Without trading, the portfolio weights will increase for the stocks in the portfolio whose returns are above the overall portfolio return.

Equation 11.2 also allows us to compute the expected return of a portfolio. Using the facts that the expectation of a sum is just the sum of the expectations and that the expectation of a known multiple is just the multiple of its expectation, we arrive at the following formula for a portfolio's expected return:

$$E[R_P] = E\left[\sum_i x_i R_i\right] = \sum_i E[x_i R_i] = \sum_i x_i E[R_i] \tag{11.3}$$

That is, the expected return of a portfolio is simply the weighted average of the expected returns of the investments within it, using the portfolio weights.

EXAMPLE 11.2

Portfolio Expected Return

Problem

Suppose you invest $10,000 in Ford stock, and $30,000 in Tyco International stock. You expect a return of 10% for Ford and 16% for Tyco. What is the expected return for your portfolio?

Solution

You have $40,000 invested in total, so your portfolio weights are 10,000 / 40,000 = 25% in Ford and 30,000 / 40,000 = 75% in Tyco. Therefore, the expected return on your portfolio is

$$E[R_P] = x_F E[R_F] + x_T E[R] = 25\% \times 0.10 + 75\% \times 0.16 = 14.5\%$$

CONCEPT CHECK

1. What is a *portfolio weight?*

2. How do we calculate the return on a portfolio?

11.2 The Volatility of a Two-Stock Portfolio

As we explained in Chapter 10, when we combine stocks in a portfolio, some of their risk is eliminated through diversification. The amount of risk that will remain depends on the degree to which the stocks are exposed to common risks. In this section we describe the statistical tools that we can use to quantify the risk stocks have in common and determine the volatility of a portfolio.

TABLE 11.1		**Returns for Three Stocks, and Portfolios of Pairs of Stocks**				
		Stock Returns			**Portfolio Returns**	
					(1)	(2)
Year		**North Air**	**West Air**	**Tex Oil**	$1/2R_N + 1/2R_W$	$1/2R_W + 1/2R_T$
1998		21%	9%	−2%	15.0%	3.5%
1999		30%	21%	−5%	25.5%	8.0%
2000		7%	7%	9%	7.0%	8.0%
2001		−5%	−2%	21%	−3.5%	9.5%
2002		−2%	−5%	30%	−3.5%	12.5%
2003		9%	30%	7%	19.5%	18.5%
Average Return		10.0%	10.0%	10.0%	10.0%	10.0%
Volatility		13.4%	13.4%	13.4%	12.1%	5.1%

Combining Risks

Let's begin with a simple example of how risk changes when stocks are combined in a portfolio. Table 11.1 shows returns for three hypothetical stocks, along with their average returns and volatilities. While the three stocks have the same volatility and average return, the pattern of their returns differs. When the airline stocks performed well, the oil stock tended to do poorly (see 1998–1999), and when the airlines did poorly, the oil stock tended to do well (2001–2002).

Table 11.1 also shows the returns for two portfolios of the stocks. The first portfolio consists of equal investments in the two airlines, North Air and West Air. The second portfolio includes equal investments in West Air and Tex Oil. The average return of both portfolios is equal to the average return of the stocks, consistent with Eq. 11.3. However, their volatilities—12.1% for portfolio 1 and 5.1% for portfolio 2—are very different from the individual stocks *and* from each other.

This example demonstrates two important phenomena. First, by combining stocks into a portfolio, we reduce risk through diversification. Because the prices of the stocks do not move identically, some of the risk is averaged out in a portfolio. As a result, both portfolios have lower risk than the individual stocks.

Second, the amount of risk that is eliminated in a portfolio depends on the degree to which the stocks face common risks and their prices move together. Because the two airline stocks tend to perform well or poorly at the same time, the portfolio of airline stocks has a volatility that is only slightly lower than that of the individual stocks. The airline and oil stocks, by contrast, do not move together; indeed, they tend to move in opposite directions. As a result, some risk is canceled out, making that portfolio much less risky.

Determining Covariance and Correlation

To find the risk of a portfolio, we need to know more than the risk and return of the component stocks: We need to know the degree to which the stocks' face common risks and their returns move together. In this section, we introduce two statistical measures, covariance and correlation, that allow us to measure the co-movement of returns.

Covariance is the expected product of the deviations of two returns from their means. The covariance between returns R_i and R_j is defined as follows:

Covariance between Returns R_i and R_j

$$Cov(R_i, R_j) = E[(R_i - E[R_i])(R_j - E[R_j])] \tag{11.4}$$

When estimating the covariance from historical data, we use the formula[1]

Estimate of the Covariance from Historical Data

$$Cov(R_i, R_j) = \frac{1}{T-1} \sum_t (R_{i,t} - \bar{R}_i)(R_{j,t} - \bar{R}_j) \tag{11.5}$$

Intuitively, if two stocks move together, their returns will tend to be above or below average at the same time, and the covariance will be positive. If the stocks move in opposite directions, one will tend to be above average when the other is below average, and the covariance will be negative.

While the sign of the covariance is easy to interpret, its magnitude is not. It will be larger if the stocks are more volatile (and so have larger deviations from their expected returns), and it will be larger the more closely the stocks move in relation to each other. In order to control for the volatility of each stock, and quantify the strength of the relationship between them, we can calculate the **correlation** between two stock returns, defined as the covariance of the returns divided by the standard deviation of each return:

$$Corr(R_i, R_j) = \frac{Cov(R_i, R_j)}{SD(R_i)\,SD(R_j)} \tag{11.6}$$

The correlation between two stocks has the same sign as their covariance, so it has a similar interpretation. Dividing by the volatilities ensures that correlation is always between -1 and $+1$, which allows us to gauge the strength of the relationship between the stocks. As Figure 11.1 shows, correlation is a barometer of the degree to which the returns share common risk and tend to move together. The closer the correlation is to $+1$,

FIGURE 11.1

Correlation

Correlation measures how returns move in relation to each other. It is between $+1$ (returns always move together) and -1 (returns always move oppositely). Independent risks have no tendency to move together and have zero correlation.

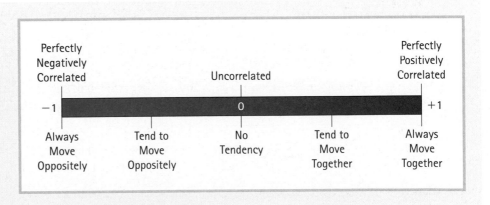

---

1. As with Eq. 10.7 for historical volatility, we divide by $T-1$ rather than by T to make up for the fact that we have used the data to compute the average returns $\bar{R}$, eliminating a degree of freedom.

the more the returns tend to move together as a result of common risk. When the correlation (and thus the covariance) equals 0, the returns are *uncorrelated;* that is, they have no tendency to move either together or in opposition of one another. Independent risks are uncorrelated. Finally, the closer the correlation is to −1, the more the returns tend to move in opposite directions.

EXAMPLE 11.3

Computing the Covariance and Correlation

Problem

Using the data in Table 11.1, what are the covariance and the correlation between North Air and West Air? Between West Air and Tex Oil?

Solution

First we compute the deviation of each return from its mean by subtracting the average return of each stock (10%) from the returns in Table 11.1. Then we compute the product of these deviations between the pairs of stocks, sum them, and divide by $T - 1 = 5$ to compute the covariance, as in Table 11.2.

From the table, we can see that North Air and West Air have a positive covariance (0.0112), indicating a tendency to move together, whereas West Air and Tex Oil have a negative covariance (−0.0128), indicating a tendency to move oppositely. We can determine the strength of these tendencies by computing the correlation, which we obtain by dividing the covariance by the standard deviation of each stock (13.4%). The correlation for North Air and West Air is 62.4%; the correlation for West Air and Tex Oil is −71.3%.

TABLE 11.2   **Computing the Covariance and Correlation Between Pairs of Stocks**

Year	Deviation from Mean			North Air and West Air	West Air and Tex Oil
	$(R_N - \bar{R}_N)$	$(R_W - \bar{R}_W)$	$(R_T - \bar{R}_T)$	$(R_N - \bar{R}_N)(R_W - \bar{R}_W)$	$(R_W - \bar{R}_W)(R_T - \bar{R}_T)$
1998	11%	−1%	−12%	−0.0011	0.0012
1999	20%	11%	−15%	0.0220	−0.0165
2000	−3%	−3%	−1%	0.0009	0.0003
2001	−15%	−12%	11%	0.0180	−0.0132
2002	−12%	−15%	20%	0.0180	−0.0300
2003	−1%	20%	−3%	−0.0020	−0.0060
Sum = $\sum_t (R_{i,t} - \bar{R}_i)(R_{j,t} - \bar{R}_j) =$				0.0558	−0.0642
Covariance: $Cov(R_i, R_j) = \dfrac{1}{T-1}$ Sum $=$				0.0112	−0.0128
Correlation: $Corr(R_i, R_j) = \dfrac{Cov(R_i, R_j)}{SD(R_i)\, SD(R_j)} =$				0.624	−0.713

EXAMPLE 11.4	The Covariance and Correlation of a Stock with Itself

Problem

What are the covariance and the correlation of a stock's return with itself?

Solution

Let R_s be the stock's return. From the definition of the covariance,

$$Cov(R_s, R_s) = E[(R_s - E[R_s])(R_s - E[R_s])] = E[(R_s - E[R_s])^2]$$
$$= Var(R_s)$$

where the last equation follows from the definition of the variance. That is, the covariance of a stock with itself is simply its variance. Then,

$$Corr(R_s, R_s) = \frac{Cov(R_s, R_s)}{SD(R_s)\,SD(R_s)} = \frac{Var(R_s)}{SD(R_s)^2} = 1$$

where the last equation follows from the definition of the standard deviation. That is, a stock's return is perfectly positively correlated with itself, as it always moves together with itself in perfect synchrony.

When will stock returns be highly correlated with each other? Stock returns will tend to move together if they are affected similarly by economic events. Thus stocks in the same industry tend to have more highly correlated returns than stocks in different industries. This tendency is illustrated in Table 11.3, which shows the volatility of individual stock returns and the correlation between them for several common stocks. Anheuser-Busch, the only representative of the beer-brewing industry, has the lowest correlation with all the stocks. Almost all of the correlations are positive, however, illustrating the general tendency of stocks to move together.

TABLE 11.3	Historical Annual Volatilities and Correlations for Selected Stocks (based on monthly returns, 1996–2004)

	Microsoft	Dell	Delta Air Lines	American Airlines	General Motors	Ford Motor	Anheuser-Busch
Volatility (Standard Deviation)	42%	54%	50%	72%	33%	37%	18%
Correlation with							
Microsoft	1.00	0.65	0.27	0.19	0.22	0.26	−0.07
Dell	0.65	1.00	0.19	0.18	0.32	0.32	0.10
Delta Air Lines	0.27	0.19	1.00	0.69	0.31	0.38	0.19
American Airlines	0.19	0.18	0.69	1.00	0.35	0.58	0.11
General Motors	0.22	0.32	0.31	0.35	1.00	0.64	0.11
Ford Motor	0.26	0.32	0.38	0.58	0.64	1.00	0.10
Anheuser-Busch	−0.07	0.10	0.19	0.11	0.11	0.10	1.00

Computing the Variance, Covariance and Correlation in Microsoft Excel

The computer spreadsheet program Excel does not compute the standard deviation, variance, covariance, and correlation consistently. The Excel function STDEV and VAR correctly use Eq. 10.7 to estimate the standard deviation and variance from historical data. But the Excel function COVAR does *not* use Eq. 11.5; instead, Excel divides by T instead of $T - 1$. Therefore, to estimate the covariance from a sample of historical returns using COVAR, you must correct the inconsistency by multiplying by the number of data points and dividing by the number of data points minus one; i.e., COVAR* $T / (T - 1)$. Alternatively, you can use the function CORREL to compute the correlation. Because the function CORREL is implemented in a way that is consistent with STDEV and VAR, you can estimate the covariance by multiplying the correlation by the standard deviation of each return.

EXAMPLE 11.5

Computing the Covariance from the Correlation

Problem

Using the data from Table 11.3, what is the covariance between Microsoft and Dell?

Solution

We can rewrite Eq. 11.6 to solve for the covariance:

$$Cov(R_{MSFT}, R_{DELL}) = Corr(R_{MSFT}, R_{DELL}) \, SD(R_{MSFT}) \, SD(R_{DELL})$$
$$= (0.65)(0.42)(0.54) = 0.1474$$

Computing a Portfolio's Variance and Volatility

We now have the tools needed to compute the variance of a portfolio. Recall from Example 11.4 that the variance of a return is equal to the covariance of a return with itself. Therefore, for a two-stock portfolio with $R_P = x_1 R_1 + x_2 R_2$,

$$
\begin{aligned}
Var(R_P) &= Cov(R_P, R_P) \\
&= Cov(x_1 R_1 + x_2 R_2, x_1 R_1 + x_2 R_2) \\
&= x_1 x_1 Cov(R_1, R_1) + x_1 x_2 Cov(R_1, R_2) + x_2 x_1 Cov(R_2, R_1) + x_2 x_2 Cov(R_2, R_2)
\end{aligned}
\tag{11.7}
$$

In the last line of Eq. 11.7, we use the fact that, as with expectations, we can change the order of the covariance with sums and multiples.[2] By combining terms and recognizing that $Cov(R_i, R_i) = Var(R_i)$, we arrive at our main result of this section:

The Variance of a Two-Stock Portfolio

$$Var(R_P) = x_1^2 Var(R_1) + x_2^2 Var(R_2) + 2x_1 x_2 Cov(R_1, R_2) \tag{11.8}$$

As always, the volatility is the square root of the variance, $SD(R_P) = \sqrt{Var(R_P)}$.

Let's check this formula for the airline and oil stocks in Table 11.1. Consider the portfolio containing shares of West Air and Tex Oil. The variance of each stock is equal to the square of its volatility, $0.134^2 = 0.018$. From Example 11.3, the covariance between

---

2. That is, $Cov(A + B, C) = Cov(A, C) + Cov(B, C)$ and $Cov(mA, B) = m \, Cov(A, B)$.

the stocks is -0.0128. Therefore, the variance of a portfolio with 50% invested in each stock is

$$Var\left(\tfrac{1}{2}R_W + \tfrac{1}{2}R_T\right) = x_W^2 Var(R_W) + x_T^2 Var(R_T) + 2x_W x_T Cov(R_W, R_T)$$

$$= \left(\tfrac{1}{2}\right)^2(0.018) + \left(\tfrac{1}{2}\right)^2(0.018) + 2\left(\tfrac{1}{2}\right)\left(\tfrac{1}{2}\right)(-0.0128)$$

$$= 0.0026$$

The volatility of the portfolio is $\sqrt{0.0026} = 5.1\%$, which corresponds to the calculation in Table 11.1. If we repeat this calculation for the North Air and West Air portfolio, the calculation is the same except for the stocks' higher covariance of 0.112, which leads to a higher volatility of 12.1%.

As we saw in Table 11.1, Eq. 11.8 shows that the variance of the portfolio depends not only on the variance of the individual stocks, but also on the covariance between them. We can also rewrite Eq. 11.8 using the stocks' volatilities and calculating the covariance from the correlation as in Example 11.5:

$$Var(R_P) = x_1^2 SD(R_1)^2 + x_2^2 SD(R_2)^2 + 2x_1 x_2 Corr(R_1, R_2) SD(R_1) SD(R_2) \quad (11.9)$$

Equations 11.8 and 11.9 demonstrate that with a positive amount invested in each stock, the more the stocks move together and the higher their covariance or correlation, the more variable the portfolio will be. The portfolio will have the greatest variance if the stocks have a perfect positive correlation of $+1$.

EXAMPLE 11.6

Computing the Volatility of a Two-Stock Portfolio

Problem

Using the data from Table 11.3, what is the volatility of a portfolio with equal amounts invested in Microsoft and Dell stock? What is the volatility of a portfolio with equal amounts invested in Dell and Delta Air Lines stock?

Solution

With portfolio weights of 50% each in Microsoft and Dell stock, from Eq. 11.9, the portfolio's variance is

$$Var(R_P) = x_{MSFT}^2 SD(R_{MSFT})^2 + x_{DELL}^2 SD(R_{DELL})^2$$

$$+ 2x_{MSFT} x_{DELL} Corr(R_{MSFT}, R_{DELL}) SD(R_{MSFT}) SD(R_{DELL})$$

$$= (0.50)^2(0.42)^2 + (0.50)^2(0.54)^2 + 2(0.50)(0.50)(0.65)(0.42)(0.54)$$

$$= 0.1907$$

The volatility is therefore $SD(R_P) = \sqrt{Var(R_P)} = \sqrt{0.1907} = 43.7\%$.

For the portfolio of Dell and Delta Air Lines (DAL) stock,

$$Var(R_P) = x_{DELL}^2 SD(R_{DELL})^2 + x_{DAL}^2 SD(R_{DAL})^2$$

$$+ 2x_{DELL} x_{DAL} Corr(R_{DELL}, R_{DAL}) SD(R_{DELL}) SD(R_{DAL})$$

$$= (0.50)^2(0.54)^2 + (0.50)^2(0.50)^2 + 2(0.50)(0.50)(0.19)(0.54)(0.50)$$

$$= 0.1610$$

The volatility in this case is $SD(R_P) = \sqrt{Var(R_P)} = \sqrt{0.1610} = 40.1\%$.

> Note that the portfolio of Dell and Delta Air Lines stock is less volatile than either of the individual stocks. It is also less volatile than the portfolio of Dell and Microsoft stock. Even though Delta stock is more volatile than Microsoft stock, its much lower correlation with Dell stock leads to greater diversification in the portfolio.

CONCEPT CHECK

1. What is the range of the correlation?

2. Does the variance of a two-stock portfolio depend only on the variances of the individual stocks?

11.3   The Volatility of a Large Portfolio

We can gain additional benefits of diversification by holding more than two stocks in our portfolio. Let's consider how to calculate the volatility of a large portfolio, and determine the amount of diversification that is possible if we hold many stocks.

Recall that the return on a portfolio of n stocks is simply the weighted average of the returns of the stocks in the portfolio:

$$R_P = x_1 R_1 + x_2 R_2 + \cdots + x_n R_n = \sum_i x_i R_i$$

Using the properties of the covariance, we can write the variance of a portfolio as follows:

$$Var(R_P) = Cov(R_P, R_P) = Cov(\Sigma_i x_i R_i, R_P) = \sum_i x_i Cov(R_i, R_P) \qquad (11.10)$$

This equation indicates that the *variance of a portfolio is equal to the weighted average covariance of each stock with the portfolio.* This expression reveals that the risk of a portfolio depends on how each stock's return moves in relation to it.

We can reduce the formula even further by replacing the second R_P with a weighted average and simplifying:

$$Var(R_P) = \sum_i x_i Cov(R_i, R_P) = \sum_i x_i Cov(R_i, \Sigma_j x_j R_j)$$

$$= \sum_i \sum_j x_i x_j Cov(R_i, R_j) \qquad (11.11)$$

This formula says that the variance of a portfolio is equal to the sum of the covariances of the returns of all pairs of stocks in the portfolio multiplied by each of their portfolio weights.[3] That is, the overall variability of the portfolio depends on the total co-movement of the stocks within it.

Diversification with an Equally Weighted Portfolio of Many Stocks

We can use Eq. 11.11 to calculate the variance of an equally weighted portfolio of size n. An **equally weighted portfolio** is a portfolio in which the same amount is invested in each stock; thus, $x_i = 1 / n$ for each stock. In this case, we have the following formula:[4]

---

3. Looking back, we can see that Eq. 11.11 generalizes the case of two stocks in Eq. 11.7.

4. For an n-stock portfolio, there are n variance terms (anytime $i = j$ in Eq. 11.11) with weight $x_i^2 = 1 / n^2$ on each, which implies a weight of $n / n^2 = 1 / n$ on the average variance. There are $n^2 - n$ covariance terms (all the terms minus the n variance terms) with weight $x_i x_j = 1 / n^2$ on each, which implies a weight of $(n^2 - n) / n^2 = 1 - 1 / n$ on the average covariance.

Variance of an Equally Weighted Portfolio of n Stocks

$$Var(R_P) = \frac{1}{n}(\text{Average Variance of the Individual Stocks})$$

$$+ \left(1 - \frac{1}{n}\right)(\text{Average Covariance between the Stocks}) \qquad (11.12)$$

Equation 11.12 demonstrates that as the number of stocks, n, grows large, the variance of the portfolio is determined primarily by the average covariance among the stocks. Consider a portfolio of stocks selected randomly from the stock market. The historical volatility of the return of a typical large firm in the stock market is about 40%, and the typical correlation between the returns of large firms is about 28%. Given these statistics, how does the volatility of an equally weighted portfolio vary with the number of stocks?

From Eq. 11.12, the volatility of an n-stock portfolio is given by

$$SD(R_P) = \sqrt{\frac{1}{n}(0.40^2) + \left(1 - \frac{1}{n}\right)(0.28 \times 0.40 \times 0.40)}$$

We graph the volatility for different numbers of stocks in Figure 11.2. Note that the volatility declines as the number of stocks in the portfolio grows. In fact, nearly half of the volatility of the individual stocks is eliminated in a large portfolio as the result of diversification. The benefit of diversification is most dramatic initially: The decrease in volatility when going from one to two stocks is much larger than the decrease when going from 100 to 101 stocks—indeed, almost all of the benefit of diversification can be achieved with about 30 stocks. Even for a very large portfolio, however, we cannot eliminate all of risk. The variance of the portfolio converges to the average covariance, so the volatility declines to $\sqrt{0.28 \times 0.4 \times 0.4} = 21.17\%$.[5]

FIGURE 11.2

Volatility of an Equally Weighted Portfolio Versus the Number of Stocks

The volatility declines as the number of stocks in the portfolio increases. Even in a very large portfolio, however, market risk remains.

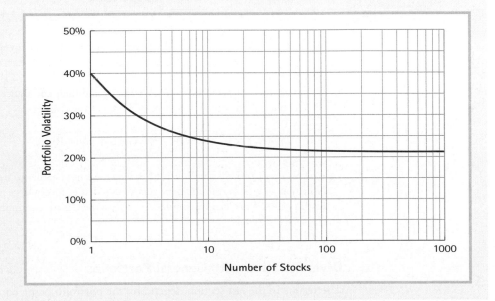

---

5. You might wonder what happens if the average covariance is negative. It turns out that while the covariance between a pair of stocks can be negative, as the portfolio grows large the average covariance cannot be negative because the returns of all stocks cannot move in opposite directions simultaneously.

EXAMPLE
11.7

Diversification Using Different Types of Stocks

Problem

Stocks within a single industry tend to have a higher correlation than stocks in different industries. Likewise, stocks in different countries have lower correlation on average than stocks within the United States. What is the volatility of a very large portfolio of stocks within an industry in which the stocks have a volatility of 40% and a correlation of 60%? What is the volatility of a very large portfolio of international stocks with a volatility of 40% and a correlation of 10%?

Solution

From Eq. 11.12, the volatility of the industry portfolio as $n \to \infty$ is given by

$$\sqrt{\text{Average Covariance}} = \sqrt{0.60 \times 0.40 \times 0.40} = 31.0\%$$

This volatility is higher than when using stocks from different industries as in Figure 11.2. Combining stocks from the same industry that are more highly correlated therefore provides less diversification. We can achieve superior diversification using international stocks. In this case,

$$\sqrt{\text{Average Covariance}} = \sqrt{0.10 \times 0.40 \times 0.40} = 12.6\%$$

Equation 11.12 can also be used to derive one of the key results that we discussed in Chapter 10: When risks are independent, all of the risk can be diversified by holding a large portfolio.

EXAMPLE
11.8

Volatility When Risks Are Independent

Problem

What is the volatility of an equally weighted average of n independent, identical risks?

Solution

If risks are independent, they are uncorrelated and their covariance is zero. Using Eq. 11.12, the volatility of an equally weighted portfolio of the risks is

$$SD(R_p) = \sqrt{Var(R_p)} = \sqrt{\tfrac{1}{n} Var(\text{Individual Risk})} = \frac{SD(\text{Individual Risk})}{\sqrt{n}}$$

This result coincides with Eq. 10.8, which we used earlier to evaluate independent risks. Note that as $n \to \infty$, the volatility goes to 0—that is, a very large portfolio will have *no* risk. In this case, all risk can be eliminated because there is no common risk.

Diversification with General Portfolios

The results in the last section depend on the portfolio being equally weighted. For a portfolio with arbitrary weights, we can rewrite Eq. 11.10 in terms of the correlation as follows:

$$Var(R_p) = \sum_i x_i Cov(R_i, R_p) = \sum_i x_i SD(R_i) SD(R_p) Corr(R_i, R_p)$$

Dividing both sides of this equation by the standard deviation of the portfolio yields the following important decomposition of the volatility of a portfolio:

Volatility of a Portfolio with Arbitrary Weights

Security i's contribution to the
volatility of the portfolio

$$SD(R_P) = \sum_i \underbrace{x_i \times SD(R_i) \times Corr(R_i, R_P)} \qquad (11.13)$$

$\uparrow$ Amount of i held $\qquad$ $\uparrow$ Total Risk of i $\qquad$ $\uparrow$ Fraction of i's risk that is common to P

Equation 11.13 states that each security contributes to the volatility of the portfolio according to its volatility, or total risk, scaled by its correlation with the portfolio, which adjusts for the fraction of the total risk that is common to the portfolio. Therefore, when combining stocks into a portfolio that puts positive weight on each stock, unless all of the stocks have a perfect positive correlation of $+1$ with the portfolio (and thus with one another), the risk of the portfolio will be lower than the weighted average volatility of the individual stocks:

$$SD(R_P) = \sum_i x_i SD(R_i) \ Corr(R_i, R_P) < \sum_i x_i SD(R_i) \qquad (11.14)$$

Contrast Eq. 11.14 with Eq. 11.3 for the expected return. The expected return of a portfolio is equal to the weighted average expected return, but the volatility of a portfolio is *less than* the weighted average volatility: We can eliminate some volatility by diversifying.

CONCEPT CHECK

1. How does the volatility of an equally weighted portfolio change as more stocks are added to it?

2. How does the volatility of a portfolio compare with the weighted average volatility of the stocks within it?

11.4 Risk Versus Return: Choosing an Efficient Portfolio

Now that we understand how to calculate the expected return and volatility of a portfolio, we can return to the main goal of the chapter and explain how an investor can create an efficient portfolio. Let's start with the simplest case—an investor who can choose between only two stocks.

Efficient Portfolios with Two Stocks

Consider Intel Corporation and the Coca-Cola Company. From 1996 to 2004, Intel stock had an average return of 25.6% on an annual basis, with a volatility of 48%. During the same period, Coca-Cola had an average return of 6.3% and a volatility of 27%. In addition, the returns of Intel and Coca-Cola were uncorrelated.[6] Suppose an investor believes these stocks will continue to perform similarly, with expected returns, volatilities, and correlation as follows:

---

6. Based on annualized monthly returns. Of course, Coca-Cola and Intel are exceptional in this regard—most stocks are positively correlated with each other.

Stock	Expected Return	Volatility	Correlation with	
			Intel	Coca-Cola
Intel	26%	50%	1.0	0.0
Coca-Cola	6%	25%	0.0	1.0

How should the investor choose a portfolio of these two stocks? Are some portfolios preferable to others?

Let's compute the expected return and volatility for different combinations of the stocks. Consider a portfolio with 40% invested in Intel stock and 60% invested in Coca-Cola stock. We can compute the expected return from Eq. 11.3 as

$$E[R_{40-60}] = x_I E[R_I] + x_C E[R_C] = 0.40(26\%) + 0.60(6\%) = 14\%$$

We can compute the variance using Eq. 11.9,

$$Var(R_{40-60}) = x_I^2 SD(R_I)^2 + x_C^2 SD(R_C)^2 + 2x_I x_C Corr(R_I, R_C) SD(R_I) SD(R_C)$$
$$= 0.40^2(0.50)^2 + 0.60^2(0.25)^2 + 2(0.40)(0.60)(0)(0.50)(0.25) = 0.0625$$

so that the volatility is $SD(R_{40-60}) = \sqrt{0.0625} = 25\%$. The results for different portfolio weights are shown in Table 11.4.

TABLE 11.4	Expected Returns and Volatility for Different Portfolios of Two Stocks

Portfolio Weights		Expected Return (%)	Volatility (%)
x_I	x_C	$E[R_P]$	$SD[R_P]$
1.00	0.00	26.0	50.0
0.80	0.20	22.0	40.3
0.60	0.40	18.0	31.6
0.40	0.60	14.0	25.0
0.20	0.80	10.0	22.3
0.00	1.00	6.0	25.0

Due to diversification, it is possible to find a portfolio with even lower volatility than either stock: Investing 20% in Intel stock and 80% in Coca-Cola stock, for example, has a volatility of only 22.3%. But knowing that investors care about volatility *and* expected return, we must consider both simultaneously. To do so, we plot the volatility and expected return of each portfolio in Figure 11.3. The portfolios from Table 11.4 are labeled with the portfolio weights. The curve (a hyperbola) represents the set of portfolios that we can create using arbitrary weights.

Faced with the choices in Figure 11.3, which ones make sense for an investor who is concerned with both the expected return and the volatility of her portfolio? Suppose the investor considers investing 100% in Coca-Cola stock. As we can see from Figure 11.3, other portfolios—such as the portfolio with 20% in Intel stock and 80% in Coca-Cola stock—make the investor better off in *both* ways: (1) They have a higher expected return,

FIGURE 11.3

Volatility Versus Expected Return for Portfolios of Intel and Coca-Cola Stock

Labels indicate portfolio weights (x_I, x_C) for Intel and Coca-Cola stocks. Portfolios on the red portion of the curve, with at least 20% invested in Intel stock, are efficient. Those on the blue portion of the curve, with less than 20% invested in Intel stock, are inefficient—an investor can earn a higher expected return with lower risk by choosing an alternative portfolio.

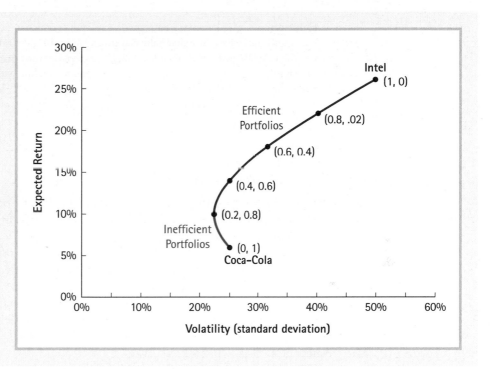

and (2) they have lower volatility. As a result, investing solely in Coca-Cola stock is not a good idea.

More generally, we say a portfolio is an **inefficient portfolio** whenever it is possible to find another portfolio that is better in terms of both expected return and volatility. Looking at Figure 11.3, a portfolio is inefficient if there are other portfolios above and to the left—that is, to the northwest—of it. Investing solely in Coca-Cola stock is inefficient, and the same is true of all portfolios with more than 80% in Coca-Cola stock (the blue part of the curve). Inefficient portfolios are not optimal for an investor. By contrast, portfolios with at least 20% in Intel stock are efficient (the red part of the curve): There is no other portfolio of the two stocks that offers a higher expected return with lower volatility.

An investor seeking high returns and low volatility should only invest in an efficient portfolio, so we can rule out inefficient portfolios because they represent inferior investment choices. However, the efficient portfolios cannot be easily ranked, because investors will choose among them based on their own preferences for return versus risk. For example, an extremely conservative investor who cares only about minimizing risk would choose the lowest-volatility portfolio (20% Intel, 80% Coca-Cola). An aggressive investor might choose to invest 100% in Intel stock—even though that approach is riskier, the investor may be willing to take that chance to earn a higher expected return.

EXAMPLE 11.9

Improving Returns with an Efficient Portfolio

Problem
Sally Ferson has invested 100% of her money in Coca-Cola stock and is seeking investment advice. She would like to earn the highest expected return possible without increasing her volatility. Which portfolio would you recommend?

Solution

In Figure 11.3, we can see that Sally can invest up to 40% in Intel stock without increasing her volatility. Because Intel stock has a higher expected return than Coca-Cola stock, she will earn higher expected returns by putting more money in Intel stock. Therefore, you should recommend that Sally put 40% of her money in Intel stock, leaving 60% in Coca-Cola stock. This portfolio has the same volatility of 25%, but an expected return of 14% rather than the 6% she has now.

The Effect of Correlation

In Figure 11.3, we assumed that the returns of Intel and Coca-Cola stocks are uncorrelated. Let's consider how the risk and return combinations in the figure would change if the correlations were different.

Correlation has no effect on the expected return of a portfolio. For example, a 40–60 portfolio will still have an expected return of 14%. However, the volatility of the portfolio will differ depending on the correlation, as we saw in Section 11.2. In particular, the lower the correlation, the lower the volatility we can obtain. In terms of Figure 11.3, as we lower the correlation and therefore the volatility of the portfolios, the curve showing the portfolios will bend to the left to a greater degree. This effect is illustrated in Figure 11.4.

When the stocks are perfectly positively correlated, the set of portfolios is identified by the straight line between them. In this extreme case (the red line in Figure 11.4), the volatility of the portfolio is equal to the weighted average volatility of the two stocks—

FIGURE 11.4

Effect on Volatility and Expected Return of Changing the Correlation between Intel and Coca-Cola Stock

This figure illustrates correlations of 1, 0.5, 0, −0.5, and −1. The lower the correlation, the lower the risk of the portfolios.

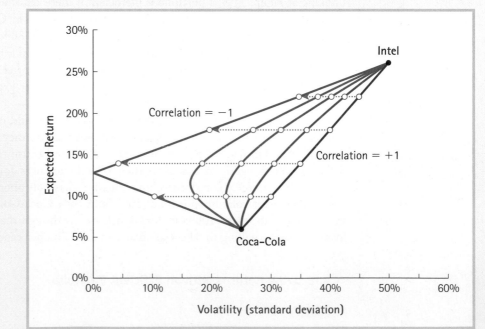

there is no diversification. When the correlation is less than 1, however, the volatility of the portfolios is reduced due to diversification, and the curve bends to the left. The reduction in risk (and the bending of the curve) becomes greater as the correlation decreases. At the other extreme of perfect negative correlation (blue line), the line again becomes straight, this time reflecting off the vertical axis. In particular, when the two stocks are perfectly negatively correlated, it becomes possible to hold a portfolio that bears absolutely no risk.

Short Sales

Thus far we have considered only portfolios in which we invest a positive amount in each stock. A positive investment in a security can be referred to as a **long position** in the security. But it is also possible to invest a *negative* amount in a stock, called a **short position**, by engaging in a **short sale**, a transaction in which you sell a stock that you do not own and then buy that stock back in the future.

Short selling is an advantageous strategy if, for example, you expect a stock price to decline in the future. In that case, you receive more upfront for the shares than you need to pay to replace them in the future. But as Example 11.10 shows, short selling can also be advantageous even if the stock price rises, as long as the portfolio is long another stock with a higher realized return.

EXAMPLE 11.10

Returns from a Short Sale

Problem

Suppose you have $20,000 in cash to invest. You decide to short sell $10,000 worth of Coca-Cola stock and invest the proceeds from your short sale, plus your $20,000, in Intel. At the end of the year, you decide to liquidate your portfolio. If the two stocks have the following realized returns, what is the return on your portfolio?

	P_0	$Div_1 + P_1$	Return
Intel	25.00	31.50	26%
Coca-Cola	40.00	42.40	6%

Solution

You short sold $10,000 or $10,000 / $40 = 250 shares of Coca-Cola stock and invested the $10,000, plus your $20,000, in Intel. That is, you purchased $30,000 or $30,000 / $25 = 1200 shares of Intel stock.

At year-end, your 1200 shares of Intel stock are worth 1200 × $31.50 = $37,800. However, you need to close your short sale by purchasing the 250 Coca-Cola shares that you sold, which costs 250 × $42.40 = $10,600. Thus your final proceeds are $37,800 − $10,600 = $27,200. Given your initial out-of-pocket expense of $20,000, you have earned a return of $7200 / $20,000 = 36%, a higher return than the return of either stock.

What are the portfolio weights corresponding to a short sale? We interpret a short sale as a negative investment in the corresponding stock. For instance, in Example 11.10, our initial investment is −$10,000 in Coca-Cola stock, and +$30,000 in Intel stock, for a

The Mechanics of a Short Sale

In mid-October 2004, Delta Air Lines stood on the verge of bankruptcy. Its only hope of avoiding bankruptcy in the near future was to reach an agreement with the pilots union to cut pilots' salaries by one-third. In the face of this crisis, the stock price had fallen by more than

any dividends that Delta would have paid him had you not borrowed his shares.*

The chart illustrates the cash flows from a short sell. First you receive the current price of the stock. Then you must pay any dividends. Finally you pay the future stock

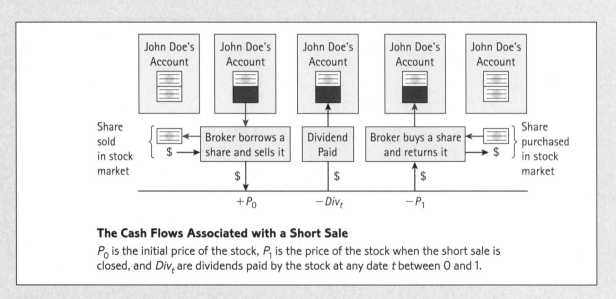

The Cash Flows Associated with a Short Sale

P_0 is the initial price of the stock, P_1 is the price of the stock when the short sale is closed, and Div_t are dividends paid by the stock at any date t between 0 and 1.

70% in the prior year. And many investors apparently felt the stock would fall further—the **short interest** (number of shares sold short) in Delta exceeded 65 million, representing more than 50% of Delta's outstanding shares.

How do you sell Delta stock if you do not own it? To short sell a stock, you must contact your broker. Your broker will try to borrow the stock from someone who currently owns it. Suppose John Doe currently holds Delta stock in a brokerage account. Your broker can lend you shares from John Doe's account so that you can sell them in the market at the current stock price. Of course, at some point you must close the short sale and return the shares to John Doe. So, you will buy the shares in the market, and your broker will replace them in John Doe's account. In the meantime, you must also pay John Doe

price. This is exactly the reverse of the cash flows you receive from buying a stock:

	Date 0	Date t	Date 1
Cash flows from buying a stock	$-P_0$	$+Div_t$	$+P_1$
Cash flows from short selling a stock	$+P_0$	$-Div_t$	$-P_1$

Because the cash flows are reversed, if you short sell a stock, rather than receiving its return, you must *pay* its return to the person you borrowed the stock from. In this way, short selling is like borrowing money at an interest rate equal to the return on the stock (which is unknown until the transaction is completed).† Investors who believed Delta stock would have a low or negative return might therefore decide to short sell the stock.

---

*In practice, John Doe may not even know his shares of the stock have been borrowed. He continues to receive dividends as before and, should he need the shares for any reason, the broker will replace them either by (1) borrowing shares from someone else or (2) forcing the short-seller to close his position and buy the shares in the market.

†Typically, the broker will charge a fee for finding the shares to borrow, and require the short-seller to deposit collateral guaranteeing the short-seller's ability to buy the stock later. The fees and the opportunity cost of depositing collateral tend to be small, so we ignore them in our analysis.

total net investment of $30,000 − $10,000 = $20,000 cash. The corresponding portfolio weights are

$$x_I = \frac{\text{Value of investment in Intel}}{\text{Total value of portfolio}} = \frac{30,000}{20,000} = 150\%$$

$$x_C = \frac{\text{Value of investment in Coca-Cola}}{\text{Total value of portfolio}} = \frac{-10,000}{20,000} = -50\%$$

Note that the portfolio weights still add up to 100%. Using these portfolio weights, we can calculate the return of the portfolio using Eq. 11.2:

$$R_P = \sum_i x_i R_i = (150\%)(26\%) + (-50\%)(6\%) = 36\%$$

All of the equations in this chapter continue to hold if we interpret short sales in this fashion. In general, we say a portfolio is short those stocks that have negative portfolio weights, and long those stocks that have positive portfolio weights.

EXAMPLE 11.11

Volatility with Short Sales

Problem
Suppose Intel stock has a volatility of 50%, Coca-Cola stock has a volatility of 25%, and the stocks are uncorrelated. What is the volatility of a portfolio that is short $10,000 of Coca-Cola and long $30,000 of Intel?

Solution
We can compute the volatility from Eq. 11.8, using portfolio weights $x_I = 150\%$ and $x_C = -50\%$. The volatility of the portfolio is

$$SD(R_P) = \sqrt{Var(R_P)} = \sqrt{x_I^2 Var(R_I) + x_C^2 Var(R_C) + 2x_I x_C Cov(R_I, R_C)}$$

$$= \sqrt{1.5^2 \times 0.50^2 + (-0.5)^2 \times 0.25^2 + 2(1.5)(-0.5)(0)} = 76.0\%$$

Note that when we allow for short sales, the volatility of the portfolio can exceed the volatility of the stocks within it.

In Figure 11.5, we show the effect on the investor's choice set when we allow for short sales. Short selling Intel to invest in Coca-Cola is not efficient (blue dashed curve)—other portfolios exist that have a higher expected return *and* a lower volatility. However, short selling Coca-Cola to invest in Intel is efficient in this case. While such a strategy leads to a higher volatility, it also provides the investor with a higher expected return. This strategy could be attractive to an aggressive investor. In general, short selling leads to higher expected returns if the stocks that are shorted are expected to have lower returns than the stocks in which the portfolio is long.

Risk Versus Return: Many Stocks

Recall from Section 11.3 that adding more stocks to a portfolio reduces risk through diversification. Let's consider the effect of adding a third stock to our portfolio, Bore Industries,

FIGURE 11.5

Portfolios of Intel and Coca-Cola Allowing for Short Sales

Labels indicate portfolio weights (x_I, x_C) for Intel and Coca-Cola stocks. Red indicates efficient portfolios, blue indicates inefficient portfolios. The dashed curves indicate positions that require shorting either Coca-Cola (red) or Intel (blue). Shorting Intel to invest in Coca-Cola is inefficient. Shorting Coca-Cola to invest in Intel is efficient and might be attractive to an aggressive investor who is seeking high expected returns.

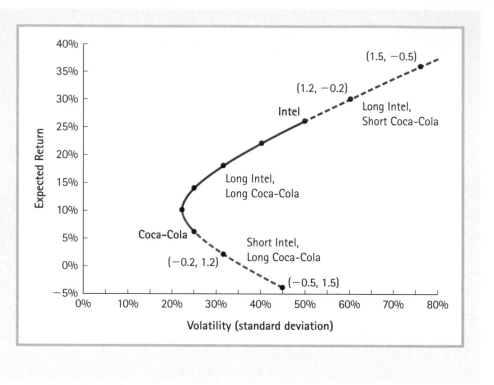

which is uncorrelated with Intel and Coca-Cola but is expected to have a very low return of 2%:

			Correlation with		
Stock	**Expected Return**	**Volatility**	**Intel**	**Coca-Cola**	**Bore Ind.**
Intel	26%	50%	1.0	0.0	0.0
Coca-Cola	6%	25%	0.0	1.0	0.0
Bore Industries	2%	25%	0.0	0.0	1.0

Figure 11.6 illustrates the portfolios that we can construct using these three stocks.

Because Bore stock is inferior to Coca-Cola stock—it has the same volatility but a lower return—you might guess that no investor would want to hold a long position in Bore. However, that conclusion ignores the diversification opportunities that Bore provides. Figure 11.6 shows the results of combining Bore with Coca-Cola or with Intel (light blue curves), or combining Bore with a 50–50 portfolio of Coca-Cola and Intel (dark blue curve).[7] We can see from the figure that some of the portfolios we obtained by combining only Intel and Coca-Cola (black curve) are inferior to these new possibilities.

When we combine Bore stock with every portfolio of Intel and Coca-Cola, and allow for short sales as well, we get an entire region of risk and return possibilities rather than just a single curve. This region is depicted as the shaded area in Figure 11.7. But note that

---

7. When a portfolio includes another portfolio, we can compute the weight of each stock by multiplying the portfolio weights. For example, a portfolio with 30% in Bore stock and 70% in the *portfolio* of (50% Intel, 50% Coca-Cola) has 30% in Bore stock, 70% × 50% = 35% in Intel stock, and 70% × 50% = 35% in Coca-Cola stock.

FIGURE 11.6

Expected Return and Volatility for Selected Portfolios of Intel, Coca-Cola, and Bore Industries Stocks

By combining Bore (B) with Intel (I), Coca-Cola (C), and portfolios of Intel and Coca-Cola, we introduce new risk and return possibilities. We can also do better than with just Coca-Cola and Intel alone (the black curve). Portfolios of Bore and Coca-Cola (B + C) and Bore and Intel (B + I) are shown in light blue in the figure. The dark blue curve is a combination of Bore with a portfolio of Intel and Coca-Cola.

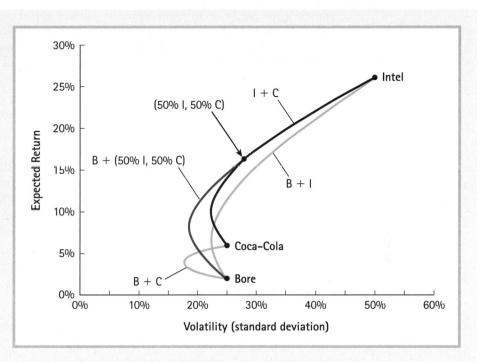

FIGURE 11.7

The Volatility and Expected Return for All Portfolios of Intel, Coca-Cola, and Bore Stock

Portfolios of all three stocks are shown, with the dark blue area showing portfolios without short sales, and the light blue area showing portfolios that include short sales. The best risk–return combinations are on the efficient frontier (red curve). The efficient frontier improves (has a higher return for each level of risk) when we move from two to three stocks.

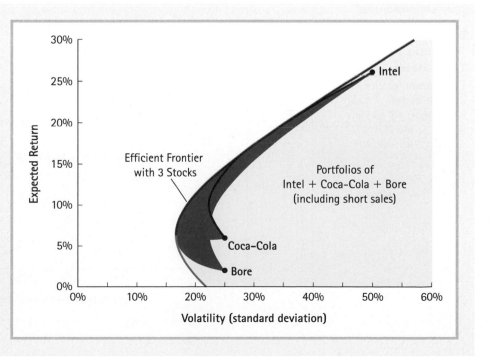

most of these portfolios are inefficient. The efficient portfolios—those offering the highest possible expected return for a given level of volatility—are those on the northwest edge of the shaded region, which we call the **efficient frontier** for these three stocks. In this case none of the stocks, on its own, is on the efficient frontier, so it would not be efficient to put all our money in a single stock.

When the set of investment opportunities increases from two to three stocks, the efficient frontier improves. Visually, the old frontier with any two stocks is located inside the new frontier. In general, adding new investment opportunities allows for greater diversification and improves the efficient frontier. Figure 11.8 uses historical data to show the effect of increasing the set from three stocks (Exxon Mobil, GE, and IBM) to ten stocks. Even though the added stocks appear to offer inferior risk–return combinations on their own, because they allow for additional diversification, the efficient frontier improves with their inclusion. Thus, to arrive at the best possible set of risk and return opportunities, we should keep adding stocks until all investment opportunities are represented. Ultimately, based on our estimates of returns, volatilities, and correlations, we can construct the efficient frontier for *all* available risky investments showing the best possible risk and return combinations that can be obtained by optimal diversification.

CONCEPT CHECK

1. How does the correlation between two stocks affect the risk and return of portfolios that combine them?

2. What is the efficient frontier, and how does it change when more stocks are used to construct portfolios?

FIGURE 11.8

Efficient Frontier with Ten Stocks Versus Three Stocks

The efficient frontier expands as new investments are added. (Based on monthly returns, 1996–2004.)

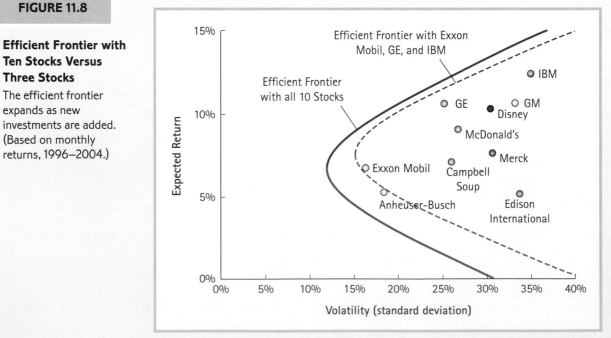

11.5 Risk-Free Saving and Borrowing

Thus far, we have considered the risk and return possibilities that result from combining risky investments into portfolios. By including all risky investments in the construction of the efficient frontier, we achieve maximum diversification.

There is another way besides diversification to reduce risk that we have not yet considered: We can keep some of our money in a safe, no-risk investment like Treasury bills. Of course, doing so will likely reduce our expected return. Conversely, if we are an aggressive investor who is seeking high expected returns, we might decide to borrow money to invest even more in the stock market. In this section we will see that the ability to choose the amount to invest in risky versus riskless securities allows us to determine the *optimal portfolio* of risky securities for an investor.

Investing in Risk-Free Securities

Consider an arbitrary risky portfolio with returns R_P. Let's look at the effect on risk and return of putting a fraction x of our money in the portfolio, while leaving the remaining fraction $(1 - x)$ in risk-free Treasury bills with a yield of r_f.

Using Eq. 11.3 and Eq. 11.8, we calculate the expected return and variance of this portfolio, whose return we will denote by R_{xP}. First, the expected return is

$$E[R_{xP}] = (1 - x)r_f + xE[R_P]$$
$$= r_f + x(E[R_P] - r_f) \qquad (11.15)$$

The first equation simply states that the expected return is the weighted average of the expected returns of Treasury bills and the portfolio. (Because we know upfront the current interest rate paid on Treasury bills, we do not need to compute an expected return for them.) The second equation rearranges the first to give a useful interpretation. Starting with an investment solely in Treasury bills, we can interpret x as the fraction of Treasury bills we have replaced with portfolio P, gaining the expected difference in their returns. This difference, $(E[R_P] - r_f)$, is the portfolio's risk premium or excess return. In summary, our expected return is equal to the risk-free rate plus a fraction of the risk premium of the portfolio based on the amount we invest in it.

Next let's compute the volatility. The volatility of the risk-free investment is zero; the risk-free rate r_f is known when we make our investment. Because our return on the risk-free investment is fixed and does not move with (or against) our portfolio, the covariance between the risk-free investment and the portfolio is also zero. Thus,

$$SD(R_{xP}) = \sqrt{(1 - x)^2 Var(r_f) + x^2 Var(R_P) + 2(1 - x)x\, Cov(r_f, R_P)}$$
$$= \sqrt{x^2 Var(R_P)}$$
$$= x\, SD(R_P) \qquad (11.16)$$

That is, the volatility is only a fraction of the volatility of the portfolio, based on the amount we invest in it.

The blue line in Figure 11.9 illustrates combinations of volatility and expected return for different choices of x. Looking at Eq. 11.15 and Eq. 11.16, as we increase the fraction x invested in P, we increase both our risk and our risk premium proportionally. Hence the line is *straight* from the risk-free investment through P.

The Risk–Return Combinations from Combining a Risk-Free Investment and a Risky Portfolio

Given a risk-free rate of 5%, the risk-free investment is represented in the graph by the point with 0% volatility and an expected return of 5%. The blue line shows the portfolios obtained by investing x in portfolio P and $(1 - x)$ in the risk-free investment. Investments with weight $x > 100\%$ in portfolio P require borrowing at the risk-free interest rate.

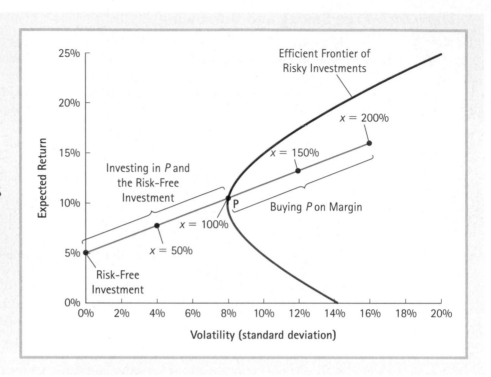

Borrowing and Buying Stocks on Margin

As we increase the fraction x invested in the portfolio P from 0 to 100%, we move along the line in Figure 11.9 from the risk-free investment to P. If we increase x beyond 100%, we get points beyond P in the graph. In this case, we are short selling the risk-free investment, so we must pay the risk-free return. That is, short selling the risk-free investment is equivalent to borrowing money at the risk-free interest rate through a standard loan.

Borrowing money to invest in stocks is referred to as **buying stocks on margin** or using leverage. A portfolio that consists of a short position in the risk-free investment is known as a *levered* portfolio. As you might expect, margin investing is a risky investment strategy. Note that the region of the blue line in Figure 11.9 with $x > 100\%$ has higher risk than the portfolio P itself. At the same time, margin investing can provide higher expected returns than investing in P using only the funds we have available.

EXAMPLE 11.12

Margin Investing

Problem

Suppose you have $10,000 in cash, and you decide to borrow another $10,000 at a 5% interest rate to invest in the stock market. You invest the entire $20,000 in portfolio Q with a 10% expected return and a 20% volatility. What is the expected return and volatility of your investment? What is your realized return if Q goes up 30% over the course of the year? What return do you realize if Q falls by 10% over the course of the year?

Solution

You have doubled your investment in Q by buying stocks on margin, so $x = 200\%$. Using Eq. 11.15 and Eq. 11.16,

$$E[R_{xQ}] = r_f + x(E[R_Q] - r_f) = 5\% + 2 \times (10\% - 5\%) = 15\%$$

$$SD(R_{xQ}) = x\,SD(R_Q) = 2 \times (20\%) = 40\%$$

You have increased both your expected return and your risk relative to the portfolio Q.

If Q goes up 30%, your investment will be worth $26,000 at year-end. However, you will owe $10,000 \times 1.05 = \$10,500$ on your loan. After repaying your loan, you will have $26,000 - \$10,500 = \$15,500$. Because you initially invested $10,000 of your own money, this is a 55% return.

If Q drops by 10%, you are left with $18,000 - \$10,500 = \$7500$, and your return is -25%.

Note that your returns are more extreme than those of the portfolio: 55% and -25% versus 30% and -10%, respectively. In fact, the range is doubled to $55\% - (-25\%) = 80\%$ from $30\% - (-10\%) = 40\%$. This doubling corresponds to the doubling of the volatility of the portfolio.

Identifying the Tangent Portfolio

Looking back at Figure 11.9, we can see that portfolio P is not the best portfolio to combine with the risk-free investment. By forming a portfolio out of the risk-free asset and a portfolio somewhat higher on the efficient frontier than portfolio P, we will get a line that is steeper than the line through P. If the line is steeper, then for any level of volatility, we will earn a higher expected return.

To earn the highest possible expected return for any level of volatility we must find the portfolio that generates the steepest possible line when combined with the risk-free investment. The slope of the line through a given portfolio P is often referred to as the **Sharpe ratio** of the portfolio:

$$\text{Sharpe Ratio} = \frac{\text{Portfolio Excess Return}}{\text{Portfolio Volatility}} = \frac{E[R_P] - r_f}{SD(R_P)} \tag{11.17}$$

The Sharpe ratio measures the ratio of reward-to-volatility provided by a portfolio.[8] The optimal portfolio to combine with the risk-free asset will be the one with the highest Sharpe ratio, as it will lead to the steepest possible line. The portfolio with the highest Sharpe ratio is the portfolio where the line with the risk-free investment just touches, and so is tangent to, the efficient frontier of risky investments, as shown in Figure 11.10. The portfolio that generates this tangent line is known as the **tangent portfolio**. All other portfolios of risky assets lie below this line. Because the tangent portfolio has the highest Sharpe ratio of any portfolio in the economy, the tangent portfolio provides the biggest reward per unit of volatility of any portfolio available.[9]

---

8. The Sharpe ratio was first introduced by William Sharpe as a measure to compare the performance of mutual funds. See William Sharpe, "Mutual Fund Performance," *Journal of Business* (January 1966): 119–138.

9. In addition to the steepness of the line in Figure 11.10, there is another interpretation to the Sharpe ratio: It is the number of standard deviations the portfolio's return would have to fall to underperform the risk-free investment. Thus, if returns are normally distributed, the portfolio with the highest Sharpe ratio can be interpreted as the portfolio with the greatest chance of earning a return above the risk-free rate.

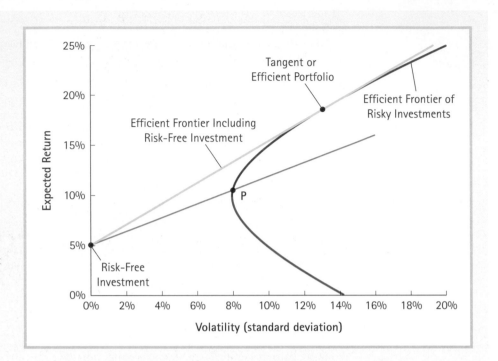

FIGURE 11.10

The Tangent or Efficient Portfolio

The tangent portfolio is the portfolio with the highest Sharpe ratio. Investments on the green line connecting the risk-free investment and the tangent portfolio provide the best risk and return tradeoff available to an investor. As a result, the tangent portfolio is also referred to as the efficient portfolio.

As is evident from Figure 11.10, combinations of the risk-free asset and the tangent portfolio provide the best risk and return tradeoff available to an investor. This observation has a striking consequence. It means that the tangent portfolio is efficient and that, once we include the risk-free investment, all efficient portfolios are combinations of the risk-free investment and the tangent portfolio. That is, no other portfolio that consists of only risky assets is efficient. Therefore, the optimal portfolio of *risky* investments no longer depends on how conservative or aggressive the investor is; every investor should invest in the tangent portfolio *independent of his or her taste for risk.* The investor's preferences will determine only *how much* to invest in the tangent portfolio versus the risk-free investment. Conservative investors will invest a small amount, choosing a portfolio on the line near the risk-free investment. Aggressive investors will invest more, choosing a portfolio that is near the tangent portfolio or even beyond it by buying stocks on margin. Both types of investors will choose to hold the *same* portfolio of risky assets, the tangent portfolio.

EXAMPLE 11.13

Optimal Portfolio Choice

Problem

Your uncle calls and asks for investment advice. Currently, he has $100,000 invested in portfolio *P* as graphed in Figure 11.10. This portfolio has an expected return of 10.5% and a volatility of 8%. Suppose the risk-free rate is 5%, and the tangent portfolio has an expected return of 18.5% and a volatility of 13%. To maximize your uncle's expected return without increasing his volatility, which portfolio would you recommend? If your uncle prefers to keep his expected return the same but minimize his risk, which portfolio would you recommend?

Solution

In either case the best portfolios are combinations of the risk-free investment and the tangent portfolio. If we invest an amount x in the tangent portfolio T, using Eq. 11.15 and Eq. 11.16 the expected return and volatility are

$$E[R_{xT}] = r_f + x(E[R_T] - r_f) = 5\% + x(18.5\% - 5\%)$$

$$SD(R_{xT}) = x\,SD(R_T) = x(13\%)$$

So, to maintain the volatility at 8%, $x = 8\% / 13\% = 61.5\%$. In this case, your uncle should invest 61.5% of his money ($61,500) in the tangent portfolio, and the remaining 38.5% ($38,500) in the risk-free investment. His expected return will then be 5% + (61.5%)(13.5%) = 13.3%, the highest possible given his level of risk.

Alternatively, to keep the expected return equal to the current value of 10.5%, x must satisfy 5% + x(13.5%) = 10.5%, so x = 40.7%. Now your uncle should invest $40,700 in the tangent portfolio and $59,300 in the risk-free investment, lowering his volatility level to (40.7%)(13%) = 5.29%, the lowest possible given his expected return.

We have achieved one of the primary goals of this chapter and explained how to identify the efficient portfolio of risky assets. The **efficient portfolio** is the tangent portfolio, the portfolio with the highest Sharpe ratio in the economy. By combining it with the risk-free investment, an investor will earn the highest possible expected return for any level of volatility he or she is willing to bear.

CONCEPT CHECK

1. Explain the concept of buying stocks on margin.

2. What is the Sharpe ratio of a portfolio?

3. What do we know about the Sharpe ratio of the efficient portfolio?

11.6   The Efficient Portfolio and the Cost of Capital

Now that we have identified the efficient portfolio, let's see how we can use it to determine the cost of capital for an investment.

How to Improve a Portfolio: Beta and the Required Return

Consider a portfolio of risky securities, P. If we invest more in this portfolio and less in the risk-free investment, our expected return and volatility will change. The Sharpe ratio of the portfolio tells us how much our expected return will increase for a given increase in volatility. The portfolio P is efficient if it has the highest possible Sharpe ratio; that is, it is efficient if it provides the largest increase in expected return possible for a given increase in volatility.

To determine whether P has the highest possible Sharpe ratio, let's consider whether we could raise its Sharpe ratio by adding more of some investment i to the portfolio. From Eq. 11.13, the contribution of investment i to the volatility of the portfolio depends on the risk that i has in common with the portfolio, which is measured by i's volatility multiplied by its correlation with P. If we purchase more of investment i by borrowing, we will earn the expected return of i minus the risk-free return. Thus adding i to the portfolio P will improve our Sharpe ratio if [10]

$$\underbrace{E[R_i] - r_f}_{\substack{\text{Additional return} \\ \text{from investment } i}} > \underbrace{SD(R_i) \times Corr(R_i, R_P)}_{\substack{\text{Incremental volatility} \\ \text{from investment } i}} \times \underbrace{\frac{E[R_P] - r_f}{SD(R_P)}}_{\substack{\text{Return per unit of volatilty} \\ \text{available from portfolio } P}} \tag{11.18}$$

To provide a further interpretation for this condition, we define the beta of an investment i with portfolio P:

Beta of Investment i with Portfolio P

$$\beta_i^P \equiv \frac{SD(R_i) \times Corr(R_i, R_P)}{SD(R_P)} = \frac{Cov(R_i, R_P)}{Var(R_P)} \tag{11.19}$$

where the second equation follows from the definition of the correlation in terms of the covariance. β_i^P measures the sensitivity of the investment i to the fluctuations of the portfolio P. That is, for each 1% change in the portfolio's excess return, the investment's excess return is expected to change by β_i^P percent due to risks that i has in common with P. With this definition, we can restate Eq. 11.18 as follows:

$$E[R_i] > r_f + \beta_i^P \times (E[R_P] - r_f)$$

Therefore increasing the amount invested in i will increase the Sharpe ratio of portfolio P if its expected return $E[R_i]$ exceeds the required return r_i, which is given by

Required Return for Investment i Given Current Portfolio P

$$r_i = r_f + \beta_i^P \times (E[R_P] - r_f) \tag{11.20}$$

The **required return** is the expected return that is necessary to compensate for the risk investment i will contribute to the portfolio. The required return for an investment i is equal to the risk-free interest rate plus a risk premium that is equal to the risk premium of the investor's current portfolio, P, scaled by β_i^P. If i's expected return exceeds this required return, then adding more of it will improve the performance of the portfolio.

EXAMPLE 11.14

The Required Return of a New Investment

Problem

You are currently invested in the Omega Fund, a broad-based fund that invests in stocks and other securities with an expected return of 15% and a volatility of 20%, as well as in risk-free Treasuries paying 3%. Your broker suggests that you add a real estate fund to your current portfolio. The real estate fund has an expected return of 9%, a volatility of 35%, and a correlation of 0.10 with the Omega Fund. Will adding the real estate fund improve your portfolio?

---

10. If $Corr(R_i, R_P)$ is positive, we can write Eq. 11.18 more intuitively as a comparison of the ratio of the gain in expected return to the incremental volatility from security i with the Sharpe ratio of the portfolio:

$$\frac{E[R_i] - r_f}{SD(R_i) \times Corr(R_i, R_P)} > \frac{E[R_P] - r_f}{SD(R_P)}$$

Solution

Let R_{re} be the return of the real estate fund and R_O be the return of the Omega Fund. From Eq. 11.19, the beta of the real estate fund with the Omega Fund is

$$\beta_{re}^O = \frac{SD(R_{re})\,Corr(R_{re}, R_O)}{SD(R_O)} = \frac{35\% \times 0.10}{20\%} = 0.175$$

We can then use Eq. 11.20 to determine the required return that makes the real estate fund an attractive addition to our portfolio:

$$r_{re} = r_f + \beta_{re}^O(E[R_O] - r_f) = 3\% + 0.175 \times (15\% - 3\%) = 5.1\%$$

The real estate fund has an expected return of 9% that exceeds the required return of 5.1%. Therefore, we can improve the performance of our current portfolio by investing some amount in the real estate fund.

Expected Returns and the Efficient Portfolio

If a security's expected return exceeds its required return given our current portfolio, then we can improve the performance of our portfolio by adding more of the security. But how much more should we add? As we buy shares of security i, its correlation with our portfolio will increase, ultimately raising its required return until $E[R_i] = r_i$. At this point our holdings of security i are optimal.

Similarly, if security i's expected return is less than the required return r_i, we should reduce our holdings of i. As we do so the correlation and the required return r_i will fall until $E[R_i] = r_i$.

Thus, if we have no restrictions on our ability to buy or sell securities that are traded in the market, we will continue to trade until the expected return of each security equals its required return—that is, until $E[R_i] = r_i$ holds for all i. At this point, no trade can possibly improve the risk–reward ratio of the portfolio, and our portfolio is the optimal, efficient portfolio. That is,

A portfolio is efficient if and only if the expected return of every available security equals its required return.

From Eq. 11.20, this result implies the following relationship between the expected return of any security and its beta with the efficient portfolio:

Expected Return of a Security

$$E[R_i] = r_i \equiv r_f + \beta_i^{eff} \times (E[R_{eff}] - r_f) \tag{11.21}$$

where R_{eff} is the return of the efficient portfolio, the portfolio with the highest Sharpe ratio of any portfolio in the economy.

EXAMPLE 11.15

Identifying the Efficient Portfolio

Problem

Consider the Omega Fund and real estate fund of Example 11.14. Suppose you have $100 million invested in the Omega Fund. In addition to this position, how much should you invest in the real estate fund to form an efficient portfolio of these two funds?

Solution

Suppose that for each \$1 invested in the Omega Fund, we borrow x_{re} dollars (or sell x_{re} worth of Treasury bill) to invest in the real estate fund. Then our portfolio has a return of $R_P = R_O + x_{re}(R_{re} - r_f)$, where R_O is the return of the Omega Fund and R_{re} is the return of the real estate fund. Table 11.5 shows the change to the expected return and volatility of our portfolio as we increase the investment x_{re} in the real estate fund, using the formulas

$$E[R_P] = E[R_O] + x_{re}(E[R_{re}] - r_f)$$

$$Var(R_P) = Var[R_O + x_{re}(R_{re} - r_f)] = Var(R_O) + x_{re}^2 Var(R_{re}) + 2x_{re}Cov(R_{re},R_O)$$

Adding the real estate fund initially improves the Sharpe ratio of the portfolio, as defined by Eq. 11.17. As we add more of the real estate fund, however, its correlation with our portfolio rises, computed as

$$Corr(R_{re},R_P) = \frac{Cov(R_{re},R_P)}{SD(R_{re})SD(R_P)} = \frac{Cov(R_{re},R_O + x_{re}(R_{re} - r_f))}{SD(R_{re})SD(R_P)}$$

$$= \frac{x_{re}Var(R_{re}) + Cov(R_{re},R_O)}{SD(R_{re})SD(R_P)}$$

The beta of the real estate fund—computed from Eq. 11.19—also rises, increasing the required return. The required return equals the 9% expected return of the real estate fund at about $x_{re} = 11\%$, which is the same level of investment that maximizes the Sharpe ratio. Thus the efficient portfolio of these two funds includes \$0.11 in the real estate fund per \$1 invested in the Omega Fund.

TABLE 11.5			**Sharpe Ratio and Required Return for Different Investments in the Real Estate Fund**			
x_{re}	$E[R_P]$	$SD(R_P)$	Sharpe Ratio	$Corr(R_{re}, R_P)$	β_{re}^P	Required Return r_{re}
0%	15.00%	20.00%	0.6000	10.0%	0.18	5.10%
4%	15.24%	20.19%	0.6063	16.8%	0.29	6.57%
8%	15.48%	20.47%	0.6097	23.4%	0.40	8.00%
10%	15.60%	20.65%	0.6103	26.6%	0.45	8.69%
11%	15.66%	20.74%	0.6104	28.2%	0.48	9.03%
12%	15.72%	20.84%	0.6103	29.7%	0.50	9.35%
16%	15.96%	21.30%	0.6084	35.7%	0.59	10.60%

Cost of Capital

In this chapter, we have focused on the optimal portfolio choice decision faced by an individual investor. The results of this section provide the link between the optimal portfolio choice and an investment's cost of capital. Intuitively, for an investor to benefit from a new investment, its expected return should exceed its required return as calculated in Eq. 11.20. The required return depends on the risk that the investment has in common

Nobel Prizes   Harry Markowitz and James Tobin

The techniques of mean-variance portfolio optimization, which allow an investor to find the portfolio with the highest expected return for any level of variance (or volatility), were developed in an article, "Portfolio Selection," published in the *Journal of Finance* in 1952 by Harry Markowitz. Markowitz's approach has evolved into one of the main methods of portfolio optimization used on Wall Street. In recognition for his contribution to the field, Markowitz was awarded the Nobel Prize for economics in 1990. The same ideas were developed concurrently by Andrew Roy in "Safety First and the Holding of Assets," published in *Econometrica* in the same year in which Markowitz's article appeared. In 1999, after winning the Nobel Prize, Markowitz wrote "I am often called the father of modern portfolio theory, but Roy can claim an equal share of this honor."* Ironically Mark Rubinstein[†] appears to have discovered another article that develops these ideas published twelve years earlier in 1940

by Bruno de Finetti in the Italian journal *Giornale dell'Instituto Italiano degli Attuari*. It has remained in obscurity perhaps because it was first translated into English in only 2004 (by Luca Barone).**

James Tobin furthered this theory with the important insight that by combining risky securities with a risk-free investment, an optimal tangent portfolio could be found that does not depend on an investor's tolerance for risk. In his article "Liquidity Preference as Behavior Toward Risk" published in the *Review of Economic Studies* in 1958, Tobin proved a "Separation Theorem," which showed that Markowitz's techniques could be applied to find the tangent portfolio, and then investors could choose their exposure to risk by varying their investments in the tangent portfolio and the risk-free investment. Tobin was awarded the Nobel Prize for economics in 1981 for his contributions to finance and economics.

---

*H. M. Markowitz, "The Early History of Portfolio Theory: 1600–1960," *Financial Analysts Journal* 55 (1999): 5–16.

[†]M. Rubinstein, "A History of the Theory of Investments," (New Jersey: John Wiley and Sons, 2006): p. 349.

**English translation forthcoming in *Journal of Investment Management*, Third Quarter, 2006.

---

with investor's current portfolio. Because the investor will optimally hold an efficient portfolio, *the appropriate risk premium for an investment can be determined from its beta with the efficient portfolio:*

Cost of Capital for Investment i

$$r_i = r_f + \beta_i^{eff} \times (E[R_{eff}] - r_f) \tag{11.22}$$

We can interpret Eq. 11.22 as follows: From Figure 11.10, the best investments available to an investor in the market are combinations of the risk-free asset and the efficient portfolio. We can construct a portfolio with the same systematic risk as the investment opportunity by investing the fraction $x = \beta_i^{eff}$ in the efficient portfolio and the fraction $(1 - x)$ in the risk-free asset. From Eq. 11.15, this portfolio has the expected return given in Eq. 11.22. Therefore, *the cost of capital of investment i is equal to the expected return of the best available portfolio in the market with the same sensitivity to systematic risk, given by Eq. 11.22.*

We derived the same expression for the cost of capital in Chapter 10. Now, however, we have a more precise definition for the efficient portfolio: It is the tangent portfolio, or the portfolio that has the highest Sharpe ratio of any portfolio in the economy. This portfolio provides the benchmark that identifies the systematic risk present in the economy. Because all other risk is diversifiable, it is an investment's beta with respect to the efficient portfolio that measures its sensitivity to systematic risk, and therefore determines its cost of capital.

INTERVIEW WITH
Jonathan Clements

Jonathan Clements is the personal-finance columnist for The Wall Street Journal. *His "Getting Going" column, launched in October 1994, now appears every Wednesday in the Journal and most Sundays in over 80 U.S. newspapers.*

QUESTION: *You have written for years on personal finance. How has academic theory influenced investor behavior?*

ANSWER: When I started writing about mutual funds in the late 1980s, investors would ask, "What are your favorite funds?" Today, they are more likely to say, "I'm looking to add a foreign-stock fund to my portfolio. Which funds in that category do you like? Or should I just index?"

We have clearly gotten away from the blind pursuit of market-beating returns, and there is more focus on portfolio construction and a growing willingness to consider indexing. That reflects the impact of academic research.

What has really influenced investors has been the academic "grunt work" of the past four decades, which has given us a decent grasp of what historical market returns look like. Thanks to that research, many ordinary investors have a better understanding of how stocks have performed relative to bonds. They realize that most actively managed stock mutual funds don't beat the market, and thus there is a case for indexing. They appreciate that different market sectors perform well at different times, so there is a real value in diversifying.

QUESTION: *Academics talk about efficient frontiers and optimal portfolios. How does that translate into advice for someone looking to build a portfolio?*

ANSWER: While academic research has influenced ordinary investors, we shouldn't overstate the case. To some extent, the research has merely codified what investors already knew intuitively. For instance, investors have always thought about risk as well as return, and they have always been inclined to diversify. The academic research may have made investors a little more rigorous in their thinking, but it didn't radically change their behavior.

Moreover, to the extent that the research doesn't fit with investors' intuition, they have clearly rejected it. Investors still behave in ways that academics would consider suboptimal. They don't build well-diversified portfolios—and then focus on the risk and return of the overall portfolio. Instead, they build moderately diversified portfolios—and then pay a lot of attention to the risk and reward of each investment they own.

QUESTION: *How does risk tolerance affect the type of portfolio a person should build?*

ANSWER: In theory, investors should hold the globally diversified all-asset "market portfolio" and then, depending on their risk tolerance, either add risk-free assets to reduce volatility or use leverage to boost returns. But almost nobody invests that way. In fact, I once tried to find out what the market portfolio looks like—and discovered that nobody knows for sure.

Among the vast majority of ordinary investors, the idea of using leverage to buy investments is an anathema. In practice, of course, many are doing just that. They hold a portfolio of assets, including stocks, bonds and real estate, and they have a heap of debt, including their mortgage, auto loans and credit-card balances. But the implication—that they effectively have a leveraged stock-market bet—would horrify most investors. Mental accounting still dominates.

While nobody seems to know what the market portfolio looks like, investors have become willing to consider a broader array of assets. In recent years, ordinary U.S. investors have increased their investment in foreign stocks, real-estate investment trusts and commodities. While there is an element of performance chasing in all this, I think the trend will continue, as people come to realize that they can lower a portfolio's risk level by adding apparently risky investments.

EXAMPLE
11.16

Computing the Cost of Capital for a Project

Problem

Alphatec is seeking to raise capital from a large group of investors to expand its operations. Suppose the S&P 500 portfolio is the efficient portfolio of risky securities (so that these investors have holdings in this portfolio). The S&P 500 portfolio has a volatility of 15% and an expected return of 10%. The investment is expected to have a volatility of 40% and a 50% correlation with the S&P 500. If the risk-free interest rate is 4%, what is the appropriate cost of capital for Alphatec's expansion?

Solution

First we determine the beta of the investment relative to the S&P 500 (the efficient portfolio):

$$\beta_A^{SP} = \frac{SD(R_A) \times Corr(R_A, R_{SP})}{SD(R_{SP})} = 0.50 \times \frac{40\%}{15\%} = 1.33$$

Then we use Eq. 11.20 to determine the required return that makes the investment an attractive addition to the investors' portfolio:

$$r_A = r_f + \beta_A^{SP} \times (E[R_{SP}] - r_f) = 4\% + 1.33 \times (10\% - 4\%) = 12\%$$

Because Alphatec's investors will require this return, this return is the appropriate cost of capital for the expansion.

CONCEPT CHECK

1. Define the required return for an investment.

2. What determines the cost of capital for an investment?

Summary

1. The portfolio weight is the initial fraction x_i of an investor's money invested in each asset. Portfolio weights add up to 1.

$$x_i = \frac{\text{Value of investment } i}{\text{Total value of portfolio}} \qquad (11.1)$$

2. The expected return of a portfolio is the weighted average of the expected returns of the investments within it, using the portfolio weights.

$$E[R_p] = \sum_i x_i E[R_i]$$

3. To find the risk of a portfolio, we need to know the degree to which stock returns move together. Covariance and correlation measure the co-movement of returns.

   a. The covariance between returns R_i and R_j is defined by

   $$Cov(R_i, R_j) = E[(R_i - E[R_i])(R_j - E[R_j])] \qquad (11.4)$$

   and is estimated from historical data using

   $$Cov(R_i, R_j) = \frac{1}{T-1} \sum_t (R_{i,t} - \bar{R}_i)(R_{j,t} - \bar{R}_j) \qquad (11.5)$$

b. The correlation is defined as the covariance of the returns divided by the standard deviation of each return. The correlation is always between -1 and $+1$. It represents the fraction of the volatility due to risk that is common to the securities.

$$Corr(R_i, R_j) = \frac{Cov(R_i, R_j)}{SD(R_i)\, SD(R_j)} \tag{11.6}$$

4. The variance of a portfolio depends on the covariance of the stocks within it.

   a. For a portfolio with two stocks, the portfolio variance is

   $$Var(R_P) = x_1^2 Var(R_1) + x_2^2 Var(R_2) + 2x_1 x_2 Cov(R_1, R_2) \tag{11.8}$$

   b. If the portfolio weights are positive, as we lower the covariance between the two stocks in a portfolio, we lower the portfolio variance.

5. The variance of an equally weighted portfolio is

$$Var(R_P) = \frac{1}{n} \text{(Average Variance of the Individual Stocks)}$$

$$+ \left(1 - \frac{1}{n}\right)\text{(Average Covariance between the Stocks)} \tag{11.12}$$

6. Diversification eliminates independent risks. The volatility of a large portfolio results from the common risk between the stocks in the portfolio.

7. Each security contributes to the volatility of the portfolio according to its total risk scaled by its correlation with the portfolio, which adjusts for the fraction of the total risk that is common to the portfolio.

$$SD(R_P) = \sum_i x_i \times SD(R_i) \times Corr(R_i, R_P) \tag{11.13}$$

8. Efficient portfolios offer investors the highest possible expected return for a given level of risk. The set of efficient portfolios is called the efficient frontier. As investors add stocks to a portfolio, the efficient portfolio improves.

   a. An investor seeking high expected returns and low volatility should invest only in efficient portfolios.

   b. Investors will choose from the set of efficient portfolios based on their own preferences for return versus risk.

9. Investors may use short sales in their portfolios. A portfolio is short those stocks with negative portfolio weights. Short selling extends the set of possible portfolios.

10. Portfolios can be formed by combining the risk-free asset with a portfolio of risky assets.

    a. The expected return for this type of portfolio is

    $$E[R_{xP}] = r_f + x(E[R_P] - r_f) \tag{11.15}$$

    b. Volatility for this type of portfolio is

    $$SD(R_{xP}) = x\, SD(R_P) \tag{11.16}$$

    c. The risk–return combinations of the risk-free investment and a risky portfolio lie on a straight line connecting the two investments.

11. The goal of an investor who is seeking to earn the highest possible expected return for any level of volatility is to find the portfolio that generates the steepest possible line when combined with the risk-free investment. The slope of this line is called the Sharpe ratio of the portfolio.

$$\text{Sharpe Ratio} = \frac{\text{Portfolio Excess Return}}{\text{Portfolio Volatility}} = \frac{E[R_P] - r_f}{SD(R_P)} \tag{11.17}$$

12. The risky portfolio with the highest Sharpe ratio is called the efficient portfolio. The efficient portfolio is the optimal combination of risky investments independent of the investor's appetite for risk. An investor can select a desired degree of risk by choosing the amount to invest in the efficient portfolio relative to the risk-free investment.

13. The beta of an investment with a portfolio is

$$\beta_i^P \equiv \frac{SD(R_i) \times Corr(R_i, R_P)}{SD(R_P)} = \frac{Cov(R_i, R_P)}{Var(R_P)} \tag{11.19}$$

Beta indicates the sensitivity of the investment's return to fluctuations in the portfolio's return.

14. Buying shares of security i improves the performance of a portfolio if its expected return exceeds the required return:

$$r_i = r_f + \beta_i^P \times (E[R_P] - r_f) \tag{11.20}$$

15. A portfolio is efficient when $E[R_i] = r_i$ for all securities. The following relationship therefore holds between beta and expected returns for traded securities:

$$E[R_i] = r_i \equiv r_f + \beta_i^{eff} \times (E[R_{eff}] - r_f) \tag{11.21}$$

16. Because the investor will optimally hold an efficient portfolio, the risk premium for an investment can be determined from its beta with the efficient portfolio:

$$r_i = r_f + \beta_i^{eff} \times (E[R_{eff}] - r_f) \tag{11.22}$$

This cost of capital of investment i is equal to the expected return of the best available portfolio in the market with the same sensitivity to systematic risk.

Key Terms

Further Reading

The following text presents in more depth optimal portfolio choice: W. F. Sharpe, *Investments* (Upper Saddle River, NJ: Prentice Hall, 1999).

Two seminal papers on optimal portfolio choice are: H. M. Markowitz, "Portfolio Selection," *Journal of Finance* 7 (March 1952): 77–91; and J. Tobin, "Liquidity Preference as Behavior Toward Risk," *Review of Economic Studies* 25 (February 1958): 65–86.

The insight that the expected return of a security is given by its beta with an efficient portfolio was first derived in the following paper: R. Roll, "A Critique of the Asset Pricing Theory's Tests," *Journal of Financial Economics* 4 (1977): 129–176.

The following paper provides a historical account of how researchers recognized the impact that short-sales constraints may have in the expected returns of assets: M. Rubinstein, "Great Moments in Financial Economics: III. Short-Sales and Stock Prices," *Journal of Investment Management* 2(1) (First Quarter 2004): 16–31.

Problems

All problems in this chapter are available in MyFinanceLab. An asterisk (*) indicates problems with a higher level of difficulty.

The Expected Return of a Portfolio

1. You are considering how to invest part of your retirement savings. You have decided to put $200,000 into three stocks: 50% of the money in GoldFinger (currently $25 / share), 25% of the money in Moosehead (currently $80 / share), and the remainder in Venture Associates (currently $2 / share). If GoldFinger stock goes up to $30 / share, Moosehead stock drops to $60 / share, and Venture Associates stock rises to $3 per share,

    a. What is the new value of the portfolio?

    b. What return did the portfolio earn?

    c. If you don't buy or sell shares after the price change, what are your new portfolio weights?

2. There are two ways to calculate the expected return of a portfolio: either calculate the expected return using the value and dividend stream of the portfolio as a whole, or calculate the weighted average of the expected returns of the individual stocks that make up the portfolio. Which return is higher?

The Volatility of a Two-Stock Portfolio

3. If the return of two stocks has a correlation of 1, what does this imply about the relative movements in the stock prices?

EXCEL 4. Using the data in the following table, estimate (a) the average return and volatility for each stock, (b) the covariance between the stocks, and (c) the correlation between these two stocks.

	Realized Returns	
Year	**Stock A**	**Stock B**
1998	−10%	21%
1999	20%	30%
2000	5%	7%
2001	−5%	−3%
2002	2%	−8%
2003	9%	25%

EXCEL   **5.**   The following spreadsheet contains monthly returns for Coca-Cola (Ticker: KO) and Exxon Mobil (Ticker: XOM) for 1990. Using these data, estimate (a) the average monthly return and volatility for each stock, (b) the covariance between the stocks, and (c) the correlation between these two stocks.

Date	KO	XOM
19900131	−10.84%	−6.00%
19900228	2.36%	1.28%
19900330	6.60%	−1.86%
19900430	2.01%	−1.90%
19900531	18.36%	7.40%
19900629	−1.22%	−0.26%
19900731	2.25%	8.36%
19900831	−6.89%	−2.46%
19900928	−6.04%	−2.00%
19901031	13.61%	0.00%
19901130	3.51%	4.68%
19901231	0.54%	2.22%

EXCEL   **6.**   Using the data from Table 11.3, what is the covariance between the stocks of American Air Lines and Delta Air Lines?

EXCEL   **7.**   Using your estimates from Problem 4, calculate the volatility (standard deviation) of a portfolio that is 70% invested in stock A and 30% invested in stock B.

EXCEL   **8.**   Using the spreadsheet from Problem 5, calculate the volatility (standard deviation) of a portfolio that is 55% invested in Coca-Cola stock and 45% invested in Exxon Mobil stock. Calculate the volatility by (a) using Eq. 11.8, (b) using Eq. 11.9, and (c) calculating the monthly returns of the portfolio and computing its volatility directly. How do your results compare?

EXCEL   ***9.**   Plot the volatility (standard deviation) of a portfolio of Coca-Cola and Exxon Mobil stocks as a function of the fraction invested in Coca-Cola. Use the spreadsheet from Problem 5. Base any statistical estimates that you need on the data in the spreadsheet.

The Volatility of a Large Portfolio

10.   How would you calculate the volatility (standard deviation) of a portfolio containing many stocks?

11.   What is the volatility (standard deviation) of a very large portfolio of equally weighted stocks within an industry in which the stocks have a volatility of 50% and a correlation of 40%?

Risk Versus Return: Choosing an Efficient Portfolio

12.   Suppose Intel's stock has an expected return of 26% and a volatility of 50%, while Coca-Cola's has an expected return of 6% and a volatility of 25%. If these two stocks were perfectly negatively correlated (i.e. their correlation coefficient is −1),

   a. Calculate the portfolio weights that remove all risk.

   b. What is the risk-free rate of interest in this economy?

For problems 13–15, suppose Johnson & Johnson and the Walgreen Company have expected returns and volatilities shown below, with a correlation of 22%.

	$E[R]$	$SD[R]$
Johnson & Johnson	7%	16%
Walgreen Company	10%	20%

13. Calculate (a) the expected return and (b) the volatility (standard deviation) of a portfolio that is equally invested in Johnson & Johnson's and Walgreen's stock.

14. Calculate (a) the expected return and (b) the volatility (standard deviation) of a portfolio that consists of a long position of $10,000 in Johnson & Johnson and a short position of $2000 in Walgreen's.

*15. Using the same data as for Problems 13 and 14, calculate the expected return and the volatility (standard deviation) of a portfolio consisting of Johnson & Johnson's and Walgreen's stocks using a wide range of portfolio weights. Plot the expected return as a function of the portfolio volatility. Using your graph, identify the range of Johnson & Johnson's portfolio weights that yield efficient combinations of the two stocks, rounded to the nearest percentage point.

Risk-Free Saving and Borrowing

*16. Suppose you have $100,000 in cash, and you decide to borrow another $15,000 at a 4% interest rate to invest in the stock market. You invest the entire $115,000 in a portfolio J with a 15% expected return and a 25% volatility.

   a. What is the expected return and volatility (standard deviation) of your investment?

   b. What is your realized return if J goes up 25% over the year?

   c. What return do you realize if J falls by 20% over the year?

17. Assume all investors want to hold a portfolio that, for a given level of volatility, has the maximum possible expected return. Explain why, when a risk-free asset exists, all investors will choose to hold the same portfolio of risky stocks.

Calculating the Beta of a Traded Security

18. You are currently invested in the Farrallon Fund, a broad-based fund of stocks and other securities with an expected return of 12% and a volatility of 25%. Currently, the risk-free rate of interest is 4%. Your broker suggests that you add a venture capital fund to your current portfolio. The venture capital fund has an expected return of 20%, a volatility of 80%, and a correlation of 0.2 with the Farrallon Fund. Calculate the required return and use it to decide whether you should add the venture capital fund to your portfolio.

19. You have noticed a market investment opportunity that, given your current portfolio, has an expected return that exceeds your required return. What can you conclude about your current portfolio?

20. Kaui Surf Boards is seeking to raise capital from a large group of investors to expand its operations. Suppose these investors currently hold the S&P 500 portfolio, which has a volatility of 15% and an expected return of 10%. The investment is expected to have a volatility of 30% and a 15% correlation with the S&P 500. If the risk-free interest rate is 4%, what is the appropriate cost of capital for Kaui Surf Boards' expansion?

Data Case

Your manager was so impressed with your work analyzing the return and standard deviations of the twelve stocks from Chapter 10 that he would like you to continue your analysis. Specifically, he wants you to update the stock portfolio by:

- Rebalancing the portfolio with the optimum weights that will provide the best risk and return combinations for the new 12-stock portfolio.

- Determining the improvement in the return and risk that would result from these optimum weights compared to the current method of equally weighting the stocks in the portfolio.

Use the Solver function in Excel to perform this analysis (the time-consuming alternative is to find the optimum weights by trial-and-error).

1. Begin with the equally weighted portfolio analyzed in Chapter 10. Establish the portfolio returns for the stocks in the portfolio using a formula that depends on the portfolio weights. Initially, these weights will all equal 1/12. You would like to allow the portfolio weights to vary, so you will need to list the weights for each stock in separate cells and establish another cell that sums the weights of the stocks. The portfolio returns for each month MUST reference these weights for Excel solver to be of any use.

2. Compute the values for the monthly mean return and standard deviation of the portfolio. Convert these values to annual numbers (as you did in Chapter 10) for easier interpretation.

3. Compute the efficient frontier when short sales are not allowed. To activate the Solver function in Excel, click the "Tools," select "Add-Ins . . .", check "Solver Add-in" in the pop-up dialog box, and then click "OK". (*Note:* You may have to install the Solver function using the Microsoft Office Disk 1 for the installation.) To set the Solver parameters:

    a. Set the target cell as the cell of interest, making it the cell that computes the (annual) portfolio standard deviation. Minimize this value.

    b. Establish the "By Changing Cells" by holding the control key and clicking in each of the 12 cells containing the weights of each stock.

    c. Add constraints by clicking on the add button next to the "Subject to the Constraints" box. One set of constraints will be the weight of each stock that is greater than or equal to zero. Calculate the constraints individually. A second constraint is that the weights will sum to one.

    d. Compute the portfolio with the lowest standard deviation for a given expected return. Start by finding this portfolio with an expected return of 5%. To do this, add a constraint that the (annual) portfolio return equals 0.05.

    e. If the parameters are set correctly, you should get a solution when you click "Solve." If there is an error, you will need to double-check the parameters, especially the constraints.

4. Record the resulting standard deviation for the "optimally weighted" portfolio with a return of 0.05 in a separate cell on the spreadsheet. Repeat step 3 to solve for the portfolio with the lowest standard deviation for several different choices of expected return: 0.1, 0.2, 0.3, and 0.4. Record these values. Plot the efficient frontier with the constraint of no short sales. To do this, create an XY Scatter Plot (similar to what you did in Chapter 10), with portfolio standard deviation on the *x*-axis and the return on the *y*-axis.

5. Redo your analysis to allow for short sales by removing the constraint that each portfolio weight is greater than or equal to zero. Use Solver to calculate the (annual) portfolio standard deviation when the annual portfolio returns are set to 0.05, 0.1, 0.2, 0.3 and 0.4. Plot the unconstrained efficient frontier on an XY Scatter Plot. How do these portfolios compare to the mean and standard deviation for the equally weighted portfolio analyzed in Chapter 10?

The Capital Asset Pricing Model

notation

r_i	required return for security i
R_i	return of security i
$E[R_i]$	expected return of security i
r_f	risk-free interest rate
β_i^P	beta of security i with respect to portfolio P
R_{xCML}	return of the CML portfolio with fraction x invested in the market
β_i^{Mkt} or β_i	beta of security i with respect to the market portfolio
$Corr(R_i, R_j)$	correlation between returns of i and j
$Cov(R_i, R_j)$	covariance between returns of i and j
P_i	price per share of security i
N_i	number of shares outstanding of security i
MV_i	total market capitalization of security i
$SD(R_i)$	standard deviation (volatility) of the return of security i
α_i	alpha of security i

When executives at Intel Corporation evaluate a capital investment project, they must estimate the appropriate cost of capital. The cost of capital should include a risk premium that compensates Intel's investors for taking on the risk of the new project. How can Intel estimate this risk premium and, therefore, the cost of capital?

In Chapter 11, we arrived at a partial answer to this question. There we showed that the cost of capital can be computed from the beta of an investment with an efficient portfolio—that is, a portfolio that has the lowest volatility possible without lowering its expected return. The difficulty with this result is that *identifying* an efficient portfolio requires information about all securities' expected returns, volatilities, and correlations, which is much more information than a corporate executive at a company such as Intel is likely to have when evaluating a project.

In this chapter, we introduce the additional assumptions of the Capital Asset Pricing Model (CAPM). Under these assumptions, the efficient portfolio can be identified as the market portfolio of all stocks and securities. The CAPM justifies the method for determining the equity cost of capital that we first proposed at the conclusion of Chapter 10, and is the main method used by most major corporations.[1]

The CAPM was proposed as a model of risk and return by William Sharpe in a 1964 paper, as well as in related papers by Jack Treynor (1962), John Lintner (1965), and Jan Mossin (1966).[2] It has become the most important model of the relationship

---

1. In a survey of CFOs, J. Graham and C. Harvey find that more than 70% rely on the CAPM ["The Theory and Practice of Corporate Finance: Evidence from the field," *Journal of Financial Economics* 60 (2001): 187–243], and F. Bruner, K. Eades, R. Harris, and R. Higgins report that 85% of a sample of large firms rely on it ["Best Practices in Estimating the Cost of Capital: Survey and Synthesis," *Financial Practice and Education* 8 (1998): 13–28].

2. W. F. Sharpe, "Capital Asset Prices: A Theory of Market Equilibrium under Conditions of Risk," *Journal of Finance* 19 (September 1964): 425–442; Jack Treynor, "Toward a Theory of the Market Value of Risky Assets," unpublished manuscript (1961); J. Lintner, "The Valuation of Risk Assets and the Selection of Risky Investments in Stock Portfolios and Capital Budgets," *Review of Economics and Statistics* 47 (February 1965): 13–37; J. Mossin, "Equilibrium in a Capital Asset Market," *Econometrica* 34 (1966): 768–783.

between risk and return. For his contributions to the theory, William Sharpe was awarded the Nobel Prize in economics in 1990.

12.1   The Efficiency of the Market Portfolio

To evaluate the NPV of an investment, we must determine the appropriate discount rate, or cost of capital, for that investment. The results we derived at the conclusion of Chapter 11 provide a link between investors' optimal portfolio choice and the cost of capital for a firm's investment project. There we showed that the expected return of any traded security is determined by its beta with the efficient portfolio:

$$E[R_i] = r_i = r_f + \beta_i^{eff} \times (E[R_{eff}] - r_f) \tag{12.1}$$

Moreover, if investors hold the efficient portfolio, then the cost of capital for any investment project is equal to its required return r_i from Eq. 12.1, again based on its beta with the efficient portfolio.

While Eq. 12.1 provides a way to calculate an investment's cost of capital, when using it we face an important challenge: How do we identify the efficient portfolio? As we saw in Chapter 11, to identify the efficient portfolio (of risky assets) we must know the expected returns, volatilities, and correlations between investments. These quantities are difficult to forecast. Furthermore, investors' beliefs may differ, and are not necessarily known by the firm. Under these circumstances, how can we determine the efficient portfolio?

To answer this question we develop the Capital Asset Pricing Model (CAPM). This model allows corporate executives to identify the efficient portfolio (of risky assets) without having any knowledge of the expected return of each security. Instead, the CAPM uses the actions of investors themselves as input. With this insight, the model identifies the efficient portfolio as the **market portfolio**—the portfolio of all stocks and securities in the market. To obtain this remarkable result, we make three assumptions regarding the behavior of investors.

The CAPM Assumptions

There are three main assumptions that underlie the CAPM. The first is a familiar one that we have adopted since Chapter 3:

Investors can buy and sell all securities at competitive market prices (without incurring taxes or transactions costs) and can borrow and lend at the risk-free interest rate.

The second assumption is that investors choose a portfolio of traded securities that offers the highest possible expected return given the level of volatility they are willing to accept:

Investors hold only efficient portfolios of traded securities—portfolios that yield the maximum expected return for a given level of volatility.

In Chapter 11, we looked at the consequences that these first two assumptions have for portfolio choice. We found that given an investor's estimates of volatilities, correlations, and expected returns, there is a unique combination of risky securities, called the efficient portfolio. By combining the efficient portfolio with risk-free borrowing or lending, the investor can obtain the highest possible expected return for whichever level of volatility the investor is prepared to accept.

Of course, there are many investors in the world, and each may have his or her own estimates of the volatilities, correlations, and expected returns of the available securities. But investors don't come up with these estimates arbitrarily; they base them on historical patterns and other information (including market prices) that is widely available to the public. If all investors use publicly available information sources, then their estimates are likely to be similar. Consequently, it is not unreasonable to consider a special case in which all investors have the same estimates concerning future investments and returns, called **homogeneous expectations**. Although investors' expectations are not completely identical in reality, assuming homogeneous expectations should be a reasonable approximation in many markets, and represents the third simplifying assumption of the CAPM:

Investors have homogeneous expectations regarding the volatilities, correlations, and expected returns of securities.

Security Demand Must Equal Supply

If investors have homogeneous expectations, then each investor will identify the same portfolio as having the highest Sharpe ratio in the economy. Thus all investors will demand the *same* efficient portfolio of risky securities, adjusting only their investment in risk-free securities to suit their particular appetite for risk. That means that each investor will hold the different risky securities in the same proportions. Without any further information, can we determine the composition this portfolio?

The answer is yes. To see why, consider what happens if we combine the portfolios held by different investors. Because all investors are holding the risky securities in the same proportions as the efficient portfolio, their combined portfolios will also reflect the same proportions as the efficient portfolio. For example, if investors have twice as much invested in stock A as in stock B, together they also have twice as much invested in A as in B. By the same logic, the combined portfolio of risky securities of *all* investors must equal the efficient portfolio.

Furthermore, because every security is owned by someone, the sum of all investors' portfolios must equal the portfolio of all risky securities available in the market, which we defined in Chapter 10 as the market portfolio. Therefore, the efficient portfolio (the portfolio that all investors hold) must be the same portfolio as the market portfolio of all risky securities.

The insight that the market portfolio is efficient is really just the statement that *demand must equal supply*. All investors demand the efficient portfolio, and the supply of securities is the market portfolio; hence the two must coincide. If some security were not part of the efficient portfolio, then no investor would want to own it, and demand for this security would not equal its supply. This security's price would fall, causing its expected return to rise until it became an attractive investment. In this way, prices in the market will adjust so that the efficient portfolio and the market portfolio coincide, and demand equals supply.

EXAMPLE 12.1	**The Market Portfolio with Two Stocks**

Problem

Suppose it is the year 2525 and there has been a great wave of mergers that has left only two large stocks remaining for investors to invest in: Western Wares and Eastern Enterprises. Western Wares and Eastern Enterprises each have 100 shares outstanding. Under the CAPM assumptions, what is the composition of the efficient portfolio?

Solution

Under the CAPM assumptions, all investors have carefully researched the stocks and are holding the efficient portfolio. At the same time, investors must be holding 100 shares of each stock in total, because these are the shares outstanding in the market. Thus, the efficient portfolio is the market portfolio, which contains 100 shares of Western Wares and 100 shares of Eastern Enterprises.

Optimal Investing: The Capital Market Line

When the CAPM assumptions hold, choosing an optimal portfolio is relatively straightforward: It is a combination of the risk-free investment and the market portfolio. We illustrate this result in Figure 12.1. As we pointed out in Chapter 11, the tangent line graphs the highest possible expected return that can be achieved for any level of volatility. When the tangent line goes through the market portfolio, it is called the **capital market line (CML)**.

Consider a portfolio on the CML, with a fraction x invested in the market portfolio and the remaining $(1 - x)$ invested in the risk-free investment. Using Eqs. 11.15 and 11.16 from Chapter 11 for combining a portfolio with risk-free borrowing and lending, the expected return and volatility of this capital market line portfolio are as follows:

$$E[R_{xCML}] = (1 - x)r_f + xE[R_{Mkt}] = r_f + x(E[R_{Mkt}] - r_f) \tag{12.2}$$

$$SD(R_{xCML}) = x\,SD(R_{Mkt}) \tag{12.3}$$

FIGURE 12.1

The Capital Market Line

When investors have homogeneous expectations, the market portfolio and the efficient portfolio coincide. Therefore the capital market line (CML), which is the line from the risk-free investment through the market portfolio, represents the highest expected return available for any level of volatility. (Also shown are individual stocks from Figure 11.8.)

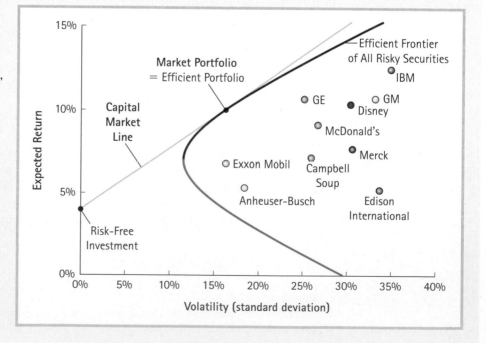

That is, the portfolio's risk premium and volatility are determined by the fraction x that is invested in the market. Recall that when x is larger than 1, the investor borrows money to increase the investment in the market. That is, the investor uses a margin loan to purchase the market portfolio.

| EXAMPLE 12.2 | **Choosing a CML Portfolio** |

Problem

Your brother-in-law's investment portfolio consists solely of $10,000 invested in McDonald's stock. Suppose the risk-free rate is 4%, McDonald's stock has an expected return of 9% and a volatility of 27%, and the market portfolio has an expected return of 10% and a volatility of 16%. Under the CAPM assumptions, which portfolio has the lowest possible volatility while having the same expected return as McDonald's stock? Which portfolio has the highest possible expected return while having the same volatility as McDonald's stock?

Solution

The CAPM assumptions imply that the best possible risk–return combinations are combinations of the risk-free investment and the market portfolio—portfolios on the capital market line. First let's find the CML portfolio that has an expected return of 9%, equal to the McDonald's return. From Eq. 12.2, we need to determine the amount x to invest in the market so that

$$9\% = E[R_{xCML}] = r_f + x(E[R_{Mkt}] - r_f) = 4\% + x(10\% - 4\%)$$

Solving for x, we get $x = 0.8333$. That is, your brother-in-law should sell his McDonald's stock and invest $8333 in the market portfolio and the remaining $1667 in the risk-free investment. Using Eq. 12.3, this portfolio has a volatility of only

$$SD(R_{xCML}) = 0.8333(16\%) = 13.3\%$$

This volatility is much lower than the volatility of McDonald's stock, and is the lowest possible volatility given an expected return of 9%.

Alternatively, we can choose the CML portfolio that matches McDonald's volatility of 27%. To do so, we use Eq. 12.3 to find x such that

$$27\% = SD(R_{xCML}) = x(16\%)$$

In this case $x = 1.6875$, so the expected return is

$$E[R_{xCML}] = 4\% + 1.6875(10\% - 4\%) = 14.1\%$$

This expected return is much higher than the expected return of McDonald's stock, and the highest possible return we can earn without increasing the volatility. To achieve this portfolio, your brother-in-law needs to sell his McDonald's stock, add (or borrow) an additional $6875, and invest $16,875 in the market portfolio.

Figure 12.2 illustrates the two alternatives to investing in McDonald's stock. Any portfolio on the capital market line between these two portfolios (that is, investing between $8333 and $16,875 in the market) will have both a higher expected return and a lower volatility than investing in McDonald's stock alone.

FIGURE 12.2

The Capital Market Line Offers the Best Possible Risk–Return Combinations

Given the assumptions in Example 12.2, portfolios with 83% to 169% invested in the market (and the rest invested or borrowed at the risk-free rate) offer a higher expected return and a lower volatility than investing 100% in McDonald's stock.

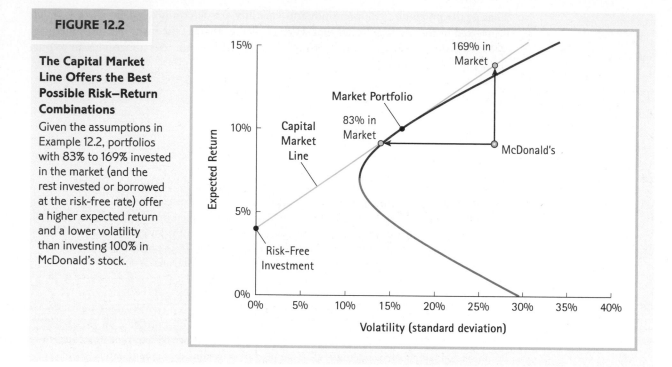

CONCEPT CHECK   1. Explain why the market portfolio is efficient according to the CAPM.

2. What is the capital market line (CML)?

12.2 Determining the Risk Premium

Under the CAPM assumptions, we can identify the efficient portfolio: It is equal to the market portfolio. More importantly, this result implies that we can determine the expected return for a security and the cost of capital of an investment opportunity by using the market portfolio as a benchmark.

Market Risk and Beta

In Eq. 12.1, we determined the expected return of an investment based on its beta with the efficient portfolio. But if the market portfolio is efficient, we can rewrite Eq. 12.1 as

$$E[R_i] = r_i = r_f + \underbrace{\beta_i^{Mkt}(E[R_{Mkt}] - r_f)}_{\text{Risk premium for security } i} \qquad (12.4)$$

In particular, the risk premium of a security is equal to the market risk premium (the amount by which the market's expected return exceeds the risk-free rate), multiplied by the amount of market risk present in the security's returns, measured by its beta with the market.

We will refer to the beta of a security with the market portfolio as simply the security's beta, and write β_i in place of β_i^{Mkt}, defined as (using Eq. 11.19)

$$\beta_i^{Mkt} \equiv \beta_i = \frac{\overbrace{SD(R_i) \times Corr(R_i, R_{Mkt})}^{\text{Volatility of } i \text{ that is common with the market}}}{SD(R_{Mkt})} = \frac{Cov(R_i, R_{Mkt})}{Var(R_{Mkt})} \qquad (12.5)$$

The beta of a security is the ratio of its volatility due to market risk to the volatility of the market as a whole.

EXAMPLE 12.3

Market and Risk-Free Betas

Problem

What is the beta of the market portfolio? What is the beta of the risk-free investment?

Solution

Using Eq. 12.5, because the correlation of a return with itself is equal to 1,

$$\text{Beta of the market portfolio} = \beta_{Mkt} = \frac{SD(R_{Mkt}) \, Corr(R_{Mkt}, R_{Mkt})}{SD(R_{Mkt})} = 1$$

Because the risk-free return is known in advance, it has no volatility and no correlation with the market. Therefore,

$$\text{Beta of the risk-free investment} = \beta_{rf} = \frac{SD(r_f) \, Corr(r_f, R_{Mkt})}{SD(R_{Mkt})} = 0$$

Under the CAPM assumptions, the market portfolio is efficient, so beta is the appropriate measure of risk to determine a security's risk premium.

EXAMPLE 12.4

Computing the Expected Return for a Stock

Problem

Suppose the risk-free return is 4% and the market portfolio has an expected return of 10% and a volatility of 16%. Campbell Soup stock has a 26% volatility and a correlation with the market of 0.33. What is Campbell Soup's beta with the market? Under the CAPM assumptions, what is its expected return?

Solution

To compute beta using Eq. 12.5:

$$\beta_{CPB} = \frac{SD(R_{CPB}) \, Corr(R_{CPB}, R_{Mkt})}{SD(R_{Mkt})} = \frac{26\% \times 0.33}{16\%} = 0.54$$

Therefore,

$$E[R_{CPB}] = r_f + \beta_{CPB}(E[R_{Mkt}] - r_f) = 4\% + 0.54(10\% - 4\%)$$

$$= 7.2\%$$

Investors will require an expected return of 7.2% to compensate for the risk associated with Campbell Soup stock.

FIGURE 12.3	The Capital Market Line and the Security Market Line

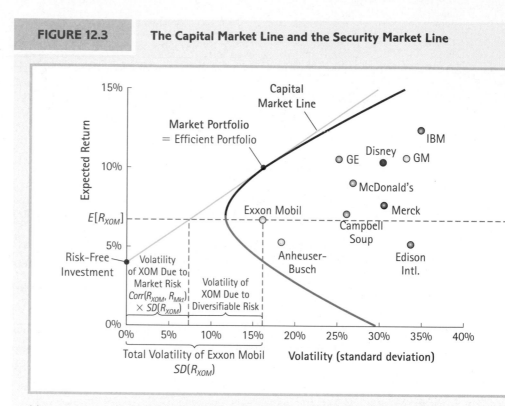

(a) The CML depicts portfolios combining the risk-free investment and the efficient portfolio, and shows the highest expected return that can be attained for each level of volatility. According to the CAPM, the market portfolio is on the CML and all other stocks and portfolios contain diversifiable risk and lie to the right of the CML, as illustrated for Exxon Mobil (XOM).

The Security Market Line

Equation 12.4 provides a justification for the method we outlined to estimate the expected return for an investment in Chapter 10. It implies that there is a linear relationship between a stock's beta and its expected return, as shown in Figure 12.3. This line is graphed in panel (b) of Figure 12.3 as the line through the risk-free investment (with a beta of 0) and the market (with a beta of 1); it is called the **security market line (SML)**.

Under the CAPM assumptions, the market portfolio is the efficient portfolio. Thus, if we plot individual securities according to their expected return and beta, the CAPM implies that they should all fall along the SML, as shown in panel (b).

Contrast this result with the capital market line shown in panel (a) of Figure 12.3, where there is no clear relationship between an individual stock's volatility and its expected return. As we illustrate for Exxon Mobil (XOM), a stock's expected return is due only to the fraction of its volatility that is common with the market—$Corr(R_{XOM}, R_{Mkt}) \times SD(R_{XOM})$; the distance of each stock to the right of the capital market line is due to its diversifiable risk. The relationship between risk and return for individual securities becomes evident only when we measure market risk rather than total risk.

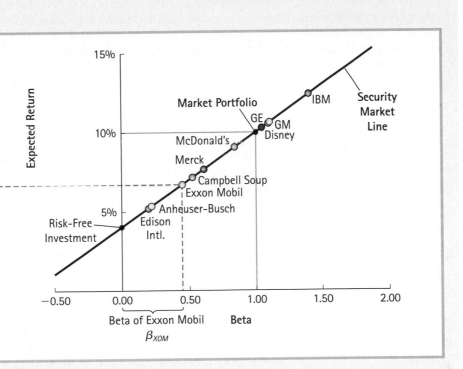

(b) The SML shows the required return for each security as a function of its beta with the market. According to the CAPM, the market portfolio is efficient, which is equivalent to the required return equaling the expected return for every security. According to the CAPM, all stocks and portfolios should lie on the SML.

EXAMPLE
12.5

A Negative-Beta Stock

Problem
Suppose the stock of Bankruptcy Auction Services, Inc. (BAS), has a negative beta of −0.30. How does its required return compare to the risk-free rate, according to the CAPM? Does this result make sense?

Solution
Because the expected return of the market is higher than the risk-free rate, Eq. 12.4 implies that the expected return of BAS will be *below* the risk-free rate. For example, if the risk-free rate is 4% and the expected return on the market is 10%,

$$E[R_{BAS}] = 4\% - 0.30(10\% - 4\%) = 2.2\%$$

(See Figure 12.3: The SML drops below r_f for $\beta < 0$.) This result seems odd: Why would investors be willing to accept a 2.2% expected return on this stock when they can invest in a safe investment and earn 4%? The answer is that a savvy investor will not hold BAS alone;

instead, she will hold it in combination with other securities as part of a well-diversified portfolio. These other securities will tend to rise and fall with the market. But because BAS has a negative beta, its correlation with the market is negative, which means that BAS tends to perform well when the rest of the market is doing poorly. Therefore, by holding BAS stock, an investor can reduce the overall market risk of her portfolio. In a sense, BAS is "recession insurance" for a portfolio, and investors will pay for this insurance by accepting a lower return.

Because the security market line applies to all securities, we can apply it to portfolios as well. For example, the market portfolio is on the SML and, according to the CAPM, other portfolios (such as mutual funds) are also on the SML. Therefore, the expected return of a portfolio should correspond to the portfolio's beta. We calculate the beta of a portfolio $R_P = \sum_i x_i R_i$ as follows:

$$\beta_P = \frac{Cov(R_P, R_{Mkt})}{Var(R_{Mkt})} = \frac{Cov\left(\sum_i x_i R_i, R_{Mkt}\right)}{Var(R_{Mkt})} = \sum_i x_i \frac{Cov(R_i, R_{Mkt})}{Var(R_{Mkt})}$$

$$= \sum_i x_i \beta_i \tag{12.6}$$

In other words, *the beta of a portfolio is the weighted average beta of the securities in the portfolio.*

EXAMPLE 12.6

The Expected Return of a Portfolio

Problem

Suppose the stock of the pharmaceutical company Pfizer (PFE) has a beta of 0.50, whereas the beta of Home Depot (HD) stock is 1.25. If the risk-free interest rate is 4%, and the expected return of the market portfolio is 10%, what is the expected return of an equally weighted portfolio of Pfizer and Home Depot stocks, according to the CAPM?

Solution

We can compute the expected return of the portfolio in two ways. First, we can use the SML to compute the expected return of each stock:

$$E[R_{PFE}] = r_f + \beta_{PFE}(E[R_{Mkt}] - r_f) = 4\% + 0.50(10\% - 4\%) = 7.0\%$$

$$E[R_{HD}] = r_f + \beta_{HD}(E[R_{Mkt}] - r_f) = 4\% + 1.25(10\% - 4\%) = 11.5\%$$

Then the expected return of the equally weighted portfolio P is

$$E[R_P] = \tfrac{1}{2}E[R_{PFE}] + \tfrac{1}{2}E[R_{HD}] = \tfrac{1}{2}(7.0\%) + \tfrac{1}{2}(11.5\%) = 9.25\%$$

Alternatively, we can compute the beta of the portfolio using Eq. 12.6:

$$\beta_P = \tfrac{1}{2}\beta_{PFE} + \tfrac{1}{2}\beta_{HD} = \tfrac{1}{2}(0.50) + \tfrac{1}{2}(1.25) = 0.875$$

We can then find the portfolio's expected return from the SML:

$$E[R_P] = r_f + \beta_P(E[R_{Mkt}] - r_f) = 4\% + 0.875(10\% - 4\%) = 9.25\%$$

Alpha

Consider the situation in Figure 12.3, and suppose new information arrives that raises the expected future return of GM and Exxon Mobil and lowers the expected future return of IBM and Anheuser-Busch. *Suppose that, if market prices remain unchanged,* this news would raise the expected return of GM and Exxon Mobil stocks by 2% and lower the expected return of IBM and Anheuser-Busch stocks by 2%, leaving the expected return of the market unchanged.[3] Figure 12.4 illustrates the effect of this change on the efficient frontier. As we can see, with the new information the market portfolio is no longer efficient. Alternative portfolios offer a higher expected return and a lower volatility than can be obtained by holding the market portfolio. Investors who are aware of this fact will want to alter their investments in order to make their portfolios efficient.

To improve the performance of their portfolios, investors who are holding the market portfolio will compare the expected return of each security with its required return from the security market line (Eq. 12.4). Figure 12.5 shows this comparison. Note that the stocks whose returns have changed are no longer on the security market line. The difference between a stock's expected return and its required return according to the security market line is called the stock's **alpha**:

$$\alpha_s = E[R_s] - r_s = E[R_s] - (r_f + \beta_s(E[R_{Mkt}] - r_f))$$

FIGURE 12.4

An Inefficient Market Portfolio

If the market portfolio is not equal to the efficient portfolio, then the market is not in the CAPM equilibrium. The figure illustrates this possibility if news is announced that raises the expected return of GM and Exxon Mobil stocks and lowers the expected return of IBM and Anheuser-Busch stocks compared to the situation depicted in Figure 12.3.

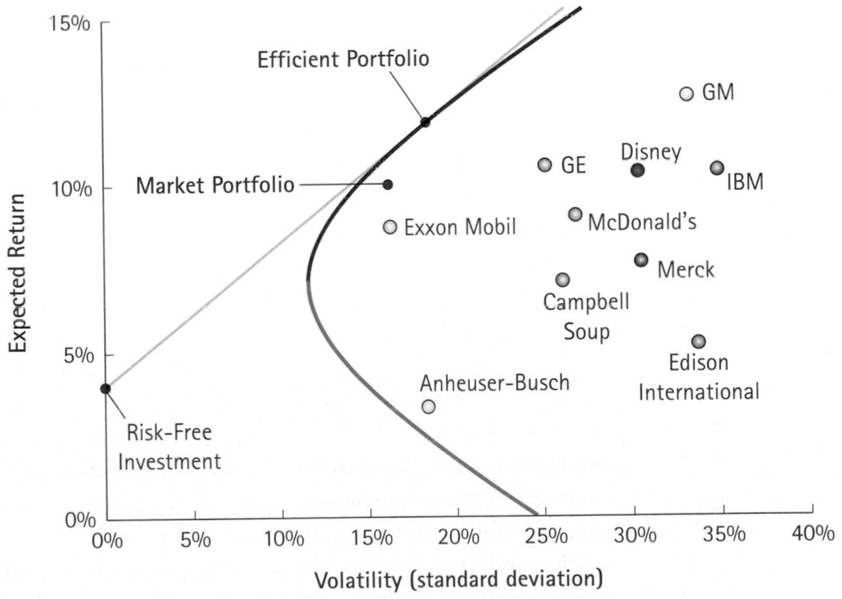

3. In general, news about GM, Exxon Mobil, IBM, and Anheuser-Busch will also change the market's expected return somewhat because these four stocks make up part of the market portfolio. For expositional simplicity, we ignore this second-order effect and assume that the changes in the expected returns in the four stocks cancel each other out in the market portfolio so that the expected return of the market remains unchanged.

Deviations from the Security Market Line

If the market portfolio is not efficient, then stocks will not all lie on the security market line. The distance of a stock above or below the security market line is the stock's alpha. We can improve upon the market portfolio by buying stocks with positive alphas and selling stocks with negative alphas.

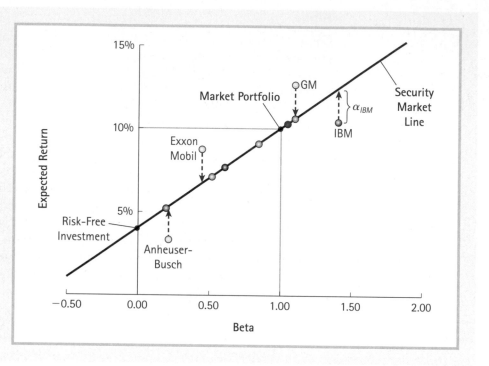

When the market portfolio is efficient, all stocks are on the security market line and have an alpha of zero. When a stock's alpha is not zero, investors can improve upon the performance of the market portfolio. As we saw in Chapter 11, the Sharpe ratio of a portfolio will increase if we buy stocks whose expected return exceeds their required return—that is, if we buy stocks with positive alphas. Similarly, we can improve the performance of our portfolio by selling stocks with negative alphas.

Faced with the situation in Figure 12.5, savvy investors who are holding the market portfolio will want to buy stock in Exxon Mobil and GM, and sell stock in Anheuser-Busch and IBM. The surge of buy orders for Exxon Mobil and GM will cause their stock prices to rise, and the surge of sell orders for Anheuser-Busch and IBM will cause their stock prices to fall. As stock prices change, so do expected returns. Recall that a stock's total return is equal to its dividend yield plus the capital gain rate. All else equal, an increase in the current stock price will lower the stock's dividend yield and future capital gain rate, thereby lowering its expected return. Thus, as savvy investors attempt to trade to improve their portfolios, they raise the price and lower the expected return of the positive-alpha stocks, and they depress the price and raise the expected return of the negative-alpha stocks, until the stocks are once again on the security market line and the market portfolio is efficient.

Summary of the Capital Asset Pricing Model

In the previous two sections, we explored the consequences of the CAPM assumptions that markets are competitive, investors choose efficient portfolios, and investors have homogeneous expectations. The CAPM leads to two major conclusions:

- *The market portfolio is the efficient portfolio.* Therefore, the best expected return–volatility combinations are portfolios on the capital market line described by Eqs. 12.2 and 12.3.
- *The risk premium for any security is proportional to its beta with the market.* Therefore, the relationship between risk and the required return is given by the security market line described by Eqs. 12.4 and 12.5.

Of course, the CAPM model is only an approximation based on rather strong assumptions. And some of its conclusions not completely accurate—it is certainly not the case that every investor holds the market portfolio, for instance. We will explore why in more detail in Chapter 13, where we also consider extensions that have been proposed to the CAPM. Nevertheless, financial economists find the qualitative intuition underlying the CAPM compelling, so it is still the most commonly used model of risk.

Many practitioners believe it sensible to *use* the CAPM and the security market line as a practical means to estimate a stock's required return and therefore a firm's equity cost of capital. In the rest of this chapter, we will explain how to implement this model. We will look more closely at the construction of the market portfolio and develop a means to estimate betas.

CONCEPT CHECK

1. What is the security market line?
2. What is a stock's alpha?

12.3 The Market Portfolio

To estimate the equity cost of capital using the CAPM, the first thing we need to do is identify the market portfolio. We have defined the market portfolio as the portfolio of *all* risky investments. But in what proportions? If you are an investor in the U.S. stock market, for example, how many shares of each security should you buy?

The answer is simple: Because the market portfolio is defined as the total supply of securities, the proportions should correspond exactly to the proportion of the total market that each security represents. Thus the market portfolio contains more of the largest stocks and less of the smallest stocks. Specifically, the investment in each security i is proportional to its **market capitalization**, which is the total market value of its outstanding shares:

$$MV_i = (\text{Number of Shares of } i \text{ Outstanding}) \times (\text{Price of } i \text{ per Share})$$
$$= N_i \times P_i \tag{12.7}$$

Value-Weighted Portfolios

A portfolio like the market portfolio, in which each security is held in proportion to its market capitalization, is called a **value-weighted portfolio**. In such a portfolio, the portfolio weights are determined as follows:

$$x_i = \frac{\text{Market Value of } i}{\text{Total Market Value of All Securities}} = \frac{MV_i}{\sum_j MV_j}$$

That is, the fraction of money invested in security i corresponds to its share of the total market value of all securities in the portfolio.

EXAMPLE 12.7	A Value-Weighted Portfolio

Problem

Suppose we have $100,000 to invest in the following stocks: Microsoft (MSFT), IBM, Wal-Mart (WMT), and Southwest Airlines (LUV). If the stock prices and number of shares outstanding are as shown in the table, what number of shares of each should we buy to construct a value-weighted portfolio?

Stock	Shares Outstanding (billions)	Stock Price ($)
MSFT	10.70	24.92
IBM	1.69	79.00
WMT	4.41	47.30
LUV	0.775	13.02

Solution

First we compute the market capitalization for each stock by multiplying the number of shares outstanding by the current price per share. For example, Microsoft has a market capitalization of 10.70 billion × $24.92 = $267 billion. Next we compute the total market capitalization for the four stocks and determine the percentage represented by each.

Stock	Market Cap ($ billions)	Percent of Total	Initial Investment	Shares Purchased	Ownership
MSFT	$267	43.1%	$43,100	1730	0.000016%
IBM	134	21.6%	21,600	273	0.000016%
WMT	209	33.7%	33,700	712	0.000016%
LUV	10	1.6%	1,600	123	0.000016%
Total	$620	100.0%	$100,000		

Based on the value weights, we can then determine the dollar amount to invest in each stock. For example, because Microsoft's market capitalization is about 43.1% of the total, we invest 43.1% × $100,000 = $43,100 in Microsoft stock. Given Microsoft's stock price of $24.92, investing $43,100 corresponds to purchasing $43,100/$24.92 = 1730 shares of Microsoft stock. We compute the number of shares for each of the other stocks similarly.

In the last column of the table, we also compute the fraction of the total number of shares outstanding that we will purchase. For Microsoft, we are buying 1730 of 10.70 billion shares, or 0.000016% of the total outstanding. Note that the percentage is the same for each stock.

In Example 12.7, we computed the number of shares purchased as a percentage of the total number of shares outstanding for each stock. Note that when buying a value-weighted portfolio, we end up purchasing the same percentage of shares of each firm. That is, a value-weighted portfolio is an **equal-ownership portfolio**: We hold an equal fraction of the total number of shares outstanding of each security in the portfolio.

This last observation is useful because it implies that to maintain a value-weighted portfolio, we do not need to trade securities and rebalance the portfolio unless the number of shares outstanding of some security changes. If the number of shares does not change, but only prices change, the portfolio will remain value weighted. Because very little trading is required to maintain it, a value-weighted portfolio is called a **passive portfolio**.

EXAMPLE 12.8

Maintaining a Value-Weighted Portfolio

Problem

Starting with the portfolio in Example 12.7, suppose that the price of Microsoft stock drops to $21 per share and Southwest Airlines' stock price rises to $26 per share. What trades are necessary to keep the portfolio value weighted?

Solution

Let's compute the value of each of the holdings:

Stock	Stock Price ($)	Shares Held	Value of Shares ($)	Percent of Portfolio
MSFT	21.00	1730	$36,330	38.3%
IBM	79.00	273	21,567	22.8%
WMT	47.30	712	33,678	35.5%
LUV	26.00	123	3,198	3.4%
		Total	$94,773	100.0%

The total value of the portfolio has dropped from $100,000 to $94,773, and each of the portfolio weights has changed. But compare the portfolio weights to the market value weights:

Stock	Shares Outstanding (billions)	Stock Price ($)	Market Cap ($ billions)	Percent of Total
MSFT	10.70	21.00	$225	38.3%
IBM	1.69	79.00	134	22.8%
WMT	4.41	47.30	209	35.5%
LUV	0.775	26.00	20	3.4%
		Total	$588	100.0%

The portfolio weights remain consistent with the market value weights. Therefore, no trades are necessary to keep the portfolio value weighted.

Common Stock Market Indexes

The CAPM says that individual investors should hold the market portfolio, a value-weighted portfolio of all risky securities in the market. What does this portfolio correspond to in practice? Is there a way to trade the market portfolio directly?

If we focus our attention on U.S. stocks, we find that several popular market indexes try to represent the performance of the U.S. stock market. A **market index** reports the value of a particular portfolio of securities. The most familiar stock index in the United States is the Dow Jones Industrial Average (DJIA), which consists of a portfolio of 30 large industrial stocks. While these stocks are chosen to be representative of different sectors of the economy, they clearly do not represent the entire market. Also, the DJIA is a price-weighted (rather than value-weighted) portfolio. A **price-weighted portfolio** holds an equal number of shares of each stock, independent of their size. Despite being non-representative of the entire market, the DJIA remains widely cited because it is one of the oldest stock market indexes (first published in 1884).

John C. Bogle founded The Vanguard Group in 1974 and created the first index mutual fund, the Vanguard 500 Index Fund, in 1975. He served as Vanguard's Chairman and Chief Executive Officer until 1996 and Senior Chairman until 2000. He is currently President of the Bogle Financial Markets Research Center.

QUESTION: *Vanguard is known for its index funds. Why is indexing as popular as it is?*

ANSWER: Indexing is popular because it works. The average mutual fund manager cannot beat the market. All fund managers like to say they will beat the market; over a decade, almost 80 percent are wrong. It's the triumph of hope over experience. Over the last 20 years, the average annual return of the S&P 500 was about 13.2%. The average equity mutual fund returned several percentage points less because of expenses, turnover costs, and initial sales charges.

To make matters worse, many fund investors also incur timing and selection penalties. They invest very little when the market's low and a lot when it is high. They buy the wrong funds—telecommunications funds, technology funds, new economy funds—at the market's high. History has shown that after costs and penalties, most mutual fund investors earned returns considerably below returns earned by the average fund. An index fund has no sales charges and an all-in cost of 0.15%, versus an all-in cost of about 3% for active equity funds. Indexing wins, only because it can't lose.

QUESTION: *As a pioneer of indexing, can you explain how theory and evidence came together in the 1970s to suggest that indexing was a smart investment strategy?*

ANSWER: The seed was planted in the 1950s when I was writing my senior thesis at Princeton on mutual funds and did studies showing that funds couldn't outperform market averages. Opportunity and motive came together when I started Vanguard in 1974. We had a company to run, and the only way to beat the market was to remove costs from the equation. I told Vanguard's directors that

I wanted to start an index fund as a way to put Vanguard on the map. Paul Samuelson recently described that creation as the equivalent of the alphabet and the wheel.

We can argue about efficient markets forever. I would say they are strongly efficient, but not perfectly so. Indexing is a smart investment strategy because it's based on the "Cost Matters Hypothesis": gross return − costs = net return to investors. We took the costs out of the equation. Beating the market is a zero sum game on average. Subtract intermediation costs, and it becomes a losing game. Indexing is not magic. It's infinite diversification, infinitely small costs, tiny portfolio turnover, and therefore high tax efficiency. But it took a long while for people to accept this idea.

QUESTION: *Exchange Traded Funds (ETFs) are growing rapidly. What are the tradeoffs between an ETF and a traditional index fund?*

ANSWER: The two are essentially the same. ETFs come in two distinct types. One is all-stock-market ETFs, like VIPERS and SPDRs (based on the S&P 500), and the others are others are sector funds—European, Asian, technology, energy sectors. I don't believe in sectors. I believe in owning the whole market. We pay selection and timing penalties when we buy sectors. ETFs also charge commissions, so the costs mount up if you want to invest a small amount each month or trade them.

There is nothing wrong with buying a SPDR or VIPER, or buying a Vanguard S&P Index fund or total stock market index fund, and holding it forever. However, people tend to hold their index funds for a long time and use ETFs largely as trading vehicles. Long-term investing and short-term speculation are opposite sides of the same coin. I believe in ETFs for buying and holding purposes—which they are rarely used for—and I don't believe in them for speculative and trading purposes.

A better representation of the entire U.S. stock market is the S&P 500, a value-weighted portfolio of 500 of the largest U.S. stocks.[4] The S&P 500 was the first widely publicized value-weighted index (S&P began publishing its index in 1923, though it was based on a smaller number of stocks at that time), and it has become a benchmark for professional investors. This index is the most commonly cited index when evaluating the overall performance of the U.S. stock market. It is also the standard portfolio used to represent "the market" when using the CAPM in practice. Even though the S&P 500 includes only 500 of the more than 7000 individual U.S. stocks in existence, because the S&P 500 includes the largest stocks, it represents more than 70% of the U.S. stock market in terms of market capitalization.

More recently created indexes, such as the Wilshire 5000, provide a value-weighted index of *all* U.S. stocks listed on the major stock exchanges.[5] While more complete than the S&P 500, and therefore more representative of the overall market, these indexes do not share the popularity of the S&P 500. This lack of popularity may in part stem from the fact that the S&P 500 and the Wilshire 5000 have very similar returns; during the 1990s, the correlation between their daily returns exceeded 98%. Given this similarity, may investors view the S&P 500 as an adequate measure of overall U.S. stock market performance.

The S&P 500 and the Wilshire 5000 indexes are both well-diversified indexes that roughly correspond to the market of U.S. stocks (with the Wilshire 5000 being somewhat more representative). Not only are these indexes widely reported, but they are also easy to invest in. Many mutual fund companies offer funds, called **index funds**, that invest in either of these portfolios. In addition, there are exchange-traded funds that represent these portfolios. An **exchange-traded fund (ETF)** is a security that trades directly on an exchange, like a stock, but represents ownership in a portfolio of stocks. For example, Standard and Poor's Depository Receipts (SPDR, nicknamed "spiders") trade on the American Stock Exchange (symbol SPY) and represent ownership in the S&P 500. Vanguard's Total Stock Market ETF (symbol VTI, nicknamed "viper") is based on the Wilshire 5000 index. By investing in an index or an exchange-traded fund, an individual investor with only a small amount to invest can easily achieve the benefits of broad diversification.

Although practitioners commonly use the S&P 500 as the market portfolio in the CAPM, no one does so because of a belief that this index is actually the market portfolio. Instead they view the index as a **market proxy**—a portfolio whose return they believe closely tracks the true market portfolio. Of course, how well the model works will depend on how closely the market proxy actually tracks the true market portfolio. We will return to this issue in Chapter 13.

CONCEPT CHECK

1. How is the weight of a stock in the market portfolio determined?

2. What is an exchange-traded fund (ETF)?

---

4. Standard and Poor's periodically replaces stocks in the index (on average about seven or eight stocks per year). While size is one criterion, Standard and Poor's also tries to maintain appropriate representation of different segments of the economy and chooses firms that are leaders in their industries. Also, from 2005, the value weights in the index are based on the number of shares available for public trading.

5. The Wilshire 5000 began with approximately 5000 stocks when it was first published in 1974. While the name has not changed, the number of stocks in the index has grown with U.S. equity markets.

12.4 Determining Beta

Having identified the S&P 500 as a market proxy, the next step in calculating the risk premium for a security is to determine the security's beta, which was defined in Eq. 12.5 as

$$\beta_i = \frac{SD(R_i)\,Corr(R_i, R_{Mkt})}{SD(R_{Mkt})} = \frac{Cov(R_i, R_{Mkt})}{Var(R_{Mkt})}$$

Beta measures the market risk of a security, as opposed to its diversifiable risk, and is the appropriate measure of the risk of a security for an investor holding the market portfolio.

One difficulty when trying to estimate beta for a security is that beta depends on the correlation and volatility of the security's and market's returns *in the future*. That is, it is based on investors' expectations. However, it is common practice to estimate beta based on the historical correlation and volatilities. This approach makes sense if a stock's beta remains relatively stable over time.

Many data sources provide estimates of beta based on historical data. Typically, these data sources estimate correlations and volatilities from two to five years of weekly or monthly returns and use the S&P 500 as the market portfolio. Table 10.6 on page 309 shows estimated betas for a number of large firms and their industries.

As we discussed in Chapter 10, the differences in betas by industry reflect the sensitivity of each industry's profits to the general health of the economy. For example, Intel and other technology stocks have high betas (near 2.0) because demand for their products usually varies with the business cycle: Companies tend to expand and upgrade their information technology infrastructure when times are good, but they cut back on these expenditures when the economy slows. In contrast, the demand for personal and household products has very little relation to the state of the economy. Firms producing these types of goods, such as Procter & Gamble, tend to have very low betas (below 0.50).

Estimating Beta from Historical Returns

In Chapter 10, we interpreted beta as the sensitivity of a security's excess return (the difference between the security's return and the risk free rate) to the overall market. Specifically,

Beta is the expected percent change in the excess return of the security for a 1% change in the excess return of the market portfolio.

That is, beta represents the amount by which risks that affect the overall market are amplified for a given stock or investment. Securities whose returns tend to move in tandem with the market on average have a beta of 1. Securities that tend to move more than the market have higher betas, while those that move less than the market have lower betas.

Let's look at Cisco Systems stock as an example. Figure 12.6 shows the monthly returns for Cisco and the monthly returns for the S&P 500 from the beginning of 1996 to 2005. Note the overall tendency for Cisco to have a high return when the market is up and a low return when the market is down. Indeed, Cisco tends to move in the same direction as the market, but with greater amplitude. The pattern suggests that Cisco's beta is larger than 1.

Rather than plot the returns over time, we can see Cisco's sensitivity to the market even more clearly by plotting Cisco's return as a function of the S&P 500 return, as shown in Figure 12.7. Each point in this figure represents the return of Cisco and the S&P 500 from one of the months in Figure 12.6. For example, in November 2002, Cisco was up

FIGURE 12.6

Monthly Returns for Cisco Stock and for the S&P 500, 1996–2005

Cisco's returns tend to move in the same direction, but with greater amplitude, than those of the S&P 500.

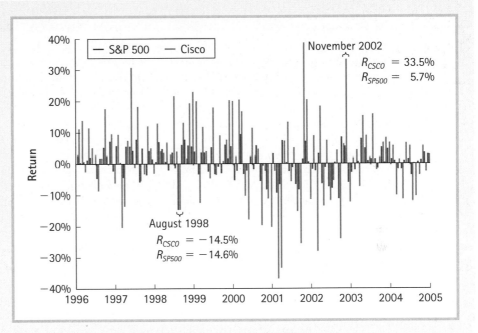

FIGURE 12.7

Scatterplot of Monthly Excess Returns for Cisco Versus the S&P 500, 1996–2005

Beta corresponds to the slope of the best-fitting line. Beta measures the expected change in Cisco's excess return per 1% change in the market's excess return. Deviations from the best-fitting line correspond to diversifiable, non-market-related risk.

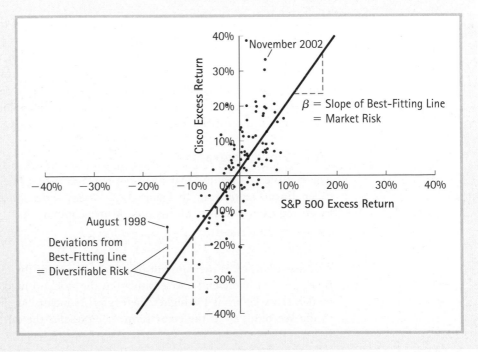

Why Not Estimate Expected Returns Directly?

If the CAPM requires us to use historical data to estimate beta and determine a security's expected return (or an investment's cost of capital), why not just use the security's historical average return as an estimate for its expected return instead? This method would certainly be simpler and more direct.

As we saw in Chapter 10, however, it is extremely difficult to infer the average return of individual stocks from historical data. For a stock with a volatility of 30%, even with 100 years of data the standard error of our estimate would be $30\% / \sqrt{100} = 3\%$ leading to 95% confidence

bounds of $\pm 6\%$. Even worse, few firms have existed for 100 years, and those that have probably bear little resemblance today to what the firms were like 100 years ago. If we use 9 years of data, the confidence bounds would be $\pm 20\%$.

At the same time, as our Cisco example shows, beta can be inferred from historical data reasonably accurately with just a few years of data. In theory at least, the CAPM can provide much more accurate estimates of expected returns for stocks than we could obtain from their historical average return.

33.5% and the S&P 500 was up 5.7%. Note the best-fitting line drawn through these points.[6]

As the scatterplot makes clear, Cisco's returns have a positive covariance with the market: Cisco tends to be up when the market is up, and vice versa. Moreover, from the best-fitting line, we can see that a 10% change in the market's return corresponds to about a 20% change in Cisco's return. That is, Cisco's return moves about two for one with the overall market, so Cisco's beta is about 2. More generally,

Beta corresponds to the slope of the best-fitting line in the plot of the security's excess returns versus the market excess return.

To fully understand this result, recall that beta measures the market risk of a security. The best-fitting line in Figure 12.7 captures the components of a security's return that can be explained by market risk factors. In any individual month, the security's returns will be higher or lower than the best-fitting line. Such deviations from the best-fitting line result from risk that is not related to the market as a whole. These deviations are zero on average in the graph, as the points above the line balance out the points below the line. This firm-specific risk is diversifiable risk that averages out in a large portfolio.

Using Linear Regression

The statistical technique that identifies the best-fitting line through a set of points is called **linear regression**. In Figure 12.7, linear regression corresponds to writing the excess return of a security as the sum of three components:

$$(R_i - r_f) = \alpha_i + \beta_i(R_{Mkt} - r_f) + \varepsilon_i \tag{12.8}$$

The first term, α_i, is the constant or intercept term of the regression. The second term, $\beta_i(R_{Mkt} - r_f)$, represents the sensitivity of the stock to market risk. For example, if the market excess return is 1% higher, there is a $\beta_i\%$ increase in the security's return. We refer to the last term, ε_i, as the **error term**: It represents the deviation from the best-fitting

---

6. By "best fitting," we mean the line that minimizes the sum of the squared deviations from the line.

line and is zero on average. (If the average error were not zero in the sample, you could improve the fit by increasing α_i.) In the CAPM, this error term corresponds to the diversifiable risk of the stock, which is unrelated to the market.

If we take expectations of both sides of Eq. 12.8, because the regression line is calculated so that average error is zero (that is, $E[\varepsilon_i] = 0$), we get

$$E[R_i] = \underbrace{r_f + \beta_i(E[R_{Mkt}] - r_f)}_{\text{Expected return for } i \text{ from the SML}} + \underbrace{\alpha_i}_{\text{Distance above / below the SML}}$$

Thus α_i measures the historical performance of the security relative to the expected return predicted by the SML. The constant term α_i is the distance the stock's average return is above or below the SML. If α_i is positive, the stock has performed better than predicted by the CAPM—its historical return is above the security market line. If α_i is negative, the stock's historical return is below the SML. Thus α_i represents a risk-adjusted performance measure for the historical returns. According to the CAPM, α_i should not be significantly different from zero.[7]

Given data for r_f, R_i, and R_{Mkt}, statistical packages for linear regression (available in most spreadsheet programs) can estimate β_i. The formula for β_i that these programs use corresponds to Eq. 12.5, where the covariance and variance are estimated from the data. If we perform this regression for Cisco using the monthly returns for 1996–2004, the estimated beta is 1.94, indicating that Cisco's returns tended to move about twice as much as the market's returns during this period. The 95% confidence interval for the estimate of beta estimate is 1.52 to 2.36. Assuming Cisco's beta remain stable over time, we would expect Cisco's beta to be in this range in the near future.

The estimate of Cisco's alpha from the regression is 1.2%. In other words, given its beta, Cisco's average monthly return was 1.2% higher than required by the security market line. The standard error of the alpha estimate is 1%, however, so that statistically the estimate is not significantly different from zero. Alphas, like expected returns, are difficult to estimate with much accuracy without a very long data series. Moreover, the alphas for individual stocks have very little persistence. Thus, although Cisco's return has exceeded its required return in the past, it may not necessarily continue to do so.

CONCEPT CHECK
1. How can a stock's beta be estimated from historical returns?
2. How is a stock's alpha defined, and what is its interpretation?

12.5 Extending the CAPM

In building the CAPM, we made no distinction between the interest rate on saving and borrowing, and we assumed that all investors had the same information about a security's risk and return. In the real world, borrowers pay higher interest rates than savers receive, and investors have different information about securities. In this section, we demonstrate that the CAPM still holds (with some qualifications) even under these considerations.

---

7. When used in this way, α_i is often referred to as Jensen's alpha. Using this regression as a test of the CAPM was introduced by F. Black, M. Jensen, and M. Scholes in "The Capital Asset Pricing Model: Some Empirical Tests." In M. Jensen, ed., *Studies in the Theory of Capital Markets.* (New York: Praeger, 1972.)

Saving Versus Borrowing Rates

In Chapter 11, we assumed that investors faced the same risk-free interest rate whether they were saving or borrowing. In practice, investors receive a lower rate when they save than they must pay when they borrow. For example, short-term margin loans from a broker are often 1% to 2% higher than the rates paid on short-term Treasury securities. Banks, pension funds, and other investors with large amounts of collateral can borrow at rates that are generally within 1% of the rate on risk-free securities, but there is still a difference. Do these differences in interest rates affect the conclusions of the CAPM?

The Efficient Frontier with Differing Saving and Borrowing Rates.

Figure 12.8 plots the risk and return possibilities when the saving and borrowing rates differ. In this graph, $r_S = 3\%$ is the rate earned on risk-free savings or lending, and $r_B = 6\%$ is the rate paid on borrowing. Each rate is associated with a different tangent portfolio, labeled T_S and T_B, respectively. A conservative investor who desires a low-risk portfolio can combine the portfolio T_S with saving at rate r_S to achieve risk and return combinations along the lower green line. An aggressive investor who desires high expected returns can invest in the portfolio T_B, using some amount of borrowed funds at rate r_B. By adjusting the amount of borrowing, the investor can achieve risk and return combinations on the upper green line. The combinations on the upper line are not as desirable as the combinations that would result if the investor could borrow at rate r_S, but the investor is unable to borrow at the lower rate. Finally, investors with intermediate preferences may choose portfolios on the red curve between T_S and T_B, which do not involve borrowing or lending.

If borrowing and lending rates differ, then, investors with different preferences will choose different portfolios of risky securities. Some will choose T_S combined with saving,

FIGURE 12.8

Tangent Portfolios with Different Saving and Borrowing Rates

Investors who save at rate r_S will invest in portfolio T_S, and investors who borrow at rate r_B will invest in portfolio T_B. Some investors may neither save nor borrow and invest in a portfolio on the efficient frontier between T_S and T_B.

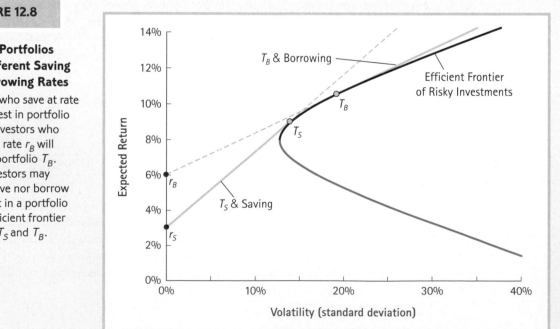

some will choose T_B combined with borrowing, and some will choose portfolios on the curve between T_S and T_B. So, the first conclusion of the CAPM—that the market portfolio is the unique efficient portfolio of risky investments—is no longer valid.

The Security Market Line with Differing Interest Rates. The more important conclusion of the CAPM for corporate finance is the security market line, which relates the risk of an investment to its required return. It turns out that the SML is still valid when interest rates differ. To see why, we make use of the following result:

A combination of portfolios on the efficient frontier of risky investments is also on the efficient frontier of risky investments.[8]

Because all investors hold portfolios on the efficient frontier between T_S and T_B, and because all investors collectively hold the market portfolio, the market portfolio must lie on the frontier between T_S and T_B. As a result, the market portfolio will be tangent for some risk-free interest rate r^* between r_S and r_B, as illustrated in Figure 12.9. Because our determination of the security market line depends only on the market portfolio being tangent for some interest rate, the SML still holds in the following form:

$$E[R_i] = r^* + \beta_i(E[R_{Mkt}] - r^*) \tag{12.9}$$

FIGURE 12.9

Market Portfolio and Determination of r^* When Saving and Borrowing Rates Differ

Because all investors choose portfolios on the efficient frontier from T_S to T_B, the market portfolio is on the efficient frontier between them. The tangent line through the market portfolio determines the interest rate r^* that can be used in the SML.

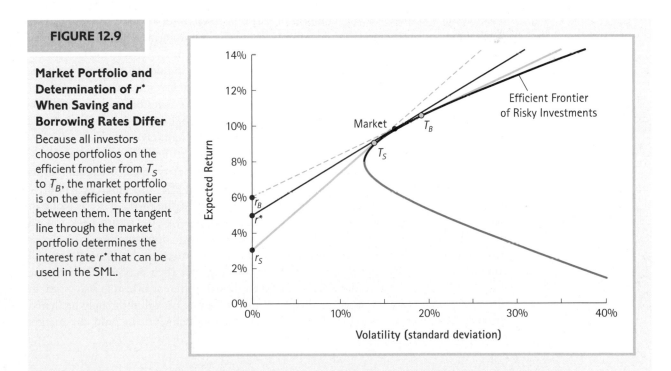

---

8. To understand this result intuitively, note that portfolios on the efficient frontier contain no diversifiable risk (otherwise we could reduce risk further without lowering the expected return). But a combination of portfolios that contain no diversifiable risk also contains no diversifiable risk, so it is also efficient.

That is, the SML holds with some rate r^* between r_S and r_B in place of r_f. The rate r^* depends on the proportion of savers and borrowers in the economy. But even without knowing those proportions, because saving and borrowing rates tend to be close to each other, r^* must be in a narrow range and we can use Eq. 12.9 to provide reasonable estimates of expected returns.[9]

We can make a similar argument regarding the choice of which risk-free rate to use. As discussed in Chapter 8, the risk-free rate varies with the investment horizon according to the yield curve. When an investor chooses her optimal portfolio, she will do so by finding the tangent line using the risk-free rate that corresponds to her investment horizon. If all investors have the same horizon, then the risk-free rate corresponding to that horizon will determine the SML. If investors have different horizons (but still have homogeneous expectations), then the SML (Eq. 12.9) will hold for some r^* on the current yield curve, with the rate depending on the proportion of investors with each investment horizon.[10]

Investor Information and Rational Expectations

We introduced the CAPM by stating its assumptions that all investors were equally sophisticated and had the same information regarding a security's expected returns, volatilities, and correlations (that is, they have homogeneous expectations). We adopted this strategy so we could focus attention on the important implications of the model, not because we believed that it is an accurate description of the world. In reality, investors have different information and spend varying amounts of effort on research for assorted stocks. Even so, there are reasons to believe that if investors do not have homogeneous expectations, the CAPM will be valid.

An important conclusion of the CAPM is that investors should hold the market portfolio combined with risk-free investments. Note that this investment advice *does not depend on the quality of an investor's information.* Even naive investors with no information can follow this investment advice. But what about sophisticated investors? As we described in Section 12.2, if the market portfolio is not efficient, savvy investors who recognize that the market portfolio is not optimal will push prices and expected returns back into balance. For example, if an investor who is researching eBay stock concludes that its expected return is above the SML and tries to buy shares of eBay, his purchase will drive up the price and lower eBay's expected return back toward the SML. If he is alone in making these trades, the investor's actions are unlikely to drive the return back toward the SML. But it is unlikely that he will be alone. If such opportunities exist, other investors will be looking out for them, too. The ones who discover this opportunity will compete with one another to capitalize on it, and together their actions will drive the price of eBay stock back to the SML. Thus, even though different investors may research different stocks, as we discussed in Chapter 9 their information will ultimately be shared through its influence on prices. Eventually, all investors will want to hold the market portfolio.

---

9. This result was shown by M. Brennan, "Capital Market Equilibrium with Divergent Borrowing and Lending Rates," *Journal of Financial and Quantitative Analysis* 6 (1971): 1197–1205.

10. The arguments in this section can be generalized further to settings in which there is no risk-free asset; see Fischer Black, "Capital Market Equilibrium with Restricted Borrowing," *Journal of Business* 45 (1972): 444–455, and Mark Rubinstein, "The Fundamental Theorem of Parameter-Preference Security Valuation," *Journal of Financial and Quantitative Analysis* 1 (1973): 61–69.

As we see, the CAPM does not require making the strong assumption of homogeneous expectations. A more plausible notion is the idea of **rational expectations**, which stipulates that

Investors may have different information regarding expected returns, correlations, and volatilities, but they correctly interpret that information and the information contained in market prices and adjust their estimates of expected returns in a rational way.

Investors may learn different information through their own research and observations. As long as they understand these differences in information and learn from other investors by observing prices, the CAPM conclusions—that the market portfolio is the efficient portfolio and that beta determines expected returns—are still true.[11] The intuition for this result is explained in Example 12.9.

EXAMPLE 12.9

How to Avoid Being Outsmarted in Financial Markets

Problem

Suppose you are an investor without access to any information regarding stocks. You know that all other investors in the market possess a great deal of information and are actively using that information to select an efficient portfolio by finding the portfolio that has the highest expected return given the level of volatility they are comfortable with. You are concerned that because of your informational disadvantage, your portfolio will underperform the portfolios of these informed investors. How can you prevent that outcome and guarantee that your portfolio will do as well as that of the average informed investor?

Solution

You can guarantee yourself the same return as the average informed investor simply by holding the market portfolio. Because the average of all investors' portfolios must equal the market portfolio (that is, demand must equal supply), if you hold the market portfolio then so must the average informed investor. To see why, suppose that the informed investors held *more* Google stock than its share of the market portfolio. For supply to equal demand, you must be holding *less* Google stock than its share of the market portfolio. But this cannot be true if you are holding the market portfolio.

Conversely, if you do not hold the market portfolio, then whatever stocks you hold more of, the informed investors hold less of, and vice versa. Because the informed investors have chosen their portfolios based on their superior information, their portfolios must be better than the market—that is, their portfolios have a positive alpha. But because your portfolio deviates from the market in precisely the opposite way, your portfolio must have a negative alpha.

Example 12.9 is very powerful. It implies that every investor, regardless of how much information he has access to, can guarantee himself an alpha of zero by holding the market portfolio (which is always on the security market line). Thus no investor should choose a portfolio with a negative alpha. However, because the average portfolio of all investors is

---

11. See, for example, P. DeMarzo and C. Skiadas, "Aggregation, Determinacy, and Informational Efficiency for a Class of Economies with Asymmetric Information," *Journal of Economic Theory* 80 (1998): 123–152.

the market portfolio, the average alpha of all investors is zero. If no investor earns a negative alpha, then no investor can earn a positive alpha, and the market portfolio must be efficient.

The only way it can be possible to earn a positive alpha and beat the market is if some investors are holding portfolios with negative alphas. Because these investors could have earned a zero alpha by holding the market portfolio, we reach the following important conclusion:

The market portfolio can be inefficient only if a significant number of investors either

1. *Misinterpret information and believe they are earning a positive alpha when they are actually earning a negative alpha, or*

2. *Care about aspects of their portfolios other than expected return and volatility, and so are willing to hold inefficient portfolios of securities.*

CONCEPT CHECK
1. Is the market portfolio the unique efficient portfolio of risky investments when saving and borrowing rates are different?

2. Under what conditions will it be possible to earn a positive alpha and beat the market?

12.6 The CAPM in Practice

The CAPM is a significant and elegant theory of the relationship between risk and return. As with all theories, we must make a number of practical choices when using the CAPM. In this section, we discuss some key considerations that arise when using the CAPM to estimate a firm's cost of capital.

Forecasting Beta

We estimate stock betas in practice by regressing past stock returns on returns of the market portfolio. Important choices in estimating beta include (1) the time horizon used, (2) the index used as the market portfolio, and (3) the method used to extrapolate from past betas to future betas.

Time Horizon.   When estimating beta by using past returns, there is a tradeoff regarding which time horizon to use to measure returns. If we use too short a time horizon, our estimate of beta will be unreliable. If we use very old data, they may be unrepresentative of the current market risk of the security. For stocks, common practice is to use at least two years of weekly return data or five years of monthly return data.[12]

The Market Proxy.   The CAPM predicts that a security's expected return depends on its beta with regard to the market portfolio of *all* risky investments available to investors.

---

12. While daily returns would provide even more sample points, we generally do not use them due to the concern—especially for smaller, less liquid stocks—that short-term factors might influence daily returns that are not representative of the longer-term risks affecting the security. Ideally, we should use a return interval equal to our investment horizon. The need for sufficient data, however, makes monthly returns the longest practical choice.

As mentioned earlier, in practice the S&P 500 is used as the market proxy. Other proxies, such as the NYSE Composite Index (a value-weighted index of all NYSE stocks), the Wilshire 5000 index of all U.S. stocks, or an even broader market index that includes both equities and fixed-income securities, are sometimes used as well. When evaluating international stocks, it is common practice to use a country or international market index.

Beta Extrapolation.   When using historical data, there is always the possibility of estimation error. Thus we should be suspicious of estimates that are extreme relative to industry norms; in fact, many practitioners prefer to use average industry betas rather than individual stock betas. In addition, evidence suggests that betas tend to regress toward the average beta of 1.0 over time.[13] For both of these reasons, many practitioners use **adjusted betas**, which are calculated by averaging the estimated beta with 1.0. For example, Bloomberg computes adjusted betas using the following formula:

$$\text{Adjusted Beta of Security } i = \tfrac{2}{3}\beta_i + \tfrac{1}{3}(1.0) \qquad (12.10)$$

The estimation methodologies of three data providers appear in Table 12.1. Each employs a unique methodology, which leads to differences in the reported betas.

TABLE 12.1	Estimation Methodologies Used by Selected Data Providers		
	Value Line	**Reuters**	**Bloomberg**
Returns	Weekly	Monthly	Weekly
Horizon	5 years	5 years	2 years
Market Index	NYSE Composite	S&P 500	S&P 500
Adjusted	Yes	No	Yes

Outliers.   The beta estimates we obtain from linear regression can be very sensitive to outliers, which are returns of unusually large magnitude. As an example, Figure 12.10 shows a scatterplot of Genentech's monthly returns versus the S&P 500 for 2002–2004. Based on these returns, we estimate a beta of 1.21 for Genentech. Looking closely at the monthly returns, however, we find two data points with unusually large returns: In April 2002, Genentech's stock price fell by almost 30%, and in May 2003, Genentech's stock price rose by almost 65%. In each case the extreme moves were a reaction to Genentech's announcement of news related to new drug development. In April 2002, Genentech reported a setback in the development of psoriasis drug Raptiva. In May 2003, the company reported the successful clinical trial of its anticancer drug Avastin. These two returns more likely represent firm-specific rather than market-wide risk. But because these large returns happened to occur during months when the market also moved in the same direction, they bias the estimate of beta that results from a standard regression. If we redo the regression replacing Genentech's returns during these two months with the average return of similar biotechnology firms during the same months, we obtain a much lower estimate

---

13. See M. Blume, "Betas and Their Regression Tendencies," *Journal of Finance* 30 (1975): 785–795.

FIGURE 12.10

Beta Estimation with and without Outliers for Genentech Using Monthly Returns for 2002–2004

Genentech's returns in April 2002 and May 2003 are largely due to firm-specific news. By replacing those returns (blue points) with industry average returns (red points), we obtain a more accurate assessment of Genentech's market risk during this period.

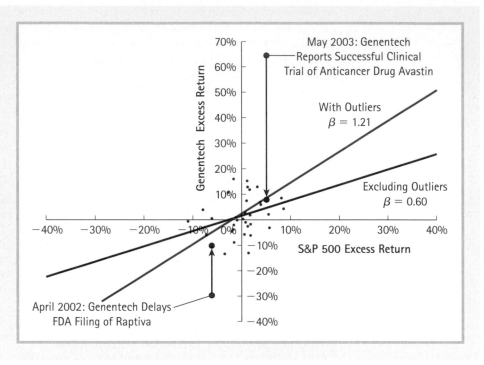

of 0.60 for Genentech's beta, as shown in Figure 12.10. This latter estimate is probably a much more accurate assessment of Genentech's market risk during this period.

There may be other reasons to exclude certain historical data as anomalous when estimating beta. For example, some practitioners advocate ignoring data from 1998–2000 to avoid distortions related to the technology, media, and telecommunications speculative bubble.[14]

Other Considerations.   When using historical returns to forecast future betas, we must be mindful of changes in the environment that might cause the future to differ from the past. For example, if a firm were to change industries, using its historical beta would be inferior to using the beta of other firms in the new industry. Also bear in mind that many practitioners analyze other information in addition to past returns, such as industry characteristics, firm size, and other financial characteristics of a firm, when they forecast betas. In the end, forecasting betas, like most types of forecasting, is as much art as science, and the best estimates require a thorough knowledge of the particulars of a firm and its industry.

The Security Market Line

In addition to beta, estimating the cost of capital from the security market line requires a risk-free interest rate and a risk-premium for the market index. We discuss next some of the considerations that determine these inputs.

---

14. For example, see A. Annema and M. H. Goedhart, "Better Betas," *McKinsey on Finance* (Winter 2003): 10–13.

The Risk-Free Interest Rate.   The risk-free interest rate is generally determined using the yields of U.S. Treasury securities, which are free from default risk. However, even U.S. Treasuries are subject to interest rate risk unless we select a maturity equal to our investment horizon. Which horizon should we choose?

As we discussed in Section 12.5, the CAPM states that we should use the risk-free interest corresponding to the investment horizon of the firm's investors. It may also be appropriate to use a rate that exceeds the rate on government bonds to account for the cost of borrowing. When surveyed, the vast majority of large firms and financial analysts report using the yields of long-term (10- to 30-year) bonds to determine the risk-free rate.[15]

The Market Risk Premium.   To determine the risk premium for a stock using the security market line, we need an estimate of the market risk premium, $E[R_{Mkt}] - r_f$. To estimate the expected return of the market, we can use a variety of approaches. For example, we can look at the historical average excess return of the market over the risk-free interest rate.[16] With this approach, it is important to use historical returns for the same market index used to calculate beta, and to compare the return over the same time horizon as that used for the risk-free interest rate.

Because we are interested in the *future* market risk premium, we again face a tradeoff in terms of the amount of data we use. As we noted in Chapter 10, it takes many years of data to produce even moderately accurate estimates of expected returns. Yet data that are very old may have little relevance for investors' expectations of the market risk premium today.

Table 12.2 reports excess returns of the S&P 500 versus one-year and ten-year Treasury rates. Since 1926, the S&P 500 has had an average return of 8.0% above the rate for one-year Treasuries. However, some evidence indicates that the market risk premium has declined over time. Since 1955, the S&P 500 has shown an excess return of only 5.7% over the rate for one-year Treasuries. Compared with ten-year Treasuries, the S&P 500 had an average excess return of only 4.5% (due primarily to the fact that ten-year Treasury bond rates tend to be higher than one-year rates). One reasonable explanation for

TABLE 12.2	Historical Excess Returns of the S&P 500 Compared to One-Year Treasury Bills and Ten-Year Treasury Notes	
Risk-free Security	**Period**	**S&P 500 Excess Return**
One-year Treasury	1926–2005	8.0%
	1955–2005	5.7%
Ten-year Treasury*	1955–2005	4.5%

*Based on a comparison of compounded returns over a ten-year holding period.

---

15. See Robert Bruner, et al., "Best Practices in Estimating the Cost of Capital: Survey and Synthesis," *Financial Practice and Education* 8 (1998): 13–28.

16. Because we are interested in the expected return, the correct average to use is the arithmetic average. See Chapter 10.

this decline is that as more investors have begun to participate in the stock market and the costs of constructing a diversified portfolio have declined, investors tend to hold less risky portfolios, so the return they require as compensation for taking on that risk has diminished. In addition, the overall volatility of the market has declined over time. Some researchers believe that the future expected returns for the market are likely to be even lower than these historical numbers, in a range of about 3–5% over Treasury bills.[17]

Using historical data to estimate the market risk premium suffers from two drawbacks. First, despite using 50 years (or more) of data, the standard errors of the estimates are large. (For example, even using data from 1926, the standard error of the excess return over one-year Treasury bills is 2.3%, implying a 95% confidence interval of ±4.6%.) Second, they are backward looking, so we cannot be sure they are representative of current expectations.

As an alternative, we can take a fundamental approach toward estimating the market risk premium. Given an assessment of firms' future cash flows, we can estimate the expected return of the market by solving for the discount rate that is consistent with the current level of the index. For example, if we use the constant expected growth model presented in Chapter 9, the expected market return is equal to

$$r_{Mkt} = \frac{Div_1}{P_0} + g = \text{Dividend Yield} + \text{Expected Dividend Growth Rate} \quad (12.11)$$

While this model is highly inaccurate for an individual firm, the assumption of constant expected growth is more reasonable when considering the overall market. If, for instance, the S&P 500 has a current dividend yield of 2%, and we assume that both earnings and dividends are expected to grow 6% per year, this model would estimate the expected return of the S&P 500 as 8%. Following such methods, researchers generally report estimates in the 3–5% range for the future equity risk premium.[18]

Evidence Regarding the CAPM

Researchers have conducted numerous studies to evaluate the performance of the CAPM. Two of the earliest and most important studies were done by Black, Jensen, and Scholes (1972) and by Fama and MacBeth (1973).[19] They compared actual average returns with those predicted by the security market line. They concluded that expected returns were related to betas, as predicted by the CAPM, rather than to other measures of risk such as the security's volatility. However, they did find some deviation from the security market line. In particular, the empirically estimated security market line is somewhat flatter than that predicted by the CAPM, as shown in Figure 12.11. That is, low-beta stocks have

---

17. See Ivo Welch, "The Equity Premium Consensus Forecast Revisited," Cowles Foundation Discussion Paper 1325 (2001), and John Graham and Campbell Harvey, "The Long-Run Equity Risk Premium," SSRN working paper (2005).

18. See, for example, Eugene Fama and Kenneth French, "The Equity Premium," *Journal of Finance* 57 (2002): 637–659; Ravi Jagannathan, Ellen McGrattan, and Anna Scherbina, "The Declining US Equity Premium," NBER working paper 8172 (2001); and Jeremy Siegel, "The Long-Run Equity Risk Premium," CFA Institute Conference proceedings *Points of Inflection: New Directions for Portfolio Management* (2004).

19. Eugene F. Fama and James MacBeth, "Risk, Return and Empirical Tests," *Journal of Political Economy* 8 (1973): 607–636.

FIGURE 12.11

Empirical SML Versus SML Predicted by CAPM (Black, Jensen, and Scholes, 1972)

Low-beta stocks tend to be somewhat above the SML, and high-beta stocks tend to be somewhat below the SML.

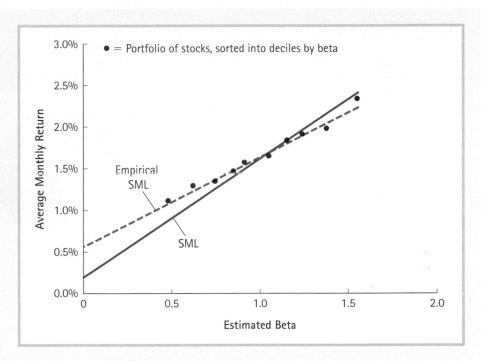

tended to perform somewhat better than the CAPM predicts, while the highest-beta stocks do worse.

While they may identify some flaws, these studies do support the qualitative conclusions of the CAPM. More recent research, however, has questioned the performance of the CAPM. A series of influential papers published in 1992 and 1993 by Eugene Fama and Kenneth French[20] argue that, based on more current data and taking other characteristics of securities into account, beta is not helpful in explaining average returns. An ongoing debate among researchers focuses on the use of more refined techniques to determine whether beta is an adequate measure of risk. (We discuss this debate further in Chapter 13, where we also describe proposed modifications to the CAPM.) Despite more than a decade of research, however, no consensus has been reached regarding the best way to improve upon the CAPM. A number of difficulties arise in resolving this debate:

- *Betas are not observed.* If betas change over time, simple historical estimates of beta are not likely to be accurate. Evidence against the CAPM may be the result of mismeasuring betas.

- *Expected returns are not observed.* Even if beta is a perfect measure of risk, average returns need not match expected returns. It takes many years of data to obtain even moderately accurate measures of the true mean of returns. Moreover, the realized average return need not match investors' expectations; for example, investors may be concerned about risks that do not come to pass.

---

20. Eugene Fama and Kenneth French, "The Cross-Section of Expected Stock Returns," *Journal of Finance* 47 (1992): 427–465; and "Common Risk Factors in the Returns on Stocks and Bonds," *Journal of Financial Economics* 33 (1993): 3–56.

FIGURE 12.12

Relative Weights of International Stock Markets by Market Capitalization, June 2004

The true market portfolio includes both domestic and international investments.

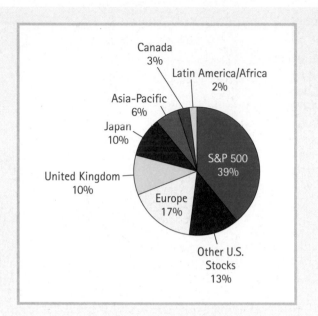

- *The market proxy is not correct.* While the S&P 500 is routinely used, it is not the true market portfolio. Although it is a reasonable proxy for the U.S. stock market, investors hold many other assets. The stock market captures less than 50% of the securities traded within the United States once government bonds, corporate bonds, and mortgage-related securities are taken into account. In addition, we should include privately held firms and real estate investments. Finally, the U.S. stock market represents only about 50% of world equity markets, as shown in Figure 12.12. Thus any failure of the CAPM may simply be the result of our failure to find a good measure of the market portfolio.[21]

Better statistical methods that attempt to address these issues, as well as allowing betas and expected returns to vary over time, may ultimately provide more conclusive evidence regarding the accuracy of the CAPM and the best ways to improve upon it.

The Bottom Line on the CAPM

While the CAPM many not be perfect, it is unlikely that a truly perfect model will be found in the foreseeable future. Furthermore, the imperfections of the CAPM may not be critical in the context of capital budgeting and corporate finance, where errors in estimating project cash flows are likely to be far more important than small discrepancies in

---

21. This observation was originally pointed out in an influential paper written by Richard Roll ["A Critique of the Asset Pricing Theory's Tests," *Journal of Financial Economics* 4 (1977): 129–176], in which he showed that because we can never know how close the portfolio we are using is to the true market portfolio, it is *impossible* to verify empirically whether the market portfolio is efficient.

Nobel Prize   William Sharpe on the CAPM

William Sharpe received the Nobel Prize in 1990 for his development of the Capital Asset Pricing Model. Here are his comments on the CAPM from a 1998 interview with Jonathan Burton:*

Portfolio theory focused on the actions of a single investor with an optimal portfolio. I said, What if everyone was optimizing? They've all got their copies of Markowitz and they're doing what he says. Then some people decide they want to hold more IBM, but there aren't enough shares to satisfy demand. So they put price pressure on IBM and up it goes, at which point they have to change their estimates of risk and return, because now they're paying more for the stock. That process of upward and downward pressure on prices continues until prices reach an equilibrium and everyone collectively wants to hold what's available. At that point, what can you say about the relationship between risk and return? The answer is that expected return is proportionate to beta relative to the market portfolio.

The CAPM was and is a theory of equilibrium. Why should anyone expect to earn more by investing in one security as opposed to another? You need to be compensated for doing badly when times are bad. The security that is going to do badly just when you need money when

times are bad is a security you have to hate, and there had better be some redeeming virtue or else who will hold it? That redeeming virtue has to be that in normal times you expect to do better. The key insight of the Capital Asset Pricing Model is that higher expected returns go with the greater risk of doing badly in bad times. Beta is a measure of that. Securities or asset classes with high betas tend to do worse in bad times than those with low betas.

The CAPM was a very simple, very strong set of assumptions that got a nice, clean, pretty result. And then almost immediately, we all said, Let's bring more complexity into it to try to get closer to the real world. People went on—myself and others—to what I call "extended" Capital Asset Pricing Models, in which expected return is a function of beta, taxes, liquidity, dividend yield, and other things people might care about.

Did the CAPM evolve? Of course. But the fundamental idea remains that there's no reason to expect reward just for bearing risk. Otherwise, you'd make a lot of money in Las Vegas. If there's reward for risk, it's got to be special. There's got to be some economics behind it or else the world is a very crazy place. I don't think differently about those basic ideas at all.

*Jonathan Burton, "Revisiting the Capital Asset Pricing Model," *Dow Jones Asset Manager* (May/June 1998): 20–28.

the cost of capital. In that sense, the CAPM may be good enough, especially relative to the effort required to implement a more sophisticated model. The CAPM remains the predominant model used in practice to determine the equity cost of capital.

Even if the CAPM is not completely correct, the security market line still provides the required return for any investment for an investor who currently holds the market index and who cares about expected return and volatility. Given the large number of investors who follow an indexing strategy, this constituency is likely to be an important one for the firm. Furthermore, the average investor must hold the market index, because the sum of all investor portfolios equals the total supply of all securities. Thus, despite its potential flaws, there are very good reasons to use the CAPM as a basis for calculating the cost of capital.

CONCEPT CHECK   1. For stocks, why do we use weekly or monthly return data to estimate beta?

2. If the CAPM is not perfect, why do we continue to use it in corporate finance?

Summary

1. Three main assumptions underlie the Capital Asset Pricing Model (CAPM):

    a. Investors trade securities at competitive market prices (without incurring taxes or transaction costs) and can borrow and lend at the risk-free rate.

    b. Investors choose efficient portfolios.

    c. Investors have homogeneous expectations regarding the volatilities, correlations, and expected returns of securities.

2. Because the supply of securities must equal the demand for securities, the CAPM implies that the market portfolio of all risky securities is the efficient portfolio.

3. The capital market line (CML) is the set of portfolios with the highest possible expected return for any level of volatility.

    a. Under the CAPM assumptions, the CML is the line through the risk-free security and the market portfolio.

    b. The expected return and volatility of a portfolio on the CML with fraction x invested in the market portfolio and the remainder invested in the risk-free asset are calculated as follows:

$$E[R_{xCML}] = (1 - x)r_f + xE[R_{Mkt}] = r_f + x(E[R_{Mkt}] - r_f) \qquad (12.2)$$

$$SD(R_{xCML}) = x\,SD(R_{Mkt}) \qquad (12.3)$$

4. Under the CAPM assumptions, the risk premium of any security is equal to the market risk premium multiplied by the beta of the security. This relationship is called the security market line (SML), and it determines the required return for an investment:

$$E[R_i] = r_i = r_f + \underbrace{\beta_i^{Mkt}(E[R_{Mkt}] - r_f)}_{\text{Risk premium for security } i} \qquad (12.4)$$

5. The beta of a security measures the amount of the security's risk that is common to the market portfolio or market risk.

    a. Beta is defined as follows:

$$\beta_i^{Mkt} \equiv \beta_i = \frac{\overbrace{SD(R_i) \times Corr(R_i, R_{Mkt})}^{\text{Volatility of } i \text{ that is common with the market}}}{SD(R_{Mkt})} = \frac{Cov(R_i, R_{Mkt})}{Var(R_{Mkt})} \qquad (12.5)$$

    b. The beta of a portfolio is the weighted-average beta of the securities in the portfolio.

6. The difference between a security's expected return and its required return from the security market line is the security's alpha. According to the CAPM:

    a. All stocks and securities should be on the security market line and have an alpha of zero.

    b. If some securities have a nonzero alpha, the market portfolio is not efficient, and its performance can be improved upon by buying securities with positive alphas and selling those with negative alphas.

7. To estimate a security's return using the CAPM, we must estimate the model's parameters.

    a. The market portfolio in theory is a value-weighted index of all risky investments. In practice, we often use a stock market index such as the S&P 500 to represent the market.

    b. To estimate beta, we often use historical returns and assume that historical values are reasonable estimates of future returns. Most data sources use five years of monthly returns to estimate beta.

    c. Beta corresponds to the slope of the best-fitting line in the plot of a security's returns versus the market's returns. We use a linear regression to find the best-fitting line.

8. If we regress a stock's excess returns against the market's excess returns, the intercept is referred to as the stock's alpha. It measures how the stock has performed historically relative to the security market line.

9. While betas tend to be stable over time, alphas do not seem to be persistent.

10. While the historical excess return of the S&P 500 has been about 8.4% more than Treasury bills since 1926, the appropriate market risk premium to use in the security market line is likely to be lower. Since 1955, the average excess return of the S&P 500 has been 5.7%, and research suggests that future excess returns are likely to be even lower.

11. When we relax some of the CAPM assumptions, most of the main results still hold.

    a. If investors borrow and lend at different rates, the SML holds in the following form:

$$r_i = r^* + \beta_i(E[R_{Mkt}] - r^*)$$

The rate r^* is between the borrowing and lending rates, and depends on the proportion of savers and borrowers in the economy.

    b. If investors have rational expectations (rather than homogeneous expectations), the market portfolio is efficient and the CAPM holds.

    c. For the market portfolio to be inefficient, a significant fraction of investors must be willing to hold negative-alpha portfolios.

12. Recent research questions the reliability of beta in explaining average returns. There are some difficulties in trying to resolve this debate, but the CAPM remains the most important method for estimating the equity cost of capital.

Key Terms

adjusted betas *p. 389*
alpha *p. 373*
capital market line (CML) *p. 366*
equal-ownership portfolio *p. 376*
error term *p. 382*
exchange-traded fund *p. 379*
homogeneous expectations *p. 365*
index funds *p. 379*
linear regression *p. 382*

market capitalization *p. 375*
market index *p. 377*
market portfolio *p. 364*
market proxy *p. 379*
passive portfolio *p. 376*
price-weighted portfolio *p. 377*
rational expectations *p. 387*
security market line (SML) *p. 370*
value-weighted portfolio *p. 375*

Further Reading

The following classic papers developed the CAPM: J. Lintner, "The Valuation of Risk Assets and the Selection of Risky Investments in Stock Portfolios and Capital Budgets," *Review of Economics and Statistics* 47 (February 1965): 13–37; J. Mossin, "Equilibrium in a Capital Asset Market," *Econometrica* 34 (1966): 768–783; W. F. Sharpe, "Capital Asset Prices: A Theory of Market Equilibrium under Conditions of Risk," *Journal of Finance* 19 (September 1964): 425–442; and J. Treynor, "Toward a Theory of the Market Value of Risky Assets," unpublished manuscript (1961).

The following articles provide some additional insights on the CAPM: F. Black, "Beta and Return," *Journal of Portfolio Management* 20 (Fall 1993): 8–18; and B. Rosenberg and J. Guy, "Beta and Investment Fundamentals," *Financial Analysts Journal* (May–June 1976): 60–72.

Although not a focus of this chapter, there is an extensive body of literature on testing the CAPM. Besides the articles mentioned in the text, here are a few others that an interested reader might want to consult: W. E. Ferson and C. R. Harvey "The Variation of Economic Risk Premiums," *Journal of Political Economy* 99 (1991): 385–415; M. R. Gibbons, S. A. Ross, and J. Shanken, "A Test of the Efficiency of a Given Portfolio," *Econometrica* 57 (1989): 1121–1152; S. P. Kothari, Jay Shanken, and Richard G. Sloan, "Another Look at the Cross-Section of Expected Stock Returns," *Journal of Finance* 50 (March 1995): 185–224; and R. A. Levy, "On the Short-Term Stationarity of Beta Coefficients," *Financial Analysts Journal* (November–December 1971): 55–62.

Problems

All problems in this chapter are available in MyFinanceLab. An asterisk (*) indicates problems with a higher level of difficulty.

The Efficiency of the Market Portfolio

1. When the CAPM correctly prices risk, the market portfolio is an efficient portfolio. Explain why.

2. Your investment portfolio consists of $15,000 invested in only one stock—Microsoft. Suppose the risk-free rate is 5%, Microsoft stock has an expected return of 12% and a volatility of 40%, and the market portfolio has an expected return of 10% and a volatility of 18%. Under the CAPM assumptions,
   a. What alternative investment has the lowest possible volatility while having the same expected return as Microsoft?
   b. What investment has the highest possible expected return while having the same volatility as Microsoft?

3. What is the volatility of the portfolio in part (a) of Problem 2?

4. What is the expected return of the portfolio in part (b) of Problem 2?

5. Plot the capital market line from the data in Problem 2 and mark the set of portfolios that dominates investing all your money in Microsoft stock—that is, the set of portfolios that has both a higher expected return and a lower volatility than investing in Microsoft stock alone.

Determining the Risk Premium

6. Suppose the risk-free return is 4% and the market portfolio has an expected return of 10% and a volatility of 16%. Johnson and Johnson Corporation (Ticker: JNJ) stock has a 20% volatility and a correlation with the market of 0.06.
   a. What is Johnson and Johnson's beta with respect to the market?
   b. Under the CAPM assumptions, what is its expected return?

7. What is the sign of the risk premium of a negative-beta stock? Explain. (Assume the risk premium of the market portfolio is positive.)

8. Suppose Intel stock has a beta of 2.16, whereas Boeing stock has a beta of 0.69. If the risk-free interest rate is 4% and the expected return of the market portfolio is 10%, what is the expected return of a portfolio that consists of 60% Intel stock and 40% Boeing stock, according to the CAPM?

*9. What is the risk premium of a zero-beta stock? Does this mean you can lower the volatility of a portfolio without changing the expected return by substituting out any zero-beta stock in a portfolio and replacing it with the risk-free asset?

The Market Portfolio

 10. Suppose all possible investment opportunities in the world are limited to the five stocks listed in the table below. What does the market portfolio consist of?

Stock	Price/Share ($)	Number of Shares Outstanding (millions)
A	10	10
B	20	12
C	8	3
D	50	1
E	45	20

EXCEL **11.** Given $100,000 to invest, construct a value-weighted portfolio of the four stocks listed below.

Stock	Price/Share ($)	Number of Shares Outstanding (millions)
Golden Seas	13	1000
Jacobs and Jacobs	22	1.25
MAG	43	30
PDJB	5	10

12. If one stock in a value-weighted portfolio goes up in price and all other stock prices remain the same, what trades are necessary to keep the portfolio value weighted?

Determining Beta

EXCEL ***13.** Go to Chapter Resources on MyFinanceLab and use the data in the spreadsheet provided to estimate the beta of Nike stock using linear regession.

EXCEL ***14.** Using the same data as in Problem 13,
  a. Estimate the alpha of Nike stock over the period covered by the data.
  b. Calculate the 95% confidence interval. Is alpha significantly different from zero?

Extending the CAPM

15. Assume that all the assumptions underlying the CAPM hold, but investors have to borrow and lend at different rates. Will all investors hold a combination of the market portfolio and risk-free borrowing or lending?

16. Assume that all the assumptions underlying the CAPM hold, but investors have to borrow and lend at different rates. Will the market portfolio be efficient?

*17. List all the conditions under which the market portfolio may not be efficient.

The CAPM in Practice

18. Describe two methods to estimate the market risk premium.

*19. Assume the CAPM is correct. Give a reason why an empirical test of the CAPM might indicate that the model does not work—that is, that stocks have alphas that are statistically significantly different from zero.

Data Case

You are still working for the budget-strapped financial planning firm. Your boss has been so impressed with your work in the Data Cases in Chapters 10 and 11 related to the stocks in the client's portfolio that he has one more request: Use the CAPM to compute expected returns for all twelve stocks in the portfolio from Chapter 10. Specifically, he would like you to calculate betas for each stock using five years of monthly data and an expected return using the historical risk premium of 4.5%. He would like you to calculate the betas using excess returns as in Eq. 12.5 with the S&P 500 as the market index and the one-month Eurodollar rate as the risk-free rate.[22] Additionally, he wants you to compute the expected return for the 12-stock portfolio beta using the equally weighted portfolio, and using one of the efficient portfolios derived from Chapter 11. In particular, you should consider the efficient portfolio from Chapter 11 with an expected return of 10%, when short selling is allowed. In preparing your analysis, you'll need to draw on your Excel data from Chapters 10 and 11.

1. Gather the monthly returns from the Chapter 10 Data Case.

2. Get the returns for the S&P 500 from Yahoo! Finance (http://finance.yahoo.com). Click on S&P 500 in the Market Summary box on the left side of the main page. Then click on "Historical Prices" on the left side of the page. Again use May 24, 2001 as the start date and May 1, 2006 as the end date to obtain the prices and remember to click "monthly". Then download those prices and add the adjusted closing prices to your spreadsheet.

3. Get the one-month Eurodollar rate from the Federal Reserve Web site (http://www.federalreserve.gov/releases/h15/data.htm). Click on Data Download. Go to Select and choose: 1.) Series type–selected interest rates 2.) Instrument–ED Eurodollar deposits (London) 3.) Maturity–1 month 4.) Frequency–monthly. Go to Format, Select Dates–From 2001 May to 2006 May, File Type–Excel. Go to download, open, and then save these rates to an Excel file.

4. Create monthly returns for the S&P 500 following the procedure you used for individual stocks. For the Eurodollar rate, convert to a monthly rate, take the yield and divide it by 100 to convert it to a decimal. Then divide the decimal by 12. The resulting rate will be the risk-free rate used in the CAPM.

5. Create separate return columns that compute the excess returns for each stock and the S&P 500. Recall that the excess return is the actual monthly return minus the risk-free rate.

6. Compute the beta of each stock using Eq. 12.5 from this chapter. Recall that Excel computes covariance as the population covariance, so you will have to compute the correlation first and then use the standard deviations of the stock and market index.

7. Using the current Eurodollar rate and the historical market risk premium, determine the expected return of each stock.

8. Determine the expected returns and portfolio betas for the equally weighted portfolio and for the efficient portfolio from Chapter 11 with an expected return of 10% when short selling is allowed.

   a. Is either portfolio "better" in terms of risk and return than the other is? Why or why not?

   b. What do the portfolio results indicate about the investment decision using the SML relative to using standard deviation?

---

22. This rate is the rate London banks charge on loans to one another. It is reflective of the institutional borrowing/lending rate, and is used as the risk-free rate in some financial applications such as derivatives pricing.

CHAPTER

13

Alternative Models
of Systematic Risk

notation

x_i portfolio weight of investment in i

R_s return of stock s

r_f risk-free rate of interest

α_s alpha of stock s

β_s^i beta of stock s with portfolio i

ε_s residual risk of stock s

w_s^i standardized weight of the ith characteristic for firm s

For the ten-year period from 1995 through 2004, the average annual return of the market portfolio of U.S. stock was 12.5%. During the same period, the smallest 10% of U.S. stocks had an annual return of almost 20%. And while the small stock portfolio was much more volatile than the market portfolio, its beta during this time period was slightly less than one. Thus, according to the CAPM, small stocks should not have outperformed the market. What accounts for this discrepancy? Was the positive alpha of small U.S. stock during this period a random occurrence, or was it indicative of potential systematic inaccuracies inherent in the CAPM? And if the CAPM is inaccurate, what alternative methods can be used to estimate a security's expected return and the cost of capital for an investment?

This chapter addresses these questions. We begin by describing several firm characteristics that seem to be related to returns. When criteria such as firm size, the book-to-market ratio, and past returns are used to form portfolios, these portfolios appear to have positive alphas—that is, they plot above the security market line. This evidence indicates that the market portfolio may not be efficient. In light of this evidence, we explain how to calculate the cost of capital if the market portfolio is not efficient. We derive an alternative model of risk—the multifactor asset pricing model. Finally, we introduce an alternative approach to estimating the cost of capital—the characteristic model of expected returns.

401

13.1   The Efficiency of the Market Portfolio

Let's begin by reviewing the results of empirical studies that have examined whether the market portfolio is efficient. As we saw in Chapter 12, the market portfolio is efficient if expected returns are related to betas according to the security market line. That is, if the market portfolio is efficient, securities should not have alphas that are significantly different from zero.

It is not difficult to find individual stocks that, *in the past*, have not plotted on the SML. For example, during the period 1996–2005, Cisco's stock had a positive alpha of 1.2% per month, but the standard error was 1%, indicating a confidence interval between −0.8% per month to 3.2% per month. The uncertainty in Cisco's alpha estimate is not exceptional. For most stocks the standard errors of the alpha estimates are large, so it is impossible to conclude that the alphas are statistically different from zero.

If the market portfolio is efficient, then all securities and portfolios must plot on the SML, not just individual stocks. Because the expected returns of large, well-diversified, portfolios can be estimated with a greater degree of accuracy, one way to construct a more powerful test of the CAPM is to see whether portfolios of stocks plot on the SML. Hence, instead of testing whether individual stocks plot on the SML, researchers have studied whether portfolios of stocks plot on this line.

To make the test of the CAPM as powerful as possible, researchers have searched for portfolios that would be most likely to have nonzero alphas. Researchers had already identified a number of characteristics that can be used to pick stocks that produce high average returns, so they used the same criteria to form their portfolios for testing purposes. Let's begin with the most widely used characteristic, market capitalization.

The Size Effect

Small stocks (those with lower market capitalizations) have higher average returns. This empirical result is called the **size effect**. Researchers have analyzed the size effect by considering the performance of portfolios based on stocks' market capitalizations. For example, Eugene Fama and Kenneth French[1] measured the excess returns of ten portfolios formed each year by collecting the smallest 10% (decile) of stocks into the first portfolio, the next 10% into the second portfolio, on up to the biggest 10% of stocks, which they formed into the tenth portfolio. Fama and French then recorded the excess return of each portfolio in each month over the following year. They repeated this process for all years in their sample. Finally, they calculated the average excess return of each portfolio and the beta of the portfolio; Figure 13.1 shows the result. As you can see, although the portfolios with higher betas yield higher returns, most portfolios plot above the security market line—all except one portfolio had a positive alpha. The most extreme effect is seen in the smallest deciles.

As is evident from Figure 13.1, even these portfolios have large standard errors—none of the alpha estimates is individually significantly different from zero—all the confidence intervals include zero. However, nine of the ten portfolios plot above the SML. If the positive alphas were due purely to statistical error, we would expect as many portfolios to appear above the line as below it. Consequently, a test of whether the alphas of all ten portfolios are jointly all equal to zero can be statistically rejected.

---

1. See Eugene Fama and Kenneth French, "The Cross-Section of Stock Returns," *Journal of Finance* 47 (1992): 427–465.

| FIGURE 13.1 | Excess Return of Size Portfolios, 1926–2005 |

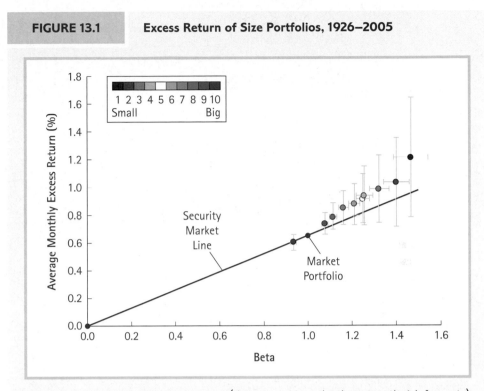

The plot shows the average excess return (the return minus the three-month risk-free rate) for ten portfolios formed in each month over 80 years using the firms' market capitalizations. The average excess return of each portfolio is plotted as a function of the portfolio's beta (estimated over the same time period). The black line is the security market line. If the market portfolio is efficient and there is no measurement error, all portfolios would plot along this line. The error bars mark the 95% confidence bands of the beta and expected excess return estimates.

Source: Data courtesy of Kenneth French.

Researchers have found similar results when they used the **book-to-market ratio**, the ratio of the book value of equity to the market value of equity, to form stocks into portfolios. Figure 13.2 demonstrates that eight out of the ten portfolios formed using the stocks' book-to-market ratios plot above the SML (i.e., have positive alphas). Once again, a joint test of whether all ten portfolios had an alpha of zero is rejected.

The size effect—the observation that small stocks (or stocks with a high book-to-market ratio) have positive alphas—was first discovered in 1981 by Rolf Banz.[2] At the time, researchers did not find the evidence to be convincing because financial economists had been *searching* the data, looking for stocks with positive alphas. As we have already pointed out, because of the existence of significant estimation error, it is always possible to find stocks with positive alphas; indeed, if we look hard enough, it is also always possible to find something these stocks have in common. As a consequence, many researchers

---

2. See R. Banz, "The Relationship between Return and Market Values of Common Stock," *Journal of Financial Economics* 9 (1981): 3–18. A similar relation between a stock's price (rather than its size) and its future return was documented earlier in M. E. Blume and F. Husic, "Price, Beta and Exchange Listing," *Journal of Finance* 28(2): 283–299.

| FIGURE 13.2 | Excess Return of Book-to-Market Portfolios, 1926–2005 |

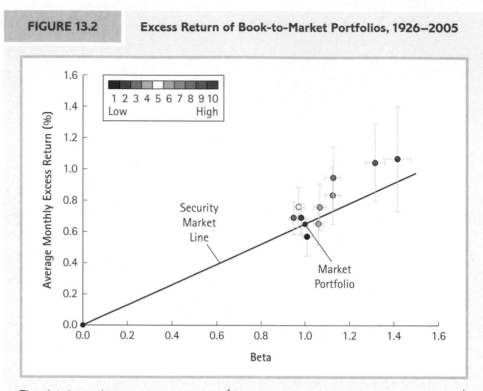

The plot shows the average excess return (the return minus the three-month risk-free rate) for ten portfolios formed in each month over 80 years using the stocks' book-to-market ratios. The average excess return of each portfolio is plotted as a function of the portfolio's beta (estimated over the same time period). The black line is the security market line. If the market portfolio is efficient and there is no measurement error, all portfolios would plot along this line. The error bars mark the 95% confidence bands of the beta and expected excess return estimates.

Source: Data courtesy of Kenneth French.

were inclined to view Banz's findings as due to a **data snooping bias**, which is the idea that given enough characteristics, it will always be possible to find some characteristic that by pure chance happens to be correlated with the estimation error of average returns.

After the publication of Banz's study, however, a theoretical reason emerged that explained the relationship between market capitalization and expected returns. Financial economists realized that when the market portfolio is not efficient, we should *expect* to observe the size effect.[3] To understand why, suppose that the market portfolio is not efficient. Some stocks will therefore plot above the SML, and some will plot below this line. Suppose we take a stock that plots above the line (i.e., has a positive alpha). All else equal, a positive alpha implies that the stock also has a relatively higher expected return. A higher expected return implies a lower price—the only way to offer a higher expected return is for investors to buy the stock's dividend stream at a lower price. A lower price means a lower market capitalization (and similarly a higher book-to-market ratio—market capitalization is in the *denominator* of the book-to-market ratio). Thus, when a financial econ-

3. See J. B. Berk, "A Critique of Size Related Anomalies," *Review of Financial Studies* 8 (1995): 275–286.

omist forms a portfolio of stocks with low market capitalizations (or high book-to-market ratios), that collection contains stocks that will likely have higher expected returns and, if the market portfolio is not efficient, positive alphas. Similarly, a stock that plots below the security market line will have a lower expected return and, therefore, a higher price, implying that it has a higher market capitalization and lower book-to-market ratio. Hence a portfolio of stocks with high market capitalizations or low book-to-market ratios will have negative alphas if the market portfolio is not efficient. Let's illustrate with a simple example.

EXAMPLE 13.1

Risk and the Market Value of Equity

Problem

Consider two firms, SM Industries and BiG Corporation, which are expected to pay the same dividend stream, $1 million per year in perpetuity. Of course, this dividend stream is expected, not guaranteed; actual dividends will depart from this number. SM's dividend stream is riskier, so its cost of capital is 14% per year. BiG's cost of capital is 10%. Which firm has the higher market value? Which firm has the higher expected return? Now assume both stocks have the same estimated beta, either because of estimation error, or because the market portfolio is not efficient. Based on this beta, the CAPM would assign an expected return of 12% to both stocks. Which firm has the higher alpha? How do the market values of the firms relate to their alphas?

Solution

The timeline of dividends is the same for both firms:

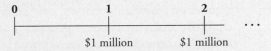

To calculate the market value of SM, we calculate the present value of its future expected dividends using the perpetuity formula and a cost of capital of 14%:

$$\text{Market Value of SM} = \frac{1}{0.14} = \$7.143 \text{ million}$$

Similarly, the market value of BiG is

$$\text{Market Value of BiG} = \frac{1}{0.10} = \$10 \text{ million}$$

SM has the lower market value, and a higher expected return (14% vs. 10%). It also has the higher alpha:

$$\alpha_{SM} = 0.14 - 0.12 = 2\%$$
$$\alpha_{BiG} = 0.10 - 0.12 = -2\%$$

Consequently, the firm with the lower market value has the higher alpha.

When the market portfolio is not efficient, theory predicts that stocks with low market capitalizations or high book-to-market ratios will have positive alphas. In light of this discovery, it became clear to most researchers that the evidence Banz uncovered was, indeed, evidence against the efficiency of the market portfolio.

Past Returns

A second criterion people have used to form portfolios with positive alphas are past stock returns. For example, for the years 1965 to 1989, Narishiman Jegadeesh and Sheridan Titman[4] ranked stocks each month by their realized returns over the prior six months. They found that the best performing stocks had positive alphas over the next six months. This is evidence against the CAPM: When the market portfolio is efficient, past returns should not predict alphas.

Over the years since the discovery of the CAPM, it has become increasingly clear to researchers and practitioners alike that by forming portfolios based on market capitalization, book-to-market ratios, and past returns, one can construct trading strategies that have a positive alpha. For example, one can buy stocks that have had past high returns and (short) sell stocks that have had past low returns. Many investors use such a **momentum strategy**. Researchers have found that this strategy is profitable. For example, Jegadeesh and Titman showed that over the period 1965–1989 it would have produced positive risk-adjusted returns of 12.83% per year.

CONCEPT CHECK   1. What is the size effect?

2. What is a momentum trading strategy?

13.2 Implication of Positive Alphas

What are the implications if trading strategies based on positive alphas really do exist? You might expect a few investors to be able to generate positive-alpha strategies because of informational advantages. But, *anyone* can implement a momentum trading strategy (it requires no special information, only knowledge of past returns) and, therefore, generate a positive alpha-investment opportunity. If the CAPM correctly computes the risk premium, an investment opportunity with a positive alpha is a positive-NPV investment opportunity, and investors should flock to invest in such strategies. In doing so they would drive down the return on these strategies; indeed, they would stop investing only when they expected the alpha of such a strategy to be zero.

The alpha of these trading strategies, however, does not appear to be zero when we examine real-world data. If, indeed, these alphas are positive, we are left to draw one of two conclusions:

1. Investors are systematically ignoring positive-NPV investment opportunities. That is, the CAPM correctly computes risk premiums, but investors are ignoring opportunities to earn extra returns without bearing any extra risk, either because they are unaware of them or because the costs to implement the strategies are larger than the NPV of undertaking them.

2. The positive-alpha trading strategies contain risk that investors are unwilling to bear but the CAPM does not capture. That is, a stock's beta with the market portfolio does not adequately measure a stock's systematic risk, and so the CAPM does not correctly compute the risk premium.

The only way a positive-NPV opportunity can exist in a market is if some barrier to entry restricts competition. In this case, it is very difficult to identify what these barriers might be. The existence of the momentum trading strategy has been widely known for at

---

4. See Narishiman Jegadeesh and Sheridan Titman, "Returns to Buying Winners and Selling Losers: Implications for Market Efficiency," *Journal of Finance* 48 (1993): 65–91.

least ten years. The fact that we are presenting this evidence in a corporate finance text-book implies that the possibility that people just don't realize that these opportunities exist is unlikely. Furthermore, the costs of implementing the strategy do not seem excessively high. Not only is the information required to form the portfolios readily available for free, but many mutual funds exist that follow both the momentum-based trading strategy and the market capitalization/book-to-market–based strategy. Hence, the first conclusion does not seem likely.

That leaves the second possibility: The market portfolio is not efficient, and therefore a stock's beta with the market is not an adequate measure of its systematic risk. Stated another way, the so called profits (positive alphas) from the trading strategy are really returns for bearing risk that investors are averse to and the CAPM does not capture. There are two reasons why the market portfolio might not be efficient. First, we might be using the wrong proxy portfolio to calculate alphas; the true market portfolio of all invested wealth might be efficient, but the proxy portfolio might not track the actual market very well. Second, even the true market portfolio may not be efficient because a significant fraction of investors might care about aspects of their portfolios other than expected return and volatility, and so would be willing to hold inefficient investment portfolios. Let's examine each possibility in turn.

Proxy Error

The true market portfolio consists of all traded investment wealth in the economy. It therefore contains much more than just stocks—it includes bonds, real estate, art, precious metals, and any other investment vehicles available. Yet, we cannot include most of these investments in the market proxy because they do not trade in competitive markets. Instead, researchers use a proxy portfolio like the S&P 500 and assume that it will be highly correlated to the true market portfolio. But what if this assumption is false?

If the true market portfolio is efficient but the proxy portfolio is not highly correlated with the true market, then the proxy will not be efficient and stocks will have nonzero alphas.[5] In this case, the alphas merely indicate that the wrong proxy is being used; they do not indicate forgone positive-NPV investment opportunities.[6]

Non-tradeable Wealth

Another possibility is that the true market portfolio is inefficient—investors might care about characteristics other than the expected returns and volatility of their portfolios. Two conditions might cause investors to care about characteristics other than the expected return and volatility of their portfolios: They might care about other measures of uncertainty (e.g., the skewness of the distribution of returns), or they might have significant wealth invested in investments that are not tradeable. Consider an investor who trades off expected return and volatility and thus picks an efficient portfolio of *all* her investments,

---

5. Richard Roll and Stephen Ross have shown that when the true market portfolio is efficient, even a small difference between the proxy and true market portfolio can lead to an insignificant relation between beta and returns. See Richard Roll and Stephen A. Ross, "On the Cross-Sectional Relation between Expected Returns and Beta," *Journal of Finance* 49(1) (March 1994): 101–121.

6. If the market proxy *is* efficient, we cannot conclude that the *true* market portfolio is efficient. Because the test of the CAPM requires finding that the *true* market portfolio is efficient, the CAPM theory is untestable. This point was first made by Richard Roll, "A Critique of the Asset Pricing Theory's Tests," *Journal of Financial Economics* 4 (1977): 129–176. Of course, from a corporate manager's perspective, whether the CAPM is testable is irrelevant—as long as an efficient portfolio can be identified, he or she can use it to compute the cost of capital.

> **COMMON MISTAKE**   **Investing in Own Company Stock**
>
> When Enron Corporation filed for bankruptcy in December 2001, 62% of the assets held in the corporation's 401(k) retirement plan consisted of shares of Enron stock.* The value of these assets had declined greatly as Enron's shares, worth $80 per share one year earlier, traded for just $0.70 one month after the bankruptcy. Consequently, the collapse of Enron not only robbed many employees of their jobs, but also wiped out their retirement savings.
>
> Why did the employees of Enron choose to hold inefficient portfolios, thereby significantly increasing their exposure to Enron's idiosyncratic risk? One explanation is that Enron made matching contributions to the plan in the form of Enron stock that it prohibited employees under the age of 50 from selling. However, according to the company, only 11% of the wealth invested in Enron stock can be traced to its matching contributions to the pension plan.
>
> Enron was not the only company that encouraged its employees to invest their pension money in company stock. Shlomo Benartzi** found that about one third of the assets of large defined-contribution retirement plans are invested in company stock.
>
> Such investment behavior is difficult to fathom. Employees, through their human capital, already have a significant fraction of their wealth tied to the fortunes of the company they work for. If anything, they should substantially underweight their investments in their own company stock. Why these employees choose to hold inefficient portfolios by further concentrating their wealth in their own company stock is a mystery. In any case, this evidence indicates that not all investors adequately diversify, and as a result hold inefficient portfolios.
>
> ___
>
> *Congressional Research Service Report for Congress, March 11, 2002.
>
> **"Excessive Extrapolation and the Allocation of 401(k) Accounts to Company Stock," *Journal of Finance* 56 (2001): 1747–1764.

whether tradeable or not. Although the entire portfolio is efficient, there is no reason why just the tradeable part of the portfolio should be efficient.

The most important example of a non-tradeable wealth is human capital.[7] People are naturally exposed to the risk in the industry in which they work. A banker working for Goldman Sachs is exposed to risk in the financial sector, while an electrical engineer working in Silicon Valley is exposed to risk in the high-tech sector. When an investor diversifies, he or she should take into account these inherent exposures. The investment banker is likely to underweight or perhaps hold a short position in financial services stocks; her job already exposes her to risk in the financial services sector. Similarly, the electrical engineer should not hold high-tech stocks. Thus, even if both investors hold efficient portfolios, their portfolios of *traded* securities need not be efficient and are unlikely to be the same. Furthermore, it is unlikely that either investor will choose to hold the market portfolio of traded securities.

If investors have a significant amount of non-tradeable wealth, this wealth will be an important part of their portfolios, but will not be part of the market portfolio of tradeable securities. In such a world, the market portfolio of tradeable securities will likely not be efficient. Indeed, researchers have found evidence that the presence of human capital can explain at least part of the reason for the inefficiency of the most commonly used market proxies.[8]

___

7. Although rare, there are innovative new markets that allow people to trade their human capital to finance their education, see Miguel Palacios, *Investing in Human Capital: A Capital Markets Approach to Student Funding,* Cambridge University Press, 2004.

8. See Ravi Jagannathan and Zhenu Wang, "The Conditional CAPM and the Cross-Sections of Expected Returns," *Journal of Finance* 51 (1996): 3–53; and Ignacio Palacios-Huerta, "The Robustness of the Conditional CAPM with Human Capital," *Journal of Financial Econometrics* 1 (2003): 272–289.

In light of the evidence against the efficiency of the market portfolio, researchers have developed alternative models of risk. In the next section we will derive the multifactor model of risk.

1. What does the existence of a positive alpha trading strategy imply?

2. If investors have a significant amount of non-tradeable (but risky) wealth, why might the market portfolio not be efficient?

13.3 Multifactor Models of Risk

In Chapter 11, we showed that the expected return of any marketable security can be written as a function of the expected return of the efficient portfolio:

$$E[R_s] = r_f + \beta_s^{eff} \times (E[R_{eff}] - r_f) \qquad (13.1)$$

When the market portfolio is not efficient, we have to find a method to identify an efficient portfolio before we can use Eq. 13.1.

As a practical matter, it is extremely difficult to identify portfolios that are efficient because we cannot measure the expected return and the standard deviation of a portfolio with great accuracy. Although we might not be able to identify the efficient portfolio itself, we know some characteristics of the efficient portfolio. First, any efficient portfolio will be well diversified. Second, an efficient portfolio can be constructed from other diversified portfolios. This latter observation may seem trivial, but it is actually quite useful: It implies that so long as an efficient portfolio can be constructed from a collection of portfolios, the collection itself can be used to measure risk. *It is not actually necessary to identify the efficient portfolio itself.* All that is required is to identify a collection of portfolios from which the efficient portfolio can be constructed.

Using Factor Portfolios

Let's keep things simple. Assume that we have identified two portfolios that we know can be combined to form an efficient portfolio; we call these portfolios **factor portfolios** and denote their returns by R_{F1} and R_{F2}. The efficient portfolio consists of some (unknown) combination of these two factor portfolios, represented by portfolio weights x_1 and x_2:

$$R_{eff} = x_1 R_{F1} + x_2 R_{F2} \qquad (13.2)$$

To see that we can use these factor portfolios to measure risk, consider regressing the excess returns of some stock s on the excess returns of *both* factors:

$$R_s - r_f = \alpha_s + \beta_s^{F1}(R_{F1} - r_f) + \beta_s^{F2}(R_{F2} - r_f) + \varepsilon_s \qquad (13.3)$$

This statistical technique is known as a **multiple regression**—it is exactly the same as the linear regression technique described in Chapter 12, except now we have two regressors, $R_{F1} - r_f$ and $R_{F2} - r_f$, whereas in Chapter 12 we only had one regressor, the excess return of the market portfolio. Otherwise the interpretation is the same. The excess return of stock s is written as the sum of a constant, α_s, plus the variation in the stock that is related to each factor, and an error term ε_s that has an expectation of zero and is uncorrelated with either factor. The error term represents the risk of the stock that is unrelated to either factor.

If the two factor portfolios can be used to construct the efficient portfolio, as in Eq. 13.2, then the constant term α_s in Eq. 13.3 is zero (up to estimation error). To see why, consider a portfolio in which we buy stock s, then sell a fraction β_s^{F1} of the first factor portfolio and β_s^{F2} of the second factor portfolio, and invest the proceeds from these sales in the risk-free investment. This portfolio, which we call P, has return

$$R_P = R_s - \beta_s^{F1} R_{F1} - \beta_s^{F2} R_{F2} + (\beta_s^{F1} + \beta_s^{F2}) r_f$$

$$= R_s - \beta_s^{F1}(R_{F1} - r_f) - \beta_s^{F2}(R_{F2} - r_f) \qquad (13.4)$$

Using Eq. 13.3 to replace R_s and simplifying, the return of this portfolio is

$$R_P = r_f + \alpha_s + \varepsilon_s \qquad (13.5)$$

That is, portfolio P has a risk premium of α_s and risk given by ε_s. Now, because ε_s is uncorrelated with each factor, it must be uncorrelated with the efficient portfolio; that is,

$$Cov(R_{eff}, \varepsilon_s) = Cov(x_1 R_{F1} + x_2 R_{F2}, \varepsilon_s)$$

$$= x_1 Cov(R_{F1}, \varepsilon_s) + x_2 Cov(R_{F2}, \varepsilon_s)$$

$$= 0 \qquad (13.6)$$

But recall from Chapter 11 that *risk that is uncorrelated with the efficient portfolio is diversifiable risk that does not command a risk premium.* Therefore, the expected return of portfolio P is r_f, which means α_s must be zero.[9]

Setting α_s equal to zero and taking expectations of both sides of Eq. 13.3, we get the following two-factor model of expected returns:

$$E[R_s] = r_f + \beta_s^{F1}(E[R_{F1}] - r_f) + \beta_s^{F2}(E[R_{F2}] - r_f) \qquad (13.7)$$

Eq. 13.7 says that the risk premium of any marketable security can be written as the sum of the risk premium of each factor multiplied by the sensitivity of the stock with that factor—the **factor betas**. Neither portfolio itself must be efficient; we just need to be able to construct the efficient portfolio out of the two portfolios.

There is nothing inconsistent between Eq. 13.7, which gives the expected return in terms of two factors, and Eq. 13.1, which gives the expected return in terms of just the efficient portfolio. *Both* equations hold; the difference between them is simply the portfolios that we use. When we use an efficient portfolio, it alone will capture all systematic risk. Consequently, we often refer to this model as a **single-factor model**. If we use more than one portfolio as factors, then together these factors will capture all systematic risk, but note that each factor in Eq. 13.7 captures different components of the systematic risk. When we use more than one portfolio to capture risk, the model is known as a **multi-factor model**. The portfolios themselves can be thought of as either a risk factor itself or a portfolio of stocks correlated with an unobservable risk factor. This particular form of the multifactor model was originally developed by Stephen Ross, although Robert Merton had developed an alternative multifactor model earlier.[10] The model is also referred to as the **Arbitrage Pricing Theory (APT)**.

---

9. That is, Eq. 13.6 implies $\beta_P^{eff} = \frac{Cov(R_{eff}, \varepsilon_s)}{Var(R_{eff})} = 0$. Substituting this result into Eq. 13.1 gives $E[R_P] = r_f$. But from Eq. 13.5, $E[R_P] = r_f + \alpha_s$, and hence $\alpha_s = 0$.

10. See Stephen A. Ross, "The Arbitrage Theory of Capital Asset Pricing," *Journal of Economic Theory* 13 (1976): 341–360; and Robert C. Merton, "An Intertemporal Capital Asset Pricing Model," *Econometrica* 41 (1973): 867–887.

Building a Multifactor Model

Although we derived Eq. 13.7 using only two portfolios, the model is easily extended to any number of portfolios. Indeed, it often makes sense to use more than two portfolios because a larger number increases the probability that an efficient portfolio can be constructed out of the portfolios. If we use N factor portfolios with returns $R_{F1}, \ldots, R_{FN}$, the expected return of asset s is given by

Multifactor Model of Risk

$$E[R_s] = r_f + \beta_s^{F1}(E[R_{F1}] - r_f) + \beta_s^{F2}(E[R_{F2}] - r_f) + \cdots + \beta_s^{FN}(E[R_{FN}] - r_f)$$

$$= r_f + \sum_{n-1}^{N} \beta_s^{Fn}(E[R_{Fn}] - r_f) \tag{13.8}$$

Here $\beta_s^1, \ldots, \beta_s^N$ are the factor betas, one for each risk factor, and have the same interpretation as the beta in the CAPM. Each factor beta is the expected percent change in the excess return of a security for a 1% change in the excess return of the factor portfolio.

We can simplify Eq. 13.8 a bit further. We can think of the expected excess return of each factor, $E[R_{Fn}] - r_f$, as the expected return of a portfolio in which we borrow the funds at rate r_f to invest in the factor portfolio. Because this portfolio costs nothing to construct (we are borrowing the funds to invest), it is called a **self-financing portfolio**. We can also construct a self-financing portfolio by going long some stocks, and going short other stocks with equal market value. In general, a self-financing portfolio is any portfolio with portfolio weights that sum to zero rather than one. If we require that all factor portfolios are self-financing (either by borrowing funds or shorting stocks), then we can rewrite Eq. 13.8 as

Multifactor Model of Risk with Self-Financing Portfolios

$$E[R_s] = r_f + \beta_s^{F1} E[R_{F1}] + \beta_s^{F2} E[R_{F2}] + \cdots + \beta_s^{FN} E[R_{FN}]$$

$$= r_f + \sum_{n=1}^{N} \beta_s^{Fn} E[R_{Fn}] \tag{13.9}$$

To recap, we have shown that it is possible to calculate the cost of capital without actually identifying the efficient portfolio using a multifactor risk model. Rather than relying on the efficiency of a single portfolio (such as the market), multifactor models rely on the weaker condition that an efficient portfolio can be constructed from a collection of well-diversified portfolios or factors. We next explain how to select the factors.

Selecting the Portfolios

In this section, we explain the method most commonly used to identify a collection of portfolios that contain the efficient portfolio. The most obvious portfolio to use in the collection is the market portfolio itself. Historically, the market portfolio has commanded a large premium over short-term risk-free investments, such as Treasury Bills. Even if the market portfolio is not efficient, it still captures at least some components of systematic risk. As Figures 13.1 and 13.2 demonstrate, even when the model fails, portfolios with higher average returns *do* tend to have higher betas. Thus the first portfolio in the collection is the return of the market portfolio less the risk-free interest rate.

How do we go about picking the other portfolios? As we pointed out earlier, trading strategies based on market capitalization, book-to-market ratios, and momentum have

INTERVIEW WITH
Rex A. Sinquefield

Rex A. Sinquefield is a director, co-founder, and former co-chairman and chief investment officer of Dimensional Fund Advisors, Inc. One of the first money managers to successfully apply the findings of academic finance to money management, he formed many of the first index funds at American National Bank of Chicago in the early 1970s.

QUESTION: *In the last 25 years, researchers have uncovered several characteristics, such as size, book-to-market ratio, and momentum, that can extend the traditional CAPM pricing model. How has this research changed the ways practitioners think about risk?*

ANSWER: Most people now realize that there are three sources of risk: general market risk, the value/growth factor, and the size risk (the risk associated with small companies). Momentum is a real conundrum. It is more a case of falling stocks continuing to fall than rising stocks continuing to rise. It primarily occurs in the small stock universe, and it's not readily exploitable. So we can set it aside. One might take it into account in running portfolios.

QUESTION: *Do you think these characteristics represent real risk characteristics or do they reflect mispricings in the market?*

ANSWER: I think this is real risk. I don't buy the idea of mispricing, or the market would have learned by now. These patterns are too systematic. They have been going on for almost 80 years in the United States and 30 years around the world. We find the size effect and the value/growth effect in almost every developed country and in emerging markets. Dimensional's core belief is that the market doesn't misvalue securities. The prices are right.

If you believe in active management, you're saying that people can make valuation judgments that are superior to the market.

QUESTION: *How does Dimensional apply these alternative pricing models in building highly diversified portfolios structured around risk factors?*

ANSWER: In building portfolios, we actually don't use the risk factors directly but instead use characteristics such as a stock's book-to-market ratio and the company's market capitalization. We use this construction technique for all types of funds, both domestic and international. These funds, which hold hundreds or even thousands of securities, track a specific part of a market. They are passive—their holdings don't vary—so they stay true to what they are doing.

Once a portfolio is built and running, we can perform multiple regression analyses, using the return history of the portfolio, to look at how the return history relates to the three risk factors. Then we can evaluate a portfolio or compare it to another portfolio.

We don't believe that money managers can consistently beat markets by picking stocks or market timing—and many studies support this. The evidence is overwhelming that markets work very, very well. Dimensional uses risk factors first to set boundaries to identify the securities according to a characteristic such as size or book-to-market. Then we are prepared to buy nearly all the securities in that category. So we don't pick stocks in the conventional sense. Second, we find that the best way to get above-market returns is to add more value or size risk. Investors can then "tilt" their portfolio to achieve above-market returns by holding value and small cap funds in above-market proportions, while recognizing this requires taking more risk.

been developed that appear to have positive alphas. A positive alpha means that the portfolios that implement the trading strategy capture risk that is not captured by the market portfolio. Hence these portfolios are good candidates for the other portfolios in a multifactor model. We will construct three additional portfolios out of the trading strategies that have produced positive risk-adjusted returns historically. The first trading strategy selects stocks based on their market capitalization, the second uses the book-to-market ratio, and the third uses past returns. We begin with the strategy that uses market capitalization.

Each year, let's place firms into one of two portfolios based on their market value of equity: Firms with market values below the median of NYSE firms in that month form an equally weighted portfolio, S, and firms above the median market value form an equally weighted portfolio, B. A trading strategy that each year buys portfolio S (small stocks) and finances this position by short selling portfolio B (big stocks) has produced positive risk-adjusted returns historically. This self-financing portfolio is widely known as the **small-minus-big (SMB) portfolio**.

A second trading strategy that has produced positive risk-adjusted returns historically uses the book-to-market ratio to select stocks. Each year firms with book-to-market ratios less than the 30th percentile of NYSE firms form an equally weighted portfolio called the low portfolio, L. Firms with book-to-market ratios greater than the 70th percentile of NYSE firms form an equally weighted portfolio called the high portfolio, H. A trading strategy that each year takes a long position in portfolio H, which it finances with a short position in portfolio L, has produced positive risk-adjusted returns. We add this self-financing portfolio (high minus low book-to-market stocks) to our collection and call it the **high-minus-low (HML) portfolio**.

The third trading strategy is a momentum strategy. Each year stocks are ranked by their return over the last one year,[11] and a portfolio is constructed that goes long the top 30% of stocks and short the bottom 30%. This trading strategy requires holding this portfolio for a year; a new self-financing portfolio is then formed and held for another year. This process is repeated annually. The resulting self-financing portfolio is known as the **prior one-year momentum (PR1YR) portfolio**.

The collection of these four portfolios—the excess return of the market ($\text{Mkt} - r_f$), SMB, HML, and PR1YR—is currently the most popular choice for the multifactor model. Using this collection, the expected return of security s is given by Eq. 13.10:

Fama-French-Carhart Factor Specification

$$E[R_s] = r_f + \beta_s^{Mkt}(E[R_{Mkt}] - r_f) + \beta_s^{SMB}E[R_{SMB}]$$
$$+ \beta_s^{HML}E[R_{HML}] + \beta_s^{PR1YR}E[R_{PR1YR}] \tag{13.10}$$

where $\beta_s^{Mkt}, \beta_s^{SMB}, \beta_s^{HML}$, and β_s^{PR1YR} are the factor betas of stock s and measure the sensitivity of the stock to each portfolio. Because the four portfolios in Eq. 13.10 were identified by Eugene Fama, Kenneth French, and Mark Carhart, we will refer to this collection of portfolios as the **Fama-French-Carhart (FFC) factor specification**.

Calculating the Cost of Capital Using the Fama-French-Carhart Factor Specification

Multifactor models have a distinct advantage over single-factor models in that it is much easier to identify a collection of portfolios that captures systematic risk than just a single portfolio. They also have an important disadvantage, however: We must estimate the expected return of each portfolio. Because expected returns are not easy to estimate, each portfolio that is added to the collection increases the difficulty of implementing the model. What makes this task especially complex is that it is unclear *which* economic risk the portfolios capture, so we cannot hope to come up with a reasonable estimate of what

---

11. Because of short-term trading effects, the most recent month's return is often dropped, so actually an 11-month return is used.

the return should be (as we did with the CAPM) based on an economic argument. If we want to implement the model, we have little choice other than to use historical average returns on the portfolios.[12]

Because the returns on the FFC portfolios are so volatile, we use 80 years of data to estimate the expected return. Table 13.1 shows the monthly average return as well as the 95% confidence bands of the FFC portfolios (we use a value-weighted portfolio of all NYSE, AMEX, and NASDAQ stocks as the proxy for the market portfolio). Even with 80 years of data, however, all of the estimates of the expected returns are imprecise.

TABLE 13.1	FFC Portfolio Average Monthly Returns, 1926–2005	
Factor Portfolio	Average Monthly Return (%)	95% Confidence Band (%)
Mkt − r_f	0.64	±0.35
SMB	0.17	±0.21
HML	0.53	±0.23
PR1YR	0.76	±0.30

Data Source: Kenneth French.

EXAMPLE 13.2

Using the FFC Factor Specification to Calculate the Cost of Capital

Problem

You are considering making an investment in a project in the food and beverages industry. You determine that the project has the same level of non-diversifiable risk as investing in Coca-Cola stock. Determine the cost of capital by using the FFC factor specification.

Solution

You decide to use data over the past five years to estimate the factor betas of Coca-Cola stock (ticker: KO). You therefore regress the monthly excess return (the realized return in each month minus the risk-free rate) of your company's stock on the return of each portfolio. The coefficient estimates are the factor betas. Here are the estimates of the four factor betas based on data from years 2000 through 2004:

$$\beta_{KO}^{Mkt} = 0.158$$
$$\beta_{KO}^{SMB} = 0.302$$
$$\beta_{KO}^{HML} = 0.497$$
$$\beta_{KO}^{PR1\,YR} = -0.276$$

12. There is a second, more subtle disadvantage to most factor models. Because factor models are designed to price traded securities, there is no guarantee that they will accurately price risks that are not currently traded (e.g., the risk associated with a new technology). In practice, it is assumed that any non-traded risk is idiosyncratic, and therefore does not command a risk premium.

Using these estimates and the current risk-free monthly rate of 5%/12 = 0.42%, you calculate the monthly expected return of investing in Coca-Cola stock:

$$E[R_{KO}] = r_f + \beta_{KO}^{Mkt}(E[R_{Mkt}] - r_f) + \beta_{KO}^{SMB}E[R_{SMB}] + \beta_{KO}^{HML}E[R_{HML}] + \beta_{KO}^{PR1\,YR}E[R_{KO}]$$

$$= 0.42\% + 0.158 \times 0.64\% + 0.302 \times 0.17\% + 0.497 \times 0.53\% - 0.276 \times 0.76\%$$

$$= 0.626\%$$

The annual expected return is 0.626% × 12 = 7.512%. The annual cost of capital of the investment opportunity is about 7.5%.

The FFC factor specification was identified a little more than ten years ago. Although it is widely used in academic literature to measure risk, much debate persists about whether it really is a significant improvement over the CAPM.[13] The one area where researchers have found that the FFC factor specification does appear to do better than the CAPM is measuring the risk of actively managed mutual funds. Researchers have found that funds with high returns in the past have positive alphas under the CAPM.[14] When Mark Carhart repeated the same test using the FFC factor specification to compute alphas, he found no evidence that mutual funds with high past returns had future positive alphas.[15]

CONCEPT CHECK

1. What is the advantage of a multifactor model over a single factor model?

2. What is the Fama-French-Carhart factor specification?

13.4 Characteristic Variable Models of Expected Returns

Calculating the cost of capital using multifactor models like the FFC factor specification or the CAPM relies on accurate estimates of risk premiums and betas. Often, however, accurately estimating these quantities is difficult. Many years of data are required to estimate risk premiums, and both risk premiums and betas may not remain stable over time. Consider, for example, the CAPM beta estimates of General Electric, General Motors, IBM, and Procter & Gamble plotted in Figure 13.3. As the figure illustrates, the beta estimate may vary substantially depending on the time period during which the beta is estimated.

Why are the betas of firms like IBM and GM so variable? One reason is statistical error. Figure 13.3 plots beta estimates, and some of the variation likely reflects measurement error. However, there is also an economic reason why firm's betas might vary—the firm itself varies. When firms make new investments in new areas or shut down unprofitable projects in old areas their risk profiles change as well.[16] Thus an economist trying

---

13. See M. Cooper, R. Gutierrez, Jr., and B. Marcum, "On the Predictability of Stock Returns in Real Time," *Journal of Business* 78 (2005): 469–500.

14. See M. Grinblatt and S. Titman, "The Persistence of Mutual Fund Performance," *Journal of Finance* 47 (1992): 1977–1984; and D. J. Hendricks, J. Patel, and R. Zeckhauser, "Hot Hands in Mutual Funds: Short-Run Persistence of Performance 1974–1988," *Journal of Finance* 4 (1993): 93–130.

15. See M. Carhart, "On Persistence in Mutual Fund Performance," *Journal of Finance* 52 (1997): 57–82.

16. For a model of the dynamics of real investment and its effect on beta, see J. B. Berk, R. C. Green, and V. Naik, "Optimal Investment, Growth Options and Security Returns," *Journal of Finance* 54 (1999): 1553–1607.

Variation of CAPM Beta in Time

The plot shows the CAPM beta estimates of General Electric (GE), General Motors (GM), IBM, and Procter & Gamble (PG). The estimates are made over the previous five years using monthly data. We use a value-weighted portfolio of all NYSE, AMEX, and NASDAQ stocks as the proxy for the market portfolio.

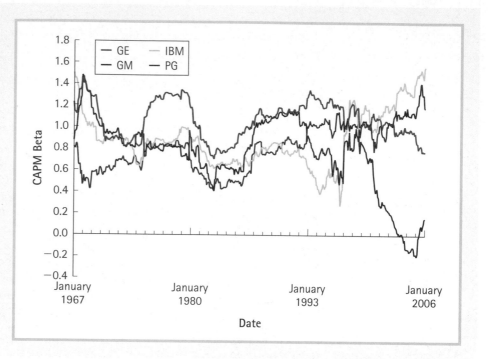

to measure a firm's beta faces an inevitable tradeoff. Using a long period of time to estimate beta reduces measurement error, but because firms evolve dynamically, old data might not reflect the current risk profile of the firm.

To address these concerns, some practitioners have developed a different approach to measuring risk, the **characteristic variable model** of returns. Rather than attempt to estimate the risk and expected return of the firm directly, this approach views firms as a portfolio of different measurable "characteristics" that together determine the firm's risk and return. If the relation between risk and these characteristics is stable over time, then a long time series can be used to estimate the risk and return associated with each characteristic. But even though the risk and return associated with each characteristic may remain stable, because the characteristics of a firm may change over time, so will the firm's risk and expected return. That is, if we view the firm as a portfolio of these characteristics, over time the portfolio weights change, and hence so does the risk of the firm.

As an example of this approach, Table 13.2 lists the characteristics that are used by one company that provides data for such an approach, MSCI Barra. The MSCI Barra model estimates risk and return based on 12 firm characteristics, together with 55 industry classifications. MSCI Barra standardizes the characteristic variables by measuring the characteristic of each firm as the number of standard deviations away the firm is from the average firm with respect to that characteristic. Table 13.3 lists these values for Coca-Cola and GE based on data from 2005. So, for example, both these firms were above average on the size characteristic, yet were below average with respect to growth. In addition to these generic characteristics Barra also includes characteristic variables that measure the weight of each firm in the sectors it produces in. For example Coca-Cola was classified as 100% in the food and beverage industry, whereas GE was classified as having 48% of its business in financial services, 29% in electrical equipment, 10% in media, 7% in medical products, and 6% in chemicals.

TABLE 13.2	Firm Characteristics Used by MSCI Barra

Characteristic	Description
Volatility	The stock's relative volatility using both long-term and short-term measures of the stock's historical beta and volatility
Momentum	The degree to which a stock has had positive excess returns in the recent past
Size	The log of the stock's market capitalization
Size non-linearity	The cube of the log of the stock's market capitalization (allows for a non-linear relationship between returns and the log of market capitalization)
Trading activity	The amount of trading in a stock based on its share turnover rate
Growth	The stock's expected future earnings growth, based on its historical growth and profitability measures
Earnings yield	Combines the stock's current, historical, and analyst-predicted earnings-to-price ratio
Value	The ratio of book value of equity to market capitalization
Earnings variability	The variability in earnings and cash flows using both historical measures and analyst predictions
Leverage	The financial leverage of a company
Currency sensitivity	The sensitivity of a company's stock return to the return on a basket of foreign currencies
Dividend yield	The stock's predicted dividend yield using the past history of dividends and the market price behavior of the stock

Once the characteristic variables have been identified and measured for each firm, the return of each characteristic can be inferred from the data. We do not observe the returns of the characteristic variables directly, but their returns in each period are estimated indirectly from firms' returns by regressing the return of all firms onto the value of the characteristic variables. Specifically, if w_s^i is the index (or weight) of stock s for characteristic or industry i, and if R_{ci} is the return associated with characteristic or industry i, then the return of stock s can be written as

The Characteristic Variable Model of Stock Returns

$$R_s = w_s^1 R_{c1} + w_s^2 R_{c2} + \cdots + w_s^N R_{cN} + \varepsilon_s \qquad (13.11)$$

There is an important difference between the characteristic variable model described by Eq. 13.11 and the multifactor models we considered earlier. In the multifactor models, the returns of the factor portfolios are observed, and we estimate the sensitivity of each stock to the different factors (the factor betas). In the characteristic variable model, the weight of each stock on each characteristic is observed, and then we estimate the return R_{cn} associated with each characteristic. Table 13.3 shows the average monthly return estimate for the MSCI Barra characteristics during 2000–2005.[17]

There are a number of ways that people use the estimated relation between the characteristic variables and returns. Perhaps the most straightforward approach is simply to use the relation to estimate each stock's expected return. That is, if you view a stock as

---

17. We thank MSCI Barra (in particular, Dan Stefek and John Taymuree) for providing these data.

TABLE 13.3		Characteristic Weight (standardized)		Characteristic Return
	Characteristic	Coca-Cola	GE	(% per month)
MSCI Barra Characteristic Weights and Return Estimates	Volatility	−0.498	−0.355	0.117
The characteristic weight of each firm is the number of standard deviations away the firm is from the average firm with respect to that characteristic. The characteristic returns are estimated as the coefficients R_{cn} in Eq. 13.11. Reported are the characteristic weights for 2005, and average characteristic returns for 2000–2005.	Momentum	−1.212	−0.216	−0.333
	Size	1.004	2.047	−0.481
	Size non-linearity	0.210	0.210	0.214
	Trading activity	−0.496	−0.577	−0.028
	Growth	−0.625	−0.204	−0.026
	Earnings yield	−0.223	−0.189	0.629
	Value	−0.665	−0.414	0.058
	Earnings variability	−0.444	−0.627	−0.057
	Leverage	−0.462	−0.158	0.045
	Currency sensitivity	−0.275	0.326	0.067
	Dividend yield	0.403	0.481	0.004

portfolio of characteristic variables, then the stock's expected return is the sum over all the variables of the amount of each characteristic variable the stock contains times the expected return of that variable:[18]

$$E[R_s] = w_s^1 E[R_{c1}] + w_s^2 E[R_{c2}] + \cdots + w_s^N E[R_{cN}] \tag{13.12}$$

Robert Haugen and Nardin Baker[19] evaluated the usefulness of the characteristic variable approach by ranking stocks based on their characteristics model; they formed stocks into 10 ranked portfolios based on their characteristics model's prediction of expected return. They then measured the return of each portfolio over the following month. If the characteristic model correctly differentiates stocks the ranking of the portfolios would be preserved by the returns—the top-ranked portfolio would have the highest return. This is exactly what Haugen and Baker found, as we illustrate in Figure 13.4.

Another approach is to use the estimated returns of the characteristic variables to estimate the covariance between pairs of stocks, or between a stock and the market index. The idea behind this approach is that if firms' characteristics change over time, the covariance between the characteristic returns may be more stable than the covariance between stocks themselves. In this case, the residual risk ε_s in Eq. 13.11 is generally assumed to be firm-specific risk, uncorrelated with the characteristic returns or the returns of other firms.

---

18. Equation 13.12 follows from Eq. 13.11 if we assume the residual risk ε_s has mean zero.

19. R. A. Haugen and N. L. Baker, "Commonality in the Determinants of Expected Stock Returns," *Journal of Financial Economics* 41 (1996): 401–439.

FIGURE 13.4

Returns of Portfolios Ranked by the Characteristic Variable Model

The figure shows the subsequent returns of portfolios formed by ranking stocks based on the characteristic variable model of returns. The portfolio of stocks ranked low subsequently had low returns, and the portfolio of stocks ranked high subsequently had high returns.

Source: Adapted from Figure 5-1 p. 52 from R. A. Haugen, *The Inefficient Market*, 2nd ed.

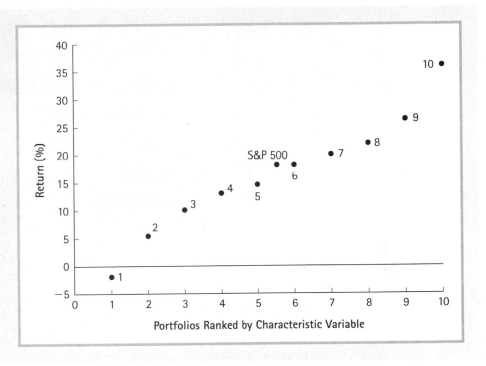

Then, by viewing each stock as a portfolio of characteristics, we can use the techniques of Chapter 11 to calculate the covariance between two different stocks i and j as

$$Cov(R_i, R_j) = \sum_{n=1}^{N} \sum_{m=1}^{N} w_i^n w_j^m Cov(R_{cn}, R_{cm}) \tag{13.13}$$

Similarly, the beta of each stock can then be calculated from the beta of the characteristic variables in the same way a beta of a portfolio can be computed from the beta of its constituent securities: The beta of a stock is equal to the weighted average of the characteristic variable betas where the weights are the amounts of each characteristic variable the stock contains. Because the amount of each characteristic variable a stock contains changes as the firm evolves in time, its beta will change accordingly to reflect its new level of risk.

CONCEPT CHECK

1. How does a characteristic variable model differ from a multifactor model of returns?

2. How are characteristic variable models used?

13.5 Methods Used in Practice

Surveying 392 CFOs, John Graham and Campbell Harvey found that 73.5% of the firms that they questioned use the CAPM to calculate the cost of capital, as indicated in Figure 13.5. They also found that larger firms were more likely to use the CAPM than were smaller firms.

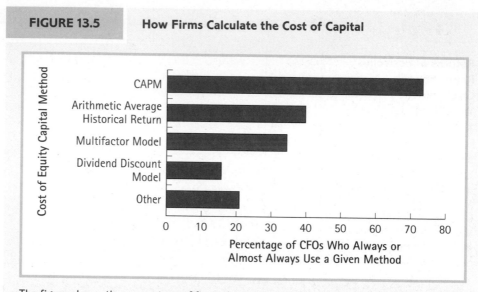

| FIGURE 13.5 | How Firms Calculate the Cost of Capital |

The figure shows the percentage of firms that use the CAPM, multifactor models, the historical average return, and the dividend discount model. Because practitioners often refer to characteristic variable models as factor models, the multifactor model characterization includes characteristic variable models. The dividend discount model is presented in Chapter 9.

Source: J. R. Graham and C. R. Harvey, "The Theory and Practice of Corporate Finance: Evidence from the Field," *Journal of Financial Economics* 60 (2001): 187–243.

What about the other techniques we covered in this chapter? Among the firms Graham and Harvey surveyed, only about one third reported using a multifactor model to calculate the cost of capital. Because practitioners often refer to the characteristic variable model as a factor model, this number likely includes both multifactor models and characteristic variable models.

Two other methods that some firms in the survey reported using are historical average returns (40%) and the dividend discount model (16%). By dividend discount model, practitioners mean Eq. 9.7 in Chapter 9: They estimate the firm's expected future growth rate and add the current dividend yield to determine the stock's expected total return.

In short, there is no clear answer to the question of which technique is used to measure risk in practice—it very much depends on the organization and the sector. It is not difficult to see why there is so little consensus in practice about which technique to use. *All the techniques we covered are imprecise.* Financial economics has not yet reached the point where we can provide a theory of expected returns that gives a precise estimate of the cost of capital. Consider, too, that all techniques are not equally simple to implement. Because the tradeoff between simplicity and precision varies across sectors, practitioners apply the techniques that best suit their particular circumstances.

When making a capital budgeting decision, the cost of capital is just one of several imprecise estimates that go into the NPV calculation. Indeed, in many cases the imprecision in the cost of capital estimate is less important than the imprecision in the estimate of future cash flows. Often the least complicated models to implement are used most often—the CAPM or even historical average returns.

CONCEPT CHECK   1. Which is the most popular method used by corporations to calculate the cost of capital?

2. What other techniques do corporations use to calculate the cost of capital?

Summary

1. The size effect refers to the observation that historically small stocks have had positive alphas compared to the predictions of the CAPM. The size effect is evidence that the market portfolio is not efficient, which suggests that the CAPM does not accurately model expected returns. Researchers find similar results using the book to market ratio instead of firm size.

2. A momentum trading strategy that goes long stocks with high past risk-adjusted returns and short stocks with low past returns also generates positive CAPM alphas, providing further evidence that the market portfolio is not efficient and that the CAPM does not accurately model expected returns.

3. Securities may have non-zero alphas if the market portfolio used is not a good proxy for the true market portfolio.

4. Two conditions might cause investors to care about characteristics other than the expected return and the volatility of their portfolios: They might care about other measures of uncertainty (e.g., the skewness of the distribution of returns), or they might have significant wealth invested in investments that are not tradeable.

5. When more than one portfolio is used to capture risk, the model is known as a multi-factor model. This model is also sometimes called the Arbitrage Pricing Theory (APT). Using a collection of N well-diversified portfolios, the expected return of stock s is

$$E[R_s] = r_f + \beta_s^{F1}(E[R_{F1}] - r_f) + \beta_s^{F2}(E[R_{F2}] - r_f) + \cdots + \beta_s^{FN}(E[R_{FN}] - r_f)$$

$$= r_f + \sum_{n=1}^{N} \beta_s^{Fn}(E[R_{Fn}] - r_f) \tag{13.8}$$

6. A simpler way to write multifactor models is to express risk premiums as the expected return on a self-financing portfolio. A self-financing portfolio is a portfolio that costs nothing to construct. By using the expected returns of self-financing portfolios, the expected return of a stock can be expressed as

$$E[R_s] = r_f + \beta_s^{F1} E[R_{F1}] + \beta_s^{F2} E[R_{F2}] + \cdots + \beta_s^{FN} E[R_{FN}]$$

$$= r_f + \sum_{n=1}^{N} \beta_s^{Fn} E[R_{Fn}] \tag{13.9}$$

7. The portfolios that are most commonly used in a multifactor model are the market portfolio (Mkt), small-minus-big (SMB) portfolio, high-minus-low (HML) portfolio, and prior one-year momentum (PR1YR) portfolio. This model is known as the Fama-French-Carhart factor specification:

$$E[R_s] = r_f + \beta_s^{Mkt}(E[R_{Mkt}] - r_f) + \beta_s^{SMB} E[R_{SMB}]$$

$$+ \beta_s^{HML} E[R_{HML}] + \beta_s^{PR1YR} E[R_{PR1YR}] \tag{13.10}$$

8. Characteristic variable models of returns associate the risk and return of the firm with the returns attributable to measurable firm characteristics.

   a. Given characteristic weights w_s^i for each stock s, the return associated with each characteristic are inferred from the regression:

$$R_s = w_s^1 R_{c1} + w_s^2 R_{c2} + \cdots + w_s^N R_{cN} + \varepsilon_s \tag{13.11}$$

   b. The expected return and beta of the firm can be calculated by interpreting the firm as a portfolio of characteristics, and using estimated returns and covariances for the characteristics.

Key Terms

Arbitrage Pricing Theory (APT) *p. 410*
book-to-market ratio *p. 403*
characteristic variable models *p. 416*
data snooping bias *p. 404*
factor betas *p. 410*
factor portfolios *p. 409*
Fama-French-Carhart (FFC) factor specification *p. 413*
high-minus-low (HML) portfolio *p. 413*

momentum strategy *p. 406*
multifactor model *p. 410*
multiple regression *p. 409*
prior one-year momentum (PR1YR) portfolio *p. 413*
self-financing portfolio *p. 411*
single-factor model *p. 410*
size effect *p. 402*
small-minus-big (SMB) portfolio *p. 413*

Further Reading

More detail on the theoretical relation between firm size and returns can be found in J. B. Berk, "Does Size Really Matter?" *Financial Analysts Journal* (September/October 1997): 12–18.

A summary of the empirical evidence on the relationship between risk-adjusted return and market value can be found in the following article: E. F. Fama and K. R. French, "The Cross-Section of Expected Stock Returns," *Journal of Finance* 47 (June 1992): 427–465.

The evidence that momentum strategies produce positive risk-adjusted returns was first published in the following article: N. Jegadeesh and S. Titman, "Returns to Buying Winners and Selling Losers: Implications for Stock Market Efficiency," *Journal of Finance* 48 (March 1993): 65–91.

The following two articles provide details on the FFC factor specification: E. F. Fama and K. R. French, "Common Risk Factors in the Returns on Stocks and Bonds," *Journal of Financial Economics* 33 (1993): 3–56; and M. Carhart, "On Persistence in Mutual Fund Performance," *Journal of Finance* 52 (March 1997): 57–82.

The first evidence that characteristic variable models could be useful in predicting firm betas was shown by W. H. Beaver, P. Kettler, and M. Scholes, "The Association between Market Determined and Accounting Determined Risk Measures," *Accounting Review* 45 (October 1970), 654–682. Readers interested in how money managers use the characteristic variable model should consult the following book: R. C. Grinold and R. N. Kahn, *Active Portfolio Management*, 2nd ed. (New York: McGraw-Hill, 1999).

Problems

A blue box (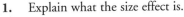) indicates problems available in MyFinanceLab. An asterisk (*) indicates problems with a higher level of difficulty.

The Efficiency of the Market Portfolio

1. Explain what the size effect is.

2. If past returns could be used to predict alphas, what implication would this have?

3. What are the implications of a trading strategy with a positive alpha?

4. Explain how to construct a positive-alpha trading strategy if stocks that have had relatively high returns in the past tend to have positive alphas and stocks that have had relatively low returns in the past tend to have negative alphas.

*5. If you can use past returns to construct a trading strategy that makes money (has a positive alpha), it is evidence that market portfolio is not efficient. Explain why.

*6. Assume all firms have the same expected dividends. If they have different expected returns, how will their market values and expected returns be related? What about the relation between their dividend yields and expected returns?

EXCEL 7. Each of the six firms in the table below is expected to pay the listed dividend payment every year in perpetuity.

Firm	Dividend ($ million)	Cost of Capital (%/Year)
S1	10	8
S2	10	12
S3	10	14
B1	100	8
B2	100	12
B3	100	14

a. Using the cost of capital in the table, calculate the market value of each firm.

b. Rank the three S firms by their market values and look at how their cost of capital is ordered. What would be the expected return for a self financing portfolio that went long on the firm with the largest market value and shorted the firm with the lowest market value? (The expected return of a self financing portfolio is the weighted average return of the consituent securities.) Repeat using the B firms.

c. Rank all six firms by their market values. How does this ranking order the cost of capital? What would be the expected return for a self financing portfolio that went long on the firm with the largest market value and shorted the firm with the lowest market value?

d. Repeat part (c) but rank the firms by the dividend yield instead of the market value. What can you conclude about the dividend yield ranking compared to the market value ranking?

Implication of Positive Alphas

8. Explain why you might expect stocks to have nonzero alphas if the proxy portfolio is not highly correlated with the true market portolio, even if the true market portfolio is efficient.

9. Explain why an employee who cares only about expected return and volatility will likely underweight the amount of money he invests in his own company's stock relative to an investor who does not work for his company.

10. Derive Eq. 13.8 using three portfolios from which the efficient portfolio can be constructed.

EXCEL **11.** Using the factor beta estimates in Table 13.4 below and the expected return estimates in Table 13.1, calculate the risk premium of General Electric stock (ticker: GE) using the FFC factor specification.

TABLE 13.4	Estimated Factor Betas		
Factor	**MSFT**	**XOM**	**GE**
MKT	1.068	0.243	0.747
SMB	−0.374	0.125	−0.478
HML	−0.814	0.144	−0.232
PR1YR	−0.226	−0.185	−0.147

EXCEL **12.** You are currently considering an investment in a project in the energy sector. The investment has the same riskiness as Exxon Mobil stock (ticker: XOM). Using the data in Table 13.1 and Table 13.4, calculate the cost of capital using the FFC factor specification if the current risk-free rate is 6% per year.

EXCEL **13.** You work for Microsoft Corporation (ticker: MSFT), and you are considering whether to develop a new software product. The risk of the investment is the same as the risk of the company. Using the data in Table 13.1 and Table 13.4, calculate the cost of capital using the FFC factor specification if the current risk-free rate is 5.5% per year.

14. You have noticed that firm betas vary, that is, firms' risk vary in time. Explain how a characteristics-based model that assumes that the expected return associated with each characteristic does not vary (is constant in time) can capture this variation and correctly price risk.

15. What variables are taken as observable (that is, are not inferred from the data) in the characteristics model of expected returns? What about in a factor of expected returns?

Capital Structure

The Law of One Price Connection. One of the fundamental questions of corporate finance is how a firm should choose the set of securities it will issue to raise capital from investors. This decision determines the firm's capital structure, which is the total amount of debt, equity, and other securities that a firm has outstanding. Does the choice of capital structure affect the value of the firm? In Chapter 14 we consider this question in a perfect capital market. There we apply the Law of One Price to show that as long as the cash flows generated by the firm's assets are unchanged, then the value of the firm—which is the total value of its outstanding securities—does not depend on its capital structure. Therefore, if capital structure has a role in determining the firm's value, it must come from important market imperfections that we explore in subsequent chapters. In Chapter 15, we analyze the role of debt in reducing the taxes a firm or its investors will pay, while in Chapter 16 we consider the costs of financial distress and changes to managerial incentives that result from leverage. Finally, in Chapter 17, we consider the firm's choice of payout policy and ask: Which is the best method for the firm to return capital to its investors? Again, the Law of One Price implies that the firm's choice to pay dividends or repurchase its stock will not affect its value in a perfect capital market. We then examine how market imperfections affect this important insight and shape the firm's optimal payout policy.

CHAPTER

14

Capital Structure in a Perfect Market

notation

PV	present value
NPV	net present value
E	market value of levered equity
D	market value of debt
U	market value of unlevered equity
A	market value of firm assets
R_D	return on debt
R_E	return on levered equity
R_U	return on unlevered equity
r_D	expected return (cost of capital) of debt
r_E	expected return (cost of capital) of levered equity
r_U	expected return (cost of capital) of unlevered equity
r_A	expected return (cost of capital) of firm assets
r_{wacc}	weighted average cost of capital
β_E	beta of levered equity
β_U	beta of unlevered equity
β_D	beta of debt
EPS	earnings per share

When a firm needs to raise new funds to undertake its investments, it must decide which type of security it will issue to investors. Even absent a need for new funds, firms can issue new securities and use the funds to repay debt or repurchase shares. What considerations should guide these decisions?

Consider the case of Dan Harris, Chief Financial Officer of Electronic Business Services (EBS), who has been reviewing plans for a major expansion of the firm. To pursue the expansion, EBS plans to raise $50 million from outside investors. One possibility is to raise the funds by selling shares of EBS stock. Due to the firm's risk, Dan estimates that equity investors will require a 10% risk premium over the 5% risk-free interest rate. That is, the company's equity cost of capital is 15%.

Some senior executives at EBS, however, have argued that the firm should consider borrowing the $50 million instead. EBS has not borrowed previously and, given its strong balance sheet, it should be able to borrow at a 6% interest rate. Does the low interest rate of debt make borrowing a better choice of financing for EBS? If EBS does borrow, will this choice affect the NPV of the expansion, and therefore change the value of the firm and its share price?

We explore these questions in this chapter in a setting of *perfect capital markets*, in which all securities are fairly priced, there are no taxes or transaction costs, and the total cash flows of the firm's projects are not affected by how the firm finances them. Although in reality capital markets are not perfect, this setting provides an important benchmark. Perhaps surprisingly, with perfect capital markets, the Law of One Price implies that the choice of debt or equity financing will *not* affect the total value of a firm, its share price, or its cost of capital. Thus, in a perfect world, EBS will be indifferent regarding the choice of financing for its expansion.

14.1 Equity Versus Debt Financing

The relative proportions of debt, equity, and other securities that a firm has outstanding constitute its **capital structure**. When corporations raise funds from outside investors, they must choose which type of security to issue. The most common choices are financing through equity alone and financing through a combination of debt and equity. We begin our discussion by considering both of these options.

Financing a Firm with Equity

Consider an entrepreneur with the following investment opportunity. For an initial investment of $800 this year, a project will generate cash flows of either $1400 or $900 next year. The cash flows depend on whether the economy is strong or weak, respectively. Both scenarios are equally likely, and are shown in Table 14.1.

TABLE 14.1	The Project Cash Flows	
Date 0	**Date 1**	
	Strong Economy	**Weak Economy**
−$800	$1400	$900

Because the project cash flows depend on the overall economy, they contain market risk. As a result, suppose investors demand a risk premium over the current risk-free interest rate of 5% to invest in this project. Suppose that given the market risk of the investment, the appropriate risk premium is 10%.

What is the NPV of this investment opportunity? Given a risk-free interest rate of 5% and a risk premium of 10%, the cost of capital for this project is 15%. Because the expected cash flow in one year is $\frac{1}{2}(\$1400) + \frac{1}{2}(\$900) = \$1150$, we get

$$NPV = -\$800 + \frac{\$1150}{1.15} = -\$800 + \$1000$$
$$= \$200$$

Thus the investment has a positive NPV.

If this project is financed using equity alone, how much would investors be willing to pay for the firm's shares? Recall from Chapter 3 that, in the absence of arbitrage, the price of a security equals the present value of its cash flows. Because the firm has no other liabilities, equity holders will receive all of the cash flows generated by the project on date 1. Hence the market value of the firm's equity today will be

$$PV(\text{equity cash flows}) = \frac{\$1150}{1.15} = \$1000$$

So, the entrepreneur can raise $1000 by selling the equity in the firm. After paying the investment cost of $800, the entrepreneur can keep the remaining $200—the project NPV—as a profit. In other words, the project's NPV represents the value to the initial owners of the firm (in this case, the entrepreneur) created by the project.

TABLE 14.2	Cash Flows and Returns for Unlevered Equity				
	Date 0	Date 1: Cash Flows		Date 1: Returns	
	Initial Value	Strong Economy	Weak Economy	Strong Economy	Weak Economy
Unlevered equity	$1000	$1400	$900	40%	−10%

What are the cash flows and returns for the shareholders who purchase the firm's equity? Equity in a firm with no debt is called **unlevered equity**. Because there is no debt, the date 1 cash flows of the unlevered equity are equal to those of the project. Given equity's initial value of $1000, shareholder's returns are either 40% or −10% as shown in Table 14.2.

The strong and weak economy outcomes are equally likely, so the expected return on the unlevered equity is $\frac{1}{2}(40\%) + \frac{1}{2}(-10\%) = 15\%$. Because the risk of unlevered equity equals the risk of the project, shareholders are earning an appropriate return for the risk they are taking.

Financing a Firm with Debt and Equity

Financing the firm exclusively with equity is not the entrepreneur's only option. She can also raise part of the initial capital using debt. Suppose she decides to borrow $500 initially, in addition to selling equity. Because the project's cash flow will always be enough to repay the debt, the debt is risk free. Thus the firm can borrow at the risk-free interest rate of 5%, and it will owe the debt holders $500 \times 1.05 = \$525$ in one year.

Equity in a firm that also has debt outstanding is called **levered equity**. Promised payments to debt holders must be made before any payments to equity holders are distributed. Given the firm's $525 debt obligation, the shareholders will receive only $1400 − $525 = $875 if the economy is strong and $900 − $525 = $375 if the economy is weak. Table 14.3 shows the cash flows of the debt, the levered equity, and the total cash flows of the firm.

What price E should the levered equity sell for, and which is the best capital structure choice for the entrepreneur? In an important paper, researchers Franco Modigliani and Merton Miller proposed an answer to this question that surprised researchers and

TABLE 14.3	Values and Cash Flows for Debt and Equity of the Levered Firm		
	Date 0	Date 1: Cash Flows	
	Initial Value	Strong Economy	Weak Economy
Debt	$500	$525	$525
Levered equity	$E = ?$	$875	$375
Firm	$1000	$1400	$900

practitioners at the time.[1] They argued that with perfect capital markets, the total value of a firm should not depend on its capital structure. Their reasoning: The firm's total cash flows still equal the cash flows of the project, and therefore have the same present value of $1000 calculated earlier (see the last line in Table 14.3). Because the cash flows of the debt and equity sum to the cash flows of the project, by the Law of One Price the combined values of debt and equity must be $1000. Therefore, if the value of the debt is $500, the value of the levered equity must be $E = \$1000 - \$500 = \$500$.

Because the cash flows of levered equity are smaller than those of unlevered equity, levered equity will sell for a lower price ($500 versus $1000). However, the fact that the equity is less valuable with leverage does not mean that the entrepreneur is worse off. She will still raise a total of $1000 by issuing both debt and levered equity, just as she did with unlevered equity alone. As a consequence, she will be indifferent between these two choices for the firm's capital structure.

The Effect of Leverage on Risk and Return

Modigliani and Miller's conclusion went against the common view, which stated that even with perfect capital markets, leverage would affect a firm's value. In particular, it was thought that the value of the levered equity would exceed $500, because the present value of its expected cash flow at 15% is

$$\frac{\frac{1}{2}(\$875) + \frac{1}{2}(\$375)}{1.15} = \$543$$

The reason this is *not* correct is that leverage increases the risk of the equity of a firm. Therefore, it is inappropriate to discount the cash flows of levered equity at the same discount rate of 15% that we used for unlevered equity. Investors in levered equity require a higher expected return to compensate for its increased risk.

Table 14.4 compares the equity returns if the entrepreneur chooses unlevered equity financing with the case in which she borrows $500 and raises an additional $500 using levered equity. Note that the returns to equity holders are very different with and without leverage. Unlevered equity has a return of either 40% or −10%, for an expected return

TABLE 14.4	Returns to Equity with and without Leverage					
	Date 0	Date 1: Cash Flows		Date 1: Returns		
	Initial Value	Strong Economy	Weak Economy	Strong Economy	Weak Economy	Expected Return
Debt	$500	$525	$525	5%	5%	**5%**
Levered equity	$500	$875	$375	75%	−25%	**25%**
Unlevered equity	$1000	$1400	$900	40%	−10%	**15%**

---

1. F. Modigliani and M. Miller, "The Cost of Capital, Corporation Finance and the Theory of Investment," *American Economic Review* 48(3) (1958): 261–297.

of 15%. But levered equity has higher risk, with a return of either 75% or −25%. To compensate for this risk, levered equity holders receive a higher expected return of 25%.

We can evaluate the relationship between risk and return more formally by computing the sensitivity of each security's return to the systematic risk of the economy. (In our simple two-state example, this sensitivity determines the security's beta; recall also our discussion of risk in Chapter 3.) Table 14.5 shows the return sensitivity and the risk premium for each security. Because the debt's return bears no systematic risk, its risk premium is zero. In this particular case, however, levered equity has twice the systematic risk of unlevered equity. As a result, levered equity holders receive twice the risk premium.

TABLE 14.5   **Systematic Risk and Risk Premiums for Debt, Unlevered Equity, and Levered Equity**

	Return Sensitivity (Systematic Risk)	Risk Premium
	$\Delta R = R(\text{strong}) - R(\text{weak})$	$E[R] - r_f$
Debt	5% − 5% = 0%	5% − 5% = 0%
Unlevered equity	40% − (−10%) = 50%	15% − 5% = 10%
Levered equity	75% − (−25%) = 100%	25% − 5% = 20%

To summarize, in the case of perfect capital markets, if the firm is 100% equity financed, the equity holders will require a 15% expected return. If the firm is financed 50% with debt and 50% with equity, the debt holders will receive a lower return of 5%, while the levered equity holders will require a higher expected return of 25% because of their increased risk. As this example shows, *leverage increases the risk of equity even when there is no risk that the firm will default.* Thus, while debt may be cheaper when considered on its own, it raises the cost of capital for equity. Considering both sources of capital together, the firm's average cost of capital with leverage is $\frac{1}{2}(5\%) + \frac{1}{2}(25\%) = 15\%$, the same as for the unlevered firm.

EXAMPLE 14.1

Leverage and the Equity Cost of Capital

Problem
Suppose the entrepreneur borrows only $200 when financing the project. According to Modigliani and Miller, what should the value of the equity be? What is the expected return?

Solution
Because the value of the firm's total cash flows is still $1000, if the firm borrows $200, its equity will be worth $800. The firm will owe $200 × 1.05 = $210 in one year. Thus, if the economy is strong, equity holders will receive $1400 − $210 = $1190, for a return of $1190 / $800 − 1 = 48.75%. If the economy is weak, equity holders will receive $900 − $210 = $690, for a return of $690 / $800 − 1 = −13.75%. The equity has an expected return of $\frac{1}{2}(48.75\%) + \frac{1}{2}(-13.75\%) = 17.5\%$.

> Note that the equity has a return sensitivity of 48.75% − (−13.75%) = 62.5%, which is 62.5% / 50% = 125% of the sensitivity of unlevered equity. Its risk premium is 17.5% − 5% = 12.5%, which is also 125% of the risk premium of the unlevered equity, so it is appropriate compensation for the risk.

CONCEPT CHECK

1. Why are the value and cash flows of levered equity less than if the firm had issued unlevered equity?

2. How does the risk and cost of capital of levered equity compare to that of unlevered equity? Which is the superior capital structure choice?

14.2 Modigliani-Miller I: Leverage, Arbitrage, and Firm Value

In the previous example, the Law of One Price implied that leverage would not affect the total value of the firm (the amount of money the entrepreneur can raise). Instead, it merely changes the allocation of cash flows between debt and equity, without altering the total cash flows of the firm. Modigliani and Miller (or simply MM) showed that this result holds more generally under a set of conditions referred to as **perfect capital markets**:

1. Investors and firms can trade the same set of securities at competitive market prices equal to the present value of their future cash flows.

2. There are no taxes, transaction costs, or issuance costs associated with security trading.

3. A firm's financing decisions do not change the cash flows generated by its investments, nor do they reveal new information about them.

Under these conditions, MM demonstrated the following result regarding the role of capital structure in determining firm value:[2]

MM Proposition I: *In a perfect capital market, the total value of a firm is equal to the market value of the total cash flows generated by its assets and is not affected by its choice of capital structure.*

MM and the Law of One Price

MM established their result with the following simple argument. In the absence of taxes or other transaction costs, the total cash flow paid out to all of a firm's security holders is equal to the total cash flow generated by the firm's assets. Therefore, by the Law of One Price, the firm's securities and its assets must have the same total market value. Thus, as long as the firm's choice of securities does not change the cash flows generated by its assets, this decision will not change the total value of the firm or the amount of capital it can raise.

We can also view MM's result in terms of the Separation Principle introduced in Chapter 3: If securities are fairly priced, then buying or selling securities has an NPV of zero and, therefore, should not change the value of a firm. The future repayments that the firm must make on its debt are equal in value to the amount of the loan it receives upfront. Thus there is no net gain or loss from using leverage, and the value of the firm is determined by the present value of the cash flows from its current and future investments.

---

2. Although it was not widely appreciated at the time, the idea that a firm's value does not depend on its capital structure was argued even earlier by John Burr Williams in his pathbreaking book, *The Theory of Investment Value* (North Holland Publishing, 1938; reprinted by Fraser Publishing, 1997).

MM and the Real World

Students often question why Modigliani and Miller's results are important if, after all, capital markets are not perfect in the real world. While it is true that capital markets are not perfect, *all* scientific theories begin with a set of idealized assumptions from which conclusions can be drawn. When we apply the theory, we must then evaluate how closely the assumptions hold, and consider the consequences of any important deviations.

As a useful analogy, consider Galileo's law of falling bodies. Galileo overturned the conventional wisdom by showing that, without friction, free-falling bodies will fall at the same rate independent of their mass. If you test this law, you will likely find it does not hold exactly. The

reason, of course, is that unless we are in a vacuum, air friction tends to slow some objects more than others.

MM's results are similar. In practice, we will find that capital structure can have an effect on firm value. But just as Galileo's law of falling bodies reveals that we must look to air friction, rather than any underlying property of gravity, to explain differences in the speeds of falling objects, MM's proposition reveals that any effects of capital structure must similarly be due to frictions that exist in capital markets. After exploring the full meaning of MM's results in this chapter, we look at the important sources of these frictions, and their consequences, in subsequent chapters.

Homemade Leverage

MM showed that the firm's value is not affected by its choice of capital structure. But suppose investors would prefer an alternative capital structure to the one the firm has chosen. MM demonstrated that in this case, investors can borrow or lend on their own and achieve the same result. For example, an investor who would like more leverage than the firm has chosen can borrow and add leverage to his or her own portfolio. When investors use leverage in their own portfolios to adjust the leverage choice made by the firm, we say that they are using **homemade leverage**. As long as investors can borrow or lend at the same interest rate as the firm,[3] homemade leverage is a perfect substitute for the use of leverage by the firm.

To illustrate, suppose the entrepreneur uses no leverage and creates an all-equity firm. An investor who would prefer to hold levered equity can do so by using leverage in his own portfolio—that is, he can buy the stock on margin, as illustrated in Table 14.6.

TABLE 14.6	Replicating Levered Equity Using Homemade Leverage		
	Date 0	Date 1: Cash Flows	
	Initial Cost	Strong Economy	Weak Economy
Unlevered equity	$1000	$1400	$900
Margin loan	−$500	−$525	−$525
Levered equity	$500	$875	$375

3. This assumption is implied by perfect capital markets because the interest rate on a loan should depend only on its risk.

If the cash flows of the unlevered equity serve as collateral for the margin loan, then the loan is risk-free and the investor should be able to borrow at the 5% rate. Although the firm is unlevered, by using homemade leverage, the investor has replicated the payoffs to the levered equity illustrated in Table 14.3, for a cost of $500. Again, by the Law of One Price, the value of levered equity must also be $500.

Now suppose the entrepreneur uses debt, but the investor would prefer to hold unlevered equity. The investor can re-create the payoffs of unlevered equity by buying both the debt *and* the equity of the firm. Combining the cash flows of the two securities produces cash flows identical to unlevered equity, for a total cost of $1000, as we see in Table 14.7.

TABLE 14.7	**Replicating Unlevered Equity by Holding Debt and Equity**		
	Date 0	Date 1: Cash Flows	
	Initial Cost	**Strong Economy**	**Weak Economy**
Debt	$500	$525	$525
Levered equity	$500	$875	$375
Unlevered equity	$1000	$1400	$900

In each case, the entrepreneur's choice of capital structure does not affect the opportunities available to investors. Investors can alter the leverage choice of the firm to suit their personal tastes either by borrowing and adding more leverage or by holding bonds and reducing leverage. With perfect capital markets, because different choices of capital structure offer no benefit to investors, they do not affect the value of the firm.

EXAMPLE 14.2

Homemade Leverage and Arbitrage

Problem
Suppose there are two firms, each with date 1 cash flows of $1400 or $900 (as in Table 14.1). The firms are identical except for their capital structure. One firm is unlevered, and its equity has a market value of $990. The other firm has borrowed $500, and its equity has a market value of $510. Does MM Proposition I hold? What arbitrage opportunity is available using homemade leverage?

Solution
MM Proposition I states that the total value of each firm should equal the value of its assets. Because these firms hold identical assets, their total values should be the same. However, the problem assumes the unlevered firm has a total market value of $990, whereas the levered firm has a total market value of $510 (equity) + $500 (debt) = $1010. Therefore, these prices violate MM Proposition I.

Because these two identical firms are trading for different total prices, the Law of One Price is violated and an arbitrage opportunity exists. To exploit it, we can borrow $500 and buy the equity of the unlevered firm for $990, re-creating the equity of the levered firm by using homemade leverage for a cost of only $990 − 500 = $490. We can then sell the equity of the levered firm for $510 and enjoy an arbitrage profit of $20.

	Date 0	Date 1: Cash Flows	
	Cash Flow	Strong Economy	Weak Economy
Borrow	$500	−$525	−$525
Buy unlevered equity	−$990	$1400	$900
Sell levered equity	$510	−$875	−$375
Total cash flow	$20	$0	$0

Note that the actions of arbitrageurs buying the unlevered firm and selling the levered firm will cause the price of the unlevered firm's stock to rise and the price of the levered firm's stock to fall until the firms' values are equal and MM Proposition I holds.

The Market Value Balance Sheet

In Section 14.1 we considered just two choices for a firm's capital structure. MM Proposition I, however, applies much more broadly to any choice of debt and equity. In fact, it applies even if the firm issues other types of securities, such as convertible debt or warrants, a type of stock option that we discuss later in the text. The logic is the same: Because investors can buy or sell securities on their own, no value is created when the firm buys or sells securities for them.

One application of MM Proposition I is the useful device known as the market value balance sheet of the firm. A **market value balance sheet** is similar to an accounting balance sheet, with two important distinctions. First, *all* assets and liabilities of the firm are included—even intangible assets such as reputation, brand name, or human capital that are missing from a standard accounting balance sheet. Second, all values are current market values rather than historical costs. On the market value balance sheet, depicted in Table 14.8, the total value of all securities issued by the firm must equal the total value of the firm's assets.

TABLE 14.8   **The Market Value Balance Sheet of the Firm**

Assets	Liabilities
Collection of Assets and Investments Undertaken by the Firm:	Collection of Securities Issued by the Firm:

Tangible Assets
  Cash
  Plant, property, and equipment
  Inventory
  (and so on)
	Debt
	  Short-term debt
	  Long-term debt
	  Convertible debt

Intangible Assets
  Intellectual property
  Reputation
  Human capital
  (and so on)
	Equity
	  Common stock
	  Preferred stock
	  Warrants (options)

Total Market Value of Firm Assets	**Total Market Value of Firm Securities**

The market value balance sheet captures the idea that value is created by a firm's choice of assets and investments. By choosing positive-NPV projects that are worth more than their initial investment, the firm can enhance its value. Holding fixed the cash flows generated by the firm's assets, however, the choice of capital structure does not change the value of the firm. Instead, it merely divides the value of the firm into different securities. Using the market value balance sheet, we can compute the value of equity as follows:

$$\text{Market Value of Equity} =$$
$$\text{Market Value of Assets} - \text{Market Value of Debt and Other Liabilities} \quad (14.1)$$

EXAMPLE 14.3

Valuing Equity When There Are Multiple Securities

Problem
Suppose our entrepreneur decides to sell the firm by splitting it into three securities: equity, $500 of debt, and a third security called a warrant that pays $210 when the firm's cash flows are high and nothing when the cash flows are low. Suppose that this third security is fairly priced at $60. What will the value of the equity be in a perfect capital market?

Solution
According to MM Proposition I, the total value of all securities issued should equal the value of the assets of the firm, which is $1000. Because the debt is worth $500 and the new security is worth $60, the value of the equity must be $440. (You can check this result by verifying that at this price, equity has a risk premium commensurate with its risk in comparison with the securities in Table 14.5.)

Application: A Leveraged Recapitalization

So far, we have looked at capital structure from the perspective of an entrepreneur who is considering financing an investment opportunity. In fact, MM Proposition I applies to capital structure decisions made at any time during the life of the firm.

Let's consider an example. Harrison Industries is currently an all-equity firm operating in a perfect capital market, with 50 million shares outstanding that are trading for $4 per share. Harrison plans to increase its leverage by borrowing $80 million and using the funds to repurchase 20 million of its outstanding shares. When a firm repurchases a significant percentage of its outstanding shares in this way, the transaction is called a **leveraged recapitalization**.

We can view this transaction in two stages. First, Harrison sells debt to raise $80 million in cash. Second, Harrison uses the cash to repurchase shares. Table 14.9 shows the market value balance sheet after each of these stages.

Initially, Harrison is an all-equity firm. That is, the market value of Harrison's equity, which is 50 million shares × $4 per share = $200 million, equals the market value of its existing assets. After borrowing, Harrison's liabilities grow by $80 million, which is also equal to the amount of cash the firm has raised. Because both assets and liabilities increase by the same amount, the market value of the equity remains unchanged.

To conduct the share repurchase, Harrison spends the $80 million in borrowed cash to repurchase $80 million ÷ $4 per share = 20 million shares. Because the firm's assets decrease by $80 million and its debt remains unchanged, the market value of the equity must also fall by $80 million, from $200 million to $120 million, for assets and liabilities to remain balanced. The share price, however, is unchanged—with 30 million shares remaining, the shares are worth $120 million ÷ 30 million shares = $4 per share, just as before.

TABLE 14.9		**Market Value Balance Sheet After Each Stage of Harrison's Leveraged Recapitalization ($ million)**			
Initial		**After Borrowing**		**After Share Repurchase**	
Assets	**Liabilities**	**Assets**	**Liabilities**	**Assets**	**Liabilities**
		Cash	Debt	Cash	Debt
		80	80	0	80
Existing assets	Equity	Existing assets	Equity	Existing assets	Equity
200	200	200	200	200	120
200	**200**	**280**	**280**	**200**	**200**
Shares outstanding (million)	50	Shares outstanding (million)	50	Shares outstanding (million)	30
Value per share	$4.00	Value per share	$4.00	Value per share	$4.00

The fact that the share price did not change should not come as a surprise. Because the firm has sold $80 million worth of new debt and purchased $80 million worth of existing equity, this zero-NPV transaction (benefits = costs) does not change the value for shareholders.

CONCEPT CHECK

1. Which choice of leverage maximizes the total market value of equity?

2. Is this choice of leverage the best capital structure choice for shareholders? Explain.

14.3 Modigliani-Miller II: Leverage, Risk, and the Cost of Capital

Modigliani and Miller showed that a firm's financing choice does not affect its value. But how can we reconcile this conclusion with the fact that the cost of capital differs for different securities? Consider again our entrepreneur from Section 14.1. When the project is financed solely through equity, the equity holders require a 15% expected return. As an alternative, the firm can borrow at the risk-free rate of 5%. In this situation, isn't debt a cheaper and better source of capital than equity?

Although debt does have a lower cost of capital than equity, we cannot consider this cost in isolation. As we saw in Section 14.1, while debt itself may be cheap, it increases the risk and therefore the cost of capital of the firm's equity. In this section, we calculate the impact of leverage on the expected return of a firm's stock, or the equity cost of capital. We then consider how to estimate the cost of capital of the firm's assets, and show that it is unaffected by leverage. In the end, the savings from the low expected return on debt, the debt cost of capital, are exactly offset by a higher equity cost of capital, and there are no net savings for the firm.

Leverage and the Equity Cost of Capital

We can use Modigliani and Miller's first proposition to derive an explicit relationship between leverage and the equity cost of capital. Let E and D denote the market value of equity and debt if the firm is levered, respectively; let U be the market value of equity if the firm is unlevered; and let A be the market value of the firm's assets. Then MM Proposition I states that

$$E + D = U = A \tag{14.2}$$

That is, the total market value of the firm's securities is equal to the market value of its assets, whether the firm is unlevered or levered.

We can interpret the first equality in Eq. 14.2 in terms of homemade leverage: By holding a portfolio of the firm's equity and debt, we can replicate the cash flows from holding unlevered equity. Because the return of a portfolio is equal to the weighted average of the returns of the securities in it, this equality implies the following relationship between the returns of levered equity (R_E), debt (R_D), and unlevered equity (R_U):

$$\frac{E}{E+D}R_E + \frac{D}{E+D}R_D = R_U \tag{14.3}$$

If we solve Eq. 14.3 for R_E, we obtain the following expression for the return of levered equity:

$$R_E = \underbrace{R_U}_{\substack{\text{Risk without}\\\text{leverage}}} + \underbrace{\frac{D}{E}(R_U - R_D)}_{\substack{\text{Additional risk}\\\text{due to leverage}}} \tag{14.4}$$

This equation reveals the effect of leverage on the return of the levered equity. The levered equity return equals the unlevered return, plus an extra "kick" due to leverage. This extra effect pushes the returns of levered equity even higher when the firm performs well ($R_U > R_D$), but makes them drop even lower when the firm does poorly ($R_U < R_D$). The amount of additional risk depends on the amount of leverage, measured by the firm's market value debt-equity ratio, D/E.

Because Eq. 14.4 holds for the realized returns, it holds for the *expected* returns as well (denoted by r in place of R). This observation leads to Modigliani and Miller's second proposition:

MM Proposition II: *The cost of capital of levered equity is equal to the cost of capital of unlevered equity plus a premium that is proportional to the market value debt-equity ratio.*

Cost of Capital of Levered Equity

$$r_E = r_U + \frac{D}{E}(r_U - r_D) \tag{14.5}$$

We can illustrate MM Proposition II for the entrepreneur's project in Section 14.1. Recall that if the firm is all-equity financed, the expected return on unlevered equity is 15% (see Table 14.4). If the firm is financed with $500 of debt, the expected return of the debt is the risk-free interest rate of 5%. Therefore, according to MM Proposition II, the expected return on equity for the levered firm is

$$r_E = 15\% + \frac{500}{500}(15\% - 5\%) = 25\%$$

This result matches the expected return calculated in Table 14.4.

EXAMPLE
14.4

Computing the Equity Cost of Capital

Problem

Suppose the entrepreneur of Section 14.1 borrows only $200 when financing the project. According to MM Proposition II, what will the firm's equity cost of capital be?

Solution

Because the firm's assets have a market value of $1000, by MM Proposition I the equity will have a market value of $800. Then, using Eq. 14.5,

$$r_E = 15\% + \frac{200}{800}(15\% - 5\%) = 17.5\%$$

This result matches the expected return calculated in Example 14.1.

Capital Budgeting and the Weighted Average Cost of Capital

If a firm is unlevered, all of the free cash flows generated by its assets are paid out to its equity holders. The market value, risk, and cost of capital for the firm's assets and its equity coincide and, therefore,

$$r_U = r_A \tag{14.6}$$

Equation 14.6 is very useful for capital budgeting. When evaluating any potential investment project, we must use a discount rate that is appropriate given the risk of the project's free cash flow. This cost of capital for the project should equal the return that is available on other investments with similar risk. If we can identify a comparison firm whose assets have the same risk as the project being evaluated, and if the firm is unlevered, Eq. 14.6 implies that we can use its equity cost of capital as the cost of capital for the project.

Of course, Eq. 14.6 applies only if the comparison firm is unlevered. If the comparison firm has debt, the increased risk due to leverage will make its equity cost of capital higher than the cost of capital of the assets and, therefore, of the project. How do we estimate r_A in this case?

The answer to this question follows from the same homemade leverage argument that we used to derive Eq. 14.3: The portfolio of a firm's equity and debt replicates the returns we would earn if it were unlevered. As a consequence, we can calculate the cost of capital of the firm's assets by computing the weighted average of the firm's equity and debt cost of capital, which we refer to as the firm's **weighted average cost of capital (WACC)**. We introduced the WACC informally in Chapter 9 as the appropriate cost of capital to use when discounting the firm's free cash flow. We now have the following formal definition:

Weighted Average Cost of Capital (No Taxes)

$$r_{wacc} \equiv \left(\begin{array}{c}\text{Fraction of Firm Value}\\\text{Financed by Equity}\end{array}\right)\left(\begin{array}{c}\text{Equity}\\\text{Cost of Capital}\end{array}\right) + \left(\begin{array}{c}\text{Fraction of Firm Value}\\\text{Financed by Debt}\end{array}\right)\left(\begin{array}{c}\text{Debt}\\\text{Cost of Capital}\end{array}\right)$$

$$= \frac{E}{E + D}r_E + \frac{D}{E + D}r_D \tag{14.7}$$

Replacing the returns in Eq. 14.3 with their expectations, and using Eq. 14.6, we obtain the following relationship:

$$r_{wacc} = r_U = r_A \tag{14.8}$$

That is, *with perfect capital markets, a firm's WACC is independent of its capital structure and is equal to its equity cost of capital if it is unlevered, which matches the cost of capital of its assets.* Therefore, if the risk of a project matches the risk of the assets of a firm, we can use the firm's WACC to estimate the appropriate cost of capital for the project.

Figure 14.1 illustrates the effect of increasing the amount of leverage in a firm's capital structure on its equity cost of capital, its debt cost of capital, and its WACC. In the figure, we measure the firm's leverage in terms of its **debt-to-value ratio**, $D/(E + D)$, which is the fraction of the firm's total value that corresponds to debt. With no debt, the WACC is equal to the unlevered equity cost of capital. As the firm borrows at the low cost of capital for debt, its equity cost of capital rises according to Eq. 14.5. The net effect is that the firm's WACC is unchanged. Of course, as the amount of debt increases, the debt becomes

---

FIGURE 14.1

WACC and Leverage with Perfect Capital Markets

As the fraction of the firm financed with debt increases, both the equity and the debt become riskier and their cost of capital rises. Yet, because more weight is put on the lower-cost debt, the weighted average cost of capital remains constant.

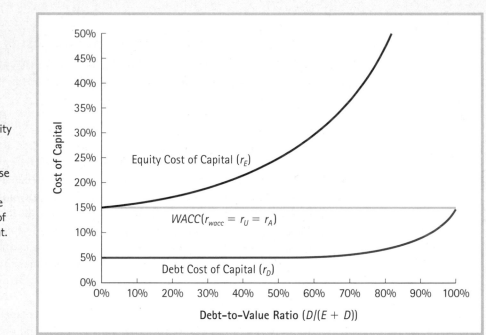

(a) Equity, debt and weighted average costs of capital for different amounts of leverage. The rate of increase of r_D and r_E, and thus the shape of the curves, depends on the characteristics of the firm's cash flows.

E	D	r_E	r_D	$\dfrac{E}{E + D}r_E + \dfrac{D}{E + D}r_D$	$= r_{wacc}$
1000	0	15.0%	5.0%	$1.0 \times 15.0\% + 0.0 \times 5.0\%$	$= 15\%$
800	200	17.5%	5.0%	$0.8 \times 17.5\% + 0.2 \times 5.0\%$	$= 15\%$
500	500	25.0%	5.0%	$0.5 \times 25.0\% + 0.5 \times 5.0\%$	$= 15\%$
100	900	75.0%	8.3%	$0.1 \times 75.0\% + 0.9 \times 8.3\%$	$= 15\%$

(b) Calculating the WACC for alternative capital structures. Data in this table correspond to the example in Section 14.1.

COMMON MISTAKE   **Is Debt Better Than Equity?**

Because debt has a lower cost of capital than equity, a common mistake is to assume that a firm can reduce its overall WACC by increasing the amount of debt financing. If this strategy works, shouldn't a firm take on as much debt as possible, at least as long as the debt is not risky?

This argument ignores the fact that even if the debt is risk free and the firm will not default, adding leverage increases the risk of the equity. Given the increase in risk, equity holders will demand a higher risk premium and, therefore, a higher expected return. The increase in the cost of equity exactly offsets the benefit of a greater reliance on the cheaper debt capital, so that the firm's overall cost of capital remains unchanged.

more risky because there is a chance the firm will default; as a result, the debt cost of capital also rises. With 100% debt, the debt would be as risky as the assets themselves (similar to unlevered equity). But even though the debt and equity costs of capital both rise when leverage is high, because more weight is put on the lower-cost debt, the WACC remains constant.

Recall from Chapter 9 that we can calculate the enterprise value of the firm by discounting its future free cash flow using the WACC. Thus, Eq. 14.8 provides the following intuitive interpretation of MM Proposition I: Although debt has a lower cost of capital than equity, leverage does not lower a firm's WACC. As a result, the value of the firm's free cash flow evaluated using the WACC does not change, and so the enterprise value of the firm does not depend on its financing choices. This observation allows us to answer the questions posed for the CFO of EBS at the beginning of this chapter: With perfect capital markets, the firm's weighted average cost of capital, and therefore the NPV of the expansion, is unaffected by how EBS chooses to finance the new investment.

EXAMPLE 14.5   **Reducing Leverage and the Cost of Capital**

Problem

The El Paso Corporation (EP) is a natural gas firm with a market debt-equity ratio of 2. Suppose its current debt cost of capital is 6%, and its equity cost of capital is 12%. Suppose also that if EP issues equity and uses the proceeds to repay its debt and reduce its debt-equity ratio to 1, it will lower its debt cost of capital to 5.5%. With perfect capital markets, what effect will this transaction have on EP's equity cost of capital and WACC?

Solution

We can calculate EP's initial WACC using Eq. 14.7:

$$r_{wacc} = \frac{E}{E+D}r_E + \frac{D}{E+D}r_D = \frac{1}{1+2}(12\%) + \frac{2}{1+2}(6\%) = 8\%$$

With perfect capital markets, EP's WACC will be unchanged by a change in its capital structure. Thus EP's unlevered cost of capital $r_U = 8\%$. We can then use Eq. 14.5 to calculate EP's equity cost of capital after the reduction in leverage:

$$r_E = r_U + \frac{D}{E}(r_U - r_D) = 8\% + \frac{1}{1}(8\% - 5.5\%) = 10.5\%$$

The reduction in leverage will cause EP's equity cost of capital to fall to 10.5%. With perfect capital markets, EP's WACC remains unchanged at $8\% = \frac{1}{2}(10.5\%) + \frac{1}{2}(5.5\%)$, and there is no net gain from this transaction.

Computing the WACC with Multiple Securities

We calculated the WACC in Eq. 14.7 assuming that the firm has issued only two types of securities (equity and debt). If the firm's capital structure is more complex, however, then the WACC is calculated by computing the weighted average cost of capital of all of the firm's securities.

EXAMPLE 14.6

WACC with Multiple Securities

Problem

Compute the WACC for the entrepreneur's project with the capital structure described in Example 14.3.

Solution

Because the firm has three securities in its capital structure (debt, equity, and the warrant), its weighted average cost of capital is the average return it must pay these three groups of investors:

$$r_{wacc} = \frac{E}{E+D+W}r_E + \frac{D}{E+D+W}r_D + \frac{W}{E+D+W}r_W$$

From Example 14.3, we know $E = 440$, $D = 500$, and $W = 60$. What are the expected returns for each security? Given the cash flows of the firm, the debt is risk free and has an expected return of $r_D = 5\%$. The warrant has an expected payoff of $\frac{1}{2}(\$210) + \frac{1}{2}(\$0) = \$105$, so its expected return is $r_w = \$105 / \$60 - 1 = 75\%$. Equity has a payoff of ($1400 - \$525 - \$210) = \$665$ when cash flows are high and ($900 - \$525) = \$375$ when cash flows are low; thus its expected payoff is $\frac{1}{2}(\$665) + \frac{1}{2}(\$375) = \$520$. The expected return for equity is then $r_E = \$520 / \$440 - 1 = 18.18\%$. We can now compute the WACC:

$$WACC = \frac{\$440}{\$1000}(18.18\%) + \frac{\$500}{\$1000}(5\%) + \frac{\$60}{\$1000}(75\%) = 15\%$$

Once again, the WACC is equal to the firm's unlevered cost of capital of 15%.

Levered and Unlevered Betas

The effect of leverage on the risk of a firm's securities can also be expressed in terms of beta.[4] Let β_E be the beta of the levered equity, β_U be the beta of equity without leverage, and β_D be the beta of the debt. Because unlevered equity is equivalent to a portfolio of debt and levered equity, and because the beta of a portfolio is the weighted average of the betas of the securities within it, we have the following relationship:

$$\beta_U = \frac{E}{E+D}\beta_E + \frac{D}{E+D}\beta_D \tag{14.9}$$

---

4. The relationship between leverage and equity betas was developed by R. Hamada in "The Effect of the Firm's Capital Structure on the Systematic Risk of Common Stocks," *Journal of Finance* 27(2) (1972): 435–452, and by M. Rubinstein in "A Mean-Variance Synthesis of Corporate Financial Theory," *Journal of Finance* 28(1) (1973): 167–181.

When we compute β_U according to Eq. 14.9, we refer to it as a firm's unlevered beta. The **unlevered beta** measures the market risk of the firm without leverage, which is equivalent to the beta of the firm's assets. The unlevered beta therefore measures the market risk of the firm's business activities, ignoring any additional risk due to leverage. In the same way that we use the WACC to estimate the cost of capital for a project, *if we are trying to estimate the unlevered beta for an investment project, we should base our estimate on the unlevered betas of firms with comparable investments.*

When a firm changes its capital structure without changing its investments, its unlevered beta will remain unaltered. However, its equity beta will change to reflect the effect of the capital structure change on its risk. Let's rearrange Eq. 14.9 to solve for β_E:

$$\beta_E = \beta_U + \frac{D}{E}(\beta_U - \beta_D) \tag{14.10}$$

Equation 14.10 is analogous to Eq. 14.5, with beta replacing the expected returns. If the firm's debt is risk free, then its beta is zero and Eq. 14.10 becomes

$$\beta_E = \beta_U + \frac{D}{E}\beta_U = \left(1 + \frac{D}{E}\right)\beta_U \tag{14.11}$$

We can see from Eq. 14.11 that leverage amplifies the market risk of a firm's assets, β_U, raising the market risk of its equity. This effect of leverage on beta explains why firms in the same industry with different capital structures can have very different equity betas even if the market risks of their business activities are very similar.

Of course, Eq. 14.11 is strictly correct only when the firm's debt is risk free. If the firm's debt is very risky, then its beta will generally be greater than zero, as firms are more likely to default during an economic downturn. Debt betas can be substantial for highly levered firms.[5] In that case, Eqs. 14.9 and 14.10 should be used.

EXAMPLE 14.7	**Airline Betas**

Problem

Estimates of equity betas and market debt-equity ratios for several airline stocks in the fall of 2005 are shown below:

Ticker	Name	Equity Beta	Debt-Equity Ratio	Debt Beta
LUV	Southwest Airlines Co.	1.13	0.15	0.00
ALK	Alaska Air Group, Inc.	1.80	1.06	0.15
SKYW	SkyWest, Inc.	1.69	1.05	0.15
MESA	Mesa Air Group, Inc.	3.27	3.52	0.30
CAL	Continental Airlines, Inc.	3.76	5.59	0.40

---

5. In principle, debt betas could be estimated using the same regression methods that we developed for equity betas in Chapter 12. In practice, however, data for the historical returns of debt securities are much more difficult to obtain, making a direct calculation of the beta for debt problematic. As a consequence, debt betas are often roughly approximated using other means. For example, given an expected return for the debt r_D (based on its yield, but adjusted downward to reflect the possibility of default), we can estimate the beta of debt using the security market line of the CAPM. Alternatively, an option pricing approach can be used, as we explain in Chapter 20.

Do the large differences in the equity betas of these firms reflect large differences in the market risk of their operations? What approximate beta would you use to evaluate projects in the airline industry?

Solution
The market risk of equity is amplified by the firm's leverage. To assess the market risk of the airlines' operations, we should consider their unlevered betas, which we compute using Eq. 14.9:

Ticker	β_E	$E/(E + D)$	β_D	$D/(E + D)$	β_U
LUV	1.13	87%	0.00	13%	0.98
ALK	1.80	49%	0.15	51%	0.96
SKYW	1.69	49%	0.15	51%	0.90
MESA	3.27	22%	0.30	78%	0.95
CAL	3.76	15%	0.40	85%	0.90

While the airlines' equity betas vary considerably, their unlevered betas are similar. Thus the differences in the market risk of their equity are primarily due to differences in their capital structures. Based on this data, an unlevered beta in the range of 0.90–0.98 would be a reasonable estimate of the market risk of projects in this industry.

Cash and Net Debt

The assets on a firm's balance sheet include any holdings of cash or risk-free securities. Because these holdings are risk-free, they reduce the risk—and therefore the required risk premium—of the firm's assets. For this reason, holding cash has the opposite effect of leverage on risk and return. In fact, we can view cash as equivalent to negative debt. If a firm holds $1 in cash and has $1 of risk-free debt, then the interest earned on the cash will equal the interest paid on the debt. The cash flows from each source cancel each other, just as if the firm held no cash and no debt.

Thus, when we are trying to evaluate a firm's business assets separate from any cash holdings, we measure the leverage of the firm in terms of its **net debt**:

$$\text{Net Debt} = \text{Debt} - \text{Cash and Risk-Free Securities} \qquad (14.12)$$

For example, we measure the market value of a firm's business assets using its enterprise value, which is equal to the market value of its equity plus its net debt. In the same way, we use the market value of the firm's net debt when computing its WACC and unlevered beta to measure the cost of capital and market risk of the firm's business assets.

Microsoft's Dividend, Cash, and Beta

In mid-2004, Microsoft had a market capitalization of more than $300 billion and nearly $60 billion in cash and short-term investments, with no debt outstanding. In November 2004, the firm used some of its cash to pay a one-time dividend of $32 billion. By paying out this cash, Microsoft *increased* its net debt from −$60 billion to −$28 billion. The effect of the dividend is equivalent to an increase in leverage: Paying out the cash will cause the beta of Microsoft's stock to be higher than it otherwise would be.

EXAMPLE
14.8

Cash and Beta

Problem

In mid-2005, Cisco Systems had no debt, total equity capitalization of $110 billion, and a beta of 2.2. Included in Cisco's assets was $16 billion in cash and risk-free securities. What was the market value of Cisco's business assets excluding its cash—that is, its enterprise value—at this time, and what was the beta of these business assets?

Solution

Because Cisco had no debt and $16 billion in cash, Cisco's net debt = 0 − $16 billion = −$16 billion. Its enterprise value was therefore $110 billion − $16 billion = $94 billion. To determine the beta of its business assets, we can apply Eq. 14.9 to compute Cisco's unlevered beta (using the fact that because Cisco's cash is risk free, its net debt has a beta of 0):

$$\beta_U = \frac{E}{E + D}\beta_E + \frac{D}{E + D}\beta_D$$

$$= \frac{110}{110 - 16}(2.20) + \frac{-16}{110 - 16}(0)$$

$$= 2.57$$

In other words, Cisco's market capitalization consists of business assets worth $94 billion plus $16 billion in cash. The business assets have a beta of 2.57. Because the cash has a beta of 0, Cisco's equity has lower market risk than its business assets, with a beta of 2.20. To check this result, note that the portfolio of Cisco's business assets plus its cash has a beta of $(94 / 110)(2.57) + (16 / 110)(0) = 2.20$.

CONCEPT CHECK

1. How do we compute the weighted average cost of capital of a firm?

2. With perfect capital markets, as a firm increases its leverage, how does its debt cost of capital change? Its equity cost of capital? Its weighted average cost of capital?

14.4 Capital Structure Fallacies

MM Propositions I and II state that with perfect capital markets, leverage has no effect on firm value or the firm's overall cost of capital. Here we take a critical look at two incorrect arguments that are sometimes cited in favor of leverage.

Leverage and Earnings per Share

Leverage can increase a firm's expected earnings per share. An argument sometimes made is that by doing so, leverage should also increase the firm's stock price.

Consider the following example. Levitron Industries (LVI) is currently an all-equity firm. It expects to generate earnings before interest and taxes (EBIT) of $10 million over the next year. Currently, LVI has 10 million shares outstanding, and its stock is trading for a price of $7.50 per share. LVI is considering changing its capital structure by borrowing $15 million at an interest rate of 8% and using the proceeds to repurchase 2 million shares at $7.50 per share.

Let's consider the consequences of this transaction in a setting of perfect capital markets. Suppose LVI has no debt. Because LVI pays no interest, and because in perfect capital markets there are no taxes, LVI's earnings would equal its EBIT. Therefore, without debt, LVI would expect earnings per share of

$$EPS = \frac{\text{Earnings}}{\text{Number of Shares}} = \frac{\$10\,\text{million}}{10\,\text{million}} = \$1$$

The new debt will obligate LVI to make interest payments each year of

$$\$15\,\text{million} \times 8\%\,\text{interest / year} = \$1.2\,\text{million / year}$$

As a result, LVI will have expected earnings after interest of

$$\text{Earnings} = \text{EBIT} - \text{Interest} = \$10\,\text{million} - \$1.2\,\text{million} = \$8.8\,\text{million}$$

The interest payments on the debt will cause LVI's total earnings to fall. But because the number of outstanding shares will also have fallen to 10 million − 2 million = 8 million shares after the share repurchase, LVI's expected earnings per share is

$$EPS = \frac{\$8.8\,\text{million}}{8\,\text{million}} = \$1.10$$

As we can see, LVI's expected earnings per share increases with leverage. This increase might appear to make shareholders better off and could potentially lead to an increase in the stock price. Yet we know from MM Proposition I that as long as the securities are fairly priced, these financial transactions have an NPV of zero and offer no benefit to shareholders. How can we reconcile these seemingly contradictory results?

The answer is that the risk of earnings has changed. We have thus far considered only *expected* earnings per share. We have not considered the consequences of this transaction on the risk of the earnings. To do so, we must determine the effect of the increase in leverage on earnings per share in a variety of scenarios.

Suppose earnings before interest payments are only $4 million. Without the increase in leverage, EPS would be $4 million ÷ 10 million shares = $0.40. With the new debt, however, earnings after interest payments would be 4 million − $1.2 million = $2.8 million, leading to earnings per share of $2.8 million ÷ 8 million shares = $0.35. So, when earnings are low, leverage will cause EPS to fall even further than it otherwise would have. Figure 14.2 presents several other scenarios.

As Figure 14.2(a) shows, if earnings before interest exceed $6 million, then EPS is higher with leverage. When earnings fall below $6 million, however, EPS is lower with leverage than without it. In fact, if earnings before interest fall below $1.2 million (the level of the interest expense), then after interest LVI will have negative EPS.

Although LVI's expected EPS rises with leverage, the risk of its EPS also increases. The increased risk can be seen because the line showing EPS with leverage in Figure 14.2(b) is steeper than the line without leverage, implying that the same fluctuation in EBIT will lead to greater fluctuations in EPS once leverage is introduced. Taken together, these observations are consistent with MM Proposition I. While EPS increases on average, this increase is necessary to compensate shareholders for the additional risk they are taking, so LVI's share price does not increase as a result of the transaction. Let's check this result in an example.

FIGURE 14.2

LVI Earnings per Share with and without Leverage

The sensitivity of EPS to EBIT is higher for a levered firm than for an unlevered firm. Thus, given assets with the same risk, the EPS of a levered firm is more volatile.

EBIT ($ million)	Unlevered EPS ($)	EBIT − Interest ($ million)	Levered EPS ($)
0	0.00	−1.2	−0.15
4	0.40	2.8	0.35
6	0.60	4.8	0.60
10	1.00	8.8	1.10
16	1.60	14.8	1.85
20	2.00	18.8	2.35

(a) Calculating earnings per share.

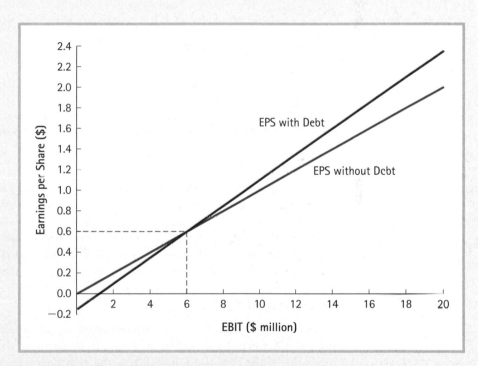

(b) LVI earnings per share for different levels of EBIT.

EXAMPLE 14.9

The MM Propositions and Earnings per Share

Problem

Assume that LVI's EBIT is not expected to grow in the future and that all earnings are paid as dividends. Use MM Propositions I and II to show that the increase in expected EPS for LVI will not lead to an increase in the share price.

Solution

Without leverage, expected earnings per share and therefore dividends are $1 each year, and the share price is $7.50. Let r_U be LVI's cost of capital without leverage. Then we can value LVI as a perpetuity:

$$P = 7.50 = \frac{Div}{r_U} = \frac{EPS}{r_U} = \frac{1.00}{r_U}$$

Therefore, LVI's current share price implies $r_U = 1/7.50 = 13.33\%$.

The market value of LVI stock without leverage is $7.50 per share × 10 million shares = $75 million. If LVI uses debt to repurchase $15 million worth of the firm's equity (that is, 2 million shares), then the remaining equity will be worth $75 million − $15 million = $60 million according to MM Proposition I. After the transaction, LVI's debt-equity ratio is $15 million ÷ $60 million = $\frac{1}{4}$. Using MM Proposition II, LVI's equity cost of capital with leverage will be

$$r_E = r_U + \frac{D}{E}(r_U - r_D) = 13.33\% + \frac{1}{4}(13.33\% - 8\%) = 14.66\%$$

Given that expected EPS is now $1.10 per share, the new value of the shares equals

$$P = \frac{1.10}{r_E} = \frac{1.10}{14.66\%} = 7.50 \text{ per share}$$

Thus, even though EPS is higher, due to the additional risk, shareholders will demand a higher return. These effects cancel out, so the price per share is unchanged.

Because the firm's earnings per share and price-earnings ratio are affected by leverage implies that we cannot reliably compare these measures across firms with different capital structures. For this reason, most analysts prefer to use performance measures and valuation multiples that are based on the firm's earnings before interest has been deducted. For example, the ratio of enterprise value to EBIT (or EBITDA) is more useful when analyzing firms with very different capital structures than is comparing their P/E ratios.

Equity Issuances and Dilution

Another often-heard fallacy is that issuing equity will dilute existing shareholders' ownership, so debt financing should be used instead. By **dilution**, the proponents of this fallacy mean that if the firm issues new shares, the cash flows generated by the firm must be divided among a larger number of shares, thereby reducing the value of each individual share. The problem with this line of reasoning is that it ignores the fact that the cash raised by issuing new shares will increase the firm's assets. Let's consider an example.

Suppose Jet Sky Airlines (JSA) is a highly successful discount airline serving the southeastern United States. It currently has no debt and 500 million shares of stock outstanding. These shares are currently trading at a price of $16. Last month the firm announced that it would expand its operations to the Northeast. The expansion will require the purchase of $1 billion of new planes, which will be financed by issuing new equity. How will the share price change when the new equity is issued today?

Based on the current share price of the firm (prior to the issue), the equity and therefore the assets of the firm have a market value of 500 million shares × $16 per share = $8 billion. Because the expansion decision has already been made and announced, in perfect capital markets this value incorporates the NPV associated with the expansion.

Suppose JSA sells 62.5 million new shares at the current price of $16 per share to raise the additional $1 billion needed to purchase the planes.

Assets ($ million)	Before Equity Issue	After Equity Issue
Cash		1000
Existing assets	8000	8000
	8000	9000
Shares outstanding (million)	500	562.5
Value per share	$16.00	$16.00

Two things happen when JSA issues equity. First, the market value of its assets grows because of the additional $1 billion in cash the firm has raised. Second, the number of shares increases. Although the number of shares has grown to 562.5 million, the value per share is unchanged: $9 billion ÷ 562.5 million shares = $16 per share.

In general, as long as the firm sells the new shares of equity *at a fair price*, there will be no gain or loss to shareholders associated with the equity issue itself. The money taken in by the firm as a result of the share issue exactly offsets the dilution of the shares. *Any gain or loss associated with the transaction will result from the NPV of the investments the firm makes with the funds raised.*

CONCEPT CHECK

1. If a change in leverage raises a firm's earnings per share, should this cause its share price to rise in a perfect market?

2. True or false: When a firm issues equity, it increases the supply of its shares in the market, which should cause its share price to fall.

14.5 MM: Beyond the Propositions

Since the publication of their original paper, Modigliani and Miller's ideas have greatly influenced finance research and practice. Perhaps more important than the specific propositions themselves is the approach that MM took to derive them. Proposition I was one of the first arguments to show that the Law of One Price could have strong implications for security prices and firm values in a competitive market; it marks the beginning of the modern theory of corporate finance.

Modigliani and Miller's work formalized a new way of thinking about financial markets that was first put forth by John Burr Williams in his 1938 book, *The Theory of Investment Value*. In it Williams argues:

If the investment value of an enterprise as a whole is by definition the present worth of all its future distributions to security holders, whether on interest or dividend account, then this value in no wise depends on what the company's capitalization is. Clearly, if a single individual or a single institutional investor owned all of the bonds, stocks and warrants issued by the corporation, it would not matter to this investor what the company's capitalization was (except for details concerning the income tax). Any earnings collected as interest could not be collected as dividends. To such an individual it would be perfectly obvious that total interest- and dividend-paying power was in no wise dependent on the kind of securities

Nobel Prize   Franco Modigliani and Merton Miller

Franco Modigliani and Merton Miller, the authors of the Modigliani-Miller Propositions, have each won the Nobel Prize in economics for their work in financial economics, including their capital structure propositions. Modigliani won the Nobel Prize in 1985 for his work on personal savings and for his capital structure theorems with Miller. Miller earned his prize in 1990 for his analysis of portfolio theory and capital structure.

Miller once described the MM propositions in an interview this way:

> People often ask: Can you summarize your theory quickly? Well, I say, you understand the M&M theorem if you know why this is a joke: The pizza delivery man comes to Yogi Berra after the game and says, "Yogi, how do you want this pizza cut, into quarters or eighths?" And Yogi says, "Cut it in eight pieces. I'm feeling hungry tonight."

Everyone recognizes that's a joke because obviously the number and shape of the pieces don't affect the size of the pizza. And similarly, the stocks, bonds, warrants, et cetera, issued don't affect the aggregate value of the firm. They just slice up the underlying earnings in different ways. *

Modigliani and Miller each won the Nobel Prize in large part for their observation that the value of a firm should be unaffected by its capital structure in perfect capital markets. While the intuition underlying the MM propositions may be as simple as slicing pizza, their implications for corporate finance are far-reaching. The propositions imply that the true role of a firm's financial policy is to deal with (and potentially exploit) financial market imperfections such as taxes and transaction costs. Modigliani and Miller's work began a long line of research into these market imperfections, which we look at over the next several chapters.

*Peter J. Tanous, *Investment Gurus* (New York: Institute of Finance, 1997).

issued to the company's owner. Furthermore no change in the investment value of the enterprise as a whole would result from a change in its capitalization. Bonds could be retired with stock issues, or two classes of junior securities could be combined into one, without changing the investment value of the company as a whole. Such constancy of investment value is analogous to the indestructibility of matter or energy: it leads us to speak of the Law of the Conservation of Investment Value, just as physicists speak of the Law of the Conservation of Matter, or the Law of the Conservation of Energy.

Thus, the results in this chapter can be interpreted more broadly as the **conservation of value principle** for financial markets: *With perfect capital markets, financial transactions neither add nor destroy value, but instead represent a repackaging of risk (and therefore return).*

The conservation of value principle extends far beyond questions of debt versus equity or even capital structure. It implies that any financial transaction that appears to be a good deal in terms of adding value either is too good to be true or is exploiting some type of market imperfection. To make sure the value is not illusory, it is important to identify the market imperfection that is the source of value. In the next several chapters we will examine different types of market imperfections and the potential sources of value that they introduce for the firm's capital structure choice and other financial transactions.

CONCEPT CHECK   **1.** Consider the questions facing Dan Harris, CFO of EBS, at the beginning of this chapter. What answers would you give based on the Modigliani-Miller Propositions? What considerations should the capital structure decision be based on?

2. State the conservation of value principle for financial markets.

Summary

1. The collection of securities a firm issues to raise capital from investors is called the firm's capital structure. Equity and debt are the securities most commonly used by firms. When equity is used without debt, the firm is said to be unlevered. Otherwise, the amount of debt determines the firm's leverage.

2. The owner of a firm should choose the capital structure that maximizes the total value of the securities issued.

3. Capital markets are said to be perfect if they satisfy three conditions:
   a. Investors and firms can trade the same set of securities at competitive market prices equal to the present value of their future cash flows.
   b. There are no taxes, transaction costs, or issuance costs associated with security trading.
   c. A firm's financing decisions do not change the cash flows generated by its investments, nor do they reveal new information about them.

4. According to MM Proposition I, with perfect capital markets the value of a firm is independent of its capital structure.
   a. With perfect capital markets, homemade leverage is a perfect substitute for firm leverage.
   b. If otherwise identical firms with different capital structures have different values, the Law of One Price would be violated and an arbitrage opportunity would exist.

5. The market value balance sheet shows that the total market value of a firm's assets equals the total market value of the firm's liabilities, including all securities issued to investors. Changing the capital structure therefore alters how the value of the assets is divided across securities, but not the firm's total value.

6. A firm can change its capital structure at any time by issuing new securities and using the funds to pay its existing investors. An example is a leveraged recapitalization in which the firm borrows money (issues debt) and repurchases shares (or pays a dividend). MM Proposition I implies that such transactions will not change the share price.

7. According to MM Proposition II, the cost of capital for levered equity is

$$r_E = r_U + \frac{D}{E}(r_U - r_D) \qquad (14.5)$$

8. Debt is less risky than equity, so it has a lower cost of capital. Leverage increases the risk of equity, however, raising the equity cost of capital. The benefit of debt's lower cost of capital is offset by the higher equity cost of capital, leaving a firm's weighted average cost of capital (WACC) unchanged with perfect capital markets:

$$r_{wacc} = \frac{E}{E+D}r_E + \frac{D}{E+D}r_D = r_U = r_A \qquad (14.7, 14.8)$$

9. The market risk of a firm's assets can be estimated by its unlevered beta:

$$\beta_U = \frac{E}{E+D}\beta_E + \frac{D}{E+D}\beta_D \qquad (14.9)$$

10. Leverage increases the beta of a firm's equity:

$$\beta_E = \beta_U + \frac{D}{E}(\beta_U - \beta_D) \qquad (14.10)$$

11. A firm's net debt is equal to its debt less its holdings of cash and other risk-free securities. We can compute the cost of capital and the beta of the firm's business assets, excluding cash, by using its net debt when calculating its WACC or unlevered beta.

12. Leverage can raise a firm's expected earnings per share, but it also increases the volatility of earnings per share. As a result, shareholders are not better off and the value of equity is unchanged.

13. As long as shares are sold to investors at a fair price, there is no cost of dilution associated with issuing equity. While the number of shares increases when equity is issued, the firm's assets also increase because of the cash raised, and the per-share value of equity remains unchanged.

14. With perfect capital markets, financial transactions are a zero-NPV activity that neither add nor destroy value on their own, but rather repackage the firm's risk and return. Capital structure—and financial transactions more generally—affect a firm's value only because of its impact on some type of market imperfection.

Key Terms

capital structure *p. 428*
conservation of value principle *p. 450*
debt-to-value ratio *p. 440*
dilution *p. 448*
homemade leverage *p. 433*
leveraged recapitalization *p. 436*
levered equity *p. 429*

market value balance sheet *p. 435*
net debt *p. 444*
perfect capital markets *p. 432*
unlevered beta *p. 443*
unlevered equity *p. 429*
weighted average cost of capital
   (WACC) *p. 439*

Further Reading

For further details on MM's argument, especially their use of the Law of One Price to derive their results, see MM's original paper: F. Modigliani and M. H. Miller, "The Cost of Capital, Corporation Finance and the Theory of Investment," *American Economic Review* 48(3) (1958): 261–297.

For a retrospective look at the work of Modigliani and Miller and its importance in corporate finance, see the collection of articles in Volume 2, Issue 4 of the *Journal of Economic Perspectives* (1988), which includes: "The Modigliani-Miller Propositions After Thirty Years," by M. Miller (pp. 99–120), "Comment on the Modigliani-Miller Propositions," by S. Ross (pp. 127–133), "Corporate Finance and the Legacy of Modigliani and Miller," by S. Bhattacharya (pp. 135–147), and "MM—Past, Present, Future," by F. Modigliani (pp. 149–158).

For an interesting interview with Merton Miller about his work, see: P. J. Tanous, *Investment Gurus* (New York: Prentice Hall Press, 1997).

For a more recent discussion of MM's contribution to the development of capital structure theory, see: R. Cookson, "A Survey of Corporate Finance ('The Party's Over' and 'Debt Is Good for You')," *The Economist* (January 27, 2001): 5–8.

A historical account of Miller-Modigliani's result is provided in these sources: P. L. Bernstein, *Capital Ideas: The Improbable Origins of Modern Wall Street* (Free Press, 1993); and M. Rubinstein, "Great Moments in Financial Economics: II. Modigliani-Miller Theorem," *Journal of Investment Management* 1(2) (2003).

Problems

All problems in this chapter are available in MyFinanceLab. An asterisk (*) indicates problems with a higher level of difficulty.

Equity Versus Debt Financing

1. Consider a project with free cash flows in one year of $130,000 or $180,000, with each outcome being equally likely. The initial investment required for the project is $100,000, and the project's cost of capital is 20%. The risk-free interest rate is 10%.

   a. What is the NPV of this project?

   b. Suppose that to raise the funds for the initial investment, the project is sold to investors as an all-equity firm. The equity holders will receive the cash flows of the project in one year. How much money can be raised in this way—that is, what is the initial market value of the unlevered equity?

   c. Suppose the initial $100,000 is instead raised by borrowing at the risk-free interest rate. What are the cash flows of the levered equity, and what is its initial value according to MM?

2. You are an entrepreneur starting a biotechnology firm. If your research is successful, the technology can be sold for $30 million. If your research is unsuccessful, it will be worth nothing. To fund your research, you need to rasie $2 million. Investors are willing to provide you with $2 million in initial capital in exchange for 50% of the unlevered equity in the firm.

   a. What is the total market value of the firm without leverage?

   b. Suppose you borrow $1 million. According to MM, what fraction of the firm's equity will you need to sell to raise the additional $1 million you need?

   c. What is the value of your share of the firm's equity in cases (a) and (b)?

3. Acort Industries owns assets that will have an 80% probability of having a market value of $50 million in one year. There is a 20% chance that the assets will be worth only $20 million. The current risk-free rate is 5%, and Acort's assets have a cost of capital of 10%.

   a. If Acort is unlevered, what is the current market value of its equity?

   b. Suppose instead that Acort has debt with a face value of $20 million due in one year. According to MM, what is the value of Acort's equity in this case?

   c. What is the expected return of Acort's equity without leverage? What is the expected return of Acort's equity with leverage?

   d. What is the lowest possible realized return of Acort's equity with and without leverage?

Modigliani-Miller I: Leverage, Arbitrage, and Firm Value

`EXCEL` 4. Suppose there are no taxes. Firm ABC has no debt, and firm XYZ has debt of $5000 on which it pays interest of 10% each year. Both companies have identical projects that generate free cash flows of $800 or $1000 each year. After paying any interest on debt, both companies use all remaining free cash flows to pay dividends each year.

   a. Fill in the table below showing the payments debt and equity holders of each firm will receive given each of the two possible levels of free cash flows.

FCF	ABC		XYZ	
---	Debt Payments	Equity Dividends	Debt Payments	Equity Dividends
$ 800				
$1000				

b. Suppose you hold 10% of the equity of ABC. What is another portfolio you could hold that would provide the same cash flows?

c. Suppose you hold 10% of the equity of XYZ. If you can borrow at 10%, what is an alternative strategy that would provide the same cash flows?

5. Suppose Alpha Industries and Omega Technology have identical assets that generate identical cash flows. Alpha Industries is an all-equity firm, with 10 million shares outstanding that trade for a price of $22 per share. Omega Technology has 20 million shares outstanding as well as debt of $60 million.

a. According to MM Proposition 1, what is the stock price for Omega Technology?

b. Suppose Omega Technology stock currently trades for $11 per share. What arbitrage opportunity is available? What assumptions are necessary to exploit this opportunity?

6. Cisoft is a highly profitable technology firm that currently has $5 billion in cash. The firm has decided to use this cash to repurchase shares from investors, and it has already announced these plans to investors. Currently, Cisoft is an all-equity firm with 5 billion shares outstanding. These shares currently trade for $12 per share. Cisoft has issued no other securities except for stock options given to its employees. The current market value of these options is $8 billion.

a. What is the market value of Cisoft's non-cash assets?

b. With perfect capital markets, what is the market value of Cisoft's equity after the share repurchase? What is the value per share?

EXCEL 7. Zetatron is an all-equity firm with 100 million shares outstanding, which are currently trading for $7.50 per share. A month ago, Zetatron announced it will change its capital structure by borrowing $100 million in short-term debt, borrowing $100 million in long-term debt, and issuing $100 million of preferred stock. The $300 million raised by these issues, plus another $50 million in cash that Zetatron already has, will be used to repurchase existing shares of stock. The transaction is scheduled to occur today. Assume perfect capital markets.

a. What is the market value balance sheet for Zetatron

i. Before this transaction?

ii. After the new securities are issued but before the share repurchase?

iii. After the share repurchase?

b. At the conclusion of this transaction, how many shares outstanding will Zetatron have, and what will the value of those shares be?

Modigliani-Miller II:
Leverage, Risk, and
the Cost of Capital

8. Explain what is wrong with the following argument: "If a firm issues debt that is risk free, because there is no possibility of default, the risk of the firm's equity does not change. Therefore, risk-free debt allows the firm to get the benefit of a low cost of capital of debt without raising its cost of capital of equity."

9. Consider the entrepreneur described in Section 14.1 (and referenced in Tables 14.1–14.3). Suppose she funds the project by borrowing $750 rather than $500.

a. According to MM Proposition I, what is the value of the equity? What are its cash flows if the economy is strong? What are its cash flows if the economy is weak?

b. What is the return of the equity in each case? What is its expected return?

c. What is the risk premium of equity in each case? What is the sensitivity of the levered equity return to systematic risk? How does its sensitivity compare to that of unlevered equity? How does its risk premium compare to that of unlevered equity?

    d. What is the debt-equity ratio of the firm in this case?

    e. What is the firm's WACC in this case?

10. Hardmon Enterprises is currently an all-equity firm with an expected return of 12%. It is considering a leveraged recapitalization in which it would borrow and repurchase existing shares.

    a. Suppose Hardmon borrows to the point that its debt-equity ratio is 0.50. With this amount of debt, the debt cost of capital is 6%. What will the expected return of equity be after this transaction?

    b. Suppose instead Hardmon borrows to the point that its debt-equity ratio is 1.50. With this amount of debt, Hardmon's debt will be much riskier. As a result, the debt cost of capital will be 8%. What will the expected return of equity be in this case?

    c. A senior manager argues that it is in the best interest of the shareholders to choose the capital structure that leads to the highest expected return for the stock. How would you respond to this argument?

11. Global Pistons (GP) has common stock with a market value of $200 million and debt with a value of $100 million. Investors expect a 15% return on the stock and a 6% return on the debt. Assume perfect capital markets.

    a. Suppose GP issues $100 million of new stock to buy back the debt. What is the expected return of the stock after this transaction?

    b. Suppose instead GP issues $50 million of new debt to repurchase stock.

        i. If the risk of the debt does not change, what is the expected return of the stock after this transaction?

        ii. If the risk of the debt increases, would the expected return of the stock be higher or lower than in part (i)?

12. Hubbard Industries is an all-equity firm whose shares have an expected return of 10%. Hubbard does a leveraged recapitalization, issuing debt and repurchasing stock, until its debt-equity ratio is 0.60. Due to the increased risk, shareholders now expect a return of 13%. Assuming there are no taxes and Hubbard's debt is risk free, what is the interest rate on the debt?

13. Hartford Mining has 50 million shares that are currently trading for $4 per share and $200 million worth of debt. The debt is risk free and has an interest rate of 5%, and the expected return of Hartford stock is 11%. Suppose a mining strike causes the price of Hartford stock to fall 25% to $3 per share. The value of the risk-free debt is unchanged. Assuming there are no taxes and the unlevered beta of Hartford's assets is unchanged, what happens to Hartford's equity cost of capital?

*14. Indell stock has a current market value of $120 million and a beta of 1.50. Indell currently has risk-free debt as well. The firm decides to change its capital structure by issuing $30 million in additional risk-free debt, and then using this $30 million plus another $10 million in cash to repurchase stock. With perfect capital markets, what will the beta of Indell stock be after this transaction?

Capital Structure Fallacies

EXCEL **15.** Yerba Industries is an all-equity firm whose stock has a beta of 1.2 and an expected return of 12.5%. Suppose it issues new risk-free debt with a 5% yield and repurchases 40% of its stock. Assume perfect capital markets.

    a. What is the beta of Yerba stock after this transaction?

    b. What is the expected return of Yerba stock after this transaction?

Suppose that prior to this transaction, Yerba expected earnings per share this coming year of $1.50, with a forward P/E ratio (that is, the share price divided by the expected earnings for the coming year) of 14.

    c. What is Yerba's expected earnings per share after this transaction? Does this change benefit shareholders? Explain.

    d. What is Yerba's forward P/E ratio after this transaction? Is this change in the P/E ratio reasonable? Explain.

16. You are CEO of a high-growth technology firm. You plan to raise $180 million to fund an expansion by issuing either new shares or new debt. With the expansion, you expect earnings next year of $24 million. The firm currently has 10 million shares outstanding, with a price of $90 per share. Assume perfect capital markets.

    a. If you raise the $180 million by selling new shares, what will the forecast for next year's earnings per share be?

    b. If you raise the $180 million by issuing new debt with an interest rate of 5%, what will the forecast for next year's earnings per share be?

    c. What is the firm's forward P/E ratio (that is, the share price divided by the expected earnings for the coming year) if it issues equity? What is the firm's forward P/E ratio if it issues debt? How can you explain the difference?

17. Zelnor, Inc., is an all-equity firm with 100 million shares outstanding currently trading for $8.50 per share. Suppose Zelnor decides to grant a total of 10 million new shares to employees as part of a new compensation plan. The firm argues that this new compensation plan will motivate employees and is a better strategy than giving salary bonuses because it will not cost the firm anything.

    a. If the new compensation plan has no effect on the value of Zelnor's assets, what will the share price of the stock be once this plan is implemented?

    b. What is the cost of this plan for Zelnor's investors? Why is issuing equity costly in this case?

Data Case

You work in the corporate finance division of The Home Depot and your boss has asked you to review the firm's capital structure. Specifically, your boss is considering changing the firm's debt level. Your boss remembers something from his MBA program about capital structure being irrelevant, but isn't quite sure what that means. You know that capital structure is irrelevant under the conditions of perfect markets and will demonstrate this point for your boss by showing that the weighted average cost of capital remains constant under various levels of debt. So, for now, suppose that capital markets are perfect as you prepare responses for your boss.

You would like to analyze relatively modest changes to Home Depot's capital structure. You would like to consider two scenarios: the firm issues $1 billion in new debt to repurchase stock, and the firm issues $1 billion in new stock to repurchase debt. Use Excel to answer the following questions using Eq. 14.5 and Eq. 14.7 from this chapter, and assuming a cost of unlevered equity (r_U) of 12 percent.

    1. Obtain the financial information you need for Home Depot.

        a. Go to Nasdaq.com (www.nasdaq.com), click on "Summary Quotes" on the left-hand side, and enter Home Depot's stock symbol (HD). Click on Go. From the Summary Quotes page, get the current stock price and number of shares outstanding.

        b. Click on "Company Financials" and the annual income statement should appear. Put the cursor in the middle of the statement, right-click your mouse, and select "Export to Microsoft Excel." (You will not need the income statement until Chapter 15, but collect all of the background data in one step.) Go back to the Nasdaq Web page and select the balance sheet. Export that to Excel as well and then cut and paste the balance sheet to the same worksheet as the income statement.

   c. To get the cost of debt for Home Depot, go to NASD BondInfo (http://www.nasdbondinfo.com). Search by symbol and enter Home Depot's symbol. The next page will contain information for all of Home Depot's outstanding and recently matured bonds. Select the latest yield on an outstanding bond with the shortest remaining maturity (the maturity date is on the line describing each issue; sometimes the list also contains recently retired bonds, so make sure not to use one of those).

2. Compute the market D/E ratio for Home Depot. Approximate the market value of debt by the book value of net debt; include both Long-Term Debt and Short-Term Debt/Current Portion of Long-Term Debt from the balance sheet and subtract any cash holdings. Use the stock price and number of shares outstanding to calculate the market value of equity.

3. Compute the cost of levered equity (r_E) for Home Depot using their current market debt-to-equity ratio and Eq. 14.5 from the chapter.

4. Compute the current weighted average cost of capital (WACC) for Home Depot using Eq. 14.7 and the existing yield on the outstanding bonds as r_D given their current debt-to-equity ratio.

5. Repeat steps 3 and 4 for the two scenarios you would like to analyze, issuing $1 billion in debt to repurchase stock, and issuing $1 billion in stock to repurchase debt. (Although you realize that the cost of debt capital (r_D) may change with changes in leverage, for these modestly small changes you decide to assume that r_D remains constant. We will explore the relation between changing leverage and changing r_D more fully in Chapter 16.) What is the market D/E ratio in each of these cases?

6. Prepare a written explanation for your boss explaining the relationship between capital structure and the cost of capital in this exercise.

7. What implicit assumptions in this exercise generate the results found in question 5? How might your results differ in the "real world"?

Debt and Taxes

notation

Int	interest expense
PV	present value
r_f	risk-free interest rate
D	market value of debt
r_E	equity cost of capital
τ_c	marginal corporate tax rate
E	market value of equity
r_{wacc}	weighted average cost of capital
r_D	debt cost of capital
V^U	value of the unlevered firm
V^L	value of the firm with leverage
τ_i	marginal personal tax rate on income from debt
τ_e	marginal personal tax rate on income from equity
τ^*	effective tax advantage of debt
τ_{ex}^*	effective tax advantage on interest in excess of EBIT

In a perfect capital market, the Law of One Price implies that all financial transactions have an NPV of zero and neither create nor destroy value. Consequently, in the previous chapter we found that the choice of debt versus equity financing does not affect the value of a firm: The funds raised from issuing debt equal the present value of the future interest and principal payments the firm will make. While leverage increases the risk and cost of capital of the firm's equity, the firm's weighted average cost of capital (WACC), total value, and share price are unaltered by a change in leverage. That is, *in a perfect capital market, a firm's choice of capital structure is unimportant.*

This statement is at odds, however, with the observation that firms invest significant resources, both in terms of managerial time and effort and investment banking fees, in managing their capital structures. In many instances, the choice of leverage is of critical importance to a firm's value and future success. As we will show, there are large and systematic variations in the typical capital structures for different industries. For example, at year-end 2004, Amgen, a biotechnology and drug company, had debt of $5 billion and a market capitalization of more than $81 billion, giving the firm a debt-equity ratio of 0.06. In constrast, Navistar International, an auto and truck manufacturer, had a debt-equity ratio of 0.95. Truck manufacturers in general have higher debt ratios than biotechnology and drug companies. If capital structure is unimportant, why do we see such consistent differences in capital structures across firms and industries? Why do managers dedicate so much time, effort, and expense to the capital structure choice?

As Modigliani and Miller made clear in their original work, capital structure does not matter in *perfect* capital markets.[1] Recall from Chapter 14 that a perfect capital market exists under the following assumptions:

1. Investors and firms can trade the same set of securities at competitive market prices equal to the present value of their future cash flows.

2. There are no taxes, transaction costs, or issuance costs associated with security trading.

3. A firm's financing decisions do not change the cash flows generated by its investments, nor do they reveal new information about them.

Thus, if capital structure *does* matter, then it must stem from a market *imperfection*. In this chapter, we focus on one such imperfection—taxes. Corporations and investors must pay taxes on the income they earn from their investments. As we will see, a firm can enhance its value by using leverage to minimize the taxes it, and its investors, pay.

15.1 The Interest Tax Deduction

Corporations must pay taxes on the income that they earn. Because they pay taxes on their profits after interest payments are deducted, interest expenses reduce the amount of corporate tax firms must pay. This feature of the tax code creates an incentive to use debt.

Let's consider the impact of interest expenses on the taxes paid by Safeway, Inc., a grocery store chain. Safeway had earnings before interest and taxes of approximately $1.25 billion in 2005, and interest expenses of about $400 million. Given Safeway's marginal corporate tax rate of 35%,[2] the effect of leverage on Safeway's earnings is shown in Table 15.1.

TABLE 15.1	Safeway's Income with and without Leverage, 2005 ($ million)	
	With Leverage	**Without Leverage**
EBIT	$1,250	$1,250
Interest expense	−400	0
Income before tax	850	1,250
Taxes (35%)	−298	−438
Net income	$552	$812

1. See F. Modigliani and M. H. Miller, "The Cost of Capital, Corporation Finance and the Theory of Investment," *American Economic Review* 48 (June 1958): 261–297. In their 1963 paper, "Corporate Income Taxes and the Cost of Capital: A Correction," *American Economic Review* 53 (June 1963): 433–443, Modigliani and Miller adjusted their analysis to incorporate taxes.

2. Safeway paid an average tax rate of approximately 33.9% in 2004, after accounting for other credits and deferrals. Because we are interested in the impact of a change in leverage, Safeway's marginal tax rate—the tax rate that would apply to additional taxable income—is relevant to our discussion.

As we can see from Table 15.1, Safeway's net income in 2005 was lower with leverage than it would have been without leverage. Thus Safeway's debt obligations reduced the value of its equity. But more importantly, the *total* amount available to *all* investors was higher with leverage:

	With Leverage	**Without Leverage**
Interest paid to debt holders	400	0
Income available to equity holders	552	812
Total available to all investors	**$952**	**$812**

With leverage, Safeway was able to pay out $952 million in total to its investors, versus only $812 million without leverage, representing an increase of $140 million.

It might seem odd that a firm can be better off with leverage even though its earnings are lower. But recall from Chapter 14 that the value of a firm is the total amount it can raise from all investors, not just equity holders. So, if the firm can pay out more in total with leverage, it will be able to raise more total capital initially.

Where does the additional $140 million come from? Looking at Table 15.1, we can see that this gain is equal to the reduction in taxes with leverage: $438 million − $298 million = $140 million. Because Safeway does not owe taxes on the $400 million of earnings it used to make interest payments, this $400 million is *shielded* from the corporate tax, providing the tax savings of 35% × $400 million = $140 million.

In general, the gain to investors from the tax deductibility of interest payments is referred to as the **interest tax shield**. The interest tax shield is the additional amount that a firm would have paid in taxes if it did not have leverage. We can calculate the amount of the interest tax shield each year as follows:

$$\text{Interest Tax Shield} = \text{Corporate Tax Rate} \times \text{Interest Payments} \qquad (15.1)$$

EXAMPLE 15.1

Computing the Interest Tax Shield

Problem
Shown below is the income statement for D.F. Builders (DFB). Given its marginal corporate tax rate of 35%, what is the amount of the interest tax shield for DFB in years 2003 through 2006?

DFB Income Statement ($ million)	2003	2004	2005	2006
Total sales	$3,369	$3,706	$4,077	$4,432
Cost of sales	−2,359	−2,584	−2,867	−3,116
Selling, general, and administrative expense	−226	−248	−276	−299
Depreciation	−22	−25	−27	−29
Operating income	762	849	907	988
Other income	7	8	10	12
EBIT	769	857	917	1,000
Interest expense	−50	−80	−100	−100
Income before tax	719	777	817	900
Taxes (35%)	−252	−272	−286	−315
Net income	**$467**	**$505**	**$531**	**$585**

Solution

From Eq. 15.1, the interest tax shield is the tax rate of 35% multiplied by the interest payments in each year:

($ million)	2003	2004	2005	2006
Interest expense	−50	−80	−100	−100
Interest tax shield (35% × interest expense)	17.5	28	35	35

CONCEPT CHECK

1. With corporate income taxes, explain why a firm's value can be higher with leverage even though its earnings are lower.

2. What is the interest tax shield?

15.2 Valuing the Interest Tax Shield

When a firm uses debt, the interest tax shield provides a corporate tax benefit each year. To determine the benefit of leverage for the value of the firm, we must compute the present value of the stream of future interest tax shields the firm will receive.

The Interest Tax Shield and Firm Value

Each year a firm makes interest payments, the cash flows it pays to investors will be higher than they would be without leverage by the amount of the interest tax shield:

$$\left(\begin{array}{c}\text{Cash Flows to Investors}\\\text{with Leverage}\end{array}\right) = \left(\begin{array}{c}\text{Cash Flows to Investors}\\\text{without Leverage}\end{array}\right) + (\text{Interest Tax Shield})$$

Figure 15.1 illustrates this relationship. Here you can see how each dollar of pretax cash flows is divided. The firm uses some fraction to pay taxes, and it pays the rest to investors. By increasing the amount paid to debt holders through interest payments, the amount of the pretax cash flows that must be paid as taxes decreases. The gain in total cash flows to investors is the interest tax shield.

Because the cash flows of the levered firm are equal to the sum of the cash flows from the unlevered firm plus the interest tax shield, by the Law of One Price the same must be true for the present values of these cash flows. Thus, letting V^L and V^U represent the value of the firm with and without leverage, respectively, we have the following change to MM Proposition I in the presence of taxes:

The total value of the levered firm exceeds the value of the firm without leverage due to the present value of the tax savings from debt:

$$V^L = V^U + PV(\text{Interest Tax Shield}) \tag{15.2}$$

Clearly, there is an important tax advantage to the use of debt financing. But how large is this tax benefit? To compute the increase in the firm's total value associated with the interest tax shield, we need to forecast how a firm's debt—and therefore its interest payments—will vary over time. Given a forecast of future interest payments, we can determine the interest tax shield and compute its present value by discounting it at a rate that corresponds to its risk.

FIGURE 15.1

The Cash Flows of the Unlevered and Levered Firm

By increasing the cash flows paid to debt holders through interest payments, a firm reduces the amount paid in taxes. The increase in total cash flows paid to investors is the interest tax shield. (Figure assumes a 40% marginal corporate tax rate.)

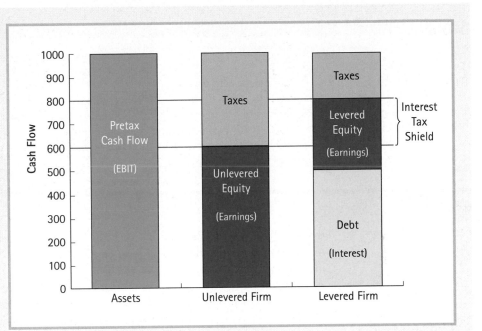

EXAMPLE 15.2

Valuing the Interest Tax Shield Without Risk

Problem

Suppose DFB plans to pay $100 million in interest each year for the next 10 years, and then repay the principal of $2 billion in year 10. These payments are risk free, and DFB's marginal tax rate will remain 35% throughout this period. If the risk-free interest rate is 5%, by how much does the interest tax shield increase the value of DFB?

Solution

In this case, the interest tax shield is 35% × $100 million = $35 million each year for the next 10 years. Therefore, we can value it as a 10-year annuity. Because the tax savings are known and not risky, we can discount them at the 5% risk-free rate:

$$PV(\text{Interest Tax Shield}) = \$35 \text{ million} \times \frac{1}{5\%}\left(1 - \frac{1}{1.05^{10}}\right)$$

$$= \$270 \text{ million}$$

The final repayment of principal in year 10 is not deductible, so it does not contribute to the tax shield.

The Interest Tax Shield with Permanent Debt

In Example 15.2 we know with certainty the firm's future tax savings. In practice, this case is rare. Typically, the level of future interest payments varies due to changes the firm makes in the amount of debt outstanding, changes in the interest rate on that debt, and the risk

Pizza and Taxes

In Chapter 14, we mentioned the pizza analogy that Merton Miller once used to describe the MM Propositions with perfect capital markets: No matter how you slice it, you still have the same amount of pizza.

We can extend this analogy to the setting with taxes, but the story is a bit different. In this case, every time the owner sells a slice of pizza to equity holders, he must give a slice to Uncle Sam as a tax payment. But if the owner sells a slice to debt holders, there is no tax. Thus, by selling more slices to debt holders than to equity holders, the revenues from a single pizza are increased. While the total amount of pizza does not change, the owner will give less away in taxes, leaving more pizza to sell to customers.

that the firm may default and fail to make an interest payment. In addition, the firm's marginal tax rate may fluctuate due to changes in the tax code and changes in the firm's income bracket.

Rather than attempting to account for all possibilities here, we will consider the special case in which the firm issues debt and plans to keep the dollar amount of debt constant forever.[3] For example, the firm might issue a perpetual consol bond, making only interest payments but never repaying the principal. More realistically, suppose the firm issues short-term debt, such as a five-year coupon bond. When the principal is due, the firm raises the money needed to pay it by issuing new debt. In this way, the firm never pays off the principal but simply refinances it whenever it comes due. In this situation, the debt is effectively permanent.

Many large firms have a policy of maintaining a certain amount of debt on their balance sheets. As old bonds and loans mature, new borrowing takes place. What is special here is that we are considering the value of the interest tax shield with a *fixed* dollar amount of outstanding debt, rather than an amount that changes with the size of the firm.

Suppose a firm borrows debt D and keeps the debt permanently. If the firm's marginal tax rate is τ_c, and if the debt is riskless with a risk-free interest rate r_f, then the interest tax shield each year is $\tau_c \times r_f \times D$, and we can value the tax shield as a perpetuity:

$$PV(\text{Interest Tax Shield}) = \frac{\tau_c \times \text{Interest}}{r_f} = \frac{\tau_c \times (r_f \times D)}{r_f}$$

$$= \tau_c \times D$$

This calculation assumes the debt is risk free and the risk-free interest rate is constant. These assumptions are not necessary, however. If the debt is fairly priced, no arbitrage implies that its market value must equal the present value of the future interest payments:[4]

$$\text{Market Value of Debt} = D = PV(\text{Future Interest Payments}) \qquad (15.3)$$

---

3. We discuss how to value the interest tax shield with more complicated leverage policies, such as maintaining a constant debt-equity or interest coverage ratio, in Chapter 18.

4. Equation 15.3 holds even if interest rates fluctuate and the debt is risky, as long as any new debt is also fairly priced. It requires only that the firm never repay the principal on the debt (it either refinances or defaults on the principal). The result follows by the same argument that we used in Chapter 9 to show that the price of equity should equal the present value of the future dividends.

If the firm's marginal tax rate is constant,[5] then we have the following general formula:

Value of the Interest Tax Shield of Permanent Debt

$$PV(\text{Interest Tax Shield}) = PV(\tau_c \times \text{ Future Interest Payments})$$
$$= \tau_c \times PV(\text{Future Interest Payments})$$
$$= \tau_c \times D \tag{15.4}$$

This formula shows the magnitude of the interest tax shield. Given a 35% corporate tax rate, it implies that for every $1 in new permanent debt that the firm issues, the value of the firm increases by $0.35.

The Weighted Average Cost of Capital with Taxes

The tax benefit of leverage can also be expressed in terms of the weighted average cost of capital. When a firm uses debt financing, the cost of the interest it must pay is offset to some extent by the tax savings from the interest tax shield. For example, suppose a firm with a 35% tax rate borrows $100,000 at 10% interest per year. Then its net cost at the end of the year is

		Year-End
Interest expense	$r \times \$100,000 =$	10,000
Tax savings	$-\tau_c \times r \times \$100,000 =$	$-3,500$
Effective after-tax cost of debt	$r \times (1 - \tau_c) \times \$100,000 =$	$6,500

The effective cost of the debt is only $6,500/$100,000 = 6.50% of the loan amount, rather than the full 10% interest. Thus, the tax deductibility of interest lowers the effective cost of debt financing for the firm. More generally,

With tax-deductible interest, the effective after-tax borrowing rate is $r(1 - \tau_c)$.[6]

In Chapter 14, we calculated the weighted average cost of capital, which is the average return that the firm must pay to its investors (equity holders and debt holders). The WACC represents the cost of capital for the free cash flow generated by the firm's assets. Because the firm's free cash flow is computed without considering the firm's leverage, we account for the benefit of the interest tax shield by calculating the WACC using the after-tax cost of debt:

Weighted Average Cost of Capital with Taxes[7]

$$r_{wacc} = \frac{E}{E + D} r_E + \frac{D}{E + D} r_D (1 - \tau_c) \tag{15.5}$$

---

5. The tax rate may not be constant if the firm's taxable income fluctuates sufficiently to change the firm's tax bracket (we discuss this possibility further in Section 15.5). If the firm's taxable income were to fall into a lower tax bracket for an extended period, the value of the tax shield would be reduced.

6. We derived this same result in Chapter 5 when considering the implications of tax-deductible interest for individuals (for example, with a home mortgage).

7. Appendix 18A.1 of Chapter 18 contains a formal derivation of this formula. Equation 15.5 assumes the interest on debt and its expected return r_D are equal, which is a reasonable approximation if the debt has very low risk and is trading near par. If not, the more precise expression for the after-tax debt cost of capital is $(r_D - \tau_c \bar{r}_D)$, where $\bar{r}_D =$ (current interest expense)/(market value of debt).

If we set the tax rate to zero in Eq. 15.5, we have precisely the formula for the WACC without taxes that we defined in Chapter 14. Relative to that case, corporate taxes lower the effective cost of debt financing, which translates into a reduction in the weighted average cost of capital. In fact, Eq. 15.5 implies

$$r_{wacc} = \underbrace{\frac{E}{E+D}r_E + \frac{D}{E+D}r_D}_{\text{Pretax WACC}} - \underbrace{\frac{D}{E+D}r_D\tau_c}_{\substack{\text{Reduction Due} \\ \text{to Interest Tax Shield}}} \qquad (15.6)$$

Thus, the reduction in the WACC increases with the amount of debt financing. The higher the firm's leverage, the more the firm exploits the tax advantage of debt, and the lower its WACC. Figure 15.2 illustrates this decline in the WACC with leverage. The figure also shows the pretax WACC, the WACC computed without taxes.

The Interest Tax Shield with a Target Debt-Equity Ratio

The decline of the WACC with leverage is an alternative way to view the tax benefits associated with debt financing. As we discuss further in Chapter 18, when a firm adjusts its leverage to maintain a target debt-equity ratio rather than maintain a permanent level of debt, we can compute its value with leverage, V^L, by discounting its free cash flow using

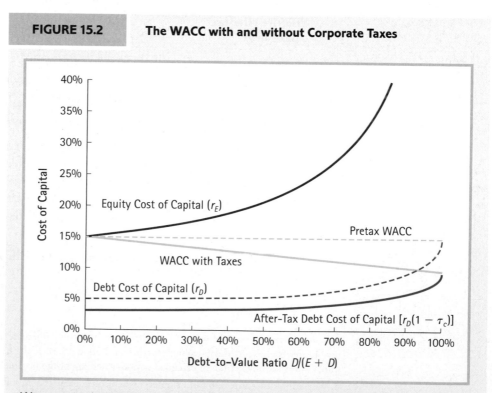

FIGURE 15.2   **The WACC with and without Corporate Taxes**

We compute the WACC as a function of leverage using Eq. 15.5. Without taxes the WACC is constant, as shown in Figure 14.1. With taxes, the WACC declines as the firm increases its reliance on debt financing and the interest tax shield grows. The figure assumes a marginal corporate income tax rate of $\tau_c = 35\%$.

the weighted average cost of capital. The value of the interest tax shield can be found by comparing V^L to the unlevered value, V^U, of the free cash flow discounted at the firm's unlevered cost of capital, the pretax WACC.[8]

<table>
<tr><td>**EXAMPLE**
15.3</td><td>**Valuing the Interest Tax Shield with a Target Debt-Equity Ratio**</td></tr>
</table>

Problem

Western Lumber Company expects to have free cash flow in the coming year of $4.25 million, and its free cash flow is expected to grow at a rate of 4% per year thereafter. Western Lumber has an equity cost of capital of 10% and a debt cost of capital of 6%, and it pays a corporate tax rate of 35%. If Western Lumber maintains a debt-equity ratio of 0.50, what is the value of its interest tax shield?

Solution

We can estimate the value of Western Lumber's interest tax shield by comparing its value with and without leverage. We compute its unlevered value by discounting its free cash flow at its pretax WACC:

$$\text{Pretax WACC} = \frac{E}{E+D}r_E + \frac{D}{E+D}r_D = \frac{1}{1+0.5}10\% + \frac{0.5}{1+0.5}6\% = 8.67\%$$

Because Western Lumber's free cash flow is expected to grow at a constant rate, we can value it as a constant growth perpetuity:

$$V^U = \frac{4.25}{8.67\% - 4\%} = \$91 \text{ million}$$

To compute Western Lumber's levered value, we calculate its WACC:

$$\text{WACC} = \frac{E}{E+D}r_E + \frac{D}{E+D}r_D(1 - \tau_c)$$

$$= \frac{1}{1+0.5}10\% + \frac{0.5}{1+0.5}6\%(1 - 0.35) = 7.97\%$$

Thus Western Lumber's value including the interest tax shield is

$$V^L = \frac{4.25}{7.97\% - 4\%} = \$107 \text{ million}$$

The value of the interest tax shield is therefore

$$PV(\text{Interest Tax Shield}) = V^L - V^U = 107 - 91 = \$16 \text{ million}$$

CONCEPT CHECK

1. With corporate taxes as the only market imperfection, how does the value of the firm with leverage differ from its value without leverage?

2. How does leverage affect a firm's weighted average cost of capital?

---

8. As we show in Chapter 18, if the firm adjusts its leverage to maintain a target debt-equity ratio or interest coverage ratio, then its pretax WACC remains constant and equal to its unlevered cost of capital. See Chapter 18 for a full discussion of the relationship between the firm's levered and unlevered costs of capital.

15.3 Recapitalizing to Capture the Tax Shield

When a firm makes a significant change to its capital structure, the transaction is called a recapitalization (or simply a "recap"). In Chapter 14, we introduced a leveraged recapitalization in which a firm issues a large amount of debt and uses the proceeds to pay a special dividend or to repurchase shares. Leveraged recaps were especially popular in the mid- to late-1980s, when many firms found that these transactions could reduce their tax payments.

Let's see how such a transaction might benefit current shareholders. Midco Industries has 20 million shares outstanding with a market price of $15 per share and no debt. Midco has had consistently stable earnings, and pays a 35% tax rate. Management plans to borrow $100 million on a permanent basis through a leveraged recap in which they would use the borrowed funds to repurchase outstanding shares. Their expectation is that the tax savings from this transaction will boost Midco's stock price and benefit shareholders. Let's see if this expectation is realistic.

The Tax Benefit

First, we examine the tax consequences of Midco's leveraged recap. Without leverage, Midco's total market value is the value of its unlevered equity. Assuming the current stock price is the fair price for the shares without leverage:

$$V^U = (20 \text{ million shares}) \times (\$15/\text{share}) = \$300 \text{ million}$$

With leverage, Midco will reduce its annual tax payments. If Midco borrows $100 million using permanent debt, the present value of the firm's future tax savings is

$$PV(\text{interest tax shield}) = \tau_c D = 35\% \times \$100 \text{ million} = \$35 \text{ million}$$

Thus the total value of the levered firm will be

$$V^L = V^U + \tau_c D = \$300 \text{ million} + \$35 \text{ million} = \$335 \text{ million}$$

This total value represents the combined value of the debt and the equity after the recapitalization. Because the value of the debt is $100 million, the value of the equity is

$$E = V^L - D = \$335 \text{ million} - \$100 \text{ million} = \$235 \text{ million}$$

While total firm value has increased, the value of equity dropped after the recap. How do shareholders benefit from this transaction?

Even though the value of the shares outstanding drops to $235 million, shareholders will also receive the $100 million that Midco will pay out through the share repurchase. In total, they will receive the full $335 million, a gain of $35 million over the value of their shares without leverage. Let's trace the details of the share repurchase and see how it leads to an increase in the stock price.

The Share Repurchase

Suppose Midco repurchases its shares at their current price of $15 per share. The firm will repurchase $100 million ÷ $15 per share = 6.67 million shares, and it will then have 20 − 6.67 = 13.33 million shares outstanding. Because the total value of equity is $235 million, the new share price is

$$\frac{\$235 \text{ million}}{13.33 \text{ million shares}} = \$17.625$$

The shareholders who keep their shares earn a capital gain of $17.625 − $15 = $2.625 per share, for a total gain of

$$\$2.625/\text{share} \times 13.33 \text{ million shares} = \$35 \text{ million}$$

In this case, the shareholders who remain after the recap receive the benefit of the tax shield. However, you may have noticed something odd in the previous calculations. We assumed that Midco was able to repurchase the shares at the initial price of $15 per share, and then demonstrated that the shares would be worth $17.625 after the transaction. Why would a shareholder agree to sell the shares for $15 when they are worth $17.625?

No Arbitrage Pricing

The previous scenario represents an arbitrage opportunity. Investors could *buy* shares for $15 immediately before the repurchase, and they could sell these shares immediately afterward at a higher price. But this activity would raise the share price above $15 even before the repurchase: Once investors know the recap will occur, the share price will rise immediately to a level that reflects the $35 million value of the interest tax shield that the firm will receive. That is, the value of the Midco's equity will rise *immediately* from $300 million to $335 million. With 20 million shares outstanding, the share price will rise to

$$\$335 \text{ million} \div 20 \text{ million shares} = \$16.75 \text{ per share}$$

Midco must offer at least this price to repurchase the shares.

With a repurchase price of $16.75, the shareholders who tender their shares and the shareholders who hold their shares both gain $16.75 − $15 = $1.75 per share as a result of the transaction. The benefit of the interest tax shield goes to all 20 million of the original shares outstanding for a total benefit of $1.75/share × 20 million shares = $35 million. In other words,

When securities are fairly priced, the original shareholders of a firm capture the full benefit of the interest tax shield from an increase in leverage.

EXAMPLE 15.4	**Alternative Repurchase Prices**

Problem

Suppose Midco announces a price at which it will repurchase $100 million worth of its shares. Show that $16.75 is the lowest price it could offer and expect shareholders to tender their shares. How will the benefits be divided if Midco offers more than $16.75 per share?

Solution

For each repurchase price, we can compute the number of shares Midco will repurchase, as well as the number of shares that will remain after the share repurchase. Dividing the $235 million total value of equity by the number of remaining shares gives Midco's new share price after the transaction. No shareholders will be willing to sell their shares unless the repurchase price is at least as high as the share price after the transaction; otherwise, they would be better off waiting to sell their shares. As the table shows, the repurchase price must be at least $16.75 for shareholders to be willing to sell rather than waiting to receive a higher price.

Repurchase Price ($/share)	Shares Repurchased (million)	Shares Remaining (million)	New Share Price ($/share)
P_R	$R = 100/P_R$	$N = 20 - R$	$P_N = 235/N$
15.00	6.67	13.33	$17.63
16.25	6.15	13.85	16.97
16.75	5.97	14.03	16.75
17.25	5.80	14.20	16.55
17.50	5.71	14.29	16.45

If Midco offers a price above $16.75, then all existing shareholders will be eager to sell their shares, because the shares will have a lower value after the transaction is completed. In this case, Midco's offer to repurchase shares will be oversubscribed and Midco will need to use a lottery or some other rationing mechanism to choose from whom it will repurchase shares. In that case, more of the benefits of the recap will go to the shareholders who are lucky enough to be selected for the repurchase.

Analyzing the Recap: The Market Value Balance Sheet

We can analyze the recapitalization using the market value balance sheet, a tool we developed in Chapter 14. It states that the total market value of a firm's securities must equal the total market value of the firm's assets. In the presence of corporate taxes, *we must include the interest tax shield as one of the firm's assets.*

We analyze the leveraged recap by breaking this transaction into steps, as shown in Table 15.2. First, the recap is announced. At this point, investors anticipate the future interest tax shield, raising the value of Midco's assets by $35 million. Next, Midco issues

TABLE 15.2	Market Value Balance Sheet for the Steps in Midco's Leveraged Recapitalization

Market Value Balance Sheet ($ million)	Initial	Step 1: Recap Announced	Step 2: Debt Issuance	Step 3: Share Repurchase
Assets				
Cash	0	0	100	0
Original assets (V^U)	300	300	300	300
Interest tax shield	0	35	35	35
Total assets	300	335	435	335
Liabilities				
Debt	0	0	100	100
Equity = Assets − Liabilities	300	335	335	235
Shares outstanding (million)	20	20	20	14.03
Price per share	$15.00	$16.75	$16.75	$16.75

$100 million in new debt, increasing both Midco's cash and liabilities by that amount. Finally, Midco uses the cash to repurchase shares at their market price of $16.75. In this step, Midco's cash declines, as does the number of shares outstanding.

Note that the share price rises at the announcement of the recap. This increase in the share price is due solely to the present value of the (anticipated) interest tax shield. Thus, even though leverage reduces the total value of equity, shareholders capture the benefits of the interest tax shield upfront.[9]

CONCEPT CHECK

1. How can shareholders benefit from a leveraged recap when it reduces the total value of equity?

2. How does the interest tax shield enter into the maket value balance sheet?

15.4 Personal Taxes

So far, we have looked at the benefits of leverage with regard to the taxes a corporation must pay. By reducing a firm's corporate tax liability, debt allows the firm to pay more of its cash flows to investors.

Unfortunately for investors, after they receive the cash flows, they are generally taxed again. For individuals, interest payments received from debt are taxed as income. Equity investors also must pay taxes on dividends and capital gains. What are the consequences to firm value of these additional taxes?

Including Personal Taxes in the Interest Tax Shield

The value of a firm is equal to the amount of money the firm can raise by issuing securities. The amount of money an investor will pay for a security ultimately depends on the benefits the investor will receive—namely, the cash flows the investor will receive *after all taxes have been paid*. Thus, just like corporate taxes, personal taxes reduce the cash flows to investors and diminish firm value. As a result, the actual interest tax shield depends on the reduction in the total taxes (both corporate and personal) that are paid.[10]

Personal taxes have the potential to offset some of the corporate tax benefits of leverage that we have described. In particular, in the United States and many other countries, interest income has historically been taxed more heavily than capital gains from equity. Table 15.3 shows recent top federal tax rates in the United States. The average rate on equity income listed in the table is an average of the top capital gains and dividend tax rates.

To determine the true tax benefit of leverage, we need to evaluate the combined effect of both corporate and personal taxes. Consider a firm with $1 of earnings before interest and taxes. The firm can either pay this $1 to debt holders as interest, or it can pay the $1 to equity holders directly, as a dividend, or indirectly, by retaining it so that shareholders receive the $1 through a capital gain. Figure 15.3 shows the tax consequences of each option.

9. We are ignoring other potential side effects of leverage, such as costs of future financial distress. We discuss such costs in Chapter 16.

10. This point was made most forcefully in yet another path-breaking article by Merton Miller, "Debt and Taxes," *Journal of Finance* 32 (1977): 261–275. See also Merton H. Miller and Myron S. Scholes, "Dividends and Taxes," *Journal of Financial Economics* (December 1978): 333–364.

| TABLE 15.3 | Top Federal Tax Rates in the United States, 1971–2005 |

Year	Corporate Tax Rate†	Personal Tax Rates*			
		Interest Income	Average Rate on Equity Income	Dividends	Capital Gains
1971–1978	48%	70%	53%	70%	35%
1979–1981	46%	70%	49%	70%	28%
1982–1986	46%	50%	35%	50%	20%
1987	40%	39%	33%	39%	28%
1988–1990	34%	28%	28%	28%	28%
1991–1992	34%	31%	30%	31%	28%
1993–1996	35%	40%	34%	40%	28%
1997–2000	35%	40%	30%	40%	20%
2001–2002	35%	39%	30%	39%	20%
2003–2005	35%	35%	15%	15%	15%

*Interest income is taxed as ordinary income. Until 2003, dividends were also taxed as ordinary income. The average tax rate on equity income is an average of dividend and capital gain tax rates (consistent with a 50% dividend payout ratio and annual realization of capital gains), where the capital gain tax rate is the long-term rate applicable to assets hold more than one year.

†The corporate rate shown is for C corporations with the highest level of income. Marginal rates can be higher for lower brackets. (For example, since 2000, the 35% tax rate applies to income levels above $18.3 million, while the tax rate for income levels between $100,000 and $335,000 is 39%.)

FIGURE 15.3

After-Tax Investor Cash Flows Resulting from $1 in EBIT

Interest income is taxed at rate τ_i for the investor. Dividend or capital gain income is taxed at rate τ_c for the corporation, and again at rate τ_e for the investor.

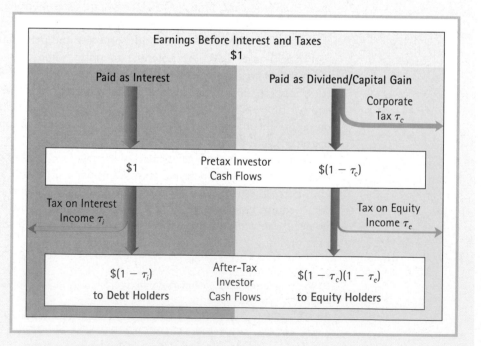

Using 2005 tax rates, debt offers a clear tax advantage with respect to corporate taxes: For every \$1 in pretax cash flows that debt holders receive, equity holders receive $\tau_c = 35\%$ less under current tax rates. But at the personal level, the income tax rate on interest income is $\tau_i = 35\%$, whereas the tax rate on equity income is only $\tau_e = 15\%$. Combining corporate and personal rates leads to the following comparison:

	After-Tax Cash Flows	Using Current Tax Rates
To debt holders	$(1 - \tau_i)$	$(1 - 0.35) = 0.65$
To equity holders	$(1 - \tau_c)(1 - \tau_e)$	$(1 - 0.35)(1 - 0.15) = 0.5525$

While a tax advantage to debt remains, it is not as large as we calculated based on corporate taxes alone. To express the comparison in relative terms, note that equity holders receive

$$\tau^* = \frac{0.65 - 0.5525}{0.65} = 15\%$$

less after taxes than debt holders. In this case, personal taxes reduce the tax advantage of debt from 35% to 15%.

In general, every \$1 received after taxes by debt holders from interest payments costs equity holders \$$(1 - \tau^*)$ on an after-tax basis, where

Effective Tax Advantage of Debt

$$\tau^* = \frac{(1 - \tau_i) - (1 - \tau_c)(1 - \tau_e)}{(1 - \tau_i)} = 1 - \frac{(1 - \tau_c)(1 - \tau_e)}{(1 - \tau_i)} \quad (15.7)$$

When there are no personal taxes, or when the personal tax rates on debt and equity income are the same ($\tau_i = \tau_e$), this formula reduces to $\tau^* = \tau_c$. But when equity income is taxed less heavily ($\tau_i > \tau_e$), then τ^* is less than τ_c.

EXAMPLE 15.5

Calculating the Effective Tax Advantage of Debt

Problem
What was the effective tax advantage of debt in 1980? In 1990?

Solution
Using Eq. 15.7 and the tax rates in Table 15.3, we can calculate

$$\tau^*_{1980} = 1 - \frac{(1 - 0.46)(1 - 0.49)}{(1 - 0.70)} = 8.2\%$$

$$\tau^*_{1990} = 1 - \frac{(1 - 0.34)(1 - 0.28)}{(1 - 0.28)} = 34\%$$

Given the tax rates at the time, the effective tax advantage of debt was much lower in 1980 than in 1990.

Figure 15.4 depicts the effective tax advantage of debt since 1971 in the United States. It has varied widely over time with changes in the tax code.

FIGURE 15.4

The Effective Tax Advantage of Debt with and without Personal Taxes, 1971–2005

After adjusting for personal taxes, the tax advantage of debt τ^* is generally below τ_c, but still positive. It has also varied widely with changes to the tax code.

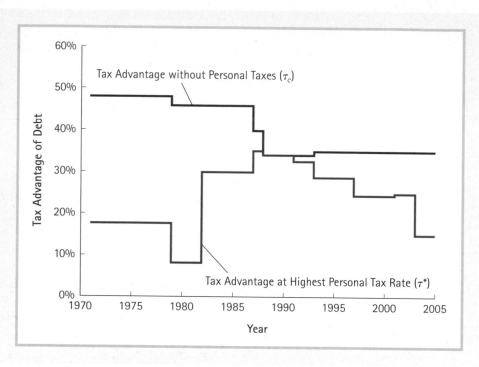

Valuing the Interest Tax Shield with Personal Taxes

How does the foregoing analysis of personal taxes affect our valuation of the debt tax shield? We postpone a detailed answer to this question until Chapter 18, and limit our discussion here to a few important observations. First, as long as $\tau^* > 0$, then despite any tax disadvantage of debt at the personal level, a net tax advantage for leverage remains. In the case of permanent debt, the value of the firm with leverage becomes

$$V^L = V^U + \tau^* D \tag{15.8}$$

Because the personal tax disadvantage of debt generally implies $\tau^* < \tau_c$, comparing Eq. 15.8 with Eq. 15.4 we see that the benefit of leverage is reduced.

Personal taxes have a similar, but indirect, effect on the firm's weighted average cost of capital. While we still compute the WACC using the corporate tax rate τ_c as in Eq. 15.5, with personal taxes the firm's equity and debt costs of capital will adjust to compensate investors for their respective tax burdens. The net result is that a personal tax disadvantage for debt causes the WACC to decline more slowly with leverage than it otherwise would.

EXAMPLE 15.6

Estimating the Interest Tax Shield with Personal Taxes

Problem

Estimate the value of Midco after its $100 million leveraged recap, accounting for personal taxes in 2005.

Solution

Given $\tau^* = 15\%$ in 2005, and given Midco's current value $V^U = \$300$ million, we estimate $V^L = V^U + \tau^* D = \$300$ million $+ 15\%(\$100$ million$) = \$315$ million. With 20 million original shares outstanding, the stock price would increase by $\$15$ million $\div$ 20 million shares $= \$0.75$ per share.

Determining the Actual Tax Advantage of Debt

In estimating the effective tax advantage of debt after taking personal taxes into account, we made several assumptions that may need adjustment when determining the actual tax benefit for a particular firm or investor.

First, with regard to the capital gains tax rate, we assumed that investors paid capital gains taxes every year. But unlike taxes on interest income or dividends, which are paid annually, capital gains taxes are paid only at the time the investor sells the stock and realizes the gain. Deferring the payment of capital gains taxes lowers the present value of the taxes, which can be interpreted as a lower *effective* capital gains tax rate. For example, given a capital gains tax rate of 15% and an interest rate of 6%, holding the asset for 10 more years lowers the effective tax rate this year to $(15\%)/1.06^{10} = 8.4\%$. Also, investors with accrued losses that they can use to offset gains face a zero effective capital gains tax rate. As a consequence, investors with longer holding periods or with accrued losses face a lower tax rate on equity income, decreasing the effective tax advantage of debt.

A second key assumption in our analysis is the computation of the tax rate on equity income τ_e. Using the average dividend and capital gains tax rate is reasonable for a firm that pays out 50% of its earnings as dividends, so that shareholder gains from additional earnings were evenly split between dividends and capital gains. For firms with much higher or much lower payout ratios, however, this average would not be accurate. For

Cutting the Dividend Tax Rate

In January 2003, President George W. Bush unveiled a proposal to boost the U.S. economy with a $674 billion tax cut plan, half of which would come from eliminating taxes on dividends. From the moment it was announced, this tax cut generated tremendous controversy.

Proponents argued that easing the tax bite on investors' dividend income would boost the stock market and stimulate the sluggish economy. Critics quickly denounced it as a tax cut for the rich. But one of the underlying motives of the plan, authored in large part by economist R. Glenn Hubbard, was to end the current distortion in tax laws that encourages companies to accumulate debt because interest is deductible but dividend payments are not.

Levying taxes both on corporate earnings and on the dividends or capital gains paid to investors is known as

double taxation. The lower rates on capital gains have provided some relief from double taxation. In 2002, however, dividends were still taxed at the same rate as ordinary income, leading to a combined tax rate in excess of 60% on dividends—one of the highest tax rates on dividends of any industrialized nation. As we have seen, this double taxation results in a tax advantage to debt financing.

Ultimately, policy makers agreed to a compromise that reduced the tax rate for individuals on both dividends (for stocks held for more than 60 days) and capital gains (for assets held for more than one year) to 15%. This compromise, set to expire in 2008, still gives a tax advantage to debt, but at a decreased level from prior years (see Figure 15.4).

example, for firms that do not pay dividends, the capital gains tax rate should be used as the tax rate on equity income.

Finally, we assumed the top marginal federal income tax rates for the investor. In reality, rates vary for individual investors, and many investors face lower rates. (We have also ignored state taxes, which vary widely by state and have an additional impact.) At lower rates, the effects of personal taxes are less substantial. Moreover, *many investors face no personal taxes.* Consider investments held in retirement savings accounts or pension funds that are not subject to taxes.[11] For these investors, the effective tax advantage of debt is $\tau^* = \tau_c$, the full corporate tax rate. This full tax advantage would also apply to securities dealers for whom interest, dividends, and capital gains are all taxed equivalently as income.

What is the bottom line? Calculating the effective tax advantage of debt accurately is extremely difficult, and this advantage will vary across firms (and from investor to investor). A firm must consider the tax bracket of its typical debt holders to estimate τ_i, and the tax bracket and holding period of its typical equity holders to determine τ_e. If, for instance, a firm's investors hold shares primarily through their retirement accounts, $\tau^* \approx \tau_c$. While τ^* is likely to be somewhat below τ_c for the typical firm, exactly how much lower is open to debate. Our calculation of τ^* in Figure 15.4 should be interpreted as a very rough guide at best.[12]

CONCEPT CHECK 1. Why is there a personal tax disadvantage of debt?

2. How does the personal tax disadvantage of debt change the value of leverage for the firm?

15.5 Optimal Capital Structure with Taxes

In Modigliani and Miller's setting of perfect capital markets, firms could use any combination of debt and equity to finance their investments without changing the value of the firm. In effect, any capital structure was optimal. In this chapter we have seen that taxes change that conclusion because interest payments create a valuable tax shield. Even after adjusting for personal taxes, the value of a firm with leverage exceeds the value of an unlevered firm, and there is a tax advantage to using debt financing.

Do Firms Prefer Debt?

Do firms show a preference for debt in practice? Figure 15.5 illustrates the net new issues of equity and debt by U.S. corporations. For equity, the figure shows the total amount of new equity issued, less the amount retired through share repurchases and acquisitions. For debt, it shows the total amount of new borrowing less the amount of loans repaid.

Figure 15.5 makes clear that when firms raise new capital from investors, they do so primarily by issuing debt. In fact, in most years aggregate equity issues are negative, meaning that firms are reducing the amount of equity outstanding by buying shares. (This

---

11. Evidence from the mid-1990s suggests that the growth in pension funds has lowered the average marginal tax rate for investors to about half the rates shown in Table 15.3. See James Poterba, "The Rate of Return to Corporate Capital and Factor Shares: New Estimates Using Revised National Income Accounts and Capital Stock Data," NBER working paper no. 6263 (1997).

12. For a discussion of methods of estimating τ^* and the need to include personal taxes, see John R. Graham, "Do Personal Taxes Affect Corporate Financing Decisions?" *Journal of Public Economics* 73 (August 1999): 147–185.

FIGURE 15.5

Net External Financing and Capital Expenditures by U.S. Corporations, 1975–2005

In aggregate, firms have raised external capital primarily by issuing debt. These funds have been used to retire equity and fund investment, but the vast majority of capital expenditures are internally funded.

Source: Federal Reserve, *Flow of Funds Accounts of the United States*, 2005.

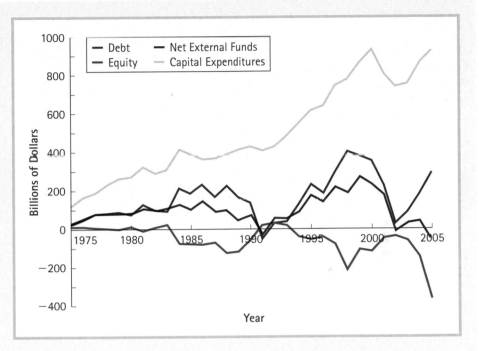

observation does not mean that *all* firms raised funds using debt. Many firms may have sold equity to raise funds. However, at the same time other firms were buying or repurchasing an equal amount so that, in aggregate, no new equity financing occurred.) The data show a clear preference for debt as a source of external financing for the total population of U.S. firms.

While firms seem to prefer debt when raising external funds, not all investment is externally funded. As Figure 15.5 also shows, capital expenditures greatly exceed firms' external financing, implying that most investment and growth is supported by internally generated funds, such as retained earnings. Thus, even though firms have not *issued* new equity, the market value of equity has risen over time as firms have grown. In fact, as shown in Figure 15.6, debt as a fraction of firm value has varied in a range from 30–45% for the average firm. The average debt-to-value ratio fell during the 1990s bull market, with the trend reversing only when the stock market and interest rates declined from 2000 through 2003.

While debt accounted for about 36% of the capital structure of the average firm in 2005, the use of debt also varied greatly by industry. Figure 15.7 shows debt as a fraction of firm value for a number of industries and the overall market. Clearly, there are large differences across industries. Firms in growth industries like biotechnology or high technology carry very little debt, whereas airlines, automakers, utilities, and financial firms have high leverage ratios. Thus the differences in the leverage ratios of Amgen and Navistar International noted in the introduction to this chapter are not unique to these firms, but rather are typical of their respective industries.

These data raise important questions. If debt provides a tax advantage that lowers a firm's weighted average cost of capital and increases firm value, why does debt make up less than half of the capital structure of most firms? And why does the leverage choice vary so much across industries? To begin to answer these questions, let's consider a bit more carefully what the optimal capital structure is from a tax perspective.

FIGURE 15.6

Debt-to-Value Ratio [*D*/(*E* + *D*)] of U.S. Firms, 1975–2005

Although firms have primarily issued debt rather than equity, the average proportion of debt in their capital structures has not increased due to the growth in value of existing equity.

Source: Compustat and Federal Reserve, *Flow of Funds Accounts of the United States*, 2005.

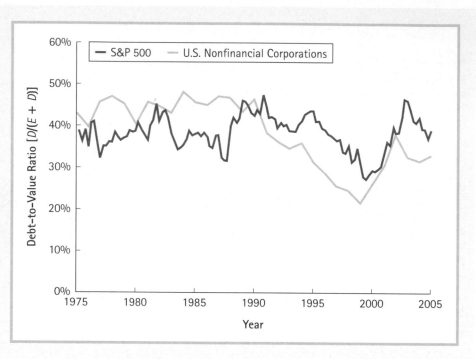

Limits to the Tax Benefit of Debt

To receive the full tax benefits of leverage, a firm need not use 100% debt financing. A firm receives a tax benefit only if it is paying taxes in the first place. That is, the firm must have taxable earnings. This constraint may limit the amount of debt needed as a tax shield.

To determine the optimal level of leverage, compare the three leverage choices shown in Table 15.4 for a firm with earnings before interest and taxes (EBIT) equal to $1000 and a corporate tax rate of $\tau_c = 35\%$. With no leverage, the firm owes tax of $350 on the full $1000 of EBIT. If the firm has high leverage with interest payments equal to $1000, then it can shield its earnings from taxes, thereby saving the $350 in taxes. Now consider a third case, in which the firm has excess leverage so that interest payments exceed EBIT. In this case, the firm has a net operating loss, but there is no increase in the tax savings. Because the firm is paying no taxes already, there is no immediate tax shield from the excess leverage.[13]

Thus no corporate tax benefit arises from incurring interest payments that regularly exceed EBIT. And, because interest payments constitute a tax disadvantage at the investor level as discussed in Section 15.4, investors will pay higher personal taxes with excess leverage, making them worse off.[14] We can quantify the tax disadvantage for excess interest

---

13. If the firm paid taxes during the prior two years, it could "carry back" the current year's net operating loss to apply for a refund of some of those taxes. Alternatively, the firm could "carry forward" the net operating loss up to 20 years to shield future income from taxes (although waiting to receive the credit reduces its present value). Thus there can be a tax benefit from interest in excess of EBIT if it does not occur on a regular basis. For simplicity, we ignore carrybacks and carryforwards in this discussion.

14. Of course, another problem can arise from having excess leverage: The firm may not be able to afford the excess interest and could be forced to default on the loan. We discuss financial distress (and its potential costs) in Chapter 16.

FIGURE 15.7

Debt-to-Value Ratio [$D/(E + D)$] for Select Industries

Debt levels are determined by book values, and equity by market values. The average debt financing for all U.S. stocks was about 36%, but note the large differences by industry.

Source: Reuters, 2005.

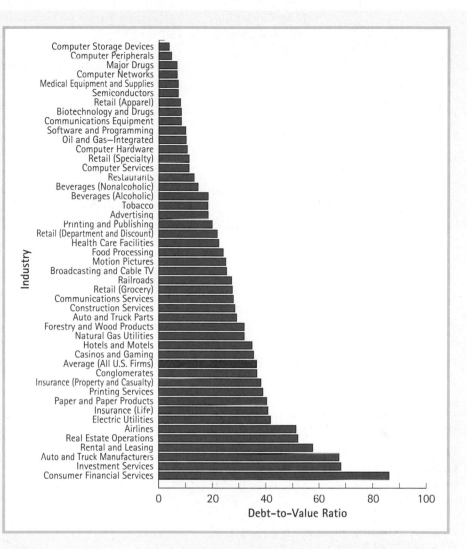

TABLE 15.4   **Tax Savings with Different Amounts of Leverage**

	No Leverage	High Leverage	Excess Leverage
EBIT	$1,000	$1,000	$1,000
Interest expense	0	−1,000	−1,100
Income before tax	1,000	0	0
Taxes (35%)	−350	0	0
Net income	650	0	−100
Tax savings from leverage	$0	$350	$350

payments by setting $\tau_c = 0$ (assuming there is no reduction in the corporate tax for excess interest payments) in Eq. 15.7 for τ^*:

$$\tau^*_{ex} = 1 - \frac{(1 - \tau_e)}{(1 - \tau_i)} = \frac{\tau_e - \tau_i}{(1 - \tau_i)} < 0 \qquad (15.9)$$

Note that τ^*_{ex} is negative because equity is taxed less heavily than interest for investors ($\tau_e < \tau_i$). At 2005 tax rates, this disadvantage is

$$\tau^*_{ex} = \frac{15\% - 35\%}{(1 - 35\%)} = -30.8\%$$

Therefore, the optimal level of leverage from a tax saving perspective is the level such that interest equals EBIT. The firm shields all of its taxable income, and it does not have any tax-disadvantaged excess interest. Figure 15.8 shows the tax savings at different levels of interest payments when EBIT equals $1000 with certainty. In this case, an interest payment of $1000 maximizes the tax savings.

Of course, it is unlikely that a firm can predict its future EBIT precisely. If there is uncertainty regarding EBIT, then with a higher interest expense there is a greater risk that interest will exceed EBIT. As a result, the tax savings for high levels of interest falls, possibly reducing the optimal level of the interest payment, as shown in Figure 15.8.[15] In general, as a firm's interest expense approaches its expected taxable earnings, the marginal tax advantage of debt declines, limiting the amount of debt the firm should use.

FIGURE 15.8

Tax Savings for Different Levels of Interest

When EBIT is known with certainty, the tax savings is maximized if the interest expense is equal to EBIT. When EBIT is uncertain, the tax savings declines for high levels of interest because of the risk that the interest payment will be in excess of EBIT.

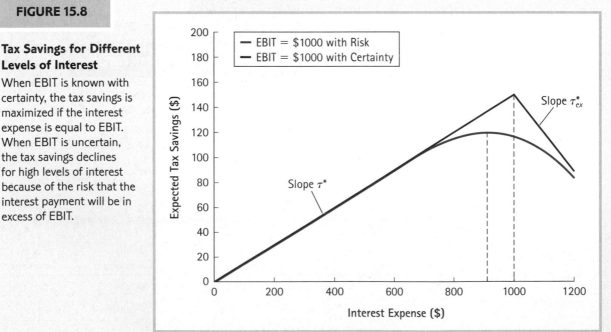

---

15. Details of how to compute the optimal level of debt when earnings are risky can be found in a paper by John Graham, "How Big Are the Tax Benefits of Debt?" *Journal of Finance* 55(5) (October 2000): 1901–1941.

Growth and Debt

In a tax-optimal capital structure, the level of interest payments depends on the level of EBIT. What does this conclusion tell us about the optimal fraction of debt in a firm's capital structure?

If we examine young technology or biotechnology firms, we often find that these firms do not have any taxable income. Their value comes mainly from the prospect that they will produce high future profits. A biotech firm might be developing drugs with tremendous potential, but it has yet to receive any revenue from these drugs. Such a firm will not have taxable earnings. In that case, a tax-optimal capital structure does not include debt. We would expect such a firm to finance its investments with equity alone. Only later, when the firm matures and becomes profitable, will it have taxable cash flows. At that time it should add debt to its capital structure.

Even for a firm with positive earnings, growth will affect the optimal leverage ratio. To avoid excess interest, this type of firm should have debt with interest payments that are below its expected taxable earnings:

$$\text{Interest} = r_D \times \text{Debt} \le \text{EBIT} \quad \text{or} \quad \text{Debt} \le EBIT/r_D$$

That is, from a tax perspective, the firm's optimal level of debt is proportional to its current earnings. However, the value of the firm's equity will depend on the growth rate of earnings: The higher the growth rate, the higher the value of equity (and equivalently, the higher the firm's price-earnings multiple). As a result, *the optimal proportion of debt in the firm's capital structure $[D/(E + D)]$ will be lower, the higher the firm's growth rate.*[16]

Other Tax Shields

Up to this point, we have assumed that interest is the only means by which firms can shield earnings from corporate taxes. But there are numerous other provisions in the tax laws for deductions and tax credits, such as depreciation, investment tax credits, carry-forwards of past operating losses, and the like. For example, many high-tech firms paid little or no taxes in the late 1990's because of tax deductions related to employee stock options (see box, next page). To the extent that a firm has other tax shields, its taxable earnings will be reduced and it will rely less heavily on the interest tax shield.[17]

The Low Leverage Puzzle

Do firms choose capital structures that fully exploit the tax advantages of debt? The results of this section imply that to evaluate this question, we should compare the level of firms' interest payments to their taxable income, rather than simply consider the fraction of debt in their capital structures. Figure 15.9 compares interest expenses and EBIT for firms in the S&P 500. It reveals two important patterns. First, firms have used debt to shield a greater percentage of their earnings from taxes in recent years than they did in the 1970s and early 1980s. This pattern mirrors the increase in the effective tax advantage of debt

16. This explanation for the low leverage of high growth firms is developed in a paper by J. L. Berens and C. J. Cuny, "The Capital Structure Puzzle Revisited," *Review of Financial Studies* 8(4) (Winter 1995): 1185–1208.

17. See H. DeAngelo and R. Masulis, "Optimal Capital Structure Under Corporate and Personal Taxation," *Journal of Financial Economics* 8 (March 1980): 3–27. For a discussion of methods to estimate a firm's marginal tax rate to account for these effects, see John R. Graham, "Proxies for the Corporate Marginal Tax Rate," *Journal of Financial Economics* 42 (April 1996): 187–221.

Employee Stock Options

Employee stock options can serve as an important tax shield for some firms. The typical employee stock option allows employees of a firm to buy the firm's stock at a discounted price (often, the price of the stock when they started employment). When an employee exercises a stock option, the firm is essentially selling shares to the employee at a discount. If the discount is large, the employee can exercise the option and earn a large profit.

The amount of the discount is a cost for the firm's equity holders because selling shares at a price below their market value dilutes the value of the firm's shares. To reflect this cost, the IRS allows firms to deduct the amount of the discount from their earnings for tax purposes. (The IRS taxes employees on the gain, so the tax burden does not go away, but moves from the firm to the employees.) Unlike the interest tax shield, the tax deduction from employee stock options does not add to the value of the firm. If the same amounts were paid to employees through salary rather than options, the firm would be able to deduct the extra salary from its taxable income as well. Until recently, however, employee stock options did not affect EBIT, so that EBIT overstated the taxable income of firms with option expenses.

During the stock market boom of the late 1990s, many technology firms and other firms that issued a large number of employee stock options were able to claim these deductions and lower their taxes relative to what one would naively have imputed from EBIT. In 2000, some of the most profitable companies in the United States (based on net income), such as Microsoft, Cisco Systems, Dell, and QUALCOMM, had *no* taxable income—using the stock option deduction, they were able to report a loss for tax purposes.[*] A recent study by J. R. Graham, M. H. Lang, and D. A. Shackelford[†] reported that in 2000, stock option deductions for the entire Nasdaq 100 exceeded aggregate pretax earnings. For these firms, there would have been no tax advantage associated with debt—which may help explain why they used little to no debt financing.

Under new accounting rules, firms are required to expense employee stock options. However, the rules for expensing the options are not the same as the tax deduction. As a consequence, even after this rule change, stock options may continue to result in a significant difference between firms' accounting income and their income for tax purposes.

[*]See M. Sullivan, "Stock Options Take $50 Billion Bite Out of Corporate Taxes," *Tax Notes* (March 18, 2002): 1396–1401.

[†]"Employee Stock Options, Corporate Taxes and Debt Policy," *Journal of Finance* 59 (2004): 1585–1618.

shown in Figure 15.4. Second, firms shield only about one-third of their earnings in this way. That is, firms have far less leverage than our analysis of the interest tax shield would predict.[18]

This low level of leverage is not unique to U.S. firms. Table 15.5 shows international leverage levels from a 1995 study by Raghuram Rajan and Luigi Zingales using 1990 data. Note that firms worldwide have similar low proportions of debt financing, with firms in the United Kingdom exhibiting especially low leverage. Also, with the exception of Italy and Canada, firms shield less than half of their taxable income using interest payments. The corporate tax codes are similar across all countries in terms of the tax advantage of debt. Personal tax rates vary more significantly, however, leading to greater variation in τ^*.

Why are firms under-leveraged? Either firms are content to pay more taxes than necessary rather than maximize shareholder value, or there is more to the capital structure story than we have uncovered so far. While some firms may deliberately choose a suboptimal capital structure, it is hard to accept that most firms are acting suboptimally. The

---

18. Additional evidence is provided by John Graham in "How Big Are the Tax Benefits of Debt?" *Journal of Finance* 55(5) (October 2000): 1901–1941, where he estimates that the typical firm exploits less than half of the potential tax benefits of debt.

FIGURE 15.9

Interest Payments as a Percentage of EBIT for S&P 500 Firms, 1975–2005

While firms have increased their use of the interest tax shield since the 1970s, they still shield less than 50% of their taxable income in this way.

Source: Compustat.

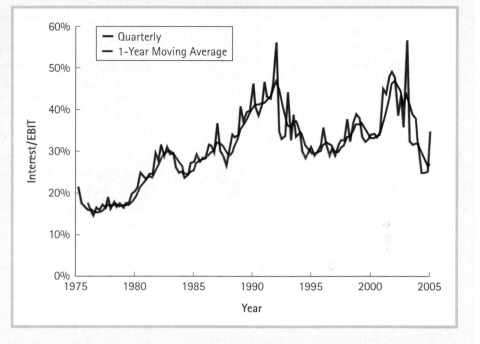

TABLE 15.5   **International Leverage and Tax Rates (1990)**

Country	$D/(E + D)$	Net of Cash $D/(E + D)$	Interest/EBIT	τ_c	τ^*
United States	28%	23%	41%	34.0%	34.0%
Japan	29%	17%	41%	37.5%	31.5%
Germany	23%	15%	31%	50.0%	3.3%
France	41%	28%	38%	37.0%	7.8%
Italy	46%	36%	55%	36.0%	18.6%
United Kingdom	19%	11%	21%	35.0%	24.2%
Canada	35%	32%	65%	38.0%	28.9%

Source: R. Rajan and L. Zingales, "What Do We Know About Capital Structure? Some Evidence from International Data," *Journal of Finance* 50(5) (December 1995): 1421–1460. Data is for median firms and top marginal tax rates.

consensus of so many managers in choosing low levels of leverage suggests that debt financing has other costs that prevent firms from using the interest tax shield fully.

Talk to financial managers and they will quickly point out a key cost of debt missing from our analysis: Increasing the level of debt increases the probability of bankruptcy. Aside from taxes, another important difference between debt and equity financing is that debt payments *must* be made to avoid bankruptcy, whereas firms have no similar obligation to pay dividends or realize capital gains. If bankruptcy is costly, these costs might offset the tax advantages of debt financing. We explore the role of financial bankruptcy costs and other market imperfections in Chapter 16.

INTERVIEW WITH
Andrew Balson

Andrew Balson is a Managing Director of Bain Capital, a leading private investment firm with nearly $40 billion in assets under management. Prior to joining the firm in 1996, he was a consultant at Bain & Company. Bain Capital specializes in leveraged buyout (LBO) transactions, in which a firm is purchased and recapitalized with debt-to-value ratios often exceeding 70%. Bain Capital has invested in many well-known companies including Domino's Pizza, Burger King, Dunkin' Brands, Sealy Mattress Company, Michael's Stores, Toys'R Us and many others. Bain Capital is a participant in the $33 billion proposed LBO of HCA Inc., the largest LBO in history.

QUESTION: *What is the role of private investment firms such as Bain Capital, and what types of firms make the best LBO candidates?*

ANSWER: Our business serves as an alternate capital market for companies that don't really belong as public companies, either during a transition period or permanently, and don't have a logical fit within another larger corporation. In that context, we've done buyouts for companies across many different industries and types. There really isn't one particular type that is best. We look for companies that are well-positioned in their industries, have advantages relative to their competitors, and provide real value to their customers. Some may be underperforming but change can enable them to turn around. Others may be performing well but could do even better. Perhaps the management team has not been given appropriate incentives, or the company has not been optimized or managed aggressively enough. Occasionally, we find a company we can buy at a low price compared to its inherent value. That was a big part of our business 10 years ago but is less so today. We pay relatively full valuations compared to the company's current earnings. What makes this work is our ability to improve current earnings or cash flow.

QUESTION: *How does leverage affect risk and return for investors?*

ANSWER: Based on my experience, if we've found interesting companies where we can change the profit trajectory, leverage will ultimately serve to magnify both the impact of the investments we make and the returns for our investors. Over the past 20 years, the Bain Capital portfolio has far outperformed any equity benchmarks. That performance comes from improved operating profits that are magnified by leverage. Growth is an important driver of our success, so we strive to create efficient capital structures that complement our strategy and enable us to invest in business opportunities. The line between too much and not enough is not distinct, however. We try to use as much debt as we can without changing how our management teams run our businesses.

QUESTION: *What are the potential tax advantages of debt, and can leverage decisions be strategic as well, affecting a firm's competitive position in the product market?*

ANSWER: In today's capital markets, we consider debt a cheaper form of capital than equity—even on a pretax basis. The tax deductibility of interest makes the net cost of debt even cheaper. While the amount of debt matters, so do the terms of the debt. Since the late 1980s, the terms of debt have changed to require less amortization and also fewer covenants, putting less financial pressure on companies. Thus we can create operating value with what traditional markets would consider relatively high leverage. Most of the high returns we earn are from improved profits, not financial engineering. A flexible debt structure enables us to invest in our businesses while at the same time enjoy the equity return benefits of leverage.

We view leverage differently from the public markets. We've run many companies successfully with high levels of leverage. When we take that company public, however, we are advised to pay off much of the debt first and run them on a relatively unlevered basis. Either we were wrong having that level of debt, or the public markets are wrong in valuing companies based on lower leverage. We believe that many public companies are miscapitalized. Our ability to use leverage in many instances makes our overall cost of capital lower than that of the public markets, even though our equity returns are higher.

CONCEPT CHECK

1. How does the growth rate of a firm affect the optimal fraction of debt in the capital structure?

2. Do firms choose capital structures that fully exploit the tax advantages of debt?

Summary

1. Because interest expense is tax deductible, leverage increases the total amount of income available to all investors.

2. The gain to investors from the tax deductibility of interest payments is called the interest tax shield.

$$\text{Interest Tax Shield} = \text{Corporate Tax Rate} \times \text{Interest Payments} \qquad (15.1)$$

3. When we consider corporate taxes, the total value of a levered firm equals the value of an unlevered firm plus the present value of the interest tax shield.

$$V^L = V^U + PV(\text{Interest Tax Shield}) \qquad (15.2)$$

4. When a firm's marginal tax rate is constant, and there are no personal taxes, the present value of the interest tax shield from permanent debt equals the tax rate times the value of the debt, $\tau_c D$.

5. The weighted average cost of capital with corporate taxes is

$$r_{wacc} - \frac{E}{E + D} r_E + \frac{D}{E + D} r_D (1 - \tau_c) \qquad (15.5)$$

Absent other market imperfections, the WACC declines with a firm's leverage.

6. When securities are fairly priced, the original shareholders of a firm capture the full benefit of the interest tax shield from an increase in leverage.

7. Personal taxes offset some of the corporate tax benefits of leverage. Every $1 received after taxes by debt holders from interest payments costs equity holders $(1 − \tau^*)$ on an after tax basis, where

$$\tau^* = 1 - \frac{(1 - \tau_c)(1 - \tau_e)}{(1 - \tau_i)} \qquad (15.7)$$

8. The optimal level of leverage from a tax-saving perspective is the level such that interest equals EBIT. In this case, the firm takes full advantage of the corporate tax deduction of interest, but avoids the tax disadvantage of excess leverage at the personal level.

9. The optimal fraction of debt, as a proportion of a firm's capital structure, declines with the growth rate of the firm.

10. The interest expense of the average firm is well below its taxable income, implying that firms do not fully exploit the tax advantages of debt.

Key Terms

interest tax shield *p. 461*

Further Reading

These are classic works in how taxation affects the cost of capital and optimal capital structure: M. King, "Taxation and the Cost of Capital," *Review of Economic Studies* 41 (1974): 21–35; M. H. Miller, "Debt and Taxes," *Journal of Finance* 32(2) (1977): 261–275; M. H. Miller and M. S. Scholes, "Dividends and Taxes," *Journal of Financial Economics* 6 (December 1978): 333–364; F. Modigliani and M. H. Miller, "Corporate Income Taxes and the Cost of Capital: A Correction," *American Economic Review* 53 (June 1963): 433–443; and J. Stiglitz, "Taxation, Corporate Financial Policy, and the Cost of Capital," *Journal of Public Economics* 2 (1973): 1–34.

For an analysis of how firms respond to tax incentives, see J. MacKie-Mason, "Do Taxes Affect Corporate Financing Decisions?" *Journal of Finance* 45(5) (1990): 1471–1493.

For a recent review of the literature of taxes and corporate finance, see J. R. Graham, "Taxes and Corporate Finance: A Review," *Review of Financial Studies* 16(4) (2003): 1075–1129.

These articles analyze in depth several issues regarding taxation and optimal capital structure: M. Bradley, G. A. Jarrell, and E. H. Kim, "On the Existence of an Optimal Capital Structure: Theory and Evidence," *The Journal of Finance* 39(3) (1984): 857–878; M. J. Brennan and E. S. Schwartz, "Corporate Income Taxes, Valuation, and the Problem of Optimal Capital Structure," *Journal of Business* 51(1) (1978): 103–114; H. DeAngelo and R. Masulis, "Optimal Capital Structure Under Corporate and Personal Taxation," *Journal of Financial Economics* 8 (March 1980): 3–29; and S. Titman and R. Wessels, "The Determinants of Capital Structure Choice," *Journal of Finance* 43(1) (1988): 1–19.

The following articles contain information on what managers say about their capital structure decisions: J. R. Graham and C. Harvey, "How Do CFOs Make Capital Budgeting and Capital Structure Decisions?" *Journal of Applied Corporate Finance* 15 (2002): 8–23; R. R. Kamath, "Long-Term Financing Decisions: Views and Practices of Financial Managers of NYSE Firms," *Financial Review* 32(2) (May 1997): 331–356; E. Norton, "Factors Affecting Capital Structure Decisions," *Financial Review* 26 (August 1991): 431–446; and J. M. Pinegar and L. Wilbricht, "What Managers Think of Capital Structure Theory: A Survey," *Financial Management* 18(4) (Winter 1989): 82–91.

For additional insight into capital structure decisions internationally, see also F. Bancel and U. R. Mittoo, "Cross-Country Determinants of Capital Structure Choice: A Survey of European Firms," *Financial Mangement* 33 (Winter 2004): 103–132; R. La Porta, F. Lopez-de-Silanes, A. Shleifer, and R. Vishny, "Legal Determinants of External Finance," *Journal of Finance* 52 (1997): 1131–1152; and L. Booth, V. Aivazian, A. Demirguq-Kunt, and V. Maksimovic, "Capital Structures in Developing Countries," *Journal of Finance* 56 (2001): 87–130.

Problems

All problems in this chapter are available in MyFinanceLab. An asterisk (*) indicates problems with a higher level of difficulty.

The Interest Tax Deduction

1. Pelamed Pharmaceuticals has EBIT of $325 million in 2006. In addition, Pelamed has interest expenses of $125 million and a corporate tax rate of 40%.

   a. What is Pelamed's 2006 net income?

   b. What is the total of Pelamed's 2006 net income and interest payments?

c. If Pelamed had no interest expenses, what would its 2006 net income be? How does it compare to your answer in part (b)?

d. What is the amount of Pelamed's interest tax shield in 2006?

2. Grommit Engineering expects to have net income next year of $20.75 million and free cash flow of $22.15 million. Grommit's marginal corporate tax rate is 35%.

a. If Grommit increases leverage so that its interest expense rises by $1 million, how will its net income change?

b. For the same increase in interest expense, how will free cash flow change?

3. Suppose the corporate tax rate is 40%. Consider a firm that earns $1000 before interest and taxes each year with no risk. The firm's capital expenditures equal its depreciation expenses each year, and it will have no changes to its net working capital. The risk-free interest rate is 5%.

a. Suppose the firm has no debt and pays out its net income as a dividend each year. What is the value of the firm's equity?

b. Suppose instead the firm makes interest payments of $500 per year. What is the value of equity? What is the value of debt?

c. What is the difference between the total value of the firm with leverage and without leverage?

d. The difference in part (c) is equal to what percentage of the value of the debt?

EXCEL 4. Braxton Enterprises currently has debt outstanding of $35 million and an interest rate of 8%. Braxton plans to reduce its debt by repaying $7 million in principal at the end of each year for the next five years. If Braxton's marginal corporate tax rate is 40%, what is the interest tax shield from Braxton's debt in each of the next five years?

Valuing the Interest Tax Shield

EXCEL 5. Your firm currently has $100 million in debt outstanding with a 10% interest rate. The terms of the loan require the firm to repay $25 million of the balance each year. Suppose that the marginal corporate tax rate is 40%, and that the interest tax shields have the same risk as the loan. What is the present value of the interest tax shields from this debt?

6. Arnell Industries has $10 million in debt outstanding. The firm will pay interest only on this debt. Arnell's marginal tax rate is expected to be 35% for the foreseeable future.

a. Suppose Arnell pays interest of 6% per year on its debt. What is its annual interest tax shield?

b. What is the present value of the interest tax shield, assuming its risk is the same as the loan?

c. Suppose instead that the interest rate on the debt is 5%. What is the present value of the interest tax shield in this case?

7. Bay Transport Systems (BTS) currently has $30 million in debt outstanding. In addition to 6.5% interest, it plans to repay 5% of the remaining balance each year. If BTS has a marginal corporate tax rate of 40%, and if the interest tax shields have the same risk as the loan, what is the present value of the interest tax shield from the debt?

8. Rumolt Motors has 30 million shares outstanding with a price of $15 per share. In addition, Rumolt has issued bonds with a total current market value of $150 million. Suppose Rumolt's equity cost of capital is 10%, and its debt cost of capital is 5%.

a. What is Rumolt's pretax weighted average cost of capital?

b. If Rumolt's corporate tax rate is 35%, what is its after-tax weighted average cost of capital?

9. Summit Builders has a market debt-equity ratio of 0.65 and a corporate tax rate of 40%, and it pays 7% interest on its debt. The interest tax shield from its debt lowers Summit's WACC by what amount?

10. Restex maintains a debt-equity ratio of 0.85, and has an equity cost of capital of 12% and a debt cost of capital of 7%. Restex's corporate tax rate is 40%, and its market capitalization is $220 million.

   a. If Restex's free cash flow is expected to be $10 million in one year, what constant expected future growth rate is consistent with the firm's current market value?

   b. Estimate the value of Restex's interest tax shield.

11. Acme Storage has a market capitalization of $100 million and debt outstanding of $40 million. Acme plans to maintain this same debt-equity ratio in the future. The firm pays an interest rate of 7.5% on its debt and has a corporate tax rate of 35%.

   a. If Acme's free cash flow is expected to be $7 million next year and is expected to grow at a rate of 3% per year, what is Acme's WACC?

   b. What is the value of Acme's interest tax shield?

Recapitalizing to
Capture the
Tax Shield

12. Milton Industries expects free cash flow of $5 million each year. Milton's corporate tax rate is 35%, and its unlevered cost of capital is 15%. The firm also has outstanding debt of $19.05 million, and it expects to maintain this level of debt permanently.

   a. What is the value of Milton Industries without leverage?

   b. What is the value of Milton Industries with leverage?

13. Kurz Manufacturing is currently an all-equity firm with 20 million shares outstanding and a stock price of $7.50 per share. Although investors currently expect Kurz to remain an all-equity firm, Kurz plans to announce that it will borrow $50 million and use the funds to repurchase shares. Kurz will pay interest only on this debt, and it has no further plans to increase or decrease the amount of debt. Kurz is subject to a 40% corporate tax rate.

   a. What is the market value of Kurz's existing assets before the announcement?

   b. What is the market value of Kurz's assets (including any tax shields) just after the debt is issued, but before the shares are repurchased?

   c. What is Kurz's share price just before the share repurchase? How many shares will Kurz repurchase?

   d. What are Kurz's market value balance sheet and share price after the share repurchase?

14. Rally, Inc., is an all-equity firm with assets worth $25 billion and 10 billion shares outstanding. Rally plans to borrow $10 billion and use these funds to repurchase shares. The firm's corporate tax rate is 35%, and Rally plans to keep its outstanding debt equal to $10 billion permanently.

   a. Without the increase in leverage, what would Rally's share price be?

   b. Suppose Rally offers $2.75 per share to repurchase its shares. Would shareholders sell for this price?

   c. Suppose Rally offers $3.00 per share, and shareholders tender their shares at this price. What will Rally's share price be after the repurchase?

   d. What is the lowest price Rally can offer and have shareholders tender their shares? What will its stock price be after the share repurchase in that case?

Personal Taxes

15. Suppose the corporate tax rate is 40%, and investors pay a tax rate of 15% on income from dividends or capital gains and a tax rate of 33.3% on interest income. Your firm decides to add debt so it will pay an additional $15 million in interest each year. It will pay this interest expense by cutting its dividend.

a. How much will debt holders receive after paying taxes on the interest they earn?

b. By how much will the firm need to cut its dividend each year to pay this interest expense?

c. By how much will this cut in the dividend reduce equity holders' annual after-tax income?

d. How much less will the government receive in total tax revenues each year?

e. What is the effective tax advantage of debt τ^*?

16. Markum Enterprises is considering permanently adding $100 million of debt to its capital structure. Markum's corporate tax rate is 35%.

a. Absent personal taxes, what is the value of the interest tax shield from the new debt?

b. If investors pay a tax rate of 40% on interest income, and a tax rate of 20% on income from dividends and capital gains, what is the value of the interest tax shield from the new debt?

*17. Garnet Corporation is considering issuing risk-free debt or risk-free preferred stock. The tax rate on interest income is 35%, and the tax rate on dividends or capital gains from preferred stock is 15%. However, the dividends on preferred stock are not deductible for corporate tax purposes, and the corporate tax rate is 40%.

a. If the risk-free interest rate for debt is 6%, what is cost of capital for risk-free preferred stock?

b. What is the after-tax debt cost of capital for the firm? Which security is cheaper for the firm?

c. Show that the after-tax debt cost of capital is equal to the preferred stock cost of capital multiplied by $(1 - \tau^*)$.

*18. Suppose the tax rate on interest income is 35%, and the average tax rate on capital gains and dividend income is 10%. How high must the marginal corporate tax rate be for debt to offer a tax advantage?

Optimal Capital Structure with Taxes

19. With its current leverage, Impi Corporation will have net income next year of $4.5 million. If Impi's corporate tax rate is 35% and it pays 8% interest on its debt, how much additional debt can Impi issue this year and still receive the benefit of the interest tax shield next year?

*20. Colt Systems will have EBIT this coming year of $15 million. It will also spend $6 million on total capital expenditures and increases in net working capital, and have $3 million in depreciation expenses. Colt is currently an all-equity firm with a corporate tax rate of 35% and a cost of capital of 10%.

a. If Colt is expected to grow by 8.5% per year, what is the market value of its equity today?

b. If the interest rate on its debt is 8%, how much can Colt borrow now and still have non-negative net income this coming year?

c. Is there a tax incentive for Colt to choose a debt-to-value ratio that exceeds 50%? Explain.

EXCEL *21. PMF, Inc., is equally likely to have EBIT this coming year of $10 million, $15 million, or $20 million. Its corporate tax rate is 35%, and investors pay a 15% tax rate on income from equity and a 35% tax rate on interest income.

a. What is the effective tax advantage of debt if PMF has interest expenses of $8 million this coming year?

b. What is the effective tax advantage of debt for interest expenses in excess of $20 million? (Ignore carryforwards.)

c. What is the expected effective tax advantage of debt for interest expenses between $10 million and $15 million? (Ignore carryforwards.)

d. What level of interest expense provides PMF with the greatest tax benefit?

Data Case

Your boss was impressed with your presentation regarding the irrelevance of capital structure from the previous chapter but, as expected, has realized that market imperfections
like taxes must be accounted for. You have now been asked to include taxes in your analysis.
Your boss knows that interest is deductible and has decided that the stock price of Home
Depot should increase if the firm increases its use of debt. Thus, your boss wants to propose
a share repurchase program using the proceeds from a new debt issue and wants to present this
plan to the CEO and perhaps to the Board of Directors.

Your boss would like you to examine the impact of two different scenarios, adding a modest
level of debt and adding a higher level of debt. In particular, your boss would like to consider
issuing $1 billion in new debt or $5 billion in new debt. In either case, Home Depot would
use the proceeds to repurchase stock.

1. Using the financial statements for Home Depot that you downloaded in Chapter 14,
   determine the average corporate tax rate for Home Depot over the last four years by
   dividing Income Tax by Earnings before Tax for each of the last four years.

2. Begin by analyzing the scenario with $1 billion in new debt. Assuming the firm plans to
   keep this new debt outstanding forever, determine the present value of the tax shield of
   the new debt. What additional assumptions did you need to make for this calculation?

3. Determine the new stock price if the $1 billion in debt is used to repurchase stock.
   a. Use the current market value of Home Depot's equity that you calculated in Chap-
      ter 14.
   b. Determine the new market value of the equity if the repurchase occurs.
   c. Determine the new number of shares and the stock price after the repurchase is
      announced.

4. What will Home Depot's D/E ratio based on book values be after it issues new debt and
   repurchases stock? What will its market value D/E ratio be?

5. Repeat stesp 2–4 for the scenario in which Home Depot issues $5 billion in debt and
   repurchases stock.

6. Based on the stock price, does the debt increase and stock repurchase appear to be a good
   idea? Why or why not? What issues might the executives of Home Depot raise that aren't
   considered in your analysis?

CHAPTER

16

Financial Distress, Managerial Incentives, and Information

notation

E	market value of equity
D	market value of debt
PV	present value
V^U	value of the unlevered firm
V^L	value of the firm with leverage
τ^*	effective tax advantage of debt

Modigliani and Miller demonstrated that capital structure does not matter in a perfect capital market. In Chapter 15, we found a tax benefit of leverage, at least up to the point that a firm's EBIT exceeds the interest payments on the debt. Yet we saw that the average U.S. firm shields only about one-third of its earnings in this way. Why don't firms use more debt?

We can gain some insight by looking at United Airlines (UAL Corporation). For the five-year period 1996 through 2000, UAL paid interest expenses of $1.7 billion, relative to EBIT of more than $6 billion. During this period, it reported a total provision for taxes on its income statement exceeding $2.2 billion. The company appeared to have a level of debt that did not fully exploit its tax shield. Even so, as a result of high fuel and labor costs, a decline in travel following the terrorist attacks of September 11, 2001, and increased competition from discount carriers, UAL filed for bankruptcy court protection in December 2002. As this case demonstrates, firms such as airlines whose future cash flows are unstable and highly sensitive to shocks in the economy run the risk of bankruptcy if they use too much leverage. The costs of bankruptcy may at least partially offset the benefits of the interest tax shield, prompting firms to use less leverage than if they were motivated by tax savings alone.

When a firm has trouble meeting its debt obligations we say the firm is in **financial distress**. In this chapter, we consider how a firm's choice of capital structure can, due to market imperfections, affect its costs of financial distress, alter managers' incentives, and signal information to investors. Each of these consequences of the capital structure decision can be significant, and each may offset the tax benefits of leverage when leverage is high. Thus these imperfections may help to explain the levels of debt that we generally observe. In addition, because their effects are likely to vary widely across different types of firms, they may help to explain the large discrepancies in leverage choices that exist across industries, as documented in the previous chapter in Figure 15.7.

16.1 Default and Bankruptcy in a Perfect Market

Debt financing puts an obligation on a firm. A firm that fails to make the required interest or principal payments on the debt is in **default**. After the firm defaults, debt holders are given certain rights to the assets of the firm. In the extreme case, the debt holders take legal ownership of the firm's assets through a process called bankruptcy. Recall that equity financing does not carry this risk. While equity holders hope to receive dividends, the firm is not legally obligated to pay them.

Thus it seems that an important consequence of leverage is the risk of bankruptcy. Does this risk represent a disadvantage to using debt? Not necessarily. As we pointed out in Chapter 14, Modigliani and Miller's results continue to hold in a perfect market even when debt is risky and the firm may default. Let's review that result by considering a hypothetical example.

Armin Industries: Leverage and the Risk of Default

Armin Industries faces an uncertain future in a challenging business environment. Due to increased competition from foreign imports, its revenues have fallen dramatically in the past year. Armin's managers hope that a new product in the company's pipeline will restore its fortunes. While the new product represents a significant advance over Armin's competitors' products, whether that product will be a hit with consumers remains uncertain. If it is a hit, revenues and profits will grow, and Armin will be worth $150 million at the end of the year. If it fails, Armin will be worth only $80 million.

Armin Industries may employ one of two alternative capital structures: (1) It can use all-equity financing or (2) it can use debt that matures at the end of the year with a total of $100 million due. Let's look at the consequences of these capital structure choices when the new product succeeds, and when it fails, in a setting of perfect capital markets.

Scenario 1: New Product Succeeds.   If the new product is successful, Armin is worth $150 million. Without leverage, equity holders own the full amount. With leverage, Armin must make the $100 million debt payment, and Armin's equity holders will own the remaining $50 million.

But what if Armin does not have $100 million in cash available at the end of the year? Even though its assets will be worth $150 million, much of that value may come from anticipated *future* profits from the new product, rather than cash in the bank. In that case, if Armin has debt, will it be forced to default?

With perfect capital markets, the answer is no. As long as the value of the firm's assets exceeds its liabilities, Armin will be able to repay the loan. Even if it does not have the cash immediately available, it can raise the cash by obtaining a new loan or by issuing new shares.

For example, suppose Armin currently has 10 million shares outstanding. Because the value of its equity is $50 million, these shares are worth $5 per share. At this price, Armin can raise $100 million by issuing 20 million new shares and use the proceeds to pay off the debt. After the debt is repaid, the firm's equity is worth $150 million. Because there is now a total of 30 million shares, the share price remains $5 per share.

This scenario shows that if a firm has access to capital markets and can issue new securities at a fair price, *then it need not default as long as the market value of its assets exceeds its liabilities.* That is, whether default occurs depends on the relative values of the firm's assets and liabilities, not on its cash flows. Many firms experience years of negative cash flows yet remain solvent.

Scenario 2: New Product Fails. If the new product fails, Armin is worth only $80 million. If the company has all-equity financing, equity holders will be unhappy but there is no immediate legal consequence for the firm. In contrast, if Armin has $100 million in debt due, it will experience financial distress. The firm will be unable to make its $100 million debt payment and will have no choice except to default. In bankruptcy, debt holders will receive legal ownership of the firm's assets, leaving Armin's shareholders with nothing. Because the assets the debt holders receive have a value of $80 million, they will suffer a loss of $20 million relative to the $100 million they were owed. Equity holders in a corporation have limited liability, so the debt holders cannot sue Armin's shareholders for this $20 million—they must accept the loss.

Comparing the Two Scenarios. Table 16.1 compares the outcome of each scenario without leverage and with leverage. Both debt and equity holders are worse off if the product fails rather than succeeds. Without leverage, if the product fails equity holders lose $150 million − $80 million = $70 million. With leverage, equity holders lose $50 million, and debt holders lose $20 million, *but the total loss is the same—$70 million. Overall, if the new product fails, Armin's investors are equally unhappy whether the firm is levered and declares bankruptcy or whether it is unlevered and the share price declines.*[1]

TABLE 16.1	Value of Debt and Equity with and without Leverage ($ million)			
	Without Leverage		**With Leverage**	
	Success	**Failure**	**Success**	**Failure**
Debt value	—	—	100	80
Equity value	150	80	50	0
Total to all investors	150	80	150	80

This point is an important one. When a firm declares bankruptcy, the news often makes headlines. Much attention is paid to the firm's poor results and the loss to investors. But the decline in value is not *caused* by bankruptcy: The decline is the same whether or not the firm has leverage. That is, if the new product fails, Armin will experience **economic distress**, which is a significant decline in the value of a firm's assets, whether or not it experiences financial distress due to leverage.

Bankruptcy and Capital Structure

With perfect capital markets, Modigliani-Miller (MM) Proposition I applies: The total value to all investors does not depend on the firm's capital structure. Investors as a group are *not* worse off because a firm has leverage. While it is true that bankruptcy results from a firm having leverage, bankruptcy alone does not lead to a greater reduction in the total value to investors. Thus there is no disadvantage to debt financing, and a firm will have the same total value and will be able to raise the same amount initially from investors with either choice of capital structure.

---

1. There is a temptation to look only at shareholders and to say they are worse off when Armin has leverage because their shares are worthless. In fact, shareholders are worse off $50 million relative to success when the firm is levered, versus $70 million without leverage. What really matters is the total value to all investors, which will determine the total amount of capital the firm can raise initially.

EXAMPLE 16.1

Bankruptcy Risk and Firm Value

Problem

Suppose the risk-free rate is 5%, and Armin's new product is equally likely to succeed or to fail. For simplicity, suppose that Armin's cash flows are unrelated to the state of the economy (i.e., the risk is diversifiable), so that the project has a beta of 0 and the cost of capital is the risk-free rate. Compute the value of Armin's securities at the beginning of the year with and without leverage, and show that MM Proposition I holds.

Solution

Without leverage, the equity is worth either $150 million or $80 million at year-end. Because the risk is diversifiable, no risk premium is necessary and we can discount the expected value of the firm at the risk-free rate to determine its value without leverage at the start of the year:[2]

$$\text{Equity (unlevered)} = V^U = \frac{\frac{1}{2}(150) + \frac{1}{2}(80)}{1.05} = \$109.52 \text{ million}$$

With leverage, equity holders receive $50 million or nothing, and debt holders receive $100 million or $80 million. Thus

$$\text{Equity (levered)} = \frac{\frac{1}{2}(50) + \frac{1}{2}(0)}{1.05} = \$23.81 \text{ million}$$

$$\text{Debt} = \frac{\frac{1}{2}(100) + \frac{1}{2}(80)}{1.05} = \$85.71 \text{ million}$$

Therefore, the value of the levered firm is $V^L = E + D = 23.81 + 85.71 = \$109.52$ million. With or without leverage, the total value of the securities is the same, verifying MM Proposition I. The firm is able to raise the same amount from investors using either capital structure.

CONCEPT CHECK

1. With perfect capital markets, under what conditions will a levered firm default?

2. Does the risk of default reduce the value of the firm?

16.2   The Costs of Bankruptcy and Financial Distress

With perfect capital markets, the *risk* of bankruptcy is not a disadvantage of debt—bankruptcy simply shifts the ownership of the firm from equity holders to debt holders without changing the total value available to all investors.

Is this description of bankruptcy realistic? No. Bankruptcy is rarely simple and straightforward—equity holders don't just "hand the keys" to debt holders the moment the firm defaults on a debt payment. Rather, bankruptcy is a long and complicated process that imposes both direct and indirect costs on the firm and its investors that the assumption of perfect capital markets ignores.

The Bankruptcy Code

We know that when a firm fails to make a required payment to debt holders, it is in default. Debt holders can then take legal action against the firm to collect payment by seizing the firm's assets. Because most firms have multiple creditors, without coordination

---

2. If the risk were not diversifiable and a risk premium were needed, the calculations here would become more complicated but the end result would not change.

it is difficult to guarantee that each creditor will be treated fairly. Moreover, because the assets of the firm might be more valuable if kept together, creditors seizing assets in a piecemeal fashion might destroy much of the remaining value of the firm.

The U.S. bankruptcy code was created to organize this process so that creditors are treated fairly and the value of the assets is not needlessly destroyed. According to the provisions of the 1978 Bankruptcy Reform Act, U.S. firms can file for two forms of bankruptcy protection: Chapter 7 or Chapter 11.

In **Chapter 7 liquidation**, a trustee is appointed to oversee the liquidation of the firm's assets through an auction. The proceeds from the liquidation are used to pay the firm's creditors, and the firm ceases to exist.

In the more common form of bankruptcy for large corporations, **Chapter 11 reorganization**, all pending collection attempts are automatically suspended, and the firm's existing management is given the opportunity to propose a reorganization plan. While developing the plan, management continues to operate the business. The reorganization plan specifies the treatment of each creditor of the firm. In addition to cash payment, creditors may receive new debt or equity securities of the firm. The value of cash and securities is generally less than the amount each creditor is owed, but more than the creditors would receive if the firm were shut down immediately and liquidated. The creditors must vote to accept the plan, and it must be approved by the bankruptcy court.[3] If an acceptable plan is not put forth, the court may ultimately force a Chapter 7 liquidation of the firm.

Direct Costs of Bankruptcy

The bankruptcy code is designed to provide an orderly process for settling a firm's debts. However, the process is still complex, time-consuming, and costly. When a corporation becomes financially distressed, outside professionals, such as legal and accounting experts, consultants, appraisers, auctioneers, and others with experience selling distressed assets, are generally hired. Investment bankers may also assist with a potential financial restructuring.

These outside experts are costly. At the time Enron entered Chapter 11 bankruptcy, it reportedly spent a record $30 million per month on legal and accounting fees, and the total cost ultimately exceeded $750 million. WorldCom paid its advisors $657 million as part of its reorganization to become MCI. Between 2003 and 2005, United Airlines paid a team of over 30 advisory firms an average of $8.6 million per month for legal and professional services related to its Chapter 11 reorganization.[4]

In addition to the money spent by the firm, the creditors may incur costs during the bankruptcy process. In the case of Chapter 11 reorganization, creditors must often wait several years for a reorganization plan to be approved and to receive payment. To ensure that their rights and interests are respected, and to assist in valuing their claims in a proposed reorganization, creditors may seek separate legal representation and professional advice.

---

3. Specifically, management holds the exclusive right to propose a reorganization plan for the first 120 days, and this period may be extended indefinitely by the bankruptcy court. Thereafter, any interested party may propose a plan. Creditors who will receive full payment or have their claims fully reinstated under the plan are deemed unimpaired, and do not vote on the reorganization plan. All impaired creditors are grouped according to the nature of their claims. If the plan is approved by creditors holding two-thirds of the claim amount in each group and a majority in the number of the claims in each group, the court will confirm the plan. Even if all groups do not approve the plan, the court may still impose the plan (in a process commonly known as a "cram down") if it deems the plan fair and equitable with respect to each group that objected.

4. Julie Johnsson, "UAL a Ch. 11 Fee Machine," *Crain's Chicago Business,* June 27, 2005.

Whether paid by the firm or its creditors, these direct costs of bankruptcy reduce the value of the assets that the firm's investors will ultimately receive. In the case of Enron, reorganization costs may approach 10% of the value of the assets. Studies typically report that the average direct costs of bankruptcy are approximately 3% to 4% of the pre-bankruptcy market value of total assets.[5] The costs are likely to be higher for firms with more complicated business operations and for firms with larger numbers of creditors, because it may be more difficult to reach agreement among many creditors regarding the final disposition of the firm's assets. Because many aspects of the bankruptcy process are independent of the size of the firm, the costs are typically higher, in percentage terms, for smaller firms. A study of Chapter 7 liquidations of small businesses found that the average direct costs of bankruptcy were 12% of the value of the firm's assets.[6]

Given the substantial legal and other direct costs of bankruptcy, firms in financial distress can avoid filing for bankruptcy by first negotiating directly with creditors. When a financially distressed firm is successful at reorganizing outside of bankruptcy; it is called a **workout**. Consequently, the direct costs of bankruptcy should not substantially exceed the cost of a workout. Another approach is a **prepackaged bankruptcy** (or "prepack"), in which a firm will *first* develop a reorganization plan with the agreement of its main creditors, and *then* file Chapter 11 to implement the plan (and pressure any creditors who attempt to hold out for better terms). With a prepack, the firm emerges from bankruptcy quickly and with minimal direct costs.[7]

Indirect Costs of Financial Distress

Aside from the direct legal and administrative costs of bankruptcy, many other *indirect* costs are associated with financial distress (whether or not the firm has formally filed for bankruptcy). While these costs are difficult to measure accurately, they are often much larger than the direct costs of bankruptcy.

Loss of Customers. Because bankruptcy may enable firms to walk away from future commitments to their customers, customers may be unwilling to purchase products whose value depends on future support or service from the firm. This problem affects many technology firms because customers may hesitate to commit to a hardware or software platform that may not be supported or upgraded in the future. Airlines face sim-

---

5. See Jerold Warner, "Bankruptcy Costs: Some Evidence," *Journal of Finance* 32 (1977): 337–347; Lawrence Weiss, "Bankruptcy Resolution: Direct Costs and Violation of Priority of Claims," *Journal of Financial Economics* 27 (1990): 285–314; Edward Altman, "A Further Empirical Investigation of the Bankruptcy Cost Question," *Journal of Finance* 39 (1984): 1067–1089; and Brian Betker, "The Administrative Costs of Debt Restructurings: Some Recent Evidence," *Financial Management* 26 (1997): 56–68. Lynn LoPucki and Joseph Doherty report that direct costs of bankruptcy may have fallen by more than 50% during the 1990s, due to a reduction in the length of time spent in bankruptcy; these authors estimate them at approximately 1.5% of firm value ("The Determinants of Professional Fees in Large Bankruptcy Reorganization Cases," *Journal of Empirical Legal Studies* 1 (2004): 111–141).

6. Robert Lawless and Stephen Ferris, "Professional Fees and Other Direct Costs in Chapter 7 Business Liquidations," *Washington University Law Quarterly* (Fall 1997): 1207–1236. For comparative international data, see K. Thorburn, "Bankruptcy Auctions: Costs, Debt Recovery and Firm Survival," *Journal of Financial Economics* 58 (2000): 337–368, and A. Raviv and S. Sundgren, "The Comparative Efficiency of Small-firm Bankruptcies: A Study of the U.S. and the Finnish Bankruptcy Codes," *Financial Management* 27 (1998): 28–40.

7. See E. Tashjian, R. C. Lease, and J. J. McConnell, "An Empirical Analysis of Prepackaged Bankruptcies," *Journal of Financial Economics* 40 (1996): 135–162.

ilar problems: Tickets are sold in advance, so customers will be reluctant to buy tickets if they believe the airline may cease operations or fail to honor their accumulated frequent-flier mileage. Manufacturers of durable goods may lose potential customers who are worried that warranties will not be honored or replacement parts will not be available. In contrast, the loss of customers is likely to be small for producers of raw materials (such as sugar or aluminum), as the value of these goods, once delivered, does not depend on the seller's continued success.[8]

Loss of Suppliers. Customers are not the only ones who retreat from a firm in financial distress. Suppliers may be unwilling to provide a firm with inventory if they fear they will not be paid. For example, Kmart Corporation filed for bankruptcy protection in January 2002 in part because the decline in its stock price scared suppliers, which then refused to ship goods. Similarly, Swiss Air was forced to shut down because its suppliers refused to fuel its planes. This type of disruption is an important financial distress cost for firms that rely heavily on trade credit.

Loss of Employees. Because firms in distress cannot offer job security with long-term employment contracts, they may have difficulty hiring new employees, and existing employees may quit or be hired away. Retaining key employees may be costly: Pacific Gas and Electric Corporation implemented a retention program costing over $80 million to retain 17 key employees while in bankruptcy.[9] This type of financial distress cost is likely to be high for firms whose value is derived largely from their human resources.

Loss of Receivables. Firms in financial distress tend to have difficulty collecting money that is owed to them. According to one of Enron's bankruptcy lawyers, "Many customers who owe smaller amounts are trying to hide from us. They must believe that Enron will never bother with them because the amounts are not particularly large in any individual case."[10] Knowing that the firm's resources are already spread thinly, debtors assume they may have an opportunity to avoid their obligations to the firm.

Fire Sales of Assets. Companies in distress may be forced to sell assets quickly to raise cash. Of course, selling assets quickly may not be optimal, which means accepting a lower price than the assets are actually worth. A study of airlines by Todd Pulvino shows that companies in bankruptcy or financial distress sell their aircraft at prices that are 15% to 40% below the prices received by financially healthy firms.[11] Discounts are also observed when distressed firms attempt to sell subsidiaries. The costs of selling assets below their value are greatest for firms with assets that lack competitive, liquid markets.

---

8. This argument was put forth by Sheridan Titman, "The Effect of Capital Structure on a Firm's Liquidation Decision," *Journal of Financial Economics* 13 (1984): 137–151. Timothy Opler and Sheridan Titman report 17.7% lower sales growth for highly leveraged firms compared to their less leveraged competitors in R&D-intensive industries during downturns ("Financial Distress and Corporate Performance," *Journal of Finance* 49 (1994): 1015–1040).

9. Rick Jurgens, "PG&E to Review Bonus Program," *Contra Costa Times,* December 13, 2003.

10. Kristen Hays, "Enron Asks Judge to Get Tough on Deadbeat Customers," *Associated Press,* August 19, 2003.

11. "Do Asset Fire-Sales Exist? An Empirical Investigation of Commercial Aircraft Transactions," *Journal of Finance* 53 (1998): 939–978, and "Effects of Bankrutpcy Court Protection on Asset Sales," *Journal of Financial Economics* 52 (1999): 151–186. For examples from other industries, see Timothy Kruse, "Asset Liquidity and the Determinants of Asset Sales by Poorly Performing Firms," *Financial Management* 31 (2002): 107–129.

Chapter 16 Financial Distress, Managerial Incentives, and Information

Delayed Liquidation. Bankruptcy protection can be used by management to delay the liquidation of a firm that should be shut down. A study by Lawrence Weiss and Karen Wruck estimates that Eastern Airlines lost more than 50% of its value while in bankruptcy because management was allowed to continue making negative-NPV investments.[12]

Costs to Creditors. Aside from the direct legal costs that creditors may incur when a firm defaults, there may be other indirect costs to creditors. If the loan to the firm was a significant asset for the creditor, default of the firm may lead to costly financial distress *for the creditor*.[13] For example, in 1998 Russia's default on its bonds led to the collapse of Long Term Capital Management (LTCM), and fears arose that some of LTCM's creditors might become distressed as well.

Overall Impact of Indirect Costs. In total, the indirect costs of financial distress may be substantial. When estimating them, however, we must remember two important points. First, we need to identify losses to total firm value (and not solely losses to equity holders or debt holders, or transfers between them). Second, we need to identify the incremental losses that are associated with financial distress, above and beyond any losses that would occur due to the firm's economic distress.[14] A study of highly levered firms by Gregor Andrade and Steven Kaplan estimated a potential loss due to financial distress of 10% to 20% of firm value.[15] We next consider the consequences of these potential costs of leverage for firm value.

CONCEPT CHECK
1. If a firm files for bankruptcy under Chapter 11 of the bankruptcy code, which party gets the first opportunity to propose a plan for the firm's reorganization?

2. Why are the losses of debt holders whose claims are not fully repaid not a cost of financial distress, whereas the loss of customers who fear the firm will stop honoring warranties is?

16.3 Financial Distress Costs and Firm Value

The costs of financial distress described in the previous section represent an important departure from Modigliani and Miller's assumption of perfect capital markets. MM assumed that the cash flows of a firm's assets do not depend on its choice of capital structure. As we have discussed, however, levered firms risk incurring financial distress costs that reduce the cash flows available to investors.

---

12. "Information Problems, Conflicts of Interest, and Asset Stripping: Ch. 11's Failure in the Case of Eastern Airlines," *Journal of Financial Economics* 48, 55–97.

13. While these costs are borne by the creditor and not by the firm, the creditor will consider these potential costs when setting the rate of the loan.

14. For an insightful discussion of this point, see Robert Haugen and Lemma Senbet, "Bankruptcy and Agency Costs: Their Significance to the Theory of Optimal Capital Structure," *Journal of Financial and Quantitative Analysis* 23 (1988): 27–38, where they also point out that the magnitude of financial distress costs can be no larger than the costs of restructuring the firm before the costs are incurred.

15. Gregor Andrade and Steven Kaplan, "How Costly Is Financial (Not Economic) Distress? Evidence from Highly Leveraged Transactions That Became Distressed," *Journal of Finance* 53 (1998): 1443–1493.

Armin Industries: The Impact of Financial Distress Costs

To illustrate how these financial distress costs affect firm value, consider again the example of Armin Industries. With all-equity financing, Armin's assets will be worth $150 million if its new product succeeds and $80 million if the new product fails. In contrast, with debt of $100 million, Armin will be forced into bankruptcy if the new product fails. In this case, some of the value of Armin's assets will be lost to bankruptcy and financial distress costs. As a result, debt holders will receive less than $80 million. We show the impact of these costs in Table 16.2, where we assume debt holders receive only $60 million after accounting for the costs of financial distress.

TABLE 16.2	Value of Debt and Equity with and without Leverage ($ million)			
	Without Leverage		**With Leverage**	
	Success	**Failure**	**Success**	**Failure**
Debt value	—	—	100	60
Equity value	150	80	50	0
Total to all investors	150	80	150	60

As Table 16.2 shows, the total value to all investors is now less with leverage than it is without leverage when the new product fails. The difference of $80 million − $60 million = $20 million is due to financial distress costs. These costs will lower the total value of the firm with leverage, and MM's Proposition I will no longer hold, as illustrated in Example 16.2.

EXAMPLE
16.2

Firm Value When Financial Distress Is Costly

Problem
Compare the current value of Armin Industries with and without leverage, given the data in Table 16.2. Assume that the risk-free rate is 5%, the new product is equally likely to succeed or fail, and the risk is diversifiable.

Solution
With and without leverage, the payments to equity holders are the same as in Example 16.1. There we computed the value of unlevered equity as $109.52 million and the value of levered equity as $23.81 million. But due to bankruptcy costs, the value of the debt is now

$$\text{Debt} = \frac{\frac{1}{2}(100) + \frac{1}{2}(60)}{1.05} = \$76.19 \text{ million}$$

The value of the levered firm is $V^L = E + D = 23.81 + 76.19 = \$100$ million, which is less than the value of the unlevered firm, $V^U = \$109.52$ million. Thus, due to bankruptcy costs, the value of the levered firm is $9.52 million less than its value without leverage. This loss equals the present value of the $20 million in financial distress costs the firm will pay if the product fails:

$$PV(\text{Financial Distress Costs}) = \frac{\frac{1}{2}(0) + \frac{1}{2}(20)}{1.05} = \$9.52 \text{ million}$$

Who Pays for Financial Distress Costs?

The financial distress costs in Table 16.2 reduce the payments to the debt holders when the new product has failed. In that case, the equity holders have already lost their investment and have no further interest in the firm. It might seem as though these costs are irrelevant from the shareholders' perspective. Why should equity holders care about costs borne by debt holders?

It is true that after a firm is in bankruptcy, equity holders care little about bankruptcy costs. But debt holders are not foolish—they recognize that when the firm defaults, they will not be able to get the full value of the assets. As a result, they will pay less for the debt initially. How much less? Precisely the amount they will ultimately give up—the present value of the bankruptcy costs.

But if the debt holders pay less for the debt, there is less money available for the firm to pay dividends, repurchase shares, and make investments. That is, this difference is money out of the equity holders' pockets. This logic leads to the following general result:

When securities are fairly priced, the original shareholders of a firm pay the present value of the costs associated with bankruptcy and financial distress.

EXAMPLE 16.3

Financial Distress Costs and the Stock Price

Problem

Suppose that at the beginning of the year, Armin Industries has 10 million shares outstanding and no debt. Armin then announces plans to issue one-year debt with a face value of $100 million and to use the proceeds to repurchase shares. Given the data in Table 16.2, what will the new share price be? As in the previous examples, assume the risk-free rate is 5%, the new product is equally likely to succeed or fail, and this risk is diversifiable.

Solution

From Example 16.1, the value of the firm without leverage is $109.52 million. With 10 million shares outstanding, this value corresponds to an initial share price of $10.952 per share. In Example 16.2, we saw that with leverage, the total value of the firm is only $100 million. In anticipation of this decline in value, the price of the stock should fall to $100 million ÷ 10 million shares = $10.00 per share on announcement of the recapitalization.

Let's check this result. From Example 16.2, due to bankruptcy costs, the new debt is worth $76.19 million. Thus, at a price of $10 per share, Armin will repurchase 7.619 million shares, leaving 2.381 million shares outstanding. In Example 16.1, we computed the value of levered equity as $23.81 million. Dividing by the number of shares gives a share price after the transaction of

$$\$23.81 \text{ million} \div 2.381 \text{ million shares} = \$10.00 \text{ per share}$$

Thus the recapitalization will cost shareholders $0.952 per share or $9.52 million in total. This cost matches the present value of financial distress costs computed in Example 16.2. Thus, although debt holders bear these costs in the end, shareholders pay the present value of the costs of financial distress upfront.

CONCEPT CHECK

1. In Examples 16.1 through 16.3, Armin incurred financial distress costs only in the event that the new product failed. Why might Armin incur financial distress costs even *before* the success or failure of the new product is known?

2. Why should shareholders be concerned about financial distress costs that will be borne by debt holders?

16.4 Optimal Capital Structure: The Tradeoff Theory

We can now combine our knowledge of the benefits of leverage from the interest tax shield (discussed in Chapter 15) with the costs of financial distress to determine the amount of debt that a firm should issue to maximize its value. The analysis presented in this section is called the **tradeoff theory** because it weighs the benefits of debt that result from shielding cash flows from taxes against the costs of financial distress associated with leverage.

According to this theory, *the total value of a levered firm equals the value of the firm without leverage plus the present value of the tax savings from debt, less the present value of financial distress costs:*

$$V^L = V^U + PV(\text{Interest Tax Shield}) - PV(\text{Financial Distress Costs}) \quad (16.1)$$

Equation 16.1 shows that leverage has costs as well as benefits. Firms have an incentive to increase leverage to exploit the tax benefits of debt. But with too much debt, they are more likely to risk default and incur financial distress costs.

Determinants of the Present Value of Financial Distress Costs

Aside from simple examples, calculating the precise present value of financial distress costs is quite complicated. Two key qualitative factors determine the present value of financial distress costs: (1) the probability of financial distress and (2) the magnitude of the costs after a firm is in distress. In Example 16.3, when Armin is levered, the present value of its financial distress costs depends on the probability that the new product will fail (50%) and the magnitude of the costs if it does fail ($20 million).

What determines each of these factors? The magnitude of the financial distress costs will depend on the relative importance of the sources of these costs discussed in Section 16.2 and is likely to vary by industry. For example, technology firms are likely to incur high costs when they are in financial distress, due to the potential for loss of customers and key personnel, as well as a lack of tangible assets that can be easily liquidated. In contrast, real estate firms are likely to have low costs of financial distress, as much of their value derives from assets that can be sold relatively easily.

The probability of financial distress depends on the likelihood that a firm will be unable to meet its debt commitments and therefore default. This probability increases with the amount of a firm's liabilities (relative to its assets). It also increases with the volatility of a firm's cash flows and asset values. Thus firms with steady, reliable cash flows, such as utility companies, are able to use high levels of debt and still have a very low probability of default. Firms whose value and cash flows are very volatile (for example, semiconductor firms) must have much lower levels of debt to avoid a significant risk of default.

Optimal Leverage

Figure 16.1 shows how the value of a levered firm, V^L, varies with the level of permanent debt, D, according to Eq. 16.1. With no debt, the value of the firm is V^U. For low levels of debt, the risk of default remains low and the main effect of an increase in leverage is an increase in the interest tax shield, which has present value $\tau^* D$, where τ^* is the effective tax advantage of debt calculated in Chapter 15. If there were no costs of financial distress, the value would continue to increase at this rate until the interest on the debt exceeds the firm's earnings before interest and taxes and the tax shield is exhausted.

FIGURE 16.1

Optimal Leverage with Taxes and Financial Distress Costs

As the level of debt, *D*, increases, the tax benefits of debt increase by τ^*D until the interest expense exceeds the firm's EBIT. The probability of default, and hence the present value of financial distress costs, also increase with *D*. The optimal level of debt, *D**, occurs when these effects balance out and V^L is maximized. *D** will be lower for firms with higher costs of financial distress.

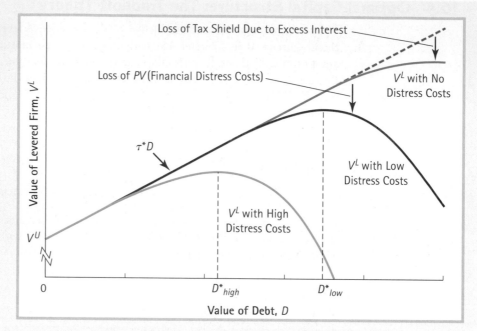

The costs of financial distress reduce the value of the levered firm, V^L. The amount of the reduction increases with the probability of default, which in turn increases with the level of the debt *D*. The tradeoff theory states that firms should increase their leverage until it reaches the level *D** for which V^L is maximized. At this point, the tax savings that result from increasing leverage are just offset by the increased probability of incurring the costs of financial distress.

Figure 16.1 also illustrates the optimal debt choices for two types of firms. The optimal debt choice for a firm with low costs of financial distress is indicated by D^*_{low}, and the optimal debt choice for a firm with high costs of financial distress is indicated by D^*_{high}. Not surprisingly, with higher costs of financial distress, it is optimal for the firm to choose lower leverage.

The tradeoff theory helps to resolve two puzzles regarding leverage that arose in Chapter 15. First, the presence of financial distress costs can explain why firms choose debt levels that are too low to fully exploit the interest tax shield. Second, differences in the magnitude of financial distress costs and the volatility of cash flows can explain the differences in the use of leverage across industries. Furthermore, the tradeoff theory can be easily extended to include other effects of leverage—which may be even more important than financial distress costs—that we discuss next.

EXAMPLE 16.4

Choosing an Optimal Debt Level

Problem

Greenleaf Industries is considering adding leverage to its capital structure. Greenleaf's managers believe they can add as much as $35 million in debt and exploit the benefits of the tax shield (for which they estimate $\tau^* = 15\%$). However, they also recognize that higher debt increases the risk of financial distress. Based on simulations of the firm's future cash flows, the CFO has made the following estimates (in millions of dollars):[16]

Debt	0	10	20	25	30	35
PV(Interest tax shield)	0.00	1.50	3.00	3.75	4.50	5.25
PV(Financial distress costs)	0.00	0.00	0.38	1.62	4.00	6.38

What is the optimal debt choice for Greenleaf?

Solution

From Eq. 16.1, the net benefit of debt is determined by subtracting *PV*(Financial distress costs) from *PV*(Interest tax shield). The net benefit for each level of debt is

Debt	0	10	20	25	30	35
Net benefit	0.00	1.50	2.62	2.13	0.50	−1.13

The level of debt that leads to the highest net benefit is $20 million. Greenleaf will gain $3 million due to tax shields, and lose $0.38 million due to the present value of distress costs, for a net gain of $2.62 million.

CONCEPT CHECK

1. Describe the tradeoff theory.

2. According to the tradeoff theory, all else being equal, which type of firm has a higher optimal level of debt: a firm with very volatile cash flows or a firm with very safe, predictable cash flows?

16.5 Exploiting Debt Holders: The Agency Costs of Leverage

In this section, we consider another way that capital structure can affect a firm's cash flows: It can alter managers' incentives and change their investment decisions. If these changes have a negative NPV, they will be costly for the firm.

The type of costs we describe in this section are examples of **agency costs**—costs that arise when there are conflicts of interest between stakeholders. Because top managers often hold shares in the firm and are hired and retained with the approval of the board of directors, which itself is elected by shareholders, managers will generally make decisions that increase the value of the firm's equity. When a firm has leverage, a conflict of interest exists if investment decisions have different consequences for the value of equity and the value of debt. Such a conflict is most likely to occur when the risk of financial distress is high. In some circumstances, managers may take actions that benefit shareholders but harm the firm's creditors and lower the total value of the firm.

We illustrate this possibility by considering a firm that is facing financial distress, Baxter Inc. Baxter has a loan of $1 million due at the end of the year. Without a change in its strategy, the market value of its assets will be only $900,000 at that time, and Baxter will default on its debt.

Over-investment

Baxter executives are considering a new strategy that seemed promising initially but appears risky after closer analysis. The new strategy requires no upfront investment, but it has only a 50% chance of success. If it succeeds, it will increase the value of the firm's assets

---

16. The PV of the interest tax shield is computed as $\tau^* D$. The PV of financial distress costs is difficult to estimate and requires option valuation techniques we introduce in Part VII of the text.

to $1.3 million. If it fails, the value of the firm's assets will fall to $300,000. Therefore, the expected value of the firm's assets under the new strategy is 50% × $1.3 million + 50% × $300,000 = $800,000, a decline of $100,000 from their value of $900,000 under the old strategy. Despite the negative expected payoff, some within the firm have suggested that Baxter should go ahead with the new strategy, in the interest of better serving its shareholders. How can shareholders benefit from this decision?

As Table 16.3 shows, if Baxter does nothing, it will ultimately default and equity holders will get nothing with certainty. Thus equity holders have nothing to lose if Baxter tries the risky strategy. If the strategy succeeds, equity holders will receive $300,000 after paying off the debt. Given a 50% chance of success, the equity holders' expected payoff is $150,000.

TABLE 16.3	Outcomes for Baxter's Debt and Equity Under Each Strategy ($ thousand)			
	Old Strategy	New Risky Strategy		
		Success	Failure	Expected
Value of assets	**900**	1300	300	**800**
Debt	**900**	1000	300	**650**
Equity	**0**	300	0	**150**

Clearly, equity holders gain from this strategy, even though it has a negative expected payoff. Who loses? The debt holders: If the strategy fails, they bear the loss. As shown in Table 16.3, if the project succeeds, debt holders are fully repaid and receive $1 million. If the project fails, they receive only $300,000. Overall, the debt holders' expected payoff is $650,000, a loss of $250,000 relative to the $900,000 they would have received under the old strategy. This loss corresponds to the $100,000 expected loss of the risky strategy and the $150,000 gain of the equity holders. Effectively, the equity holders are gambling with the debt holders' money.

This example illustrates a general point: *When a firm faces financial distress, shareholders can gain by making sufficiently risky investments, even if they have negative NPV.*[17] This result leads to an **over-investment problem**: Shareholders have an incentive to invest in risky negative-NPV projects. But a negative-NPV project destroys value for the firm overall. Anticipating this bad behavior, security holders will pay less for the firm initially. This cost is likely to be highest for firms that can easily increase the risk of their investments.

Under-investment

Suppose Baxter does not pursue the risky strategy. Instead, the firm's managers consider an attractive investment opportunity that requires an initial investment of $100,000 and will generate a risk-free return of 50%. That is, it has the following cash flows (in thousands of dollars):

17. This problem is also referred to as *asset substitution:* After issuing debt, equity holders have an incentive to substitute risky investments for safe ones. See Michael Jensen and William Meckling, "Theory of the Firm: Managerial Behavior, Agency Costs and Ownership Structure," *Journal of Financial Economics* 3 (1976): 305–360.

If the current risk-free rate is 5%, this investment clearly has a positive NPV. The only problem is that Baxter does not have the cash on hand to make the investment.

Could Baxter raise the $100,000 by issuing new equity? Unfortunately, it cannot. Suppose equity holders were to contribute the $100,000 in new capital required. Their payoff at the end of the year is shown in Table 16.4.

TABLE 16.4	Outcomes for Baxter's Debt and Equity with and without the New Project ($ thousand)	
	Without New Project	**With New Project**
Existing assets	900	900
New project		150
Total firm value	900	1050
Debt	900	1000
Equity	0	50

Thus, if equity holders contribute $100,000 to fund the project, they get back only $50,000. The other $100,000 from the project goes to the debt holders, whose payoff increases from $900,000 to $1 million. Because the debt holders receive most of the benefit, this project is a negative-NPV investment opportunity for equity holders, even though it offers a positive NPV for the firm.

This example illustrates another general point: *When a firm faces financial distress, it may choose not to finance new, positive-NPV projects.*[18] In this case, there is an **under-investment problem**: Shareholders choose to not invest in a positive-NPV project. This failure to invest is costly for debt holders and for the overall value of the firm, because it is giving up the NPV of the missed opportunities. The cost is highest for firms that are likely to have profitable future growth opportunities requiring large investments.

Cashing Out

When a firm faces financial distress, shareholders have an incentive not to invest and to withdraw money from the firm if possible. As an example, suppose Baxter has equipment it can sell for $25,000 at the beginning of the year. It will need this equipment to continue normal operations during the year; without it, Baxter will have to shut down some operations and the firm will be worth only $800,000 at year-end. Although selling the equipment reduces the value of the firm by $100,000, if it is likely that Baxter will default at year-end, this cost would be borne by the debt holders. So, equity holders gain if Baxter sells the equipment and uses the $25,000 to pay an immediate cash dividend. This incentive to liquidate assets at prices below their actual value is another form of under-investment that occurs when a firm faces financial distress.

Agency Costs and the Value of Leverage

These examples illustrate how leverage can encourage managers and shareholders to act in ways that reduce firm value. In each case, the equity holders benefit at the expense of the debt holders. But, as with financial distress costs, it is the shareholders of the firm who

---

18. This cost of debt, also referred to as *debt overhang*, was formalized by Stewart Myers, "Determinants of Corporate Borrowing," *Journal of Financial Economics* 5 (1977): 147–175.

ultimately bear these agency costs. When a firm initially chooses to add leverage to its capital structure, the decision has two effects on the share price. First, the share price benefits from equity holders' ability to exploit debt holders in times of distress. Second, the debt holders recognize this possibility and pay less for the debt when it is issued, reducing the amount the firm can distribute to shareholders. Because debt holders lose more than shareholders gain from these activities, the net effect is a reduction in the initial share price of the firm. The amount of this reduction will correspond to the negative NPV of the decisions.

These agency costs of debt can arise only if there is some chance the firm will default and impose losses on its debt holders. The magnitude of the agency costs increases with the risk, and therefore the amount, of the firm's debt. Agency costs, therefore, represent another cost of increasing the firm's leverage that will affect the firm's optimal capital structure choice.

EXAMPLE 16.5

Agency Costs and the Amount of Leverage

Problem
Would the agency costs described previously arise if Baxter had less leverage and owed $400,000 rather than $1 million?

Solution
If Baxter makes no new investments or changes to its strategy, the firm will be worth $900,000. Thus the firm will remain solvent and its equity will be worth $900,000 − $400,000 = $500,000.

If Baxter takes the risky strategy, its assets will be worth either $1.3 million or $300,000, so equity holders will receive $900,000 or $0. In this case, the equity holders' expected payoff with the risky project is only $450,000. Thus equity holders will reject the risky strategy.

What about under-investment? If Baxter raises $100,000 from equity holders to fund a new investment that increases the value of assets by $150,000, the equity will be worth

$$\$900,000 + \$150,000 - \$400,000 = \$650,000$$

This is a gain of $150,000 over the $500,000 equity holders would receive without the investment. Because their payoff has gone up by $150,000 for a $100,000 investment, they will be willing to invest in the new project.

Similarly, Baxter has no incentive to cash out and sell equipment to pay a dividend. If the firm pays the dividend, equity holders receive $25,000 today. But their future payoff declines to $800,000 − $400,000 = $400,000. Thus they give up $100,000 in one year for a $25,000 gain today. For any reasonable discount rate, this is a bad deal and stockholders will reject the dividend.

Debt Maturity and Covenants

Several things can be done to mitigate the agency costs of debt. First, note that the magnitude of agency costs likely depends on the maturity of debt. With long-term debt, equity holders have more opportunities to profit at the debt holders' expense before the debt matures. Thus agency costs are smallest for short-term debt.[19] For example, if Baxter's debt were due today, the firm would be forced to default or renegotiate with debt holders

---

19. See Shane Johnson, "Debt Maturity and the Effects of Growth Opportunities and Liquidity on Leverage," *Review of Financial Studies* 16 (March 2003): 209–236, for empirical evidence supporting this hypothesis.

before it could increase risk, fail to invest, or cash out. However, by relying on short-term debt the firm will be obligated to repay or refinance its debt more frequently. Short-term debt may also increase the firm's risk of financial distress and its associated costs.

Second, as a condition of making a loan, creditors often place restrictions on the actions that the firm can take. Such restrictions are referred to as **debt covenants**. Covenants may limit the firm's ability to pay large dividends or the types of investments that the firm can make. These covenants are often designed to prevent management from exploiting debt holders, so they may help to reduce agency costs. Conversely, because covenants hinder management flexibility, they have the potential to get in the way of positive NPV opportunities and so can have costs of their own.[20]

CONCEPT CHECK

1. What is the purpose of debt covenants in a bond contract?

2. Why would debt holders desire covenants that restrict the firm's ability to pay dividends, and why might shareholders also benefit from this restriction?

16.6 Motivating Managers: The Agency Benefits of Leverage

In Section 16.5, we took the view that managers act in the interests of the firm's equity holders, and we considered the potential conflicts of interest between debt holders and equity holders when a firm has leverage. Of course, managers also have their own personal interests, which may differ from those of both equity holders and debt holders. Although managers often do own shares of the firm, in most large corporations they own only a very small fraction of the outstanding shares. And while the shareholders, through the board of directors, have the power to fire managers, they rarely do so unless the firm's performance is exceptionally poor.[21]

This separation of ownership and control creates the possibility of **management entrenchment**; facing little threat of being fired and replaced, managers are free to run the firm in their own best interests. As a result, managers may make decisions that benefit themselves at investors' expense. In this section, we consider how leverage can provide incentives for managers to run the firm more efficiently and effectively. The benefits we describe in this section, in addition to the tax benefits of leverage, give the firm an incentive to use debt rather than equity financing.

Concentration of Ownership

One advantage of using leverage is that it allows the original owners of the firm to maintain their equity stake. As major shareholders, they will have a strong interest in doing what is best for the firm. Next we consider an example of such a situation.

Ross Jackson is the owner of a successful furniture store. He plans to expand by opening several new stores. Ross can either borrow the funds needed for expansion or raise the money by selling shares in the firm. If he issues equity, he will need to sell 40% of the firm to raise the necessary funds.

---

20. For an analysis of the costs and benefits of bond covenants, see C. W. Smith and J. B. Warner, "On Financial Contracting: An Analysis of Bond Covenants," *Journal of Financial Economics* (June 1979): 117–161.

21. See, for example, Jerold Warner, Ross Watts, and Karen Wruck, "Stock Prices and Top Management Changes," *Journal of Financial Economics* 20 (1988): 461–492.

If Ross uses debt, he retains ownership of 100% of the firm's equity. As long as the firm does not default, any decision Ross makes that increases the value of the firm by $1 increases the value of his own stake by $1. But if Ross issues equity, he retains only 60% of the equity. Thus Ross gains only $0.60 for every $1 increase in firm value.

The difference in Ross's ownership stake changes his incentives in running the firm. Suppose the value of the firm depends largely on Ross's personal effort. Ross is then likely to work harder, and the firm will be worth more, if he receives 100% of the gains rather than only 60%.

Another effect of issuing equity is Ross's temptation to enjoy corporate perks, such as a large office with fancy artwork, a corporate limo and driver, a corporate jet, or a large expense account. With leverage, Ross is the sole owner and will bear the full cost of these perks. But with equity, Ross bears only 60% of the cost; the other 40% will be paid for by the new equity holders. Thus, with equity financing, it is more likely that Ross will overspend on these luxuries.

The costs of reduced effort and excessive spending on perks are another form of agency cost. These agency costs arise in this case due to the dilution of ownership that occurs when equity financing is used. Who pays these agency costs? As always, if securities are fairly priced, the original owners of the firm pay the cost. In our example, Ross will find that if he chooses to issue equity, the new investors will discount the price they will pay to reflect Ross's lower effort and increased spending on perks. In this case, using leverage can benefit the firm by preserving ownership concentration and avoiding these agency costs.[22]

Reduction of Wasteful Investment

While ownership is often concentrated for small, young firms, ownership typically becomes diluted over time as a firm grows. First, the original owners of the firm may retire, and the new managers likely will not hold a large ownership stake. Second, firms often need to raise more capital for investment than can be sustained using debt alone (recall the discussion of debt capacity and growth in Chapter 15). Third, owners will often choose to sell off their stakes and invest in a well-diversified portfolio to reduce risk.[23] As a result, for large U.S. firms, most CEOs own less than 1% of their firms' shares.

With such low ownership stakes, the potential for conflict of interest between managers and equity holders is high. Appropriate monitoring and standards of accountability are required to prevent abuse. While most successful firms have implemented appropriate mechanisms to protect shareholders, each year scandals are revealed in which managers have acted against shareholders' interests.

While overspending on personal perks may be a problem for large firms, these costs are likely to be small relative to the overall value of the firm. A more serious concern for large corporations is that managers may make large, unprofitable investments: Bad investment

---

22. This potential benefit of leverage is discussed by Michael Jensen and William Meckling, "Theory of the Firm: Managerial Behavior, Agency Costs and Ownership Structure," *Journal of Financial Economics* 3 (1976): 305–360. Note also that because managers who own a large block of shares are more difficult to replace, increased ownership concentration may also lead to increased entrenchment and reduce incentives; see Randall Morck, Andrei Shleifer, and Robert W. Vishny, "Management Ownership and Market Valuation," *Journal of Financial Economics* 20 (1988): 293–315.

23. According to a recent study, original owners tend to reduce their stake by more than 50% within nine years after the firm becomes a public company (Branko Urošević, "Essays in Optimal Dynamic Risk Sharing in Equity and Debt Markets," Ph.D. thesis, 2002, University of California, Berkeley).

Excessive Perks and Corporate Scandals

While most CEOs and managers exercise proper restraint when spending shareholders' money, there have been some highly publicized exceptions in the corporate scandals that have come to light.

Former Enron CFO Andrew Fastow reportedly used complicated financial transactions to enrich himself with at least $30 million of shareholder money. Tyco Corporation's ex-CEO Dennis Kozlowski will be remembered for his $6000 shower curtain, $6300 sewing basket, and $17 million Fifth Avenue condo, all paid for with Tyco funds. In total, he and former CFO Mark Swartz were convicted of pilfering $600 million from company coffers.* Former WorldCom CEO Bernie Ebbers, who was convicted for his role in the firm's $11 billion accounting scandal, borrowed more than $400 million from the company at favorable terms from late 2000 to early 2002. Among other things, he used the money from these loans to give gifts to friends and family, as well as build a house.† John Rigas and his son Timothy, former CEO and CFO of Adelphia Communications, were convicted of stealing $100 million from the firm as well as hiding $2 billion in corporate debt.

But these are certainly exceptional cases. And they were not, in and of themselves, the cause of the firms' downfalls, but rather a symptom of a broader problem of a lack of oversight and accountability within these firms, together with an opportunistic attitude of the managers involved.

*Melanie Warner, "Exorcism at Tyco," *Fortune Magazine,* April 28, 2003, p. 106.

†Andrew Backover, "Report Slams Culture at WorldCom," *USA Today,* November 5, 2002, p. 1B.

---

decisions have destroyed many otherwise successful firms. But what would motivate managers to make negative-NPV investments?

Some financial economists explain a manager's willingness to engage in negative-NPV investments as *empire building*. According to this view, managers prefer to run large firms rather than small ones, so they will take on investments that increase the size—rather than the profitability—of the firm. One potential reason for this preference is that managers of large firms tend to earn higher salaries, and they may also have more prestige and garner greater publicity than managers of small firms. As a result, managers may expand (or fail to shut down) unprofitable divisions, pay too much for acquisitions, make unnecessary capital expenditures, or hire unnecessary employees.

Another reason that managers may over-invest is that they are overconfident. Even when managers attempt to act in shareholders' interests, they may make mistakes. Managers tend to be bullish on the firm's prospects and so may believe that new opportunities are better than they actually are. They may also become committed to investments the firm has already made and continue to invest in projects that should be cancelled.[24]

For managers to engage in wasteful investment, they must have the cash to invest. This observation is the basis of the **free cash flow hypothesis**, the view that wasteful spending is more likely to occur when firms have high levels of cash flow in excess of what is needed to make all positive-NPV investments and payments to debt holders.[25] Only

---

24. For evidence of the relationship between CEO overconfidence and investment distortions, see Ulrike Malmendier and Geoffrey Tate, "CEO Overconfidence and Corporate Investment," *Journal of Finance* 60 (2005): 2661–2700. See also J. B. Heaton "Managerial Optimism and Corporate Finance," *Financial Management* 31 (2002): 33–45; and Richard Roll, "The Hubris Hypothesis of Corporate Takeovers," *Journal of Business* 59 (1986): 197–216.

25. The hypothesis that excess cash flow induces empire building was put forth by M. Jensen, "Agency Costs of Free Cash Flow, Corporate Finance, and Takeovers," *American Economic Review* 76 (1986): 323–329.

when cash is tight will managers be motivated to run the firm as efficiently as possible. According to this hypothesis, leverage increases firm value because it commits the firm to making future interest payments, thereby reducing excess cash flows and wasteful investment by managers.[26]

A related idea is that leverage can reduce the degree of managerial entrenchment because managers are more likely to be fired when a firm faces financial distress. Managers who are less entrenched may be more concerned about their performance and less likely to engage in wasteful investment. In addition, when the firm is highly levered, creditors themselves will closely monitor the actions of managers, providing an additional layer of management oversight.[27]

Leverage and Commitment

Leverage may also tie managers' hands and commit them to pursue strategies with greater vigor than they would without the threat of financial distress. For example, when American Airlines was in labor negotiations with its unions in April 2003, the firm was able to win wage concessions by explaining that higher costs would push it into bankruptcy. (A similar situation enabled Delta Airlines to persuade its pilots to accept a 33% wage cut in November 2004.) Without the threat of financial distress, American's managers might not have reached agreement with the union as quickly or achieved the same wage concessions.[28]

A firm with greater leverage may also become a fiercer competitor and act more aggressively in protecting its markets because it cannot risk the possibility of bankruptcy. This commitment to aggressive behavior can scare off potential rivals. (This argument could work in reverse: A firm weakened by too much leverage might become so financially fragile that it crumbles in the face of competition, allowing other firms to erode its markets.)[29]

CONCEPT CHECK

1. In what ways might managers benefit by overspending on acquisitions?

2. How might shareholders use the firm's capital structure to prevent this problem?

---

26. Of course, if the firm did not generate sufficient free cash flow, managers could also raise new capital for wasteful investment. But new investors would be reluctant to contribute to such an endeavor and would offer unfavorable terms. In addition, raising external funds would likely attract greater scrutiny and public criticism regarding the investment.

27. See for example M. Harris and A. Raviv, "Capital Structure and the Informational Role of Debt," *Journal of Finance* 45 2 (1990): 321–349.

28. See E. C. Perotti and K. E. Spier, "Capital Structure as a Bargaining Tool: The Role of Leverage in Contract Renegotiation," *American Economic Review* (December 1993): 1131–1141. Debt can also affect a firm's bargaining power with its suppliers; see S. Dasgupta and K. Sengupta, "Sunk Investment, Bargaining and Choice of Capital Structure," *International Economic Review* (February 1993): 203–220; and O. H. Sarig, "The Effect of Leverage on Bargaining with a Corporation," *Financial Review* 33 (February 1998): 1–16. Debt may also enhance a target's bargaining power in a control contest; see M. Harris and A. Raviv, "Corporate Control Contests and Capital Structure," *Journal of Financial Economics* (March 1988): 55–86; and R. Israel, "Capital Structure and the Market for Corporate Control: The Defensive Role of Debt Financing," *Journal of Finance* (September 1991): 1391–1409.

29. This idea was formalized by James Brander and Tracy Lewis, "Oligopoly and Financial Structure: The Limited Liability Effect," *American Economic Review* 76 (1986): 956–970. In an empirical study, Judy Chevalier finds that leverage reduces the competitiveness of supermarket firms ["Capital Structure and Product-Market Competition: Empirical Evidence from the Supermarket Industry," *American Economic Review* 85 (1995): 415–435]. Patric Bolton and David Scharfstein discuss the effects of not having deep pockets in "A Theory of Predation Based on Agency Problems in Financial Contracting," *American Economic Review* 80 (1990): 93–106.

16.7 Agency Costs and the Tradeoff Theory

We can now adjust Eq. 16.1 for the value of the firm to include the costs and benefits of the incentives that arise when the firm has leverage. This more complete equation is shown below:

$$V^L = V^U + PV(\text{Interest Tax Shield}) - PV(\text{Financial Distress Costs})$$
$$- PV(\text{Agency Costs of Debt}) + PV(\text{Agency Benefits of Debt}) \quad (16.2)$$

The net effect of the costs and benefits of leverage on the value of a firm is illustrated in Figure 16.2. With no debt, the value of the firm is V^U. As the debt level increases, the firm benefits from the interest tax shield (which has present value $\tau^* D$). The firm also benefits from improved incentives for management, which reduce wasteful investment and perks. If the debt level is too large, however, firm value is reduced due to the loss of tax benefits (when interest exceeds EBIT), financial distress costs, and the agency costs of leverage. The optimal level of debt, D^*, balances the costs and benefits of leverage.

The Optimal Debt Level

It is important to note that the relative magnitudes of the different costs and benefits of debt vary with the characteristics of the firm. Likewise, the optimal level of debt varies. As an example, let's contrast the optimal capital structure choice for two types of firms.

R&D-Intensive Firms.   Firms with high R&D costs and future growth opportunities typically maintain low debt levels. These firms tend to have low current free cash flows, so they need little debt to provide a tax shield or to control managerial spending. In addition, they tend to have high human capital, so there will be large costs as a result of financial

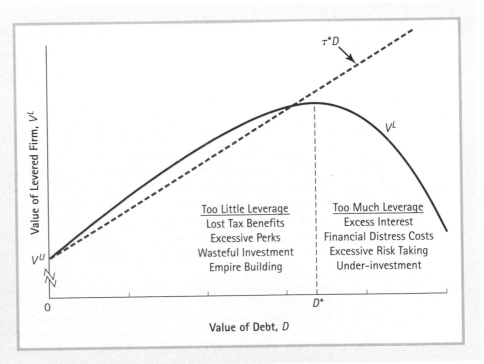

FIGURE 16.2

Optimal Leverage with Taxes, Financial Distress, and Agency Costs

As the level of debt, *D*, increases, the value of the firm increases from the interest tax shield as well as improvements in managerial incentives. If leverage is too high, however, the present value of financial distress costs, as well as the agency costs from debt holder–equity holder conflicts, dominates and reduces firm value. The optimal level of debt, *D**, balances these benefits and costs of leverage.

distress. Also, these firms may find it easy to increase the risk of their business strategy (by pursuing a riskier technology) and often need to raise additional capital to fund new investment opportunities. Thus their agency costs of debt are also high. Biotechnology and technology firms often maintain less than 10% leverage.

Low-Growth, Mature Firms. Mature, low-growth firms with stable cash flows and tangible assets often fall into the high-debt category. These firms tend to have high free cash flows with few good investment opportunities. Thus the tax shield and incentive benefits of leverage are likely to be high. With tangible assets, the financial distress costs of leverage are likely to be low, as the assets can be liquidated for close to their full value. Examples of low-growth industries in which firms typically maintain greater than 20% leverage include real estate, utilities, and supermarket chains.

Debt Levels in Practice

The tradeoff theory explains how firms *should* choose their capital structures to maximize value to current shareholders. However, these results need not coincide with what firms actually *do* in practice. Keep in mind that, like investment decisions, capital structure decisions are made by managers who have their own incentives. Proponents of the **management entrenchment theory** of capital structure believe that managers choose a capital structure to avoid the discipline of debt and maintain their own job security. Thus managers seek to *minimize* leverage to prevent the job loss that would accompany financial distress. Managers are constrained from using too little debt, however, to keep shareholders happy. If managers sacrifice too much firm value, disgruntled shareholders may try to replace them or sell the firm to an acquirer. Under this hypothesis, firms will have leverage that is less than the optimal level D^* in Figure 16.2, and increase it toward D^* only in response to a takeover threat or the threat of shareholder activism.[30]

CONCEPT CHECK
1. Describe how the management entrenchment can affect the value of the firm.

2. Coca-Cola Enterprises is almost 50% debt financed, while Amgen, a biotechnology firm, is less than 10% debt financed. Why might these firms choose such different capital structures?

16.8 Asymmetric Information and Capital Structure

Throughout this chapter, we have assumed that managers, stockholders, and creditors have the same information. We have also assumed that securities are fairly priced: The firm's shares and debt are priced according to their true underlying value. These assumptions may not always be accurate in practice. Managers' information about the firm and its future cash flows is likely to be superior to that of outside investors—there is **asymmetric information** between managers and investors. In this section, we consider how asymmetric information may motivate managers to alter a firm's capital structure.

---

30. See Jeffrey Zwiebel, "Dynamic Capital Structure Under Managerial Entrenchment," *American Economic Review* 86 (1996): 1197–1215; Luigi Zingales and Walter Novaes, "Capital Structure Choice When Managers are in Control: Entrenchment versus Efficiency," *Journal of Business* 76 (2002): 49–82; and Erwan Morellec, "Can Managerial Discretion Explain Observed Leverage Ratios," *Review of Financial Studies* 17 (2004): 257–294; Jonathan Berk, Richard Stanton, and Josef Zechner, "Human Capital, Bankruptcy and Capital Structure," working paper, 2006.

Leverage as a Credible Signal

Consider the plight of Kim Smith, CEO of Beltran International, who believes her company's stock is undervalued. Market analysts and investors are concerned that several of Beltran's key patents will expire soon, and that new competition will force Beltran to cut prices or lose customers. Smith believes that new product innovations and soon-to-be-introduced manufacturing improvements will keep Beltran ahead of its competitors and enable it to sustain its current profitability well into the future. She seeks to convince investors of Beltran's promising future and to increase Beltran's current stock price.

One potential strategy is to launch an investor relations campaign. Smith can issue press releases, describing the merits of the new innovations and the manufacturing improvements. But Smith knows that investors may be skeptical of these press releases if their claims cannot be verified. After all, managers, much like politicians, have an incentive to sound optimistic and confident about what they can achieve.

Because investors expect her to be biased, to convince the market Smith must take actions that give credible signals of her knowledge of the firm. That is, she must take actions that the market understands she would be unwilling to do unless her statements were true. This idea is more general than manager–investor communication; it is at the heart of much human interaction. We call it the **credibility principle**:

Claims in one's self-interest are credible only if they are supported by actions that would be too costly to take if the claims were untrue.

This principle is the essence behind the adage, "Actions speak louder than words."

One way a firm can credibly convey its strength to investors is by making statements about its future prospects that investors and analysts can ultimately verify. Because the penalties for intentionally deceiving investors are large,[31] investors will generally believe such statements.

For example, suppose Smith announces that pending long-term contracts from the U.S., British, and Japanese governments will increase revenues for Beltran by 30% next year. Because this statement can be verified after the fact, it would be costly to make it if untrue. For deliberate misrepresentation, the U.S. Securities and Exchange Commission (SEC) would likely fine the firm and file charges against Smith. The firm could also be sued by its investors. These large costs would likely outweigh any potential benefits to Smith and Beltran for temporarily misleading investors and boosting the share price. Thus investors will likely view the announcement as credible.

But what if Beltran cannot yet reveal specific details regarding its future prospects? Perhaps the contracts for the government orders have not yet been signed or cannot be disclosed for other reasons. How can Smith credibly communicate her positive information regarding the firm?

One strategy is to commit the firm to large future debt payments. If Smith is right, then Beltran will have no trouble making the debt payments. But if Smith is making false claims and the firm does not grow, Beltran will have trouble paying its creditors and will experience financial distress. This distress will be costly for the firm and also for Smith, who will likely lose her job. Thus Smith can use leverage as a way to convince investors that she does have information that the firm will grow, even if she cannot provide verifiable details about the sources of growth. Investors know that Beltran would be at risk of

---

31. The Sarbanes-Oxley Act of 2002 increased the penalties for securities fraud to include up to ten years of imprisonment.

defaulting without growth opportunities, so they will interpret the additional leverage as a credible signal of the CEO's confidence. The use of leverage as a way to signal good information to investors is known as the **signaling theory of debt**.[32]

EXAMPLE 16.6

Debt Signals Strength

Problem

Suppose that Beltran currently uses all-equity financing, and that Beltran's market value in one year's time will be either $100 million or $50 million depending on the success of the new strategy. Currently, investors view the outcomes as equally likely, but Smith has information that success is virtually certain. Will leverage of $25 million make Smith's claims credible? How about leverage of $55 million?

Solution

If leverage is substantially less than $50 million, Beltran will have no risk of financial distress regardless of the outcome. As a result, there is no cost of leverage even if Smith does not have positive information. Thus leverage of $25 million would not be a credible signal of strength to investors.

However, leverage of $55 million is likely to be a credible signal. If Smith has no positive information, there is a significant chance that Beltran will face bankruptcy under this burden of debt. Thus Smith would be unlikely to agree to this amount of leverage unless she is certain about the firm's prospects.

Issuing Equity and Adverse Selection

Suppose a used-car dealer tells you he is willing to sell you a nice-looking sports car for $5000 less than its typical price. Rather than feel lucky, perhaps your first reaction should be one of skepticism: If the dealer is willing to sell it for such a low price, there must be something wrong with the car—it is probably a "lemon."

The idea that buyers will be skeptical of a seller's motivation for selling was formalized by George Akerlof.[33] Akerlof showed that if the seller has private information about the quality of the car, then his *desire to sell* reveals the car is probably of low quality. Buyers are therefore reluctant to buy except at heavily discounted prices. Owners of high-quality cars are reluctant to sell because they know buyers will think they are selling a lemon and offer only a low price. Consequently, the quality and prices of cars sold in the used-car market are both low. This result is referred to as **adverse selection**: The selection of cars sold in the used-car market is worse than average.

Adverse selection extends beyond the used-car market. In fact, it applies in any setting in which the seller has more information than the buyer. Adverse selection leads to the **lemons principle**:

When a seller has private information about the value of a good, buyers will discount the price they are willing to pay due to adverse selection.

---

32. Such a theory is developed by Stephen Ross, "The Determination of Financial Structure: The Incentive-Signalling Approach," *Bell Journal of Economics* 8 (1977): 23–40.

33. "The Market for Lemons: Quality, Uncertainty, and the Market Mechanism," *Quarterly Journal of Economics* 84 (1970): 488–500.

Nobel Prize   The 2001 Nobel Prize in Economics

In 2001, George Akerlof, Michael Spence, and Joseph Stiglitz jointly received the Nobel Prize in economics for their analyses of markets with asymmetric information and adverse selection. In this chapter, we discuss the implications of their theory for firm capital structure. This theory, however, has much broader applications. As described on the Nobel Prize Web site (www.nobelprize.org):

Many markets are characterized by asymmetric information: Actors on one side of the market have much better information than those on the other. Borrowers know more *than lenders about their repayment prospects, managers and boards know more than shareholders about the firm's profitability, and prospective clients know more than insurance companies about their accident risk. During the 1970s, this year's Laureates laid the foundation for a general theory of markets with asymmetric information. Applications have been abundant, ranging from traditional agricultural markets to modern financial markets. The Laureates' contributions form the core of modern information economics.*

© The Nobel Foundation

We can apply this principle to the market for equity.[34] Suppose the owner of a start-up company tells you that his firm is a wonderful investment opportunity—and then offers to sell you 70% of his stake in the firm. He states that he is selling *only* because he wants to diversify. Although you appreciate this desire, you also suspect the owner may be eager to sell such a large stake because he has negative information about the firm's future prospects. That is, he may be trying to cash out before the bad news becomes known.[35]

As with the used-car dealer, a firm owner's desire to sell equity may lead you to question how good an investment opportunity it really is. Based on the lemons principle, you therefore reduce the price you are willing to pay. This discount of the price due to adverse selection is a potential cost of issuing equity, and it may make owners with good information refrain from issuing equity.

EXAMPLE 16.7

Adverse Selection in Equity Markets

Problem
Zycor stock is worth either $100 per share, $80 per share, or $60 per share. Investors believe each case is equally likely, and the current share price is equal to the average value of $80.

Suppose the CEO of Zycor announces he will sell most of his holdings of the stock to diversify. Diversifying is worth 10% of the share price—that is, the CEO would be willing to receive 10% less than the shares are worth to achieve the benefits of diversification. If investors believe the CEO knows the true value, how will the share price change if he tries to sell? Will the CEO sell at the new share price?

---

34. This observation is due to Hayne Leland and David Pyle, "Information Asymmetries, Financial Structure and Financial Intermediation," *Journal of Finance* 32 (1977): 371–387.

35. Again, if the owner of the firm (or the car, in the earlier example) has very specific information that can be verified ex-post, there are potential legal consequences for not revealing that information to a buyer. Generally, however, there is a great deal of subtle information the seller might have that would be impossible to verify.

Solution

If the true value of the shares were $100, the CEO would not be willing to sell at the market price of $80 per share, which would be 20% below their true value. So, if the CEO tries to sell, shareholders can conclude the shares are worth either $80 or $60. In that case, share price should fall to the average value of $70. But again, if the true value were $80, the CEO would be willing to sell for $72, but not $70 per share. So, if he still tries to sell, investors will know the true value is $60 per share. Thus the CEO will sell only if the true value is the lowest possible price, $60 per share. If the CEO knows the firm's stock is worth $100 or $80 per share, he will not sell.

In explaining adverse selection, we considered an owner of a firm selling his or her *own* shares. What if a manager of the firm decides to sell securities on the *firm's* behalf? If the securities are sold at a price below their true value, the buyer's windfall represents a cost for the firm's current shareholders. Acting on behalf of the current shareholders, the manager may be unwilling to sell.[36]

Let's consider a simple example. Gentec is a biotech firm with no debt, and its 20 million shares are currently trading at $10 per share, for a total market value of $200 million. Based on the prospects for one of Gentec's new drugs, management believes the true value of the company is $300 million, or $15 per share. Management believes the share price will reflect this higher value after the clinical trials for the drug are concluded next year.

Gentec has already announced plans to raise $60 million from investors to build a new research lab. It can raise the funds today by issuing 6 million new shares at the current price of $10 per share. In that case, after the good news comes out, the value of the firm's assets will be $300 million (from the existing assets) plus $60 million (new lab), for a total value of $360 million. With 26 million shares outstanding, the new share price will be $360 million ÷ 26 million shares = $13.85 per share.

But suppose Gentec waits for the good news to come out and the share price to rise to $15 *before* issuing the new shares. At that time, the firm will be able to raise the $60 million by selling 4 million shares. The firm's assets will again be worth a total of $360 million, but Gentec will have only 24 million shares outstanding, which is consistent with the share price of $360 million ÷ 24 million shares = $15 per share.

Thus issuing new shares when management knows they are underpriced is costly for the original shareholders. Their shares will be worth only $13.85 rather than $15. As a result, if Gentec's managers care primarily about the firm's current shareholders, they will be reluctant to sell securities at a price that is below their true value. If they believe the shares are underpriced, managers will prefer to wait until after the share price rises to issue equity.

This preference not to issue equity that is underpriced leads us to the same lemons problem we had before: Managers who know securities have a high value will not sell, and those who know they have a low value will sell. Due to this adverse selection, investors will be willing to pay only a low price for the securities. The lemons problem creates a

---

36. Stewart Myers and Nicholas Majluf demonstrated this result, and a number of its implications for capital structure, in an influential paper, "Corporate Financing and Investment Decisions When Firms Have Information that Investors Do Not Have," *Journal of Financial Economics* 13 (1984): 187–221.

cost for firms that need to raise capital from investors to fund new investments. If they try to issue equity, investors will discount the price they are willing to pay to reflect the possibility that managers are privy to bad news.

Implications for Equity Issuance

Adverse selection has a number of important implications for equity issuance. First and foremost, the lemons principle directly implies that

1. *The stock price declines on the announcement of an equity issue.*

When a firm issues equity, it signals to investors that its equity may be overpriced. As a result, investors are willing to pay less for the equity and the stock price declines. Numerous studies have confirmed this result, finding that the stock price falls about 3% on average on the announcement of an equity issue by a publicly traded firm in the United States.[37]

As was true for Gentec, managers issuing equity have an incentive to delay the issue until any news that might positively affect the stock price becomes public. In contrast, there is no incentive to delay the issue if managers expect negative news to come out. These incentives lead to the following pattern:

2. *The stock price tends to rise prior to the announcement of an equity issue.*

This result is also supported empirically, as illustrated in Figure 16.3 using data from a study by Deborah Lucas and Robert McDonald.[38] They found that stocks with equity issues outperformed the market by almost 50% in the year and a half prior to the announcement of the issue.

Managers may also try to avoid the price decline associated with adverse selection by issuing equity at times when they have the smallest informational advantage over investors. For example, because a great deal of information is released to investors at the time of earnings announcements, equity issues are often timed to occur immediately after these announcements. That is,

3. *Firms tend to issue equity when information asymmetries are minimized, such as immediately after earnings announcements.*[39]

Implications for Capital Structure

Because managers find it costly to issue equity that is underpriced, they may seek alternative forms of financing. While debt issues may also suffer from adverse selection, because the value of low-risk debt is not very sensitive to managers' private information about the firm (but is instead determined mainly by interest rates), the degree of underpricing

---

37. See, for example, Paul Asquith and David Mullins, "Equity Issues and Offering Dilution," *Journal of Financial Economics* 15 (1986): 61–89; Ronald Masulis and Ashok Korwar, "Seasoned Equity Offerings: An Empirical Investigation," *Journal of Financial Economics* 15 (1986): 91–118; and Wayne Mikkelson and Megan Partch, "Valuation Effects of Security Offerings and the Issuance Process," *Journal of Financial Economics* 15 (1986): 31–60.

38. "Equity Issues and Stock Price Dynamics," *Journal of Finance* 45 (1990): 1019–1043.

39. In a 1991 study, Robert Korajczyk, Deborah Lucas, and Robert McDonald confirmed this timing and reported that the negative stock price reaction is smallest immediately after earnings announcements, and becomes larger as the amount of time since the last earnings announcement increases ["The Effect of Information Releases on the Pricing and Timing of Equity Issues," *Review of Financial Studies* 4 (1991): 685–708].

FIGURE 16.3

Stock Returns Before and After an Equity Issue

Stocks tend to rise (relative to the market) before an equity issue is announced. Upon announcement, stock prices fall on average. This figure shows the average return relative to the market before and after announcements using data from Deborah Lucas and Robert McDonald, "Equity Issues and Stock Price Dynamics," *Journal of Finance* 45 (1990): 1019–1043.

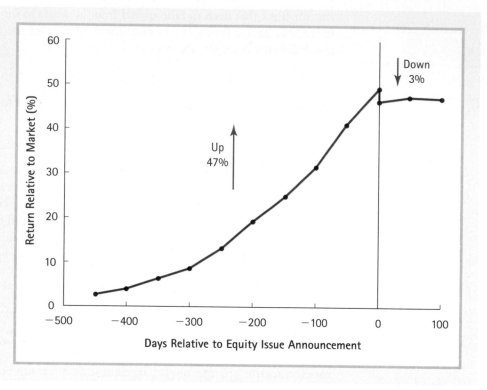

will tend to be smaller for debt than for equity. Of course, a firm can avoid underpricing altogether by financing investment using its cash (retained earnings) when possible. Thus

Managers who perceive the firm's equity is underpriced will have a preference to fund investment using retained earnings, or debt, rather than equity.

The converse to this statement is also true: Managers who perceive the firm's equity to be overpriced will prefer to issue equity, as opposed to issuing debt or using retained earnings, to fund investment. However, due to the negative stock price reaction when issuing equity, it is less likely that equity will be overpriced. In fact, absent other motives to issue equity, if both managers and investors behave rationally, the price drop upon announcement may be sufficient to deter managers from issuing equity except as a last resort.

The idea that managers will prefer to use retained earnings first, and will issue new equity only as a last resort, is often referred to as the **pecking order hypothesis**, put forth by Stewart Myers.[40] While difficult to test directly, this hypothesis is consistent with the aggregate data on corporate financing in Figure 16.4, which shows that firms tend to be net repurchasers (rather than issuers) of equity, whereas they are issuers of debt. Moreover, the vast majority of investment is funded by retained earnings, with net external financing amounting to less than 30% of capital expenditures in most years. These observations can also be consistent with the tradeoff theory of capital structure, however, and there is substantial evidence that firms do not follow a *strict* pecking order, as firms often issue equity even when borrowing is possible.[41]

---

40. Stewart Myers, "The Capital Structure Puzzle," *Journal of Finance* 39 (1984): 575–592.

41. See, for example, Mark Leary and Michael Roberts, "Financial Slack and Tests of the Pecking Order's Financing Hierarchy," working paper, University of Pennsylvania, 2004.

FIGURE 16.4

Aggregate Sources of Funding for Capital Expenditures, U.S. Corporations

In aggregate, firms tend to repurchase equity and issue debt. But more than 70% of capital expenditures are funded from retained earnings.

Source: Federal Reserve Flow of Funds.

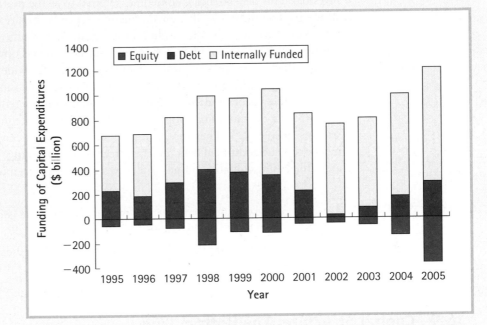

E X A M P L E
16.8

The Pecking Order of Financing Alternatives

Problem

Axon Industries needs to raise $10 million for a new investment project. If the firm issues one-year debt, it may have to pay an interest rate of 7%, although Axon's managers believe that 6% would be a fair rate given the level of risk. However, if the firm issues equity, they believe the equity may be underpriced by 5%. What is the cost to current shareholders of financing the project out of retained earnings, debt, and equity?

Solution

If the firm spends $10 million out of retained earnings, rather than paying that money out to shareholders as a dividend, the cost to shareholders is $10 million. Using debt costs the firm $10 × (1.07) = $10.7 million in one year, which has a present value based on management's view of the firm's risk of $10.7 ÷ (1.06) = $10.094 million. Finally, if equity is underpriced by 5%, then to raise $10 million the firm will need to issue $10.5 million in new equity. Thus, the cost to existing shareholders will be $10.5 million. Comparing the three, retained earnings are the cheapest source of funds, followed by debt, and finally by equity.

Aside from a general preference for using retained earnings or debt as a source of funding rather than equity, adverse selection costs do not lead to a clear prediction regarding a firm's overall capital structure. Instead, these costs imply that managers' choice of financing will depend, in addition to the other costs and benefits discussed in this chapter, on whether they believe the firm is currently underpriced or overpriced by investors. This dependence is sometimes referred to as the **market timing** view of capital structure: The firm's overall capital structure depends in part on the market conditions that existed when it sought funding in the past. As a result, similar firms in the same industry might end up with very different, but nonetheless optimal, capital structures.[42]

Indeed, even the pecking order hypothesis does not provide a clear prediction regarding capital structure on its own. While it argues that firms should prefer to use retained earnings, then debt, and then equity as funding sources, retained earnings are merely another form of equity financing (they increase the value of equity while the value of debt remains unchanged). Therefore, firms might have low leverage either because they are unable to issue additional debt and are forced to rely on equity financing or because they are sufficiently profitable to finance all investment using retained earnings.

CONCEPT CHECK

1. How does asymmetric information explain the negative stock price reaction to the announcement of an equity issue?

2. Why might firms prefer to fund investments using retained earnings or debt rather than issuing equity?

16.9 Capital Structure: The Bottom Line

Over the past three chapters, we have examined a number of factors that might influence a firm's choice of capital structure. What is the bottom line for a financial manager?

The most important insight regarding capital structure goes back to Modigliani and Miller: With perfect capital markets, a firm's security choice alters the risk of the firm's equity, but it does not change its value or the amount it can raise from outside investors. Thus the optimal capital structure depends on market imperfections, such as taxes, financial distress costs, agency costs, and asymmetric information.

Of all the different possible imperfections that drive capital structure, the most clear-cut, and possibly the most significant, is taxes. The interest tax shield allows firms to repay investors and avoid the corporate tax. Each dollar of permanent debt financing provides the firm with a tax shield worth τ^* dollars, where τ^* is the effective tax advantage of debt. For firms with consistent taxable income, this benefit of leverage is important to consider.

While firms should use leverage to shield their income from taxes, how much of their income should they shield? If leverage is too high, there is an increased risk that a firm may not be able to meet its debt obligations and will be forced to default. While the risk of default is not itself a problem, financial distress may lead to other consequences that reduce the value of the firm. Firms must, therefore, balance the tax benefits of debt against the costs of financial distress.

Agency costs and benefits of leverage are also important determinants of capital structure. Too much debt can motivate managers and equity holders to take excessive risks or under-invest in a firm. When free cash flows are high, too little leverage may encourage wasteful spending. This effect may be especially important for firms in countries lacking

---

42. For evidence suggestive of the idea that firms' capital structures result from past attempts to time the equity market, see Jeffrey A. Wurgler and Malcolm P. Baker, "Market Timing and Capital Structure," *Journal of Finance* 57 (2002): 1–32.

strong protections for investors against self-interested managers.[43] When agency costs are significant, short-term debt may be the most attractive form of external financing.

A firm must also consider the potential signaling and adverse selection consequences of its financing choice. Because bankruptcy is costly for managers, increasing leverage can signal managers' confidence in the firm's ability to meet its debt obligations. When managers have different views regarding the value of securities, managers can benefit current shareholders by issuing securities that are the most overpriced. However, investors will respond to this incentive by lowering the price they are willing to pay for securities that the firm issues, leading to negative price reaction when a new issue is announced. This effect is most pronounced for equity issues, because the value of equity is most sensitive to the manager's private information. To avoid this "lemons cost," firms should rely first on retained earnings, then debt, and finally equity. This pecking order of financing alternatives will be most important when managers are likely to have a great deal of private information regarding the value of the firm.

Finally, it is important to recognize that because actively changing a firm's capital structure (for example, by selling or repurchasing shares or bonds) entails transactions costs, firms may be unlikely to change their capital structures unless they depart significantly from the optimal level. As a result, most changes to a firm's debt-equity ratio are likely to occur passively, as the market value of the firm's equity fluctuates with changes in the firm's stock price.

CONCEPT CHECK

1. Consider the differences in leverage across industries shown in Figure 15.7. To what extent can you account for these differences?

2. What are some reasons firms might depart from their optimal capital structure, at least in the short run?

Summary

1. In the Modigliani-Miller setting, leverage may result in bankruptcy, but bankruptcy alone does not reduce the value of the firm. With perfect capital markets, bankruptcy shifts ownership from the equity holders to debt holders without changing the total value available to all investors.

2. U.S. firms can file for bankruptcy protection under the provisions of the 1978 Bankruptcy Reform Act.
   a. In a Chapter 7 liquidation, a trustee oversees the liquidation of the firm's assets.
   b. In a Chapter 11 reorganization, management attempts to develop a reorganization plan that will improve operations and maximize value to investors. If the firm cannot successfully reorganize, it may be liquidated under Chapter 7 bankruptcy.

3. Bankruptcy is a costly process that imposes both direct and indirect costs on a firm and its investors.
   a. Direct costs include the costs of experts and advisors such as lawyers, accountants, appraisers, and investment bankers hired by the firm or its creditors during the bankruptcy process.

43. See Joseph Fan, Sheridan Titman, and Garry Twite, "An International Comparison of Capital Structure and Debt Maturity Choices," working paper, University of Texas–Austin, 2003.

   b. Indirect costs include the loss of customers, suppliers, employees, or receivables during bankruptcy. Firms also incur indirect costs when they need to sell assets at distressed prices.

4. When securities are fairly priced, the original shareholders of a firm pay the present value of the costs associated with bankruptcy and financial distress.

5. According to the tradeoff theory, the total value of a levered firm equals the value of the firm without leverage plus the present value of the tax savings from debt minus the present value of financial distress costs:

$$V^L = V^U + PV(\text{Interest Tax Shield}) - PV(\text{Financial Distress Costs}) \qquad (16.1)$$

   Optimal leverage is the level of debt that maximizes V^L.

6. Agency costs arise when there are conflicts of interest between stakeholders. When a firm faces financial distress:

   a. Shareholders can gain by undertaking a negative-NPV project if it is sufficiently risky.

   b. A firm may be unable to finance new, positive-NPV projects.

   c. Shareholders have an incentive to liquidate assets at prices below their market values and distribute the proceeds as a dividend.

7. Leverage has agency benefits and can improve incentives for managers to run a firm more efficiently and effectively.

   a. Leverage can benefit a firm by preserving ownership concentration. Managers with higher ownership concentration are more likely to work hard and less likely to consume corporate perks.

   b. Leverage reduces the likelihood that a firm will pursue wasteful investments.

   c. The threat of financial distress may commit managers more fully to pursue strategies that improve operations.

8. The tradeoff theory may be extended to include agency costs. The value of a firm, including agency costs and benefits, is:

$$V^L = V^U + PV(\text{Interest Tax Shield}) - PV(\text{Financial Distress Costs})$$
$$- PV(\text{Agency Costs of Debt}) + PV(\text{Agency Benefits of Debt}) \qquad (16.2)$$

   Optimal leverage is the level of debt that maximizes V^L.

9. When managers have better information than investors, there is asymmetric information. Given asymmetric information, managers may use leverage as a credible signal to investors of the firm's ability to generate future free cash flow.

10. According to the lemons principle, when managers have private information about the value of a firm, investors will discount the price they are willing to pay for a new equity issue due to adverse selection.

11. Managers are more likely to sell equity when they know a firm is overvalued. As a result,

   a. The stock price declines when a firm announces an equity issue.

   b. The stock price tends to rise prior to the announcement of an equity issue because managers tend to delay equity issues until after good news becomes public.

   c. Firms tend to issue equity when information asymmetries are minimized.

   d. Managers who perceive that the firm's equity is underpriced will have a preference to fund investment using retained earnings, or debt, rather than equity. This result is called the pecking order hypothesis.

Key Terms

adverse selection *p. 514*	lemons principle *p. 514*
agency costs *p. 503*	management entrenchment *p. 507*
asymmetric information *p. 512*	management entrenchment theory *p. 512*
Chapter 7 liquidation *p. 495*	market timing *p. 520*
Chapter 11 reorganization *p. 495*	over-investment problem *p. 504*
credibility principle *p. 513*	pecking order hypothesis *p. 518*
debt covenants *p. 507*	prepackaged bankruptcy *p. 496*
default *p. 492*	signaling theory of debt *p. 514*
economic distress *p. 493*	tradeoff theory *p. 501*
financial distress *p. 491*	under-investment problem *p. 505*
free cash flow hypothesis *p. 509*	workout *p. 496*

Further Reading

For a survey of alternative theories of capital structure, see M. Harris and A. Raviv, "The Theory of Capital Structure," *Journal of Finance* 46 (1991): 197–355. For a textbook treatment, see J. Tirole, *The Theory of Corporate Finance*, Princeton University Press, 2005.

In this chapter we did not discuss how firms dynamically manage their capital structures. Although this topic is beyond the scope of this book, interested readers can consult the following papers: R. Goldstein, N. Ju, and H. Leland, "An EBIT-Based Model of Dynamic Capital Structure," *Journal of Business* 74 (2001): 483–512; O. Hart and J. Moore, "Default and Renegotiation: A Dynamic Model of Debt," *Quarterly Journal of Economics* 113(1) (1998): 1–41; C. A. Hennessy and T. M. Whited, "Debt Dynamics," *Journal of Finance* 60(3) (2005): 1129–1165; and H. Leland, "Agency Costs, Risk Management, and Capital Structure," *Journal of Finance* 53(4) (1998): 1213–1243.

For an empirical study of how firms' capital structures evolve in response to changes in their stock price, and how these dynamics relate to existing theories, see I. Welch, "Capital Structure and Stock Returns," *Journal of Political Economy* 112(1) (2004): 106–131. See also I. Strebulaev, "Do Tests of Capital Structure Theory Mean What They Say?" working paper, Stanford Universty, 2006, for an analysis of the importance of adjustment costs in interpreting firms' capital structure choices.

Readers interested in the results of empirical test of the pecking order theory can consult E. Fama and K. R. French, "Testing Tradeoff and Pecking Order Predictions About Dividends and Debt," *Review of Financial Studies* 15(1): 1–33; M. Z. Frank and V. K. Goyal, "Testing the Pecking Order Theory of Capital Structure," *Journal of Financial Economics* 67(2) (2003): 217–248; and L. Shyam-Sunder and S. C. Myers, "Testing Static Tradeoff Against Pecking Order Models of Capital Structure," *Journal of Financial Economics* 51(2) (1999): 219–244.

Problems

All problems in this chapter are available in MyFinanceLab. An asterisk (*) indicates problems with a higher level of difficulty.

Default and Bankruptcy in a Perfect Market

EXCEL   **1.** Gladstone Corporation is about to launch a new product. Depending on the success of the new product, Gladstone may have one of four values next year: $150 million, $135 million,

$95 million, and $80 million. These outcomes are all equally likely, and this risk is diversifiable. Gladstone will not make any payouts to investors during the year. Suppose the risk-free interest rate is 5% and assume perfect capital markets.

a. What is the initial value of Gladstone's equity without leverage?

Now suppose Gladstone has zero-coupon debt with a $100 million face value due next year.

b. What is the initial value of Gladstone's debt?

c. What is the yield-to-maturity of the debt? What is its expected return?

d. What is the initial value of Gladstone's equity? What is Gladstone's total value with leverage?

2. Baruk Industries has no cash and a debt obligation of $36 million that is now due. The market value of Baruk's assets is $81 million, and the firm has no other liabilities. Assume perfect capital markets.

a. Suppose Baruk has 10 million shares outstanding. What is Baruk's current share price?

b. How many new shares must Baruk issue to raise the capital needed to pay its debt obligation?

c. After repaying the debt, what will Baruk's share price be?

**The Costs of Bankruptcy
and Financial Distress**

3. When a firm defaults on its debt, debt holders often receive less than 50% of the amount they are owed. Is the difference between the amount debt holders are owed and the amount they receive a *cost* of bankruptcy?

4. Which type of firm is more likely to experience a loss of customers in the event of financial distress:

a. Campbell Soup Company or Intuit, Inc. (a maker of accounting software)?

b. Allstate Corporation (an insurance company) or Reebok International (a footwear and clothing firm)?

5. Which type of asset is more likely to be liquidated for close to its full market value in the event of financial distress:

a. An office building or a brand name?

b. Product inventory or raw materials?

c. Patent rights or engineering "know-how"?

**Financial Distress Costs
and Firm Value**

EXCEL 6. As in Problem 1, Gladstone Corporation is about to launch a new product. Depending on the success of the new product, Gladstone may have one of four values next year: $150 million, $135 million, $95 million, and $80 million. These outcomes are all equally likely, and this risk is diversifiable. Suppose the risk-free interest rate is 5% and that, in the event of default, 25% of the value of Gladstone's assets will be lost to bankruptcy costs. (Ignore all other market imperfections, such as taxes.)

a. What is the initial value of Gladstone's equity without leverage?

Now suppose Gladstone has zero-coupon debt with a $100 million face value due next year.

b. What is the initial value of Gladstone's debt?

c. What is the yield-to-maturity of the debt? What is its expected return?

d. What is the initial value of Gladstone's equity? What is Gladstone's total value with leverage?

Suppose Gladstone has 10 million shares outstanding and no debt at the start of the year.

e. If Gladstone does not issue debt, what is its share price?

f. If Gladstone issues debt of $100 million due next year and uses the proceeds to repurchase shares, what will its share price be? Why does your answer differ from that in part (e)?

7. Kohwe Corporation plans to issue equity to raise $50 million to finance a new investment. After making the investment, Kohwe expects to earn free cash flows of $10 million each year. Kohwe currently has 5 million shares outstanding, and it has no other assets or opportunities. Suppose the appropriate discount rate for Kohwe's future free cash flows is 8%, and the only capital market imperfections are corporate taxes and financial distress costs.

   a. What is the NPV of Kohwe's investment?

   b. What is Kohwe's share price today?

Suppose Kohwe borrows the $50 million instead. The firm will pay interest only on this loan each year, and it will maintain an outstanding balance of $50 million on the loan. Suppose that Kohwe's corporate tax rate is 40%, and expected free cash flows are still $10 million each year.

   c. What is Kohwe's share price today if the investment is financed with debt?

Now suppose that with leverage, Kohwe's expected free cash flows will decline to $9 million per year due to reduced sales and other financial distress costs. Assume that the appropriate discount rate for Kohwe's future free cash flows is still 8%.

   d. What is Kohwe's share price today given the financial distress costs of leverage?

Optimal Capital Structure: The Tradeoff Theory

8. Hawar International is a shipping firm with a current share price of $5.50 and 10 million shares outstanding. Suppose Hawar announces plans to lower its corporate taxes by borrowing $20 million and repurchasing shares.

   a. With perfect capital markets, what will the share price be after this announcement?

Suppose that Hawar pays a corporate tax rate of 30%, and that shareholders expect the change in debt to be permanent.

   b. If the only imperfection is corporate taxes, what will the share price be after this announcement?

   c. Suppose the only imperfections are corporate taxes and financial distress costs. If the share price rises to $5.75 after this announcement, what is the PV of financial distress costs Hawar will incur as the result of this new debt?

9. Marpor Industries has no debt and expects to generate free cash flows of $16 million each year. Marpor believes that if it permanently increases its level of debt to $40 million, the risk of financial distress may cause it to lose some customers and receive less favorable terms from its suppliers. As a result, Marpor's expected free cash flows with debt will be only $15 million per year. Suppose Marpor's tax rate is 35%, the risk-free rate is 5%, the expected return of the market is 15%, and the beta of Marpor's free cash flows is 1.10 (with or without leverage).

   a. Estimate Marpor's value without leverage.

   b. Estimate Marpor's value with the new leverage.

10. Real estate purchases are often financed with at least 80% debt. Most corporations, however, have less than 50% debt financing. Provide an explanation for this difference using the trade-off theory.

Exploiting Debt Holders: The Agency Costs of Leverage

11. Dynron Corporation's primary business is natural gas transportation using its vast gas pipeline network. Dynron's assets currently have a market value of $150 million. The firm is exploring the possibility of raising $50 million by selling part of its pipeline network and investing the

$50 million in a fiber-optic network to generate revenues by selling high-speed network bandwidth. While this new investment is expected to increase profits, it will also substantially increase Dynron's risk. If Dynron is levered, would this investment be more or less attractive to equity holders than if Dynron had no debt?

12. Consider a firm whose only asset is a plot of vacant land, and whose only liability is debt of $15 million due in one year. If left vacant, the land will be worth $10 million in one year. Alternatively, the firm can develop the land at an upfront cost of $20 million. The developed land will be worth $35 million in one year. Suppose the risk-free interest rate is 10%, assume all cash flows are risk-free, and assume there are no taxes.

   a. If the firm chooses not to develop the land, what is the value of the firm's equity today? What is the value of the debt today?

   b. What is the NPV of developing the land?

   c. Suppose the firm raises $20 million from equity holders to develop the land. If the firm develops the land, what is the value of the firm's equity today? What is the value of the firm's debt today?

   d. Given your answer to part (c), would equity holders be willing to provide the $20 million needed to develop the land?

EXCEL 13. Zymase is a biotechnology start-up firm. Researchers at Zymase must choose one of three different research strategies. The payoffs (after-tax) and their likelihood for each strategy are shown below. The risk of each project is diversifiable.

Strategy	Probability	Payoff ($ million)
A	100%	75
B	50%	140
	50%	0
C	10%	300
	90%	40

   a. Which project has the highest expected payoff?

   b. Suppose Zymase has debt of $40 million due at the time of the project's payoff. Which project has the highest expected payoff for equity holders?

   c. Suppose Zymase has debt of $110 million due at the time of the project's payoff. Which project has the highest expected payoff for equity holders?

   d. If management chooses the strategy that maximizes the payoff to equity holders, what is the expected agency cost to the firm from having $40 million in debt due? What is the expected agency cost to the firm from having $110 million in debt due?

*Motivating Managers:
The Agency Benefits
of Leverage*

14. You own your own firm, and you want to raise $30 million to fund an expansion. Currently, you own 100% of the firm's equity, and the firm has no debt. To raise the $30 million solely through equity, you will need to sell two-thirds of the firm. However, you would prefer to maintain at least a 50% equity stake in the firm to retain control.

   a. If you borrow $20 million, what fraction of the equity will you need to sell to raise the remaining $10 million? (Assume perfect capital markets.)

   b. What is the smallest amount you can borrow to raise the $30 million without giving up control? (Assume perfect capital markets.)

15. Empire Industries forecasts net income this coming year as shown below (in thousands of dollars):

EBIT	$1,000
Interest expense	0
Income before tax	1,000
Taxes	−350
Net income	$650

Approximately $200,000 of Empire's earnings will be needed to make new, positive-NPV investments. Unfortunately, Empire's managers are expected to waste 10% of its net income on needless perks, pet projects, and other expenditures that do not contribute to the firm. All remaining income will be returned to shareholders through dividends and share repurchases.

a. What are the two benefits of debt financing for Empire?

b. By how much would each $1 of interest expense reduce Empire's dividend and share repurchases?

c. What is the increase in the *total* funds Empire will pay to investors for each $1 of interest expense?

EXCEL 16. Ralston Enterprises has assets that will have a market value in one year as shown below:

Probability	1%	6%	24%	38%	24%	6%	1%
Value ($ million)	70	80	90	100	110	120	130

That is, there is a 1% chance the assets will be worth $70 million, a 6% chance the assets will be worth $80 million, and so on. Suppose the CEO is contemplating a decision that will benefit her personally but will reduce the value of the firm's assets by $10 million. The CEO is likely to proceed with this decision unless it substantially increases the firm's risk of bankruptcy.

a. If Ralston has debt due of $75 million in one year, the CEO's decision will increase the probability of bankruptcy by what percentage?

b. What level of debt provides the CEO with the biggest incentive not to proceed with the decision?

**Agency Costs and the
Tradeoff Theory**

EXCEL 17. If it is managed efficiently, Remel Inc. will have assets with a market value of $50 million, $100 million, or $150 million next year, with each outcome being equally likely. However, managers may engage in wasteful empire building, which will reduce the firm's market value by $5 million in all cases. Managers may also increase the risk of the firm, changing the probability of each outcome to 50%, 10%, and 40%, respectively.

a. What is the expected value of Remel's assets if it is run efficiently?

Suppose managers will engage in empire building unless that behavior increases the likelihood of bankruptcy. They will choose the risk of the firm to maximize the expected payoff to equity holders.

b. Suppose Remel has debt due in one year as shown below. For each case, indicate whether managers will engage in empire building, and whether they will increase risk. What is the expected value of Remel's assets in each case?

i. $44 million   iii. $90 million

ii. $49 million   iv. $99 million

    c. Suppose the tax savings from the debt, after including investor taxes, is equal to 10% of the expected payoff of the debt. The proceeds from the debt, as well as the value of any tax savings, will be paid out to shareholders immediately as a dividend when the debt is issued. Which debt level in part (b) is optimal for Remel?

18. Which of the following industries have low optimal debt levels according to the tradeoff theory? Which have high optimal levels of debt?

    a. Tobacco firms

    b. Accounting firms

    c. Mature restaurant chains

    d. Lumber companies

    e. Cell phone manufacturers

19. According to the managerial entrenchment theory, managers choose capital structure so as to preserve their control of the firm. On the one hand, debt is costly for managers because they risk losing control in the event of default. On the other hand, if they do not take advantage of the tax shield provided by debt, they risk losing control through a hostile takeover.

    Suppose a firm expects to generate free cash flows of $90 million per year, and the discount rate for these cash flows is 10%. The firm pays a tax rate of 40%. A raider is poised to take over the firm and finance it with $750 million in permanent debt. The raider will generate the same free cash flows, and the takeover attempt will be successful if the raider can offer a premium of 20% over the current value of the firm. What level of permanent debt will the firm choose, according to the managerial entrenchment hypothesis?

Asymmetric Information and Capital Structure

20. Info Systems Technology (IST) manufacturers microprocessor chips for use in appliances and other applications. IST has no debt and 100 million shares outstanding. The correct price for these shares is either $14.50 or $12.50 per share. Investors view both possibilities as equally likely, so the shares currently trade for $13.50.

    IST must raise $500 million to build a new production facility. Because the firm would suffer a large loss of both customers and engineering talent in the event of financial distress, managers believe that if IST borrows the $500 million, the present value of financial distress costs will exceed any tax benefits by $20 million. At the same time, because investors believe that managers know the correct share price, IST faces a lemons problem if it attempts to raise the $500 million by issuing equity.

    a. Suppose that if IST issues equity, the share price will remain $13.50. To maximize the long-term share price of the firm once its true value is known, would managers choose to issue equity or borrow the $500 million if

        i. They know the correct value of the shares is $12.50?

        ii. They know the correct value of the shares is $14.50?

    b. Given your answer to part (a), what should investors conclude if IST issues equity? What will happen to the share price?

    c. Given your answer to part (a), what should investors conclude if IST issues debt? What will happen to the share price in that case?

    d. How would your answers change if there were no distress costs, but only tax benefits of leverage?

21. During the internet boom of the late 1990's, the stock prices of many internet firms soared to extreme heights. As CEO of such a firm, if you believed your stock was significantly overvalued, would using your stock to acquire non-internet stocks be a wise idea, even if you had to pay a small premium over their fair market value to make the acquisition?

*22.   "We R Toys" (WRT) is considering expanding into new geographic markets. The expansion will have the same business risk as WRT's existing assets. The expansion will require an initial investment of $50 million and is expected to generate perpetual EBIT of $20 million per year. After the initial investment, future capital expenditures are expected to equal depreciation, and no further additions to net working capital are anticipated.

WRT's existing capital structure is composed of $500 million in equity and $300 million in debt (market values), with 10 million equity shares outstanding. The unlevered cost of capital is 10%, and WRT's debt is risk free with an interest rate of 4%. The corporate tax rate is 35%, and there are no personal taxes.

    a. WRT initially proposes to fund the expansion by issuing equity. If investors were not expecting this expansion, and if they share WRT's view of the expansion's profitability, what will the share price be once the firm announces the expansion plan?

    b. Suppose investors think that the EBIT from WRT's expansion will be only $4 million. What will the share price be in this case? How many shares will the firm need to issue?

    c. Suppose WRT issues equity as in part (b). Shortly after the issue, new information emerges that convinces investors that management was, in fact, correct regarding the cash flows from the expansion. What will the share price be now? Why does it differ from that found in part (a)?

    d. Suppose WRT instead finances the expansion with a $50 million issue of permanent risk-free debt. If WRT undertakes the expansion using debt, what is its new share price once the new information comes out? Comparing your answer with that in part (c), what are the two advantages of debt financing in this case?

Payout Policy

For many years, Microsoft Corporation chose to distribute cash to investors primarily by repurchasing its own stock. During the five fiscal years ending June 2004, for example, Microsoft spent an average of $5.4 billion per year on share repurchases. Microsoft began paying dividends to investors in 2003, with what CFO John Connors called "a starter dividend" of $0.08 per share. Then, on July 20, 2004, Microsoft stunned financial markets by announcing plans to pay the largest single cash dividend payment in history, a one-time dividend of $32 billion, or $3 per share, to all shareholders of record on November 17, 2004. In addition to this dividend, Microsoft announced plans to repurchase up to $30 billion of its stock over the next four years and pay regular quarterly dividends at an annual rate of $0.32 per share.

When a firm's investments generate free cash flow, the firm must decide how to use that cash. If the firm has new positive-NPV investment opportunities, it can reinvest the cash and increase the value of the firm. Many young, rapidly growing firms reinvest 100% of their cash flows in this way. But mature, profitable firms such as Microsoft often find that they generate more cash than they need to fund all of their attractive investment opportunities. When a firm has excess cash, it can hold those funds as part of its cash reserves or pay the cash out to shareholders. If the firm decides to follow the latter approach, it has two choices: It can pay a dividend or it can repurchase shares from current owners. These decisions represent the firm's payout policy.

In this chapter, we show that, as with capital structure, a firm's payout policy is shaped by market imperfections, such as taxes, agency costs, transaction costs, and asymmetric information between managers and investors. We look at why some firms prefer to pay dividends, whereas others pay no dividends at all and rely exclusively on share repurchases. In addition, we explore why some firms retain cash and build up large reserves, while others tend to pay out their excess cash.

17.1   Distributions to Shareholders

Figure 17.1 illustrates the alternative uses of free cash flow.[1] The way a firm chooses between these alternatives is referred to as its **payout policy**. We begin our discussion of a firm's payout policy by considering the choice between paying dividends and repurchasing shares. In this section, we examine the details of these methods of paying cash to shareholders.

Dividends

A public company's board of directors determines the amount of the firm's dividend. The board sets the amount per share that will be paid and decides when the payment will occur. The date on which the board authorizes the dividend is the **declaration date**. After the board declares the dividend, the firm is legally obligated to make the payment.

The firm will pay the dividend to all shareholders of record on a specific date, set by the board, called the **record date**. Because it takes three business days for shares to be registered, only shareholders who purchase the stock at least three days prior to the record date receive the dividend. As a result, the date two business days prior to the record date is known as the **ex-dividend date**; anyone who purchases the stock on or after the ex-dividend date will not receive the dividend. Finally, on the **payable date** (or **distribution date**), which is generally about a month after the record date, the firm mails dividend checks to the registered shareholders. Figure 17.2 shows these dates for Microsoft's $3.00 dividend.

Most companies that pay dividends pay them at regular, quarterly intervals. Companies typically adjust the amount of their dividends gradually, with little variation in the amount of the dividend from quarter to quarter. Occasionally, a firm may pay a one-time, **special dividend** that is usually much larger than a regular dividend, as was Microsoft's

---

FIGURE 17.1

Uses of Free Cash Flow

A firm can retain its free cash flow, either investing or accumulating it, or pay out its free cash flow through a dividend or share repurchase. The choice between these options is determined by the firm's payout policy.

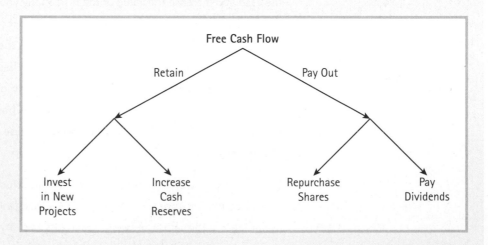

---

1. Strictly speaking, Figure 17.1 is for an all equity firm. For a levered firm, we would begin with the firm's free cash flow to equity, which we define in Chapter 18 as free cash flow less (after-tax) payments to debt holders.

FIGURE 17.2 **Important Dates for Microsoft's Special Dividend**

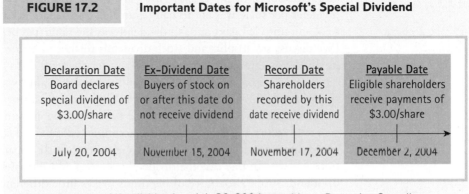

Microsoft declared the dividend on July 20, 2004, payable on December 2 to all shareholders of record on November 17. Because the record date was November 17, the ex-dividend date was two days earlier, or November 15, 2004.

$3.00 dividend in 2004. Figure 17.3 shows the dividends paid by GM from 1983 to 2006. In addition to regular dividends, GM paid special dividends in December 1997 and again in May 1999 (associated with spin-offs of subsidiaries, discussed further in Section 17.7).

Notice that GM split its stock in March 1989 so that each owner of one share received a second share. This kind of transaction is called a 2-for-1 stock split. More generally, in a **stock split** or **stock dividend**, the company issues additional shares rather than cash to

FIGURE 17.3

Dividend History for GM Stock, 1983–2006

Since 1983, GM has paid a regular dividend each quarter. GM paid additional special dividends in December 1997 and May 1999, and had a 2-for-1 stock split in March 1989.

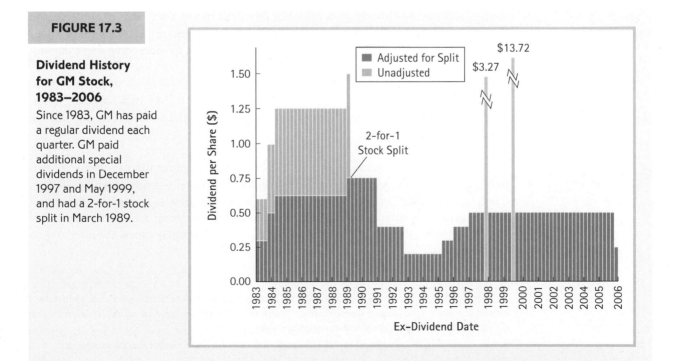

its shareholders. In the case of GM's stock split, the number of shares doubled, but the dividend per share was cut in half (from $1.50 per share to $0.75 per share), so that the total amount GM paid out as a dividend was the same just before and just after the split. (We discuss stock splits and stock dividends further in Section 17.7.) While GM raised its dividends throughout the 1980s, it cut its dividend during the recession in the early 1990s. GM raised its dividends again in the late 1990s, but was forced to cut its dividend again in early 2006 when it encountered financial difficulties.

Dividends are a cash outflow for the firm. From an accounting perspective, dividends generally reduce the firm's current (or accumulated) retained earnings. In some cases, dividends are attributed to other accounting sources, such as paid-in capital or the liquidation of assets. In this case the dividend is known as a **return of capital** or a **liquidating dividend**. While the source of the funds makes little difference to a firm or to investors directly, there is a difference in tax treatment: A return of capital is taxed as a capital gain rather than as a dividend for the investor.[2]

Share Repurchases

An alternative way to pay cash to investors is through a share repurchase or buyback. In this kind of transaction, the firm uses cash to buy shares of its own outstanding stock. These shares are generally held in the corporate treasury, and they can be resold if the company needs to raise money in the future. We now examine three possible transaction types for a share repurchase.

Open Market Repurchase.   An **open market repurchase** is the most common way that firms repurchase shares. A firm announces its intention to buy its own shares in the open market, and then proceeds to do so over time like any other investor. The firm may take a year or more to buy the shares, and it is not obligated to repurchase the full amount it originally stated. Also, the firm must not buy its shares in a way that might appear to manipulate the price. For example, SEC guidelines recommend that the firm not purchase more than 25% of the average daily trading volume in its shares on a single day, nor make purchases at the market open or within 30 minutes of the close of trade.[3]

While open market share repurchases represent about 95% of all repurchase transactions,[4] other methods are available to a firm that wants to buy back its stock. These methods are used when a firm wishes to repurchase a substantial portion of its shares, often as part of a recapitalization.

Tender Offer.   A firm can repurchase shares through a **tender offer** in which it offers to buy shares at a prespecified price during a short time period—generally within 20 days. The price is usually set at a substantial premium (10%–20% is typical) to the current market price. The offer often depends on shareholders tendering a sufficient number of shares. If shareholders do not tender enough shares, the firm may cancel the offer and no buyback occurs.

---

2. There is also a difference in the accounting treatment. A cash dividend reduces the cash and retained earnings shown on the balance sheet, whereas a return of capital reduces paid-in capital. This accounting difference has no direct economic consequence, however.

3. SEC Rule 10b-18, introduced in 1983, defines guidelines for open market share repurchases.

4. G. Grullon and D. Ikenberry, "What Do We Know About Stock Repurchases?" *Journal of Applied Corporate Finance* 13(1) (2000): 31–51.

A related method is the **Dutch auction** share repurchase, in which the firm lists different prices at which it is prepared to buy shares, and shareholders in turn indicate how many shares they are willing to sell at each price. The firm then pays the lowest price at which it can buy back its desired number of shares.

Targeted Repurchase.   A firm may also purchase shares directly from a major shareholder in a **targeted repurchase**. In this case the purchase price is negotiated directly with the seller. A targeted repurchase may occur if a major shareholder desires to sell a large number of shares but the market for the shares is not sufficiently liquid to sustain such a large sale without severely affecting the price. Under these circumstances, the shareholder may be willing to sell shares back to the firm at a discount to the current market price. Alternatively, if a major shareholder is threatening to take over the firm and remove its management, the firm may decide to eliminate the threat by buying out the shareholder—often at a large premium over the current market price. This type of transaction is called **greenmail**.

CONCEPT CHECK

1. How is a stock's ex-dividend date determined, and what is its significance?

2. What is a Dutch auction share repurchase?

17.2 Comparison of Dividends and Share Repurchases

If a corporation decides to pay cash to shareholders, it can do so through either dividend payments or share repurchases. How do firms choose between these alternatives? In this section, we show that in the perfect capital markets setting of Modigliani and Miller, the method of payment does not matter.

Consider the case of Genron Corporation, a hypothetical firm. Genron has $20 million in excess cash and no debt. The firm expects to generate additional free cash flows of $48 million per year in subsequent years. If Genron's unlevered cost of capital is 12%, then the enterprise value of its ongoing operations is

$$\text{Enterprise Value} = PV(\text{Future FCF}) = \frac{\$48 \text{ million}}{12\%} = \$400 \text{ million}$$

Including the cash, Genron's total market value is $420 million.

Genron's board is meeting to decide how to pay out its $20 million in excess cash to shareholders. Some board members have advocated using the $20 million to pay a $2 cash dividend for each of Genron's 10 million outstanding shares. Others have suggested repurchasing shares instead of paying a dividend. Still others have proposed that Genron raise additional cash and pay an even larger dividend today, in anticipation of the high future free cash flows it expects to receive. Will the amount of the current dividend affect Genron's share price? Which policy would shareholders prefer?

Let's analyze the consequences of each of these three alternative policies and compare them in a setting of perfect capital markets.

Alternative Policy 1: Pay Dividend with Excess Cash

Suppose the board opts for the first alternative and uses all excess cash to pay a dividend. With 10 million shares outstanding, Genron will be able to pay a $2 dividend immediately. Because the firm expects to generate future free cash flows of $48 million per year, it anticipates paying a dividend of $4.80 per share each year thereafter. The board declares the dividend and sets the record date as December 14, so that the ex-dividend date is December 12. Let's compute Genron's share price just before and after the stock goes ex-dividend.

The fair price for the shares is the present value of the expected dividends given Genron's equity cost of capital. Because Genron has no debt, its equity cost of capital equals its unlevered cost of capital of 12%. Just before the ex-dividend date, the stock is said to trade **cum-dividend** ("with the dividend") because anyone who buys the stock will be entitled to the dividend. In this case,

$$P_{cum} = \text{Current Dividend} + PV(\text{Future Dividends}) = 2 + \frac{4.80}{0.12} = 2 + 40 = \$42$$

After the stock goes ex-dividend, new buyers will not receive the current dividend. At this point the share price will reflect only the dividends in subsequent years:

$$P_{ex} = PV(\text{Future Dividends}) = \frac{4.80}{0.12} = \$40$$

The share price will drop on the ex-dividend date, December 12. The amount of the price drop is equal to the amount of the current dividend, $2. We can also determine this change in the share price using the market value balance sheet (values in millions of dollars):

	December 11 (Cum-Dividend)	December 12 (Ex-Dividend)
Cash	20	0
Other assets	400	400
Total market value	420	400
Shares (millions)	10	10
Share price	**$42**	**$40**

As the market value balance sheet shows, the share price falls when a dividend is paid because the reduction in cash decreases the market value of the firm's assets. Although the stock price falls, holders of Genron stock do not incur a loss overall. Before the dividend, their stock was worth $42. After the dividend, their stock is worth $40 and they hold $2 in cash from the dividend, for a total value of $42.[5]

The fact that the stock price falls by the amount of the dividend also follows from the assumption that no opportunity for arbitrage exists. If it fell by less than the dividend, an investor could earn a profit by buying the stock just before it goes ex-dividend and selling it just after, as the dividend would more than cover the capital loss on the stock. Similarly, if the stock price fell by more than the dividend, an investor could profit by selling the stock just before it goes ex-dividend and buying it just after. Therefore, no arbitrage implies

In a perfect capital market, when a dividend is paid, the share price drops by the amount of the dividend when the stock begins to trade ex-dividend.

---

5. For simplicity, we have ignored the short delay between the ex-dividend date and the payable date of the dividend. In reality, the shareholders do not receive the dividend immediately, but rather the *promise* to receive it within several weeks. The stock price adjusts by the present value of this promise, which is effectively equal to the amount of the dividend unless interest rates are extremely high.

Alternative Policy 2: Share Repurchase (No Dividend)

Suppose that Genron does not pay a dividend this year, but instead uses the $20 million to repurchase its shares on the open market. How will the repurchase affect the share price?

With an initial share price of $42, Genron will repurchase $20 million ÷ $42 per share = 0.476 million shares, leaving only 10 − 0.476 = 9.524 million shares outstanding. Once again, we can use Genron's market value balance sheet to analyze this transaction:

	December 11 (Before Repurchase)	December 12 (After Repurchase)
Cash	20	0
Other assets	400	400
Total market value of assets	420	400
Shares (millions)	10	9.524
Share price	**$42**	**$42**

In this case, the market value of Genron's assets falls when the company pays out cash, but the number of shares outstanding also falls. The two changes offset each other, so the share price remains the same.

Genron's Future Dividends.   We can also see why the share price does not fall after the share repurchase by considering the effect on Genron's future dividends. In future years, Genron expects to have $48 million in free cash flow, which can be used to pay a dividend of $48 million ÷ 9.524 million shares = $5.04 per share each year. Thus, with a share repurchase, Genron's share price today is

$$P_{rep} = \frac{5.04}{0.12} = \$42$$

In other words, by not paying a dividend today and repurchasing shares instead, Genron is able to raise its dividends *per share* in the future. The increase in future dividends compensates shareholders for the dividend they give up today. This example illustrates the following general conclusion about share repurchases:

In perfect capital markets, an open market share repurchase has no effect on the stock price, and the stock price is the same as the cum-dividend price if a dividend were paid instead.

Investor Preferences.   Would an investor prefer that Genron issue a dividend or repurchase its stock? Both policies lead to the same *initial* share price of $42. But is there a difference in shareholder value *after* the transaction? Consider an investor who currently holds 2000 shares of Genron stock. Assuming the investor does not trade the stock, the investor's holdings after a dividend or share repurchase are as follows:

Dividend	Repurchase
$40 × 2000 = $80,000 stock	$42 × 2000 = $84,000 stock
$ 2 × 2000 = $ 4000 cash	

In either case, the value of the investor's portfolio is $84,000 immediately after the transaction. The only difference is the distribution between cash and stock holdings. Thus it

| COMMON MISTAKE | **Repurchases and the Supply of Shares** |

There is a misconception that when a firm repurchases its own shares, the price rises due to the decrease in the supply of shares outstanding. This intuition follows naturally from the standard supply and demand analysis taught in microeconomics. Why does that analysis not apply here?

When a firm repurchases its own shares, two things happen. First, the supply of shares is reduced. At the same time, however, the value of the firm's assets declines when it spends its cash to buy the shares. If the firm repurchases its shares at their market price, these two effects offset each other, leaving the share price unchanged.

This result is similar to the dilution fallacy discussed in Chapter 14: When a firm issues shares at their market price, the share price does not fall due to the increase in supply. The increase in supply is offset by the increase in the firm's assets that results from the cash it receives from the issuance.

might seem the investor would prefer one approach or the other based on whether she needs the cash.

But if Genron repurchases shares and the investor wants cash, she can raise cash by selling shares. For example, she can sell $4000 \div $42 per share = 95 shares to raise about $4000 in cash. She will then hold 1905 shares, or $1905 \times $42 \approx $80,000 in stock. Thus, in the case of a share repurchase, by selling shares an investor can create a *homemade dividend*.

Similarly, if Genron pays a dividend and the investor does not want the cash, she can use the $4000 proceeds of the dividend to purchase 100 additional shares at the ex-dividend share price of $40 per share. As a result she will hold 2100 shares, worth $2100 \times $40 = $84,000.[6]

We summarize these two cases below:

Dividend + Buy 100 shares	Repurchase + Sell 95 shares
$40 \times 2100 = $84,000 stock	$42 \times 1905 \approx $80,000 stock
	$42 \times 95 \approx $\ \ 4000 cash

By selling shares or reinvesting dividends, the investor can create any combination of cash and stock desired. As a result, the investor is indifferent between the various payout methods the firm might employ:

In perfect capital markets, investors are indifferent between the firm distributing funds via dividends or share repurchases. By reinvesting dividends or selling shares, they can replicate either payout method on their own.

Alternative Policy 3: High Dividend (Equity Issue)

Let's look at a third possibility for Genron. Suppose the board wishes to pay an even larger dividend than $2 per share right now. Is that possible and, if so, will the higher dividend make shareholders better off?

Genron plans to pay $48 million in dividends starting next year. Suppose the firm wants to start paying that amount today. Because it has only $20 million in cash today,

---

6. In fact, many firms allow investors to register for a dividend reinvestment program, or *DRIP*, which automatically reinvests any dividends into new shares of the stock.

Genron needs an additional $28 million to pay the larger dividend now. It could raise cash by scaling back its investments. But if the investments have positive NPV, reducing them would lower firm value. An alternative way to raise more cash is to borrow money or sell new shares. Let's consider an equity issue. Given a current share price of $42, Genron could raise $28 million by selling $28 million ÷ $42 per share = 0.67 million shares. Because this equity issue will increase Genron's total number of shares outstanding to 10.67 million, the amount of the dividend per share each year will be

$$\frac{\$48 \text{ million}}{10.67 \text{ million shares}} = \$4.50 \text{ per share}$$

Under this new policy, Genron's cum-dividend share price is

$$P_{cum} = 4.50 + \frac{4.50}{0.12} = 4.50 + 37.50 = \$42$$

As in the previous examples, the initial share value is unchanged by this policy, and increasing the dividend has no benefit to shareholders.

EXAMPLE 17.1

Homemade Dividends

Problem

Suppose Genron does not adopt the third alternative policy, and instead pays a $2 dividend per share today. Show how an investor holding 2000 shares could create a homemade dividend of $4.50 per share × 2000 shares = $9000 per year on her own.

Solution

If Genron pays a $2 dividend, the investor receives $4000 in cash and holds the rest in stock. To receive $9000 in total today, she can raise an additional $5000 by selling 125 shares at $40 per share just after the dividend is paid. In future years, Genron will pay a dividend of $4.80 per share. Because she will own 2000 − 125 = 1875 shares, the investor will receive dividends of 1875 × $4.80 = $9000 per year from then on.

Modigliani–Miller and Dividend Policy Irrelevance

In our analysis we considered three possible dividend policies for the firm: (1) pay out all cash as a dividend, (2) pay no dividend and use the cash instead to repurchase shares, or (3) issue equity to finance a larger dividend. These policies are illustrated in Table 17.1.

TABLE 17.1	**Genron's Dividends per Share Each Year Under the Three Alternative Policies**				
		\multicolumn{4}{c}{**Dividend Paid ($ per share)**}			
	Initial Share Price	**Year 0**	**Year 1**	**Year 2**	**...**
Policy 1:	$42.00	2.00	4.80	4.80	...
Policy 2:	$42.00	0	5.04	5.04	...
Policy 3:	$42.00	4.50	4.50	4.50	...

COMMON MISTAKE   The Bird in the Hand Fallacy

"A bird in the hand is worth two in the bush."

The **bird in the hand hypothesis** states that firms choosing to pay higher current dividends will enjoy higher stock prices because shareholders prefer current dividends to future ones (with the same present value).

According to this view, alternative policy 3 would lead to the highest share price for Genron.

Modigliani and Miller's response to this view is that with perfect capital markets, shareholders can generate an equivalent homemade dividend at any time by selling shares. Thus the dividend choice of the firm should not matter.*

*The bird in the hand hypothesis is proposed in Lintner and Gordon's early studies of dividend policy. See M. J. Gordon, "Optimal Investment and Financing Policy," *Journal of Finance* 18(2) (1963): 264–272, and J. Lintner, "Dividends, Earnings, Leverage, Stock Prices and the Supply of Capital to Corporations," *Review of Economics and Statistics* 44(3) (1962): 243–269.

Table 17.1 shows an important tradeoff: If Genron pays a higher *current* dividend per share, it will pay lower *future* dividends per share. For example, if the firm raises the current dividend by issuing equity, it will have more shares and therefore smaller free cash flows per share to pay dividends in the future. If the firm lowers the current dividend and repurchases its shares, it will have fewer shares in the future, so it will be able to pay a higher dividend per share. The net effect of this tradeoff is to leave the total present value of all future dividends, and hence the current share price, unchanged.

The logic of this section matches that in our discussion of capital structure in Chapter 14. There we explained that in perfect capital markets, buying and selling equity and debt are zero-NPV transactions that do not affect firm value. Moreover, any choice of leverage by a firm could be replicated by investors using homemade leverage. As a result, the firm's choice of capital structure is irrelevant.

Here we have established the same principle for a firm's choice of a dividend. Regardless of the amount of cash the firm has on hand, it can pay a smaller dividend (and use the remaining cash to repurchase shares) or a larger dividend (by selling equity to raise cash). Because buying or selling shares is a zero-NPV transaction, such transactions have no effect on the initial share price. Furthermore, shareholders can create a homemade dividend of any size by buying or selling shares themselves.

Modigliani and Miller developed this idea in another influential paper published in 1961.[7] As with their result on capital structure, it went against the conventional wisdom that dividend policy could change a firm's value and make its shareholders better off even absent market imperfections. We state here their important proposition:

MM Dividend Irrelevance: *In perfect capital markets, holding fixed the investment policy of a firm, the firm's choice of dividend policy is irrelevant and does not affect the initial share price.*

7. See M. Modigliani and M. Miller, "Dividend Policy, Growth, and the Valuation of Shares," *Journal of Business* 34(4) (1961): 411–433. See also J. B. Williams, *The Theory of Investment Value* (Cambridge, MA: Harvard University Press, 1938).

Dividend Policy with Perfect Capital Markets

The examples in this section illustrate the idea that by using share repurchases or equity issues a firm can easily alter its dividend payments. Because these transactions do not alter the value of the firm, neither does dividend policy.

This result may at first seem to contradict the idea that the price of a share should equal the present value of its future dividends. As our examples have shown, however, a firm's choice of dividend today affects the dividends it can afford to pay in the future in an offsetting fashion. Thus, while dividends *do* determine share prices, a firm's choice of dividend policy does not.

As Modigliani and Miller make clear, the value of a firm ultimately derives from its underlying free cash flow. A firm's free cash flow determines the level of payouts that it can make to its investors. In a perfect capital market, whether these payouts are made through dividends or share repurchases does not matter. Of course, in reality capital markets are not perfect. As with capital structure, it is the imperfections in capital markets that should determine the firm's payout policy.

CONCEPT CHECK

1. Explain the misconception that when a firm repurchases its own shares, the price rises due to the decrease in the supply of shares outstanding.

2. In a perfect capital market, how important is the firm's decision to pay dividends versus repurchase shares?

17.3 The Tax Disadvantage of Dividends

As with capital structure, taxes are an important market imperfection that influence a firm's decision to pay dividends or repurchase shares.

Taxes on Dividends and Capital Gains

Shareholders typically must pay taxes on the dividends they receive. They must also pay capital gains taxes when they sell their shares. Table 17.2 shows the history of U.S. tax rates applied to dividends and long-term capital gains for investors in the highest tax bracket.

Do taxes affect investors' preferences for dividends versus share repurchases? When a firm pays a dividend, shareholders are taxed according to the dividend tax rate. If the firm repurchases shares instead, and shareholders sell shares to create a homemade dividend, the homemade dividend will be taxed according to the capital gains tax rate. If dividends are taxed at a higher rate than capital gains, which has been true until the most recent change to the tax code, shareholders will prefer share repurchases to dividends.[8] As we saw in Chapter 15, recent changes to the tax code have equalized the tax rates on dividends and capital gains. But because long-term investors can defer the capital gains tax until they sell, there is still a tax advantage for share repurchases over dividends.

The higher tax rate on dividends also makes it undesirable for a firm to raise funds to pay a dividend. Absent taxes and issuance costs, if a firm raises money by issuing shares and then gives that money back to shareholders as a dividend, shareholders are no better

---

8. Not all countries tax dividends at a higher rate than capital gains. In Germany, for example, dividends are taxed at a lower rate than capital gains for most classes of investors.

TABLE 17.2	Long-Term Capital Gains Versus Dividend Tax Rates in the United States, 1971–2005

Year	Capital Gains	Dividends
1971–1978	35%	70%
1979–1981	28%	70%
1982–1986	20%	50%
1987	28%	39%
1988–1990	28%	28%
1991–1992	28%	31%
1993–1996	28%	40%
1997–2000	20%	40%
2001–2002	20%	39%
2003–*	15%	15%

*The current tax rates are set to expire in 2008 unless they are extended by Congress. The tax rates shown are for financial assets held for one year. For assets held less than one year, capital gains are taxed at the ordinary income tax rate (currently 35% for the highest bracket); the same is true for dividends if the assets are held for less than 61 days. Because the capital gains tax is not paid until the asset is sold, for assets held for longer than one year the *effective* capital gains tax rate is equal to the present value of the rate shown, when discounted by the after-tax risk-free interest rate for the additional number of years the asset is held.

or worse off—they get back the money they put in. When dividends are taxed at a higher rate than capital gains, however, this transaction hurts shareholders because they will receive less than their initial investment.

EXAMPLE 17.2

Issuing Equity to Pay a Dividend

Problem
Suppose a firm raises $10 million from shareholders and uses this cash to pay them $10 million in dividends. If the dividend is taxed at a 40% rate, and if capital gains are taxed at a 15% rate, how much will shareholders receive after taxes?

Solution
Shareholders will owe 40% of $10 million, or $4 million in dividend taxes. Because the value of the firm will fall when the dividend is paid, shareholders' capital gain on the stock will be $10 million less when they sell, lowering their capital gains taxes by 15% of $10 million or $1.5 million. Thus, in total, shareholders will pay $4 million − $1.5 million = $2.5 million in taxes, and they will receive back only $7.5 million of their $10 million investment.

Optimal Dividend Policy with Taxes

When the tax rate on dividends exceeds the tax rate on capital gains, shareholders will pay lower taxes if a firm uses share repurchases for all payouts rather than dividends. This tax savings will increase the value of a firm that uses share repurchases rather than dividends.

FIGURE 17.4

The Declining Use of Dividends

This figure shows the percentage of U.S. firms each year that made payouts to shareholders. The shaded regions show the firms that used dividends exclusively, repurchases exclusively, or both. Note the trend away from the use of dividends over time, with firms that made payouts showing a greater reliance on share repurchases, together with a sharp decrease in the percentage of firms making payouts of any kind.
Source: Compustat.

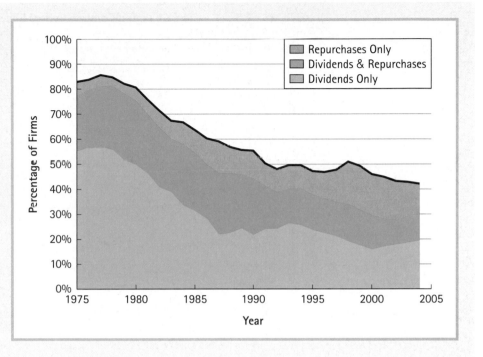

We can also express the tax savings in terms of a firm's equity cost of capital. Firms that use dividends will have to pay a higher pre-tax return to offer their investors the same after-tax return as firms that use share repurchases.[9] As a result, the optimal dividend policy when the dividend tax rate exceeds the capital gain tax rate is to *pay no dividends at all*.

While firms do still pay dividends, substantial evidence shows that many firms have recognized their tax disadvantage. For example, prior to 1980, most firms used dividends exclusively to distribute cash to shareholders (see Figure 17.4). But by 2000, only 16% of firms relied on dividends. At the same time, 30% of all firms (and more than 65% of firms making payouts to shareholders) used share repurchases exclusively or in combination with dividends. The trend away from dividends has reversed slightly, however, since 2000.[10]

We see a more dramatic trend if we consider the relative magnitudes of both forms of corporate payouts. Figure 17.5 shows the relative importance of share repurchases as a proportion of total payouts to shareholders. While dividends accounted for more than 80% of corporate payouts until the early 1980s, the importance of share repurchases grew dramatically in the mid-1980s. Repurchase activity slowed during the 1990–1991 recession,

---

9. For an extension of the CAPM that includes investor taxes, see M. Brennan, "Taxes, Market Valuation and Corporation Financial Policy," *National Tax Journal* 23(4) (1970): 417–427.

10. See G. Grullon and R. Michaely, "Dividends, Share Repurchases, and the Substitution Hypothesis," *Journal of Finance* 57(4) (2002): 1649–1684, and E. Fama and K. French, "Disappearing Dividends: Changing Firm Characteristics or Lower Propensity to Pay?" *Journal of Financial Economics* 60(3) (2001): 3–43. For an examination of the changing trend since 2000, see B. Julio and D. Ikenberry, "Reappearing Dividends," *Journal of Applied Corporate Finance* 16(4) (2004): 89–100.

| FIGURE 17.5 | The Changing Composition of Shareholder Payouts |

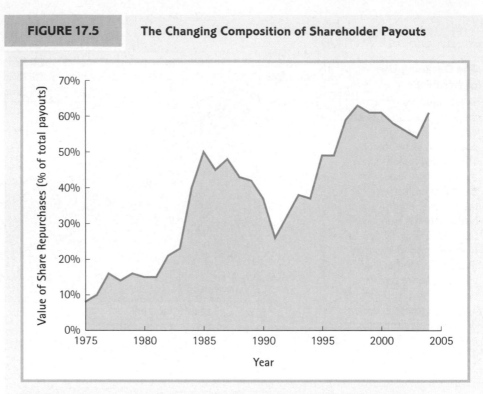

This figure shows the value of share repurchases as a percentage of total payouts to shareholders (dividends and repurchases). Although initially small, the total dollar amount of share repurchases has grown faster than dividends, so that by the late 1990s share repurchases surpassed dividends to become the largest form of corporate payouts for U.S. industrial firms.

Source: Compustat/CRSP data for U.S. firms, excluding financial firms and utilities. Data provided by A. Dittmar and R. Dittmar, "Stock Repurchase Waves: An Examination of the Trends in Aggregate Corporate Payout Policy," Working Paper, 2006, University of Michigan.

but by the end of the 1990s repurchases exceeded the value of dividend payments for U.S. industrial firms.[11]

While this evidence is indicative of the growing importance of share repurchases as a part of firms' payout policies, it also shows that dividends remain a key form of payouts to shareholders. The fact that firms continue to issue dividends despite their tax disadvantage is often referred to as the **dividend puzzle**.[12] In the next section, we consider some factors that may mitigate this tax disadvantage. In Section 17.6, we examine alternative motivations for using dividends based on asymmetric information.

CONCEPT CHECK

1. What is the optimal dividend policy when the dividend tax rate exceeds the capital gain tax rate?

2. What is the dividend puzzle?

---

11. For further evidence that repurchases are replacing dividends, see A. Dittmar and R. Dittmar, "Stock Repurchase Waves: An Examination of the Trends in Aggregate Corporate Payout Policy," Working Paper, 2006, University of Michigan.

12. See F. Black, "The Dividend Puzzle," *Journal of Portfolio Management* 2 (1976): 5–8.

17.4 Dividend Capture and Tax Clienteles

While many investors have a tax preference for share repurchases rather than dividends, the strength of that preference depends on the difference between the dividend tax rate and the capital gains tax rate that they face. Tax rates vary by income, by jurisdiction, and by whether the stock is held in a retirement account. Because of these differences, firms may attract different groups of investors depending on their dividend policy. In this section, we look in detail at the tax consequences of dividends as well as investor strategies that may reduce the impact of dividend taxes on firm value.

The Effective Dividend Tax Rate

To compare investor preferences, we must quantify the combined effects of dividend and capital gains taxes to determine an effective dividend tax rate for an investor. For simplicity, consider an investor who buys a stock today just before it goes ex-dividend, and sells the stock just after.[13] By doing so, the investor will qualify for, and capture, the dividend. If the stock pays a dividend of amount Div, and the investor's dividend tax rate is τ_d, then her after-tax cash flow from the dividend is $Div(1 - \tau_d)$.

In addition, because the price just before the stock goes ex-dividend, P_{cum}, exceeds the price just after, P_{ex}, the investor will expect to incur a capital loss on her trade. If her tax rate on capital gains is τ_g, her after-tax loss is $(P_{cum} - P_{ex})(1 - \tau_g)$.

The investor therefore earns a profit by trading to capture the dividend if the after-tax dividend exceeds the after-tax capital loss. Conversely, if the after-tax capital loss exceeds the after-tax dividend, the investor benefits by selling the stock just before it goes ex-dividend and buying it afterward, thereby avoiding the dividend. In other words, there is an arbitrage opportunity unless the price drop and dividend are equal after taxes:

$$(P_{cum} - P_{ex})(1 - \tau_g) = Div(1 - \tau_d) \tag{17.1}$$

We can write Eq. 17.1 in terms of the share price drop as

$$P_{cum} - P_{ex} = Div \times \left(\frac{1 - \tau_d}{1 - \tau_g}\right) = Div \times \left(1 - \frac{\tau_d - \tau_g}{1 - \tau_g}\right) = Div \times (1 - \tau_d^*) \tag{17.2}$$

where we define τ_d^* to be the **effective dividend tax rate**:

$$\tau_d^* = \left(\frac{\tau_d - \tau_g}{1 - \tau_g}\right) \tag{17.3}$$

The effective dividend tax rate τ_d^* measures the additional tax paid by the investor per dollar of after-tax capital gains income that is instead received as a dividend.[14]

---

13. We could equally well consider a long-term investor deciding between selling the stock just before or just after the ex-dividend date. The analysis would be identical (although the applicable tax rates will depend on the holding period).

14. Elton and Gruber first identified and found empirical support for Eq. 17.2. See E. Elton and M. Gruber, "Marginal Stockholder Tax Rates and the Clientele Effect," *Review of Economics and Statistics* 52(1) (1970): 68–74. For investor reaction to major tax code changes see J. L. Koski, "A Microstructure Analysis of Ex-Dividend Stock Price Behavior Before and After the 1984 and 1986 Tax Reform Acts," *Journal of Business* 69 (1996):313–338.

| E X A M P L E 17.3 | **Changes in the Effective Dividend Tax Rate** |

Problem

Consider an individual investor in the highest U.S. tax bracket who plans to hold a stock for one year. What was the effective dividend tax rate for this investor in 2002? How did the effective dividend tax rate change in 2003? (Ignore state taxes.)

Solution

From Table 17.2, in 2002 we have $\tau_d = 39\%$ and $\tau_g = 20\%$. Thus

$$\tau_d^* = \frac{0.39 - 0.20}{1 - 0.20} = 23.75\%$$

This indicates a significant tax disadvantage of dividends; each $1 of dividends is worth only $0.7625 in capital gains. However, after the 2003 tax cut, $\tau_d = 15\%$, $\tau_g = 15\%$, and

$$\tau_d^* = \frac{0.15 - 0.15}{1 - 0.15} = 0\%$$

Therefore, the 2003 tax cut eliminated the tax disadvantage of dividends for a one-year investor.

Tax Differences Across Investors

The effective dividend tax rate τ_d^* for an investor depends on the tax rates the investor faces on dividends and capital gains. These rates differ across investors for a variety of reasons.

Income Level. Investors with different levels of income fall into different tax brackets and face different tax rates.

Investment Horizon. Capital gains on stocks held less than one year, and dividends on stocks held for less than 61 days, are taxed at higher ordinary income tax rates. Long-term investors can defer the payment of capital gains taxes (lowering their effective capital gains tax rate even further). Investors who plan to bequeath stocks to their heirs avoid the capital gains tax altogether.

Tax Jurisdiction. U.S. investors are subject to state taxes that differ by state. For example, New Hampshire imposes a 5% tax on income from interest and dividends, but no tax on capital gains. Foreign investors in U.S. stocks are subject to 30% withholding for dividends they receive (unless that rate is reduced by a tax treaty with their home country). There is no similar withholding for capital gains.

Type of Investor or Investment Account. Stocks held by individual investors in a retirement account are not subject to taxes on dividends or capital gains.[15] Similarly, stocks held through pension funds or nonprofit endowment funds are not subject to dividend or capital gains taxes. Corporations that hold stocks are able to exclude 70% of dividends they receive from corporate taxes, but are unable to exclude capital gains.[16]

To illustrate, consider four different investors: (1) a "buy and hold" investor who holds the stock in a taxable account and plans to transfer the stock to her heirs, (2) an investor

---

15. While taxes (or penalties) may be owed when the money is withdrawn from the retirement account, these taxes do not depend on whether the money came from dividends or capital gains.

16. Corporations can exclude 80% if they own more than 20% of the shares of the firm paying the dividend.

who holds the stock in a taxable account but plans to sell it in one year, (3) a pension fund, and (4) a corporation. Under the current maximum U.S. federal tax rates, the effective dividend tax rate for each would be

1. Buy and hold individual investor: $\tau_d = 15\%$, $\tau_g = 0$, and $\tau_d^* = 15\%$

2. One-year individual investor: $\tau_d = 15\%$, $\tau_g = 15\%$, and $\tau_d^* = 0$

3. Pension fund: $\tau_d = 0$, $\tau_g = 0$, and $\tau_d^* = 0$

4. Corporation: Given a corporate tax rate of 35%, $\tau_d = (1 - 70\%) \times 35\% = 10.5\%$, $\tau_g = 35\%$, and $\tau_d^* = -38\%$

As a result of their different tax rates, these investors have varying preferences regarding dividends. Long-term investors are more heavily taxed on dividends, so they would prefer share repurchases to dividend payments. One-year investors, pension funds, and other non-taxed investors have no tax preference for share repurchases over dividends; they would prefer a payout policy that most closely matches their cash needs. For example, a non-taxed investor who desires current income would prefer high dividends so as to avoid the brokerage fees and other transaction costs of selling the stock.

Finally, the negative effective dividend tax rate for corporations implies that corporations enjoy a tax *advantage* associated with dividends. For this reason, a corporation that chooses to invest its cash will prefer to hold stocks with high dividend yields.

Clientele Effects

Table 17.3 summarizes the different preferences across investor groups. These differences in tax preferences create **clientele effects**, in which the dividend policy of a firm is optimized for the tax preference of its investor clientele. Individuals in the highest tax brackets have a preference for stocks that pay no or low dividends, whereas tax-free investors and corporations have a preference for stocks with high dividends. In this case, a firm's dividend policy is optimized for the tax preference of its investor clientele.

TABLE 17.3	**Differing Dividend Policy Preferences Across Investor Groups**	
Investor Group	**Dividend Policy Preference**	**Proportion of Investors**
Individual investors	Tax disadvantage for dividends Prefer share repurchase	~52%
Institutions, pension funds, retirement accounts	No tax preference Prefer dividend policy that matches income needs	~47%
Corporations	Tax advantage for dividends	~1%

Source: Proportions based on *Federal Reserve Flow of Funds Accounts*, 2003.

Evidence supports the existence of tax clienteles. For example, Franklin Allen and Roni Michaely[17] report that in 1996 individual investors held 54% of all stocks by market value, yet received only 35% of all dividends paid, indicating that individuals tend to hold

---

17. F. Allen and R. Michaely, "Payout Policy," in *Handbook of the Economics of Finance: Corporate Finance Volume* 1A, Chapter 7, Elsevier, Amsterdam, The Netherlands (2003) (ed: G. M. Constantinides, M. Harris, R. M. Stulz).

stocks with low dividend yields. Of course, the fact that high-tax investors receive any dividends at all implies that the clienteles are not perfect—dividend taxes are not the only determinants of investors' portfolios.

Another clientele strategy is a dynamic clientele effect, also called the **dividend-capture theory**.[18] This theory states that absent transaction costs, investors can trade shares at the time of the dividend so that non-taxed investors receive the dividend. That is, non-taxed investors need not hold the high-dividend-paying stocks all the time; it is necessary only that they hold them when the dividend is actually paid.

An implication of this theory is that we should see large volumes of trade in a stock around the ex-dividend day, as high-tax investors sell and low-tax investors buy the stock in anticipation of the dividend, and then reverse those trades just after the ex-dividend date. Consider Figure 17.6, which illustrates the price and volume for the stock of Value Line, Inc., during 2004. On April 23, Value Line announced it would use its accumulated cash to pay a special dividend of $17.50 per share, with an ex-dividend date of May 20.

FIGURE 17.6   **Volume and Share Price Effects of Value Line's Special Dividend**

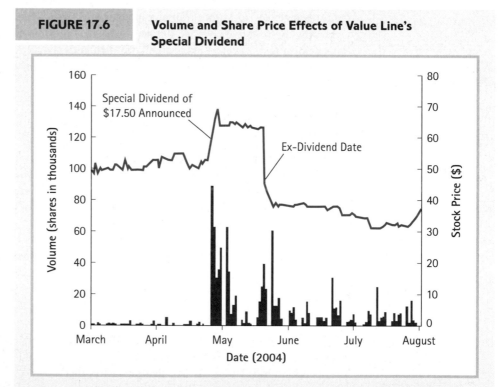

On announcement of the special dividend of $17.50 per share, Value Line's share price rose, as did the volume of trade. The share price dropped by $17.91 on the ex-dividend date, and the volume gradually declined over the following weeks. This pattern of volume is consistent with non-taxed investors buying the stock before the ex-dividend date and selling it afterward. (We consider reasons for the jump in the stock price on the announcement of the dividend in Sections 17.5 and 17.6.)

---

18. This idea is developed by A. Kalay, "The Ex-Dividend Day Behavior Of Stock Prices: A Reexamination of the Clientele Effect," *Journal of Finance* 37(4) (1982): 1059–1070. See also J. Boyd and R. Jagannathan, "Ex-Dividend Price Behavior of Common Stocks," *Review of Financial Studies* 7(4) (1994): 711–741, who discuss the complications that arise with multiple tax clienteles.

Note the substantial increase in the volume of trade around the time of the special dividend. The volume of trade in the month following the special dividend announcement was more than 25 times the volume in the month prior to the announcement. In the three months following the announcement of the special dividend, the cumulative volume exceeded 65% of the total shares available for trade.

While this evidence supports the dividend-capture theory, it is also true that many high-tax investors continue to hold stocks even when dividends are paid. For a small ordinary dividend, the transaction costs and risks of trading the stock probably offset the benefits associated with dividend capture.[19] Large increases in volume, as in the case of Value Line, tend to be associated with large special dividends. Thus, while clientele effects and dividend-capture strategies reduce the relative tax disadvantage of dividends, they do not eliminate it.[20]

CONCEPT CHECK

1. Under what conditions will investors have a tax preference for share repurchases rather than dividends?

2. What does the dividend-capture theory imply about the volume of trade in a stock around the ex-dividend day?

17.5 Payout Versus Retention of Cash

Looking back at Figure 17.1, we have thus far considered only one aspect of a firm's payout policy: the choice between paying dividends and repurchasing shares. But how should a firm decide the amount it should pay out to shareholders and the amount it should retain?

To answer this question, we must first consider what the firm will do with cash that it retains. It can invest the cash in new projects or in financial instruments. We will demonstrate that in the context of perfect capital markets, once a firm has taken all positive-NPV investments, it is indifferent between saving excess cash and paying it out. But once we consider market imperfections, there is a tradeoff: Retaining cash can reduce the costs of raising capital in the future, but it can also increase taxes and agency costs.

Retaining Cash with Perfect Capital Markets

If a firm retains cash, it can use those funds to invest in new projects. If new positive-NPV projects are available, this decision is clearly the correct one. Making positive-NPV investments will create value for the firm's investors, whereas saving the cash or paying it out

---

19. The risk of the dividend-capture strategy is the risk that the stock price may fluctuate for reasons unrelated to the dividend before the transaction can be completed. See J. Koski and R. Michaely, "Prices, Liquidity, and the Information Content of Trades," *Review of Financial Studies* 13(3) (2000): 659–696, who demonstrate that in some cases the risk can be eliminated by negotiating a purchase and sale simultaneously, but with settlement dates before and after the ex-dividend date. In this case the amount of dividend-related volume is greatly increased.

20. These effects are one reason it is difficult to find evidence that the equity cost of capital increases with dividend yields as one would expect if long-term investors are an important clientele. While evidence was found by R. Litzenberger and K. Ramaswamy ["The Effects of Personal Taxes and Dividends on Capital Asset Prices: Theory and Empirical Evidence," *Journal of Financial Economics* 7(2) (1979): 163–195], this evidence is contradicted by the results of F. Black and M. Scholes ["The Effects of Dividend Yield and Dividend Policy on Common Stock Prices and Returns," *Journal of Financial Economics* 1(1) (1974): 1–22]. A. Kalay and R. Michaely provide an explanation for the differing results of these studies and do not find a significant impact of dividend yields on expected returns ["Dividends and Taxes: A Reexamination," *Financial Management* 29(2) (2000): 55–75].

will not. However, once the firm has already taken all positive-NPV projects, any additional projects it takes on are zero or negative-NPV investments. Taking on negative-NPV investments will reduce shareholder value, as the benefits of such investments do not exceed their costs.

Of course, rather than waste excess cash on negative-NPV projects, a firm can hold the cash in the bank or use it to purchase financial assets. The firm can then pay the money to shareholders at a future time or invest it when positive-NPV investment opportunities become available.

What are the advantages and disadvantages of retaining cash and investing in financial securities? In perfect capital markets, buying and selling securities is a zero-NPV transaction, so it should not affect firm value. Shareholders can make any investment a firm makes on their own if the firm pays out the cash. Thus it should not be surprising that with perfect capital markets, the retention versus payout decision—just like the dividend versus share repurchase decision—is irrelevant.

EXAMPLE 17.4	**Delaying Dividends with Perfect Markets**

Problem

Barston Mining has $100,000 in excess cash. Barston is considering investing the cash in one-year Treasury bills paying 6% interest, and then using the cash to pay a dividend next year. Alternatively, the firm can pay a dividend immediately and shareholders can invest the cash on their own. In a perfect capital market, which option will shareholders prefer?

Solution

If Barston pays an immediate dividend, the shareholders receive $100,000 today. If Barston retains the cash, at the end of one year the company will be able to pay a dividend of

$$\$100,000 \times (1.06) = \$106,000$$

This payoff is the same as if shareholders had invested the $100,000 in Treasury bills themselves. In other words, the present value of this future dividend is exactly $106,000 ÷ (1.06) = $100,000. Thus shareholders are indifferent about whether the firm pays the dividend immediately or retains the cash.

As Example 17.4 illustrates, there is no difference for shareholders if the firm pays the cash immediately or retains the cash and pays it out at a future date. This example provides yet another illustration of Modigliani and Miller's fundamental insight regarding financial policy irrelevance in perfect capital markets:

MM Payout Irrelevance: *In perfect capital markets, if a firm invests excess cash flows in financial securities, the firm's choice of payout versus retention is irrelevant and does not affect the initial share price.*

Thus, the decision of whether to retain cash depends on market imperfections, which we turn to next.

Taxes and Cash Retention

Example 17.4 assumed perfect capital markets, and so ignored the effect of taxes. How would our result change with taxes?

EXAMPLE 17.5	Retaining Cash with Corporate Taxes

Problem

Suppose Barston must pay corporate taxes at a 35% rate on the interest it will earn from the one-year Treasury bill paying 6% interest. Would pension fund investors (who do not pay taxes on their investment income) prefer that Barston use its excess cash to pay the $100,000 dividend immediately or retain the cash for one year?

Solution

If Barston pays an immediate dividend, shareholders receive $100,000 today. If Barston retains the cash for one year, it will earn an after-tax return on the Treasury bills of

$$6\% \times (1 - 0.35) = 3.90\%$$

Thus, at the end of the year, Barston will pay a dividend of $100,000 \times (1.039) = $103,900.

This amount is less than the $106,000 the investors would have earned if they had invested the $100,000 in Treasury bills themselves. Because Barston must pay corporate taxes on the interest it earns, there is a tax disadvantage to retaining cash. Pension fund investors will therefore prefer that Barston pays the dividend now.

As Example 17.5 shows, corporate taxes make it costly for a firm to retain excess cash. This effect is the very same effect we identified in Chapter 15 with regard to leverage: When a firm pays interest, it receives a tax deduction for that interest, whereas when a firm receives interest, it owes taxes on the interest. As we discussed in Chapter 14, cash is equivalent to *negative* leverage, so the tax advantage of leverage implies a tax disadvantage to holding cash.

EXAMPLE 17.6	Microsoft's Special Dividend

Problem

In the introduction to this chapter, we described Microsoft's special dividend of $3 per share, or $32 billion, during late 2004. If Microsoft had instead retained that cash permanently, what would the present value of the additional taxes paid be?

Solution

If Microsoft retained the cash, the interest earned on it would be subject to a 35% corporate tax rate. Because the interest payments are risk free, we can discount the tax payments at the risk-free interest rate under the assumption that Microsoft's marginal corporate tax rate will remain constant (or that any changes to it have a beta of zero). Thus, the present value of the tax payments on Microsoft's additional interest income would be

$$\frac{\$32 \text{ billion} \times r_f \times 35\%}{r_f} = \$32 \text{ billion} \times 35\% = \$11.2 \text{ billion}$$

So, on a per share basis, Microsoft's tax savings from paying out the cash rather than retaining it is $3 \times 35\% = $1.05 per share.

Adjusting for Investor Taxes

The decision to pay out versus retain cash may also affect the taxes paid by shareholders. While pension and retirement fund investors are tax exempt, most individual investors must pay taxes on interest, dividends, and capital gains. How do investor taxes affect the tax disadvantage of retaining cash?

We illustrate the tax impact with a simple example. Consider a firm whose only asset is $100 in cash, and suppose all investors face identical tax rates. Let's compare the option of paying out this cash as an immediate dividend of $100 with the option of retaining the $100 permanently and using the interest earned to pay dividends.

Suppose the firm pays out its cash immediately as a dividend and shuts down. Because the ex-dividend price of the firm is zero (it has shut down), using Eq. 17.2 we find that before the dividend is paid the firm has a share price of

$$P_{cum} = P_{ex} + Div_0 \times \left(\frac{1 - \tau_d}{1 - \tau_g}\right) = 0 + 100 \times \left(\frac{1 - \tau_d}{1 - \tau_g}\right) \quad (17.4)$$

This price reflects the fact that the investor will pay tax on the dividend at rate τ_d, but will receive a tax credit (at capital gains tax rate τ_g) for the capital loss when the firm shuts down.

Alternatively, the firm can retain the cash and invest it in Treasury bills, earning interest at rate r_f each year. After paying corporate taxes on this interest at rate τ_c, the firm can pay a perpetual dividend of

$$Div = 100 \times r_f \times (1 - \tau_c)$$

each year and retain the $100 in cash permanently. What price will an investor pay for the firm in this case? The investor's cost of capital is the after-tax return that she could earn by investing in Treasury bills on her own: $r_f \times (1 - \tau_i)$, where τ_i is the investor's tax rate on interest income. Because the investor must pay taxes on the dividends as well, the value of the firm if it retains the $100 is[21]

$$P_{retain} = \frac{Div \times (1 - \tau_d)}{r_f \times (1 - \tau_i)} = \frac{100 \times r_f \times (1 - \tau_c) \times (1 - \tau_d)}{r_f \times (1 - \tau_i)}$$

$$= 100 \times \frac{(1 - \tau_c)(1 - \tau_d)}{(1 - \tau_i)} \quad (17.5)$$

Comparing Eqs. 17.5 and 17.4,

$$P_{retain} = P_{cum} \times \frac{(1 - \tau_c)(1 - \tau_g)}{(1 - \tau_i)} = P_{cum} \times (1 - \tau^*_{retain}) \quad (17.6)$$

where τ^*_{retain} measures the effective tax disadvantage of retaining cash:

$$\tau^*_{retain} = \left[1 - \frac{(1 - \tau_c)(1 - \tau_g)}{(1 - \tau_i)}\right] \quad (17.7)$$

---

21. There is no capital gains tax consequence in this case because the share price will remain the same each year.

Because the dividend tax will be paid whether the firm pays the cash immediately or retains the cash and pays the interest over time, the dividend tax rate does not affect the cost of retaining cash in Eq. 17.7.[22] The intuition for Eq. 17.7 is that when a firm retains cash, it must pay corporate tax on the interest it earns. In addition, the investor will owe capital gains tax on the increased value of the firm. In essence, the interest on retained cash is taxed twice. If the firm paid the cash to its shareholders instead, they could invest it and be taxed only once on the interest that they earn. The cost of retaining cash therefore depends on the combined effect of the corporate and capital gains taxes, compared to the single tax on interest income. Using 2005 tax rates (see Table 15.3), $\tau_c = \tau_i = 35\%$ and $\tau_g = 15\%$, we get an effective tax disadvantage of retained cash of $\tau^*_{retain} = 15\%$. Thus, after adjusting for investor taxes, there remains a substantial tax *disadvantage* for the firm to retaining excess cash.

Issuance and Distress Costs

If there is a tax disadvantage to retaining cash, why do some firms accumulate large cash balances? Generally, they retain cash balances to cover potential future cash shortfalls. For example, if there is a reasonable likelihood that future earnings will be insufficient to fund future positive-NPV investment opportunities, a firm may start accumulating cash to make up the difference. This motivation is especially relevant for firms that may need to fund large-scale research and development projects or large acquisitions.

The advantage of holding cash to cover future potential cash needs is that this strategy allows a firm to avoid the transaction costs of raising new capital (through new debt or equity issues). The direct costs of issuance range from 1% to 3% for debt issues and from 3.5% to 7% for equity issues. There can also be substantial indirect costs of raising capital due to the agency and adverse selection (lemons) costs discussed in Chapter 16. A firm must therefore balance the tax costs of holding cash with the potential benefits of not having to raise external funds in the future. Firms with very volatile earnings may also build up cash reserves to enable them to weather temporary periods of operating losses. By holding sufficient cash, these firms can avoid financial distress and its associated costs.

Agency Costs of Retaining Cash

There is no benefit to shareholders when a firm holds cash above and beyond its future investment or liquidity needs, however. In fact, in addition to the tax cost, there are likely to be agency costs associated with having too much cash in the firm. As discussed in Chapter 16, when firms have excessive cash, managers may use the funds inefficiently by

22. Equation 17.7 also holds if the firm uses share repurchases instead of dividends in both cases or uses the same mix of dividends and share repurchases. However, if the firm initially retains cash by cutting back only on share repurchases, and then later uses the cash to pay a mix of dividends and repurchases, then we would replace τ_g in Eq. 17.7 with the average tax rate on dividends and capital gains, $\tau_e = \alpha\tau_d + (1 - \alpha)\tau_g$, where α is the proportion of dividends versus repurchases. In that case, τ^*_{retain} equals the effective tax disadvantage of debt τ^* we derived in Eq. 15.7, where we implicitly assumed that debt was used to fund a share repurchase (or to avoid an equity issue), and that the future interest payments displaced a mix of dividends and share repurchases. Using τ_g here is sometimes referred to as the "new view" or "trapped-equity" view of retained earnings; see, for example, A. J. Auerbach, "Tax Integration and the 'New View' of the Corporate Tax: A 1980s Perspective," *Proceedings of the National Tax Association–Tax Institute of America* (1981): 21–27. Using τ_e corresponds to the "traditional view"; see, for example, J. M. Poterba and L. H. Summers, "Dividend Taxes, Corporate Investment, and 'Q'," *Journal of Public Economics*, 22 (1983): 135–167.

continuing money-losing pet projects, paying excessive executive perks, or over-paying for acquisitions. Leverage is one way to reduce a firm's excess cash; dividends and share repurchases perform a similar role by taking cash out of the firm.

Thus paying out excess cash through dividends or share repurchases can boost the stock price by reducing managers' ability and temptation to waste resources. For example, the roughly $10 increase in Value Line's stock price on the announcement of its special dividend, shown in Figure 17.6, likely corresponds to the perceived tax benefits and reduced agency costs that would result from the transaction.

EXAMPLE 17.7

Cutting Negative-NPV Growth

Problem

Rexton Oil is an all-equity firm with 100 million shares outstanding. Rexton has $150 million in cash and expects future free cash flows of $65 million per year. Management plans to use the cash to expand the firm's operations, which will in turn increase future free cash flows by 12%. If the cost of capital of Rexton's investments is 10%, how would a decision to use the cash for a share repurchase rather than the expansion change the share price?

Solution

If Rexton uses the cash to expand, its future free cash flows will increase by 12% to $65 million × 1.12 = $72.8 million per year. Using the perpetuity formula, its market value will be $72.8 million ÷ 10% = $728 million, or $7.28 per share.

If Rexton does not expand, the value of its future free cash flows will be $65 million ÷ 10% = $650 million. Adding the cash, Rexton's market value is $800 million, or $8.00 per share. If Rexton repurchases shares, there will be no change to the share price: It will repurchase $150 million ÷ $8.00 / share = 18.75 million shares, so it will have assets worth $650 million with 81.25 million shares outstanding, for a share price of $650 million ÷ 81.25 million shares = $8.00 / share.

In this case, cutting investment and growth to fund a share repurchase increases the share price by $0.72 per share. The reason is the expansion has a negative NPV: It costs $150 million, but increases future free cash flows by only $7.8 million, for an NPV of

$$-\$150 \text{ million} + \$7.8 \text{ million} / 10\% = -\$72 \text{ million, or } -\$0.72 \text{ per share}$$

Ultimately, firms should choose to retain cash for the same reasons they would use low leverage[23]—to preserve financial slack for future growth opportunities and to avoid financial distress costs. These needs must be balanced against the tax disadvantage of holding cash and the agency cost of wasteful investment. It is not surprising, then, that high-tech and biotechnology firms, which typically choose to use little debt, also tend to retain and accumulate large amounts of cash. See Table 17.4 for a list of some U.S. firms with large cash balances.

As with capital structure decisions, however, payout policies are generally set by managers whose incentives may differ from those of shareholders. Managers may prefer to retain and maintain control over the firm's cash rather than pay it out. The retained cash can be used to fund investments that are costly for shareholders but have benefits for

---

23. As discussed in Chapter 14, we can view excess cash as negative debt. As a consequence, the trade-offs from holding excess cash are very similar to those involved in the capital structure decision.

TABLE 17.4	Firms with Large Cash Balances		
Ticker	Company	Cash ($ billion)	Percentage of Market Capitalization
MSFT	Microsoft	34.7	12%
PFE	Pfizer	22.2	12%
MRK	Merck	15.6	21%
MOT	Motorola	14.8	25%
INTC	Intel	12.8	11%
HPQ	Hewlett-Packard	12.0	13%

Source: Yahoo! Finance, April 2006.

managers (for instance, pet projects and excessive salaries), or it can simply be held as a means to reduce leverage and the risk of financial distress that could threaten managers' job security. According to the managerial entrenchment theory of payout policy, managers pay out cash only when pressured to do so by the firm's investors.[24]

CONCEPT CHECK

1. Is there an advantage for a firm to retain its cash instead of paying it out to shareholders in perfect capital markets?

2. How do corporate taxes affect the decision of a firm to retain excess cash?

17.6 Signaling with Payout Policy

One market imperfection that we have not yet considered is asymmetric information. When managers have better information than investors regarding the future prospects of the firm, their payout decisions may signal this information. In this section, we look at managers' motivations when setting a firm's payout policy, and we evaluate what these decisions may communicate to investors.

Dividend Smoothing

Firms can change dividends at any time, but in practice they vary the sizes of their dividends relatively infrequently. For example, General Motors (GM) has changed the amount of its regular dividend only seven times over a 20-year period. Yet during that same period, GM's earnings varied widely, as shown in Figure 17.7.

The pattern seen with GM is typical of most firms that pay dividends. Firms adjust dividends relatively infrequently, and dividends are much less volatile than earnings. This practice of maintaining relatively constant dividends is called **dividend smoothing**. Firms also increase dividends much more frequently than they cut them. For example, from 1971

---

24. Recall from Section 16.7 that the managerial entrenchment theory of capital structure argued that managers choose low leverage to avoid the discipline of debt and preserve their job security. Applied to payout policy, the same theory implies that managers will reduce leverage further by choosing to hold too much cash.

FIGURE 17.7

GM's Earnings and Dividends per Share, 1985–2006

Compared to GM's earnings, its dividend payments have remained relatively stable. (Data adjusted for splits, earnings exclude extraordinary items.)

Source: Compustat and CapitalIQ.

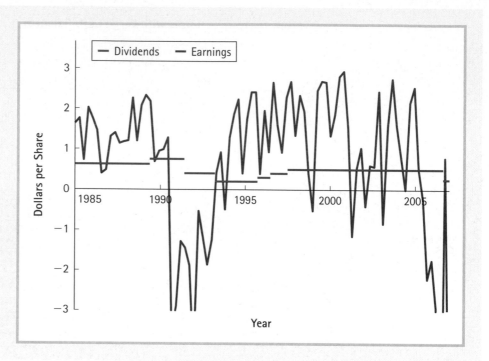

to 2001, only 5.4% of dividend changes were decreases.[25] In a classic survey of corporate executives, John Lintner[26] suggested that these observations resulted from (1) management's belief that investors prefer stable dividends with sustained growth, and (2) management's desire to maintain a long-term target level of dividends as a fraction of earnings. Thus firms raise their dividends only when they perceive a long-term sustainable increase in the expected level of future earnings, and cut them only as a last resort.[27]

How can firms keep dividends smooth as earnings vary? As we have already discussed, firms can maintain almost any level of dividend in the short run by adjusting the number of shares they repurchase or issue and the amount of cash they retain. However, due to the tax and transaction costs of funding a dividend with new equity issues, managers do not wish to commit to a dividend that the firm cannot afford to pay out of regular earnings. For this reason, firms generally set dividends at a level they expect to be able to maintain based on the firm's earnings prospects.

Dividend Signaling

If firms smooth dividends, the firm's dividend choice will contain information regarding management's expectations of future earnings. When a firm increases its dividend, it sends a positive signal to investors that management expects to be able to afford the higher div-

---

25. F. Allen and R. Michaely, "Payout Policy," in G. Constantinides, M. Harris, and R. Stulz, eds., *Handbook of the Economics of Finance* (2003).

26. J. Lintner, "Distribution of Incomes of Corporations Among Dividends, Retained Earnings and Taxes," *American Economic Review* 46 (1956): 97–113.

27. While perhaps a good description of how firms *do* set their dividends, as we have shown in this chapter there is no clear reason why firms *should* smooth their dividends, nor convincing evidence that investors prefer this practice.

Royal & SunAlliance's Dividend Cut

In some quarters, Julian Hance must have seemed like a heretic. On November 8, 2001, the finance director of Royal & SunAlliance, a U.K.-based insurance group with £12.6 billion (€20.2 billion) in annual revenue, did the unthinkable—he announced that he would cut the firm's dividend.

Many observers gasped at the decision. Surely, they argued, cutting the dividend was a sign of weakness. Didn't companies only cut their dividend when profits were falling?

Quite the contrary, countered Hance. With insurance premiums rising around the world, particularly following the World Trade Center tragedy, Royal & SunAlliance believed that its industry offered excellent growth opportunities.

"The outlook for business in 2002 and beyond makes a compelling case for reinvesting capital in the business rather than returning it to shareholders," explains Hance.

The stock market agreed with him, sending Royal & SunAlliance's shares up 5% following its dividend news. "Cutting the dividend is a positive move," observes Matthew Wright, an insurance analyst at Credit Lyonnais. "It shows the company expects future profitability to be good."

Source: Justin Wood, CFO Europe.com, December 2001.

---

idend for the foreseeable future. Conversely, when managers cut the dividend, it may signal that they have given up hope that earnings will rebound in the near term and so need to reduce the dividend to save cash. The idea that dividend changes reflect managers' views about a firm's future earnings prospects is called the **dividend signaling hypothesis**.

Studies of the market's reaction to dividend changes are consistent with this hypothesis. For example, during the period 1967–1993, firms that raised their dividend by 10% or more saw their stock prices rise by 1.34% after the announcement, while those that cut their dividend by 10% or more experienced a price decline of −3.71%.[28] The average size of the stock price reaction increases with the magnitude of the dividend change, and is larger for dividend cuts.[29]

Dividend signaling is similar to the use of leverage as a signal that we discussed in Chapter 16. Increasing debt signals that management believes the firm can afford the future interest payments, in the same way that raising the dividend signals the firm can afford to maintain the dividends in the future. However, while cutting the dividend is costly for managers in terms of their reputation and the reaction of investors, it is by no means as costly as failing to make debt payments. As a consequence, we would expect dividend changes to be a somewhat weaker signal than leverage changes. Indeed, empirical studies have found average stock price increases of more than 10% when firms replace equity with debt, and decreases of 4% to 10% when firms replace debt with equity.[30]

---

28. See G. Grullon, R. Michaely, and B. Swaminathan, "Are Dividend Changes a Sign of Firm Maturity?" *Journal of Business* 75(3) (2002): 387–424. The effects are even larger for dividend initiations (+3.4%) and omissions (−7%), according to studies by R. Michaely, R. Thaler, and K. Womack, "Price Reactions to Dividend Initiations and Omissions: Overreaction or Drift?" *Journal of Finance* 50(2) (1995): 573–608, and similar results by P. Healy and K. Palepu, "Earnings Information Conveyed by Dividend Initiations and Omissions," *Journal of Financial Economics* 21(2) (1988): 149–176.

29. Not all of the evidence is consistent with dividend signaling, however. For example, it has been difficult to document a relationship between dividend changes and realized future earnings [S. Benartzi, R. Michaely and R. Thaler, "Do Changes in Dividends Signal the Future or the Past?" *Journal of Finance* 52(3) (1997): 1007–1034].

30. C. Smith, "Raising Capital: Theory and Evidence," in D. Chew, ed., *The New Corporate Finance* (McGraw-Hill, 1993).

While an increase of a firm's dividend may signal management's optimism regarding its future cash flows, it might also signal a lack of investment opportunities. For example, Microsoft's move to initiate dividends in 2003 was largely seen as a result of its declining growth prospects as opposed to a signal about its increased future profitability.[31] Conversely, a firm might cut its dividend to exploit new positive-NPV investment opportunities. In this case, the dividend decrease might lead to a positive—rather than negative—stock price reaction (see the box on Royal and SunAlliance's dividend cut on page 557). In general, we must interpret dividends as a signal in the context of the type of new information managers are likely to have.

Signaling and Share Repurchases

Share repurchases, like dividends, may also signal managers' information to the market. However, several important differences distinguish share repurchases and dividends. First, managers are much less committed to share repurchases than to dividend payments. As we noted earlier, when firms announce authorization for an open market share repurchase, they generally announce the maximum amount they plan to spend on repurchases. The actual amount spent, however, may be far less. Also, it may take several years to complete the share repurchase.[32] Second, unlike with dividends, firms do not smooth their repurchase activity from year to year. As a result, announcing a share repurchase today does not necessarily represent a long-term commitment to repurchase shares. In this regard, share repurchases may be less of a signal than dividends about future earnings of a firm.

A third key difference between dividends and share repurchases is that the cost of a share repurchase depends on the market price of the stock. If managers believe the stock is currently over-valued, a share repurchase will be costly to the firm. That is, buying the stock at its current (over-valued) price is a negative-NPV investment. By contrast, repurchasing shares when managers perceive the stock to be under-valued is a positive-NPV investment. Managers will clearly be more likely to repurchase shares if they believe the stock to be under-valued.

Thus share repurchases may signal that managers believe the firm to be under-valued (or at least not severely over-valued). Share repurchases are a credible signal that the shares are under-priced, because if they are over-priced a share repurchase is costly for current shareholders. If investors believe that managers have better information regarding the firm's prospects and act on behalf of current shareholders, then investors will react favorably to share repurchase announcements.

In a 2004 survey, 87% of CFOs agreed that firms should repurchase shares when their stock price is a good value relative to its true value.[33] Investors also appear to interpret share repurchases as a positive signal. The average market price reaction to the announcement of an open market share repurchase program is about 3% (with the size of the reac-

---

31. See "An End to Growth?" *The Economist* (July 22, 2004): 61.

32. See C. Stephens and M. Weisbach, "Actual Share Reacquisitions in Open-Market Repurchase Programs," *Journal of Finance* 53(1) (1998): 313–333, for an analysis of how firms' actual repurchases compare to their announced plans. For details of how share repurchase programs are implemented, see D. Cook, L. Krigman, and J. Leach, "On the Timing and Execution of Open Market Repurchases," *Review of Financial Studies* 17(2) (2004): 463–498.

33. A. Brav, J. Graham, C. Harvey, and R. Michaely, "Payout Policy in the 21st Century," *Journal of Financial Economics* 77(3) (2005): 483–527.

tion increasing in the portion of shares outstanding sought).[34] The reaction is much larger for fixed-price tender offers (12%) and Dutch auction share repurchases (8%).[35] Recall that these methods of repurchase are generally used for very large repurchases conducted in a very short timeframe and are often part of an overall recapitalization. Also, the shares are repurchased at a premium to the current market price. Thus tender offers and Dutch auction repurchases are even stronger signals than open market repurchases that management views the current share price as under-valued.

EXAMPLE 17.8

Share Repurchases and Market Timing

Problem

Clark Industries has 200 million shares outstanding, a current share price of $30, and no debt. Clark's management believes that the shares are under-priced, and that the true value is $35 per share. Clark plans to pay $600 million in cash to its shareholders by repurchasing shares at the current market price. Suppose that soon after the transaction is completed, new information comes out that causes investors to revise their opinion of the firm and agree with management's assessment of Clark's value. What is Clark's share price after the new information comes out? How would the share price differ if Clark waited until after the new information came out to repurchase the shares?

Solution

Clark's initial market cap is $30/share × 200 million shares = $6 billion, of which $600 million is cash and $5.4 billion corresponds to other assets. At the current share price, Clark will repurchase $600 million ÷ $30/share = 20 million shares. The market value balance sheet before and after the transaction is shown below (in millions of dollars):

	Before Repurchase	After Repurchase	After New Information
Cash	600	0	0
Other assets	5,400	5,400	6,400
Total market value of assets	6,000	5,400	6,400
Shares (millions)	200	180	180
Share Price	**$30**	**$30**	**$35.56**

According to management, Clark's initial market capitalization should be $35/share × 200 million shares = $7 billion, of which $6.4 billion would correspond to other assets. As the market value balance sheet shows, after the new information comes out Clark's share price will rise to $35.56.

If Clark waited for the new information to come out before repurchasing the shares, it would buy shares at a market price of $35 per share. Thus it would repurchase only 17.1 million shares. The share price after the repurchase would be $6.4 billion ÷ 182.9 shares = $35.

---

34. See D. Ikenberry, J. Lakonishok, and T. Vermaelen, "Market Underreaction to Open Market Share Repurchases," *Journal of Financial Economics* 39(2) (1995): 181–208, and G. Grullon and R. Michaely, "Dividends, Share Repurchases, and the Substitution Hypothesis," *Journal of Finance* 57(4) (2002): 1649–1684.

35. R. Comment and G. Jarrell, "The Relative Signaling Power of Dutch-Auction and Fixed-Price Self-tender Offers and Open-Market Share Repurchases," *Journal of Finance* 46(4) (1991): 1243–1271.

> Hence, by repurchasing shares while the stock is under-priced, the ultimate share price will be $0.56 higher, for a total gain of $0.56 × 180 million shares = $100 million. This gain equals the gain from buying 20 million shares at a price that is $5 below their true value. It comes at the expense of shareholders who sold shares for $30/share as part of the repurchase.
>
> As this example shows, the gain from buying shares when the stock is under-priced leads to an increase in the firm's long-run share price. Similarly, buying shares when the stock is over-priced will reduce the long-run share price. The firm may therefore try to time its repurchases appropriately. Anticipating this strategy, shareholders may interpret a share repurchase as a signal that the firm is undervalued.

CONCEPT CHECK

1. What possible signals does a firm give when it cuts its dividend?

2. Would managers be more likely to repurchase shares if they believe the stock is under- or over-valued?

17.7 Stock Dividends, Splits, and Spin-offs

In this chapter, we have focused on a firm's decision to pay cash to its shareholders. But a firm can pay another type of dividend that does not involve cash: a stock dividend. In this case, each shareholder who owns the stock before it goes ex-dividend receives additional shares of stock of the firm itself (a stock split) or of a subsidiary (a spin-off). Here we briefly review these two types of transactions.

Stock Dividends and Splits

If a company declares a 10% stock dividend, each shareholder will receive one new share of stock for every 10 shares already owned. Stock dividends of 50% or higher are generally referred to as stock splits. For example, with a 50% stock dividend, each shareholder will receive one new share for every two shares owned. Because a holder of two shares will end up holding three new shares, this transaction is also called a 3 : 2 ("3-for-2") stock split. Similarly, a 100% stock dividend is equivalent to a 2 : 1 stock split.

With a stock dividend, a firm does not pay out any cash to shareholders. As a result, the total market value of the firm's assets and liabilities, and therefore of its equity, is unchanged. The only thing that is different is the number of shares outstanding. The stock price will therefore fall because the same total equity value is now divided over a larger number of shares.

Let's illustrate a stock dividend for Genron. Suppose Genron paid a 50% stock dividend (a 3 : 2 stock split) rather than a cash dividend. Table 17.5 shows the market value balance sheet and the resulting share price before and after the stock dividend.

A shareholder who owns 100 shares before the dividend has a portfolio worth $42 × 100 = $4200. After the dividend, the shareholder owns 150 shares worth $28, giving a portfolio value of $28 × 150 = $4200. (Note the important difference between a stock split and a share issuance: When the company issues shares, the number of shares increases, but the firm also raises cash to add to its existing assets. If the shares are sold at a fair price, the stock price should not change.)

Unlike cash dividends, stock dividends are not taxed. Thus, from both the firm's and shareholders' perspectives, there is no real consequence to a stock dividend. The number

TABLE 17.5	Cum and Ex-Dividend Share Price for Genron with a 50% Stock Dividend ($ million)	
	December 11 (Cum-Dividend)	December 12 (Ex-Dividend)
Cash	20	20
Other assets	400	400
Total market value of assets	420	420
Shares (millions)	10	15
Share price	$42	$28

of shares is proportionally increased and the price per share is proportionally reduced so that there is no change in value.

Why, then, do companies pay stock dividends or split their stock? The typical motivation for a stock split is to keep the share price in a range thought to be attractive to small investors. Stocks generally trade in lots of 100 shares, and in any case do not trade in units less than one share. As a result, if the share price rises significantly, it might be difficult for small investors to afford one share, let alone 100. Making the stock more attractive to small investors can increase the demand for and the liquidity of the stock, which may in

Berkshire Hathaway's A & B Shares

Many managers split their stock to keep the price affordable for small investors, making it easier for them to buy and sell the stock. Warren Buffett, chairman and chief executive of Berkshire Hathaway, disagrees. As he commented in Berkshire's 1983 annual report: "We are often asked why Berkshire does not split its stock . . . we want [shareholders] who think of themselves as business owners with the intention of staying a long time. And, we want those who keep their eyes focused on business results, not market prices." In its 40-year history, Berkshire Hathaway has never split its stock.

As a result of Berkshire Hathaway's strong performance and the lack of stock splits, the stock price climbed. By 1996, it exceeded $30,000 per share. Because this price was much too expensive for some small investors, several financial intermediaries created unit investment trusts whose only investment was Berkshire shares. (Unit investment trusts are similar to mutual funds, but their investment portfolio is fixed.) Investors could buy smaller interests in these trusts, effectively owning Berkshire stock with a much lower initial investment.

In response, in February 1996 Buffett announced the creation of a second class of Berkshire Hathaway stock, the Class B shares. Each owner of the original shares (now called Class A shares) was offered the opportunity to convert each A share into 30 B shares. "We're giving shareholders a do-it-yourself split, if they care to do it," Buffett said. Through the B shares, investors could own Berkshire stock with a smaller investment, and they would not have to pay the extra transaction costs required to buy stock through the unit trusts.

In May 2006, the price of one share of Berkshire Hathaway Class A shares was more than $92,000 per share.*

*We should note that Buffet's logic for not splitting the stock is a bit puzzling. Why should letting the stock price rise to a very high level attract a "better" investor clientele compared to splitting the stock and keeping its price in a more typical range? And if an extremely high stock price were advantageous, Buffet could have obtained it much sooner through a reverse split of the stock.

John Connors was Senior Vice President and Chief Financial Officer of Microsoft. He retired in 2005 and is now a partner at Ignition Partners, a Seattle venture capital firm.

QUESTION: *Microsoft declared a dividend for the first time in 2003. What goes into the decision of a company to initiate a dividend?*

ANSWER: Microsoft was in a unique position. The company had never paid a dividend and was facing shareholder pressure to do something with its $60 billion cash buildup. The company considered five key questions in developing its distribution strategy:

1. Can the company sustain payment of a cash dividend in perpetuity and increase the dividend over time? Microsoft was confident it could meet that commitment and raise the dividend in the future.

2. Is a cash dividend a better return to stockholders than a stock buyback program? These are capital structure decisions: Do we want to reduce our shares outstanding? Is our stock attractively priced for a buyback, or do we want to distribute the cash as a dividend? Microsoft had plenty of capacity to issue a dividend *and* continue a buyback program.

3. What is the tax effect of a cash dividend versus a buyback to the corporation and to shareholders? From a tax perspective to shareholders, it was largely a neutral decision in Microsoft's case.

4. What is the psychological impact on investors, and how does it fit the story of the stock for investors? This is a more qualitative factor. A regular ongoing dividend put Microsoft on a path to becoming an attractive investment for income investors.

5. What are the public relations implications of a dividend program? Investors don't look to Microsoft to hold cash but to be a leader in software development and provide equity growth. So they viewed the dividend program favorably.

QUESTION: *How does a company decide whether to increase its dividend, have a special dividend, or repurchase its stock to return capital to investors?*

ANSWER: The decision to increase the dividend is a function of cash flow projections. Are you confident that you have adequate cash flow to sustain this and future increases? Once you increase the dividend, investors expect future increases as well. Some companies establish explicit criteria for dividend increases. In my experience as a CFO, the analytic framework involves a set of relative comparables. What are the dividend payouts and dividend yields of the market in general and of your peer group, and where are we relative to them? We talk to significant investors and consider what is best for increasing shareholder value long-term.

A special dividend is a very efficient form of cash distribution that generally involves a nonrecurring situation, such as the sale of a business division or a cash award from a legal situation. Also, companies without a comprehensive distribution strategy use special dividends to reduce large cash accumulations. For Microsoft, the 2004 special dividend and announcement of the stock dividend and stock buyback program resolved the issue of what to do with all the cash and clarified our direction going forward.

QUESTION: *What other factors go into dividend decisions?*

ANSWER: Powerful finance and accounting tools help us to make better and broader business decisions. But these decisions involve as much psychology and market thinking as math. You have to consider non-quantifiable factors such as the psychology of investors. Not long ago, everyone wanted growth stocks; no one wanted dividend-paying stocks. Now dividend stocks are in vogue. You must also take into account your industry and what the competition is doing. In many tech companies, employee ownership in the form of options programs represents a fairly significant percentage of fully diluted shares. Dividend distributions reduce volatility of stock and hence the value of options.

At the end of the day, you want to be sure that your cash distribution strategy helps your overall story with investors.

turn boost the stock price. On average, announcements of stock splits are associated with a 2% increase in the stock price.[36]

Most firms use splits to keep their share prices from exceeding $100. From 1990 to 2000, Cisco Systems split its stock nine times, so that one share purchased at the IPO split into 288 shares. Had it not split, Cisco's share price at the time of its last split in March 2000 would have been 288 × $72.19, or $20,790.72.

Firms also do not want their stock prices to fall too low. First, a stock price that is very low raises transaction costs for investors. For example, the spread between the bid and ask price for a stock has a minimum size of one tick ($0.01 for the NYSE and Nasdaq exchanges) independent of the stock price. In percentage terms, the tick size is larger for stocks with a low price than for stocks with a high price. Also, exchanges require stocks to maintain a minimum price to remain listed on an exchange (for example, the NYSE and Nasdaq require listed firms to maintain a price of at least $1 per share).

If the price of the stock falls too low, a company can engage in a **reverse split** and reduce the number of shares outstanding. For example, in a 1:10 reverse split, every 10 shares of stock are replaced with a single share. As a result, the share price increases tenfold. Reverse splits became necessary for many dot-coms after the Internet bust in 2000. Infospace.com, for instance, split 2:1 three times in 1999 through 2000, but was forced to implement a 1:10 reverse split in 2002 when its share price dropped below $0.40.

Through a combination of splits and reverse splits, firms can keep their share prices in any range they desire. As Figure 17.8 shows, almost all firms have stock prices below $100 per share, with most firms' prices being between $5 and $60 per share.

Spin-offs

Rather than pay a dividend using cash or shares of its own stock, a firm can also distribute shares of a subsidiary in a transaction referred to as a **spin-off**. Non-cash special dividends are commonly used to spin off assets or a subsidiary as a separate company. For example, after selling 15% of Monsanto Corporation in an IPO in October 2000, Pharmacia Corporation announced in July 2002 that it would spin off its remaining 85% holding of Monsanto Corporation. The spin-off was accomplished through a special dividend in which each Pharmacia shareholder received 0.170593 share of Monsanto per share of Pharmacia owned. After receiving the Monsanto shares, Pharmacia shareholders could trade them separately from the shares of the parent firm.

On the distribution date of August 13, 2002, Monsanto shares traded for an average price of $16.21. Thus the value of the special dividend was

$$0.170593 \text{ Monsanto shares} \times \$16.21 \text{ per share} = \$2.77 \text{ per share}$$

A shareholder who initially owned 100 shares of Pharmacia stock would receive 17 shares of Monsanto stock, plus cash of 0.0593 × $16.21 = $0.96 in place of the fractional shares.

---

36. S. Nayak and N. Prabhala, "Disentangling the Dividend Information in Splits: A Decomposition Using Conditional Event-Study Methods," *Review of Financial Studies* 14(4) (2001): 1083–1116. For evidence that stock splits are successful at attracting individual investors, see R. Dhar, W. Goetzmann, and N. Zhu, "The Impact of Clientele Changes: Evidence from Stock Splits," *Yale ICF Working Paper* no. 03-14 (2004). While splits seem to increase the number of shareholders, evidence of their impact on liquidity is mixed; see, for example, T. Copeland, "Liquidity Changes Following Stock Splits," *Journal of Finance* 34(1) (1979): 115–141, and J. Lakonishok and B. Lev, "Stock Splits and Stock Dividends: Why, Who and When," *Journal of Finance* 42(4) (1987): 913–932.

FIGURE 17.8

Distribution of Stock Prices for NYSE Firms (April 2005)

By using splits and reverse splits, most firms keep their share prices between $5 and $60 to reduce transaction costs for investors.

Source: Reprinted from Reuters, 2005.

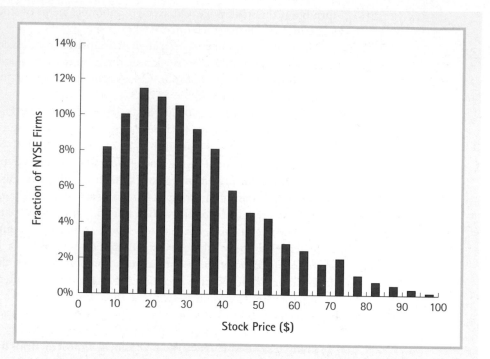

Alternatively, Pharmacia could have sold the shares of Monsanto and distributed the cash to shareholders as a cash dividend. The transaction Pharmacia chose offers two advantages over that strategy: (1) It avoids the transaction costs associated with such a sale, and (2) the special dividend is not taxed as a cash distribution. Instead, Pharmacia shareholders who received Monsanto shares are liable for capital gains tax only at the time they sell the Monsanto shares.[37]

Here we have considered only the methods of distributing the shares of the firm that has been spun off, either by paying a stock dividend or by selling the shares directly and then distributing (or retaining) the cash. The decision of whether to do the spin-off in the first place raises a new question: When is it better for two firms to operate as separate entities, rather than as a single combined firm? The issues that arise in addressing this question are the same as those that arise in the decision to merge two firms, which we discuss further in Chapter 28.

CONCEPT CHECK

1. What is the difference between a stock dividend and a stock split?
2. What is the main purpose of a reverse split?

---

37. The capital gain is computed by allocating a fraction of the cost basis of the Pharmacia shares to the Monsanto shares received. Because Pharmacia was trading at an ex-dividend price of $42.54 on the distribution date, the special dividend amounted to 6.1% = 2.77 / (2.77 + 42.54) of total value. Thus the original cost basis of the Pharmacia stock was divided by allocating 6.1% to the Monsanto shares and the remaining 93.9% to the Pharmacia shares.

Summary

1. When a firm wants to distribute cash to its shareholders, it can pay a cash dividend or it can repurchase shares.

   a. Most companies pay regular, quarterly dividends. Sometimes firms announce one-time, special dividends.

   b. Firms repurchase shares using an open market repurchase, a tender offer, a Dutch auction repurchase, or a targeted repurchase.

2. On the declaration date, firms announce that they will pay dividends to all shareholders of record on the record date. The ex-dividend date is the first day on which the stock trades without the right to an upcoming dividend; it is usually two trading days prior to the record date. Dividend checks are mailed on the payment date.

3. In a stock split or a stock dividend, a company distributes additional shares rather than cash to shareholders.

4. In perfect capital markets, the stock price falls by the amount of the dividend when a dividend is paid. An open market share repurchase has no effect on the stock price, and the stock price is the same as the cum-dividend price if a dividend were paid instead.

5. The Modigliani-Miller dividend irrelevance proposition states that in perfect capital markets, holding fixed the investment policy of a firm, the firm's choice of dividend policy is irrelevant and does not affect the initial share price.

6. In reality, capital markets are not perfect, and market imperfections affect firm dividend policy.

7. Taxes are an important market friction that affects dividend policy.

   a. Considering taxes as the only market imperfection, when the tax rate on dividends exceeds the tax rate on capital gains, the optimal dividend policy is for firms to pay no dividends. Firms should use share repurchases for all payouts.

   b. The effective dividend tax rate, τ_d^*, measures the net tax cost to the investor per dollar of dividend income received.

$$\tau_d^* = \left(\frac{\tau_d - \tau_g}{1 - \tau_g} \right) \qquad (17.3)$$

   The effective dividend tax rate varies across investors for several reasons, including income level, investment horizon, tax jurisdiction, and type of investment account.

   c. Different investor taxes create clientele effects, in which the dividend policy of a firm suits the tax preference of its investor clientele.

8. Modigliani-Miller payout policy irrelevance says that, in perfect capital markets, if a firm invests excess cash flows in financial securities, the firm's choice of payout versus retention is irrelevant and does not affect the initial share price.

9. Corporate taxes make it costly for a firm to retain excess cash. Even after adjusting for investor taxes, retaining excess cash brings a substantial tax disadvantage for a firm.

10. Even though there is a tax disadvantage to retaining cash, some firms accumulate cash balances. Cash balances help firms minimize the transaction costs of raising new capital when they have future potential cash needs. However, there is no benefit to shareholders from firms holding cash in excess of future investment needs.

11. In addition to the tax disadvantage of holding cash, agency costs may arise, as managers may be tempted to spend excess cash on inefficient investments and perks. Without pressure from shareholders, managers may choose to horde cash to spend in this way or as a means of reducing a firm's leverage and increasing their job security.

12. Dividends and share repurchases help minimize the agency problem of wasteful spending when a firm has excess cash.

13. Firms typically maintain relatively constant dividends. This practice is called dividend smoothing.

14. The idea that dividend changes reflect managers' views about firms' future earnings prospects is called the dividend signaling hypothesis.

   a. Managers usually increase dividends only when they are confident the firm will be able to afford higher dividends for the foreseeable future.

   b. When managers cut the dividend, it may signal that they have lost hope that earnings will improve.

15. Share repurchases may be used to signal positive information, as repurchases are more attractive if management believes the stock is under-valued at its current price.

16. With a stock dividend, shareholders receive either additional shares of stock of the firm itself (a stock split) or shares of a subsidiary (a spin-off). The stock price generally falls proportionally with the size of the split.

17. A reverse split decreases the number of shares outstanding, and therefore results in a higher share price.

Key Terms

bird in the hand hypothesis *p. 540*
clientele effect *p. 547*
cum-dividend *p. 536*
declaration date *p. 532*
dividend puzzle *p. 544*
dividend signaling hypothesis *p. 557*
dividend smoothing *p. 555*
dividend-capture theory *p. 548*
Dutch auction *p. 535*
effective dividend tax rate *p. 545*
ex-dividend date *p. 532*
greenmail *p. 535*
liquidating dividend *p. 534*

open market repurchase *p. 534*
payable date (distribution date) *p. 532*
payout policy *p. 532*
record date *p. 532*
return of capital *p. 534*
reverse split *p. 563*
special dividend *p. 532*
spin-off *p. 563*
stock dividend *p. 533*
stock split *p. 533*
targeted repurchase *p. 535*
tender offer *p. 534*

Further Reading

Readers interested in delving deeper into the issues covered in this chapter might want to begin with the following comprehensive review of the literature on payout policy: F. Allen and R. Michaely, "Payout Policy," in G. Constantinides, M. Harris, and R. Shulz, eds., *Handbook of the Economics of Finance*, Chapter 7 (Elsevier, 2003).

The literature on payout policy is extensive. It is impossible, given the space requirements, to cover all the relevant further readings here. Nevertheless, readers interested in specific issues might find the following articles interesting:

On the information content of payout policy: K. L. Dewenter and V. A. Warther, "Dividends, Asymmetric Information, and Agency Conflicts: Evidence from a Comparison of the Dividend Policies of Japanese and U.S. Firms," *Journal of Finance* 53(3) (1998): 879–904; E. Dyl and R. Weigand, "The Information Content of Dividend Initiations: Additional Evidence," *Financial Management* 27(3) (1998): 27–35; and G. Grullon and R. Michaely, "The Information Content of Share Repurchase Programs," *Journal of Finance* 59(2) (2004): 651–680.

On the decision corporations make between dividends and share repurchases: L. S. Bagwell and J. B. Shoven, "Cash Distributions to Shareholders," *Journal of Economic Perspectives* 3(3) (1989): 129–140; M. J. Barclay and C.W. Smith, "Corporate Payout Policy: Cash Dividends Versus Open-Market Repurchases," *Journal of Financial Economics* 22(1) (1988): 61–82; A. Dittmar, "Why Do Firms Repurchase Stock?" *Journal of Business* 73(3) (2000): 331–355; G. W. Fenn and N. Liang, "Corporate Payout Policy and Managerial Stock Incentives," *Journal of Financial Economics* 60(1) (2001): 45–72; W. Guay and J. Harford, "The Cash-Flow Permanence and Information Content of Dividend Increases Versus Repurchases," *Journal of Financial Economics* 57(3) (2000): 385–415; M. Jagannathan, C. P. Stephens, and M. Weisbach, "Financial Flexibility and the Choice Between Dividends and Stock Repurchases," *Journal of Financial Economics* 57(3) (2000): 355–384; K. Kahle, "When a Buyback Isn't a Buyback: Open Market Repurchases and Employee Options," *Journal of Financial Economics* 63(2) (2002): 235–261; and M. Rozeff, "How Companies Set Their Dividend Payout Ratios," in Joel M. Stern and Donald H. Chew, eds., *The Revolution in Corporate Finance* (New York: Basil Blackwell, 1986).

On tax clienteles: F. Allen, A. E. Bernardo, and I. Welch, "A Theory of Dividends Based on Tax Clienteles," *Journal of Finance* 55(6) (2000): 2499–2536.

On the timing of share repurchases: P. Brockman and D. Y. Chung, "Managerial Timing and Corporate Liquidity: Evidence from Actual Share Repurchases," *Journal of Financial Economics* 61(3) (2001): 417–448; and D. O. Cook, L. Krigman, and J. C. Leach, "On the Timing and Execution of Open Market Repurchases," *Review of Financial Studies* 17(2) (2004): 463–498.

Problems

All problems in this chapter are available in MyFinanceLab.

Distributions to Shareholders

1. ABC Corporation announced that it will pay a dividend to all shareholders of record as of Monday, April 3, 2006. It takes three business days of a purchase for the new owners of a share of stock to be registered.

   a. When is the last day an investor can purchase ABC stock and still get the dividend payment?

   b. When is the ex-dividend day?

2. Describe the different mechanisms available to a firm to use to repurchase shares.

Comparison of Dividends and Share Repurchases

3. Natsam Corporation has $250 million of excess cash. The firm has no debt and 500 million shares outstanding with a current market price of $15 per share. Natsam's board has decided to pay out this cash as a one-time dividend.

    a. What is the ex-dividend price of a share in a perfect capital market?

    b. If the board instead decided to use the cash to do a one-time share repurchase, in a perfect capital market what is the price of the shares once the repurchase is complete?

    c. In a perfect capital market, which policy (in part a or b) makes investors in the firm better off?

4. Suppose the board of Natsam Corporation decided to do the share repurchase in Problem 3(b), but you, as an investor, would have preferred to receive a dividend payment. How can you leave yourself in the same position as if the board had elected to make the dividend payment instead?

5. Suppose you work for Oracle Corporation, and part of your compensation takes the form of stock options. The value of the stock option is equal to the difference between Oracle's stock price and an exercise price of $10 per share at the time that you exercise the option. As an option holder, would you prefer that Oracle use dividends or share repurchases to pay out cash to shareholders? Explain.

The Tax Disadvantage of Dividends

6. The HNH Corporation will pay a constant dividend of $2 per share, per year, in perpetuity. Assume all investors pay a 20% tax on dividends and that there is no capital gains tax. The cost of capital for investing in HNH stock is 12%.

    a. What is the price of a share of HNH stock?

    b. Assume that management makes a surprise announcement that HNH will no longer pay dividends but will use the cash to repurchase stock instead. What is the price of a share of HNH stock now?

Dividend Capture and Tax Clienteles

7. What was the effective dividend tax rate for a U.S. investor in the highest tax bracket who planned to hold a stock for one year in 1981? How did the effective dividend tax rate change in 1982 when the Reagan tax cuts took effect? (Ignore state taxes.)

8. The dividend tax cut passed in 2003 lowered the effective dividend tax rate for a U.S. investor in the highest tax bracket to a historic low. During which other periods in the last 35 years was the effective dividend tax rate as low?

9. On Monday, November 15, 2004, TheStreet.Com reported: "An experiment in the efficiency of financial markets will play out Monday following the expiration of a $3.08 dividend privilege for holders of Microsoft." The story went on: "The stock is currently trading ex-dividend both the special $3 payout and Microsoft's regular 8-cent quarterly dividend, meaning a buyer doesn't receive the money if he acquires the shares now." Microsoft stock ultimately opened for trade at $27.34 on the ex-dividend date (November 15), down $2.63 from its previous close.

    a. Assuming that this price drop resulted only from the dividend payment (no other information affected the stock price that day), what does this decline in price imply about the effective dividend tax rate for Microsoft?

    b. Based on this information, which investors are most likely to be the marginal investors (the ones who determine the price) in Microsoft stock?

        i. Long-term individual investors

        ii. One-year individual investors

        iii. Pension funds

        iv. Corporations

10. At current tax rates, which investors are most likely to hold a stock that has a high dividend yield?

    a. Individual investors

    b. Pension funds

    c. Mutual funds

    d. Corporations

11. A stock that you know is held by long-term individual investors paid a large one-time dividend. You notice that the price drop on the ex-dividend date is about the size of the dividend payment. You find this relationship puzzling given the tax disadvantage of dividends. Explain how the dividend-capture theory might account for this behavior.

Payout Versus Retention of Cash

EXCEL 12. Assume capital markets are perfect. Kay Industries currently has $100 million invested in short-term Treasury securities paying 7%, and it pays out the interest payments on these securities as a dividend. The board is considering selling the Treasury securities and paying out the proceeds as a one-time dividend payment.

    a. If the board went ahead with this plan, what would happen to the value of Kay stock upon the announcement of a change in policy?

    b. What would happen to the value of Kay stock on the ex-dividend date of the one-time dividend?

    c. Given these price reactions, will this decision benefit investors?

EXCEL 13. Redo Problem 12 but assume that Kay must pay a corporate tax rate of 35%, and investors pay no taxes.

EXCEL 14. Redo Problem 12 but assume that investors pay a 15% tax on dividends but no capital gains taxes or taxes on interest income, and Kay does not pay corporate taxes.

15. Use the data in Table 15.3 to calculate the tax disadvantage of retained cash in

    a. 1998.

    b. 1976.

Signaling with Payout Policy

16. Explain under which conditions an increase in the dividend payment can be interpreted as a signal of

    a. Good news.

    b. Bad news.

17. Why is an announcement of a share repurchase considered a positive signal?

EXCEL *18. AMC Corporation currently has an enterprise value of $400 million and $100 million in excess cash. The firm has 10 million shares outstanding and no debt. Suppose AMC uses its excess cash to repurchase shares. After the share repurchase, news will come out that will change AMC's enterprise value to either $600 million or $200 million.

    a. What is AMC's share price prior to the share repurchase?

    b. What is AMC's share price after the repurchase if its enterprise value goes up? What is AMC's share price after the repurchase if its enterprise value declines?

    c. Suppose AMC waits until after the news comes out to do the share repurchase. What is AMC's share price after the repurchase if its enterprise value goes up? What is AMC's share price after the repurchase if its enterprise value declines?

d. Suppose AMC management expects good news to come out. Based on your answers to parts (b) and (c), if management desires to maximize AMC's ultimate share price, will they undertake the repurchase before or after the news comes out? When would management undertake the repurchase if they expect bad news to come out?

e. Given your answer to part (d), what effect would you expect an announcement of a share repurchase to have on the stock price? Why?

Stock Dividends, Splits, and Spin-offs

EXCEL **19.** Suppose the stock of Host Hotels & Resorts is currently trading for $20 per share.

a. If Host issued a 20% stock dividend, what will its new share price be?

b. If Host does a 3 : 2 stock split, what will its new share price be?

c. If Host does a 1 : 3 reverse split, what will its new share price be?

20. Explain why most companies choose to pay stock dividends (split their stock).

21. When might it be advantageous to undertake a reverse stock split?

22. After the market close on May 11, 2001, Adaptec, Inc., distributed a dividend of shares of the stock of its software division, Roxio, Inc. Each Adaptec shareholder received 0.1646 share of Roxio stock per share of Adaptec stock owned. At the time, Adaptec stock was trading at a price of $10.55 per share (cum-dividend), and Roxio's share price was $14.23 per share. In a perfect market, what would Adaptec's ex-dividend share price be after this transaction?

Data Case

In your role as a consultant at a wealth management firm, you have been assigned a very powerful client who holds one million shares of Amazon.com purchased on February 28, 2003. In researching Amazon, you discovered that they are holding a large amount of cash, which was surprising since the firm has only relatively recently begun operating at a profit. Additionally, your client is upset that the Amazon stock price has been somewhat stagnant as of late. The client is considering approaching the Board of Directors with a plan for half of the cash the firm has accumulated, but can't decide whether a share repurchase or a special dividend would be best. You have been asked to determine which initiative would generate the greatest amount of money after taxes, assuming that with a share repurchase your client would keep the same proportion of ownership. Because both dividends and capital gains are taxed at the same rate (15%), your client has assumed that there is no difference between the repurchase and the dividend. To confirm, you need to "run the numbers" for each scenario.

1. Go to the Nasdaq homepage (www.nasdaq.com), enter the symbol for Amazon (AMZN), and click "Summary Quote."

   a. Record the current price and the number of shares outstanding.

   b. Click on company financials and then select the balance sheet. Right-click with the cursor in the middle of the balance sheet and select "Export to Microsoft Excel."

2. Using one-half of the most recent cash and cash equivalents reported on the balance sheet (in thousands of dollars), compute the following:

   a. The number of shares that would be repurchased given the current market price.

   b. The dividend per share that could be paid given the total number of shares outstanding.

3. Go to Yahoo! Finance (http://finance.yahoo.com) to obtain the price at which your client purchased the stock on February 28, 2003.

   a. Enter the symbol for Amazon and click "Get Quotes."

   b. Click "Historical Prices," enter the date your client purchased the stock as the start date and the end date, and hit enter. Record the adjusted closing price.

4. Compute the total cash that would be received by your client under the repurchase and the dividend both before taxes and after taxes.

5. The calculation in the last step reflects your client's immediate cash flow and tax liability, but it does not consider the final payoff for the client after any shares not sold in a repurchase are liquidated. To incorporate this feature, you first decide to see what happens if the client sells all remaining shares of stock immediately after the dividend or the repurchase. Assume that the stock price will fall by the amount of the dividend if a dividend is paid. What are the client's total after-tax cash flows (considering both the payout and the capital gain) under the repurchase of the dividend in this case?

6. Under which program would your client be better off before taxes? Which program is better after taxes, assuming the remaining shares are sold immediately after the dividend is paid?

7. Because your client is unlikely to sell all 1 million shares today, at the time of dividend/repurchase, you decide to consider two longer holding periods: Assume that under both plans the client sells all remaining shares of stock 5 years later, or the client sells 10 years later. Assume that the stock will return 10% per year going forward. Also assume that Amazon will pay no other dividends over the next 10 years.

   a. What would the stock price be after 5 years or 10 years if a dividend is paid now?

   b. What would the stock price be after 5 years or 10 years if Amazon repurchases shares now?

   c. Calculate the total after-tax cash flows at both points in time (when the dividend payment or the share repurchase takes place, and when the rest of the shares are sold) for your client if the remaining shares are sold in 5 years under both initiatives. Compute the difference between the cash flows under both initiatives at each point in time. Repeat assuming the shares are sold in 10 years.

8. Repeat Question 7 assuming the stock will return 20% per year going forward. What do you notice about the difference in the cash flows under the two initiatives when the return is 20% and 10%?

9. Calculate the NPV of the difference in the cash flows under both holding period assumptions for a range of discount rates. Based on your answer to Question 8, what is the correct discount rate to use?

Valuation

The Law of One Price Connection.   In this part of the text we return to the topic of valuation and integrate our understanding of risk, return, and the firm's choice of capital structure. Chapter 18 combines the knowledge of the first five parts of the text and develops the three main methods for capital budgeting with leverage and market imperfections: The weighted average cost of capital (WACC) method, the adjusted present value (APV) method, and the flow-to-equity (FTE) method. While the Law of One Price guarantees that all three methods ultimately lead to the same assessment of value, we will identify conditions that can make one method easiest to apply. Chapter 19 applies Chapter 18's methods of valuation to value a corporation in the context of a leveraged acquisition. Chapter 19 thus serves as a capstone case that illustrates how all the concepts developed to date in the text are used to make complex real-world financial decisions.

Capital Budgeting and Valuation with Leverage

In mid-2006, General Electric Company had a market capitalization of approximately $350 billion. With debt of close to $370 billion, GE's total enterprise value was $720 billion, making it the most valuable business in the world, with almost twice the value of its closest rival. GE's businesses include power generation and air transportation equipment, health care and medical equipment, consumer appliances, consumer and commercial financing and insurance, as well as entertainment through its affiliate, NBC Universal. With a debt-equity ratio exceeding 50%, leverage is clearly part of GE's business strategy. How should a firm that uses leverage, like GE, incorporate the costs and benefits associated with leverage into its capital budgeting decisions? And how should a firm adjust for the differences in risk, and debt capacity, associated with its different business activities?

We introduced capital budgeting in Chapter 7. There we outlined the following basic procedure: First we estimate the incremental free cash flow generated by the project; then we discount the free cash flow based on the project's cost of capital to determine the NPV. While that basic procedure is correct, in this chapter we discuss complexities that were absent from our earlier analysis, integrating the lessons from Parts IV and V of the text into our capital budgeting framework. In particular, we address how to estimate the appropriate cost of capital for a project and explore how the financing decision of the firm can affect both the cost of capital and the set of cash flows that we ultimately discount.

In this chapter, we introduce the three main methods for capital budgeting with leverage and market imperfections: the weighted average cost of capital (WACC) method, the adjusted present value (APV) method, and the flow-to-equity (FTE) method. While their details differ, when appropriately applied each method produces the same estimate of an investment's (or firm's) value. The choice of method is thus guided by which is the simplest to use in a given setting.

Throughout this chapter, we focus on the intuition and implementation of the main capital budgeting methods. The appendix to the chapter provides additional details about the justification for and assumptions behind some of the results we use in the chapter. It also introduces advanced computational techniques that can be used in Excel to solve for leverage and value simultaneously.

18.1   Overview

We introduce the three main methods of capital budgeting in Sections 18.2 through 18.4. To illustrate these methods and the relationships between them most clearly, we apply each method to a single example in which we have made a number of simplifying assumptions:

1. *The project has average risk.* We assume initially that the market risk of the project is equivalent to the average market risk of the firm's investments. In that case, the project's cost of capital can be assessed based on the risk of the firm.

2. *The firm's debt-equity ratio is constant.* We initially consider a firm that adjusts its leverage continuously to maintain a constant debt-equity ratio in terms of market values. This policy determines the amount of debt the firm will take on when it accepts a new project. It also implies that the risk of the firm's equity and debt, and therefore its weighted average cost of capital, will not fluctuate due to leverage changes.

3. *Corporate taxes are the only imperfection.* We assume initially that at the firm's debt-equity ratio the main effect of leverage on valuation is due to the corporate tax shield. We ignore personal taxes and issuance costs, and we assume that other imperfections (such as financial distress or agency costs) are not significant at the level of debt chosen.

While these assumptions are special, they are also a reasonable approximation for many projects and firms. The first assumption is likely to fit typical projects of firms with investments concentrated in a single industry. In that case, the market risk of both the project and the firm will primarily depend on the sensitivity of the industry to the overall economy. The second assumption, while unlikely to hold exactly, reflects the fact that firms tend to increase their levels of debt as they grow larger; some may even have an explicit target for their debt-equity ratio. Finally, for firms without very high levels of debt, the interest tax shield is likely to be the most important market imperfection affecting the capital budgeting decision. Hence, the third assumption is a reasonable starting point to begin our analysis.

Of course, while these three assumptions may be a reasonable approximation in many situations, there are certainly projects and firms for which they do not apply. The remainder of the chapter therefore relaxes these assumptions and shows how to generalize the methods to more complicated settings. In Section 18.5, we adjust these methods for projects whose risk or debt capacity is substantially different from the rest of the firm. These adjustments are especially important for multidivisional firms, such as GE. In Section 18.6, we consider alternative leverage policies for the firm (rather than maintaining a constant debt-equity ratio) and adapt the APV method to handle such cases. We consider the consequence of other market imperfections, such as issuance, distress, and agency costs, on valuation in Section 18.7. Finally, in Section 18.8, we investigate a number of advanced topics, including periodically adjusted leverage policies and the effect of investor taxes.

1. Describe three simplifying assumptions that we make in valuing a project.

2. In what scenario is a project's risk likely to match the risk of the firm overall?

18.2 The Weighted Average Cost of Capital Method

A project's cost of capital depends on its risk. When the market risk of the project is similar to the average market risk of the firm's investments, then its cost of capital is equivalent to the cost of capital for a portfolio of all of the firm's securities; that is, the project's cost of capital is equal to the firm's weighted average cost of capital (WACC). As we showed in Chapter 15, the WACC incorporates the benefit of the interest tax shield by using the firm's *after-tax* cost of capital for debt:

$$r_{wacc} = \frac{E}{E + D} r_E + \frac{D}{E + D} r_D (1 - \tau_c) \qquad (18.1)$$

In this formula,

E = market value of equity r_E = equity cost of capital

D = market value of debt (net of cash) r_D = debt cost of capital

τ_c = marginal corporate tax rate

For now, we assume that the firm maintains a constant debt-equity ratio and that the WACC calculated in Eq. 18.1 remains constant over time.[1] Because the WACC incorporates the tax savings from debt, we can compute the *levered value* of an investment, which is its value including the benefit of interest tax shields given the firm's leverage policy, by discounting its future free cash flow using the WACC. Specifically, if FCF_t is the expected free cash flow of an investment at the end of year t, then the investment's initial levered value, V_0^L, is[2]

$$V_0^L = \frac{FCF_1}{1 + r_{wacc}} + \frac{FCF_2}{(1 + r_{wacc})^2} + \frac{FCF_3}{(1 + r_{wacc})^3} + \cdots \qquad (18.2)$$

The intuition for the WACC method is that the firm's weighted average cost of capital represents the average return the firm must pay to its investors (both debt and equity holders) on an after-tax basis. Thus, to be profitable, a project should generate an expected return of at least the firm's weighted average cost of capital.

Using the WACC to Value a Project

Let's apply the WACC method to value a project. Avco, Inc., is a manufacturer of custom packaging products. Avco is considering introducing a new line of packaging, the RFX series, that will include an embedded radio-frequency identification (RFID) tag, which is a miniature radio antenna and transponder that allows a package to be tracked much more efficiently and with fewer errors than standard bar codes.

---

1. In Section 18.8 we consider the case in which the WACC changes over time due to changes in leverage.

2. See Appendix Section 18A.1 for a formal justification of this result.

Avco engineers expect the technology used in these products to become obsolete after four years. During the next four years, however, the marketing group expects annual sales of $60 million per year for this product line. Manufacturing costs and operating expenses are expected to be $25 million and $9 million, respectively, per year. Developing the product will require upfront R&D and marketing expenses of $6.67 million, together with a $24 million investment in equipment. The equipment will be obsolete in four years and will be depreciated via the straight-line method over that period. Avco bills the majority of its customers in advance, and it expects no net working capital requirements for the project. Avco pays a corporate tax rate of 40%. Using this information, the spreadsheet in Table 18.1 projects the project's expected free cash flow.

TABLE 18.1 SPREADSHEET	Expected Free Cash Flow from Avco's RFX Project					
Year	0	1	2	3	4	
Incremental Earnings Forecast ($ million)						
1 Sales	—	60.00	60.00	60.00	60.00	
2 Cost of Goods Sold	—	(25.00)	(25.00)	(25.00)	(25.00)	
3 Gross Profit	—	35.00	35.00	35.00	35.00	
4 Operating Expenses	(6.67)	(9.00)	(9.00)	(9.00)	(9.00)	
5 Depreciation	—	(6.00)	(6.00)	(6.00)	(6.00)	
6 EBIT	(6.67)	20.00	20.00	20.00	20.00	
7 Income Tax at 40%	2.67	(8.00)	(8.00)	(8.00)	(8.00)	
8 Unlevered Net Income	(4.00)	12.00	12.00	12.00	12.00	
Free Cash Flow						
9 Plus: Depreciation	—	6.00	6.00	6.00	6.00	
10 Less: Capital Expenditures	(24.00)	—	—	—	—	
11 Less: Increases in NWC	—	—	—	—	—	
12 Free Cash Flow	(28.00)	18.00	18.00	18.00	18.00	

The market risk of the RFX project is expected to be similar to that for the company's other lines of business. Thus we can use Avco's equity and debt to determine the weighted average cost of capital for the new project. Table 18.2 shows Avco's current market value balance sheet and equity and debt costs of capital. Avco has built up $20 million in cash for investment needs, so that its *net* debt is $D = 320 - 20 = \$300$ million. Avco's enterprise value, which is the market value of its non-cash assets, is $E + D = \$600$ million. Avco intends to maintain a similar (net) debt-equity ratio for the foreseeable future, including any financing related to the RFX project.

TABLE 18.2	Avco's Current Market Value Balance Sheet ($ million) and Cost of Capital Without the RFX Project

Assets		Liabilities		Cost of Capital	
Cash	20	Debt	320	Debt	6%
Existing Assets	600	Equity	300	Equity	10%
Total Assets	620	Total Liabilities and Equity	620		

With this capital structure, Avco's weighted average cost of capital is

$$r_{wacc} = \frac{E}{E+D}r_E + \frac{D}{E+D}r_D(1-\tau_c) = \frac{300}{600}(10.0\%) + \frac{300}{600}(6.0\%)(1-0.40)$$
$$= 6.8\%$$

We can determine the value of the project, including the tax shield from debt, by calculating the present value of its future free cash flows, V_0^L, using the WACC:

$$V_0^L = \frac{18}{1.068} + \frac{18}{1.068^2} + \frac{18}{1.068^3} + \frac{18}{1.068^4} = \$61.25 \text{ million}$$

Because the upfront cost of launching the product line is only $28 million, this project is a good idea—taking the project results in an NPV of $61.25 - 28 = \$33.25$ million for the firm.

Summary of the WACC Method

To summarize, the key steps in the WACC valuation method are as follows:

1. Determine the free cash flow of the investment.
2. Compute the weighted average cost of capital using Eq. 18.1.
3. Compute the value of the investment, including the tax benefit of leverage, by discounting the free cash flow of the investment using the WACC.

In many firms, the corporate treasurer performs the second step, calculating the firm's WACC. This rate can then be used throughout the firm as the companywide cost of capital for new investments *that are of comparable risk to the rest of the firm and that will not alter the firm's debt-equity ratio.* Employing the WACC method in this way is very simple and straightforward. As a result, it is the method that is most commonly used in practice for capital budgeting purposes.

EXAMPLE 18.1

Valuing an Acquisition Using the WACC Method

Problem
Suppose Avco is considering the acquisition of another firm in its industry that specializes in custom packaging. The acquisition is expected to increase Avco's free cash flow by $3.8 million the first year, and this contribution is expected to grow at a rate of 3% per year from then on. Avco has negotiated a purchase price of $80 million. After the transaction, Avco will adjust its capital structure to maintain its current debt-equity ratio. If the acquisition has similar risk to the rest of Avco, what is the value of this deal?

Solution
The free cash flows of the acquisition can be valued as a growing perpetuity. Because its risk matches the risk for the rest of Avco, and because Avco will maintain the same debt-equity ratio going forward, we can discount these cash flows using the WACC of 6.8%. Thus the value of the acquisition is

$$V^L = \frac{3.8}{6.8\% - 3\%} = \$100 \text{ million}$$

Given the purchase price of $80 million, the acquisition has an NPV of $20 million.

Implementing a Constant Debt-Equity Ratio

Thus far we have simply assumed the firm adopted a policy of keeping its debt-equity ratio constant. In fact, an important advantage of the WACC method is that you do not need to know how this leverage policy is implemented to make the capital budgeting decision. Nevertheless, keeping the debt-equity ratio constant has implications for how the firm's total debt will change with new investment. For example, Avco currently has a debt-equity ratio of 300 / 300 = 1 or, equivalently, a debt-to-value ratio $[D/(E + D)]$ of 50%. To maintain this ratio, the firm's new investments must be financed with debt equal to 50% of their market value.

By undertaking the RFX project, Avco adds new assets to the firm with initial market value $V_0^L = \$61.25$ million. Therefore, to maintain its debt-to-value ratio, Avco must add 50% × 61.25 = \$30.625 million in new debt.[3] Avco can add this debt either by reducing cash or by borrowing and increasing debt. Suppose Avco decides to spend its \$20 million in cash and borrow an additional \$10.625 million. Because only \$28 million is required to fund the project, Avco will pay the remaining 30.625 − 28 = \$2.625 million to shareholders through a dividend (or share repurchase). Table 18.3 shows Avco's market value balance sheet with the RFX project in this case.

TABLE 18.3	Avco's Current Market Value Balance Sheet (\$ million) with the RFX Project		
Assets		**Liabilities**	
Cash	—	Debt	330.625
Existing Assets	600.00		
RFX Project	61.25	Equity	330.625
Total Assets	661.25	Total Liabilities and Equity	661.25

This financing plan maintains Avco's 50% debt-to-value ratio. The market value of Avco's equity increases by 330.625 − 300 = \$30.625 million. Adding the dividend of \$2.625 million, the shareholders' total gain is 30.625 + 2.625 = \$33.25 million, which is exactly the NPV we calculated for the RFX project.

In general, we define an investment's **debt capacity**, D_t, as the amount of debt at date t that is required to maintain the firm's target debt-to-value ratio, d. If V_t^L is the project's levered continuation value on date t—that is, the levered value of its free cash flow after date t—then

$$D_t = d \times V_t^L \tag{18.3}$$

We compute the debt capacity for the RFX project in the spreadsheet in Table 18.4. Starting with the project's free cash flow, we compute its levered continuation value at

---

3. We can also evaluate the project's debt as follows: Of the \$28 million upfront cost of the project, 50% (\$14 million) will be financed with debt. In addition, the project generates an NPV of \$33.25 million, which will increase the market value of the firm. To maintain a debt-equity ratio of 1, Avco must add debt of 50% × 33.25 = \$16.625 million at the time when the NPV of the project is anticipated (which could occur before the new investment is made). Thus the total new debt is 14 + 16.625 = \$30.625 million.

each date (line 2) by discounting the future free cash flow at the WACC as in Eq. 18.2. Because the continuation value at each date includes the value of all subsequent cash flows, it is even simpler to compute the value at each date by working backward from period 4, discounting next period's free cash flow and continuation value:

$$\overbrace{\phantom{FCF_{t+1} + V_{t+1}^L}}^{\text{Value of } FCF \text{ in year } t+2 \text{ and beyond}}$$

$$V_t^L = \frac{FCF_{t+1} + V_{t+1}^L}{1 + r_{wacc}} \tag{18.4}$$

Once we have computed the project's value V_t^L at each date, we apply Eq. 18.3 to compute the project's debt capacity at each date (line 3). As the spreadsheet shows, the project's debt capacity declines each year, and falls to zero by the end of year 4.

TABLE 18.4 SPREADSHEET	Continuation Value and Debt Capacity of the RFX Project over Time					
Year	0	1	2	3	4
Project Debt Capacity ($ million)						
1 Free Cash Flow	(28.00)	18.00	18.00	18.00	18.00
2 Levered Value, V^L (at r_{wacc} = 6.8%)	61.25	47.41	32.63	16.85	—
3 Debt Capacity (at d = 50%)	30.62	23.71	16.32	8.43	—

EXAMPLE 18.2

Debt Capacity for an Acquisition

Problem

Suppose Avco proceeds with the acquisition described in Example 18.1. How much debt must Avco use to finance the acquisition and still maintain its debt-to-value ratio? How much of the acquisition cost must be financed with equity?

Solution

From the solution to Example 18.1, the market value of the assets acquired in the acquisition, V^L, is $100 million. Thus, to maintain a 50% debt-to-value ratio, Avco must increase its debt by $50 million. The remaining $30 million of the $80 million acquisition cost will be financed with new equity. In addition to the $30 million in new equity, the value of Avco's existing shares will increase in value by the $20 million NPV of the acquisition, so in total the market value of Avco's equity will rise by $50 million.

CONCEPT CHECK

1. Describe the key steps in the WACC valuation method.

2. What is the intuition of using the WACC method to value a project?

18.3 The Adjusted Present Value Method

The **adjusted present value (APV)**, method is an alternative valuation method in which we determine the levered value V^L of an investment by first calculating its *unlevered value* V^U, which is its value without any leverage, and then adding the value of the interest tax shield and deducting any costs that arise from other market imperfections:

The APV Formula

$$V^L = APV = V^U + PV(\text{Interest Tax Shield})$$
$$- PV(\text{Financial Distress, Agency, and Issuance Costs}) \qquad (18.5)$$

The APV method is the approach we described in Chapter 16 to determine the optimal level of debt according to the tradeoff theory.[4] For now, we focus solely on the corporate tax benefits of debt and defer the discussion of other consequences of leverage to Section 18.7. As Eq. 18.5 shows, the APV method incorporates the value of the interest tax shield directly, rather than by adjusting the discount rate as in the WACC method. Let's demonstrate the APV method by returning to Avco's RFX project.

The Unlevered Value of the Project

From the free cash flow estimates in Table 18.1, the RFX project has an upfront cost of $28 million, and it generates $18 million per year in free cash flow for the next four years. The first step in the APV method is to calculate the value of these free cash flows using the project's cost of capital if it were financed without leverage.

What is the project's unlevered cost of capital? Because the RFX project has similar risk to Avco's other investments, its unlevered cost of capital is the same as for the firm as a whole. We demonstrated in Chapter 14 that with perfect markets, we could undo a firm's leverage by recombining its equity and debt in a portfolio. In that case, Avco's **unlevered cost of capital** is a weighted average of its equity and debt costs of capital:

Unlevered Cost of Capital with a Target Leverage Ratio

$$r_U = \frac{E}{E + D} r_E + \frac{D}{E + D} r_D = \text{Pretax WACC} \qquad (18.6)$$

In Chapter 14, we derived Eq. 18.6 in a world without taxes; in Appendix Section 18A.2, we show that *Eq. 18.6 holds with taxes for firms that adjust their debt to maintain a target leverage ratio.* A **target leverage ratio** means that the firm adjusts its debt proportionally to the project's value or its cash flows, so that a constant debt-equity ratio is a special case.[5]

Equation 18.6 states that the firm's unlevered cost of capital is equal to its *pretax* weighted average cost of capital—that is, using the pretax cost of debt, r_d, rather than its after-tax cost, $r_d(1 - \tau_c)$. Because we will value the tax shield separately, with the APV method we do not include the benefit of the tax shield in the discount rate as we do in the WACC method.

Applying Eq. 18.6 to Avco, we find its unlevered cost of capital to be

$$r_U = 0.50 \times 10.0\% + 0.50 \times 6.0\% = 8.0\%$$

Avco's unlevered cost of capital is less than its equity cost of capital of 10.0% (which includes the financial risk of leverage), but is more than its WACC of 6.8% (which incorporates the tax benefit of leverage).

---

4. For the application of the APV to capital budgeting, see S. C. Myers, "Interactions of Corporate Financing and Investment Decisions—Implications for Capital Budgeting," *Journal of Finance* 29(1) (1974): 1–25.

5. More generally, we can allow the target ratio to change over time. See Appendix Section 18A.2 for further details.

Given our estimate of the unlevered cost of capital r_U and the project's free cash flows, we calculate the project's value without leverage:

$$V^U = \frac{18}{1.08} + \frac{18}{1.08^2} + \frac{18}{1.08^3} + \frac{18}{1.08^4} = \$59.62 \text{ million}$$

Valuing the Interest Tax Shield

The value of the unlevered project, V^U, calculated above does not include the value of the tax shield provided by the interest payments on debt. Given the project's debt capacity from Table 18.4, we can estimate the expected interest payments and the tax shield as shown in the spreadsheet in Table 18.5. The interest paid in year t is estimated based on the amount of debt outstanding at the end of the prior year:

$$\text{Interest paid in year } t = r_D \times D_{t-1} \tag{18.7}$$

The interest tax shield is equal to the interest paid multiplied by the corporate tax rate τ_c.

TABLE 18.5 SPREADSHEET	Expected Debt Capacity, Interest Payments, and Interest Tax Shield for Avco's RFX Project					
Year	0	1	2	3	4
Interest Tax Shield ($ million)						
1 Debt Capacity, D_t		30.62	23.71	16.32	8.43	—
2 Interest Paid (at $r_D = 6\%$)		—	1.84	1.42	0.98	0.51
3 Interest Tax Shield (at $\tau_c = 40\%$)		—	0.73	0.57	0.39	0.20

To compute the present value of the interest tax shield, we need to determine the appropriate cost of capital. Because Avco maintains a fixed debt-equity ratio, the actual level of the project's debt depends on the continuation value of the project, which will fluctuate continuously with market conditions. Thus the interest tax shields shown in Table 18.5 are expected values, and the true amount of the interest tax shield each year will vary with the cash flows of the project. If the project does well, its value will be higher, it will support more debt, and the interest tax shield will be higher. If the project goes poorly, its value will fall, Avco will reduce its debt level, and the interest tax shield will be lower. In Appendix Section 18A.2, we show that because the tax shield will fluctuate with the growth of the project:

When the firm maintains a target leverage ratio, its future interest tax shields have similar risk to the project's cash flows, so they should be discounted at the project's unlevered cost of capital.

For Avco's RFX project, we have

$$PV(\text{interest tax shield}) = \frac{0.73}{1.08} + \frac{0.57}{1.08^2} + \frac{0.39}{1.08^3} + \frac{0.20}{1.08^4} = \$1.63 \text{ million}$$

While we have used the unlevered cost of capital r_U to discount the tax shield in this case, the correct discount rate for the interest tax shield depends critically on the firm's leverage policy. In Section 18.5 we consider the case in which the debt levels are fixed in advance (and so do not fluctuate with the cash flows of the project), which implies that the tax shield has a lower risk than the project itself.

To determine the value of the project with leverage, we add the value of the interest tax shield to the unlevered value of the project:[6]

$$V^L = V^U + PV(\text{interest tax shield}) = 59.62 + 1.63 = \$61.25 \text{ million}$$

Again, given the $28 million initial investment required, the RFX project has an NPV with leverage of $61.25 - 28 = \$33.25$ million, which matches precisely the value we computed in Section 18.2 using the WACC approach.

Summary of the APV Method

To determine the value of a levered investment using the APV method, we proceed as follows:

1. Determine the investment's value without leverage, V^U, by discounting its free cash flows at the unlevered cost of capital, r_U. With a constant debt-equity ratio, r_U may be estimated using Eq. 18.6.

2. Determine the present value of the interest tax shield.
   a. Determine the expected interest tax shield: Given expected debt D_t on date t, the interest tax shield on date $t + 1$ is $\tau_c r_D D_t$.[7]
   b. Discount the interest tax shield. If a constant debt-equity ratio is maintained, using r_U is appropriate.

3. Add the unlevered value, V^U, to the present value of the interest tax shield to determine the value of the investment with leverage, V^L.

The APV method is more complicated than the WACC method because we must compute two separate valuations: the unlevered project and the interest tax shield. Furthermore, in this example, to determine the project's debt capacity for the interest tax shield calculation, we relied on the calculation in Table 18.4, *which depended on the value of the project.* Thus, we need to know the debt level to compute the APV, but with a constant debt-equity ratio we need to know the project's value to compute the debt level. As a result, implementing the APV approach with a constant debt-equity ratio requires solving for the project's debt and value *simultaneously.* (See Appendix Section 18A.3 for an example of this calculation.)

Despite its complexity, the APV method has some advantages. As we shall see in Section 18.5, it can be easier to apply than the WACC method when the firm does not maintain a constant debt-equity ratio. The APV approach also explicitly values the market imperfections and therefore allows managers to measure their contribution to value. In the case of Avco's RFX project, the benefit of the interest tax shield is relatively small. Even if tax rates were to change, or if Avco decided for other reasons not to increase its debt,

---

6. Because we are using the same discount rate for the free cash flow and the tax shield, the cash flows of the project and the tax shield can be combined first and then discounted at the rate r_U. The combined cash flows are also referred to as the capital cash flows (CCF): CCF = FCF + Interest Tax Shield. This method is known as the CCF or "compressed APV" method [see S. Kaplan and R. Ruback, "The Valuation of Cash Flow Forecasts: An Empirical Analysis," *Journal of Finance* 50(4) (1995): 1059–1093; and R. Ruback, "Capital Cash Flows: A Simple Approach to Valuing Risky Cash Flows," *Financial Management* 31(2) (2002): 85-103].

7. The return on the debt need not come solely from interest payments, so this value is an approximation. The same approximation is implicit in the definition of the WACC (see also footnote 26 in Appendix Section 18A.1).

the profitability of the project would not be jeopardized. However, this need not always be the case. Consider again the acquisition in Example 18.1, where the APV method makes clear that the gain from the acquisition crucially depends on the interest tax shield.

EXAMPLE 18.3

Using the APV Method to Value an Acquisition

Problem

Consider again Avco's acquisition from Examples 18.1 and 18.2. The acquisition will contribute $3.8 million in free cash flows the first year, which will grow by 3% per year thereafter. The acquisition cost of $80 million will be financed with $50 million in new debt initially. Compute the value of the acquisition using the APV method, assuming Avco will maintain a constant debt-equity ratio for the acquisiton.

Solution

First, we compute the value without leverage. Given Avco's unlevered cost of capital of r_U = 8%, we get

$$V^U = 3.8 \, / \, (8\% - 3\%) = \$76 \text{ million}$$

Avco will add new debt of $50 million initially to fund the acquisition. At a 6% interest rate, the interest expense the first year is 6% × 50 = $3 million, which provides an interest tax shield of 40% × 3 = $1.2 million. Because the value of the acquisition is expected to grow by 3% per year, the amount of debt the acquisition supports—and, therefore, the interest tax shield—is expected to grow at the same rate. The present value of the interest tax shield is

$$PV(\text{interest tax shield}) = 1.2 \, / \, (8\% - 3\%) = \$24 \text{ million}$$

The value of the acquisition with leverage is given by the APV:

$$V^L = V^U + PV(\text{interest tax shield}) = 76 + 24 = \$100 \text{ million}$$

This value is identical to the value computed in Example 18.1 and implies an NPV of 100 − 80 = $20 million for the acquisition. Without the benefit of the interest tax shield, the NPV would be 76 − 80 = −$4 million.

CONCEPT CHECK

1. Describe the adjusted present value (APV) method.

2. At what rate should we discount the interest tax shield when a firm maintains a target leverage ratio?

18.4 The Flow-to-Equity Method

In the WACC and APV methods, we value a project based on its free cash flow, which is computed ignoring interest and debt payments. Some students find these methods confusing because, if the goal is to determine the benefit of the project to shareholders, it seems to them that we should focus on the cash flows that *shareholders* will receive.

In the **flow-to-equity (FTE)** valuation method, we explicitly calculate the free cash flow available to equity holders *taking into account all payments to and from debt holders*. The cash flows to equity holders are then discounted using the *equity* cost of capital.[8] Despite this difference in implementation, the FTE method produces the same assessment of the project's value as the WACC or APV methods.

---

8. The FTE approach is very similar to the total payout method for valuing the firm described in Chapter 9. In that method, we value the total dividends and repurchases that the firm pays to shareholders.

Calculating the Free Cash Flow to Equity

The first step in the FTE method is to determine the project's **free cash flow to equity (FCFE)**. The FCFE is the free cash flow that remains after adjusting for interest payments, debt issuance, and debt repayment. The spreadsheet shown in Table 18.6 calculates the FCFE for Avco's RFX project.

TABLE 18.6 SPREADSHEET	Expected Free Cash Flows to Equity from Avco's RFX Project					
Year		0	1	2	3	4
Incremental Earnings Forecast ($ million)						
1	Sales	—	60.00	60.00	60.00	60.00
2	Cost of Goods Sold	—	(25.00)	(25.00)	(25.00)	(25.00)
3	**Gross Profit**	—	35.00	35.00	35.00	35.00
4	Operating Expenses	(6.67)	(9.00)	(9.00)	(9.00)	(9.00)
5	Depreciation	—	(6.00)	(6.00)	(6.00)	(6.00)
6	**EBIT**	(6.67)	20.00	20.00	20.00	20.00
7	Interest Expense	—	(1.84)	(1.42)	(0.98)	(0.51)
8	**Pretax Income**	(6.67)	18.16	18.58	19.02	19.49
9	Income Tax at 40%	2.67	(7.27)	(7.43)	(7.61)	(7.80)
10	**Net Income**	(4.00)	10.90	11.15	11.41	11.70
Free Cash Flow to Equity						
11	Plus: Depreciation	—	6.00	6.00	6.00	6.00
12	Less: Capital Expenditures	(24.00)	—	—	—	—
13	Less: Increases in NWC	—	—	—	—	—
14	Plus: Net Borrowing	30.62	(6.92)	(7.39)	(7.89)	(8.43)
15	**Free Cash Flow to Equity**	2.62	9.98	9.76	9.52	9.27

Comparing the FCFE estimates in Table 18.6 with the free cash flow estimates in Table 18.1, we notice two changes. First, we deduct interest expenses (computed in Table 18.5) on line 7, before taxes. As a consequence, we compute the incremental net income of the project on line 10, rather than its *unlevered* net income as we do when computing free cash flows. The second change appears on line 14, where we add the proceeds from the firm's net borrowing activity. These proceeds are positive when the firm issues debt; they are negative when the firm reduces its debt by repaying principal. For the RFX project, Avco issues $30.62 million in debt initially. At date 1, however, the debt capacity of the project falls to $23.71 million (see Table 18.4), so that Avco must repay $30.62 - 23.71 = \$6.91$ million of the debt.[9] In general, given the project's debt capacity D_t,

$$\text{Net Borrowing at Date } t = D_t - D_{t-1} \tag{18.8}$$

As an alternative to Table 18.6, we can compute a project's FCFE directly from its free cash flow. Because interest payments are deducted before taxes in line 7, we adjust the firm's FCF by their after-tax cost. We then add net borrowing to determine FCFE:

Free Cash Flow to Equity

$$FCFE = FCF - \underbrace{(1 - \tau_c) \times (\text{Interest Payments})}_{\text{After-tax interest expense}} + (\text{Net Borrowing}) \tag{18.9}$$

---

9. The $0.01 million difference in the spreadsheet is due to rounding.

We illustrate this alternative calculation for Avco's RFX project in Table 18.7. Note that the project's FCFE is lower than its FCF in years 1 through 4 due to the interest and principal payments on the debt. In year 0, however, the proceeds from the loan more than offset the negative free cash flow, so FCFE is positive (and equal to the dividend we calculated in Section 18.2).

TABLE 18.7 SPREADSHEET	Computing FCFE from FCF for Avco's RFX Project					
	Year	0	1	2	3	4
Free Cash Flow to Equity ($ million)						
1 Free Cash Flow		(28.00)	18.00	18.00	18.00	18.00
2 After-tax Interest Expense		—	(1.10)	(0.85)	(0.59)	(0.30)
3 Net Borrowing		30.62	(6.92)	(7.39)	(7.89)	(8.43)
4 **Free Cash Flow to Equity**		2.62	9.98	9.76	9.52	9.27

Valuing Equity Cash Flows

The project's free cash flow to equity shows the expected amount of additional cash the firm will have available to pay dividends (or conduct share repurchases) each year. Because these cash flows represent payments to equity holders, they should be discounted at the project's equity cost of capital. Given that the risk and leverage of the RFX project are the same as for Avco overall, we can use Avco's equity cost of capital of $r_E = 10.0\%$ to discount the project's FCFE:

$$NPV(FCFE) = 2.62 + \frac{9.98}{1.10} + \frac{9.76}{1.10^2} + \frac{9.52}{1.10^3} + \frac{9.27}{1.10^4} = \$33.25 \text{ million}$$

The value of the project's FCFE represents the gain to shareholders from the project. It is identical to the NPV we computed using the WACC and APV methods.

Why isn't the project's NPV lower now that we have deducted interest and debt payments from the cash flows? Recall that these costs of debt are offset by cash received when the debt is issued. Looking back at Table 18.6, the cash flows from debt in lines 7 and 14 have an NPV of zero assuming the debt is fairly priced.[10] In the end, the only effect on value comes from a reduction in the tax payments, leaving the same result as with the other methods.

---

10. The interest and principal payments for the RFX project are as follows:

	Year	0	1	2	3	4
1 Net Borrowing		30.62	(6.92)	(7.39)	(7.89)	(8.43)
2 Interest Expense		—	(1.84)	(1.42)	(0.98)	(0.51)
3 **Cash Flow from Debt**		30.62	(8.76)	(8.81)	(8.87)	(8.93)

Because these cash flows have the same risk as the debt, we discount them at the debt cost of capital of 6% to compute their NPV:

$$30.62 + \frac{-8.76}{1.06} + \frac{-8.81}{1.06^2} + \frac{-8.87}{1.06^3} + \frac{-8.93}{1.06^4} = 0.$$

Summary of the Flow-to-Equity Method

The key steps in the flow-to-equity method for valuing a levered investment are as follows:

1. Determine the free cash flow to equity of the investment using Eq. 18.9.
2. Determine the equity cost of capital, r_E.
3. Compute the equity value, E, by discounting the free cash flow to equity using the equity cost of capital.

Applying the FTE method was simplified in our example because the project's risk and leverage matched the firm's, and the firm's equity cost of capital was expected to remain constant. Just as with the WACC, however, this assumption is reasonable only if the firm maintains a constant debt-equity ratio. If the debt-equity ratio changes over time, the risk of equity—and, therefore, its cost of capital—will change as well.

In this setting, the FTE approach has the same disadvantage associated with the APV approach: We need to compute the project's debt capacity to determine interest and net borrowing before we can make the capital budgeting decision. For this reason, in most settings the WACC is easier to apply. The FTE method can offer an advantage when calculating the value of equity for the entire firm, if the firm's capital structure is complex and the market values of other securities in the firm's capital structure are not known. In that case the FTE method allows us to compute the value of equity directly. In contrast, the WACC and APV methods compute the firm's enterprise value, so that a separate valuation of the other components of the firm's capital structure is needed to determine the value of equity. Finally, by emphasizing a project's implication for equity, the FTE method may be viewed as a more transparent method for discussing a project's benefit to shareholders—a managerial concern.

EXAMPLE 18.4

Using the FTE Method to Value an Acquisition

Problem

Consider again Avco's acquisition from Examples 18.1 through 18.3. The acquisition will contribute $3.8 million in free cash flows the first year, growing by 3% per year thereafter. The acquisition cost of $80 million will be financed with $50 million in new debt initially. What is the value of this acquisition using the FTE method?

Solution

Because the acquisition is being financed with $50 million in new debt, the remaining $30 million of the acquisition cost must come from equity:

$$FCFE_0 = -80 + 50 = -\$30 \text{ million}$$

In one year, the interest on the debt will be 6% × 50 = $3 million. Because Avco maintains a constant debt-equity ratio, the debt associated with the acquisition is also expected to grow at a 3% rate: 50 × 1.03 = $51.5 million. Therefore, Avco will borrow an additional 51.5 − 50 = $1.5 million in one year.

$$FCFE_1 = +3.8 - (1 - 0.40) \times 3 + 1.5 = \$3.5 \text{ million}$$

After year 1, FCFE will also grow at a 3% rate. Using the cost of equity $r_E = 10\%$, we compute the NPV:

$$NPV(FCFE) = -30 + 3.5 / (10\% - 3\%) = \$20 \text{ million}$$

This NPV matches the result we obtained with the WACC and APV methods.

What Counts as "Debt"?

Firms often have many types of debt as well as other liabilities, such as leases. Practitioners use different guidelines to determine which to include as debt when computing the WACC. Some use only long-term debt. Others use both long-term and short-term debt, plus lease obligations. Students are often confused by these different approaches and are left wondering: Which liabilities should be included as debt?

In fact, any choice will work if done correctly. We can view the WACC and FTE methods as special cases of a more general approach in which we *value the after-tax cash flows from a set of the firm's assets and liabilities by discounting them at the after-tax weighted average cost of capital of the firm's remaining assets and liabilities.* In the WACC method, the FCF does not include the interest and principal payments on debt, so debt is included in the calculation of the weighted average cost of capital. In the FTE method, the FCFE incorporates the after-tax cash flows to and from debt holders, so debt is excluded from the weighted average cost of capital (which is simply the equity cost of capital).

Other combinations are also possible. For example, long-term debt can be included in the weighted average cost of capital, and short-term debt can be included as part of the cash flows. Similarly, other assets (such as cash) or liabilities (such as leases) can be included either in the weighted average cost of capital or as part of the cash flow. All such methods, if applied consistently, will lead to an equivalent valuation. Typically, the most convenient choice is the one for which the assumption of a constant debt-to-value ratio is a reasonable approximation.

CONCEPT CHECK

1. Describe the key steps in the flow to equity method for valuing a levered investment.

2. Does the flow to equity method produce the same assessment of the project's value as the WACC and APV methods?

18.5 Project-Based Costs of Capital

Up to this point we have assumed that both the risk and the leverage of the project under consideration matched those characteristics for the firm as a whole. This assumption allowed us, in turn, to assume that the cost of capital for a project matched the cost of capital of the firm.

In the real world, specific projects often differ from the average investment made by the firm. Consider General Electric Company, discussed in the introduction to this chapter. Projects in its health care division are likely to have different market risk than projects in air transportation equipment or at NBC Universal. Projects may also vary in the amount of leverage they will support—for example, acquisitions of real estate or capital equipment are often highly levered, whereas investments in intellectual property are not. In this section, we show how to calculate the cost of capital for the project's cash flows when a project's risk and leverage differ from those for the firm overall.

Estimating the Unlevered Cost of Capital

We begin by explaining how to calculate the unlevered cost of capital of a project with market risk that is very different from the rest of the firm. Suppose Avco launches a new plastics manufacturing division that faces different market risks than its main packaging business. What unlevered cost of capital would be appropriate for this division?

We can estimate r_U for the plastics division by looking at other single-division plastics firms that have similar business risks. For example, suppose two firms are comparable to the plastics division and have the following characteristics:

Firm	Equity Cost of Capital	Debt Cost of Capital	Debt-to-Value Ratio, $D/(E + D)$
Comparable #1	12.0%	6.0%	40%
Comparable #2	10.7%	5.5%	25%

Assuming that both firms maintain a target leverage ratio, we can estimate the unlevered cost of capital for each competitor by using the pretax WACC from Eq. 18.6:

$$\text{Competitor 1: } r_U = 0.60 \times 12.0\% + 0.40 \times 6.0\% = 9.6\%$$

$$\text{Competitor 2: } r_U = 0.75 \times 10.7\% + 0.25 \times 5.5\% = 9.4\%$$

Based on these comparable firms, we estimate an unlevered cost of capital for the plastics division of about 9.5%.[11] With this rate in hand, we can use the APV approach to calculate the value of Avco's investment in plastic manufacturing. To use either the WACC or FTE method, however, we need to estimate the project's equity cost of capital, which will depend on the incremental debt the firm will take on as a result of the project.

Project Leverage and the Equity Cost of Capital

Suppose the firm will fund the project according to a target leverage ratio. This leverage ratio may differ from the firm's overall leverage ratio, as different divisions or types of investments may have different optimal debt capacities. We can rearrange terms in Eq. 18.6 to get the following expression for the equity cost of capital:[12]

$$r_E = r_U + \frac{D}{E}(r_U - r_D) \tag{18.10}$$

Equation 18.10 shows that the project's equity cost of capital depends on its unlevered cost of capital, r_U, and the debt-equity ratio of the incremental financing that will be put in place to support the project. For example, suppose that Avco plans to maintain an equal mix of debt and equity financing as it expands into plastics manufacturing, and it expects its borrowing cost to remain at 6%. Given its 9.5% unlevered cost of capital, the plastics division's equity cost of capital is

$$r_E = 9.5\% + \frac{0.50}{0.50}(9.5\% - 6\%) = 13.0\%$$

Once we have the equity cost of capital, we can use Eq. 18.1 to determine the division's WACC:

$$r_{WACC} = 0.50 \times 13.0\% + 0.50 \times 6.0\% \times (1 - 0.40) = 8.3\%$$

Based on these estimates, Avco should use a WACC of 8.3% for the plastics division, compared to the WACC of 6.8% for the packaging division that we calculated in Section 18.2.

---

11. If we are using the CAPM to estimate expected returns, this procedure is equivalent to unlevering the betas of comparable firms using Eq. 14.9:

$$\beta_U = [E/(E + D)]\beta_E + [D/(D + E)]\beta_D.$$

12. In a CAPM setting, Eq. 18.10 is equivalent to relevering the beta according to Eq. 14.10.

In fact, we can combine Eqs. 18.1 and 18.10 to obtain a direct formula for the WACC when the firm maintains a target leverage ratio for the project. If d is the project's debt-to-value ratio, $D/(E + D)$, then[13]

Project-Based WACC Formula

$$r_{wacc} = r_U - d\tau_c r_D \qquad (18.11)$$

For example, in the case of Avco's plastics division:

$$r_{wacc} = 9.5\% - 0.50 \times 0.40 \times 6\% = 8.3\%$$

EXAMPLE 18.5

Computing Divisional Costs of Capital

Problem

Hasco Corporation is a multinational provider of lumber and milling equipment. Currently, Hasco's equity cost of capital is 12.7%, and its borrowing cost is 6%. Hasco has traditionally maintained a 40% debt-to-value ratio. Hasco engineers have developed a GPS-based inventory control tracking system, which the company is considering developing commercially as a separate division. Management views the risk of this investment as similar to that of other technology companies' investments, with comparable firms typically having an unlevered cost of capital of 15%. Suppose Hasco plans to finance the new division using 10% debt financing (a constant debt-to-value ratio of 10%) with a borrowing rate of 6%, and its corporate tax rate is 35%. Estimate the unlevered, equity, and weighted average costs of capital for each division.

Solution

For the lumber and milling division, we can use the firm's current equity cost of capital r_E = 12.7% and debt-to-value ratio of 40%. Then

$$r_{wacc} = 0.60 \times 12.7\% + 0.40 \times 6\% \times (1 - 0.35) = 9.2\%$$
$$r_U = 0.60 \times 12.7\% + 0.40 \times 6\% = 10.0\%$$

For the technology division, we estimate its unlevered cost of capital using comparable firms: $r_U = 15\%$. Because Hasco's technology division will support 10% debt financing,

$$r_E = 15\% + \frac{0.10}{0.90}(15\% - 6\%) = 16\%$$
$$r_{wacc} = 15\% - 0.10 \times 0.35 \times 6\% = 14.8\%$$

Note that the cost of capital is quite different across the two divisions.

Determining the Incremental Leverage of a Project

To determine the equity or weighted average cost of capital for a project, we need to know the amount of debt to associate with the project. For capital budgeting purposes, the project's financing is the *incremental* financing that results if the firm takes on the project.

---

13. We can derive Eq. 18.11 even more simply by comparing the WACC and pretax WACC in Eqs. 18.1 and 18.6. This formula for the WACC was proposed by R. Harris and J. Pringle, "Risk Adjusted Discount Rates: Transition from the Average Risk Case," *Journal of Financial Research* 8(3) (1985): 237–244.

COMMON MISTAKE   **Re-levering the WACC**

When computing the WACC using its definition in Eq. 18.1, always remember that the equity and debt costs of capital, r_E and r_D, will change for different choices of the firm's leverage ratio. For example, consider a firm with a debt-to-value ratio of 25%, a debt cost of capital of 6.67%, an equity cost of capital of 12%, and a tax rate of 40%. From Eq. 18.1, its current WACC is

$$r_{wacc} = 0.75(12\%) + 0.25(6.67\%)(1 - 0.40)$$
$$= 10\%$$

Suppose the firm increases its debt-to-value ratio to 50%. It is tempting to conclude that its WACC will fall to

$$0.50(12\%) + 0.50(6.67\%)(1 - 0.40) = 9\%$$

In fact, when the firm increases leverage, its equity and debt cost of capital will rise. To compute the new WACC correctly, we must first determine the firm's unlevered cost of capital from Eq. 18.6:

$$r_U = 0.75(12\%) + 0.25(6.67\%) = 10.67\%$$

If the firm's debt cost of capital rises to 7.34% with the increase in leverage, then from Eq. 18.10 its equity cost of capital will rise as well:

$$r_E = 10.67\% + \frac{0.50}{0.50}(10.67\% - 7.34\%) = 14\%$$

Using Eq. 18.1, with the new equity and debt cost of capital, we can correctly compute the new WACC:

$$r_{wacc} = 0.50(14\%) + 0.50(7.34\%)(1 - 0.40)$$
$$= 9.2\%$$

We can also calculate the new WACC using Eq. 18.11:

$$r_{wacc} = 10.67 - 0.50(0.40)(7.34\%) = 9.2\%$$

Note that if we fail to incorporate the effect of an increase in leverage on the firm's equity and debt costs of capital, we will overestimate the reduction in its WACC.

That is, it is the change in the firm's total debt (net of cash) with the project versus without the project.

The incremental financing of a project need not correspond to the financing that is directly tied to the project. As an example, suppose a project involves buying a new warehouse, and the purchase of the warehouse is financed with a mortgage for 90% of its value. However, if the firm has an overall policy to maintain a 40% debt-to-value ratio, it will reduce debt elsewhere in the firm once the warehouse is purchased in an effort to maintain that ratio. In that case, the appropriate debt-to-value ratio to use when evaluating the warehouse project is 40%, not 90%.

Here are some important concepts to remember when determining the project's incremental financing.

Cash Is Negative Debt. A firm's leverage should be evaluated based on its debt net of any cash. Thus, if an investment will reduce the firm's cash holdings, it is equivalent to the firm adding leverage. Similarly, if the positive free cash flow from a project will increase the firm's cash holdings, then this growth in cash is equivalent to a reduction in the firm's leverage.

A Fixed Payout Policy Implies 100% Debt Financing. Consider a firm whose dividend payouts and expenditures on share repurchases are set in advance and will not be affected by a project's free cash flow. In this case, the only source of financing is *debt*— any cash requirement of the project will be funded using the firm's cash or borrowing, and any cash that the project produces will be used to repay debt or increase the firm's cash. As a result, the incremental effect of the project on the firm's financing is to change the level of debt, so this project is 100% debt financed (that is, its debt-to-value ratio $d = 1$). If the firm's payout policy is fixed for the life of a project, the appropriate WACC for the project is $r_U - \tau_c r_D$. This case can be relevant for a highly levered firm that devotes its free cash flow to paying down its debt or for a firm that is hoarding cash.

Optimal Leverage Depends on Project _and_ Firm Characteristics.   Projects with safer cash flows can support more debt before they increase the risk of financial distress for the firm. But, as we discussed in Part V of the text, the likelihood of financial distress that a firm can bear depends on the magnitude of the distress, agency, and asymmetric information costs that it may face. These costs are not specific to a project, but rather depend on the characteristics of the entire firm. As a consequence, the optimal leverage for a project will depend on the characteristics of both the project and the firm.

Safe Cash Flows Can Be 100% Debt Financed.   When an investment has risk-free cash flows, a firm can offset these cash flows 100% with debt and leave its overall risk unchanged. If it does so, the appropriate discount rate for safe cash flows is $r_D(1 - \tau_c)$.

EXAMPLE 18.6

Debt Financing at Cisco Systems

Problem

In mid-2005, Cisco Systems held more than $16 billion in cash and securities and no debt. Consider a project with an unlevered cost of capital of $r_U = 12\%$. Suppose Cisco's payout policy is fixed during the life of this project, so that the free cash flow from the project will affect only Cisco's cash balance. If Cisco earns 4% interest on its cash holdings and pays a 35% corporate tax rate, what cost of capital should Cisco use to evaluate the project?

Solution

Because the inflows and outflows of the project change Cisco's cash balance, the project is financed by 100% debt; that is, $d = 1$. The appropriate cost of capital for the project is

$$r_{wacc} = r_U - \tau_c r_D = 12\% - 0.35 \times 4\% = 10.6\%$$

Note that the project is effectively 100% debt financed, even though Cisco itself had no debt.

CONCEPT CHECK

1. How do we estimate a project's unlevered cost of capital when the project's risk is different from that of a firm?

2. What is the incremental debt associated with a project?

18.6 APV with Other Leverage Policies

To this point, we have assumed that the incremental debt of a project is set to maintain a constant debt-equity (or, equivalently, debt-to-value) ratio. While a constant debt-equity ratio is a convenient assumption that simplifies the analysis, not all firms adopt this leverage policy. In this section, we consider two alternative leverage policies: constant interest coverage and predetermined debt levels.

When we relax the assumption of a constant debt-equity ratio, the equity cost of capital and WACC for a project will change over time as the debt-equity ratio changes. As a result, the WACC and FTE method are difficult to implement (see Section 18.8 for further details). The APV method, however, is relatively straightforward to use and is therefore the preferred method with alternative leverage policies.

Constant Interest Coverage Ratio

As discussed in Chapter 15, if a firm is using leverage to shield income from corporate taxes, then it will adjust its debt level so that its interest expenses grow with its earnings. In this case, it is natural to specify the firm's incremental interest payments as a target fraction, k, of the project's free cash flow:[14]

$$\text{Interest Paid in Year } t = k \times FCF_t \tag{18.12}$$

When the firm keeps its interest payments to a target fraction of its FCF, we say it has a **constant interest coverage ratio**.

To implement the APV approach, we must compute the present value of the tax shield under this policy. Because the tax shield is proportional to the project's free cash flow, it has the same risk as the project's cash flow and so should be discounted at the same rate—that is, the unlevered cost of capital, r_U. But the present value of the project's free cash flow at rate r_U is the unlevered value of the project. Thus

$$PV(\text{Interest Tax Shield}) = PV(\tau_c k \times FCF) = \tau_c k \times PV(FCF)$$

$$= \tau_c k \times V^U \tag{18.13}$$

That is, with a constant interest coverage policy, the value of the interest tax shield is proportional to the project's unlevered value. Using the APV method, the value of the project with leverage is given by the following formula:

Levered Value with a Constant Interest Coverage Ratio

$$V^L = V^U + PV(\text{Interest Tax Shield}) = V^U + \tau_c k \times V^U$$

$$= (1 + \tau_c k)V^U \tag{18.14}$$

For example, we calculated the unlevered value of Avco's RFX project as $V^U = \$59.62$ million in Section 18.3. If Avco targets interest to be 20% of its free cash flow, the value with leverage is $V^L = [1 + 0.4 (20\%)]\, 59.62 = \$64.39$ million. (This result differs from the value of $61.25 million for the project that we calculated in Section 18.3, where we assumed a different leverage policy of a 50% debt-to-value ratio.)

Equation 18.14 provides a simple rule to determine an investment's levered value based on a leverage policy that may be appropriate for many firms.[15] Note also that if the investment's free cash flows are expected to grow at a constant rate, then the assumption of constant interest coverage and a constant debt-equity ratio are equivalent, as in Example 18.7.

---

14. It might be even better to specify interest as a fraction of taxable earnings. Typically, however, taxable earnings and free cash flows are roughly proportional, so the two specifications are very similar. Also, for Eq. 18.12 to hold exactly, the firm must adjust debt continuously throughout the year. We will relax this assumption in Section 18.8 to a setting in which the firm adjusts debt periodically based on its expected level of future free cash flow (see Example 18.10).

15. J. Graham and C. Harvey report that a majority of firms target a credit rating when issuing debt ["The Theory and Practice of Corporate Finance: Evidence from the Field," *Journal of Financial Economics* 60 (2001)]. The interest coverage ratios are important determinants of credit ratings. Firms and rating agencies also consider the *book* debt-equity ratio, which often fluctuates in tandem with a firm's cash flows, rather than with its market value. (For example, book equity increases when the firm invests in physical capital to expand, which generally results in higher cash flows.)

| EXAMPLE 18.7 | **Valuing an Acquisition with Target Interest Coverage** |

Problem

Consider again Avco's acquisition from Examples 18.1 and 18.2. The acquisition will contribute $3.8 million in free cash flows the first year, growing by 3% per year thereafter. The acquisition cost of $80 million will be financed with $50 million in new debt initially. Compute the value of the acquisition using the APV method assuming Avco will maintain a constant interest coverage ratio for the acquisition.

Solution

Given Avco's unlevered cost of capital of $r_U = 8\%$, the acquisition has an unlevered value of

$$V^U = 3.8 / (8\% - 3\%) = \$76 \text{ million}$$

With $50 million in new debt and a 6% interest rate, the interest expense the first year is 6% × 50 = $3 million, or $k = \text{Interest}/FCF = 3/3.8 = 78.95\%$. Because Avco will maintain this interest coverage, we can use Eq. 18.14 to compute the levered value:

$$V^L = (1 + \tau_c k) V^U = [1 + 0.4(78.95\%)]76 = \$100 \text{ million}$$

This value is identical to the value computed using the WACC method in Example 18.1, where we assumed a constant debt-equity ratio.

Predetermined Debt Levels

Rather than set debt according to a target debt-equity ratio or interest coverage level, a firm may adjust its debt according to a fixed schedule that is known in advance. Suppose, for example, that Avco plans to borrow $30.62 million and then will reduce the debt on a fixed schedule to $20 million after one year, to $10 million after two years, and to zero after three years. The RFX project will have no other consequences for Avco's leverage, regardless of its success. How can we value an investment like this one when its future *debt levels*, rather than the *debt-equity ratio*, are known in advance?

Because the debt levels are known, we can immediately compute the interest payments and the corresponding interest tax shield, as shown in Table 18.8.

| TABLE 18.8 SPREADSHEET | **Interest Payments and Interest Tax Shield Given a Fixed Debt Schedule for Avco's RFX Project** |

Year	0	1	2	3	4
Interest Tax Shield ($ million)					
1 Debt Capacity, D_t	30.62	20.00	10.00	—	—
2 Interest Paid (at $r_D = 6\%$)		1.84	1.20	0.60	—
3 Interest Tax Shield (at $\tau_c = 40\%$)		0.73	0.48	0.24	—

At what rate should we discount this tax shield to determine the present value? In Section 18.3, we used the project's unlevered cost of capital because the amount of debt—and, therefore, the tax shield—fluctuated with the value of the project itself and so had similar risk. However, with a fixed debt schedule, the amount of the debt will not fluctuate. In this case, the tax shield is less risky than the project, so it should be discounted at a lower rate. Indeed, the risk of the tax shield is similar to the risk of the debt payments. We therefore advise the following general rule:[16]

When debt levels are set according to a fixed schedule, we can discount the predetermined interest tax shields using the debt cost of capital, r_D.

In Avco's case, $r_D = 6\%$:

$$PV(\text{Interest Tax Shield}) = \frac{0.73}{1.06} + \frac{0.48}{1.06^2} + \frac{0.24}{1.06^3} = \$1.32 \text{ million}$$

We then combine the value of the tax shield with the unlevered value of the project (which we already computed in Section 18.3) to determine the APV:

$$V^L = V^U + PV(\text{Interest Tax Shield}) = 59.62 + 1.32 = \$60.94 \text{ million}$$

The value of the interest tax shield computed here, \$1.32 million, differs from the value of \$1.63 million we computed in Section 18.3 based on constant debt-equity ratio. Comparing the firm's debt in the two cases, we see that it is paid off more rapidly in Table 18.8 than in Table 18.4. Also, because the debt-equity ratio for the project changes over time in this example, the project's WACC also changes, making it difficult—though not impossible—to apply the WACC method to this case. We show how to do so, and verify that we get the same result, as part of the advanced topics in Section 18.8.

A particularly simple example of a predetermined debt level occurs when the firm has permanent fixed debt, maintaining the same level of debt forever. We discussed this debt policy in Section 15.2 and showed that if the firm maintains a fixed level of debt, D, the value of the tax shield is $\tau_c \times D$.[17] Hence the value of the levered project in this case is

Levered Value with Permanent Debt

$$V^L = V^U + \tau_c \times D \tag{18.15}$$

A Cautionary Note. When debt levels are predetermined, the firm will not adjust its debt based on fluctuations to its cash flows or value. Therefore, we are no longer in a setting in which the firm maintains a target leverage ratio, so Eqs. 18.6, 18.10, and 18.11 do not apply. For example, if we compute the WACC using Eq. 18.11 and apply it in the case of permanent debt, the value we estimate will *not* be consistent with Eq. 18.15. To obtain the correct result, we need to use a more general version of Eq. 18.11, which we provide in Eq. 18.21 in Section 18.8.

A Comparison of Methods

We have introduced three methods for valuing levered investments: WACC, APV, and FTE. How do we decide which method to use in which circumstances?

When used consistently, each method produces the same valuation for the investment. Thus the choice of method is largely a matter of convenience. As a general rule, the WACC method is the easiest to use when the firm will maintain a fixed debt-to-value

---

16. The risk of the tax shield is not literally equivalent to that of the debt payments, because it is based on only the interest portion of the payments and is subject to the risk of fluctuations in the firm's marginal tax rate. Nevertheless, this assumption is a reasonable approximation absent much more detailed information.

17. Because the interest tax shield is $\tau_c r_D D$ in perpetuity, using the discount rate r_D we get $PV(\text{Interest Tax Shield}) = \tau_c r_D D / r_D = \tau_c D$.

ratio over the life of the investment. For alternative leverage policies, the APV method is usually the most straightforward approach. The FTE method is typically used only in complicated settings for which the values of other securities in the firm's capital structure or the interest tax shield are themselves difficult to determine.

CONCEPT CHECK

1. What condition must the firm meet to have a constant interest coverage policy?

2. What is the appropriate discount rate for tax shields when the debt schedule is fixed in advance?

18.7 Other Effects of Financing

The WACC, APV, and FTE methods determine the value of an investment incorporating the tax shields associated with leverage. However, as we discussed in Chapter 16, some other potential imperfections are associated with leverage. In this section, we investigate ways to adjust our valuation to account for imperfections such as issuance costs, security mispricing, personal taxes, and financial distress and agency costs.

Issuance and Other Financing Costs

When a firm takes out a loan or raises capital by issuing securities, the banks that provide the loan or underwrite the sale of the securities charge fees. Table 18.9 lists the typical fees for common transactions. The fees associated with the financing of the project are a cost that should be included as part of the project's required investment, reducing the NPV of the project.

TABLE 18.9	Typical Issuance Costs for Different Securities, as a Percentage of Proceeds	
Financing Type		**Underwriting Fees**
Bank loans		< 2%
Corporate bonds		
Investment grade		1–2%
Non-investment grade		2–3%
Equity issues		
Initial public offering		8–9%
Seasoned equity offering		5–6%

Source: Data based on typical underwriting, legal, and accounting fees for $50 million transaction. See, e.g., I. Lee, S. Lochhead, J. Ritter, and Q. Zhao, "The Cost of Raising Capital," *Journal of Financial Research* 19(1) (1996): 59–74.

For example, suppose a project has a levered value of $20 million and requires an initial investment of $15 million. To finance the project, the firm will borrow $10 million and fund the remaining $5 million by reducing dividends. If the bank providing the loan charges fees (after any tax deductions) totaling $200,000, the project NPV is

$$NPV = V^L - (\text{Investment}) - (\text{After Tax Issuance Costs}) = 20 - 15 - 0.2 = \$4.8 \text{ million}$$

Airline Loan Guarantees after September 11, 2001

On September 22, 2001, President George W. Bush signed into law the Air Transportation Safety and System Stabilization Act, which established the Air Transportation Stabilization Board (ATSB). The ATSB was authorized to distribute $5 billion in cash and issue up to $10 billion in federal loan guarantees. The purpose of the loan guarantees was to enable air carriers to obtain credit at a time when it was difficult for them to do so otherwise, so that they could make the investments necessary to maintain a safe, efficient, and viable commercial avia-

tion system in the United States in the aftermath of the September 11 tragedy. U.S. Airways received the largest loan guarantee of $900 million, and America West Airlines received the second largest, for $380 million. These loan guarantees protect creditors in the event of an airline's default, and they therefore enabled the airlines to obtain loans at a lower interest rate than they would without the guarantee. Because of the lower interest rate on the loans, the loans obtained with the help of the federal guarantee had a positive NPV for the airlines.

Security Mispricing

With perfect capital markets, all securities are fairly priced and issuing securities is a zero-NPV transaction. However, as discussed in Chapter 16, sometimes management may believe that the securities they are issuing are priced at less than (or more than) their true value. If so, the NPV of the transaction, which is the difference between the actual money raised and the true value of the securities sold, should be included in the value of the project. For example, if the financing of the project involves an equity issue, and if management believes that the equity will sell at a price that is less than its true value, this mispricing is a cost of the project for the *existing* shareholders.[18] It can be deducted from the project NPV in addition to other issuance costs.

When a firm borrows funds, a mispricing scenario arises if the interest rate charged differs from the rate that is appropriate given the actual risk of the loan. For example, a firm may pay an interest rate that is too high if news that would improve its credit rating has not yet become public. With the WACC method, the cost of the higher interest rate will result in a higher weighted average cost of capital and a lower value for the investment. With the APV method, we must add to the value of the project the NPV of the loan cash flows when evaluated at the "correct" rate that corresponds to their actual risk.[19]

EXAMPLE 18.8

Valuing a Loan

Problem

Gap, Inc., is considering borrowing $100 million to fund an expansion of its stores. Given investors' uncertainty regarding its prospects, Gap will pay a 6% interest rate on this loan. The firm's management knows, however, that the actual risk of the loan is extremely low and that the appropriate rate on the loan is 5%. Suppose the loan is for five years, with all principal being repaid in the fifth year. If Gap's marginal corporate tax rate is 40%, what is the net effect of the loan on the value of the expansion?

---

18. New shareholders, of course, benefit from receiving the shares at a low price.

19. We must also use the correct rate for r_D when levering or unlevering the cost of capital.

Solution

Shown below are the cash flows (in $ millions) and interest tax shields of a fair loan, at a 5% interest rate, and of the above-market rate loan Gap will receive, with a 6% interest rate. For each loan, we compute both the NPV of the loan cash flows and the present value of the interest tax shields, using the correct rate $r_D = 5\%$.

	Year	0	1	2	3	4	5
1	Fair Loan	100.00	(5.00)	(5.00)	(5.00)	(5.00)	(105.00)
2	Interest Tax Shield		2.00	2.00	2.00	2.00	2.00
3	At $r_D = 5\%$:						
4	NPV(Loan Cash Flows)	0.00					
5	PV(Interest Tax Shield)	8.66					
6	Actual Loan	100.00	(6.00)	(6.00)	(6.00)	(6.00)	(106.00)
7	Interest Tax Shield		2.40	2.40	2.40	2.40	2.40
8	At $r_D = 5\%$:						
9	NPV(Loan Cash Flows)	(4.33)					
10	PV(Interest Tax Shield)	10.39					

For the fair loan, note that the NPV of the loan cash flows is zero. Thus the benefit of the loan on the project's value is the present value of the interest tax shield of $8.66 million. For the actual loan, the higher interest rate increases the value of the interest tax shield but implies a negative NPV for the loan cash flows. The combined effect of the loan on the project's value is

$$NPV(\text{Loan Cash Flows}) + PV(\text{Interest Tax Shield}) = -4.33 + 10.39 = \$6.06 \text{ million}$$

While leverage is still valuable due to the tax shields, paying the higher interest rate reduces its benefit to the firm by $8.66 - 6.06 = \$2.60$ million.

Financial Distress and Agency Costs

As discussed in Chapter 16, one consequence of debt financing is the possibility of financial distress and agency costs. Because these costs affect the future free cash flows that will be generated by the project, they can be incorporated directly into the estimates of the project's expected free cash flows. When the debt level—and, therefore, the probability of financial distress—is high, the expected free cash flow will be reduced by the expected costs associated with financial distress and agency problems. Conversely, as discussed in Chapter 16, lower levels of debt may improve management's incentives and increase the firm's free cash flow.

Financial distress and agency costs also have consequences for the cost of capital. For example, financial distress is more likely to occur when economic times are bad. As a result, the costs of distress cause the value of the firm to fall further in a market downturn. Financial distress costs therefore tend to increase the sensitivity of the firm's value to market risk, raising the *unlevered* cost of capital for highly levered firms.

How do we incorporate these effects into the valuation methods described in this chapter? First, we must adjust the free cash flow estimates to include expected distress and agency costs. Second, because these costs also affect the systematic risk of the cash flows, the unlevered cost of capital, r_U, will no longer be independent of the firm's leverage.[20] Let's consider an example.

---

20. Indeed, calling r_U the *unlevered* cost of capital is, in this case, somewhat of a misnomer. It is the appropriate discount rate for the free cash flows ignoring any tax benefits of leverage, but including financial distress and agency consequences of leverage.

**EXAMPLE
18.9**

Valuing Distress Costs

Problem

Your firm currently has no leverage, and it expects to generate free cash flows of $10 million per year in perpetuity. The firm's current (unlevered) cost of capital is 10%, and its marginal corporate tax rate is 35%. You would like to determine whether adding leverage would increase the firm's value. Simulating the firm's future cash flows, you have estimated the likelihood and cost of financial distress with different levels of permanent debt and have produced the following estimates:

Debt Level, D	0	20	40	60	80
$E(FCF)$	10.0	9.9	9.8	9.5	9.0
r_U	10.0%	10.5%	11.0%	11.8%	13.0%

Based on this information, which level of permanent debt is optimal for the firm?

Solution

Because the debt level is known, the simplest course of action is to apply the APV method. The unlevered value of the firm can be computed as a perpetuity, $V^U = E(FCF) / r_U$. With permanent debt, the value of the tax shield is $\tau_c D$. Adding these together yields the estimate of the firm's levered value:

Debt Level, D	0	20	40	60	80
$V^U = E(FCF) / r_U$	100.0	94.3	89.1	80.5	69.2
$PV(ITS) = \tau_c D$	0.0	7.0	14.0	21.0	28.0
$V^L = V^U + \tau_c D$	100.0	101.3	103.1	101.5	97.2

Of the debt levels shown here, the value of the firm is maximized with $D = \$40$ million. This debt level provides the best tradeoff of tax benefits versus financial distress and agency costs.

An alternative method of incorporating financial distress and agency costs is to first value the project ignoring these costs, and then value the incremental cash flows associated with financial distress and agency problems separately. Because these costs tend to occur only when a firm is in (or near) default, valuing them is best done using the option valuation techniques introduced in Part VII of the text.

CONCEPT CHECK
1. How do we deal with issuance costs and security mispricing costs in our assessment of a project's value?
2. How would financial distress and agency costs affect a firm's use of leverage?

18.8 Advanced Topics in Capital Budgeting

In the previous sections, we have highlighted the most important methods for capital budgeting with leverage and demonstrated their application in common settings. In this section, we consider several more complicated scenarios and show how our tools can be extended to these cases. First, we consider leverage policies in which firms keep debt fixed in the short run, but adjust to a target leverage ratio in the long run. Second, we look at the relationship between a firm's equity and unlevered cost of capital for alternative leverage policies. Third, we implement the WACC and FTE methods when the firm's debt-equity ratio changes over time. We then conclude the section by incorporating the effects of personal taxes.

Periodically Adjusted Debt

To this point, we have considered leverage policies in which debt is either adjusted continuously to a target leverage ratio[21] or set according to a fixed plan that will never change. As Figure 18.1 shows, most real-world firms do not, in fact, appear to adjust debt levels continuously to maintain a target leverage ratio at all times. (See also Figure 15.6 in Chapter 15 for the behavior of aggregate leverage ratios over time.) Instead, most firms allow the debt-equity ratio of the firm to stray from the target and periodically adjust leverage to bring it back into line with the target. We next consider the effect of such a debt policy.

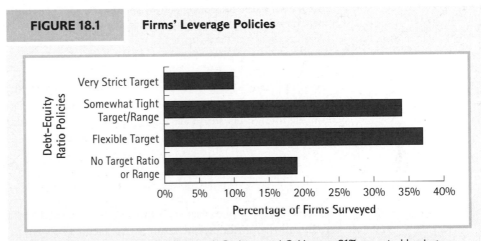

FIGURE 18.1   **Firms' Leverage Policies**

Of 392 CFOs surveyed by Professors J. Graham and C. Harvey, 81% reported having a target debt-equity ratio. However, only 10% of respondents viewed the target as set in stone. Most were willing to let the debt-equity ratio of the firm stray from the target and periodically adjust leverage to bring it back into line.

Source: J. R. Graham and C. Harvey, "The Theory and Practice of Corporate Finance: Evidence from the Field," *Journal of Financial Economics* 60 (2001): 187–243.

Suppose the firm adjusts its leverage every s periods, as shown in Figure 18.2. Then the firm's interest tax shields up to date s are predetermined, so they should be discounted at rate r_D. In contrast, interest tax shields that occur after date s depend on future adjustments the firm will make to its debt, so they are risky. If the firm will adjust the debt according to a target debt-equity ratio or interest coverage level, then the future interest tax shields should be discounted at rate r_D for the periods that they are known, but at rate r_U for all earlier periods when they are still risky.

---

21. While we have simplified our exposition earlier in the chapter by calculating debt and interest payments on an annual basis, the formulas we have used in the case of a constant debt-equity or interest coverage ratio are based on the assumption that debt changes during the year.

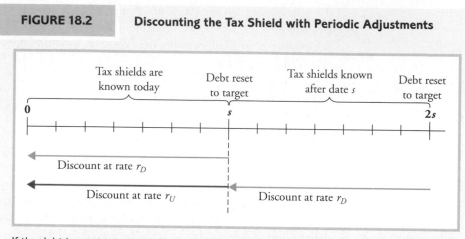

| FIGURE 18.2 | **Discounting the Tax Shield with Periodic Adjustments** |

If the debt is reset to a target leverage ratio every *s* periods, then interest tax shields within the first *s* periods are known and should be discounted at rate r_D. Interest tax shields that occur after date *s* are not yet known, so they should be discounted at rate r_D for the periods when they will be known and at rate r_U for earlier periods.

An important special case is when the debt is adjusted annually. In that case, the expected interest expense on date *t*, Int_t, is known as of date $t - 1$. Therefore, we discount the interest tax shield at rate r_D for one period, from date *t* to $t - 1$ (because it will be known at that time), and then discount it from date $t - 1$ to 0 at rate r_U:

$$PV(\tau_c \times Int_t) = \frac{\tau_c \times Int_t}{(1 + r_U)^{t-1}(1 + r_D)} = \frac{\tau_c \times Int_t}{(1 + r_U)^t} \times \left(\frac{1 + r_U}{1 + r_D}\right) \quad (18.16)$$

Equation 18.16 implies that we can value the tax shield by discounting it at rate r_U as before, and then multiply the result by the factor $(1 + r_U) / (1 + r_D)$ to account for the fact that the tax shield is known one year in advance.

This same adjustment can be applied to other valuation methods as well. For example, when the debt is adjusted annually rather than continuously to a target debt-to-value ratio *d*, the project-based WACC formula of Eq. 18.11 becomes,[22]

$$r_{wacc} = r_U - d\tau_c r_D \frac{1 + r_U}{1 + r_D} \quad (18.17)$$

Similarly, when the firm sets debt annually based on its expected future free cash flow, the constant interest coverage model in Eq. 18.14 becomes

$$V^L = \left(1 + \tau_c k \frac{1 + r_U}{1 + r_D}\right) V^U \quad (18.18)$$

Example 18.10 illustrates these methods in a constant growth setting.

---

22. This formula for the WACC was proposed by J. A. Miles and J. R. Ezzell, "The Weighted Average Cost of Capital, Perfect Capital Markets and Project Life: A Clarification," *Journal of Financial and Quantitative Analysis* 15(3) (1980): 719–730.

| EXAMPLE 18.10 | **Annual Debt Ratio Targeting** |

Problem

Celmax Corporation expects free cash flows this year of $7.36 million and a future growth rate of 4% per year. The firm currently has $30 million in debt outstanding. This leverage will remain fixed during the year, but at the end of each year Celmax will increase or decrease its debt to maintain a constant debt-equity ratio. Celmax pays 5% interest on its debt, pays a corporate tax rate of 40%, and has an unlevered cost of capital of 12%. Estimate Celmax's value with this leverage policy.

Solution

Using the APV approach, the unlevered value is $V^U = 7.36 / (12\% - 4\%) = \$92.0$ million. In the first year, Celmax will have an interest tax shield of $\tau_c\, r_D\, D = 0.40 \times 5\% \times \$30$ million $= \$0.6$ million. Because Celmax will adjust its debt after one year, the tax shields are expected to grow by 4% per year with the firm. The present value of the interest tax shield is therefore

$$PV(\text{Interest Tax Shield}) = \underbrace{\frac{0.6}{(12\% - 4\%)}}_{\substack{PV\,\text{at rate } r_U}} \times \underbrace{\left(\frac{1.12}{1.05}\right)}_{\substack{\text{Debt is set 1 year}\\\text{in advance}}} = \$8.0 \text{ million}$$

Therefore, $V^L = V^U + PV(\text{Interest Tax Shield}) = 92.0 + 8.0 = \$100.0$ million.

We can also apply the WACC method. From Eq. 18.17, Celmax's WACC is

$$r_{wacc} = r_U - d\tau_c r_D \frac{1 + r_U}{1 + r_D} = 12\% - \frac{30}{100}(0.40)(5\%)\frac{1.12}{1.05}$$

$$= 11.36\%$$

Therefore, $V^L = 7.36 / (11.36\% - 4\%) = \$100$ million.

Finally, the constant interest coverage model can be applied (in this setting with constant growth, a constant debt-equity ratio implies a constant interest coverage ratio). Given interest of $5\% \times \$30$ million $= \$1.50$ million this year, from Eq. 18.18

$$V^L - \left(1 + \tau_c k \frac{1 + r_U}{1 + r_D}\right) V^U$$

$$= \left(1 + 0.40 \times \frac{1.50}{7.36} \times \frac{1.12}{1.05}\right) 92.0 = \$100 \text{ million}$$

Leverage and the Cost of Capital

The relationship between leverage and the project's costs of capital in Eqs. 18.6, 18.10, and 18.11 relies on the assumption that the firm maintains a target leverage ratio. That relationship holds because in that case the interest tax shields have the same risk as the firm's cash flows. But when debt is set according to a fixed schedule for some period of time, the interest tax shields for the scheduled debt are known, relatively safe cash flows. These safe cash flows will reduce the effect of leverage on the risk of the firm's equity. To account for this effect, we should deduct the value of these "safe" tax shields from the debt—in the same way that we deduct cash—when evaluating a firm's leverage. That is, if T^s is the present value of the interest tax shields from predetermined debt, the risk of a firm's equity will depend on its *debt net of the predetermined tax shields:*

$$D^s = D - T^s \qquad (18.19)$$

We show in Appendix Section 18A.2 that Eqs. 18.6 and 18.10 continue to apply with D replaced by D^s, so that the more general relationship between the unlevered and equity costs of capital are related as follows:

Leverage and the Cost of Capital with a Fixed Debt Schedule

$$r_U = \frac{E}{E + D^s} r_E + \frac{D^s}{E + D^s} r_D \text{ or, equivalently, } r_E = r_U + \frac{D^s}{E}(r_U - r_D) \qquad (18.20)$$

We can also combine Eq. 18.20 with the definition of the WACC in Eq. 18.1 and generalize the project-based WACC formula in Eq. 18.11:

Project WACC with a Fixed Debt Schedule

$$r_{wacc} = r_U - d\tau_c[r_D + \phi(r_U - r_D)] \qquad (18.21)$$

where $d = D / (D + E)$ is the debt-to-value ratio, and $\phi = T^s / (\tau_c D)$ is a measure of the permanence of the debt level, D. Here are three cases commonly used in practice, which differ according to the frequency with which the debt is assumed to adjust to the growth of the investment:[23]

1. Continuously adjusted debt: $T^s = 0$, $D^s = D$, and $\phi = 0$

2. Annually adjusted debt: $T^s = \dfrac{\tau_c r_D D}{1 + r_D}$, $D^s = D\left(1 - \tau_c \dfrac{r_D}{1 + r_D}\right)$, and $\phi = \dfrac{r_D}{1 + r_D}$

3. Permanent debt: $T^s = \tau_c D$, $D^s = D(1 - \tau_c)$, and $\phi = 1$

Finally, note that unless d and ϕ remain constant over time, the WACC and equity cost of capital must be computed period by period.

EXAMPLE 18.11

APV and WACC with Permanent Debt

Problem

International Paper Company is considering the acquisition of additional forestland in the southeastern United States. The wood harvested from the land will generate free cash flows of $4.5 million per year, with an unlevered cost of capital of 7%. As a result of this acquisition, International Paper will permanently increase its debt by $30 million. If International Paper's tax rate is 35%, what is the value of this acquisition using the APV method? Verify this result using the WACC method.

---

23. Case 1 reduces to the Harris-Pringle formula (see footnote 13), case 2 is the Miles-Ezzell formula (see footnote 22), and case 3 is equivalent to the Modigliani-Miller-Hamada formula with permanent debt. See F. Modigliani and M. Miller, "Corporate Income Taxes and the Cost of Capital: A Correction," *American Economic Review* 53(3) (1963): 433–443; and R. Hamada, "The Effect of a Firm's Capital Structure on the Systematic Risks of Common Stocks," *Journal of Finance* 27(2) (1972): 435–452.

Solution

Using the APV method, the unlevered value of the land is $V^U = FCF/r_U = 4.5/0.07 = 64.29 million. Because the debt is permanent, the value of the tax shield is $\tau_c D = 0.35(30) = 10.50$. Therefore, $V^L = 64.29 + 10.50 = \$74.79$ million.

To use the WACC method, we apply Eq. 18.21 with $\phi = T^s/(\tau_c D) = 1$ and $d = 30/74.79 = 40.1\%$. Therefore, the WACC for the investment is

$$r_{wacc} = r_U - d\tau_c r_U = 7\% - 0.401 \times 0.35 \times 7\% = 6.017\%$$

and $V^L = 4.5/0.06017 = \$74.79$ million.

The WACC or FTE Method with Changing Leverage

When a firm does not maintain a constant debt-equity ratio for a project, the APV method is generally the most straightforward method to apply. The WACC and FTE methods become more difficult to use because when the proportion of debt financing changes, the project's equity cost of capital and WACC will not remain constant over time. With a bit of care, however, these methods can still be used (and, of course, will lead to the same result as the APV method).

As an example, the spreadsheet in Table 18.10 computes the equity cost of capital and WACC for the RFX project each year given the fixed debt schedule shown in line 3. The value of the project with leverage using the APV method is computed in line 7 as the total of the unlevered value and the value of the tax shield. With the project's equity value and net debt D^s in hand, we can use Eq. 18.20 to calculate the project's equity cost of capital each year (line 11). Note that the equity cost of capital declines over time as the project's leverage ratio D^s/E declines. By year 3, the debt is fully repaid and the equity cost of capital equals the unlevered cost of capital of 8%.

TABLE 18.10 SPREADSHEET	Adjusted Present Value and Cost of Capital for Avco's RFX Project with a Fixed Debt Schedule					
Year		0	1	2	3	4
Unlevered Value ($ million)						
1 Free Cash Flow		(28.00)	18.00	18.00	18.00	18.00
2 Unlevered Value, V^U (at $r_u = 8.0\%$)		59.62	46.39	32.10	16.67	—
Interest Tax Shield						
3 Debt Schedule, D_t		30.62	20.00	10.00	—	—
4 Interest Paid (at $r_D = 6\%$)		—	1.84	1.20	0.60	—
5 Interest Tax Shield (at $\tau_c = 40\%$)		—	0.73	0.48	0.24	—
6 Tax Shield Value, T^s (at $r_D = 6.0\%$)		1.32	0.67	0.23	—	—
Adjusted Present Value						
7 Levered Value, $V^L = V^U + T^s$		60.94	47.05	32.33	16.67	—
Effective Leverage and Cost of Capital						
8 Equity, $E = V^L - D$		30.32	27.05	22.33	16.67	—
9 Effective Debt, $D^s = D - T^s$		29.30	19.33	9.77	—	—
10 Effective Debt-Equity Ratio, D^s/E		0.966	0.715	0.438	0.000	
11 Equity Cost of Capital, r_E		9.93%	9.43%	8.88%	8.00%	
12 WACC, r_{wacc}		6.75%	6.95%	7.24%	8.00%	

Given the project's equity cost of capital, we compute its WACC using Eq. 18.1 in line 12. For example, at the beginning of the project,

$$r_{wacc} = \frac{E}{E+D}r_E + \frac{D}{E+D}r_D(1-\tau_c)$$

$$= \frac{30.32}{60.94}9.93\% + \frac{30.62}{60.94}6\%(1-0.40) = 6.75\%$$

Note that as the leverage of the project falls, its WACC rises, until it eventually equals the unlevered cost of capital of 8% when the project debt is fully repaid at year 3.

Once we have computed the WACC or the equity cost of capital, we can value the project using the WACC or FTE method. Because the cost of capital changes over time, we must use a different discount rate each year when applying these methods. For example, using the WACC method, the levered value each year is computed as

$$V_t^L = \frac{FCF_{t+1} + V_{t+1}^L}{1 + r_{wacc}(t)} \tag{18.22}$$

where $r_{wacc}(t)$ is the project's WACC in year t. This calculation is shown in Table 18.11. Note that the levered value matches the result from the APV method (line 7 in Table 18.10). The same approach can be used when applying the FTE method.[24]

| TABLE 18.11 SPREADSHEET | WACC Method for Avco's RFX Project with a Fixed Debt Schedule |

WACC Method ($ millions)	Year	0	1	2	3	4
1 Free Cash Flow		(28.00)	18.00	18.00	18.00	18.00
2 WACC, r_{wacc}		6.75%	6.95%	7.24%	8.00%	
3 Levered Value V^L (at r_{wacc})		60.94	47.05	32.33	16.67	—

Personal Taxes

As we discussed in Chapter 15, leverage has tax consequences for both investors and for corporations. For individuals, interest income from debt is generally taxed more heavily than income from equity (capital gains and dividends). So how do personal taxes affect our valuation methods?

If investors are taxed on the income they receive from holding equity or debt, it will raise the return they require to hold those securities. That is, the equity and debt cost of capital in the market *already* reflects the effects of investor taxes. As a result, *the WACC method does not change in the presence of investor taxes*; we can continue to compute the WACC according to Eq. 18.1 and compute the levered value as in Section 18.2.

---

24. You will notice, however, that we used the APV to compute the debt-equity ratio each period, which we needed to calculate r_E and r_{wacc}. If we had not already solved for the APV, we would need to determine the project's value and WACC simultaneously, using the approach described in Appendix Section 18A.3.

The APV approach, however, requires modification in the presence of investor taxes because it requires that we compute the unlevered cost of capital. This computation *is* affected by the presence of investor taxes. Let τ_e be the tax rate investors pay on equity income (dividends) and τ_i be the tax rate investors pay on interest income. Then, given an expected return on debt r_D, define r_D^* as the expected return on equity income that would give investors the same after-tax return:

$$r_D^* (1 - \tau_e) = r_D (1 - \tau_i)$$

So

$$r_D^* \equiv r_D \frac{(1 - \tau_i)}{(1 - \tau_e)} \tag{18.23}$$

Because the unlevered cost of capital is for a hypothetical firm that is all equity, investors' tax rates on income for such a firm are the equity rates, so we must use the rate r_D^* when computing the unlevered cost of capital. Therefore, Eq. 18.20 becomes

Unlevered Cost of Capital with Personal Taxes

$$r_U = \frac{E}{E + D^s} r_E + \frac{D^s}{E + D^s} r_D^* \tag{18.24}$$

Next, we must compute the interest tax shield using the effective tax advantage of debt, τ^*, in place of τ_c. The effective tax rate τ^* incorporates the investors' tax rate on equity income, τ_e, and on interest income, τ_i, and was defined in Chapter 15 as follows:

$$\tau^* = 1 - \frac{(1 - \tau_c)(1 - \tau_e)}{(1 - \tau_i)} \tag{18.25}$$

We then calculate the interest tax shield using tax rate τ^* and interest rate r_D^*:

$$\text{Interest Tax Shield in Year } t = \tau^* \times r_D^* \times D_{t-1} \tag{18.26}$$

Finally we discount the interest tax shields at rate r_U if the firm maintains a target leverage ratio or at rate r_D^* if the debt is set according to a predetermined schedule.[25]

EXAMPLE 18.12

Using the APV Method with Personal Taxes

Problem

Apex Corporation has an equity cost of capital of 14.4% and a debt cost of capital of 6%, and the firm maintains a debt-equity ratio of 1. Apex is considering an expansion that will contribute $4 million in free cash flows the first year, growing by 4% per year thereafter. The expansion will cost $60 million and will be financed with $40 million in new debt initially with a constant debt-equity ratio maintained thereafter. Apex's corporate tax rate is 40%; the tax rate on interest income is 40%; and the tax rate on equity income is 20%. Compute the value of the expansion using the APV method.

---

25. If the debt is permanent, for example, the value of the tax shield is $\tau^* r_D^* D / r_D^* = \tau^* D$, as shown in Chapter 15.

Solution

First, we compute the value without leverage. From Eq. 18.23, the debt cost of capital of 6% is equivalent to an equity rate of

$$r_D^* = r_D \frac{1 - \tau_i}{1 - \tau_e} = 6\% \times \frac{1 - 0.40}{1 - 0.20} = 4.5\%$$

Because Apex maintains a constant debt-equity ratio, $D^s = D$ and Apex's unlevered cost of capital is, using Eqs. 18.23 and 18.24,

$$r_U = \frac{E}{E + D^s} r_E + \frac{D^s}{E + D^s} r_D^* = 0.50 \times 14.4\% + 0.50 \times 4.5\% = 9.45\%$$

Therefore, $V^U = 4 / (9.45\% - 4\%) = \$73.39$ million.

From Eq. 18.25, the effective tax advantage of debt is

$$\tau^* = 1 - \frac{(1 - \tau_c)(1 - \tau_e)}{(1 - \tau_i)} = 1 - \frac{(1 - 0.40)(1 - 0.20)}{(1 - 0.40)} = 20\%$$

Apex will add new debt of \$40 million initially, so from Eq. 18.26 the interest tax shield is $20\% \times 4.5\% \times 40 = \$0.36$ million the first year (note that we use r_D^* here). With a growth rate of 4%, the present value of the interest tax shield is

$$PV(\text{Interest Tax Shield}) = 0.36 / (9.45\% - 4\%) = \$6.61 \text{ million}$$

Therefore the value of the expansion with leverage is given by the APV:

$$V^L = V^U + PV(\text{Interest Tax Shield}) = 73.39 + 6.61 = \$80 \text{ million}$$

Given the cost of \$60 million, the expansion has an NPV of \$20 million.

Let's check this result using the WACC method. Note that the expansion has the same debt-to-value ratio of $40/80 = 50\%$ as the firm overall. Thus its WACC is equal to the firm's WACC:

$$r_{wacc} = \frac{E}{E + D} r_E + \frac{D}{E + D} r_D (1 - \tau_c)$$

$$= 0.50 \times 14.4\% + 0.50 \times 6\% \times (1 - 0.40) = 9\%$$

Therefore, $V^L = 4 / (9\% - 4\%) = \$80$ million, as before.

As the Example 18.12 illustrates, the WACC method is much simpler to apply than the APV method in the case with investor taxes. More significantly, the WACC approach does not require knowledge of investors' tax rates. This fact is important because in practice, estimating the marginal tax rate of the investor can be very difficult.

If the investment's leverage or risk does not match the firm's, then investor tax rates are required even with the WACC method, as we must unlever and/or re-lever the firm's cost of capital using Eq. 18.24. When the investor's tax rate on interest income exceeds that on equity income, an increase in leverage will lead to a smaller reduction in the WACC (see Problem 25).

CONCEPT CHECK

1. When a firm has pre-determined tax shields, how do we measure its net debt when calculating its unlevered cost of capital?

2. If the firm's debt-equity ratio changes over time, can the WACC method still be applied?

Summary

1. The key steps in the WACC valuation method are as follows:

   a. Determine the unlevered free cash flows of the investment.

   b. Compute the weighted average cost of capital:

   $$r_{wacc} = \frac{E}{E+D}r_E + \frac{D}{E+D}r_D(1 - \tau_c) \qquad (18.1)$$

   c. Compute the value with leverage, V^L, by discounting the free cash flows of the investment using the WACC.

2. To determine the value of a levered investment using the APV method, proceed as follows:

   a. Determine the investment's value without leverage, V^U, by discounting its free cash flows at the unlevered cost of capital, r_U.

   b. Determine the present value of the interest tax shield.

      i. Given debt D_t on date t, the tax shield on date $t + 1$ is $\tau_c r_D D_t$.

      ii. If the debt level varies with the investment's value or free cash flow, use discount rate r_U. If the debt is predetermined, discount the tax shield at rate r_D.

   c. Add the unlevered value V^U to the present value of the interest tax shield to determine the value of the investment with leverage, V^L.

3. The key steps in the flow-to-equity method for valuing a levered investment are as follows:

   a. Determine the free cash flow to equity of the investment:

   $$FCFE = FCF - (1 - \tau_c) \times (\text{Interest Payments}) + (\text{Net Borrowing}) \qquad (18.9)$$

   b. Compute the equity value, E, by discounting the free cash flow to equity using the equity cost of capital.

4. The unlevered and equity costs of capital are related as follows:

   $$r_U = \frac{E}{E+D^s}r_E + \frac{D^s}{E+D^s}r_D \text{ or, equivalently, } r_E = r_U + \frac{D^s}{E}(r_U - r_D)$$

   where

   a. $D^s = D$, the firm's net debt, if the firm maintains a target leverage ratio (see Eqs. 18.6 and 18.10).

   b. If some of the firm's debt is predetermined, then $D^s = D - T^s$, where T^s is the value of predetermined interest tax shields (see Eq. 18.20).

5. If a project's risk is different from that of the firm as a whole, we must estimate its cost of capital separately from the firm's cost of capital. We estimate the project's unlevered cost of capital by looking at the unlevered cost of capital for other firms with similar market risk as the project.

6. If $d = D / (D + E)$ is the debt-to-value ratio of the project,

   a. Its WACC is equal to $r_{wacc} = r_U - d\tau_c r_D$, if the firm maintains a target leverage ratio (see Eq. 18.11).

   b. If some of the tax shields are predetermined, then

   $$r_{wacc} = r_U - d\tau_c[r_D + \phi(r_U - r_D)] \qquad (18.21)$$

   where $\phi = T^s / (\tau_c D)$ reflects the permanence of the debt level.

7. When assessing the leverage associated with a project, we must consider its incremental impact on the debt, net of cash balances, of the firm overall and not just the specific financing used for that investment.

8. A firm has a constant interest coverage policy if it sets debt to maintain its interest expenses as a fraction, k, of free cash flow. The levered value of a project with such a leverage policy is $V^L = (1 + \tau_c k) V^U$.

9. If a firm chooses to keep the level of debt at a constant level, D, permanently, then the levered value of a project with such a leverage policy is $V^L = V^U + \tau_c \times D$.

10. In general, the WACC method is the easiest to use when a firm has a target debt-equity ratio that it plans to maintain over the life of the investment. For other leverage policies, the APV method is usually the most straightforward method.

11. Issuance costs and any costs or gains from mispricing of issued securities should be included in the assessment of a project's value.

12. If a firm adjusts its debt annually to a target leverage ratio, the value of the interest tax shield is enhanced by the factor $(1 + r_U) / (1 + r_D)$.

13. Financial distress costs are likely to (1) lower the expected free cash flow of a project and (2) raise its unlevered cost of capital. Taking these effects into account, together with other agency and asymmetric information costs, may limit a firm's use of leverage.

14. The WACC method does not need to be modified to account for investor taxes. For the APV method, we use the interest rate

$$r_D^* \equiv r_D \frac{(1 - \tau_i)}{(1 - \tau_e)} \tag{18.23}$$

in place of r_D and we replace τ_c with the effective tax rate:

$$\tau^* = 1 - \frac{(1 - \tau_c)(1 - \tau_e)}{(1 - \tau_i)} \tag{18.25}$$

Key Terms

adjusted present value (APV) *p. 581*
constant interest coverage ratio *p. 594*
debt capacity *p. 580*
flow to equity (FTE) *p. 585*

free cash flow to equity (FCFE) *p. 586*
target leverage ratio *p. 582*
unlevered cost of capital *p. 582*

Further Reading

For a further treatment of the valuation with leverage, see: T. Copeland, T. Koller, and J. Murrin, *Valuation: Measuring and Managing the Value of Companies,* 3rd ed. (New York: McGraw-Hill, 2000); and S. P. Pratt, R. F. Reilly, and R. P. Schweihs, *Valuing a Business: The Analysis and Appraisal of Closely Held Companies,* 4th ed. (New York: McGraw-Hill, 2000).

For a more detailed treatment of the issues discussed in this chapter, the interested reader will find these articles useful: E. R. Arzac and L. R. Glosten, "A Reconsideration of Tax Shield Valuation," *European Financial Management* 11(4) (2005): 453–461; R. S. Harris and J. J. Pringle, "Risk-Adjusted Discount Rates—Extensions from the Average-Risk Case," *Journal of Financial Research* 8(3) (1985): 237–244; I. Inselbag and H. Kaufold, "Two DCF Approaches in Valuing Companies Under Alternative Financing Strategies (and How to Choose Between Them)," *Journal of Applied Corporate Finance* 10(1) (1997): 114–122;

T. A. Luehrman, "Using APV: A Better Tool for Valuing Operations," *Harvard Business Review* 75 (May–June 1997): 145–154; J. A. Miles and J. R. Ezzell, "The Weighted Average Cost of Capital, Perfect Capital Markets, and Project Life: A Clarification," *Journal of Financial and Quantitative Analysis* 15(3) (1980): 719–730; J. A. Miles and J. R. Ezzell, "Reformulation Tax Shield Valuation: A Note," *Journal of Finance* 40(5) (1985): 1485–1492; R. Ruback, "Capital Cash Flows: A Simple Approach to Valuing Risky Cash Flows," *Financial Management* 31(2) (2002): 85–104; and R. A. Taggart, "Consistent Valuation and Cost of Capital Expressions with Corporate and Personal Taxes," *Financial Management* 20(3) (1991): 8–20.

Problems

All problems in this chapter are available in MyFinanceLab. An asterisk (*) indicates problems with a higher level of difficulty.

Overview

1. Explain whether each of the following projects is likely to have risk similar to the average risk of the firm.

   a. The Clorox Company considers launching a new version of Armor All designed to clean and protect notebook computers.

   b. Google, Inc., plans to purchase real estate to expand its headquarters.

   c. Target Corporation decides to expand the number of stores it has in the southeastern United States.

   d. GE decides to open a new Universal Studios theme park in China.

2. Suppose Caterpillar, Inc., has 665 million shares outstanding with a share price of $74.77, and $25 billion in debt. If in three years, Caterpillar has 700 million shares outstanding trading for $83 per share, how much debt will Caterpillar have if it maintains a constant debt-equity ratio?

3. In 2006, Intel Corporation had a market capitalization of $112 billion, debt of $2.2 billion, cash of $9.1 billion, and EBIT of more than $11 billion. If Intel were to increase its debt by $1 billion and use the cash for a share repurchase, which market imperfections would be most relevant for understanding the consequence for Intel's value? Why?

The Weighted Average Cost of Capital Method

4. Suppose Goodyear Tire and Rubber Company is considering divesting one of its manufacturing plants. The plant is expected to generate free cash flows of $1.5 million per year, growing at a rate of 2.5% per year. Goodyear has an equity cost of capital of 8.5%, a debt cost of capital of 7%, a marginal corporate tax rate of 35%, and a debt-equity ratio of 2.6. If the plant has average risk and Goodyear plans to maintain a constant debt-equity ratio, what after-tax amount must it receive for the plant for the divestiture to be profitable?

5. Suppose Lucent Technologies has an equity cost of capital of 10%, market capitalization of $10.8 billion, and an enterprise value of $14.4 billion. Suppose Lucent's debt cost of capital is 6.1% and its marginal tax rate is 35%.

   a. What is Lucent's WACC?

   b. If Lucent maintains a constant debt-equity ratio, what is the value of a project with average risk and the following expected free cash flows?

Year	0	1	2	3
FCF	−100	50	100	70

   c. If Lucent maintains its debt-equity ratio, what is the debt capacity of the project in part (b)?

6. Acort Industries has 10 million shares outstanding and a current share price of $40 per share. It also has long-term debt outstanding. This debt is risk free, is four years away from maturity, has annual coupons with a coupon rate of 10%, and a $100 million face value. The first of the remaining coupon payments will be due in exactly one year. The riskless interest rates for all maturities are constant at 6%. Acort has EBIT of $106 million, which is expected to remain constant each year. New capital expenditures are expected to equal depreciation and equal $13 million per year, while no changes to net working capital are expected in the future. The corporate tax rate is 40%, and Acort is expected to keep its debt-equity ratio constant in the future (by either issuing additional new debt or buying back some debt as time goes on).

    a. Based on this information, estimate Acort's WACC.

    b. What is Acort's equity cost of capital?

The Adjusted Present Value Method

7. Suppose Goodyear Tire and Rubber Company has an equity cost of capital of 8.5%, a debt cost of capital of 7%, a marginal corporate tax rate of 35%, and a debt-equity ratio of 2.6. Suppose Goodyear maintains a constant debt-equity ratio.

    a. What is Goodyear's WACC?

    b. What is Goodyear's unlevered cost of capital?

    c. Explain, intuitively, why Goodyear's unlevered cost of capital is less than its equity cost of capital and higher than its WACC.

8. You are a consultant who was hired to evaluate a new product line for Markum Enterprises. The upfront investment required to launch the product line is $10 million. The product will generate free cash flow of $750,000 the first year, and this free cash flow is expected to grow at a rate of 4% per year. Markum has an equity cost of capital of 11.3%, a debt cost of capital of 5%, and a tax rate of 35%. Markum maintains a debt-equity ratio of 0.40.

    a. What is the NPV of the new product line (including any tax shields from leverage)?

    b. How much debt will Markum initially take on as a result of launching this product line?

    c. How much of the product line's value is attributable to the present value of interest tax shields?

9. Consider Lucent's project in Problem 5.

    a. What is Lucent's unlevered cost of capital?

    b. What is the unlevered value of the project?

    c. What are the interest tax shields from the project? What is their present value?

    d. Show that the APV of Lucent's project matches the value computed using the WACC method.

The Flow-to-Equity Method

10. Consider Lucent's project in Problem 5.

    a. What is the free cash flow to equity for this project?

    b. What is its NPV computed using the FTE method? How does it compare with the NPV based on the WACC method?

11. In year 1, AMC will earn $2000 before interest and taxes. The market expects these earnings to grow at a rate of 3% per year. The firm will make no net investments (that is, capital expenditures will equal depreciation) or changes to net working capital. Assume that the corporate tax rate equals 40%. Right now, the firm has $5000 in risk-free debt. It plans to keep a constant ratio of debt to equity every year, so that on average the debt will also grow by 3% per year. Suppose the risk-free rate equals 5%, and the expected return on the market equals 11%. The asset beta for this industry is 1.11.

a. If AMC were an all-equity (unlevered) firm, what would its market value be?

b. Assuming the debt is fairly priced, what is the amount of interest AMC will pay next year? If AMC's debt is expected to grow by 3% per year, at what rate are its interest payments expected to grow?

c. Even though AMC's debt is *riskless* (the firm will not default), the future growth of AMC's debt is uncertain, so the exact amount of the future interest payments is risky. Assuming the future interest payments have the same beta as AMC's assets, what is the present value of AMC's interest tax shield?

d. Using the APV method, what is AMC's total market value, V^L? What is the market value of AMC's equity?

e. What is AMC's WACC? (*Hint:* Work backward from the FCF and V^L.)

f. Using the WACC method, what is the expected return for AMC equity?

g. Show that the following holds for AMC: $\beta_A = \dfrac{E}{D+E}\beta_E + \dfrac{D}{D+E}\beta_D$.

h. Assuming that the proceeds from any increases in debt are paid out to equity holders, what cash flows do the equity holders expect to receive in one year? At what rate are those cash flows expected to grow? Use that information plus your answer to part (f) to derive the market value of equity using the FTE method. How does that compare to your answer in part (d)?

Project-Based Costs of Capital

12. Prokter and Gramble (PG) has historically maintained a debt-equity ratio of approximately 0.20. Its current stock price is $50 per share, with 2.5 billion shares outstanding. The firm enjoys very stable demand for its products, and consequently it has a low equity beta of 0.50 and can borrow at 4.20%, just 20 basis points over the risk-free rate of 4%. The expected return of the market is 10%, and PG's tax rate is 35%.

    a. This year, PG is expected to have free cash flows of $6.0 billion. What constant expected growth rate of free cash flow is consistent with its current stock price?

    b. PG believes it can increase debt without any serious risk of distress or other costs. With a higher debt-equity ratio of 0.50, it believes its borrowing costs will rise only slightly to 4.50%. If PG announces that it will raise its debt-equity ratio to 0.5 through a leveraged recap, determine the increase in the stock price that would result from the anticipated tax savings.

13. Amarindo, Inc. (AMR), is a newly public firm with 10 million shares outstanding. You are doing a valuation analysis of AMR. You estimate its free cash flow in the coming year to be $15 million, and you expect the firm's free cash flows to grow by 4% per year in subsequent years. Because the firm has only been listed on the stock exchange for a short time, you do not have an accurate assessment of AMR's equity beta. However, you do have beta data for UAL, another firm in the same industry:

	Equity Beta	Debt Beta	Debt-Equity Ratio
UAL	1.5	0.30	1

AMR has a much lower debt-equity ratio of 0.30, which is expected to remain stable, and its debt is risk free. AMR's corporate tax rate is 40%, the risk-free rate is 5%, and the expected return on the market portfolio is 11%.

    a. Estimate AMR's equity cost of capital.

    b. Estimate AMR's share price.

EXCEL   **14.** Remex (RMX) currently has no debt in its capital structure. The beta of its equity is 1.50. For each year into the indefinite future, Remex's free cash flow is expected to equal $25 million. Remex is considering changing its capital structure by issuing debt and using the proceeds to buy back stock. It will do so in such a way that it will have a 30% debt-equity ratio after the change, and it will maintain this debt-equity ratio forever. Assume that Remex's debt cost of capital will be 6.5%. Remex faces a corporate tax rate of 35%. Except for the corporate tax rate of 35%, there are no market imperfections. Assume that the CAPM holds, the risk-free rate of interest is 5%, and the expected return on the market is 11%.

a. Using the information provided, fill in the table below:

	Debt-Equity Ratio	Debt Cost of Capital	Equity Cost of Capital	Weighted Average Cost of Capital
Before change in capital structure	0	N/A		
After change in capital structure	0.30	6.5%		

b. Using the information provided and your calculations in part (a), determine the value of the tax shield acquired by Remex if it changes its capital structure in the way it is considering.

APV with Other
Leverage Policies

15. Tybo Corporation adjusts its debt so that its interest expenses are 20% of its free cash flow. Tybo is considering an expansion that will generate free cash flows of $2.5 million this year and is expected to grow at a rate of 4% per year from then on. Suppose Tybo's marginal corporate tax rate is 40%.

a. If the unlevered cost of capital for this expansion is 10%, what is its unlevered value?

b. What is the levered value of the expansion?

c. If Tybo pays 5% interest on its debt, what amount of debt will it take on initially for the expansion?

d. What is the debt-to-value ratio for this expansion? What is its WACC?

e. What is the levered value of the expansion using the WACC method?

EXCEL   **16.** You are on your way to an important budget meeting. In the elevator, you review the project valuation analysis you had your summer associate prepare for one of the projects to be discussed:

	0	1	2	3	4
EBIT		10.0	10.0	10.0	10.0
Interest (5%)		−4.0	−4.0	−3.0	−2.0
Earnings Before Taxes		6.0	6.0	7.0	8.0
Taxes		−2.4	−2.4	−2.8	−3.2
Depreciation		25.0	25.0	25.0	25.0
Cap Ex	−100.0				
Additions to NWC	−20.0				20.0
Net New Debt	80.0	0.0	−20.0	−20.0	−40.0
FCFE	−40.0	28.6	8.6	9.2	9.8
NPV at 11% Equity Cost of Capital	5.9				

Looking over the spreadsheet, you realize that while all of the cash flow estimates are correct, your associate used the flow-to-equity valuation method and discounted the cash flows using the *company's* equity cost of capital of 11%. However, the project's incremental leverage is very different from the company's historical debt-equity ratio of 0.20: For this project, the company will instead borrow $80 million upfront and repay $20 million in year 2, $20 million in year 3, and $40 million in year 4. Thus the *project's* equity cost of capital is likely to be higher than the firm's, not constant over time—invalidating your associate's calculation.

Clearly, the FTE approach is not the best way to analyze this project. Fortunately, you have your calculator with you, and with any luck you can use a better method before the meeting starts.

  a. What is the present value of the interest tax shield associated with this project?
  b. What are the free cash flows of the project?
  c. What is the best estimate of the project's value from the information given?

17. Your firm is considering building a $600 million plant to manufacture HDTV circuitry. You expect operating profits (EBITDA) of $145 million per year for the next ten years. The plant will be depreciated on a straight-line basis over ten years (assuming no salvage value for tax purposes). After ten years, the plant will have a salvage value of $300 million (which, since it will be fully depreciated, is then taxable). The project requires $50 million in working capital at the start, which will be recovered in year 10 when the project shuts down. The corporate tax rate is 35%. All cash flows occur at the end of the year.

  a. If the risk-free rate is 5%, the expected return of the market is 11%, and the asset beta for the consumer electronics industry is 1.67, what is the NPV of the project?
  b. Suppose that you can finance $400 million of the cost of the plant using ten-year, 9% coupon bonds sold at par. This amount is incremental new debt associated specifically with this project and will not alter other aspects of the firm's capital structure. What is the value of the project, including the tax shield of the debt?

Other Effects of Financing

EXCEL 18. DFS Corporation is currently an all-equity firm, with assets with a market value of $100 million and 4 million shares outstanding. DFS is considering a leveraged recapitalization to boost its share price. The firm plans to raise a fixed amount of permanent debt (i.e., the outstanding principal will remain constant) and use the proceeds to repurchase shares. DFS pays a 35% corporate tax rate, so one motivation for taking on the debt is to reduce the firm's tax liability. However, the upfront investment banking fees associated with the recapitalization will be 5% of the amount of debt raised. Adding leverage will also create the possibility of future financial distress or agency costs; shown below are DFS's estimates for different levels of debt:

Debt amount ($ million):	0	10	20	30	40	50
Present value of expected distress and agency costs ($ million):	0.0	−0.3	−1.8	−4.3	−7.5	−11.3

  a. Based on this information, which level of debt is the best choice for DFS?
  b. Estimate the stock price once this transaction is announced.

19. Your firm is considering a $150 million investment to launch a new product line. The project is expected to generate a free cash flow of $20 million per year, and its unlevered cost of capital is 10%. To fund the investment, your firm will take on $100 million in permanent debt.

  a. Suppose the marginal corporate tax rate is 35%. Ignoring issuance costs, what is the NPV of the investment including any tax benefits of leverage?

b. Suppose your firm will pay a 2% underwriting fee when issuing the debt. It will raise the remaining $50 million by issuing equity. In addition to the 5% underwriting fee for the equity issue, you believe that your firm's current share price of $40 is $5 per share less than its true value. What is the NPV of the investment in this case? (Assume all fees are on an after-tax basis.)

20. Consider Avco's RFX project from Section 18.3. Suppose that Avco is receiving government loan guarantees that allow it to borrow at the 6% rate. Without these guarantees, Avco would pay 6.5% on its debt.

   a. What is Avco's unlevered cost of capital given its true debt cost of capital of 6.5%?

   b. What is the unlevered value of the RFX project in this case? What is the present value of the interest tax shield?

   c. What is the NPV of the loan guarantees? (*Hint:* Because the actual loan amounts will fluctuate with the value of the project, discount the expected interest savings at the unlevered cost of capital.)

   d. What is the levered value of the RFX project, including the interest tax shield and the NPV of the loan guarantees?

Advanced Topics in Capital Budgeting

21. Arden Corporation is considering an investment in a new project with an unlevered cost of capital of 9%. Arden's marginal corporate tax rate is 40%, and its debt cost of capital is 5%.

   a. Suppose Arden adjusts its debt continuously to maintain a constant debt-equity ratio of 50%. What is the appropriate WACC for the new project?

   b. Suppose Arden adjusts its debt once per year to maintain a constant debt-equity ratio of 50%. What is the appropriate WACC for the new project now?

   c. Suppose the project has free cash flows of $10 million per year, which are expected to decline by 2% per year. What is the value of the project in parts (a) and (b) now?

22. XL Sports is expected to generate free cash flows of $10.9 million per year. XL has permanent debt of $40 million, a tax rate of 40%, and an unlevered cost of capital of 10%.

   a. What is the value of XL's equity using the APV method?

   b. What is XL's WACC? What is XL's equity value using the WACC method?

   c. If XL's debt cost of capital is 5%, what is XL's equity cost of capital?

   d. What is XL's equity value using the FTE method?

EXCEL *23. Propel Corporation plans to make a $50 million investment, initially funded completely with debt. The free cash flows of the investment and Propel's incremental debt from the project are shown below:

Year	0	1	2	3
Free cash flows	−50	40	20	25
Debt	50	30	15	0

Propel's incremental debt for the project will be paid off according to the predetermined schedule shown. Propel's debt cost of capital is 8%, and its tax rate is 40%. Propel also estimates an unlevered cost of capital for the project of 12%.

   a. Use the APV method to determine the levered value of the project at each date and its initial NPV.

   b. Calculate the WACC for this project at each date. How does the WACC change over time? Why?

   c. Compute the project's NPV using the WACC method.

d. Compute the equity cost of capital for this project at each date. How does the equity cost of capital change over time? Why?

e. Compute the project's equity value using the FTE method. How does the initial equity value compare with the NPV calculated in parts (a) and (c)?

*24. Gartner Systems has no debt and an equity cost of capital of 10%. Gartner's current market capitalization is $100 million, and its free cash flows are expected to grow at 3% per year. Gartner's corporate tax rate is 35%. Investors pay tax rates of 40% on interest income and 20% on equity income.

a. Suppose Gartner adds $50 million in permanent debt, and uses the proceeds to repurchase shares. What will Gartner's levered value be in this case?

b. Suppose instead Gartner decides to maintain a 50% debt-to-value ratio going forward. If Gartner's debt cost of capital is 6.67%, what will Gartner's levered value be in this case?

EXCEL *25. Revtek, Inc., has an equity cost of capital of 12% and a debt cost of capital of 6%. Revtek maintains a constant debt-equity ratio of 0.5, and its tax rate is 35%.

a. What is Revtek's WACC given its current debt-equity ratio?

b. Assuming no personal taxes, how will Revtek's WACC change if it increases its debt-equity ratio to 2 and its debt cost of capital remains at 6%?

c. Now suppose investors pay tax rates of 40% on interest income and 15% on income from equity. How will Revtek's WACC change if it increases its debt-equity ratio to 2 in this case?

d. Provide an intuitive explanation for the difference in your answers to parts (b) and (c).

Data Case

Toyota Motor Company is expanding the production of their gas-electric hybrid drive systems and plans to begin production in the United States. To enable the expansion they are contemplating investing $1.5 billion in a new plant with an expected ten-year life. The anticipated free cash flows from the new plant would be $220 million the first year of operation and grow by 10% for each of the next two years and then 5% per year for the remaining seven years. As a newly hired MBA in the capital budgeting division you have been asked to evaluate the new project using the WACC, Adjusted Present Value, and Flow-to-Equity methods. You will compute the appropriate costs of capital and the net present values with each method. Because this is your first major assignment with the firm, they want you to demonstrate that you are capable of handling the different valuation methods. You must seek out the information necessary to value the free cash flows but will be provided some directions to follow. (This is an involved assignment, but at least you don't have to come up with the actual cash flows for the project!)

1. Go to MarketWatch.com (www.marketwatch.com) and get the quote for Toyota (symbol: TM).

a. Click on "Financials." The income statements for the last four fiscal years will appear. Place the cursor in the middle of the statements and right-click the mouse. Select "Export to Microsoft Excel."

b. Go back to the Web page and select "Balance Sheets" from the top of the page. Repeat the download procedure for the balance sheets, then copy and paste them into the same worksheet as the income statements.

c. Click on "Historical Quote" in the left column, and find Toyota's stock price for the last day of the month at the end of each of the past four fiscal years. Record the stock price on each date in your spreadsheet.

2. Create a timeline in Excel with the free cash flows for the ten years of the project.

3. Determine the WACC using Eq. 18.1.

   a. For the cost of debt, r_D:

      i. Go to NasdBondInfo.com (www.nasdbondinfo.com) and click to search by symbol. Enter Toyota's symbol and press enter.

      ii. Find the yield for the Toyota Motor Credit Corp. bond with a maturity of 1/25/2016. Enter the yield on your spreadsheet as an estimate of Toyota's debt cost of capital.

   b. For the cost of equity, r_E:

      i. Get the yield on the ten-year U.S. Treasury Bond from Yahoo! Finance (http://finance.yahoo.com). Scroll down to the Market Summary. Enter that yield as the risk-free rate.

      ii. Find the beta for Toyota from Nasdaq.com. Enter the symbol for Toyota and click on "Summary Quote." The beta for Toyota will be listed there.

      iii. Use a market risk premium of 4.50% to compute r_E using the CAPM.

   c. Determine the values for E and D from Eq. 18.1 for Toyota and the debt-to-value and equity-to-value ratios.

      i. To compute the net debt for Toyota add the long-term debt and the short-term debt and subtract cash and cash equivalents for each year on the balance sheet.

      ii. Multiply the historical stock prices by the "Basic Weighted Shares Outstanding" data in the income statement to compute Toyota's market capitalization at the end of each fiscal year.

      iii. Compute Toyota's enterprise value at the end of each fiscal year by combining the values obtained for its equity market capitalization and its net debt.

      iv. Compute Toyota's debt-to-value ratio at the end of each year by dividing its net debt by its enterprise value. Use the average ratio from the last four years as an estimate for Toyota's target debt-to-value ratio.

   d. Determine Toyota's tax rate by dividing the income tax by earnings before tax for each year. Take the average of the four rates as Toyota's marginal corporate tax rate.

   e. Compute the WACC for Toyota using Eq. 18.1.

4. Compute the NPV of the hybrid engine expansion given the free cash flows you calculated using the WACC method of valuation.

5. Determine the NPV using the Adjusted Present Value Method, and also using the Flow-to-Equity method. In both cases, assume Toyota maintains the target leverage ratio you computed in Question 3(c).

6. Compare the results under the three methods and explain how the resulting NPVs are achieved under each of the three different methods.

| CHAPTER 18 APPENDIX | **Foundations and Further Details** |

In this appendix we look at the foundations for the WACC method, and for the relationship between a firm's levered and unlevered costs of capital. We also address how we can solve for a firm's leverage policy and value simultaneously.

18A.1   Deriving the WACC Method

The WACC can be used to value a levered investment, as in Eq. 18.2 on page 577. Consider an investment that is financed by both debt and equity. Because equity holders require an expected return of r_E on their investment and debt holders require a return of r_D, the firm will have to pay investors a total of

$$E(1 + r_E) + D(1 + r_D) \tag{18A.1}$$

next year. What is the value of the investment next year? The project generates free cash flows of FCF_1 at the end of the year. In addition, the interest tax shield of the debt provides a tax savings of $\tau_c \times$ (interest on debt) $\approx \tau_c\, r_D\, D$.[26] Finally, if the investment will continue beyond next year, it will have a continuation value of V_1^L. Thus, to satisfy investors, the project cash flows must be such that

$$E(1 + r_E) + D(1 + r_D) = FCF_1 + \tau_c r_D D + V_1^L \tag{18A.2}$$

Because $V_0^L = E + D$, we can write the WACC definition in Eq. 18.1 as

$$r_{wacc} = \frac{E}{V_0^L} r_E + \frac{D}{V_0^L} r_D (1 - \tau_c) \tag{18A.3}$$

If we move the interest tax shield to the left side of Eq. 18A.2, we can use the definition of the WACC to rewrite Eq. 18A.2 as follows:

$$\underbrace{E(1 + r_E) + D[1 + r_D(1 - \tau_c)]}_{V_0^L(1 + r_{wacc})} = FCF_1 + V_1^L \tag{18A.4}$$

---

26. The return on the debt r_D need not come solely from interest payments. If C_t is the coupon paid and D_t is the market value of the debt in period t, then in period t, r_D is defined as

$$r_D = \frac{E[\text{Coupon Payment} + \text{Capital Gain}]}{\text{Current Price}} = \frac{E[C_{t+1} + D_{t+1} - D_t]}{D_t}$$

The return that determines the firm's interest expense is

$$\bar{r}_D = \frac{E[C_{t+1} + \overline{D}_{t+1} - \overline{D}_t]}{D_t}$$

where $\overline{D}_t$ is the value of the debt on date t according to a fixed schedule set by the tax code based on the difference between the bond's initial price and its face value, which is called the bond's *original issue discount* (OID). (If the bond is issued at par and the firm will not default on the next coupon, then $\overline{D}_t = \overline{D}_{t+1}$ and $\bar{r}_D = C_{t+1} / D_t$, which is the bond's *current yield*.) Thus the true after-tax cost of debt is $(r_D - \tau_c \bar{r}_D)$. In practice, the distinction between r_D and $\bar{r}_D$ is often ignored, and the after-tax cost of debt is computed as $r_D(1 - \tau_c)$. Also, the debt's yield to maturity is often used in place of r_D. Because the yield to maturity ignores default risk, it generally overstates r_D and therefore the WACC.

Dividing by $(1 + r_{wacc})$, we can express the value of the investment today as the present value of next period's free cash flows and continuation value:

$$V_0^L = \frac{FCF_1 + V_1^L}{1 + r_{wacc}} \tag{18A.5}$$

In the same way, we can write the value in one year, V_1^L, as the discounted value of the free cash flows and continuation value of the project in year 2. If the WACC is the same next year, then

$$V_0^L = \frac{FCF_1 + V_1^L}{1 + r_{wacc}} = \frac{FCF_1 + \dfrac{FCF_2 + V_2^L}{1 + r_{wacc}}}{1 + r_{wacc}} = \frac{FCF_1}{1 + r_{wacc}} + \frac{FCF_2 + V_2^L}{(1 + r_{wacc})^2} \tag{18A.6}$$

By repeatedly replacing each continuation value, and *assuming the WACC remains constant*, we can derive Eq. 18.2:[27]

$$V_0^L = \frac{FCF_1}{1 + r_{wacc}} + \frac{FCF_2}{(1 + r_{wacc})^2} + \frac{FCF_3}{(1 + r_{wacc})^3} + \cdots \tag{18A.7}$$

That is, *the value of a levered investment is the present value of its future free cash flows using the weighted average cost of capital.*

18A.2   The Levered and Unlevered Cost of Capital

In this appendix, we derive the relationship between the levered and unlevered cost of capital for the firm. Suppose an investor holds a portfolio of all of the equity and debt of the firm. Then the investor will receive the free cash flows of the firm plus the tax savings from the interest tax shield. These are the same cash flows an investor would receive from a portfolio of the unlevered firm (which generates the free cash flows) and a separate "tax shield" security that paid the investor the amount of the tax shield each period. Because these two portfolios generate the same cash flows, by the Law of One Price they have the same market values:

$$V^L = E + D = V^U + T \tag{18A.8}$$

where T is the present value of the interest tax shield. Equation 18A.8 is the basis of the APV method. Because these portfolios have equal cash flows, they must also have identical expected returns, which implies

$$Er_E + Dr_D = V^U r_U + Tr_T \tag{18A.9}$$

where r_T is the expected return associated with the interest tax shields. The relationship between r_E, r_D, and r_U will depend on the expected return r_T, which is determined by the risk of the interest tax shield. Let's consider the two cases discussed in the text.

Target Leverage Ratio

Suppose the firm adjusts its debt continuously to maintain a target debt-to-value ratio, or a target ratio of interest to free cash flow. We show below that in this case, the risk of the interest

---

27. This expansion is the same approach we took in Chapter 9 to derive the discounted dividend formula for the stock price.

tax shield will be equal to that of the firm's free cash flow, so $r_T = r_U$. With this observation, Eq. 18A.9 becomes

$$Er_E + Dr_D = V^U r_U + T r_U = (V^U + T) r_U$$
$$= (E + D) r_U \tag{18A.10}$$

Dividing by $(E + D)$ leads to Eq. 18.6 on page 582.

Predetermined Debt Schedule

Suppose some of the firm's debt is set according to a predetermined schedule that is independent of the growth of the firm. Suppose the value of the tax shield from the scheduled debt is T^s, and the remaining value of the tax shield $T - T^s$ is from debt that will be adjusted according to a target leverage ratio. Because the risk of the interest tax shield from the scheduled debt is similar to the risk of the debt itself, Eq. 18A.9 becomes

$$Er_E + Dr_D = V^U r_U + T r_T = V^U r_U + (T - T^s) r_U + T^s r_D \tag{18A.11}$$

Subtracting $T^s r_D$ from both sides, and using $D^s = D - T^s$,

$$Er_E + D^s r_D = (V^U + T - T^s) r_U = (V^L - T^s) r_U$$
$$= (E + D^s) r_U \tag{18A.12}$$

Dividing by $(E + D^s)$ leads to Eq. 18.20 on page 604.

Risk of the Tax Shield with a Target Leverage Ratio

The previous analysis relied on the fact that with a target leverage ratio, it is reasonable to assume that $r_T = r_U$. Why should this be the case?

We define a target leverage ratio as a setting in which the firm adjusts its debt at date t to be a proportion $d(t)$ of the investment's value, or a proportion $k(t)$ of its free cash flow. (The target ratio for either policy need not be constant over time, but can vary according to a predetermined schedule.)

With either policy, the value at date t of the incremental tax shield from the project's free cash flow at a later date s, FCF_s, is proportional to the value of the cash flow $V_t^L(FCF_s)$. The assumption $r_T = r_U$ therefore follows as long as all cash flows have the same market risk between $t - 1$ and t; that is, when discounting $V_t^L(FCF_s)$ to period $t - 1$, the cost of capital does not depend on s (a standard assumption in capital budgeting).[28]

18A.3 Solving for Leverage and Value Simultaneously

When we use the APV method, we need to know the debt level to compute the interest tax shield and determine the project's value. But if a firm maintains a constant debt-to-value ratio, we need to know the project's value to determine the debt level. How can we apply the APV method in this case?

When a firm maintains a constant leverage ratio, to use the APV method we must solve for the debt level and the project value simultaneously. While complicated to do by hand, it is (fortunately) easy to do in Excel. We begin with the spreadsheet shown in Table 18A.1, which illustrates the standard APV calculation outlined in Section 18.3 of the text. For now, we have just inserted arbitrary values for the project's debt capacity in line 3.

---

28. If the risk of the individual cash flows differs, then r_T will be a weighted average of the unlevered costs of capital of the individual cash flows, with the weights depending on the schedule d or k. See P. DeMarzo, "A Note on Discounting Tax Shields and the Unlevered Cost of Capital," a working paper, 2006.

TABLE 18A.1 SPREADSHEET   **Adjusted Present Value for Avco's RFX Project with Arbitrary Debt Levels**

Year	0	1	2	3	4
Unlevered Value ($ million)					
1 Free Cash Flow	(28.00)	18.00	18.00	18.00	18.00
2 Unlevered Value, V^U (at $r_u = 8.0\%$)	59.62	46.39	32.10	16.67	—
Interest Tax Shield					
3 Debt Capacity (arbitrary)	30.00	20.00	10.00	5.00	—
4 Interest Paid (at $r_d = 6\%$)	—	1.80	1.20	0.60	0.30
5 Interest Tax Shield (at $\tau_c = 40\%$)	—	0.72	0.48	0.24	0.12
6 Tax Shield Value, T (at $r_u = 8.0\%$)	1.36	0.75	0.33	0.11	—
Adjusted Present Value					
7 Levered Value, $V^L = V^U + T$	60.98	47.13	32.42	16.78	—

Note that the debt capacity specified in line 3 is not consistent with a 50% debt-to-value ratio for the project. For example, given the value of $60.98 million in year 0, the initial debt capacity should be 50% × $60.98 million = $30.49 million in year 0. But if we change each debt capacity in line 3 to a *numerical* value that is 50% of the value in line 7, the interest tax shield and the project's value will change, and we will still not have a 50% debt-to-value ratio.

The solution is to enter in line 3 a *formula* that sets the debt capacity to be 50% of the project's value in line 7 in the same year. Now line 7 depends on line 3, and line 3 depends on line 7, creating a circular reference in the spreadsheet (and you will most likely receive an error message). By changing the calculation option in Excel to calculate the spreadsheet iteratively (Tools > Options menu, Calculation Tab, and check the Iteration box), Excel will keep calculating until the values in line 3 and line 7 of the spreadsheet are consistent, as shown in Table 18A.2.

TABLE 18A.2 SPREADSHEET   **Adjusted Present Value for Avco's RFX Project with Debt Levels Solved Iteratively**

Year	0	1	2	3	4
Unlevered Value ($ million)					
1 Free Cash Flow	(28.00)	18.00	18.00	18.00	18.00
2 Unlevered Value, V^U (at $r_u = 8.0\%$)	59.62	46.39	32.10	16.67	—
Interest Tax Shield					
3 Debt Capacity (at $d = 50\%$)	30.62	23.71	16.32	8.43	—
4 Interest Paid (at $r_d = 6\%$)	—	1.84	1.42	0.98	0.51
5 Interest Tax Shield (at $\tau_c = 40\%$)	—	0.73	0.57	0.39	0.20
6 Tax Shield Value, T (at $r_u = 8.0\%$)	1.63	1.02	0.54	0.19	—
Adjusted Present Value					
7 Levered Value, $V^L = V^U + T$	61.25	47.41	32.63	16.85	—

The same method can be applied when using the WACC method with known debt levels. In that case, we need to know the project's value to determine the debt-to-value ratio and compute the WACC, and we need to know the WACC to compute the project's value. Again, we can use iteration within Excel to determine simultaneously the project's value and debt-to-value ratio.

Valuation and Financial Modeling: A Case Study

notation

R_s	return on security s
r_f	risk-free rate
α_s	the alpha of security s
β_s	the beta of security s
R_{mkt}	return of the market portfolio
$E[R_{mkt}]$	expected return of the market portfolio
ε_s	the regression error term
β_U	the beta of an unlevered firm
β_E	the beta of the equity of a levered firm
β_D	the beta of the debt of a levered firm
r_U	unlevered cost of capital
V_T^L	continuing value of a project at date T
FCF_t	free cash flow at date t
r_{wacc}	weighted average cost of capital
g	growth rate
V^U	unlevered value
T^s	predetermined tax shield value
r_D	debt cost of capital

The goal of this chapter is to apply the financial tools we have developed thus far to demonstrate how they are used in practice to build a valuation model of a firm. In this chapter, we will value a hypothetical firm, Ideko Corporation. Ideko is a privately held designer and manufacturer of specialty sports eyewear based in Chicago. In mid-2005, its owner and founder, June Wong, has decided to sell the business, after having relinquished management control about four years ago. As a partner in PKK Investments, you are investigating purchasing the company. If a deal can be reached, the acquisition will take place at the end of the current fiscal year. In that event, PKK plans to implement operational and financial improvements at Ideko over the next five years, after which it intends to sell the business.

Ideko has total assets of $87 million and annual sales of $75 million. The firm is also quite profitable, with earnings this year of almost $7 million, for a net profit margin of 9.3%. You believe a deal could be struck to purchase Ideko's equity at the end of this fiscal year for an acquisition price of $150 million, which is almost double Ideko's current book value of equity. Is this price reasonable?

We begin the chapter by estimating Ideko's value using data for comparable firms. We then review PKK's operating strategies for running the business after the acquisition, to identify potential areas for improvements. We build a financial model to project cash flows that reflect these operating improvements. These cash flow forecasts enable us to value Ideko using the APV model introduced in Chapter 18 and estimate the return on PKK's investment. Finally, we explore the sensitivity of the valuation estimates to our main assumptions.

19.1 Valuation Using Comparables

As a result of preliminary conversations with Ideko's founder, you have estimates of Ideko's income and balance sheet information for the current fiscal year shown in Table 19.1. Ideko currently has debt outstanding of $4.5 million, but it also has a substantial cash balance. To obtain your first estimate of Ideko's value, you decide to value Ideko by examining comparable firms.

TABLE 19.1 SPREADSHEET	**Estimated 2005 Income Statement and Balance Sheet Data for Ideko Corporation**

Income Statement ($ 000)	Year 2005	Balance Sheet ($ 000)	Year 2005
1 Sales	75,000	Assets	
2 Cost of Goods Sold		1 Cash and Equivalents	12,664
3 Raw Materials	(16,000)	2 Accounts Receivable	18,493
4 Direct Labor Costs	(18,000)	3 Inventories	6,165
5 Gross Profit	41,000	4 Total Current Assets	37,322
6 Sales and Marketing	(11,250)	5 Property, Plant, and Equipment	49,500
7 Administrative	(13,500)	6 Goodwill	–
8 EBITDA	16,250	7 Total Assets	86,822
9 Depreciation	(5,500)	Liabilities and Stockholders' Equity	
10 EBIT	10,750	8 Accounts Payable	4,654
11 Interest Expense (net)	(75)	9 Debt	4,500
12 Pretax Income	10,675	10 Total Liabilities	9,154
13 Income Tax	(3,736)	11 Stockholders' Equity	77,668
14 Net Income	6,939	12 Total Liabilities and Equity	86,822

A quick way to gauge the reasonableness of the proposed price for Ideko is to compare it to that of other publicly traded firms using the method of comparable firms introduced in Chapter 9. For example, at a price of $150 million, Ideko's price-earnings (P/E) ratio is 150,000 / 6939 = 21.6, roughly equal to the market average P/E ratio in mid-2005.

It is even more informative to compare Ideko to firms in a similar line of business. Although no firm is exactly comparable to Ideko in terms of its overall product line, three firms with which it has similarities are Oakley, Inc., Luxottica Group, and Nike, Inc. The closest competitor is Oakley, which also designs and manufactures sports eyewear. Luxottica Group is an Italian eyewear maker, but much of its business is prescription eyewear; it also owns and operates a number of retail eyewear chains. Nike is a manufacturer of specialty sportswear products, but it concentrates in footwear. You also decide to compare Ideko to a portfolio of firms in the sporting goods industry.

A comparison of Ideko's proposed valuation to this peer set, as well as to the average firm in the sporting goods industry, appears in Table 19.2. The table not only lists P/E ratios, but also shows each firm's enterprise value (EV) as a multiple of sales and EBITDA (earnings before interest, taxes, depreciation, and amortization). Recall that enterprise value is the total value of equity plus net debt, where net debt is debt less cash and investments in marketable securities that are not required as part of normal operations. Ideko has $4.5 million in debt, and you estimate that it holds $6.5 million of cash in excess of its working capital needs. Thus Ideko's enterprise value at the proposed acquisition price is 150 + 4.5 − 6.5 = $148 million.

TABLE 19.2	Ideko Financial Ratios Comparison, Mid-2005				
Ratio	Ideko (Proposed)	Oakley, Inc.	Luxottica Group	Nike, Inc.	Sporting Goods Industry
P/E	21.6×	24.8×	28.0×	18.2×	20.3×
EV/Sales	2.0×	2.0×	2.7×	1.5×	1.4×
EV/EBITDA	9.1×	11.6×	14.4×	9.3×	11.4×
EBITDA/Sales	21.7%	17.0%	18.5%	15.9%	12.1%

At the proposed price, Ideko's P/E ratio is low relative to those of Oakley and Luxottica, although it is somewhat above the P/E ratios of Nike and the industry overall. The same can be said for Ideko's valuation as a multiple of sales. Thus, based on these two measures, Ideko looks "cheap" relative to Oakley and Luxottica, but is priced at a premium relative to Nike and the average sporting goods firm. The deal stands out, however, when you compare Ideko's enterprise value relative to EBITDA. The acquisition price of just over nine times EBITDA is below that of all of the comparable firms as well as the industry average. Ideko's low EBITDA multiple is a result of its high profit margins: At $16,250 / 75,000 = 21.7\%$, its EBITDA margin exceeds that of all of the comparables.

While Table 19.2 provides some reassurance that the acquisition price is reasonable compared to other firms in the industry, it by no means establishes that the acquisition is a good investment opportunity. As with any such comparison, the multiples in Table 19.2 vary substantially. Furthermore, they ignore important differences such as the operating efficiency and growth prospects of the firms, and they do not reflect PKK's plans to improve Ideko's operations. To assess whether this investment is attractive requires a careful analysis both of the operational aspects of the firm and of the ultimate cash flows the deal is expected to generate and the return that should be required.

EXAMPLE 19.1

Valuation by Comparables

Problem

What range of acquisition prices for Ideko is implied by the range of multiples for P/E, EV/Sales, and EV/EBITDA in Table 19.2?

Solution

For each multiple, we can find the highest and lowest values across all three firms and the industry portfolio. Applying each multiple to the data for Ideko in Table 19.1 yields the following results:

	Range		Price ($ million)	
Multiple	Low	High	Low	High
P/E	18.2×	28.0×	126.3	194.3
EV/Sales	1.4×	2.7×	107.0	204.5
EV/EBITDA	9.3×	14.4×	153.1	236.0

For example, Nike has the lowest P/E multiple of 18.2. Multiplying this P/E by Ideko's earnings of $6.94 million gives a value of $18.2 \times 6.94 = \$126.3$ million. The highest multiple of enterprise value to sales is 2.7 (Luxottica); at this multiple, Ideko's enterprise value is $2.7 \times 75 = \$202.5$ million. Adding Ideko's excess cash and subtracting its debt implies a purchase price of $202.5 + 6.5 - 4.5 = \$204.5$ million. The above table demonstrates that while comparables provide a useful benchmark, they cannot be relied upon for a precise estimate of value.

CONCEPT CHECK

1. What is the purpose of the valuation using comparables?

2. If the valuation using comparables indicates the acquisition price is reasonable compared to other firms in the industry, does it establish that the acquisition is a good investment opportunity?

19.2 The Business Plan

While comparables provide a useful starting point, whether this acquisition is a successful investment for PKK depends on Ideko's post-acquisition performance. Thus it is necessary to look in detail at Ideko's operations, investments, and capital structure, and to assess its potential for improvements and future growth.

Operational Improvements

On the operational side, you are quite optimistic regarding the company's prospects. The market is expected to grow by 5% per year, and Ideko produces a superior product. Ideko's market share has not grown in recent years because current management has devoted insufficient resources to product development, sales, and marketing. Conversely, Ideko has overspent on administrative costs. Indeed, Table 19.1 reveals that Ideko's current administrative expenses are $13,500 / 75,000 = 18\%$ of sales, a rate that exceeds its expenditures on sales and marketing (15% of sales). This is in stark contrast to its rivals, which spend less on administrative overhead than they do on sales and marketing.

PKK plans to cut administrative costs immediately and redirect resources to new product development, sales, and marketing. By doing so, you believe Ideko can increase its market share from 10% to 15% over the next five years. The increased sales demand can be met in the short run using the existing production lines by increasing overtime and running some weekend shifts. Once the growth in volume exceeds 50%, however, Ideko will need to undertake a major expansion to increase its manufacturing capacity.

The spreadsheet in Table 19.3 shows sales and operating cost assumptions for the next five years based on this plan. In the spreadsheet, numbers in blue represent data that has been entered, whereas numbers in black are calculated based on the data provided. For example, given the current market size of 10 million units and an expected growth rate of 5% per year, the spreadsheet calculates the expected market size in years 1 through 5. Also shown is the expected growth in Ideko's market share.

Note that Ideko's average selling price is expected to increase because of a 2% inflation rate each year. Likewise, manufacturing costs are expected to rise. Raw materials are forecast to increase at a 1% rate and, although you expect some productivity gains, labor costs will rise at a 4% rate due to additional overtime. The table also shows the reallocation of resources from administration to sales and marketing over the five-year period.

TABLE 19.3 SPREADSHEET	Ideko Sales and Operating Cost Assumptions						

	Year	2005	2006	2007	2008	2009	2010
Sales Data	**Growth/Year**						
1 Market Size	(000 units) 5.0%	10,000	10,500	11,025	11,576	12,155	12,763
2 Market Share	1.0%	10.0%	11.0%	12.0%	13.0%	14.0%	15.0%
3 Average Sales Price	($/unit) 2.0%	75.00	76.50	78.03	79.59	81.18	82.81
Cost of Goods Data							
4 Raw Materials	($/unit) 1.0%	16.00	16.16	16.32	16.48	16.65	16.82
5 Direct Labor Costs	($/unit) 4.0%	18.00	18.72	19.47	20.25	21.06	21.90
Operating Expense and Tax Data							
6 Sales and Marketing	(% sales)	15.0%	16.5%	18.0%	19.5%	20.0%	20.0%
7 Administrative	(% sales)	18.0%	15.0%	15.0%	14.0%	13.0%	13.0%
8 Tax Rate		35.0%	35.0%	35.0%	35.0%	35.0%	35.0%

EXAMPLE 19.2

Production Capacity Requirements

Problem
Based on the data in Table 19.3, what production capacity will Ideko require each year? When will an expansion be necessary?

Solution
Production volume each year can be estimated by multiplying the total market size and Ideko's market share in Table 19.3:

	Year	2005	2006	2007	2008	2009	2010
Production Volume (000 units)							
1 Market Size		10,000	10,500	11,025	11,576	12,155	12,763
2 Market Share		10.0%	11.0%	12.0%	13.0%	14.0%	15.0%
3 Production Volume (1 × 2)		1,000	1,155	1,323	1,505	1,702	1,914

Based on this forecast, production volume will exceed its current level by 50% by 2008, necessitating an expansion then.

Capital Expenditures: A Needed Expansion

The spreadsheet in Table 19.4 shows the forecast for Ideko's capital expenditures over the next five years. Based on the estimates for capital expenditures and depreciation, this spreadsheet tracks the book value of Ideko's plant, property, and equipment starting from its level at the beginning of 2005. Note that investment is expected to remain at its current level over the next two years, which is roughly equal to the level of depreciation. Ideko will expand its production during this period by using its existing plant more efficiently. In 2008, however, a major expansion of the plant will be necessary, leading to a large increase in capital expenditures in 2008 and 2009.

The depreciation entries in Table 19.4 are based on the appropriate depreciation schedule for each type of property. Those calculations are quite specific to the nature of the property and are not detailed here. The depreciation shown will be used for tax purposes.[1]

---

1. Firms often maintain separate books for accounting and tax purposes, and they may use different depreciation assumptions for each. Because depreciation affects cash flows through its tax consequences, tax depreciation is more relevant for valuation.

TABLE 19.4 SPREADSHEET		Ideko Capital Expenditure Assumptions					
	Year	2005	2006	2007	2008	2009	2010
Fixed Assets and Capital Investment ($ 000)							
1 Opening Book Value		50,000	49,500	49,050	48,645	61,781	69,102
2 Capital Investment		5,000	5,000	5,000	20,000	15,000	8,000
3 Depreciation		(5,500)	(5,450)	(5,405)	(6,865)	(7,678)	(7,710)
4 Closing Book Value		49,500	49,050	48,645	61,781	69,102	69,392

Working Capital Management

To compensate for its weak sales and marketing efforts, Ideko has sought to retain the loyalty of its retailers in part by maintaining a very lax credit policy. This policy affects Ideko's working capital requirements: For every extra day that customers take to pay, another day's sales revenue is added to accounts receivable (rather than received in cash). From Ideko's current income statement and balance sheet (Table 19.1), we can estimate the number of days of receivables:

$$\text{Accounts Receivable Days} = \frac{\text{Accounts Receivable (\$)}}{\text{Sales Revenue (\$ / yr)}} \times 365 \text{ days / yr}$$

$$= \frac{18,493}{75,000} \times 365 \text{ days} = 90 \text{ days} \qquad (19.1)$$

The standard for the industry is 60 days, and you believe that Ideko can tighten its credit policy to achieve this goal without sacrificing sales.

You also hope to improve Ideko's inventory management. Ideko's balance sheet in Table 19.1 lists inventory of $6.164 million. Of this amount, approximately $2 million corresponds to raw materials, while the rest is finished goods. Given raw material expenditures of $16 million for the year, Ideko currently holds $(2 / 16) \times 365 = 45.6$ days worth of raw material inventory. While maintaining a certain amount of inventory is necessary to avoid production stoppages, you believe that, with tighter controls of the production process, 30 days worth of inventory will be adequate.

Capital Structure Changes: Levering Up

With little debt, excess cash, and substantial earnings, Ideko appears to be significantly underleveraged. You plan to greatly increase the firm's debt, and have obtained bank commitments for loans of $100 million should an agreement be reached. These term loans will have an interest rate of 6.8%, and Ideko will pay interest only during the next five years. The firm will seek additional financing in 2008 and 2009 associated with the expansion of its manufacturing plant, as shown in the spreadsheet in Table 19.5. While Ideko's credit quality should improve over time, the steep slope of the yield curve suggests interest rates may increase, and so on balance you expect Ideko's borrowing rate to remain at 6.8%.

Given Ideko's outstanding debt, its interest expense each year is computed as[2]

$$\text{Interest in Year } t = \text{Interest Rate} \times \text{Ending Balance in Year } (t - 1) \qquad (19.2)$$

The interest on the debt will provide a valuable tax shield to offset Ideko's taxable income.

---

2. Equation 19.2 assumes that changes in debt occur at the end of the year. If debt changes during the year, it is more accurate to compute interest expenses based on the average level of debt during the year.

TABLE 19.5 SPREADSHEET	Ideko's Planned Debt and Interest Payments						
Year	2005	2006	2007	2008	2009	2010	
Debt and Interest Table ($ 000)							
1 Outstanding Debt		100,000	100,000	100,000	115,000	120,000	120,000
2 Interest on Term Loan	6.80%		(6,800)	(6,800)	(6,800)	(7,820)	(8,160)

In addition to the tax benefit, the loan will allow PKK to limit its investment in Ideko and preserve its capital for other investments and acquisitions. The sources and uses of funds for the acquisition are shown in the Table 19.6 spreadsheet. In addition to the $150 million purchase price for Ideko's equity, $4.5 million will be used to repay Ideko's existing debt. With $5 million in advisory and other fees associated with the transaction, the acquisition will require $159.5 million in total funds. PKK's sources of funds include the new loan of $100 million as well as Ideko's own excess cash (which PKK will have access to). Thus PKK's required equity contribution to the transaction is $159.5 - 100 - 6.5 = \$53$ million.

TABLE 19.6 SPREADSHEET	Sources and Uses of Funds for the Ideko Acquisition		
Acquisition Financing ($ 000)			
Sources		Uses	
1 New Term Loan	100,000	Purchase Ideko Equity	150,000
2 Excess Ideko Cash	6,500	Repay Existing Ideko Debt	4,500
3 PKK Equity Investment	53,000	Advisory and Other Fees	5,000
4 Total Sources of Funds	159,500	Total Uses of Funds	159,500

CONCEPT CHECK

1. What are the different operational improvements PKK plans to make?

2. Why is it necessary to consider these improvements to assess whether the acquisition is attractive?

19.3 Building the Financial Model

The value of any investment opportunity arises from the future cash flows it will generate. To estimate the cash flows resulting from the investment in Ideko, we begin by projecting Ideko's future earnings. We then consider Ideko's working capital and investment needs and estimate its free cash flow. With these data in hand, we can forecast Ideko's balance sheet and statement of cash flows.

Forecasting Earnings

We can forecast Ideko's income statement for the five years following the acquisition based on the operational and capital structure changes proposed. This income statement is often referred to as a **pro forma** income statement, because it is not based on actual data but rather depicts the firm's financials under a given set of hypothetical assumptions. The pro forma income statement translates our expectations regarding the operational improvements PKK can achieve at Ideko into consequences for the firm's earnings.

To build the pro forma income statement, we begin with Ideko's sales. Each year, sales can be calculated from the estimates in Table 19.3 as follows:

$$\text{Sales} = \text{Market Size} \times \text{Market Share} \times \text{Average Sales Price} \qquad (19.3)$$

For example, in 2006, Ideko has projected sales of 10.5 million $\times$ 11% $\times$ 76.5 = $88.358 million. The spreadsheet in Table 19.7 shows Ideko's current (2005) sales as well as projections for five years after the acquisition (2006–2010).

The next items in the income statement detail the cost of goods sold. The raw materials cost can be calculated from sales as

$$\text{Raw Materials} = \text{Market Size} \times \text{Market Share} \times \text{Raw Materials per Unit} \qquad (19.4)$$

In 2006, the cost of raw materials is 10.5 million $\times$ 11% $\times$ 16.16 = $18.665 million. The same method can be applied to determine the direct labor costs. Sales, marketing, and administrative costs can be computed directly as a percentage of sales. For example:

$$\text{Sales and Marketing} = \text{Sales} \times (\text{Sales and Marketing \% of Sales}) \qquad (19.5)$$

Therefore, sales and marketing costs are forecast to be $88.358 million $\times$ 16.5% = $14.579 million in 2006.

TABLE 19.7 SPREADSHEET	Pro Forma Income Statement for Ideko, 2005–2010					
Year	2005	2006	2007	2008	2009	2010
Income Statement ($ 000)						
1 Sales	75,000	88,358	103,234	119,777	138,149	158,526
2 Cost of Goods Sold						
3 Raw Materials	(16,000)	(18,665)	(21,593)	(24,808)	(28,333)	(32,193)
4 Direct Labor Costs	(18,000)	(21,622)	(25,757)	(30,471)	(35,834)	(41,925)
5 **Gross Profit**	41,000	48,071	55,883	64,498	73,982	84,407
6 Sales and Marketing	(11,250)	(14,579)	(18,582)	(23,356)	(27,630)	(31,705)
7 Administrative	(13,500)	(13,254)	(15,485)	(16,769)	(17,959)	(20,608)
8 **EBITDA**	16,250	20,238	21,816	24,373	28,393	32,094
9 Depreciation	(5,500)	(5,450)	(5,405)	(6,865)	(7,678)	(7,710)
10 **EBIT**	10,750	14,788	16,411	17,508	20,715	24,383
11 Interest Expense (net)	(75)	(6,800)	(6,800)	(6,800)	(7,820)	(8,160)
12 **Pretax Income**	10,675	7,988	9,611	10,708	12,895	16,223
13 Income Tax	(3,736)	(2,796)	(3,364)	(3,748)	(4,513)	(5,678)
14 **Net Income**	**6,939**	**5,193**	**6,247**	**6,960**	**8,382**	**10,545**

Deducting these operating expenses from Ideko's sales, we can project EBITDA over the next five years as shown in Table 19.7. Subtracting the depreciation expenses we estimated in Table 19.4, we arrive at Ideko's earnings before interest and taxes. We next deduct interest expenses according to the schedule given in Table 19.5.[3] The final expense is the corporate income tax, which we computed using the tax rate in Table 19.3 as

$$\text{Income Tax} = \text{Pretax Income} \times \text{Tax Rate} \qquad (19.6)$$

---

3. This interest expense should be offset by any interest earned on investments. As we discuss later in this chapter, we assume that Ideko does not invest its excess cash balances, but instead pays them out to its owner, PKK. Thus net interest expenses are solely due to Ideko's outstanding debt.

After income taxes, we are left with Ideko's projected pro forma net income as the bottom line in Table 19.7. Based on our projections, net income will rise by 52% from $6.939 million to $10.545 million at the end of five years, though it will drop in the near term due to the large increase in interest expense from the new debt.

Forecasting Income

Problem
By what percentage is Ideko's EBITDA expected to grow over the five-year period? By how much would it grow if Ideko's market share remained at 10%?

Solution
EBITDA will increase from $16.25 million to $32.09 million, or $(32.09 / 16.25) - 1 = 97\%$, over the five years. With a 10% market share rather than a 15% market share, sales will be only $(10\% / 15\%) = 66.7\%$ of the forecast in Table 19.7. Because Ideko's operating expenses are proportional to its sales, its expenses and EBITDA will also be 66.7% of the current estimates. Thus EBITDA will grow to $66.7\% \times 32.09 = \$21.40$ million, which is an increase of only $(21.40 / 16.25) - 1 = 32\%$.

Working Capital Requirements

The spreadsheet in Table 19.8 lists Ideko's current working capital requirements and forecasts the firm's future working capital needs. (See Chapter 26 for a further discussion of working capital requirements and their determinants.) This forecast includes the plans to tighten Ideko's credit policy, speed up customer payments, and reduce Ideko's inventory of raw materials.

TABLE 19.8 SPREADSHEET	Ideko's Working Capital Requirements		
	Year	2005	>2005
Working Capital Days			
Assets	Based on:	Days	Days
1 Accounts Receivable	Sales Revenue	90	60
2 Raw Materials	Raw Materials Costs	45	30
3 Finished Goods	Raw Materials + Labor Costs	45	45
4 Minimum Cash Balance	Sales Revenue	30	30
Liabilities			
5 Wages Payable	Direct Labor + Admin Costs	15	15
6 Other Accounts Payable	Raw Materials + Sales and Marketing	45	45

Based on these working capital requirements, the spreadsheet in Table 19.9 forecasts Ideko's net working capital (NWC) over the next five years. Each line item in the spreadsheet is found by computing the appropriate number of day's worth of the corresponding revenue or expense from the income statement (Table 19.7). For example, accounts receivable in 2006 is calculated as[4]

4. If products are highly seasonal, large fluctuations in working capital may occur over the course of the year. When these effects are important, it is best to develop forecasts on a quarterly or monthly basis so that the seasonal effects can be tracked.

$$\text{Accounts Receivable} = \text{Days Required} \times \frac{\text{Annual Sales}}{365 \text{ days / yr}}$$

$$= 60 \text{ days} \times \frac{\$88.358 \text{ million / yr}}{365 \text{ days / yr}} = \$14.525 \text{ million} \quad (19.7)$$

Similarly, Ideko's inventory of finished goods will be $45 \times (18.665 + 21.622) / 365 = \$4.967$ million.

TABLE 19.9 SPREADSHEET	Ideko's Net Working Capital Forecast						
Year	2005	2006	2007	2008	2009	2010
Working Capital ($ 000)							
Assets							
1 Accounts Receivable		18,493	14,525	16,970	19,689	22,709	26,059
2 Raw Materials		1,973	1,534	1,775	2,039	2,329	2,646
3 Finished Goods		4,192	4,967	5,838	6,815	7,911	9,138
4 Minimum Cash Balance		6,164	7,262	8,485	9,845	11,355	13,030
5 Total Current Assets		30,822	28,288	33,067	38,388	44,304	50,872
Liabilities							
6 Wages Payable		1,294	1,433	1,695	1,941	2,211	2,570
7 Other Accounts Payable		3,360	4,099	4,953	5,938	6,900	7,878
8 Total Current Liabilities		4,654	5,532	6,648	7,879	9,110	10,448
Net Working Capital							
9 Net Working Capital (5 − 8)		26,168	22,756	26,419	30,509	35,194	40,425
10 Increase in Net Working Capital			(3,412)	3,663	4,089	4,685	5,231

Table 19.9 also lists Ideko's minimum cash balance each year. This balance represents the minimum level of cash needed to keep the business running smoothly, allowing for the daily variations in the timing of income and expenses. Firms generally earn little or no interest on these balances, which are held in cash or in a checking or short-term savings accounts. As a consequence, we account for this opportunity cost by including the minimal cash balance as part of the firm's working capital.

We assume that Ideko will earn no interest on this minimal balance. (If it did, this interest would reduce the firm's net interest expense in the income statement.) We also assume that Ideko will pay out as dividends all cash not needed as part of working capital. Therefore, Ideko will hold no excess cash balances or short-term investments above the minimal level reported in Table 19.9. If Ideko were to retain excess funds, these balances would be included as part of its financing strategy (reducing its net debt), and not as part of working capital.[5]

Ideko's net working capital for each year is computed in Table 19.9 as the difference between the forecasted current assets and current liabilities. Increases in net working capital represent a cost to the firm. Note that as a result of the improvements in accounts receivable and inventory management, Ideko will reduce its net working capital by more than $3.4 million in 2006. After this initial savings, working capital needs will increase in conjunction with the growth of the firm.

---

5. Firms often hold excess cash in anticipation of future investment needs or possible cash shortfalls. Because Ideko can rely on PKK to provide needed capital, excess cash reserves are unnecessary.

Forecasting Free Cash Flow

We now have the data needed to forecast Ideko's free cash flows over the next five years. Ideko's earnings are available from the income statement (Table 19.7), as are its depreciation and interest expenses. Capital expenditures are available from Table 19.4, and changes in net working capital can be found in Table 19.9. We combine these items to estimate the free cash flows in the spreadsheet in Table 19.10.

TABLE 19.10 SPREADSHEET	Ideko's Free Cash Flow Forecast					
Year	2005	2006	2007	2008	2009	2010
Free Cash Flow ($ 000)						
1 Net Income		5,193	6,247	6,960	8,382	10,545
2 Plus: After-Tax Interest Expense		4,420	4,420	4,420	5,083	5,304
3 Unlevered Net Income		9,613	10,667	11,380	13,465	15,849
4 Plus: Depreciation		5,450	5,405	6,865	7,678	7,710
5 Less: Increases in NWC		3,412	(3,663)	(4,089)	(4,685)	(5,231)
6 Less: Capital Expenditures		(5,000)	(5,000)	(20,000)	(15,000)	(8,000)
7 Free Cash Flow of Firm		13,475	7,409	(5,845)	1,458	10,328
8 Plus: Net Borrowing		—	—	15,000	5,000	—
9 Less: After-Tax Interest Expense		(4,420)	(4,420)	(4,420)	(5,083)	(5,304)
10 Free Cash Flow to Equity		9,055	2,989	4,735	1,375	5,024

To compute Ideko's free cash flow, which excludes cash flows associated with leverage, we first adjust net income by adding back the after-tax interest payments associated with the net debt in its capital structure:[6]

$$\text{After-Tax Interest Expense} =$$
$$(1 - \text{Tax Rate}) \times (\text{Interest on Debt} - \text{Interest on Excess Cash}) \quad (19.8)$$

Because Ideko has no excess cash, its after-tax interest expense in 2006 is $(1 - 35\%) \times 6.8 = \$4.42$ million, providing unlevered net income of $5.193 + 4.42 = \$9.613$ million. We could also compute the unlevered net income in Table 19.10 by starting with EBIT and deducting taxes. In 2006, for example, EBIT is forecasted as $14.788 million, which amounts to $14.788 \times (1 - 35\%) = \$9.613$ million after taxes.

To compute Ideko's free cash flow from its unlevered net income, we add back depreciation (which is not a cash expense), and deduct Ideko's increases in net working capital and capital expenditures. The free cash flow on line 7 of Table 19.10 shows the cash the firm will generate for its investors, both debt and equity holders. While Ideko will generate substantial free cash flow over the next five years, the level of free cash flow varies substantially from year to year. It is highest in 2006 (due mostly to the large reduction in working capital) and is forecasted to be negative in 2008 (when the plant expansion will begin).

To determine the free cash flow to equity, we first add Ideko's net borrowing (that is, increases to net debt):

$$\text{Net Borrowing in Year } t = \text{Net Debt in Year } t - \text{Net Debt in Year } (t - 1) \quad (19.9)$$

---

6. If Ideko had some interest income or expenses from working capital, we would *not* include that interest here. We adjust only for interest that is related to the firm's *financing*—that is, interest associated with debt and *excess* cash (cash not included as part of working capital).

Ideko will borrow in 2008 and 2009 as part of its expansion. We then deduct the after-tax interest payments that were added in line 2.

As shown in the last line of Table 19.10, during the next five years Ideko is expected to generate a positive free cash flow to equity, which will be used to pay dividends to PKK. The free cash flow to equity will be highest in 2006; by 2010, PKK will recoup a significant fraction of its initial investment.

<table>
<tr><td>**EXAMPLE**
19.4</td><td colspan="2">**Leverage and Free Cash Flow**</td></tr>
</table>

Problem

Suppose Ideko does not add leverage in 2008 and 2009, but instead keeps its debt fixed at $100 million until 2010. How would this change in its leverage policy affect its expected free cash flow? How would it affect the free cash flow to equity?

Solution

Because free cash flow is based on unlevered net income, it will not be affected by Ideko's leverage policy. Free cash flow to equity will be affected, however. Net borrowing will be zero each year, and the firm's after-tax interest expense will remain at the 2006 level of $4.42 million:

Year	2005	2006	2007	2008	2009	2010
Free Cash Flow ($ 000)						
1 Free Cash Flow of Firm		13,475	7,409	(5,845)	1,458	10,328
2 Plus: Net Borrowing		—	—	—	—	—
3 Less: After-Tax Interest Expense		(4,420)	(4,420)	(4,420)	(4,420)	(4,420)
4 Free Cash Flow to Equity		9,055	2,989	(10,265)	(2,962)	5,908

In this case, Ideko will have a negative free cash flow to equity in 2008 and 2009. That is, without additional borrowing, PKK will have to invest additional capital in the firm to fund the expansion.

The Balance Sheet and Statement of Cash Flows (Optional)

The information we have calculated so far can be used to project Ideko's balance sheet and statement of cash flows through 2010. While these statements are not critical for our valuation, they often prove helpful in providing a more complete picture of how a firm will grow during the forecast period. These statements for Ideko are shown in the spreadsheets in Tables 19.11 and 19.12.

On the balance sheet (Table 19.11), current assets and liabilities come from the net working capital spreadsheet (Table 19.9). The inventory entry on the balance sheet includes both raw materials and finished goods. Property, plant, and equipment information comes from the capital expenditure spreadsheet (Table 19.4), and the debt comes from Table 19.5. The goodwill entry arises from the difference in the acquisition price and Ideko's initial book value of equity in Table 19.1:[7]

$$\text{New Goodwill} = \text{Acquisition Price} - \text{Existing Book Value of Equity} \quad (19.10)$$

---

7. There are a number of potential complications to the goodwill calculation that we ignore here. In particular, transaction fees directly attributable to the acquisition (but not to the debt issue) would generally be included in the purchase price. Also, in some cases a portion of the purchase price can be allocated to intangible assets as opposed to goodwill.

Given the acquisition price of $150 million, the new goodwill is $150 - 77.668 =$ $72.332 million. The stockholders' equity of $48 million in 2005 arises from PKK's initial equity contribution of $50 million (the $150 million purchase price less $100 million financed with debt) less the $2 million in dividends paid ($6.5 million in excess cash less $4.5 million in debt repaid). The stockholders' equity increases each year through retained earnings (net income less dividends) and new capital contributions. Dividends after 2005 are taken from the free cash flow to equity given in Table 19.10. (If free cash flow to equity were negative in any year, it would appear as a capital contribution in line 14 of the balance sheet.) As a check on the calculations, note that the balance sheet does, indeed, balance: Total assets equal total liabilities and equity.[8]

TABLE 19.11 SPREADSHEET	Pro Forma Balance Sheet for Ideko, 2005–2010					

Year	2005	2006	2007	2008	2009	2010
Balance Sheet ($ 000)						
Assets						
1 Cash and Cash Equivalents	6,164	7,262	8,485	9,845	11,355	13,030
2 Accounts Receivable	18,493	14,525	16,970	19,689	22,709	26,059
3 Inventories	6,165	6,501	7,613	8,854	10,240	11,784
4 **Total Current Assets**	30,822	28,288	33,067	38,388	44,304	50,872
5 Property, Plant, and Equipment	49,500	49,050	48,645	61,781	69,102	69,392
6 Goodwill	72,332	72,332	72,332	72,332	72,332	72,332
7 **Total Assets**	152,654	149,670	154,044	172,501	185,738	192,597
Liabilities						
8 Accounts Payable	4,654	5,532	6,648	7,879	9,110	10,448
9 Debt	100,000	100,000	100,000	115,000	120,000	120,000
10 **Total Liabilities**	104,654	105,532	106,648	122,879	129,110	130,448
Stockholders' Equity						
11 Starting Stockholders' Equity		48,000	44,138	47,396	49,621	56,628
12 Net Income		5,193	6,247	6,960	8,382	10,545
13 Dividends	(2,000)	(9,055)	(2,989)	(4,735)	(1,375)	(5,024)
14 Capital Contributions	50,000	—	—	—	—	—
15 **Stockholders' Equity**	48,000	44,138	47,396	49,621	56,628	62,149
16 **Total Liabilities and Equity**	152,654	149,670	154,044	172,501	185,738	192,597

Ideko's book value of equity will decline in 2006, as Ideko reduces its working capital and pays out the savings as part of a large dividend. The firm's book value will then rise as it expands. Ideko's book debt-equity ratio will decline from $100,000 / 48,000 = 2.1$ to $120,000 / 62,149 = 1.9$ during the five-year period.

The statement of cash flows in Table 19.12 starts with net income. Cash from operating activities includes depreciation as well as changes to working capital items (other than cash) from Table 19.9. Cash from investing activities includes the capital expenditures in Table 19.4. Cash from financing activities includes net borrowing from Table 19.10,

---

8. In Table 19.11, goodwill is assumed to remain constant. If the transaction were structured as an acquisition of assets (as opposed to stock), the goodwill would be amortizable over 15 years for tax reporting as specified in section 197 of Internal Revenue Code. For financial accounting purposes, goodwill is not amortized but is subject to an impairment test at least once a year as specified in FASB 142, so the amount of goodwill may change over time (though any changes in goodwill due to impairment have no tax accounting consequences).

**TABLE 19.12
SPREADSHEET**   **Pro Forma Statement of Cash Flows for Ideko, 2005–2010**

	Year	2005	2006	2007	2008	2009	2010
	Statement of Cash Flows ($ 000)						
1	Net Income		5,193	6,247	6,960	8,382	10,545
2	Depreciation		5,450	5,405	6,865	7,678	7,710
3	Changes in Working Capital						
4	Accounts Receivable		3,968	(2,445)	(2,719)	(3,020)	(3,350)
5	Inventory		(336)	(1,112)	(1,242)	(1,385)	(1,544)
6	Accounts Payable		878	1,116	1,231	1,231	1,338
7	**Cash from Operating Activities**		15,153	9,211	11,095	12,885	14,699
8	Capital Expenditures		(5,000)	(5,000)	(20,000)	(15,000)	(8,000)
9	Other Investment		–	–	–	–	–
10	**Cash from Investing Activities**		(5,000)	(5,000)	(20,000)	(15,000)	(8,000)
11	Net Borrowing		–	–	15,000	5,000	–
12	Dividends		(9,055)	(2,989)	(4,735)	(1,375)	(5,024)
13	Capital Contributions		–	–	–	–	–
14	**Cash from Financing Activities**		(9,055)	(2,989)	10,265	3,625	(5,024)
15	**Change in Cash** (7 + 10 + 14)		**1,098**	**1,223**	**1,360**	**1,510**	**1,675**

and dividends or capital contributions determined by the free cash flow to equity in Table 19.10. As a final check on the calculations, note that the change in cash and cash equivalents on line 15 equals the change in the minimum cash balance shown on the balance sheet (Table 19.11).

CONCEPT CHECK

1. What is a pro forma income statement?

2. How do we calculate the firm's free cash flow, and the free cash flow to equity?

19.4 Estimating the Cost of Capital

To value PKK's investment in Ideko, we need to assess the risk associated with Ideko and estimate an appropriate cost of capital. Because Ideko is a private firm, we cannot use its own past returns to evaluate its risk, but must instead rely on comparable publicly traded firms. In this section, we use data from the comparable firms identified earlier to estimate a cost of capital for Ideko.

Our approach is as follows. First, we use the techniques developed in Part IV of the text to estimate the equity cost of capital for Oakley, Luxottica Group, and Nike. We then estimate the unlevered cost of capital for each firm based on its capital structure. The unlevered cost of capital of the comparable firms are next used to estimate Ideko's unlevered cost of capital. Once we have this estimate, we can use Ideko's capital structure to determine its equity cost of capital or WACC, depending on the valuation method employed.

CAPM-Based Estimation

To determine an appropriate cost of capital, we must first determine the appropriate measure of risk. PKK's investment in Ideko will represent a large fraction of its portfolio. As a consequence, PKK itself is not well diversified. But PKK's investors are primarily pension funds and large institutional investors which are themselves well diversified and which evaluate their performance relative to the market as a benchmark. Thus you decide that estimating market risk using the CAPM approach is justified.

Using the CAPM, we can estimate the equity cost of capital for each comparable firm based on the beta of its equity. As outlined in Chapter 12, the standard approach to estimating an equity beta is to determine the historical sensitivity of the stock's returns to the market's returns by using linear regression to estimate the slope coefficient in the equation:

$$R_s - r_f = \alpha_s + \beta_s \underbrace{(R_{mkt} - r_f)}_{\substack{\text{Excess return} \\ \text{of market portfolio}}} + \varepsilon_s \tag{19.11}$$

$$\underbrace{}_{\substack{\text{Excess return} \\ \text{of stock } s}}$$

As a proxy for the market portfolio, we will use a value-weighted portfolio of all NYSE, AMEX, and Nasdaq stocks. With data from 2000 to 2004, we calculate the excess return—the realized return minus the yield on a one-month Treasury security—for each firm and for the market portfolio. We then estimate the equity beta for each firm by regressing its excess return onto the excess return of the market portfolio. We perform the regression for both monthly returns and ten-day returns. The estimated equity betas, together with their 95% confidence intervals, are shown in Table 19.13.

TABLE 19.13	Equity Betas with Confidence Intervals for Comparable Firms			
	Monthly Returns		**Ten-Day Returns**	
Firm	**Beta**	**95% C.I.**	**Beta**	**95% C.I.**
Oakley	1.99	1.2 to 2.8	1.37	0.9 to 1.9
Luxottica	0.56	0.0 to 1.1	0.86	0.5 to 1.2
Nike	0.48	−0.1 to 1.0	0.69	0.4 to 1.0

While we would like to assess risk and, therefore, estimate beta based on longer horizon returns (consistent with our investors' investment horizon), the confidence intervals we obtain using monthly data are extremely wide. These confidence intervals narrow somewhat when we use ten-day returns. In any case, the results make clear that a fair amount of uncertainty persists when we estimate the beta for an individual firm.

Unlevering Beta

Given an estimate of each firm's equity beta, we next "unlever" the beta based on the firm's capital structure. Here we use Eq. 14.9 (which is equivalent, in terms of returns, to calculating the pretax WACC as in Eq. 18.6):

$$\beta_U = \left(\frac{\text{Equity Value}}{\text{Enterprise Value}} \right) \beta_E + \left(\frac{\text{Net Debt Value}}{\text{Enterprise Value}} \right) \beta_D \tag{19.12}$$

Recall that we must use the *net* debt of the firm—that is, we must subtract any cash from the level of debt—so we use the enterprise value of the firm as the sum of debt and equity in the formula.[9] Table 19.14 shows the capital structure for each comparable firm. Oakley has no debt, while Luxottica has about 17% debt in its capital structure. Nike holds cash that exceeds its debt, leading to a negative net debt in its capital structure.

TABLE 19.14	Capital Structure and Unlevered Beta Estimates for Comparable Firms				
Firm	$\dfrac{E}{E+D}$	$\dfrac{D}{E+D}$	β_E	β_D	β_U
Oakley	1.00	0.00	1.50	—	1.50
Luxottica	0.83	0.17	0.75	0	0.62
Nike	1.05	−0.05	0.60	0	0.63

Table 19.14 also estimates the unlevered beta of each firm. Here we have used an equity beta for each firm within the range of the results from Table 19.13. Given the low or negative debt levels for each firm, assuming a beta for debt of zero is a reasonable approximation. We then compute an unlevered beta for each firm according to Eq. 19.12.

The range of the unlevered betas for these three firms is large. Both Luxottica and Nike have relatively low betas, presumably reflecting the relative noncyclicality of their core businesses (prescription eyewear for Luxottica and athletic shoes for Nike). Oakley has a much higher unlevered beta, perhaps because the high-end specialty sports eyewear it produces is a discretionary expense for most consumers.

Ideko's Unlevered Cost of Capital

The data from the comparable firms provides guidance to us for estimating Ideko's unlevered cost of capital. Ideko's products are not as high end as Oakley's eyewear, so their sales are unlikely to vary as much with the business cycle as Oakley's sales do. However, Ideko does not have a prescription eyewear division, as Luxottica does. Ideko's products are also fashion items rather than exercise items, so we expect Ideko's cost of capital to be closer to Oakley's than to Nike's or Luxottica's. We therefore use 1.20 as our preliminary estimate for Ideko's unlevered beta, which is somewhat above the average of the comparables in Table 19.14.

We use the security market line of the CAPM to translate this beta into a cost of capital for Ideko. In mid-2005, one-year Treasury rates were approximately 4%; we use this rate for the risk-free interest rate. We also need an estimate of the market risk premium. Since 1960, the average annual return of the value-weighted market portfolio of U.S. stocks has exceeded that of one-year Treasuries by approximately 5%. However, this estimate is a backward-looking number. As we mentioned in Chapter 12, some researchers believe that future stock market excess returns are likely to be lower than this historical average. To be conservative in our valuation of Ideko, we will use 5% as the expected market risk premium.

---

9. Recall from Chapter 18 that Eq. 19.12 assumes that the firm will maintain a target leverage ratio. If the debt is expected to remain fixed for some period, we should also deduct the value of the predetermined tax shields from the firm's net debt.

Based on these choices, our estimate of Ideko's unlevered cost of capital is

$$r_U = r_f + \beta_U(E[R_{mkt}] - r_f) = 4\% + 1.20(5\%)$$
$$= 10\%$$

Of course, as our discussion has made clear, this estimate contains a large amount of uncertainty. Thus we will include sensitivity analysis with regard to the unlevered cost of capital in our analysis.

EXAMPLE 19.5

Estimating the Unlevered Cost of Capital

Problem

Using the monthly equity beta estimates for each firm in Table 19.13, what range of unlevered cost of capital estimates is possible?

Solution

Oakley has the highest equity beta of 1.99, which is also its unlevered beta (it has no debt). With this beta, the unlevered cost of capital would be $r_U = 4\% + 1.99(5\%) = 13.95\%$. At the other extreme, given its capital structure, Luxottica's equity beta of 0.56 implies an unlevered beta of $(0.56)(0.83) = 0.46$. With this beta, the unlevered cost of capital would be $r_U = 4\% + 0.46(5\%) = 6.3\%$.

As with any analysis based on comparables, experience and judgment are necessary to come up with a reasonable estimate of the unlevered cost of capital. In this case, our choice would be guided by industry norms, an assessment of which comparable is closest in terms of market risk, and possibly knowledge of how cyclical Ideko's revenues have been historically.

CONCEPT CHECK

1. How do we estimate a firm's unlevered cost of capital using data from comparable publicly traded firms?

2. What is a standard approach to estimate an equity beta?

19.5 Valuing the Investment

Thus far, we have forecasted the first five years of cash flows from PKK's investment in Ideko, and we have estimated the investment's unlevered cost of capital. In this section, we combine these inputs to estimate the value of the opportunity. The first step is to develop an estimate of Ideko's value at the end of our five-year forecast horizon. To do so, we consider both a multiples approach and a discounted cash flow (DCF) valuation using the WACC method. Given Ideko's free cash flow and continuation value, we then estimate its total enterprise value in 2005 using the APV method. Deducting the value of debt and PKK's initial investment from our estimate of Ideko's enterprise value gives the NPV of the investment opportunity. In addition to NPV, we look at some other common metrics, including IRR and cash multiples.

The Multiples Approach to Continuation Value

Practitioners generally estimate a firm's continuation value (also called the terminal value) at the end of the forecast horizon using a valuation multiple. While forecasting cash flows explicitly is useful in capturing those specific aspects of a company that distinguish the firm from its competitors in the short run, in the long run firms in the same industry typically have similar expected growth rates, profitability, and risk. As a consequence, multiples are likely to be relatively homogeneous across firms. Thus applying a multiple is potentially as reliable as estimating the value based on an explicit forecast of distant cash flows.

Of the different valuation multiples available, the EBITDA multiple is most often used in practice. In most settings, the EBITDA multiple is more reliable than sales or earnings multiples because it accounts for the firm's operating efficiency and is not affected by leverage differences between firms. We estimate the continuation value using an EBITDA multiple as follows:

$$\text{Continuation Enterprise Value at Forecast Horizon} =$$
$$\text{EBITDA at Horizon} \times \text{EBITDA Multiple at Horizon} \quad (19.13)$$

From the income statement in Table 19.7, Ideko's EBITDA in 2010 is forecast to be $32.09 million. If we assume its EBITDA multiple in 2010 is unchanged from the value of 9.1 that we calculated at the time of the original purchase, then Ideko's continuation value in 2010 is 32.09 × 9.1 = $292.05 million. This calculation is shown in the spreadsheet in Table 19.15. Given Ideko's outstanding debt of $120 million in 2010, this estimate corresponds to an equity value of $172.05 million.

TABLE 19.15 SPREADSHEET	Continuation Value Estimate for Ideko		

Continuation Value: Multiples Approach ($ 000)			
1 EBITDA in 2010	32,094	Common Multiples	
2 EBITDA multiple	9.1×	EV/Sales	1.8×
3 **Continuation Enterprise Value**	**292,052**	P/E (levered)	16.3×
4 Debt	(120,000)	P/E (unlevered)	18.4×
5 **Continuation Equity Value**	**172,052**		

Table 19.15 also shows Ideko's sales and P/E multiples based on this continuation value. The continuation value is 1.8 times Ideko's 2010 sales, and the equity value is 16.3 times Ideko's 2010 earnings. Because the P/E multiple is affected by leverage, we also report Ideko's **unlevered P/E ratio**, which is calculated as its continuing enterprise value divided by its unlevered net income in 2010 (listed in Table 19.10). Ideko would have this P/E ratio if it had no debt in 2010, so this information is useful when comparing Ideko to unlevered firms in the industry.

We can use the various multiples to assess the reasonableness of our estimated continuation value. While the value-to-sales ratio is high compared to the overall sporting goods industry, these multiples are otherwise low relative to the comparables in Table 19.2, and we would consider this estimate of Ideko's continuation value as reasonable (if not relatively conservative).

The Discounted Cash Flow Approach to Continuation Value

One difficulty with relying solely on comparables when forecasting a continuation value is that we are comparing *future* multiples of the firm with *current* multiples of its competitors. In 2010, the multiples of Ideko and the comparables we have chosen may all be very different, especially if the industry is currently experiencing abnormal growth. To guard against such a bias, it is wise to check our estimate of the continuation value based on fundamentals using a discounted cash flow approach.

To estimate a continuation value in year T using discounted cash flows, we assume a constant expected growth rate, g, and a constant debt-equity ratio. As explained in Chapter 18, when the debt-equity ratio is constant, the WACC valuation method is the simplest to apply:

$$\text{Enterprise Value in Year } T = V_T^L = \frac{FCF_{T+1}}{r_{wacc} - g} \tag{19.14}$$

To estimate free cash flow in year $T + 1$, recall that free cash flow is equal to unlevered net income plus depreciation, less capital expenditures and increases in net working capital (see Table 19.10):

$$FCF_{T+1} = \text{Unlevered Net Income}_{T+1} + \text{Depreciation}_{T+1}$$
$$- \text{ Increases in NWC}_{T+1} - \text{ Capital Expenditures}_{T+1} \tag{19.15}$$

Suppose the firm's sales are expected to grow at a nominal rate g. If the firm's operating expenses remain a fixed percentage of sales, then its unlevered net income will also grow at rate g. Similarly, the firm's receivables, payables, and other elements of net working capital will grow at rate g.

What about capital expenditures? The firm will need new capital to offset depreciation; it will also need to add capacity as its production volume grows. Given a sales growth rate g, we may expect that the firm will need to expand its investment in fixed assets at the same rate. In that case,[10]

$$\text{Capital Expenditures}_{T+1} = \text{Depreciation}_{T+1} + g \times \text{Fixed Assets}_T$$

Thus, given a growth rate of g for the firm, we can estimate its free cash flow as

$$FCF_{T+1} = (1 + g) \times \text{Unlevered Net Income}_T - g \times \text{Net Working Capital}_T$$
$$- g \times \text{Fixed Assets}_T \tag{19.16}$$

Together, Eqs. 19.14 and 19.16 allow us to estimate a firm's continuation value based on its long-run growth rate.

EXAMPLE 19.6

A DCF Estimate of the Continuation Value

Problem

Estimate Ideko's continuation value in 2010 assuming a future expected growth rate of 5%, a future debt-to-value ratio of 40%, and a debt cost of capital of 6.8%.

---

10. Here, fixed assets are measured according to their book value net of accumulated depreciation. This level of capital expenditures is required to maintain the firm's ratio of sales to fixed assets (also called its fixed asset turnover ratio). However, a number of factors could affect the required level of capital expenditures needed to sustain a given growth rate. For example, some amount of revenue growth may be accommodated through productivity gains (or be the result of inflation), rather than an increase in fixed assets. Also, the book value of the firm's fixed assets may misrepresent the cost of adding new assets (one could consider market value instead). Absent knowledge of these details, the approach taken here provides a reasonable estimate.

Solution

In 2010, Ideko's unlevered net income is forecasted to be \$15.849 million (Table 19.10), with working capital of \$40.425 million (Table 19.9). It has fixed assets of \$69.392 million (Table 19.4). From Eq. 19.16, we can estimate Ideko's free cash flow in 2011:

$$FCF_{2011} = (1.05)(15.849) - (5\%)(40.425) - (5\%)(69.392) = \$11.151 \text{ million}$$

This estimate represents nearly an 8% increase over Ideko's 2010 free cash flow of \$10.328 million. It exceeds the 5% growth rate of sales due to the decline in the required additions to Ideko's net working capital as its growth rate slows.

With a debt-to-value ratio of 40%, Ideko's WACC can be calculated from Eq. 18.11:

$$r_{wacc} = r_U - d\,\tau_c\,r_D = 10\% - 0.40(0.35)\,6.8\% = 9.05\%$$

Given the estimate of Ideko's free cash flow and WACC, we can estimate Ideko's continuation value in 2010:

$$V^L_{2010} = \frac{11.151}{9.05\% - 5\%} = \$275.33 \text{ million}$$

This continuation value represents a terminal EBITDA multiple of 275.33 / 32.09 = 8.6.

Both the multiples approach and the discounted cash flow approach are useful in deriving a realistic continuation value estimate. Our recommendation is to combine both approaches, as we do in Table 19.16. As shown in the spreadsheet, our projected EBITDA multiple of 9.1 can be justified according the discounted cash flow method with a nominal long-term growth rate of about 5.3%.[11] Given an inflation rate of 2%, this nominal rate represents a real growth rate of about 3.3%. This implied growth rate is another important reality check for our continuation value estimate. If it is much higher than our expectations of long-run growth for the industry as a whole, we should be more skeptical of the estimate being used.

TABLE 19.16 SPREADSHEET   **Discounted Cash Flow Estimate of Continuation Value, with Implied EBITDA Multiple**

Continuation Value: DCF and EBITDA Multiple ($ 000)			
1 Long-Term Growth Rate	5.3%		
2 Target D/(E + D)	40.0%		
3 Projected WACC	9.05%		
Free Cash Flow in 2011			
4 Unlevered Net Income	16,695	Continuation Enterprise Value	292,052
5 Less: Increase in NWC	(2,158)		
6 Less: Increase in Fixed Assets*	(3,705)	Implied EBITDA Multiple	9.1×
7 Free Cash Flow	10,832		

*The increase in fixed assets equals the difference between capital expenditures and depreciation, and so subtracting this amount is equivalent to adding back depreciation and subtracting capital expenditures.

11. The exact nominal growth rate needed to match an EBITDA multiple of 9.1 is 5.33897%, which can be found using Solver in Excel.

| COMMON MISTAKE | Continuation Values and Long-Run Growth |

The continuation value is one of the most important estimates when valuing a firm. A common mistake is to use an overly optimistic continuation value, which will lead to an upward bias in the estimated current value of the firm. Here are several pitfalls to beware of:

Using multiples based on current high growth rates. Continuation value estimates are often based on current valuation multiples of existing firms. But if these firms are currently experiencing high growth that will eventually slow down, their multiples can be expected to decline over time. In this scenario, if we estimate a continuation value based on today's multiples without accounting for this decline as growth slows, the estimate will be biased upward.

Ignoring investment necessary for growth. When using the discounted cash flow method, we cannot assume that $FCF_{T+1} = FCF_T (1 + g)$ if the firm's growth rate has changed between T and $T + 1$. Whenever the growth rate changes, expenditures on working and fixed capital will be affected, and we must take this effect into account as we do in Eq. 19.16.

Using unsustainable long-term growth rates. When using the discounted cash flow method, we must choose a long-term growth rate for the firm. By choosing a high rate, we can make the continuation value estimate extremely high. In the long run, however, firms cannot continue to grow faster than the overall economy. Thus we should be suspicious of long-term growth rates that exceed the expected rate of GDP growth, which has averaged between 3% and 4% in *real* terms (that is, not including inflation) in the United States over the past several decades.

APV Valuation of Ideko Equity

Our estimate of Ideko's continuation value summarizes the value of the firm's free cash flow beyond the forecast horizon. We can combine it with our forecast for free cash flow through 2010 (Table 19.10, line 7) to estimate Ideko's value today. Recall from Chapter 18 that because the debt is paid on a fixed schedule during the forecast period, the APV method is the easiest valuation method to apply.

The steps to estimate Ideko's value using the APV method are shown in the spreadsheet in Table 19.17. First, we compute Ideko's unlevered value V^U, which is the firm's value if we were to operate the company without leverage during the forecast period and sell it for its continuation value at the end of the forecast horizon. Thus the final value in 2010 would be the continuation value we estimated in Table 19.15. The value in earlier periods includes the free cash flows paid by the firm (from Table 19.10) discounted at the unlevered cost of capital r_U that we estimated in Section 19.4:

$$V_{t-1}^U = \frac{FCF_t + V_t^U}{1 + r_U} \tag{19.17}$$

Next, we incorporate Ideko's interest tax shield during the forecast horizon. The interest tax shield equals the tax rate of 35% (Table 19.3) multiplied by Ideko's scheduled interest payments (see Table 19.5). Because the debt levels are predetermined, we compute the value T^s of the tax shield by discounting the tax savings at the debt interest rate, $r_D = 6.80\%$:

$$T_{t-1}^s = \frac{\text{Interest Tax Shield}_t + T_t^s}{1 + r_D} \tag{19.18}$$

Combining the unlevered value and the tax shield value gives the APV, which is Ideko's enterprise value given the planned leverage policy. By deducting debt, we obtain our estimate for the value of Ideko's equity during the forecast period.

TABLE 19.17 SPREADSHEET	APV Estimate of Ideko's Initial Equity Value						
	Year	2005	2006	2007	2008	2009	2010
APV Method ($ 000)							
1 Free Cash Flow			13,475	7,409	(5,845)	1,458	10,328
2 Unlevered Value V^u		202,732	209,530	223,075	251,227	274,891	292,052
3 Interest Tax Shield			2,380	2,380	2,380	2,737	2,856
4 Tax Shield Value T^s		10,428	8,757	6,972	5,067	2,674	—
5 APV: $V^L = V^u + T^s$		213,160	218,287	230,047	256,294	277,566	292,052
6 Debt		(100,000)	(100,000)	(100,000)	(115,000)	(120,000)	(120,000)
7 Equity Value		113,160	118,287	130,047	141,294	157,566	172,052

Thus our estimate for Ideko's initial enterprise value is $213 million, with an equity value of $113 million. As PKK's initial cost to acquire Ideko's equity is $53 million (see Table 19.6), based on these estimates the deal looks attractive, with an NPV of $113 million − $53 million = $60 million.

A Reality Check

At this point, it is wise to step back and assess whether our valuation results make sense. Does an initial enterprise value of $213 million for Ideko seem reasonable compared to the values of other firms in the industry?

Here again, multiples are helpful. Let's compute the initial valuation multiples that would be implied by our estimated enterprise value of $213 million and compare them to Ideko's closest competitors as we did in Table 19.2. Table 19.18 provides our results.

Naturally, the valuation multiples based on the estimated enterprise value of $213 million, which would correspond to a purchase price of $215 million given Ideko's existing debt and excess cash, are higher than those based on a purchase price of $150 million. They are now at the top end or somewhat above the range of the values of the other firms that we used for comparison. While these multiples are not unreasonable given the operational improvements that PKK plans to implement, they indicate that our projections may be somewhat optimistic and depend critically on PKK's ability to achieve the operational improvements it plans.

COMMON MISTAKE   **Missing Assets or Liabilities**

When computing the enterprise value of a firm from its free cash flows, remember that we are valuing only those assets and liabilities whose cash flow consequences are included in our projections. Any "missing" assets or liabilities must be added to the APV estimate to determine the value of equity. In this case, we deduct the firm's debt and add any excess cash or other marketable securities that have not been included (for Ideko, excess cash has already been paid out and will remain at zero, so

no adjustment is needed). We also adjust for any other assets or liabilities that have not been explicitly considered. For example, if a firm owns vacant land, or if it has patents or other rights whose potential cash flows were not included in the projections, the value of these assets must be accounted for separately. The same is true for liabilities such as stock option grants, potential legal liabilities, leases (if the lease payments were not included in earnings), or underfunded pension liabilities.

TABLE 19.18	**Ideko Financial Ratios Comparison, Mid-2005, Based on Discounted Cash Flow Estimate Versus Proposed Purchase Price**					

Ratio	Ideko (Estimated Value)	Ideko (Purchase Price)	Oakley, Inc.	Luxottica Group	Nike, Inc.	Sporting Goods
P/E	31.0×	21.6×	24.8×	28.0×	18.2×	20.3×
EV/Sales	2.8×	2.0×	2.0×	2.7×	1.5×	1.4×
EV/EBITDA	13.1×	9.1×	11.6×	14.4×	9.3×	11.4×

Our estimated initial EBITDA multiple of 13.1 also exceeds the multiple of 9.1 that we assumed for the continuation value. Thus our estimate forecasts a decline in the EBITDA multiple, which is appropriate given our expectation that growth will be higher in the short run. If the multiple did not decline, we should question whether our continuation value is too optimistic.

IRR and Cash Multiples

While the NPV method is the most reliable method when evaluating a transaction like PKK's acquisition of Ideko, real-world practitioners often use IRR and the *cash multiple* (or multiple of money) as alternative valuation metrics. We discuss both of these methods in this section.

To compute the IRR, we must compute PKK's cash flows over the life of the transaction. PKK's initial investment in Ideko, from Table 19.6, is $53 million. PKK will then receive cash dividends from Ideko based on the free cash flow to equity reported in Table 19.10. Finally, we assume that PKK will sell its equity share in Ideko at the end of five years, receiving the continuation equity value. We combine these data to determine PKK's cash flows in the spreadsheet in Table 19.19. Given the cash flows, we compute the IRR of the transaction, which is 33.3%.

TABLE 19.19 SPREADSHEET	**IRR and Cash Multiple for PKK's Investment in Ideko**						

	Year	2005	2006	2007	2008	2009	2010
IRR and Cash Multiple							
1 Initial Investment		(53,000)					
2 Free Cash Flow to Equity			9,055	2,989	4,735	1,375	5,024
3 Continuation Equity Value							172,052
4 PKK Cash Flows		(53,000)	9,055	2,989	4,735	1,375	177,077
5 IRR		33.3%					
6 Cash Multiple		3.7×					

While an IRR of 33.3% might sound attractive, it is not straightforward to evaluate in this context. To do so, we must compare it to the appropriate cost of capital for PKK's investment. Because PKK holds an equity position in Ideko, we should use Ideko's equity cost of capital. Of course, Ideko's leverage ratio changes over the five-year period, which

Joseph L. Rice, III is a founding partner and Chairman of Clayton, Dubilier & Rice (CD&R). Since its formation in 1978, the firm has invested more than $6 billion in 38 businesses with an aggregate trans-action value in excess of $40 billion.

QUESTION: *How has private equity business changed since you began in the industry?*

ANSWER: The term "private equity" is very broad and today can cover virtually every kind of investing, short of investing in the stock or bond markets. The buyout business represents a significant component of the private equity market. Since I started in 1966, I've seen many changes as the asset class has matured. In the 1960s and 1970s, the buyout business had relatively little following. Limited capital availability kept transactions small, and we relied on unconventional funding sources. The total purchase price of my first transaction was approximately $3 million, financed through a secured bank line and from individuals contributing amounts ranging from $25,000 to $50,000. In contrast, recently we bought Hertz from Ford for approximately $15 billion.

As the industry has evolved, the attractive returns generated from buyout investments has attracted broader interest from both institutions and high net worth individuals. Buyout firms apply a variety of value creation models, including financial engineering, multiple arbitrage, and industry sector bets, such as technology or healthcare. Today there is more focus on generating returns from improving business performance—which has always been CD&R's underlying investment approach. The character of the businesses that we buy has also changed. Traditionally, this was an asset-heavy business, with much of the financing coming from banks that lent against percentages of inventory and receivables and the liquidation value of hard assets. Now it's become more of a cash flow business.

QUESTION: *What makes a company a good buyout candidate?*

ANSWER: We look to acquire good businesses at fair prices. Acquiring non-core, underperforming divisions of large companies and making them more effective has been a fertile investment area for CD&R. These divestiture buyouts tend to be complex and require experience and patience to execute. For example, we were in discussions with Ford management for three years prior to leading the Hertz division acquisition.

After running a series of projections based on information from management, we develop a capital structure designed to insure the viability of the acquisition candidate. We are relatively unconcerned with EPS but are very return conscious, focusing on cash and creating long-term shareholder value. We must also believe that we can generate a return on equity that meets our standards and justifies our investors' commitments to us.

We also acquire businesses confronting strategic issues where our operating expertise can bring value, such as Kinko's, a great brand franchise that we reorganized and expanded. We prefer service and distribution businesses to large manufacturers because of the wage differential between Asia and the United States and Europe. We also prefer businesses with a diversity of suppliers and customers and where there are multiple levers under our control to improve operating performance.

QUESTION: *Post acquisition, what is the role of the private equity firm?*

ANSWER: CD&R brings both a hands-on ownership style and capital. After closing a transaction, we assess current management's capability to do the job our investment case calls for. If necessary, we build and strengthen the management team. Then we work with them to determine the appropriate strategy to produce outstanding results. Finally, we aggressively pursue productivity, cost reduction, and growth initiatives to enhance operating and financial performance. At Kinko's, we restructured 129 separate S-corporations into one centralized corporation and installed a new management team. Our key strategic decision was transforming Kinko's from a loose confederation of consumer and small business-oriented copy shops into a highly networked company serving major corporations. In the end, that is what made the company an attractive acquisition for FedEx in 2004.

will change the risk of its equity. Thus there is no single cost of capital to compare to the IRR.[12]

The spreadsheet in Table 19.19 also computes the cash multiple for the transaction. The **cash multiple** (also called the multiple of money or absolute return) is the ratio of the total cash received to the total cash invested. The cash multiple for PKK's investment in Ideko is

$$\text{Cash Multiple} = \frac{\text{Total Cash Received}}{\text{Total Cash Invested}}$$

$$= \frac{9055 + 2989 + 4735 + 1375 + 177{,}077}{53{,}000} = 3.7 \quad (19.19)$$

That is, PKK expects to receive a return that is 3.7 times its investment in Ideko. The cash multiple is a common metric used by investors in transactions such as this one. It has an obvious weakness: The cash multiple does not depend on the amount of time it takes to receive the cash, nor does it account for the risk of the investment. It is therefore useful only for comparing deals with similar time horizons and risk.

CONCEPT CHECK

1. What are the main methods of estimating the continuation value of the firm at the end of the forecast horizon?

2. What are the potential pitfalls of analyzing a transaction like this one based on its IRR or cash multiple?

19.6 Sensitivity Analysis

Any financial valuation is only as accurate as the estimates on which it is based. Before concluding our analysis, it is important to assess the uncertainty of our estimates and to determine their potential impact on the value of the deal.

Once we have developed the spreadsheet model for PKK's investment in Ideko, it is straightforward to perform a sensitivity analysis to determine the impact of changes in different parameters on the deal's value. For example, the spreadsheet in Table 19.20 shows the sensitivity of our estimates of the value of PKK's investment to changes in our assumptions regarding the exit EBITDA multiple that PKK obtains when Ideko is sold, as well as Ideko's unlevered cost of capital.

TABLE 19.20 SPREADSHEET	Sensitivity Analysis for PKK's Investment in Ideko					
Exit EBITDA Multiple	6.0	7.0	8.0	9.1	10.0	11.0
Implied Long-Run Growth Rate	1.60%	3.43%	4.53%	**5.34%**	5.81%	6.21%
Ideko Enterprise Value ($ million)	151.4	171.3	191.2	**213.2**	231.1	251.0
PKK Equity Value ($ million)	51.4	71.3	91.2	**113.2**	131.1	151.0
PKK IRR	14.8%	22.1%	28.0%	**33.3%**	37.1%	40.8%
Unlevered Cost of Capital	9.0%	10.0%	11.0%	12.0%	13.0%	14.0%
Implied Long-Run Growth Rate	3.86%	5.34%	6.81%	8.29%	9.76%	11.24%
Ideko Enterprise Value ($ million)	222.1	**213.2**	204.7	196.7	189.1	181.9
PKK Equity Value ($ million)	122.1	**113.2**	104.7	96.7	89.1	81.9

12. See the appendix to this chapter for a calculation of Ideko's annual equity cost of capital.

In our initial analysis, we assumed an exit EBITDA multiple of 9.1. Table 19.20 shows that each 1.0 increase in the multiple represents about $20 million in initial value.[13] PKK will break even on its $53 million investment in Ideko with an exit multiple of slightly more than 6.0. The table also shows, however, that an exit multiple of 6.0 is consistent with a future growth rate for Ideko of less than 2%, which is even less than the expected rate of inflation and probably unrealistically low.

Table 19.20 also illustrates the effect of a change to our assumption about Ideko's unlevered cost of capital. A higher unlevered cost of capital reduces the value of PKK's investment; yet, even with a rate as high as 14%, the equity value exceeds PKK's initial investment. However, if the unlevered cost of capital exceeds 12%, the implied long-term growth rate that justifies the assumed exit EBITDA multiple of 9.1 is probably unrealistically high. Thus, if we believe the unlevered cost of capital falls within this range, we should lower our forecast for the exit EBITDA multiple, which will further reduce the value of PKK's equity. Conversely, if we are confident in our estimate of the exit multiple, this analysis lends further support to our choice for the unlevered cost of capital.

The exercises at the end of this chapter continue the sensitivity analysis by considering different levels of market share growth and changes to working capital management.

CONCEPT CHECK

1. What is the purpose of the sensitivity analysis?

2. Table 19.20 shows the sensitivity analysis for PKK's investment in Ideko. Based on the exit EBITDA multiple, do you recommend the acquisition of Ideko?

Summary

1. Valuation using comparables may be used as a preliminary way to estimate the value of a firm.

2. The value of an investment ultimately depends on the firm's future cash flows. To estimate cash flows, it is first necessary to look at a target firm's operations, investments, and capital structure to assess the potential for improvements and growth.

3. A financial model may be used to project the future cash flows from an investment.

   a. A pro forma income statement projects the firm's earnings under a given set of hypothetical assumptions.

   b. The financial model should also consider future working capital needs and capital expenditures to estimate future free cash flows.

   c. Based on these estimates, we can forecast the balance sheet and statement of cash flows.

4. To value an investment, we need to assess its risk and estimate an appropriate cost of capital. One method for doing so is to use the CAPM.

   a. Use the CAPM to estimate the equity cost of capital for comparable firms, based on their equity betas.

   b. Given an estimate of each comparable firm's equity beta, unlever the beta based on the firm's capital structure.

   c. Use the CAPM and the estimates of unlevered betas for comparable firms to estimate the unlevered cost of capital for the investment.

---

13. In fact, we can calculate this directly as the present value of Ideko's projected EBITDA in 2010: ($32.094 million) / (1.10^5) = $19.928 million.

5. In addition to forecasting cash flows for a few years, we need to estimate the firm's continuation value at the end of the forecast horizon.

   a. One method is to use a valuation multiple based on comparable firms.

   b. To estimate a continuation value in year T using discounted cash flows, it is common practice to assume a constant expected growth rate g and a constant debt-equity ratio:

$$\text{Enterprise Value in Year } T = V_T^L = \frac{FCF_{T+1}}{r_{wacc} - g} \tag{19.14}$$

6. Given the forecasted cash flows and an estimate of the cost of capital, the final step is to combine these inputs to estimate the value of the opportunity. We may use the valuation methods described in Chapter 18 to calculate firm value.

7. While the NPV method is the most reliable approach for evaluating an investment, practitioners often use the IRR and cash multiple as alternative valuation metrics.

   a. We use the cash flows over the lifetime of the investment to calculate the IRR.

   b. The cash multiple for an investment is the ratio of the total cash received to the total cash invested:

$$\text{Cash Multiple} = \frac{\text{Total Cash Received}}{\text{Total Cash Invested}} \tag{19.19}$$

8. Sensitivity analysis is useful for evaluating the uncertainty of estimates used for valuation, and the impact of this uncertainty on the value of the deal.

Key Terms

cash multiple (multiple of money, absolute return) *p. 647*

pro forma *p. 629*
unlevered P/E ratio *p. 640*

Further Reading

These books are a good reference for those readers who want to go into more detail on the issues involved in the valuation and financial modeling of companies and projects: T. Copeland, T. Koller, and J. Murrin, *Valuation: Measuring and Managing the Value of Companies*, 3rd ed. (Hoboken, NJ: John Wiley & Sons, 2000); S. Z. Benninga and O. Sarig, *Corporate Finance: A Valuation Approach* (New York: McGraw-Hill/Irwin, 1996); E. R. Arzac, *Valuation for Mergers, Buyouts and Restructuring* (Hoboken, NJ: John Wiley & Sons, 2004); and S. P. Pratt, R. F. Reilly, and R. P. Schweihs, *Valuing a Business: The Analysis and Appraisal of Closely Held Companies*, 4th ed. (New York: McGraw-Hill, 2000).

Problems

An asterisk (*) indicates problems with a higher level of difficulty.

Valuation Using Comparables

1. You would like to compare Ideko's profitability to its competitors' profitability using the EBITDA/sales multiple. Given Ideko's current sales of $75 million, use the information in Table 19.2 to compute a range of EBITDA for Ideko assuming it is run as profitably as its competitors.

2. Assume that Ideko's market share will increase by 0.5% per year rather than the 1% used in the chapter. What production capacity will Ideko require each year? When will an expansion become necessary (when production volume will exceed the current level by 50%)?

3. Under the assumption that Ideko market share will increase by 0.5% per year, you determine that the plant will require an expansion in 2010. The cost of this expansion will be $15 million. Assuming the financing of the expansion will be delayed accordingly, calculate the projected interest payments and the amount of the projected interest tax shields (assuming that the interest rates on the term loans remain the same as in the chapter) through 2010.

 4. Under the assumption that Ideko's market share will increase by 0.5% per year (and the investment and financing will be adjusted as described in Problem 3), you project the following depreciation:

Year	2005	2006	2007	2008	2009	2010
Fixed Assets and Capital Investment ($ 000)						
2 New Investment	5,000	5,000	5,000	5,000	5,000	20,000
3 Depreciation	(5,500)	(5,450)	(5,405)	(5,365)	(5,328)	(6,795)

Using this information, project net income through 2010 (that is, reproduce Table 19.7 under the new assumptions).

EXCEL 5. Under the assumptions that Ideko's market share will increase by 0.5% per year (implying that the investment, financing, and depreciation will be adjusted as described in Problems 3 and 4) and that the forecasts in Table 19.8 remain the same, calculate Ideko's working capital requirements though 2010 (that is, reproduce Table 19.9 under the new assumptions).

EXCEL 6. Under the assumptions that Ideko's market share will increase by 0.5% per year (implying that the investment, financing, and depreciation will be adjusted as described in Problems 3 and 4) but that the projected improvements in net working capital do not transpire (so the numbers in Table 19.8 remain at their 2005 levels through 2010), calculate Ideko's working capital requirements though 2010 (that is, reproduce Table 19.9 under these assumptions).

EXCEL 7. Forecast Ideko's free cash flow (reproduce Table 19.10), assuming Ideko's market share will increase by 0.5% per year; investment, financing, and depreciation will be adjusted accordingly; and the projected improvements in working capital occur (that is, under the assumptions in Problem 5).

EXCEL 8. Forecast Ideko's free cash flow (reproduce Table 19.10), assuming Ideko's market share will increase by 0.5% per year; investment, financing, and depreciation will be adjusted accordingly; and the projected improvements in working capital do *not* occur (that is, under the assumptions in Problem 6).

EXCEL *9. Reproduce Ideko's balance sheet and statement of cash flows, assuming Ideko's market share will increase by 0.5% per year; investment, financing, and depreciation will be adjusted accordingly; and the projected improvements in working capital occur (that is, under the assumptions in Problem 5).

EXCEL *10. Reproduce Ideko's balance sheet and statement of cash flows, assuming Ideko's market share will increase by 0.5% per year; investment, financing, and depreciation will be adjusted accordingly; and the projected improvements in working capital do *not* occur (that is, under the assumptions in Problem 6).

Estimating the Cost
of Capital

11. Calculate Ideko's unlevered cost of capital when Ideko's unlevered beta is 1.1 rather than 1.2, and all other required estimates are the same as in the chapter.

12. Calculate Ideko's unlevered cost of capital when the market risk premium is 6% rather than 5%, the risk-free rate is 5% rather than 4%, and all other required estimates are the same as in the chapter.

Valuing the Investment

13. Using the information produced in the income statement in Problem 4, use EBITDA as a multiple to estimate the continuation value in 2010, assuming the current value remains unchanged (reproduce Table 19.15). Infer the EV/sales and the unlevered and levered P/E ratios implied by the continuation value you calculated.

14. How does the assumption on future improvements in working capital affect your answer to Problem 13?

15. Approximately what expected future long-run growth rate would provide the same EBITDA multiple in 2010 as Ideko has today (i.e., 9.1)? Assume that the future debt-to-value ratio is held constant at 40%; the debt cost of capital is 6.8%; Ideko's market share will increase by 0.5% per year until 2010; investment, financing, and depreciation will be adjusted accordingly; and the projected improvements in working capital occur (that is, the assumptions in Problem 5).

16. Approximately what expected future long-run growth rate would provide the same EBITDA multiple in 2010 as Ideko has today (i.e., 9.1). Assume that the future debt-to-value ratio is held constant at 40%; the debt cost of capital is 6.8%; Ideko's market share will increase by 0.5% per year; investment, financing, and depreciation will be adjusted accordingly; and the projected improvements in working capital do *not* occur (that is, the assumptions in Problem 6).

17. Using the APV method, estimate the value of Ideko and the NPV of the deal using the continuation value you calculated in Problem 13 and the unlevered cost of capital estimate in Section 19.4. Assume that the debt cost of capital is 6.8%; Ideko's market share will increase by 0.5% per year until 2010; investment, financing, and depreciation will be adjusted accordingly; and the projected improvements in working capital occur (that is, the assumptions in Problem 5).

18. Using the APV method, estimate the value of Ideko and the NPV of the deal using the continuation value you calculated in Problem 13 and the unlevered cost of capital estimate in Section 19.4. Assume that the debt cost of capital is 6.8%; Ideko's market share will increase by 0.5% per year; investment, financing, and depreciation will be adjusted accordingly; and the projected improvements in working capital do *not* occur (that is, the assumptions in Problem 6).

19. Use your answers from Problems 17 and 18 to infer the value today of the projected improvements in working capital under the assumptions that Ideko's market share will increase by 0.5% per year and that investment, financing, and depreciation will be adjusted accordingly.

Compensating Management

The success of PKK's investment critically depends on its ability to execute the operational improvements laid out in its business plan. PKK has learned from experience that it is much more likely to achieve its goals if the management team responsible for implementing the changes is given a strong incentive to succeed. PKK therefore considers allocating 10% of Ideko's equity to a management incentive plan. This equity stake would be vested over the next five years, and it would provide Ideko's senior executives with a strong financial interest in the success of the venture. What is the cost to PKK of providing this equity stake to the management team? How will this incentive plan affect the NPV of the acquisition?

To determine the value of the acquisition to PKK, we must include the cost of the 10% equity stake granted to management. Because the grant vests after five years, management will not receive any of the dividends paid by Ideko during that time. Instead, management will receive the equity in five years time, at which point we have estimated the value of Ideko's equity to be $172 million (see Table 19.15). Thus the cost of management's stake in 2010 is equal to 10% × $172 million = $17.2 million according to our estimate. We must determine the present value of this amount today.

Because the payment to the managers is an equity claim, to compute its present value we must use an equity cost of capital. We take an FTE valuation approach to estimate the cost of management's share in Ideko, shown in the spreadsheet in Table 19A1.

To compute Ideko's equity cost of capital r_E, we use Eq. 18.20, which applies when the debt levels of the firm follow a known schedule:

$$r_E = r_U + \frac{D - T^s}{E}(r_U - r_D)$$

Using the debt, equity, and tax shield values from the spreadsheet in Table 19.17 to compute the effective leverage ratio $(D - T^s) / E$, we compute r_E each year as shown in the spreadsheet. We then compute the cost of management's equity share by discounting at this rate:

$$\text{Cost of Management's Share}_t = \frac{\text{Cost of Management's Share}_{t+1}}{1 + r_E(t)} \tag{19A.1}$$

Once we have determined the cost of management's equity share, we deduct it from the total value of Ideko's equity (from Table 19.17) to determine the value of PKK's share of Ideko's equity, shown as the last line of the spreadsheet. Given the initial cost of the acquisition to PKK of $53 million, PKK's NPV from the investment, including the cost of management's compensation, is $103.58 million − $53 million = $50.58 million.

TABLE 19A.1 SPREADSHEET	FTE Estimate of the Cost of Management's Share and PKK's Equity Value					
Year	2005	2006	2007	2008	2009	2010
Management/PKK Share ($ 000)						
1 Management Payoff (10% share)						17,205
2 Effective Leverage $(D - T^s)/E$	0.792	0.771	0.715	0.778	0.745	
3 Equity Cost of Capital r_E	12.53%	12.47%	12.29%	12.49%	12.38%	
4 Cost of Management's Share	(9,576)	(10,777)	(12,120)	(13,610)	(15,309)	(17,205)
5 Ideko Equity Value	113,160	118,287	130,047	141,294	157,566	172,052
6 PKK Equity	103,583	107,511	117,927	127,684	142,256	154,847

Glossary

10-K The annual form that U.S. companies use to file their financial statements with the U.S. Securities and Exchange Commission (SEC).

10-Q The quarterly reporting form that U.S. companies use to file their financial statements with the U.S. Securities and Exchange Commission (SEC).

absolute return *See* cash multiple.

accounts payable The amounts owed to creditors for products or services purchased with credit.

accounts payable days An expression of a firm's accounts payable in terms of the number of days' worth of cost of goods sold that the accounts payable represents.

accounts receivable Amounts owed to a firm by customers who have purchased goods or services on credit.

accounts receivable days An expression of a firm's accounts receivable in terms of the number of days' worth of sales that the accounts receivable represents.

adjusted betas A beta that has been adjusted toward 1 to account for estimation error.

adjusted present value (APV) A valuation method to determine the levered value of an investment by first calculating its unlevered value (its value without any leverage) and then adding the value of the interest tax shield and deducting any costs that arise from other market imperfections

adverse selection The idea that when the buyers and sellers have different information, the average quality of assets in the market will differ from the average quality overall.

after-tax interest rate Reflects the amount of interest an investor can keep after taxes have been deducted.

agency costs Costs that arise when there are conflicts of interest between a firm's stakeholders.

alpha The difference between a stock's expected return and its required return according to the security market line.

amortization A charge that captures the change in value of acquired assets. Like depreciation, amortization is not an actual cash expense.

amortizing loan A loan on which the borrower makes monthly payments that include interest on the loan plus some part of the loan balance.

annual percentage rate (APR) Indicates the amount of interest earned in one year without the effect of compounding.

annual report The yearly summary of business sent by U.S. public companies to their shareholders that accompanies or includes the financial statement.

annuity A stream of equal periodic cash flows over a specified time period. These cash flows can be inflows of returns earned on investments or outflows of funds invested to earn future returns.

annuity spreadsheet An Excel spreadsheet that can compute any one of the five variables of *NPER, RATE, PV, PMT,* and *FV.* Given any four input variables the spreadsheet computes the fifth.

APR *See* annual precentage rate.

APT *See* Arbitrage Pricing Theory.

APV *See* adjusted present value.

arbitrage The practice of buying and selling equivalent goods or portfolios to take advantage of a price difference.

arbitrage opportunity Any situation in which it is possible to make a profit without taking any risk or making any investment.

Arbitrage Pricing Theory (APT) A model that uses more than one portfolio to capture systematic risk. The portfolios themselves can be thought of as either the risk factor itself or a portfolio of stocks correlated with an unobservable risk factor. Also referred to as a multifactor model.

ask price The price at which a market maker or specialist is willing to sell a security.

assets The cash, inventory, property, plant and equipment, and other investments a company has made.

asymmetric information A situation in which parties have different information. It can arise when, for example, managers have superior information to investors regarding the firm's future cash flows.

auditor A neutral third party that corporations are required to hire that checks the annual financial statements to ensure they are prepared according to GAAP, and to verify that the information is reliable.

average annual return The arithmetic average of an investment's realized returns for each year.

balance sheet A list of a firm's assets and liabilities that provides a snapshot of the firm's financial position at a given point in time.

beta (β) The expected percent change in the excess return of a security for a 1% change in the excess return of the market (or other benchmark) portfolio.

bid price The price at which a market maker or specialist is willing to buy a security.

bid-ask spread The amount by which the ask price exceeds the bid price.

bird in the hand hypothesis The thesis that firms choosing to pay higher current dividends will enjoy higher stock prices because shareholders prefer current dividends to future ones (with the same present value).

board of directors A group elected by shareholders that has the ultimate decision-making authority in the corporation.

bond A security sold by governments and corporations to raise money from investors today in exchange for the promised future payment.

bond certificate   States the terms of a bond as well as the amounts and dates of all payments to be made.

book-to-market ratio   The ratio of the book value of equity to the market value of equity.

book value   The acquisition cost of an asset less its accumulated depreciation.

book value of equity   The difference between the book value of a firm's assets and its liabilities; also called stockholders' equity, it represents the net worth of a firm from an accounting perspective.

break-even   The level for which an investment has an NPV of zero.

break-even analysis   A calculation of the value of each parameter for which the NPV of the project is zero.

buying stocks on margin (leverage)   Borrowing money to invest in stocks.

"C" corporations   Corporations that have no restrictions on who owns their shares or the number of shareholders, and therefore cannot qualify for subchapter S treatment and are subject to direct taxation.

CAGR   *See* compound annual growth rate.

cannibalization   When sales of a firm's new product displace sales of one of its existing products.

Capital Asset Pricing Model (CAPM)   An equilibrium model of the relationship between risk and return that characterizes a security's expected return based on its beta with the market portfolio.

capital budget   Lists all of the projects that a company plans to undertake during the next period.

capital budgeting   The process of analyzing investment opportunities and deciding which ones to accept.

capital expenditures   Purchases of new property, plant, and equipment.

capital gain   The amount by which the sale price of an asset exceeds its initial purchase price.

capital gain rate   An expression of capital gain as a percentage of the initial price of the asset.

capital (finance) lease   Long-term lease contract that obligates a firm to make regular lease payments in exchange for the use of an asset. Viewed as an acquisition for accounting purposes, the lessee lists the asset on its balance sheet and incurs depreciation expenses. The lessee also lists the present value of the future lease payments as a liability, and deducts the interest portion of the lease payment as an interest expense.

capital market line (CML)   When plotting expected returns versus volatility, the line from the risk-free investment through the efficient portfolio of risky stocks (the portfolio that has the highest possible Sharpe Ratio). In the context of the CAPM, it is the line from the risk-free investment through the market portfolio. It shows the highest possible expected return that can be obtained for any given volatility.

capital structure   The relative proportions of debt, equity, and other securities that a firm has outstanding.

CAPM   *See* Capital Asset Pricing Model.

carryback or carryforward   *See* tax loss carryforwards and carrybacks.

cash multiple (multiple of money, absolute return)   The ratio of the total cash received to the total cash invested.

Chapter 11 reorganization   A common form of bankruptcy for large corporations in which all pending collection attempts are automatically suspended, and the firm's existing management is given the opportunity to propose a reorganization plan. While developing the plan, management continues to operate the business as usual. The creditors must vote to accept the plan, and it must be approved by the bankruptcy court. If an acceptable plan is not put forth, the court may ultimately force a Chapter 7 liquidation of the firm.

Chapter 7 liquidation   A provision of the U.S. bankruptcy code in which a trustee is appointed to oversee the liquidation of a firm's assets through an auction. The proceeds from the liquidation are used to pay the firm's creditors, and the firm ceases to exist.

characteristic variable   An observable characteristic of a firm, such as its market price, price-earnings ratio, or book-to-market ratio, that implicitly captures risk factors that affect the firm's future returns.

characteristic variable models   An approach to measuring risk that views firms as a portfolio of different measurable characteristics that together determine the firm's risk and return.

chief executive officer or CEO   The person charged with running the corporation by instituting the rules and policies set by the board of directors.

clean price   A bond's cash price less an adjustment for accrued interest, the amount of the next coupon payment that has already accrued.

clientele effect   When the dividend policy of a firm reflects the tax preference of its investor clientele.

CML   *See* capital market line.

common risk   Perfectly correlated risk.

competitive market   A market in which goods can be bought and sold at the same price.

compound annual growth rate (CAGR)   The geometric average of an investment's realized annual returns.

compounding   Computing the return on an investment over a long horizon by multiplying the return factors associated with each intervening period.

compound interest   The effect of earning "interest on interest."

conservation of value principle   With perfect capital markets, financial transactions neither add nor destroy value, but instead represent a repackaging of risk (and therefore return).

consol   A bond that promises its owner a fixed cash flow every year, forever.

constant dividend growth model   A model for valuing a stock by viewing its dividends as a constant growth perpetuity.

constant interest coverage ratio   When a firm keeps its interest payments equal to a target fraction of its free cash flows.

continuation value   The current value of all future free cash flow from continuing a project or investment.

continuous compounding   The compounding of interest every instant (an infinite number of times per year).

convertible bonds   Corporate bonds with a provision that gives the bondholder an option to convert each bond owned into a fixed number of shares of common stock.

corporate bonds   Bonds issued by a corporation.

corporation   A legally defined, artificial being, separate from its owners.

correlation   The covariance of the returns divided by the standard deviation of each return; a measure of the common risk shared by stocks that does not depend on their volatility.

cost of capital   The expected return available on securities with equivalent risk and term to a particular investment.

coupon bonds   Bonds that pay regular coupon interest payments up to maturity, when the face value is also paid.

coupon-paying yield curve   A plot of the yield of coupon bonds of different maturities.

coupon rate   Determines the amount of each coupon payment of a bond. The coupon rate, expressed as an APR, is set by the issuer and stated on the bond certificate.

coupons   The promised interest payments of a bond.

covariance   The expected product of the deviation of each return from its mean.

credibility principle   The principle that claims in one's self-interest are credible only if they are supported by actions that would be too costly to take if the claims were untrue.

credit rating   A rating assigned by a rating agency that assesses the likelihood that a borrower will default.

credit risk   The risk of default by the issuer of any bond that is not default free; it is an indication that the bond's cash flows are not known with certainty.

credit spread   The difference between the risk-free interest rate on U.S. Treasury notes and the interest rates on all other loans. The magnitude of the credit spread will depend on investors' assessment of the likelihood that a particular firm will default.

cum dividend   When a stock trades before the ex-dividend date, entitling anyone who buys the stock to the dividend.

current assets   Cash or assets that could be converted into cash within one year. This category includes marketable securities, accounts receivable, inventories, and pre-paid expenses such as rent and insurance.

current liabilities   Liabilities that will be satisfied within one year. They include accounts payable, notes payable, short-term debt, current maturities of long-term debt, salary or taxes owed, and deferred or unearned revenue.

current ratio   The ratio of current assets to current liabilities.

data snooping bias   The idea that given enough characteristics, it will always be possible to find some characteristic that by pure chance happens to be correlated with the estimation error of a regression.

debt capacity   The amount of debt at a particular date that is required to maintain the firm's target debt-to-value ratio.

debt cost of capital   The cost of capital, or expected return, that a firm must pay on its debt.

debt covenants   Conditions of making a loan in which creditors place restrictions on actions that a firm can take.

debt holders   Individuals or institutions who have lent money to a firm.

debt-equity ratio   The ratio of a firm's total amount of short- and long-term debt (including current maturities) to the value of its equity, which may be calculated based on market or book values.

debt-to-value ratio   The fraction of a firm's enterprise value that corresponds to debt.

declaration date   The date on which a public company's board of directors authorizes the payment of a dividend.

default   When a firm fails to make the required interest or principal payments on its debt, or violates a debt covenant.

default spread   *See* credit spread.

deferred taxes   An asset or liability that results from the difference between a firm's tax expenses as reported for accounting purposes, and the actual amount paid to the taxing authority.

depreciation   A yearly deduction a firm makes from the value of its fixed assets (other than land) over time according to a depreciation schedule that depends on an asset's life span.

depreciation tax shield   The tax savings that result from the ability to deduct depreciation.

diluted EPS   A firm's disclosure of its potential for dilution from options it has awarded which shows the earnings per share the company would have if the stock options were exercised.

dilution   An increase in the total number of shares that will divide a fixed amount of earnings; often occurs when stock options are exercised or convertible bonds are converted.

dilution fallacy   The idea that issuing shares will, on its own, reduce the value of existing shares.

dirty price (invoice price)   A bond's actual cash price.

discount   The amount by which a cash flow exceeds its present value.

discounted free cash flow model   A method for estimating a firm's enterprise value by discounting its future free cash flow.

discount factor   The value today of a dollar received in the future.

discounting   Finding the equivalent value today of a future cash flow by multiplying by a discount factor, or equivalently, dividing by 1 plus the discount rate.

discount rate   The rate used to discount a stream of cash flows; the cost of capital of a stream of cash flows.

distribution date   *See* payable date.

diversifiable risk   *See* firm-specific risk.

diversification   The averaging of independent risks in a large portfolio.

dividend-capture theory   The theory that absent transaction costs, investors can trade shares at the time of the dividend so that non-taxed investors receive the dividend.

dividend-discount model   A model that values shares of a firm according to the present value of the future dividends the firm will pay.

dividend payments   Payments made at the discretion of the corporation to its equity holders.

dividend payout rate   The fraction of a firm's earnings that the firm pays as dividends each year.

dividend puzzle   When firms continue to issue dividends despite their tax disadvantage.

dividend signaling hypothesis   The idea that dividend changes reflect managers' views about a firm's future earnings prospects.

dividend smoothing   The practice of maintaining relatively constant dividends.

dividend yield   The expected annual dividend of a stock divided by its current price. The dividend yield is the percentage return an investor expects to earn from the dividend paid by the stock.

duration   The sensitivity of a bond's price to changes in interest rates. The value-weighted average maturity of a bond's cash flows.

Dutch auction   A share repurchase method in which the firm lists different prices at which it is prepared to buy shares, and shareholders in turn indicate how many shares they are willing to sell at each price. The firm then pays the lowest price at which it can buy back its desired number of shares.

EAR   *See* effective annual rate.

earnings per share (EPS)   A firm's net income divided by the total number of shares outstanding.

EBIT   A firm's earnings before interest and taxes are deducted.

EBIT break-even   The level of sales for which a project's EBIT is zero.

EBITDA   A computation of a firm's earnings before interest, taxes, depreciation, and amortization are deducted.

economic distress   A significant decline in the value of a firm's assets, whether or not the firm experiences financial distress due to leverage.

economic profit   The difference between revenue and the opportunity cost of all resources consumed in producing that revenue, including the opportunity cost of capital.

Economic Value Added (EVA)   The cash flows of project less a capital charge that reflects the opportunity cost of the capital invested, as well as any capital consumed.

effective annual rate (EAR)   The total amount of interest that will be earned at the end of one year.

effective dividend tax rate   The effective dividend tax rate measures the additional tax paid by the investor per dollar of after-tax capital gain income that is instead received as a dividend.

efficient capital market   When the cost of capital of an investment depends only on its systematic risk, and not its diversifiable risk.

efficient frontier   The set of portfolios that can be formed from a given set of investments with the property that each portfolio has the highest possible expected return that can be attained without increasing its volatility.

efficient markets hypothesis   The idea that competition among investors works to eliminate all positive-NPV trading opportunities. It implies that securities will be fairly priced, based on their future cash flows, given all information that is available to investors.

efficient portfolio   A portfolio that contains only systematic risk. An efficient portfolio cannot be diversified further; there is no way to reduce the volatility of the portfolio without lowering its expected return. The efficient portfolio is the tangent portfolio, the portfolio with the highest Sharpe ratio in the economy.

empirical distribution   A plot showing the frequency of outcomes based on historical data.

enterprise value   The total market value of a firm's equity and debt, less the value of its cash and marketable securities. It measures the value of the firm's underlying business.

EPS   *See* earnings per share.

equally weighted portfolio   A portfolio in which the same dollar amount is invested in each stock.

equal-ownership portfolio   A portfolio containing an equal fraction of the total number of shares outstanding of each security in the portfolio. Equivalent to a value-weighted portfolio.

equity   The collection of all the outstanding shares of a corporation.

equity cost of capital   The expected rate of return available in the market on other investments with equivalent risk to the firm's shares.

equity holder (also shareholder or stockholder)   An owner of a share of stock in a corporation.

error term   Represents the deviation from the best-fitting line in a regression. It is zero on average and uncorrelated with any regressors.

EVA®   *See* Economic Value Added.

EVA investment rule   Accept any investment opportunity in which the present value of all future EVA's is positive.

evergreen credit   A revolving line of credit with no fixed maturity.

excess return   The difference between the average return for an investment and the average return for a risk-free investment.

exchange-traded fund   A security that trades directly on an exchange, like a stock, but represents ownership in a portfolio of stocks.

ex-dividend date   A date, two days prior to a dividend's record date, on or after which anyone buying the stock will not be eligible for the dividend.

expected (mean) return   A computation for the return of a security based on the average payoff expected.

face value   The notional amount of a bond used to compute its interest payments. The face value of the bond is generally due at the bond's maturity. Also called par value or principal amount.

factor beta   The sensitivity of the stock's excess return to the excess return of a factor portfolio, as computed in a multifactor regression.

factor portfolios   Portfolios that can be combined to form an efficient portfolio.

Fama-French-Carhart (FFC) factor specification   A multi-factor model of risk and return in which the factor portfolios are the market, small-minus-big, high-minus-low, and PR1YR portfolios identified by Fama, French, and Carhart.

FCFE   *See* free cash flow to equity.

federal funds rate   The overnight loan rate charged by banks with excess reserves at a Federal Reserve bank (called federal funds) to banks that need additional funds to meet reserve requirements. The federal funds rate is influenced by the Federal Reserve's monetary policy, and itself influences other interest rates in the market.

FFC factor specification   *See* Fama-French-Carhart factor specification.

financial distress   When a firm has difficulty meeting its debt obligations.

financial option   A contract that gives its owner the right (but not the obligation) to purchase or sell an asset at a fixed price at some future date.

financial security   An investment opportunity that trades in a financial market.

financial statements   Firm-issued (usually quarterly and annually) accounting reports with past performance information.

firm-specific, idiosyncratic, unsystematic, unique, or diversifiable risk   Fluctuations of a stock's return that are due to firm-specific news and are independent risks unrelated across stocks.

flow to equity (FTE)   A valuation method that calculates the free cash flow available to equity holders taking into account all payments to and from debt holders. The cash flows to equity holders are then discounted using the equity cost of capital.

forward earnings   A firm's anticipated earnings over the coming 12 months.

forward P/E   A firm's price-earnings (P/E) ratio calculated using forward earnings.

free cash flow   The incremental effect of a project on a firm's available cash.

free cash flow hypothesis   The view that wasteful spending is more likely to occur when firms have high levels of cash flow in excess of what is needed after making all positive-NPV investments and payments to debt holders.

free cash flow to equity (FCFE)   The free cash flow that remains after adjusting for interest payments, debt issuance, and debt repayment.

FTE   *See* flow to equity.

future value   The value of a cash flow that is moved forward in time.

GAAP   *See* Generally Accepted Accounting Principles.

general lien   *See* floating lien.

Generally Accepted Accounting Principles (GAAP)   A common set of rules and a standard format for public companies to use when they prepare their financial reports.

goodwill   The difference between the price paid for a company and the book value assigned to its assets.

greenmail   When a firm avoids a threat of takeover and removal of its management by a major shareholder by buying out the shareholder, often at a large premium over the current market price.

gross profit   The third line of an income statement that represents the difference between a firm's sales revenues and its costs.

growing annuity   A stream of cash flows paid at regular intervals and growing at a constant rate, up to some final date.

growing perpetuity   A stream of cash flows that occurs at regular intervals and grows at a constant rate forever.

growth stocks   Firms with high market-to-book ratios.

high-minus-low (HML) portfolio   An annually updated portfolio that is long stocks with high book-to-market ratios and short stocks with low book-to-market ratios.

high-yield bonds   Bonds below investment grade which trade with a high yield to maturity to compensate investors for their high risk of default.

HML portfolio   *See* high-minus-low portfolio.

homemade leverage   When investors use leverage in their own portfolios to adjust the leverage choice made by a firm.

homogeneous expectations   A theoretical situation in which all investors have the same estimates concerning future investment returns.

hostile takeover   A situation in which an individual or organization, sometimes referred to as a corporate raider, purchases a large fraction of a target corporation's stock and in doing so gets enough votes to replace the target's board of directors and its CEO.

hurdle rate   A higher discount rate created by the hurdle rate rule. If a project can jump the hurdle with a positive NPV at this higher discount rate, then it should be undertaken.

idiosyncratic risk   *See* firm-specific risk.

income statement   A list of a firm's revenues and expenses over a period of time.

incremental earnings   The amount by which a firm's earnings are expected to change as a result of an investment decision.

incremental IRR investment rule   Applies the IRR rule to the difference between the cash flows of two mutually exclusive alternatives (the *increment* to the cash flows of one investment over the other).

independent risk   Risks that bear no relation to each other. If risks are independent, then knowing the outcome of one provides no information about the other. Independent risks are always uncorrelated, but the reverse need not be true.

index funds   Mutual funds that invest in stocks in proportion to their representation in a published index, such as the S&P 500 or Wilshire 5000.

inefficient portfolio   Describes a portfolio for which it is possible to find another portfolio that has higher expected return and lower volatility.

interest coverage ratio   An assessment by lenders of a firm's leverage. Common ratios consider operating income, EBIT, or EBITDA as a multiple of the firm's interest expenses.

interest rate factor   One plus the interest rate, it is the rate of exchange between dollars today and dollars in the future.

interest tax shield   The reduction in taxes paid due to the tax deductibility of interest payments.

internal rate of return (IRR)   The interest rate that sets the net present value of the cash flows equal to zero.

internal rate of return (IRR) investment rule   A decision rule that accepts any investment opportunity where IRR exceeds the opportunity cost of capital. This rule is only optimal in special circumstances, and often leads to errors if misapplied.

inventories   A firm's raw materials as well as its work-in-progress and finished goods.

inventory days   An expression of a firm's inventory in terms of the number of days' worth or cost of goods sold that the inventory represents.

investment-grade bonds   Bonds in the top four categories of creditworthiness with a low risk of default.

invoice price   *See* dirty price.

IRR   *See* internal rate of return.

IRR investment rule   *See* internal rate of return investment rule.

junk bonds   Bonds in one of the bottom five categories of creditworthiness (below investment grade) that have a high risk of default.

Law of One Price   In competitive markets, securities or portfolios with the same cash flows must have the same price.

lemons principle   When a seller has private information about the value of a good, buyers will discount the price they are willing to pay due to adverse selection.

leverage   The amout of debt held in a portfolio or issued by a firm. *See also* buying stocks on margin.

leverage ratio   A measure of leverage obtained by looking at debt as proportion of value, or interest payments as a proportion of cash flows.

leveraged recapitalization   When a firm uses borrowed funds to pay a large special dividend or repurchase a significant amount of its outstanding shares.

levered equity   Equity in a firm with outstanding debt.

liabilities   A firm's obligations to its creditors.

limited liability   When an investor's liability is limited to her initial investment.

limited liability company (LLC)   A limited partnership without a general partner.

limited partnership   A partnership with two kinds of owners, general partners and limited partners.

linear regression   The statistical technique that identifies the best-fitting line through a set of points.

liquid   Describes an investment that can easily be turned into cash because it can be sold immediately at a competitive market price.

liquidating dividend   A return of capital to shareholders from a business operation that is being terminated.

liquidation   Closing down a business and selling off all its assets; often the result of the business declaring bankruptcy.

liquidation value   The value of a firm after its assets are sold and liabilities paid.

LLC   *See* limited liability company.

long position   A positive investment in a security.

long-term debt   Any loan or debt obligation with a maturity of more than a year.

MACRS depreciation   The most accelerated cost recovery system allowed by the IRS. Based on the recovery period, MACRS depreciation tables assign a fraction of the purchase price that the firm can depreciate each year.

management discussion and analysis (MD&A)   A preface to the financial statements in which a company's management discusses the recent year (or quarter), providing a background on the company and any significant events that may have occurred.

management entrenchment   A situation arising as the result of the separation of ownership and control in which managers may make decisions that benefit themselves at investors' expense.

management entrenchment theory   A theory that suggests managers choose a capital structure to avoid the discipline of debt and maintain their own job security.

marginal corporate tax rate   The tax rate a firm will pay on an incremental dollar of pre-tax income.

marketable securities   Short-term, low-risk investments that can be easily sold and converted to cash (such as money market investments, like government debt, that mature within a year).

market capitalization   The total market value of equity; equals the market price per share times the number of shares.

market index   The market value of a broad-based portfolio of securities.

market makers   Individuals on the trading floor of a stock exchange who match buyers with sellers.

market portfolio   A value-weighted portfolio of all shares of all stocks and securities in the market.

market proxy   A portfolio whose return is believed to closely track the true market portfolio.

market risk   *See* systematic risk.

market-to-book ratio (price-to-book [PB] ratio)   The ratio of a firm's market (equity) capitalization to the book value of its stockholders' equity.

market value balance sheet   similar to an accounting balance sheet, with two key distinctions: First, all assets and liabilities of the firm are included, even intangible assets such as reputation, brand name, or human capital that are missing from a standard accounting balance sheet; second, all values are current market values rather than historical costs.

maturity date   The final repayment date of a bond.

MD&A   *See* management discussion and analysis.

method of comparables   An estimate of the value of a firm based on the value of other, comparable firms or other investments that are expected to generate very similar cash flows in the future.

momentum strategy   Buying stocks that have had past high returns, and (short) selling stocks that have had past low returns.

multifactor model   A model that uses more than one risk factor to capture risk. Also referred to as Arbitrage Pricing Theory (APT).

multiple of money   *See* cash multiple.

multiple regression   A regression with more than one independent variable.

mutually exclusive projects   Projects that compete with one another; by accepting one, the others cannot be accepted.

net debt   Total debt outstanding minus any cash balances.

net income or earnings   The last or "bottom line" of a firm's income statement that is a measure of the firm's income over a given period of time.

net present value (NPV)   The difference between the present value of a project or investment's benefits and the present value of its costs.

Net Present Value (NPV) Investment Rule   When making an investment decision, take the alternative with the highest NPV. Choosing this alternative is equivalent to receiving its NPV in cash today.

net profit margin   The ratio of net income to revenues, it shows the fraction of each dollar in revenues that is available to equity holders after the firm pays interest and taxes.

net working capital   The difference between a firm's current assets and current liabilities that represents the capital available in the short term to run the business.

95% confidence interval   A confidence interval gives a range of values which is likely to include an unknown parameter. If independent samples are taken repeatedly from the same population, then the true parameter will lie outside the 95% confidence interval 5% of the time. For a normal distribution, the interval corresponds to approximately 2 standard deviations on both sides of the mean.

no-arbitrage price   In a normal market, when the price of a security equals the present value of the cash flows paid by the security.

nominal interest rates   Interest rates quoted by banks and other financial institutions that indicate the rate at which money will grow if invested for a certain period of time.

normal market   A competitive market in which there are no arbitrage opportunities.

NPV   *See* net present value.

NPV Investment Rule   *See* Net Present Value Investment Rule.

NPV Decision Rule   When choosing among investment alternatives, take the alternative with the highest NPV. Choosing this alternative is equivalent to receiving its NPV in cash today.

off-balance sheet transactions   Transactions or arrangements that can have a material impact on a firm's future performance yet do not appear on the balance sheet.

on-the-run bonds   The most recently issued treasury security of a particular original maturity.

open market repurchase   When a firm repurchases shares by buying its shares in the open market.

operating income   A firm's gross profit less its operating expenses.

operating margin   The ratio of operating income to revenues, it reveals how much a company has earned from each dollar of sales before interest and taxes are deducted.

opportunity cost   The value a resource could have provided in its best alternative use.

opportunity cost of capital   The best available expected return offered in the market on an investment of comparable risk and term to the cash flow being discounted; the return the investor forgoes on an alternative investment of equivalent riskiness and term when the investor takes on a new investment.

overhead expenses   Those expenses associated with activities that are not directly attributable to a single business activity but instead affect many different areas of a corporation.

over-investment problem   When a firm faces financial distress, shareholders can gain at the expense of bondholders by taking a negative-NPV project, if it is sufficiently risky.

par   A price at which coupon bonds trade that is equal to their face value.

partnership   A sole proprietorship with more than one owner.

passive portfolio   A portfolio that is not rebalanced in response to price changes.

payable date (distribution date)   A date, generally within a month after the record date, on which a firm mails dividend checks to its registered stockholders.

payback investment rule   The simplest investment rule. Only projects that pay back their initial investment within the payback period are undertaken.

payback period   A specified amount of time used in the payback investment rule. Only investments that pay back their initial investment within this amount of time are undertaken.

payout policy   The way a firm chooses between the alternative ways to pay cash out to equity holders.

P/E   *See* price-earnings ratio.

pecking order hypothesis   The idea that managers will prefer to fund investments by first using retained earnings, then debt and equity only as a last resort.

perfect capital markets   A set of conditions in which investors and firms can trade the same set of securities at competitive market prices with no frictions such as taxes, transaction costs, issuance costs, asymmetric information, or agency costs.

perpetuity   A stream of equal cash flows that occurs at regular intervals and lasts forever.

portfolio weights   The fraction of the total investment in a portfolio held in each individual investment in the portfolio.

premium   A price at which coupon bonds trade that is greater than their face value. Also, the price a firm pays to purchase insurance, allowing the firm to exchange a random future loss for a certain upfront expense.

prepackaged bankruptcy   A method for avoiding many of the legal and other direct costs of bankruptcy in which a firm first develops a reorganization plan with the agreement of its main creditors, and then files Chapter 11 to implement the plan.

present value (PV)   The value of a cost or benefit computed in terms of cash today.

pretax WACC   The weighted average cost of captial computed using the pretax cost of debt; it can be used to estimate the unlevered cost of captial for a firm that maintains a target leverage ratio.

price-earnings ratio (P/E)   The ratio of the market value of equity to the firm's earnings, or its share price to its earnings per share.

price-to-book (PB) ratio   *See* market-to-book ratio.

price-weighted portfolio   A portfolio that holds an equal number of shares of each stock, independent of their size.

principal or face value   The notational amount used to compute a bond's interest payments; in many cases also the final principal payment on the maturity date of a bond.

principal-agent problem   A problem that arises when employees in control (the agents) act in their own interest rather than in the interest of the owners (the principals).

PR1YR   *See* prior one-year momentum portfolio.

prior one-year momentum (PR1YR) portfolio   A self-financing portfolio that goes long on the top 30% of stocks with the highest prior year returns, and short on the 30% with the lowest prior year returns, each year.

private company   A company whose shares do not trade on a public market.

probability distribution   A graph that provides the probability of every possible discrete state.

profitability index   Measures the NPV per unit of resource consumed.

pro forma   Describes a statement that is not based on actual data but rather depicts a firm's financials under a given set of hypothetical assumptions.

project externalities   Indirect effects of a project that may increase or decrease the profits of other business activities of a firm.

public companies   Those corporations whose stock is traded on a stock market or exchange, providing shareholders the ability to quickly and easily convert their investments in to cash.

pure discount bonds   Zero-coupon bonds.

PV   *See* present value.

quick ratio   The ratio of current assets other than inventory to current liabilities.

rational expectations   The idea that investors may have different information regarding expected returns, correlations, and volatilities, but they correctly interpret that information and the information contained in market prices and adjust their estimates of expected returns in a rational way.

real interest rate   The rate of growth of purchasing power after adjusting for inflation.

realized return   The return that actually occurs over a particular time period.

record date   When a firm pays a dividend, only shareholders of record on this date receive the dividend.

regression   A statistical technique that estimates a linear relationship between two variables (the dependent and independent variable) by fitting a line that minimizes the squared distance between the data and the line.

required return   The expected return of an investment that is necessary to compensate for the risk of undertaking the investment.

retained earnings   The difference between a firm's net income and the amount it spends on dividends.

retention rate   The fraction of a firm's current earnings that the firm retains.

return   The difference between the selling price and purchasing price of an asset plus any cash distributions expressed as a percentage of the buying price.

return of capital   When a firm, instead of paying dividends out of current earnings (or accumulated retained earnings), pays dividends from other sources, such as paid-in capital or the liquidation of assets.

return on assets (ROA)   The ratio of net income to the total book value of the firm's assets.

return on equity (ROE)   The ratio of a firm's net income to the book value of its equity.

reverse split   When the price of a company's stock falls too low and the company reduces the number of outstanding shares.

risk aversion   When investors prefer to have a safe future payment rather than an uncertain one of the same expected amount.

risk-free interest rate   The interest rate at which money can be borrowed or lent without risk over a given period.

risk premium   Represents the additional return that investors expect to earn to compensate them for a security's risk.

ROA   *See* return on assets.

ROE   *See* return on equity.

"S" corporations   Those corporations that elect subchapter S tax treatment and are allowed, by the U.S. Internal Revenue Tax code, an exemption from double taxation.

scenario analysis   An important capital budgeting tool that determines how the NPV varies as a number of the underlying assumptions are changed simultaneously.

security market line (SML)   The pricing implication of the CAPM, it specifies a linear relation between the risk premium of a security and its beta with the market portfolio.

self-financing portfolio   A portfolio that costs nothing to construct.

sensitivity analysis   An important capital budgeting tool that determines how the NPV varies as a single underlying assumption is changed.

Separation Principle   In a perfect market, the NPV of an investment decision can be evaluated separately from any financial transactions a firm is considering.

shareholder (also stockholder or equity holder)   An owner of a share of stock in a corporation.

shareholders' equity, stockholders' equity   An accounting measure of a firm's net worth that represents the difference between the firm's assets and its liabilities.

share repurchase   A situation in which a firm uses cash to buy back its own stock.

Sharpe ratio   The excess return of an asset divided by the volatility of the return of the asset; a measure of the reward per unit risk.

short interest   The number of shares sold short.

short position   A negative amount invested in a stock.

short sale   Selling a security you do not own.

signaling theory of debt   The use of leverage as a way to signal information to investors.

simple interest   Interest earned without the effect of compounding.

single-factor model   A model using an efficient portfolio, capturing all systemic risk alone.

size effect   The observation that small stocks (or stocks with a high book-to-market ratio) have higher returns.

small-minus-big (SMB) portfolio   A portfolio resulting from a trading strategy that each year buys a small market value portfolio and finances that position by selling short a large market value portfolio.

SMB portfolio   *See* small-minus-big portfolio.

SML   *See* security market line.

sole proprietorship   A business owned and run by one person.

special dividend   A one-time dividend payment a firm makes that is usually much larger than a regular dividend.

specialists   Individuals on the trading floor of the NYSE who match buyers with sellers; also called market makers.

speculative bonds   Bonds in one of the bottom five categories of creditworthiness that have a high risk of default.

spin-off   When a firm sells a subsidiary by selling shares in the subsidiary alone.

spot interest rates   Default-free, zero-coupon yields.

standard deviation   A common method used to measure the risk of a probability distribution, it is the square root of the variance, the expected squared deviation from the mean.

standard error   The standard deviation of the estimated value of the mean of the actual distribution around its true value; that is, it is the standard deviation of the average return.

statement of cash flows   An accounting statement that shows how a firm has used the cash it earned during a set period.

statement of stockholders' equity   An accounting statement that breaks down the stockholders' equity computed on the balance sheet into the amount that came from issuing new shares versus retained earnings.

stock   The ownership or equity of a corporation divided into shares.

stock dividend   *See* stock split.

stockholder (also shareholder or equity holder)   An owner of a share of stock or equity in a corporation.

stockholder's equity   *See* shareholder's equity.

stock exchanges (stock markets)   *See* stock markets.

stock markets (also stock exchanges)   Organized markets on which the shares of many corporations are traded.

stock options   A form of compensation a firm gives to its employees that gives them the right to buy a certain number of shares of stock by a specific date at a specific price.

stock split (stock dividend)   When a company issues a dividend in shares of stock rather than cash to its shareholders.

straight-line depreciation   A method of depreciation in which an asset's cost is divided equally over its life.

stream of cash flows   A series of cash flows lasting several periods.

sunk cost   Any unrecoverable cost for which a firm is already liable.

systematic, undiversifiable, or market risk   Fluctuations of a stock's return that are due to market-wide news representing common risk.

tangent portfolio   A portfolio with the highest Sharpe ratio; the point of tangency to the efficient frontier of a line drawn from the risk-free asset; the market portfolio if the CAPM holds.

targeted repurchase   When a firm purchases shares directly from a specific shareholder.

target leverage ratio   When a firm adjusts its debt proportionally to a project's value or its cash flows (where the proportion need not remain constant). A constant market debt-equity ratio is a special case.

tax loss carryforwards and carrybacks   Two features of the U.S. tax code that allow corporations to take losses during a current year and offset them against gains in nearby years. Since 1997, companies can "carry back" losses for two years and "carry forward" losses for 20 years.

tender offer   A public announcement of an offer to all existing security holders to buy back a specified amount of outstanding securities at a prespecified price over a prespecified period of time.

term   The time remaining until the final repayment date of a bond.

terminal value (*See also* continuation value)   The value of a project's remaining free cash flows beyond the forecast horizon. This amount represents the market value (as of the last forecast period) of the free cash flow from the project at all future dates.

term structure   The relationship between the investment term and the interest rate.

timeline   A linear representation of the timing of (potential) cash flows.

time value of money   The difference in value between money today and money in the future; also, the observation that two cash flows at two different points in time have different values.

total payout model   A firm's total payouts to equity holders (i.e., all the cash distributed as dividends and stock repurchases) are discounted and then divided by the current number of shares outstanding to determine the share price.

total return   The sum of a stock's dividend yield and its capital gain rate.

trade credit   The difference between receivables and payables that is the net amount of a firm's capital consumed as a result of those credit transactions; the credit that a firm extends to its customers.

tradeoff theory   The firm picks its capital structure by trading off the benefits of the tax shield from debt against the costs of financial distress and agency costs.

trailing earnings   A firm's earnings over the prior 12 months.

trailing P/E   The computation of a firm's P/E using its trailing earnings.

transaction cost   In most markets, an expense such as a broker commission and the bid-ask spread investors must pay in order to trade securities.

Treasury bills   Zero-coupon bonds, issued by the U.S. government, with a maturity of up to one year.

Treasury bonds   A type of U.S. Treasury coupon securities, currently traded in financial markets, with original maturities of more than ten years.

Treasury notes   A type of U.S. Treasury coupon securities, currently traded in financial markets, with original maturities from one to ten years.

under-investment problem   A situation in which equity holders choose not to invest in a postive NPV project because the firm is in financial distress and the value of undertaking the investment opportunity will accrue to bondholders rather than themselves.

undiversifiable risk   *See* systematic risk.

unique risk   *See* firm-specific risk.

unlevered beta   Measures the risk of a firm were it unlevered; beta of the firm's assets; measures the market risk of the firm's business activities, ignoring any additional risk due to leverage.

unlevered cost of capital   The cost of capital of a firm, were it unlevered; for a firm that maintains a target leverage ratio, it can be estimated as the weighted average cost of capital computed without taking into account taxes (pre-tax WACC).

unlevered equity   Equity in a firm with no debt.

unlevered net income   Net income plus after-tax interest expense.

unlevered P/E ratio   The enterprise value of a firm divided by its unlevered net income in a particular year.

unsystematic risk   *See* firm-specific risk.

valuation multiple   A ratio of a firm's value to some measure of the firm's scale or cash flow.

value additivity   A relationship determined by the Law of One Price, in which the price of an asset that consists of other assets must equal the sum of the prices of the other assets.

value stocks   Firms with low market-to-book ratios.

value-weighted portfolio   A portfolio in which each security is held in proportion to its market capitalization. Also called an equal-ownership portfolio, because it consists of the same fraction of the outstanding shares of each security.

variance   A method to measure the risk of a probability distribution, it is the expected squared deviation from the mean.

volatility   The standard deviation of a return.

WACC   *See* weighted average coast of capital.

weighted average cost of capital (WACC)   The average of a firm's equity and after-tax cost of capital, weighted by the fraction of the firm's enterprise value that corresponds to equity and debt, respectively. Discounting free cash flows using the WACC computes their vaule including the interest tax shield.

workout   A method for avoiding a declaration of bankruptcy in which a firm in financial distress negotiates directly with its creditors to reorganize.

yield curve   A plot of bond yields as a function of the bonds' maturity date.

yield to maturity (YTM)   The IRR of an investment in a bond that is held to its maturity date.

YTM   *See* yield to maturity.

zero-coupon bond   A bond that makes only one payment at maturity.

zero-coupon yield curve   A plot of the yield of risk-free zero-coupon bonds (STRIPS) as a function of the bond's maturity date.

Index

Page numbers in boldface refer to boldface terms in the text. Figures, tables, examples, and boxed text are indicated by italicized *f, t, e,* and *b.*

KEY EQUATIONS